FIREARMS IDENTIFICATION

J. HOWARD MATHEWS

Firearms Identification

VOLUME I The laboratory examination of small arms, rifling

characteristics in hand guns, and notes on automatic pistols

With a Foreword by Julian S. Hatcher, Maj. Gen., U.S. Army, Retired

CHARLES C THOMAS • PUBLISHER
Springfield • Illinois • U.S.A.

Published and Distributed Throughout the World by
CHARLES C THOMAS • PUBLISHER
BANNERSTONE HOUSE
301–327 East Lawrence Avenue, Springfield, Illinois, U.S.A.

© *1962 by* CHARLES C THOMAS • PUBLISHER
ISBN 0–398–02355–7

Library of Congress Catalog Card Number: 71–180107

First Printing, 1962

Second Printing, 1973

With THOMAS BOOKS *careful attention is given to all details of
manufacturing and design. It is the Publisher's desire to present books
that are satisfactory as to their physical qualities and artistic possibilities
and appropriate for their particular use.* THOMAS BOOKS *will be true
to those laws of quality that assure a good name and good will.*

Printed in the United States of America

Composed by Superior Typesetting, St. Louis, Missouri and
printed by Meriden Gravure Company, Meriden, Connecticut

Foreword

Dr. J. H. Mathews, a 1903 graduate of the University of Wisconsin, with later Master's and Doctor's degrees from Harvard, is one of the real pioneers in criminal investigation work involving firearms identification. His first criminal case was in 1923 and involved the metallographic analysis of certain parts of a bomb which had killed one person and badly injured another. As a result of his success in this case, other cases, including firearms examinations and identifications, soon came to his laboratory and, as his well-deserved reputation in this work spread, the demand for his services rose until he now has a record of several hundred important cases successfully completed and can be considered one of the world's outstanding experts in this field. For 16 years he was a member of the Madison, Wisconsin, Police and Fire Commission, and for a time he was president of that body.

During World War I, Professor Mathews served 18 months in the Ordnance Department of the U.S. Army, and from 1919 until his retirement in 1952 he was a Professor in the University of Wisconsin, with the duties of Chairman of the Department of Chemistry and Director of the Course in Chemistry. Besides being a Past-President of the Madison Rotary Club, the Madison Professional Men's Club, and of the Madison University Club, he is also a founder of the professional chemical fraternity Alpha Chi Sigma, a Fellow of the A.A.A.S., and a long time member of the American Chemical Society as well as the organizer of the first Annual Colloid Symposium.

Dr. Mathews is the possessor of a superbly equipped laboratory devoted to firearms identification work containing many instruments designed by him and employing techniques which he developed or discovered in nearly 40 years of work in this field. Several of his cases have attracted international as well as national attention, and his work has been highly commended by the Chief Justice of the Supreme Court of Wisconsin in a Supreme Court decision, by the Wisconsin Bar Association, and by international experts. He has lectured widely on scientific criminal identification and has given a course of lectures on this subject each year for 15 years at the University of Wisconsin. Since his "retirement" on July 1, 1952, he has been putting in full time working at his hobby of improving the methods of criminal identification by scientific methods.

Early in his work along this line, he found that the data on the characteristics of various makes of hand firearms were unsatisfactory in quantity, woefully incomplete in many instances, incorrect in others, and not only inadequate but scattered and hard to refer to.

In an attempt to remedy this condition and obtain some of the data which he urgently needed in his own investigations, he began to collect and tabulate such information as width of lands, width and number of grooves of rifling, twist of rifling, diameter of bore and grooves, and various other important dimensions which the criminal investigator would be likely to need to know.

The task turned out to be colossal, for he soon found that many makers of pistols and revolvers had no fixed specifications for these things, and that the dimensions varied from gun to gun and from year to year. Others had specifications which might or might not be adhered to. In other words, he found that rather than to depend on published tabulations he had to obtain actual samples of every pistol and revolver available, make his own measurements, and construct his own tabulations.

This monumental task proved to be most difficult of accomplishment, involving as it did the collecting of information from all over the world and then the checking and verifying of this information by actual measurements made on sample guns which were often extremely difficult to obtain. The instruments used are described in detail in this book.

During the course of this part of the work, Dr. Mathews managed to obtain the loan of over 2100 different pistols or revolvers originating in 23 countries. His new book gives the rifling data taken by him in his own laboratory for all these guns, plus photographs of both sides of over 1100 different guns taken by him and some 900 gun photos from other sources. He has also included well over 100 photographs of rim fire firing pin impressions.

Besides all this tabular and illustrative matter, the book contains a meticulously complete text on the techniques and instrumentation of criminal firearms identification, all of which is copiously illustrated.

This treatise should also be of great interest and value to gun collectors, present and future. The number of photographs of hand guns far exceeds that to be found in any book heretofore published and many arms are shown here for the first time in any book of reference. Supplementing these numerous and unusual photographs, the section entitled "Miscellaneous Notes on Automatic Pistols," containing a large amount of hitherto unpublished information, will be of particular interest to collectors of such arms.

The publication of this splendid reference work will be an event of the utmost importance in the field of firearms identification.

Julian S. Hatcher, Maj. Gen., U. S. Army, Retired
Technical Editor, *The American Rifleman*
Washington, D. C.   April 21, 1960

Acknowledgment

To give credit to all the individuals and organizations that have been of assistance in furnishing information, firearms, and counsel during the several years in which material for this publication has been accumulating would be quite impossible.

The data resulting from measurements and photographs of firearms (both made by me) could not have been obtained without the cooperation of a great many persons too numerous to mention individually. Such a list would include literally scores of my former students as well as many other friends who learned of my work. Special mention, however, should be made of some, including the following: General Julian S. Hatcher, Technical Editor of The American Rifleman, who made available his own private collection and that of the National Rifle Association; Clark E. Kauffman, a private collector of Leesburg, Florida, who furnished well over three hundred specimens; Col. G. B. Jarrett of the Ordnance Corps at Aberdeen, who, with the permission of the Chief of Ordnance, sent me every item requested from the Aberdeen Museum; B. D. Munhall and the H. P. White Laboratory of Bel Air, Md., who also sent me every specimen asked for from their extensive collection; Dr. W. C. McKern, Director, and Eldon G. Wolff, Curator, of the Milwaukee Public Museum who made available all items desired from the famous Nunnemacher Collection; the Wisconsin State Historical Society Museum, which contains the Rosebush Collection of firearms; Sidney Aberman, a private collector in Pittsburgh; Sam Smith, a private collector of Markesan, Wis.; H. C. Harrison, Assistant Director of the Laboratories for Scientific Criminal Investigation of the University of Rhode Island; the Police Departments of Milwaukee, Madison, and La Crosse in Wisconsin, and those of Cincinnati, Minneapolis, and St. Paul; the Laboratory of Criminal Investigation, U.S. Army, Fort Gordon, Ga.; and the Pittsburgh and Allegheny County Crime Laboratory. I am especially indebted to the Wisconsin State Crime Laboratory, as all guns acquired by this laboratory are made available to me. Charles W. Wilson, Superintendent, Joseph C. Wilimovsky, Jr., Associate Superintendent, and Allan Wilimovsky, Firearms Examiner, have all been most coöperative.

I also wish to express appreciation for the assistance given me by Jack Krcma, Firearms Examiner in the Attorney General's Laboratory for the Province of Ontario, Toronto, Canada. Through him certain valuable material and a number of photographs have been made available. His assistance with the Czech guns has been particularly helpful.

For much of the technical and historical material in Part III I am particularly indebted to Donald Bady of Forest Hills, N. Y., a well-known authority on firearms, whose assistance has been invaluable. I am also deeply indebted to Burt D. Munhall and the H. P. White Laboratory, and to Joseph C. Wilimovsky, Jr., for valuable historical information.

Mention should be made of the coöperation of many manufacturers and dealers, too numerous to mention individually, who have furnished catalogs, circulars, and information by correspondence. Firms such as Webley and Scott, Ltd., Smith and Wesson, the Bausch and Lomb Optical Co., and the American Optical Co. deserve special mention for the excellent photographs they have furnished, as does also A. W. Sijthoff of Leiden for permission to use several illustrations taken from Kersten's *Munitie en Wapens*. Acknowledgment is also made to Verlag J. Neumann-Neudamm, Melsungen, Germany, for illustrations taken from Bock's *Moderne Faustfeuerwaffen*.

Valuable information concerning arms formerly made in Spain was furnished by the Banco Oficiel de Pruebas de Armas de Fuego, in Eibar, and by the late José Maria Fernandez Ladreda, Director General de Industria y Material, of the Ministerio del Ejército, in Madrid, and by his successor, Joaquin Gomez-Pantoja.

J. H. M.

Contents

Volume I of Three Volumes

Introduction

Firearms identifications are of interest to those engaged in law enforcement and to gun collectors, but from quite different points of view. The law enforcement officer is chiefly concerned with bringing to justice persons who have committed crimes, while the collector is interested in guns because of a fascination that only a gun collector can fully understand. Both need to know all that they can learn about firearms and it is hoped that the material here presented will be useful to both groups. The work makes no pretense of being a complete treatise on firearms investigations or a manual of identification procedures, nor does it pretend to be complete as to measurements and photographs that might have been made. It does attempt to set forth the principles of firearms identification from the standpoint of the markings which may be found on fired bullets and shells. Large areas of the general subject were intentionally omitted. In addition to the very considerable amount of material presented here, the author knows of many hand guns of which he could not obtain specimens, and no doubt there are many makes and models of guns of which he has never heard. It is believed, however, that the types likely to be encountered are fairly well covered.

The justification for the publication of this work, if one is needed, is that it contains much material that is unavailable elsewhere and it presents a more nearly complete account of rifling characteristics *as they actually exist* than has ever before been compiled. The data here presented represent actual performance rather than manufacturers' specifications. The book also represents, to a certain extent at least, the fulfillment of a desire to pass on to others some of the basic information accumulated over a considerable number of years, in the hope that they will find it useful.

For over thirty years the author has devoted considerable time to the making of firearms identifications and to other applications of scientific methods of crime investigations for the law enforcement agencies of the State of Wisconsin. As his position was that of Professor of Chemistry and Director of the Course in Chemistry at the State University this work constituted an "extracurricular" activity, but one which seemed important because no one else in his state was doing it, it needed to be done, and the law enforcement agencies, from the police officer on the beat to the State Supreme Court, appreciated the service. This activity arose from the fact that the state, at that time, had made no provision for scientific investigations of crimes other than the employment of a State Toxicologist (for a few years), and there were urgent demands for such work.

The author's work along these lines began in 1923 when he assisted in the solution of the Magnuson bomb case, in which metallographic evidence was used for the first time in a murder case. Soon thereafter he was importuned to study the evidence in a homicide involving the use of a rifle. At this time Calvin Goddard was the only man in the country really qualified to make such investigations on a truly scientific basis, but the local authorities felt that they could not afford to pay his fees—particularly, it is presumed, if they could get a professor from the state university to do it for next to nothing! The work was undertaken, with no other equipment than that to be found in a well-equipped laboratory of physical chemistry (cameras, microscopes, measuring devices, etc.), and it resulted in securing a confession of the murder during the course of the trial. The publicity resulting from these two cases brought others and it was soon realized that special equipment must be purchased and built to handle cases properly.

As the comparison microscope had just been introduced by Goddard for work in the firearms field, for which (unfortunately, as he and others later agreed) he coined the name "forensic ballistics," an attempt was made through him to acquire one of these instruments, but one of his associates (Waite) objected to his giving out any information. An appeal to the Bausch and Lomb Optical Company, however, brought results and the author's laboratory soon received the first instrument that they made for firearms identifications. As time went on, more and more equipment was added until a fairly well-equipped laboratory, containing some instruments that were unique, was available.

It was realized very early, however, that the state should have a State Crime Laboratory, well equipped and adequately staffed, to handle the many types of work that come up in criminal cases and a recommendation to this effect was made to the Wisconsin State Bar Association at their annual meeting in 1925. A resolution was adopted unanimously directing that a bill be introduced in the next session of the Legislature calling for the establishment of a State Crime Laboratory. The bill was introduced, but because of inadequate support it did not receive favorable action. This process was repeated at each session of the Legislature until favorable action was taken, and in 1947 the laboratory became an actuality with Charles M. Wilson, formerly an associate of Goddard at the Northwestern University Crime Laboratory and later Director of the Chicago Police Laboratory, as Superintendent. Since the establishment of this laboratory the author has done little work in the way of investigations but has had an opportunity, especially since his official retirement from his professorship at the university in 1952, to devote himself to research in the field of firearms investigations.

Much has been said and written about the identification of the type, make, and model of a firearm from "class characteristics," which involves a knowledge of the rifling specifications (and practices) used by different manufacturers, and of special features of construction which affect the markings to be found on fired shells. Because of differences of opinion and because of the unavailability of exact data concerning rifling characteristics as they actually exist, it seemed to the author that someone should make a comprehensive set of measurements on hand arms, covering all of the many makes, types, and models as far as the availability of specimens permitted. This was found to be quite an undertaking because many of the guns made in the last 75 or 100 years are still in existence and still usable and because many hundreds of thousands of cheap foreign-made guns were imported into this country, particularly after World War I. Therefore, no pretense of completeness is made. No measurements were made on rifles, which would have been desirable, although they are not as frequently used in the commission of crimes. But this would have extended the study by several years.

To start the work, methods for making the desired measurements were developed and the necessary equipment was either purchased or constructed. Three things soon became apparent: (a) many manufacturers who have exact specifications do not follow them closely, (b) many manufacturers apparently had no specifications, and (c) the author had a big job on his hands! As the work proceeded it was realized that here was a golden opportunity to secure photographs and information on guns that would be useful to collectors as well as to firearms examiners, so from that point on photographs were made of all the different makes and models that came to the laboratory for measurement. Unfortunately this procedure was not used right from the start and some interesting guns were returned to their owners without being photographed.

The determination of the names of the actual manufacturers of many foreign guns has been a task of great difficulty, and in a number of cases it has been impossible. Often a foreign-made gun may carry only the name of a dealer or his trade mark, and sometimes it may bear no marking whatever. To complicate things further, different manufacturers have used the same name for guns that are quite unlike in construction as well as for some that appear to be copies of each other or of some other well-known firearm. Many of these guns, particularly those made in Belgium and Spain, were made in little shops, perhaps in the workmen's homes, and were sold to dealers who put their names on them. For example, a number of Spanish automatics have been encountered which bear the inscription on the slide: FABRIQUE D'ARMES DE GUERRE DE GRANDE PRECISION— EIBAR, SPAIN. As a matter of fact, no manufacturing company of that name ever existed. This was exclusively an exporting company and not a manufacturer. Many other cases might be cited for guns made in Spain and in Germany. Of course this practice is not limited to Europe. It is a common practice in this country and has been for a hundred years or more. Scores of examples might be cited not only of guns bearing names that give no clue as to their maker, but also of guns bearing names of "manufacturers" that never existed. Some Spanish manufacturers not only made guns but also sold guns made by others, and it is difficult to ascertain which guns they actually manufactured. It is clear that Garate, Anitua y Cia. in Eibar was one of these as they certainly did not make all the guns that bear their trade mark. In Belgium the same practice was followed. L. Ancion Marx is a good example of a firm (and there were many others) who not only made some revolvers but who marketed a good many that they did not make. These were made, wholly or sometimes in part, in little shops and even in private homes in the city of Liége and in the surrounding country, particularly the upland of Herve, northeast of Liége. In the early part of the century this part of Belgium was a "beehive of activity" for firearms manufacture.

Now practically all of this industry is gone. During World Wars I and II the Germans destroyed all of the firearms industry in Belgium that they did not need for their own use, and Franco wiped out the industry in Spain when he came into power and decreed that there should be only three manufacturers of automatic pistols and only one of revolvers. (Fortunately, he made good choices as to who should be allowed to make firearms.*) Thus the manufacture of revolvers in these countries has virtually ceased, but many hundreds of thousands of guns made earlier are probably still in existence. And as long as they exist, and they are rather "nonperishable," they will be a problem to firearms examiners, though perhaps a joy to collectors.

It might be thought that reliable information as to the names of firearms manufacturers could be obtained from the Government Proof Houses, but this is not the case because, in the course of war and revolution, their records have been destroyed. So they are of little help. The amount of reliable information from Government Ministries is also quite limited, perhaps for the same reason and because of changing personnel. Some of the manufacturers who are still in existence have been very helpful, but they too are

often unable to give specific information that is desired concerning products made long ago. The Spanish and Belgian patents have been of some assistance, but they do not give much information as to the actual manufacturers.

The word "patent" as it relates to Spanish firearms is likely to be confusing. Unpatented arms may be marked "patent" or "patented." Where a patent number does appear it may refer to the general design of the arm, or to some design feature or to the trade mark or trade name. The legitimate design patents are usually prefaced by "Co." (for Concedido) and during the period 1915 to 1922, when there was a virtual epidemic of new Spanish pistols, these patent numbers ranged from 60,000 to 71,000. Trade mark patents usually bear the prefix "Mar." (for Marca) and in the same period they ran from 30,000 to 40,000. But these designating prefixes do not appear on the firearms, only in the patent literature. There is still another type of number that was applied to design models, roughly equivalent to the German D.R.G.M. (Deutsche Reich Gebrauch Muster). These do not seem to have a pattern and all of them center in the range 2,000 to 4,000 for the period 1915 to 1922. Some of these apply to pistols.

As pointed out, the number appearing on a Spanish firearm may relate to one of several kinds of patents, and only a search of the Spanish patents will reveal which it is. Some examples are the following:

1. The number 39,391 is a patent number appearing on the slide of all Colonial pistols examined. A study of Spanish patents reveals that Pat. Mar. 39.391 was issued in November 1920 to Etxezarraga Abaitua y Cia. of Eibar.

2. The patent number appearing on the slides of some specimens of the Libia is 69.094. This turns out to be Pat. Co. 69.094, issued to Beistegui Hermanos of Eibar on Feb. 19, 1919, and is a design patent covering automatic pistols without respect to any trade name. A later patent, not appearing on the pistol, is Mar. 36.386, issued to Beistegui Hermanos on Oct. 1, 1919, and covers the trade name Libia for use on automatic pistols and revolvers.

3. The JO-LO-AR bears the numbers 68027 and 70235. Both turn out to be design patents. Pat. Co. 68.027 was issued to D. Toribio Arrizabalaga y Ibarzabal on Jan. 8, 1919. Pat. Co. 70.235 was issued to D. José de L. Arnaiz on September 12, 1919. According to the Eibar Proof House, and other sources, the pistol was actually produced by Hijos de Calixto Arrizabalaga in Eibar. The 6.35 mm. SHARP SHOOTER (some are marked SHARP SOOTER), made by the same firm, bears the patent number 68,027. This pistol bears a close resemblance to the JO-LO-AR. It is

*Bonifacio Echeverria, S.A., in Eibar, pistols only (Star); Unceta y Cia., in Guernica, pistols only (Astra); and Gabilondo y Cia., in Elgoibar, pistols (Llama) and revolvers (Ruby). In 1958 Astra-Unceta y Cia. announced the manufacture of a .22 caliber revolver, the Cadix, so the original edict of Franco must have been modified. The company states that they will "make them in larger bores sometime in the future."

probable (but not confirmed) that the name JO-LO-AR was derived from the name of D. José de L. Arnaiz, to whom the second patent (No. 70,235) was issued.

Trade marks are often very helpful in identifying guns. But here again we have the same problem, i.e., Is a particular trade mark on a gun that of a dealer or that of a manufacturer, or perhaps of both? Garate, Anitua y Cia., already mentioned, is a good example. Although they made guns, their trade mark is found on guns that they definitely did not make. In spite of these uncertainties we believe that trade marks and other identification marks do have some value and we have taken the opportunities presented to accumulate a large number of them and to reproduce them here. There are some which we have not been able to identify, but perhaps someone else may be able to. No doubt we have identified some dealers' marks as those of manufacturers, and vice versa.

Despite these and other difficulties, considerable information has been accumulated, enough to warrant publication, we believe. Certainly there are many omissions, due to lack of information, and no doubt there are errors. In a number of cases our sources of information disagree.

Since quite a number of makes and many models of hand guns have not been available for measurement and photographing, there are important gaps in our information. To fill these gaps, in part at least, a collection of photographs from other sources has been made and many of these photographs are here reproduced. While it cannot be expected that all of the makes and models of hand guns that have been made in the past century can be photographed and published in a single volume, it is hoped that the information presented here is sufficient to be useful to both law enforcement agencies and collectors. It will be noted that very few of the revolvers made in the U.S. in the last quarter century are shown. This omission was deliberate because these firearms are so well known, or the information is so easily obtainable elsewhere.

Part IV of Volume II contains the photographs taken by the author. Chapter 1, Volume II, is devoted to automatic pistols and Chapter 2, Volume II, to revolvers and nonautomatic pistols. These are, in each case, arranged by caliber and alphabetized according to name and model of the arm. The name and location of the manufacturer (or source) are also given, where known. Serial numbers are also given as they help to date an arm or model. Both sides of each arm are shown, together with a scale.

Part V of Volume II consists of reproductions of photographs and illustrations of hand guns, most of which have been unavailable to the author, and are arranged alphabetically. These were obtained from various sources: donated or purchased photographs, loaned photographs or negatives, catalog and circular illustrations issued by manufacturers, etc.

The work of measuring and photographing hand guns is continuing and considerable new material has accumulated since this book went to press. Of necessity it has been omitted.

PART I

Laboratory identification
of a firearm

Principles involved

While there are many questions that come up in firearms investigations, the two that come up most frequently are: (1) What kind of a gun was used, and (2) was this particular gun used? Both of these questions involve a study of the markings which are left on the fired bullet or cartridge, or both. On each there will be two types of markings: *repetitive* and *accidental*. The accidental markings may have some relation to the investigation (instances of which will be mentioned later) but are of no value in identifying a particular weapon or make and model, since they are not formed regularly in the operation of the gun. Repetitive marks, on the other hand, are very useful because they show identity of performance. Experience has shown that no two firearms, even those of the same make and model and made consecutively by the same tools, will produce the same markings on a bullet or a cartridge. There will, of course, be a "family resemblance"—e.g., the bullets will have (approximately) the same diameter, same number and widths of grooves, same pitch and direction of slant of rifling marks. Technically expressed, the guns have the same "rifling characteristics," but, while the markings may be sufficiently alike to characterize the make (and even model) of the gun, they are not sufficiently alike as to be considered "identical" and are not likely to confuse an expert. These "Class Characteristics" have now been measured for a very large number of guns and the results are set forth later.

On the other hand, bullets fired through the *same* rifled barrel and cartridge cases (usually called shells) fired in the *same* gun may be expected to show an "identity"* of markings which is peculiar to this particular firearm and to no other.

These markings serve then to identify a particular rifled barrel because that barrel has an individuality possessed by no other barrel. In 1926 at Springfield Arsenal a very interesting and conclusive experiment was made. Four barrels were rifled one after the other with the same rifling tools in an attempt to produce barrels as alike as possible. Bullets were fired through each barrel and compared. It was found that no two barrels matched completely; each had a distinct and separate individuality. Some time later Goddard fired 500 rounds through a machine gun and found that even bullet No. 500 could be matched with bullet No. 1, indicating that the individuality of a barrel persists. The results of these two early experiments have been confirmed over and over again in identification practice and are now generally accepted. Similarly, the markings produced on the head of a fired cartridge (shell) often can give valuable information as to the type and make of gun used and often can identify the particular gun when located.

Rifling methods

Modern rifles, revolvers, and pistols have barrels

---

*The words identity and identical as used in firearms investigations do not mean that the markings on two bullets two objects are ever identical in the absolute sense. Just as no or on two shells are absolutely alike in every particular. No two persons are alike, no two objects made by man or by nature are absolutely alike. So the term "identity" is a relative one.

which are "rifled," i.e., they have spiral grooves in the inner surface, the purpose of which is to cause the bullet to acquire a rapid spin on its longitudinal axis, the gyroscopic effect of which keeps the bullet from "yawing" or "tumbling" in flight. This method of improving the accuracy of the flight of a bullet has been used for hundreds of years and no one knows just when the principle was first discovered. These grooves in the bore of the barrel and the lands (ridges) between them constitute the rifling. In present-day hand guns the pitch (or twist, as it is called) of the rifling is uniform from one end of the barrel to the other. Many years ago certain manufacturers used a "gain twist" in which the angle of twist increased from breech to muzzle. This will be discussed in a later section.

While the method whereby the grooves were first produced seems not to be definitely known, it can be said that until fairly recently there have been two methods in general use for producing rifling. These methods are the "scrape cutter" method and the "hook cutter" method. Most of the weapons the firearms examiner will encounter have been rifled by one of these two methods, and mostly by the second. However, this situation will change as many firearms now being made are being rifled by newer methods which have the advantage of being more rapid.

Fig. 1. Section of a "scrape" cutter. For rifling barrels with an even number of grooves, two (opposite) scrapers were used.

A typical scraping device is shown in Figure 1. It consists of a rod, slightly smaller than the bore of the gun, into which is set either one or two curved, hardened steel scrapers the height of which can be adjusted between successive passages through the barrel. If an odd number of grooves is to be cut, a single scraper is used. If an even number, two scrapers placed opposite each other may be used. Of course an even number can be cut with a single scraper, one at a time. The operation is a very slow one, particularly if five or six grooves are to be formed by a single cutter. Some of the finest rifling ever done has been done by the scrape-cutter method.

In European practice there seems to have been more variation in the application of the scrape-cutter method. It seems that the following variations of

rifling head construction have been used: (1) Two single curved cutting blades, each of which is an integral part of the surface of a plate that fits closely into slots that are placed opposite each other in the rifling head, so that two grooves are cut simultaneously. (2) Four cutting blades, two on each plate set "tandem" to each other so that the second cutter follows in the groove made by the first one, thus deepening the groove, the plates being set into slots opposite each other in the rifling head. Thus two opposite grooves are cut simultaneously but deeper than in (1). There is evidence that in some cases three cutters were set in tandem (in each of the two oppositely placed plates) so as to increase still more the speed of the rifling operation. (3) Two cutters

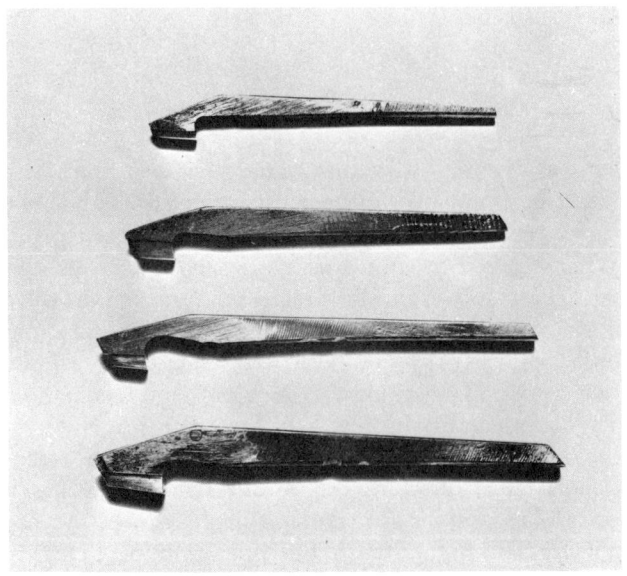

Fig. 2. Four "hooks" used in the hook cutter method of rifling a barrel.

The cutting edge of the hook, which has been filed to exact dimensions, projects through a slot in a rod whose diameter is slightly less than that of the bore to be rifled. The height to which the cutting edge protrudes is adjusted by a screw at the end of the rod.

The rod is pulled through the bore and on each pass a very small amount of metal is removed. Each groove is started with the same adjustment of the cutter. After all have been started the cutting edge is set up a bit and the process repeated on all grooves. This is done again and again until all the grooves are cut to the proper depth. This may take as many as 80 passes for each groove in the rifling of a first-class gun.

Since the hooks wear away during the cutting operation they have to be replaced frequently to keep within the tolerances that have been set in the specifications. Some manufacturers pay little attention to their "specifications," however.

The hooks shown are for .25, .32, .38, and .45 calibers.

on each of two plates set opposite to each other, but instead of being set in tandem they are set apart (with respect to the longitudinal axis of the rifling tool) a distance equal to the desired width of the land. Thus, when this assembly is pulled through the barrel four equally spaced grooves are cut simultaneously. (4) Three cutters arranged symmetrically in the rifling head so as to cut three equally spaced grooves simultaneously. To get the second set of three grooves the barrel or the rifling head is indexed into the proper position so that the completed job will have six equally spaced grooves.

In each of the above procedures a wedge-shaped rod (or shim) is pushed in a bit automatically at each rifling stroke so that for each passage the cutters are raised the desired amount, the process being repeated until the desired depth of groove is attained. The cutting edges in each case above are formed by milling away the steel of the plate so as to leave the curved cutter with the desired shape, height, and angle.

In the "hook cutter" method, a cutter with the general shape of a crochet hook (Fig. 2) is set into a recess or slot in a rod (Fig. 3) which is a bit smaller than the bore of the barrel. The height of the cutting edge of the "hook" can be adjusted by turning an adjusting screw at the end of the rod. On each pass through the barrel a fraction of a thousandth of an inch of steel is removed, and as the

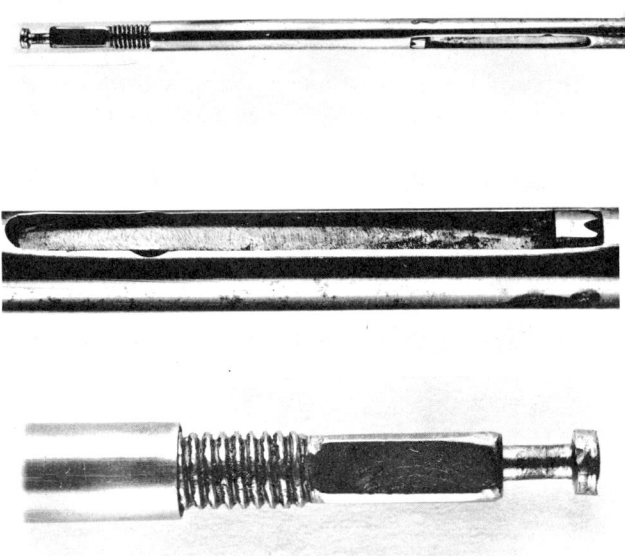

Fig. 3. The hook cutter. *Top:* Section of cutter for .22 caliber. *Middle:* Enlarged view of hook section. *Bottom:* Enlarged view of adjusting screw.

barrel is given a steady rotation at a predetermined rate a very shallow spiral groove is formed, having the width of the cutting edge. The barrel is then positioned so as to cut a second shallow groove parallel to the first one, and this process is repeated until all of the grooves have been started. Since they are not yet of the desired depth the cutting edge of the "hook" is now raised a bit and each groove is cut a bit deeper. The process is repeated again and again until all the grooves have been cut to the desired depth—amounting to a few thousandths of an inch. In the cheaper guns only 20 or so passes are used for making each groove, whereas on a finely made firearm as many as 80 or more might be used. Here again the process is exacting and time consuming, and for these reasons newer methods of rifling are coming into general use. In theory each groove is cut to very exact dimensions. All lands are supposed to be equal in width and all grooves are supposed to be of equal width and depth, but actually this perfection is never obtained and some manufacturers pay little attention to specifications.

Whether a scrape cutter or a hook cutter is used, a microscopic examination with sufficient magnification of the cutting edge would reveal the fact that the edge is not truly smooth. It would have nicks in it, just as the blade of a dull knife has them, the only difference being that they are smaller. No matter how much care is used in the honing operation nicks will still be present and they result in serrations or ridges being formed in the bottom of the groove made by the cutter.

It must be remembered, also, that the steel used in barrels is not absolutely homogeneous and there will be some areas of the surface which are harder than others. The cutter will not act the same on these areas with different hardnesses and this will result in inequalities in the surface. Also, tiny chips of metal from the cutting operation may produce inequalities in the action of the cutter. No matter how these inequalities are produced, unless they are removed they will tend to make repetitive marks on bullets because the bullets are of softer material. Various methods are used to remove these inequalities.

Some manufacturers perform a "lapping" operation after all the grooves have been cut. A lead plug is cast on the end of a rod placed in the barrel. This, of course, insures a good fit. Then, with a mixture of oil and fine emery powder as a lubricant and polishing agent, the plug is pushed back and forth through the barrel. Finally a mirror-like surface is produced and most of the inequalities in the surface, produced in the boring, reaming, and rifling processes, are

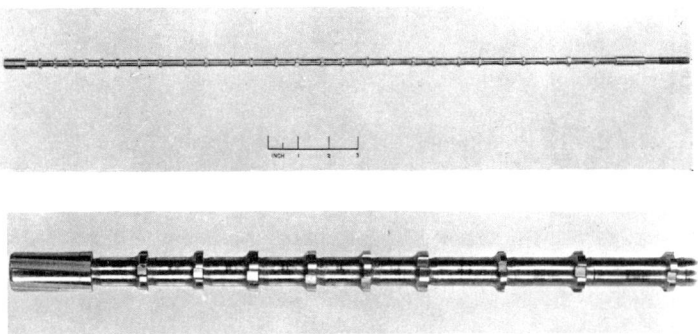

Fig. 4. Broach for cutting rifling. Upper view shows the entire tool, about 23″ in length, with 27 cutters. The lower view shows a section enlarged.

removed. A new, lapped barrel will leave fewer and smaller markings on a bullet fired through it than will an unlapped one, but marks will still be present and identification will normally be possible.

Next to be mentioned is the broaching process which is now used by several American firearms manufacturers and some in Europe as well. As somewhat of an oversimplification, a broach may be thought of as a rod upon which there are 25 to 30 hardened steel rings, each one being slightly greater in diameter than the preceding one and having slots of the proper size cut into it at equal intervals, thus forming a series (or "gang") of cutters, each of which has the same number of lands and grooves. (Figs. 4, 5) The lands on the cutters produce grooves in the

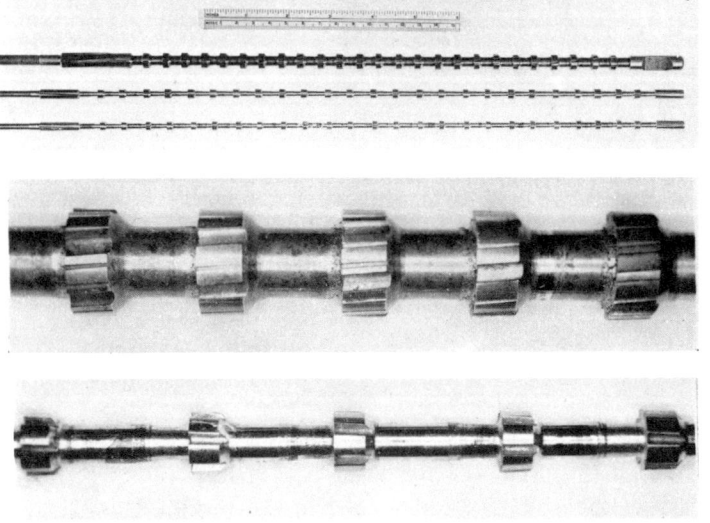

Fig. 5. Broaches for cutting rifling. Top views show three entire broaches: A .38 cal. Colt broach and two H & R broaches, all 16 inches long and having 25 cutters.
Enlarged views of short sections of the Colt broach and one of the H & R broaches are shown in the lower part of the figure.

barrel and all grooves are cut to the desired depth during a single passage of the series or gang of cutters through the barrel. Each successive cutter must be perfectly aligned so that its lands will follow the grooves made by the preceding (smaller) cutter. This is a simplified description of the process but will serve to illustrate the principle.

The broaches require much skill in their preparation but each broach is capable of rifling a large number of barrels and the operation time has been reduced to such an extent that one machine can rifle several hundred barrels in a working day. Also, many more can be rifled with a broach than with a single scrape cutter or hook cutter because the broach has many more cutting edges and the wear on each edge is consequently less than that on a single cutter.

It might be thought that since many barrels are rifled with the same broach, all the barrels would have lands and grooves which are exactly alike and that it would be impossible for the firearms examiner to distinguish between bullets fired from them. This, however, is not the case. Each rifled barrel still possesses an individuality which is expressed in the markings made on bullets fired through it. This is due in considerable part to the fact that there is one thing in common in all three of the methods of rifling so far discussed. In all cases the preparation of the bore of the barrel to be rifled is essentially the same. A hole of suitable diameter is bored from end to end through the piece of stock that is to become the barrel. Since the surface so produced is too rough it has to be reamed in order to smooth it sufficiently. In this process of reaming, the movement is transverse to the axis of the barrel and if a cross section of the barrel is examined microscopically at this point a multitude of small lines (scorings) running crosswise of the bore will be observed. In the succeeding rifling operation a portion only of these transverse lines will be removed, i.e., in the areas where the grooves are cut. They will still be present on the lands. If a cross section of a rifled barrel is examined (Fig. 6) it will be seen that there are two sets of lines or tiny scratches, those on the lands running transversely and another set at the bottom of the grooves running longitudinally. There will frequently be defects in the surface of the lands in the barrel due to scoring by chips produced in the broaching operation, and it appears that the broach has a tendency to "ride the lands" and produce changes thereon. Any inequality in the surface of the barrel with which the bullet comes in contact may produce a scratch or serration on a bullet fired through it, and since the greater pressure against the bullet is produced by the lands on the barrel the most

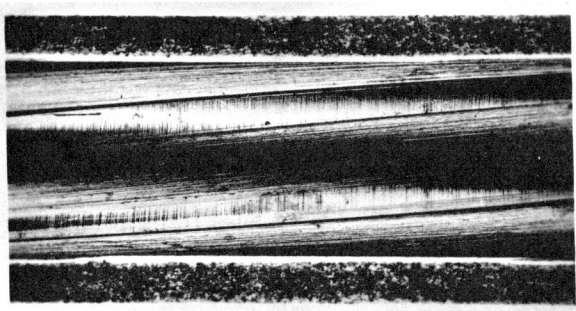

Fig. 6. Section of barrel rifled with a "hook" cutter. Longitudinal marks due to rifling tool. Transverse marks due to drill.

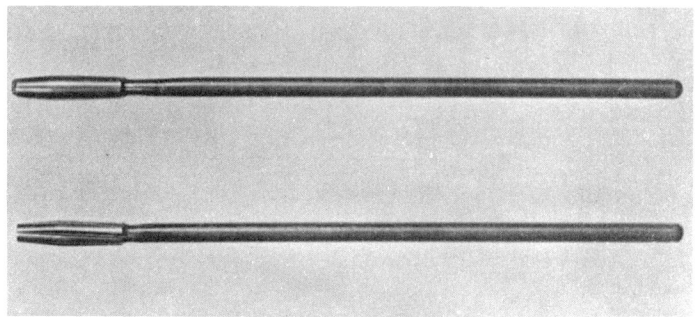

Fig. 7. Rifling buttons. *Upper:* Bore button swage. *Lower:* Groove button swage.

prominent markings are likely to be found at the bottom of the grooves on the bullet. However, if the bullet fits quite tightly longitudinal striations will be found on the lands of the bullet also, caused by the scraping of the bullet along the bottom of the grooves of the rifling. In many of the more cheaply made guns, particularly those made in the 1910–1935 period in Spain and Belgium, the reaming operation apparently was omitted, or was so poorly done that it might just as well have been omitted. Many of the cheaply made American guns also belong in this category. Since at one time an American revolver could be purchased for $1.50 one could not expect much! Unfortunately many of these are still in circulation.

Another system for rifling barrels is fast coming into favor and some believe that it may eventually replace completely the broaching process as it should produce a barrel in which the rifling will have a longer life since it causes a hardening of the surface which comes into contact with the bullet. The process seems to have been used first in Germany but has been the subject of considerable experimentation in the U.S. and is in use by at least two manufacturers. It is also being used in other countries.

This process is known as the swaging method. When a plug of extreme hardness (called a "button") is forced through a barrel the bore of which is slightly smaller than the button, the metal of the barrel flows slightly under this very high pressure and the bore is slightly increased (Fig. 7). Because of the elasticity of the metal of the barrel the bore will not be quite as great in diameter as the button itself, but it will be greater than it was before the swaging operation. If the button has a very smooth surface and is very hard, the newly produced bore will be very smooth, of very uniform diameter, and it will have a harder surface because of the increased density of the metal produced by the compression it

has undergone. This is said to be superior to the reaming operation, particularly as the latter is usually performed. The grooves are formed in a similar operation, but with a torpedo-shaped button made of tungsten carbide, or other similar material of extreme hardness, which is provided with lands and grooves that are the negative of those to be produced in the barrel. As this passes through the barrel it causes a further compressing of the steel as well as producing rifling grooves. If both button reaming and button rifling procedures are used all of the interior surfaces of the barrel will be hardened and all will be exceptionally smooth. Any striations present, either on the lands or in the grooves, will run longitudinally through the barrel (Figs. 7, 8). Steels which are so hard that they give trouble when other rifling methods are used can be rifled by the swaging method. The making of a suitable button requires great skill because of the extreme hardness of the material and because it must have very precise dimensions to function properly; but once formed the same button may be used for the rifling of thousands of barrels. Because of the extreme hardness of the material, diamond-grinding processes must be used in forming them.

Because of less wear on the cutting edges in the broach and button methods, the lands and grooves in barrels rifled successively by one of these methods will be more alike than those in barrels rifled by the scrape-cutter or hook-cutter method. Indeed, many of the major markings (scorings, striations, etc.—particularly along the edges of the grooves) may be repeated from barrel to barrel, and the widths of the

Fig. 8. Rifling button used for .22 cal. rifles.

7

lands and grooves, though practically never exactly the same in a barrel, will show the same sequence of variations in barrels rifled by the same broach or button. Consequently, the examiner must be on guard, as it is then no longer possible to rely either upon agreeing sequences of land or groove widths or on the recurrence of striations or gouges on the edges of the grooves on a fired bullet. He must resort to closer examinations, often with higher magnifications than formerly necessary. Fortunately for the examiner, barrels rifled by these newer methods (and having nearly identical characteristics) still do have individuality, and as the gun is used (and abused) each barrel will develop more individuality.

Still another method of producing rifling, though it is doubtful whether it will come into general use for firearms of good quality, is also a swaging method, but a quite different one. In this method a tightly fitting mandrel of very hard steel, bearing a negative form of the rifling desired, is pushed into the bore of the barrel after the reaming operation and the barrel is then compressed onto the mandrel under very high pressure so that the steel flows into the grooves in the mandrel, filling them completely, thus forming a set of lands and grooves in the barrel. This method was used to some extent during World War II in the production of the M-3 submachine gun. Hard steel, such as is used in high powered rifles and good grades of hand guns, does not lend itself to this process, and the method has many difficulties.

The removal of the mandrel from the barrel appears to be a tricky job and during its removal the rifling is likely to be damaged somewhat. Here again experience has shown that every barrel produced has an individuality and bullets fired from different barrels can be easily distinguished.

To increase the rate of production of rifled barrels a cold forming process, known as the "hammer" process, was developed in Europe by a Dr. Appel, and this process has been introduced into the United States since World War II. It is being used by Appel Process, Inc., in Detroit, Michigan.

In this method a steel tube is passed over a short mandrel, composed of very hard steel, which bears a negative impression of the rifling desired. As the tube advances on the mandrel, multiple hammers pound the metal of the tube into the grooves of the mandrel. The degree of twist of the rifling so produced is determined by the pitch of the lands and grooves on the mandrel. The perfection of the rifling will depend on the perfection of the mandrel and on how perfectly the grooves in the mandrel are filled.

This is a swaging process but it differs from the one previously described in that the metal is caused

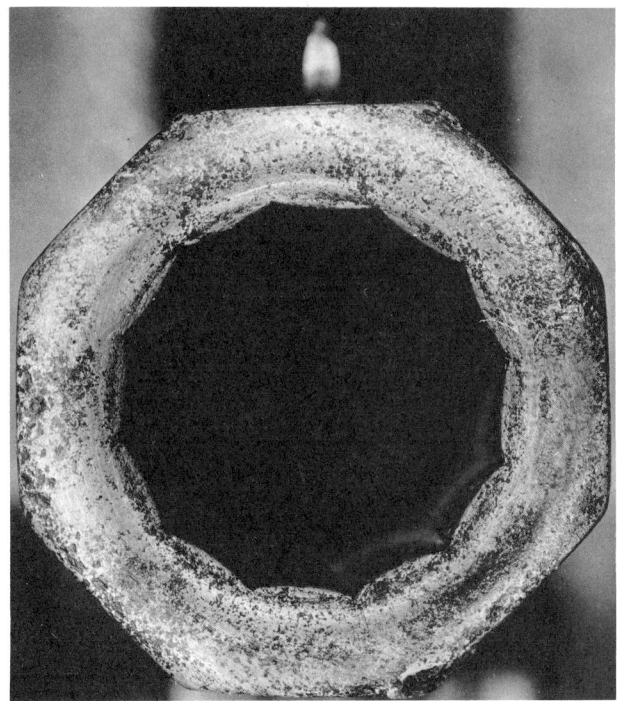

Fig. 9. An unusual type of rifling. 12 rounded lands. Galand revolver.

to flow under the pressure produced by hammers, in an automatic machine, rather than by pressing a tube onto a mandrel by the application of a very high pressure, applied more uniformly. It would appear that the process would have some of the disadvantages experienced in the preceding process, notably the necessity of using a soft, malleable steel which would be quite unsuited for use in any but the cheaper, small-caliber arms. It doubtless has one decided advantage over the preceding process in that the mandrel used is relatively short and the difficulty of removing the long mandrel from the completed rifled tube would be eliminated.

A very curious type of rifling, which has been encountered only in the Galand revolver, is that shown in Fig. 9. How this was produced is not known. The twelve convex lands would not seem to be as effective as the rifling generally used.

Another unusual type of rifling is that which was used in the .22 cal. single-shot Hamilton rifle, which was patented by Clarence J. Hamilton and Coelle Hamilton, U.S. Patent No. 600,725, dated October 30, 1900.

In the completed barrel the bore is a dodecagon, i.e., the rifling consists of twelve chords approximately equal in length, as shown in Fig. 10. Actually the chords vary in length (in one specimen at least) from 0.046 to 0.052 inch, though presumably they

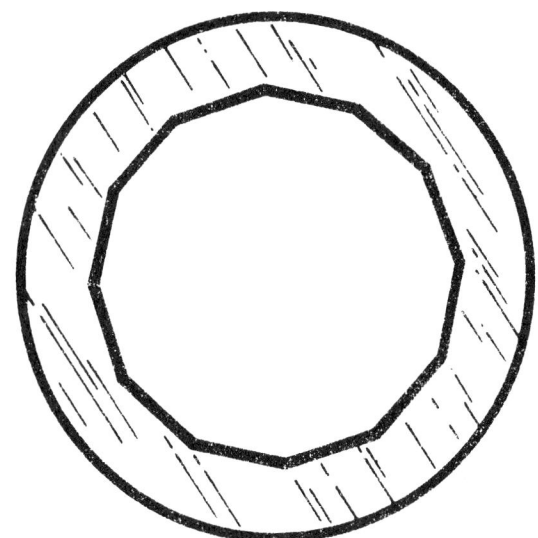

Fig. 10. Unusual type of rifling used in .22 cal. Hamilton rifle, Mod. 15. Bore is a dodecagon in cross section. Rifled sleeve is of bronze.

were intended to be equal. In the usual sense there are no lands and grooves.

This peculiar rifling was produced by slipping a seamless brass tube tightly over a steel mandrel which had the negative profile of the desired shape and subjecting the tube to powerful pressure in a suitable press. This compressed the brass into the desired shape and, according to the patent, "hardens the brass" due to the considerable pressure applied. After the brass tube had been pressed into its new shape a steel tube was sweated on to give added strength. In a variation of procedure, a heavier brass tube was taken and pressed into the desired shape, and no steel tube was used. The first procedure was preferred, however. Barrels longer than the mandrel were produced by taking a longer brass tube and pressing it in sections, being careful to have some overlap so that the bore would be uniform.

The gun was produced from about 1902 to 1908, and apparently in several different models. In Mod. 15 the barrel is but 8 inches in length although the over-all length is 27½ inches, the bolt being actually longer than the barrel. While the gun is only of historical interest, the manner of producing the rifling is of special interest as it seems to have been a forerunner of one of the modern procedures used in rifling gun barrels.

Bullet identifications

Markings on the bullet

When a bullet, either plain lead or jacketed, passes through a rifled barrel under high pressure, the bullet tends to expand and fill the whole cross section of the barrel. The bullet should be of such size that it does this, in order to follow the rifling as it should, to prevent loss of pressure, and to prevent erosion of the inner surfaces of the barrel by escaping gases. The more completely the bullet fills the cross section of the barrel the more distinctive the markings will be and the better the matchings of rifling marks. Inequalities in the steel surfaces of both lands and grooves will then score the bullet as it passes through the barrel under pressure, and it will show useful markings not only in the grooves (made by the lands of the barrel) but also on the lands, where the pressure was less. The ideal case is that in which all grooves and lands on the fired bullet have markings which show an individuality which is repetitive, i.e., will be found on all bullets fired from this barrel, so that every groove and land can be "matched." Needless to say such perfection is rarely met! In some cases the examiner will be lucky, because of mutilation of the bullet, to get one match that is sufficiently convincing to enable him to express a positive opinion. In the case of jacketed bullets the situation where all lands and grooves can be matched is very rarely met because, the greater hardness of the jacketing material prevents the metal from being forced into the grooves sufficiently to fill the whole cross section. Indeed, it frequently happens that the lands of the bullet will show few if any markings of sufficiently repetitive character to enable one to get a matching that carries any conviction.

A good example of bullet markings (at least about as good an example as one can ordinarily hope to get) is shown in Fig. 11.* Such matchings of markings on both grooves and lands is not to be expected in the case of jacketed bullets, and rarely even on lead bullets. From what has been said, however, it must not be inferred that bullet matchings on lead bullets are superior in quality to those to be found on jacketed bullets. As a matter of fact the markings on jacketed bullets (generally in the grooves, however) are usually of better quality than those produced on lead bullets because the jacket is of harder metal.

Because of the greater hardness of the jacket, fine engravings produced in the passage of the bullet through the barrel are less likely to be wiped off. But, if the bullet is too small it may not follow the rifling sufficiently to produce repetitive markings. Obviously if the bullet slips there will be a confusion of markings, as two bullets are not likely to slip in the same manner. (A case in point is one where a man was killed by a .30-30 bullet fired in a .32 cal. rifle. Repetitive marks on test bullets could not be obtained. Fortunately, however, the case was solved by comparison of the markings on the head of the evidence shell with those made on test shells.) If a bullet is only slightly smaller than it should be, it may skid as it enters the rifled part of the bore of an automatic and then settle down and follow the rifling. In such a case the marks may be of the same character as the skid marks found on bullets fired from revolvers. Very frequently a bullet, particularly a jacketed one, while showing good markings in the

*Many other examples of bullet matchings will be shown later.

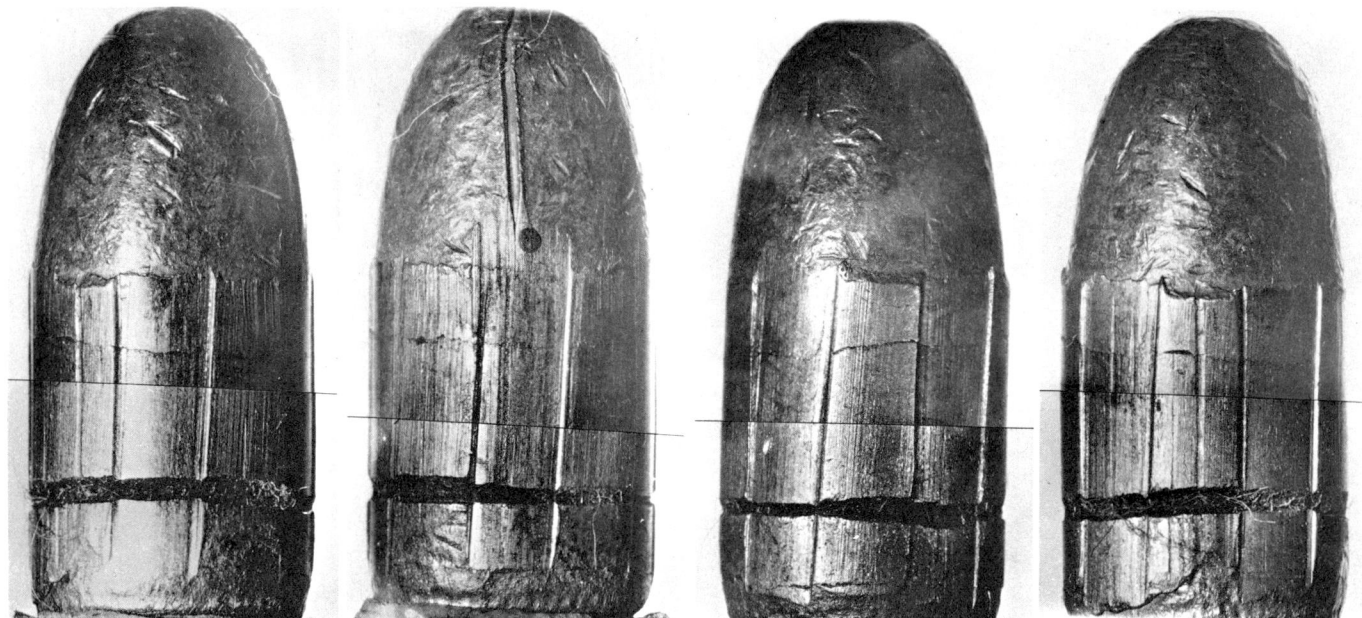

Fig. 11. Comparison camera photos showing four matchings found on a pair of bullets fired from a .38 cal. S & W revolver.

grooves will show little or no marking on the lands because the bullet did not expand sufficiently or was not of proper size in the first place.

In addition to the markings made by the rifling, marks may be made when the bullet strikes the forcing cone (if one is present) and by irregularities that exist at the muzzle. Some foreign-made guns have no chamfering of the rifling or forcing cone and the rifling begins abruptly. The diameter of the bore of the rifled section is less than that just preceding it. The ends of the lands, being sharp (not chamfered), dig into the bullet as it strikes them. In some makes of guns the barrel is constricted at the muzzle, probably caused in the operation of producing the crown. This constriction has an important bearing on the marks that have previously been put on the bullet as it passed through the major portion of the barrel. Previously made markings may be removed and new ones put on. Barrels are frequently found to be "burred" at the muzzle due to accident or some misuse and these burrs may dig into the bullet, producing distinctive marks in the form of longitudinal gouges. When such gouges are found one should examine the muzzle for the presence of burrs.

Frequently the examiner will find a gun that has a bulge in the barrel. These bulges are caused by firing a bullet through a barrel which has an obstruction in it—usually a bullet that has lodged. When a bullet is fired through a bulged barrel it will have two sets of rifling marks which, being out of phase because of failure to follow the rifling through the bulged zone, will be superimposed on each other to some extent and may cause considerable confusion.

When a bullet is fired from a revolver it usually will show slippage or "skid" marks, the grooves being wider at the nose end of the bullet than at the base end. This skidding of the bullet occurs when the bullet strikes the lands of the barrel after acquiring a high velocity during passage from the cartridge to the rifling. Because of the high inertia it has thus acquired, it resists the attempts of the lands to cause it to take a rotational motion; hence, it skids.

Skidding seldom is observed on bullets fired from automatic pistols. It naturally occurs most prominently where the bullet is traveling at a high velocity when it hits the lands. But this does not happen in an automatic, since the bullet, before firing, is practically in contact with the lands. Therefore, it starts into the rifling with comparatively little inertia and follows the lands from the start.

Revolvers which are poorly made or those which are very much worn may have cylinders which are not properly in alignment with the bore of the barrel and in such cases there will be "shaving of lead." An example of this is shown in Fig. 70. This shaving of lead may or may not cause difficulty in identification of a gun. If the performance is repetitive there will be no difficulty, but if it is not repetitive, of course, there will be. If the cylinder is very loose the alignment with the bore of the barrel will be capricious and trouble will be caused. Usually the difficulty is

11

overcome by firing many test bullets instead of the customary three.

Nonrepetitive markings of another type are likely to be encountered and care must be taken that confusion is not caused by their presence. These are tiny scratches, parallel to the axis of the bullet, produced when the bullet is forced out of a shell into which it has been held by the crimping of the mouth of the shell into a cannelure on the bullet, or by points of the shell casing having been peened into the bullet, or even by a simple tight fit of the bullet in the mouth of the shell. These may exist in great number and occasionally some of them may not be removed by the passage of the bullet through the barrel. Since they are so short it may be difficult to determine the fact that they are parallel to the axis of the bullet rather than to the marks made by the rifling and, consequently, they can be mistaken for rifling marks. A bullet which has been forcibly pulled from a shell will, of course, show these marks.

In some of the cheap foreign guns, particularly those made in Spain and Belgium before the Spanish Revolution and World War II, the rifling was very poorly done. Not only were there transverse scrapings on the top of the lands but there were also deep scratches or gouges in the rifling grooves, caused by using cutters which had nicks in their cutting edges. If such gouges are present in a barrel they will produce markings on bullets fired through that barrel. If the nicks in the cutter are rather prominent, several almost identical gouges may be produced in each barrel groove, and a bullet fired through such a barrel might have several very similar markings on *each* land. When this occurs, pseudo or illusory matchings of one bullet against another could be obtained, i.e., one land might be matched with several others on the same bullet, provided *other* differentiating markings were absent. Fortunately each groove and land in a rifled barrel usually does have sufficient individuality to prevent an experienced examiner from going astray.

Short barrels can be, and sometimes are, made by cutting the required length from a longer rifled barrel, and the U.S. 45 once had barrels made in pairs which were then cut apart to form single barrels. In the former case the barrels will have the same class characteristics but each will have an individuality which expresses itself on bullets fired through it. In the case of the U.S. 45 the two barrels will have the same class characteristics, even though they are reversed when completed. Each will have a high individuality because the inequalities produced in the processes will also be reversed in order.

Firing test bullets

In firing test bullets it is good practice to use the same make of ammunition as that submitted as evidence, preferably ammunition taken from the gun itself when confiscated or in possession of the suspect. This will not only help to assure similarity, which often is important because of variations in the same brand as well as in different brands, but it will also meet the objections of opposing counsel who will very likely raise the question as to the similarity of test ammunition. If one does not obtain good matchings when using similar ammunition it is of course permissible to experiment with other makes of ammunition to see whether better matching of markings can be obtained. If they can be so obtained, they are good evidence because they could not be produced by any other gun, no matter what ammunition was used. Bullet markings are influenced not only by the presence of rust, particles of grit or other foreign matter, metal particles torn off bullets previously fired, etc., but also by the material of the bullet and coatings thereon. Bullets made from highly hardened lead will show markings somewhat different from those made from soft lead. Bullets made from zinc or solder would show little evidence of rifling marks. Lubaloy-coated bullets will show markings different from those on plain lead bullets.

Some investigators recommend that reduced powder charges be used to get test bullets, particularly when high powered cartridges are being fired, maintaining that the markings on bullets are not affected by the strength of the charge. Some have even resorted to pushing bullets through a barrel to get test bullets. Others view the matter very differently. Certainly wherever test bullets of suitable quality can be obtained by not reducing the charge the normal ammunition should be used. It is felt that a reduced charge should be used only in those cases where it is absolutely impossible to get a satisfactory test bullet otherwise, and one probably never should resort to pushing bullets through the bore for the purpose of getting a test bullet.

Collecting test bullets

Obviously it is important to collect test bullets in such a manner that additional marks will not be put on them after they leave the muzzle of the barrel. The most common procedure is to fire bullets from low powered guns into clean cotton waste, or into cotton batting. For high powered guns, such as many rifles, a better procedure is to fire them into oiled sawdust. The author uses a wooden box, 8 by 8 inches by 6 feet, set horizontally and open at the top. One end is also open and over this is placed a sheet of thin cardboard or heavy paper, through which the bullet is fired. Vertical sheets of cardboard or paper are placed as partitions across the box at intervals of 14 to 16 inches and the box is filled with sawdust which has been sifted to remove any pieces of wood or other undesirable material and then mixed with lubricating oil. The amount of oil used should be such that when a handful of the sawdust is squeezed tightly oil will exude. After the test bullet is fired, the paper partitions are removed one by one, from the firing end, until an unperforated one is found. The sawdust in the section in front of this is then scooped out and placed on a large (2- × 2-foot) sieve made of ¼-inch-mesh galvanized wire. The bullet is soon found.

A number of examiners use tanks filled with water, some being set horizontally and others vertically. Excellent results are reported. The vertical tank, with a cone-shaped bottom to direct the falling bullet into a wire basket which can be removed from the top of the tank or into a large gate valve at the bottom of the cone which, upon rotation, allows the bullet to fall out with a minimum loss of water, would seem preferable to the horizontal tank. The latter takes up much more floor space, the removal of the fired bullet is not so simple, and the firing must be through a self-sealing membrane of some kind to avoid a considerable loss of water. To prevent the growth of organisms in the water a small amount of bichloride of mercury or a little toluene may be added.

A rather unusual procedure for catching fired bullets is to fire them into a block of ice. Lead bullets of .22 cal. when fired into ice retain even the microscopic markings put on them by the gun and they show no perceptible deformation. The heat and pressure of the bullet cause the ice to melt, and the bullet decelerates without damage to its shape or to its surface markings. (Fig. 12) This is not a practical method for routine work but might be of use in special situations.

Methods of comparison

Before the advent of the comparison microscope in firearms identifications in the 1920's, and for some time thereafter, bullet matchings (and shell-matchings also) were sometimes made by other methods now seldom used. Sometimes a convincing identification of a bullet could be made by measuring in sequence the widths of the grooves on the evidence and test bullets and comparing them. These

measurements were made with a filar micrometer (Fig. 13), an instrument readily obtainable. This is a special device placed at the top of a compound microscope. It has a scale and a cross hair which moves along this scale (or, as in the Spencer microscope, a scale which moves) as a calibrated drum is turned. One observes the bullet through the scale. The drum is rotated (clockwise, to avoid lost motion)

Fig. 12. Unusual bullet-collecting medium. Lead bullets of .22 cal. were fired into a block of ice. Heat and pressure caused the ice to melt and little if any deformation occurred. The matchings shown (comparison camera) are better than those ordinarily obtained for .22 cal. lead bullets collected in the usual manner.

Fig. 13. Filar micrometer eyepiece. (Photo by courtesy of Bausch & Lomb.)

until the cross hair is lined up with one edge of the groove and a reading of its position taken. Then a similar setting is made and reading taken on the opposite side of the groove. The difference is a measure of the width of the groove. The micrometer has to be calibrated before use, against an accurate scale placed on the stage of the microscope. Any change in the tube length (i.e., the distance between objective and eyepiece) destroys the calibration since it changes the magnification, so it is safest to recalibrate every time the micrometer is used. When properly used it is quite accurate. However, as will be discussed later, we now have better methods of measuring groove widths.

The width of each groove on the bullet is measured, proceeding clockwise, in sequence around the bullet, and the readings are then tabulated in order. If there is one groove on the evidence bullet and on the test bullet that is unusual in any way (as to width or marking) this may be called No. 1 for each bullet, and the readings then fall into order. One example of several identifications which were made by the author previous to 1925 is shown in Table 1.

TABLE 1
Widths of grooves
(Measurements made with the filar micrometer)

Grooves on fatal bullets		Grooves on test bullets		
Bullet X	Bullet Y	Bullet 1	Bullet 2	Bullet 3
.038 in.	.038 in.	.038 in.	.038 in.	.038 in.
.031 "	.031 "	.031 "	.031 "	.031 "
.034 "	.034 "	.033 "	.033 "	.033 "
.031 "	.031 "	.032 "	.031 "	.032 "
.032 "	.032 "	.032 "	.031 "	.032 "
.033 "	.033 "	.033 "	.033 "	.033 "

Note: The technique illustrated in this table is not only outmoded, because of the adoption of the comparison microscope which affords a much more positive means of identification, but would be inapplicable in these days when so many barrels are rifled by either the broaching or the button-swaging process. Barrels rifled successively with the same broach (or button) will have rifling grooves (and lands) which will show the same sequence of widths, thus making it impossible to say which of several barrels (rifled with the same tool) was the one from which a particular bullet was fired.

Two fatal bullets and a revolver taken from the suspect were submitted for examination. Three test bullets were fired into cotton waste, and the grooves on all five bullets were measured. All the bullets were very unusual as to the variation of the widths of the rifling grooves—which was an additional point in favor of the identification. The suspect confessed. Naturally this method cannot be used unless a sequence of measurements can be made, and often one does not have such a sequence because the bullet may be deformed too much.

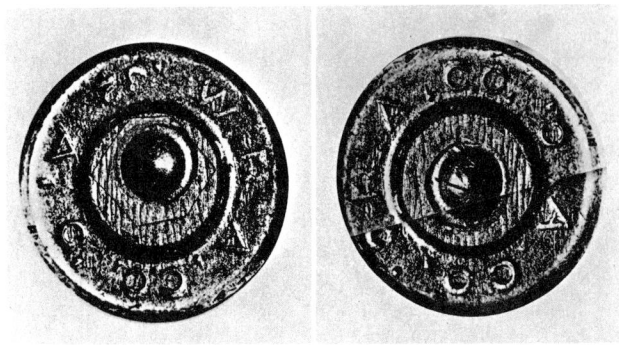

Fig. 14. Method of interchange. (Applied to photos in Fig. 26.) *Left:* A portion of the photo of the Lowell Test Shell has been cut out and placed on the Evidence Shell. *Right:* A portion of the photo of the Evidence Shell has been placed on the upper part of the Lowell Test Shell.

Another method of identification used in the pre-comparison-microscope days was known as the method of interchange, which apparently originated in France—a method which required much skill, patience, and time. The evidence bullet was set up in front of a long-focus camera provided with a short-focus lens in order to get good magnification. Illumination was adjusted so as to bring out to best advantage the details of the markings on the bullet. If the bullet had six grooves, six pictures were taken, in sequence. The bullet was rotated and carefully positioned so that each succeeding groove occupied the same position on the ground glass as the preceding one. It is important that the angle of view be the same. Usually the groove, being the bearer of the best markings, occupied the exact center of the ground glass. Once established, the illumination was kept the same for all six exposures. Then the evidence bullet was replaced by a test bullet and a sequence of six pictures was made in the same manner, using the same illumination throughout. After prints were made from the properly numbered negatives, sections of the test pictures were cut out and placed on the appropriate evidence pictures to see if the markings matched. If portions of two photos (one of the evidence bullet, the other of a test bullet) when placed in juxtaposition were found to have a sufficient number of lines which were continuous across the boundary, the pictures were said to be matched.

In addition to being time consuming and tricky the method has the disadvantage that one never knows what degree of success he has had until all the pictures are taken and compared. Unless the bullets are placed in exactly the right position when photographed, the results will be disappointing. Figs. 14

Fig. 15. Matching by method of interchange.

No. 1. Photo of head of fatal shell. (Cut in half for interchange.)

No. 2. Photo of head of test shell fired in suspect gun.

No. 3. Upper half of photo No. 1 superimposed on lower half of photo No. 2.

No. 4. Upper half of photo No. 2 superimposed on lower half of photo No. 1.

This method, now considered obsolete, originated with the noted French criminologist Balthazard in 1912 when he applied it to the identification of fired bullets.

and 15 show an application of this "method of interchange" as applied to the identification of shell heads through a comparison of breechblock markings. The method is much easier to apply in the case of shell heads because a whole series of pictures is not needed. It is of course necessary that the shells be placed in the same position and that they be illuminated the same, from the same direction and angle. Some experimentation will be necessary to determine the best angle for the illumination. Markings are made more distinct by using a low angle of illumina- 15 tion at right angles to scratches that may be present on the object being photographed.

Modern comparisons are usually made by the comparison microscope which for many years has been the standard method. This instrument and the comparison camera will be described in a later section. In these instruments portions of each object being examined can be brought into juxtaposition either in the optical field of the microscope or on the ground glass of a specially constructed camera and no pictures are made until a matching of characteristic features in the two areas under observation is found.

Additional markings and objects attached to fired bullets

Other things that happen to a bullet may be of use in special instances. Frequently when a lead bullet passes through cloth an impression of the weave will be found on the end of the bullet and this may be compared with those experimentally made by firing similar bullets from the suspect gun through the cloth under simulated conditions. This may indicate which of two or more bullets that were fired was the one that passed completely through a body—a very important point when two guns were involved in the shooting. Bullets are frequently fired through window screens also, and may be studied similarly. (Fig. 16) Objects, often minute, found

Fig. 16. Nose end of a .22 cal. lead bullet which had been fired through a wire window screen.

attached to or imbedded in the surface of a bullet may add useful information. These might be bits of plaster or of wood, glass particles, hair, fibers of various kinds, and many others. Fig. 17 illustrates an

interesting case. A hermit, while eating his evening meal alone in his cabin, was killed by a rifle bullet fired through an open window, the bullet passing entirely through his body. A search of the wall opposite the window disclosed a .38 cal. bullet imbedded therein. The bullet was removed and brought

Fig. 17. Embedded fibers tell a story. During investigation of the murder of a hermit two bullets were found embedded in a wall, near each other. The bullets were of different caliber, and there was only one bullet hole through the body. Examination of the .35 cal. bullet disclosed blue cotton and white wool fibers embedded in the exposed lead of the nose end. Deceased had been wearing a blue denim jacket and a white wool undershirt. The .38 cal. lead bullet showed no such fibers but did show some mold in the cannelure indicating that it must have been fired at least several days previously.

to the laboratory. Examination showed the surface to be oxidized uniformly over its entire surface, and a small amount of a fungus was found growing in the cannelure. It was obvious that this bullet had been fired at some time previous to the murder, because sufficient time had not elapsed for these effects to have been produced. A further search was made by the officers after they were told they had brought the wrong bullet, and a soft-nosed copper-jacketed bullet was discovered in the wall. Examination of this bullet showed it to be the murder bullet because tiny, blue cotton fibers from the hermit's blue denim jacket and white wool fibers from his underwear were found imbedded in the exposed lead on the nose end of the bullet. Police officers, sheriffs, and others who have anything to do with crime investigations should be informed that evidence bullets should be handled properly so that important evidence which may be clinging to them may not be lost, and also that the often delicately engraved markings on them will not be removed by carelessness. A soft lead bullet was once brought to the author by a sheriff who had carried it around in his trousers pocket with his loose change for several days!

While black powder ammunition is no longer made, it must be remembered that many cartridges loaded with it are still in existence and that much of it is still usable. A bullet which has been propelled by black powder will be smudged on the base, whereas the modern ammunition produces no such smudging. Another thing to remember is the fact that there are many rim fire cartridges still in existence, other than those of .22 cal., which are still usable in rim fire revolvers, many of which are also still in existence. Another type of marking, which, so far as the author knows, is produced only by the Magnum cartridge, is the pitting which will be found on the base of the bullet and which is due to the type of powder used.

Class characteristics

It will be well at this point to discuss what are known as "class characteristics," as the term applies to rifling. Class characteristics are those features which, because of the differences laid down in the specifications of different manufacturers, will (if actually followed in the processes of manufacture) often give a promising clue to the make and model of the gun from which the evidence bullet was fired. These characteristics are:

1. The land (bore) and groove diameters
2. The direction of the rifling twist
3. The number of lands and grooves
4. The width of the lands and grooves
5. The degree of twist of the rifling
6. Depth of grooves.

1. Bore diameter and caliber

The term caliber ("nominal caliber" would be a more proper term) refers to the diameter of the bore of a rifle, revolver, or pistol. It is not used in the case of shotguns, with the exception of the little .410. Actually it is a rather general term, as it does not, except in a few cases, actually describe the diameter of the bore. For example, taking data from a single manufacturer, the specified bore diameters at the muzzle for Colt automatic pistols and revolvers (as of 1945) are given in Table 2. From the values given in this table (which are typical) it is clear that the terms ".32 cal.," ".38 cal.," and, especially, ".44

cal." are not precise terms, since they often differ markedly from the actual bore diameters.

TABLE 2

Bore diameters for Colt pistols and revolvers
(1945 specifications)

Caliber and name of gun	Bore at muzzle end	
	Minimum	Maximum
S-22 Colt Auto	.214	.215
N-25 " "	.243	.244
M-32 " "	.304	.305
L-38 " "	.348	.349
M-380 " "	.348	.349
O-45 " "	.442	.444
O-455 Eley Colt Auto	.450	.451
Camp Perry Model	.214	.215
G-22 Police Pos. Target	.214	.215
H-32 " " "	.304	.305
A-32 Pocket Positive	.304	.305
B-32 Police Positive	.304	.305
D 32/20 Police Pos. Spec.	.304	.305
C-38 Police Positive	.346	.347
D-38 Police Pos. Spec.	.346	.347
I-38 Officers Mod. Tar.	.346	.347
E 32/20 Colt Army Spec.	.304	.305
E-38 " " "	.346	.347
E 38/40 " " "	.394	.395
E-41 " " "	.394	.395
P-32/20 Single Action Army	.304	.305
P-38/40 " " "	.394	.395
P-44 " " "	.419	.420
P-45 " " "	.444	.445
J-41 New Service Target	.394	.395
J-44 & 44/40 " " "	.419	.420
J-45 " " "	.444	.445
J-455 " " "	.444	.445
F-38/40 New Service	.394	.395
F-44 & 44/40 " "	.419	.420
F-45 " "	.444	.445

Estimations of caliber and number of grooves— Ordinarily there is little difficulty in determining the caliber of a fired bullet and the number of grooves thereon but this is not invariably the case. Frequently a bullet will be found to be so badly mutilated, distorted, or even fragmented that the customary measurements and observations do not suffice.

If the bullet appears not to have lost any of its metal it can be weighed and from this an "educated guess" can be made as to its caliber and type. An extensive table of bullet weights for different types of bullets has been prepared by Munhall, and by permission this table is reproduced in Appendix No. III. While it cannot be expected to give the answer in every instance, due to the many variations in bullet weights (past and present) for bullets made by a host of manufacturers in many countries, the table may often prove to give a good lead and frequently the definite answer.

In those cases where a bullet has obviously lost some of its original metal, as very often happens, this procedure obviously cannot be used. In such cases a different procedure, also developed by Munhall, may be used. This is based on the measurement of the combined widths of a groove and an adjoining land, provided that one groove and land are in sufficiently good condition to be measured. Methods for making such measurements are described under Instrumentation.

The table prepared by Munhall for this procedure is reproduced (by courtesy) in Appendix No. IV, together with an explanation as to how the table was constructed and how it is to be used. While it may not be infallible, it will be found to be useful.

2. Direction of rifling twist

Obviously there are but two possibilities here, but they are extremely important because a bullet having grooves which slant to the left ("Colt Type") could not have been fired from a gun having rifling that slants to the right ("S and W Type"), quite apart from any other features. Every firearms examiner of experience has probably had police officers or sheriffs bring in a gun and a bullet which clearly show right hand twist for one and left hand for the other. The only U.S. manufacturer who now uses left hand twist is the Colt Company, and they use it exclusively. In years gone by, several other manufacturers used left hand twist or both kinds and even some early Colt revolvers show right hand twist. Hopkins and Allen and Forehand Arms Co. used both. A number of European manufacturers use left hand twist but the majority do not. And some use both. The Colt automatic has been copied in several countries, but these copies usually have rifling with right hand twist.

3. Number of lands and grooves

In American-made hand guns the most common numbers of lands and grooves are 5 and 6, though others have been used. Hopkins and Allen, Plant's Mfg. Co., D. Moore, Remington (.50 cal. 1867 Navy Pistol), American Standard Tool Co., Iver Johnson, and others have used three-groove rifling, but no guns in current production have three grooves. Two-groove rifling was used for the M-3 Machine Gun during World War II, but apparently never has been used in pistols or revolvers, and probably will not be. Four-groove rifling is very uncommon in U.S.-made hand guns but the Schall Company used it in their .22 cal. pistol. In foreign countries four-groove rifling

is still common though several have changed to six-groove. Seven-groove rifling is no longer used in the U.S., although it was used in the Mod. 51 Remington automatic pistol, in a number of early Colt pistols, and by the Metropolitan Arms Co. Abroad it has been used extensively by Webley and Scott in England, and was also used in some of the Belgian Francotte revolvers. Eight-groove rifling has been found in a 7.7 mm. Bittner made in Austria and in a 9.4 mm. German revolver marked J. H. Damm. Eight-groove rifling was used in the Schmeisser Mod. 2 for pistols whose serial numbers were less than 105,000 at which point six-groove rifling was adopted. Both the "Luna" and the "Tell" models of the .22 cal. Büchel Free Pistol made by Ernst Friederich Büchel at Zella-Mehlis, Germany, had eight lands and grooves. The .22 cal. Simson rifle (German) had eight grooves. And the Modelo Corla .22 automatic made by Fabbrica de Armas Zaragoza in Mexico also had eight, but as only 65 were made they are not likely to be encountered. Nine-groove rifling has been found in a "British Bull Dog" revolver of unknown make, ten grooves are used in the Wamo single-shot pistol, and twelve-groove rifling has been found only in the Galand revolver. The Marlin rifle now has 16, 20, or 22 grooves; but to date this new system of "microgrooving" has not been used in a revolver or automatic pistol. Most examiners probably hope that it will not be! As manufacturers do change the number of lands and grooves at times one must not assume, because he finds a specimen to have a certain number, that all guns of the same make will be rifled in the same manner.

4. Widths of lands and grooves

The widths of lands and grooves show a great variation, even for guns having the same number of grooves. Here again each reputable manufacturer has adopted certain specifications and tolerances but often these appear to be "window dressing" as they are not always closely followed, and, indeed, some manufacturers appear not to have had any specifications to be followed. This question of widths is dealt with at length in a later chapter.

Suffice it to say here that some guns have grooves and lands which are equal in width, some have lands which are narrower than the grooves, and others have lands which are wider than the grooves. Some claim that the lands should be wide in order that the bullet may have more bearing surface upon which to ride, with groove depths just sufficient to insure rotation. Others claim that it is necessary to have rather narrow lands in order that they will bite into the bullet to prevent slippage. As will be seen later there is considerable difference in the same make and model even in the finer target pistols, which are especially designed for accuracy. One is thus led to the conclusion that considerable difference in land widths is allowable as long as certain limits are not exceeded.

The width of a land in a gun can be determined by measuring the width of its impression on a bullet passed through it. The width of a groove in the gun cannot be so determined, i.e., by measuring the width of a land on the bullet, because the whole cross section of the bore may not have been filled, and because the land in a gun is usually wedge shaped in cross section.

5. *Degree of twist of the rifling*

In the degree of twist of the rifling one again finds a great variation from manufacturer to manufacturer. Many revolvers made a great many years ago had much less twist than those made currently. Quite a number of makes used a twist of over 30 inches (for one complete turn of the rifling), and some even more. An Iver Johnson "American Bull Dog" had one turn in 40.9 inches; a "New Colt 38" had one in 48.3 inches; "Col. Le Mat's Pat. Rev.," one in 55.7; a "Maynard Tape Primer" revolver, one in 88.8; a Colt Mod. 1848, one in 120.0; and a "Sterling," one in 360! At the other extreme we have an "Ortgies" with one turn in 7.1 inches; an Austrian "Rast" with one in 6.0 inches; and a 7.65 mm. Chinese imitation of the F.N.-1900 Mod. Browning that had one in 5.7 inches. As in the case of land widths, a manufacturer may change his specifications for twist from time to time. The better manufacturers do not often change, however. Because of the relative constancy in the production of this particular characteristic and because it is the one characteristic of a barrel that does not change materially in use, it is unfortunate that it cannot be used more frequently in bullet identification. The difficulty is that the angle of rifling on a fired bullet is so difficult to measure with the accuracy necessary to have any meaning. This matter is discussed at length in another chapter.

6. *Depth of grooves*

The depth of the grooves on a fired bullet has little application to the problem of identification of a firearm. While it is fairly easy to determine by measurement the depth of the grooves in a rifled barrel it is very difficult to measure the depth of a groove on a fired bullet, and even where measurements are possible they ordinarily have little meaning. If all fired bullets were undamaged and perfectly symmetrical and if each represented precisely the cross section of the barrel, measurements could be made and they would have some significance. But these bullets do not exist. No two bullets, even when fired successively, will be the same in every particular.

Very seldom does a bullet fill completely the cross section of the barrel through which it is fired and unless the metal of the bullet is pressed to the very bottom of the groove even an accurate measurement on the bullet would have no significance. In practice it is found that a series of measurements of groove depths made on different grooves of the same fired bullet will show differences and since the characteristic which is being measured is a matter of only a few thousandths of an inch the variations are proportionately large. The majority of bullets brought to the laboratory show some degree of mutilation and many of them show extreme mutilation.

Different makes of guns do have a considerable variation in groove depths despite statements and inferences to the contrary in some textbooks, and these differences have some qualitative significance. Groove depths may vary from 0.002 to 0.010 inch, and even more in some of the older guns. Here again manufacturers lay down a specification as to the depth of grooves. One manufacturer specifies the same groove depth for over 30 models of all calibers made from .22 to .45. Actually these specifications are not strictly followed, and probably there is no reason why they should be.

The statements made above may seem to present a very discouraging picture as to the value of class characteristics, though such is not intended. As a matter of fact, class characteristics are often very useful indeed, but all are by no means of equal value. Caliber (bore diameter), number of lands and grooves, and the direction of the twist are the ones most often used. Widths of grooves on the bullet (indicating the widths of lands in the gun) could probably be used more than they are. If one has no equipment for making precise measurements he can at least use the alternate method, described later, which requires only a stage micrometer slide and the comparison microscope. In the use of class characteristics to locate a gun one must be careful not to go too far in his predictions as to the make and model of gun that must be found. The fact is, as will be seen by examining the data presented in a later section, there may be several makes and models of firearms that have rifling characteristics that are nearly alike. If, for example, one has a bullet with characteristics indicating that it was (or could have been) fired from a Smith and Wesson, he will be wise in saying that the bullet was fired from an S & W 19 *or* from some other gun having similar rifling characteristics. In firearms investigations one should be very careful not to make positive statements that may backfire.

Some general observations regarding bullets

Before the advent of smokeless powder, plain lead or lead hardened by the addition of small amounts of antimony or tin (or both) was used for bullet making. But with the higher velocities attainable with this new powder, "metal fouling" became a serious problem, and this led to the use of surface coating of the lead bullets with some harder metal. Bullets for low powered .22 cal. rifles are still made of plain lead alloy, or they may have an extremely thin protective coating of copper or of some copper alloy which not only hardens but also lubricates the bullet and reduces metal fouling. This thin coating

Fig. 18. Remains of jacketed bullet. This portion of a soft-nosed jacketed bullet was taken from a body. No lead was recovered. The markings on the copper jacket served to identify the gun from which it had been fired.

(or gilding) is not to be confused with the "jacketing" of bullets with a metal casing. Many years ago bullets were lubricated by putting grease on their exterior surfaces, but now lubrication, when used, is done by putting the lubricant in a depressed ring (called a cannelure) around that portion of the bullet which is within the case, so that it is held in place and the exterior of the cartridges is free from grease. These cannelures also enable the maker to produce a longer bullet without increasing its weight unduly, and they are frequently used to help hold the bullet in proper position by having the end of the case crimped into one of them. Holding the bullet in proper position is important because if the bullet is set back too far into the case the pressure of firing may be dangerously increased, and if it should move forward and become loosened it would not feed properly into the mechanism of the gun. In some cases, particularly in the older types, there was a shoulder on the lead bullet which prevented the bullet from setting back farther into the case. Jacketed bullets may be held in place in a number of ways. The end of the case may be crimped into a cannelure on the bullet; the case itself may have a cannelure against which the end of the bullet is tightly pressed; the bullet may fit so snugly that it will stay in place; or points (usually three in number) may be "peened" into the case so as to produce increased friction.

Metal-jacketed bullets are now standard for high powered rifles and for use in automatic pistols and machine guns. And they are widely used in revolvers. Many varieties have been developed and a collection of all types is a necessary part of the equipment of a crime laboratory. Unlike the gilded lead bullets, where the coating is not more than 0.0002 inch thick, the jackets are from 0.020 to 0.030 inch in thickness.

For use in automatics the jacketing covers the whole forward end of the bullet and the only exposed lead is in the center of the base end. For hunting purposes the jacket may cover all of the bullet except a portion of the nose end. These "soft nosed" bullets expand on striking flesh and cause more destruction of the tissues, thus increasing their effectiveness (Fig. 18). "Hollow point" bullets are completely jacketed with the exception of a small hole at the point. These open up upon striking flesh and are very destructive to tissues. All bullets for military use are fully covered at the nose end. They may have a rounded nose or they may be very pointed, to produce greater penetration. A steel (or other hard metal) point may be set into the nose end of this type of bullet to further increase penetration.

In the case of both hollow-point and soft-nosed bullets, instances will be met frequently where the only portion of the bullet received by the examiner will be the jacket—the lead core having been completely expelled. Since the rifling marks are on the jacket, this loss of the lead is of no particular importance. For some high powered rifles the velocity of the bullet may be so great that it practically explodes when it strikes an animal (or any other object) and no large fragments of the bullet may be found. Then very small fragments of the jacket should be searched for, because even a tiny piece may carry identifying markings.

Bullets designed for automatic pistols (of caliber higher than .22) are fully metal-jacketed at the nose end, because exposed lead would likely lead to malfunctions. The finding of such bullets (i.e., bullets designed for use in automatic pistols) does not necessarily mean that they were actually fired from an automatic pistol, however. Cartridges designed for automatics *can* be fired from some revolvers and vice versa, although the practice is not a common one. The only exception to the last statement is the case where "half moon" clips are used to hold .45 cal. A.C.P. cartridges so that they may be used in a revolver in spite of the absence of a projecting rim. All .22 cal. automatic pistols are designed to function with the same ammunition as is commonly used in revolvers, single shot pistols, and rifles.

The jacketing material may be of copper or cupro-nickel, both of which are much harder than lead. Steel jackets are used to some extent in Europe but are not made in the U.S.—except for experimental purposes. Jacketed bullets do not require lubrication and do not (ordinarily) produce metal fouling. Metal fouling does occur to some extent with the "gilded" type of coating, although the protective coating (and

lubrication) prevents it considerably. Metal fouling presents a serious problem to the firearms examiner. If a test bullet is fired through a barrel which has become fouled subsequent to the passage of the evidence bullet through it, the markings on the test and evidence bullets may be quite different. Also, if the evidence bullet was fired through a fouled barrel which subsequently had been cleared of all fouling (previous to the firing of a test bullet), the evidence and test bullets might be impossible to match. Naturally the difficulty depends on the degree of fouling.

The "gilded" bullets (such as Lubaloy-coated) are in general more difficult to match than either the plain lead bullets or the jacketed ones. Plain lead bullets, as pointed out elsewhere, expand because of the pressure behind them and the frictional resistance produced by the walls of the barrel, and, consequently, they tend to fill the whole cross section of the barrel. This, together with the relative softness of the lead, causes the bullet to take good distinctive markings on both the lands and grooves. The "gilded" bullets, which present a somewhat harder surface, may not fill the whole cross section, at least not with the same pressure, and the markings may not be so well engraved on the bullet. Another difficulty arises due to "flaking" of the gilded surface, which presents a mottled appearance that interferes not only with the visual comparison but also with photography. The metal-jacketed bullets, having a harder surface, do not completely fill the cross section of the barrel. They may have excellent markings in the grooves but little or no markings on the lands. This disadvantage is offset by the fact that the engraved marks on a jacketed bullet are less susceptible to damage than those on the softer lead bullet.

Cartridge identifications

Markings on the cartridge

Cartridges, especially those fired in automatic or repeating firearms, often show repetitive marks which are useful in the identification of the type (and sometimes the make) of weapon used and of the individual arm when test cartridges fired in it are compared with an evidence cartridge.

Impressions that are made by file marks, tool marks, or other inequalities on the surface of the breechblock when a shell sets back against it under high pressure are likely to be more reproducible than marks made by the sliding of a bullet over a slightly rough surface, such as the interior of a rifled barrel. The former resembles the process of printing from fixed type, or that of die stamping, whereas the markings on bullets are made by a process more like that of making tool marks where the tool slides while in contact with the surface.

The size, shape, and location of extractor and ejector marks, the type of breechblock mark, the presence of magazine scratches, etc. are all important in helping to determine the type and make (and possibly the model) of a gun used. In the case of rim fire ammunition, the size, shape, and location of the firing pin impression is of value in determining the make of arm used. This will be discussed later.

The individual weapon in which a cartridge was fired can often be determined by comparison of the markings on the evidence shell with those produced by the suspect arm on test shells. Here again it is important that the same make of ammunition be used as that in the evidence submitted. In fact it is even more important here than in the case of bullet comparisons, because small differences in thickness or in the composition of the primer or in the composition of the brass of the shell head will make marked differences in the distinctness of the marks produced.

In many cases ammunition of the same make as that of the evidence shell will be found in the possession of the suspect. These cartridges are the ones that are preferably used to secure test shells, as they are more likely to have been made from the same batches of metal (i.e., primer and case). Not all ammunition of the same make will be made of metals having the same degree of hardness, and one cannot say definitely that the confiscated cartridges were made of metals from the same batches as those used in making the evidence shell, although the probability is great that such was the case. Therefore, if reproducible and matching marks are not present on test shells it is quite proper to use other cartridges of the same or even of different makes of ammunition, because if the marks on the evidence shell can be reproduced on *any* ammunition it is sufficient proof that one has the right gun. Naturally it is more satisfying if one can testify in court that he used ammunition of the same make as that of the evidence shell and found in possession of the suspect.

Sometimes primers have protective coatings and if the evidence shall has such a coating a cartridge having a primer similarly coated should be used. Frequently good, well-defined marks present on an evidence shell will not be present on a test shell or, if present, may be poorly defined when a different make of ammunition is used. This may be due to differences in the primer or it may also be due to differences in powder pressures. The higher the pressure the more distinct the marks are likely to be. Since many of the cartridges used in crime cases were made years ago it is imperative that the firearms examiner have available a collection of old ammunition as well as of that currently in production.

Rim fire firing pin marks

The most distinguishing mark to be found on a rim fire shell is the impression of the firing pin. Breechblock marks are almost never present, unless the new "magnum" cartridge is used. Extractor marks may be present (although not necessarily so) on shells that are ejected in the process of firing. As these are the ones most likely to be found at the scene of a shooting they are naturally the ones in which we are most interested. Occasionally extractor marks are sufficiently repetitive and distinctive in character to permit matching under the comparison microscope, consequently they should always be looked for. Ejector marks are less likely to be found, and when present they are rarely amenable to profitable comparison with the microscope. However, the position of the ejector mark and the extractor mark (if such marks be present) with respect to the location of the firing pin impression is important and will be discussed later.

Frequently the details of a firing pin impression will show characteristic features which are repetitive, and in such cases matchings will be possible. These comparisons are usually made with the comparison microscope but can also (though less conveniently) be made with the comparison camera; and with either instrument photographic recordings of what one sees can be made. Figs. 19 and 20 show examples of such comparisons.

The term "firing pin" as used here includes the various devices which are used to cause the shell to fire. In some cases the firing pin is an integral part of a hammer, in others it may be a separate entity hinged to the face of the hammer, or it may be an actual pin or rod (spring loaded or not) driven forward by a spring-actuated hammer or some other spring-actuated system. In any case the end of the "firing pin" strikes the edge of the shell causing a detonation which sets fire to the powder, and in so doing it leaves a more or less perfect facsimile impression of the face of the pin on or near the rim of the shell. These impressions are often excellent.

Fortunately for the investigator, different manufacturers have different ideas concerning the best shape and size for the end of the pin. As long as each manufacturer sticks to a definite form and size of pin for each model of gun he produces, and many do quite consistently over a considerable period, the firing pin impression is an important characteristic. If frequent changes are made its value is lessened. As long as it remains unchanged it may help the examiner to (1) give police officers some idea as to

Fig. 19. Matching of rim fire firing pin impressions. Occasionally the impressions made by a firing pin on a rim fire shell are sufficiently well defined and so repetitive as to permit matching them with the comparison microscope or the comparison camera. Two such matchings are shown.

Three shells (A, B, & C) were fired in the same Remington rifle. The left photo shows Shell A (top) matched with Shell B. At the right is shown the matching of Shell C (top) with Shell A. The photos were made with the comparison camera.

Fig. 20. Matching of rim fire firing pin marks (comparison microscope photo). Matchings of this quality are rarely found on .22 cal. rim fire shells. Inasmuch as they are conclusive evidence a search for matchings should always be made.

what make or makes of guns are possibilities in the case and (2), in cases where guns are submitted for examination, it may help to eliminate a suspect gun or guns. In one instance in the author's experience eleven .22 cal. repeating rifles were submitted for examination in connection with a shooting case.

Fig. 21. Illustrating variation in point of impact of firing pin. (See text for discussion.)

All eleven could quickly be eliminated because none of them produced the characteristic firing pin impression found on the evidence shells.

Since there are fairly distinct shapes of firing pin impressions they may be classified as to type. The H. P. White Laboratory, for example, uses the following classification: *Bar* (extending across shell head), *Rectangular, Round, Semicircular,* and *Special.* In addition, the approximate vertical and horizontal dimensions are noted. Still other classifications are possible, such as: *Bar, Rectangular (Square), Rectangular (Narrow), Rectangular (Broad), Round (Large), Round (Small), Semicircular (Large), Semicircular (Small),* and *Special.* The term *Special* is used for those which do not conform to any of the previous types, and, as a matter of fact, they are comparatively rare.

With respect to classifications such as the foregoing, some words of caution are necessary. If all of

Fig. 22. Semicircular firing pin impressions. The impression on this shell, fired in an Iver Johnson D.A. Model 1900 revolver, would be classed as "Semicircular." However, the impression of the firing pin made on a thin sheet of copper (shown at the left) shows that the pin actually has a rectangular striking surface, rounded at the lower end. Since only this lower portion of the pin strikes the rim of the shell a semicircular effect is produced. Such vagaries are frequently encountered.

the marks made by a given firing pin were always alike as to shape and dimensions, the situation would be quite simple, but, unfortunately, this ideal situation does not exist. If a new clean gun is used, with the same ammunition, and if the shell is properly seated in the chamber, the marks should be quite repetitive in shape, location, and dimensions. In a much-used gun, or in one poorly made, the pin may not strike in exactly the same place (Fig. 21). The length of a rectangular firing pin impression will thus be affected, and a round-faced pin could produce either round or semicircular impressions of different sizes (Fig. 22). The size, and to some extent the shape, of a firing pin impression will depend on the depth of penetration of the pin (Fig. 23). Frequently a cartridge at the moment of firing is not seated firmly against the shoulder of the chamber, and "normal" depth of penetration will not be achieved. This obviously will affect the dimensions of the impression, be the pin of the round-end or rectangular-faced type. The latter are usually somewhat wedge shaped (to add strength); consequently, a deeper impression will be both wider and longer. Firing pins having rounded ends or flat circular ends are frequently tapered and here again the size of the impression will depend on the depth of penetration. If the cartridge does not fit the chamber snugly the point of impact of the firing pin on successive shots fired will not necessarily be the same, and the size (particularly the vertical dimension) of the impres-

Fig. 23. Semicircular firing pin impressions. The two shells were fired in an Iver Johnson "Supershot Sealed Eight" revolver. Impressions made by the same firing pin on a piece of sheet copper are shown below and demonstrate that the end of the pin is circular and flat. Most semicircular impressions are caused by the end of a round pin striking on the edge of the rim of the shell, as was the case here illustrated.

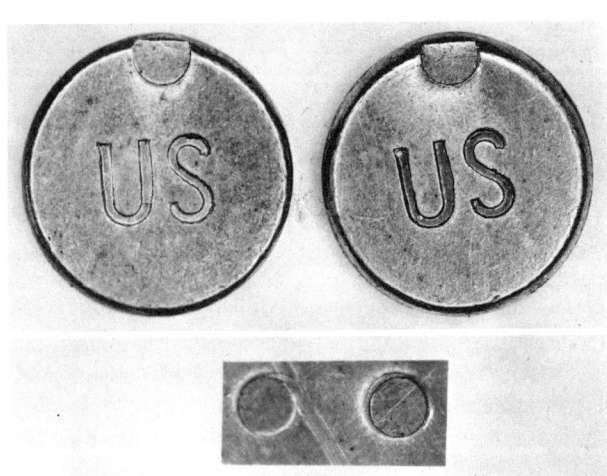

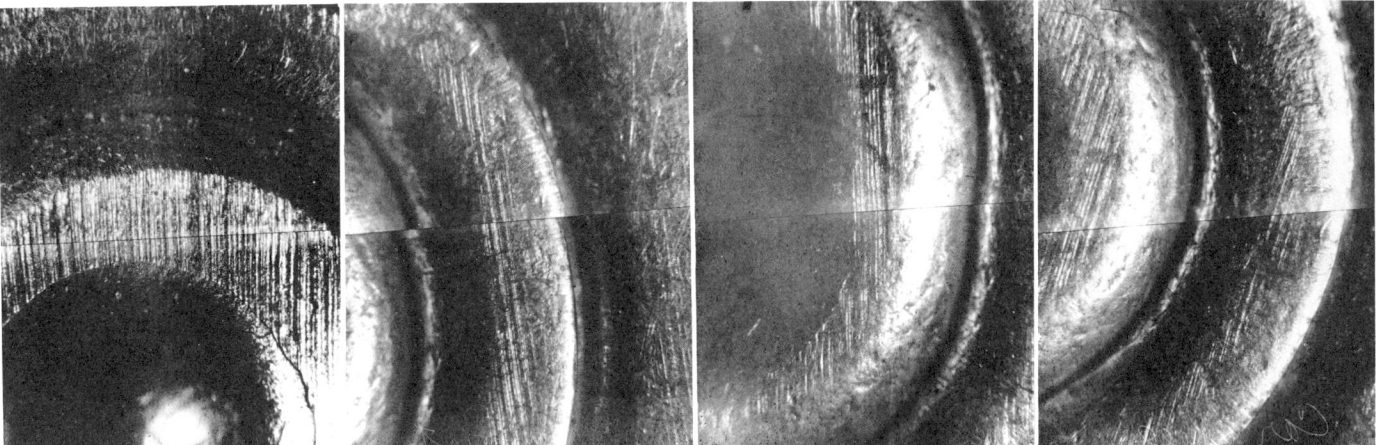

Fig. 24. Matching of breechblock marks (comparison microscope photos). All four of these matches were obtained on the same pair of shells. Test shell above line of separation in each case.

sions will not be uniform. A pin having a round (circular) face may produce either a circular or semicircular impression depending on how near it strikes the edge of the rim of the shell. Most semicircular impressions are made by pins having rounded or flat circular faces.

Another factor of importance is the ammunition used. Firing pin impressions on shells of different makes may show distinct differences. It is well known that even pure copper does not always have the same degree of hardness because of different treatments to which it may have been subjected. Copper from different sources may have different degrees of hardness due to small impurities. Furthermore, the depth of penetration depends on the thickness of the metal in the head of the shell, and this may vary from manufacturer to manufacturer.

In making comparisons of firing pin impressions on test and evidence shells it is therefore highly recommended that, whenever possible, the same ammunition be used (from the same lot when possible). It is also apparent from what has been said above that several shells should be fired for comparisons. It is recommended that at least three be fired and compared with each other. If the impressions on these are all alike it may be assumed that the evidence shell should show the same marking if actually fired from the gun in question. If significant variations appear in the firing pin impressions on the three test shells more test shells should then be fired. If, after comparing a considerable number, none are found with markings that closely resemble the evidence shell marking one can safely conclude that he does not have the right weapon.

As has been mentioned, the locations of the extractor and ejector marks may be of considerable importance. Just to cite one example, suppose we had to distinguish between two guns—a Winchester Model 74 Self-loading rifle and a Winchester Model 75 Bolt Action rifle, both of which are possibilities in our theoretical case. The information given by the firing pin impressions alone is not conclusive, but there are important differences with respect to extractor and ejector markings. If the Mod. 74 test shell is oriented so that the firing pin impression is at the 12 o'clock position, the extractor mark will be at 3 o'clock and the ejector mark at 9 o'clock. If the test shell from the Mod. 75 is similarly oriented, with the firing pin impression at 12 o'clock, two extractor marks should be present, one at 3 o'clock and the other at 9 o'clock, and the ejector mark will be at about 6 o'clock. A comparison of the evidence shell with the test shells should enable one to determine which of the two guns (if either) may have fired the evidence shell. If the evidence shell shows two extractor marks and an ejector mark at the 6 o'clock position we can safely eliminate the Mod. 74 if none of a series of test shells show these markings. Of course, this does not prove that this particular Mod. 75 rifle was used.

A file of photographs of rim fire firing pin impressions, containing as extensive a coverage as possible, is an important asset to a crime investigation laboratory. While drawings and reproduced photographs are useful, original photographs are preferable. These should show the shell heads at least 1½ inches in diameter in order that the details of impressions may be sufficiently distinct. In taking such photographs proper lighting is essential. The author prefers to use the large Silvermann illuminator, which consists of a circular tungsten-filament lamp (about 2½ inches in diameter) set into a circular reflector through which

25

the reflected light passes from the shell head to the camera lens. This gives a very even illumination without shadows.

Because of possible variations in the appearance of firing pin impressions made by the same pin, it is recommended that, in building up such a file, three

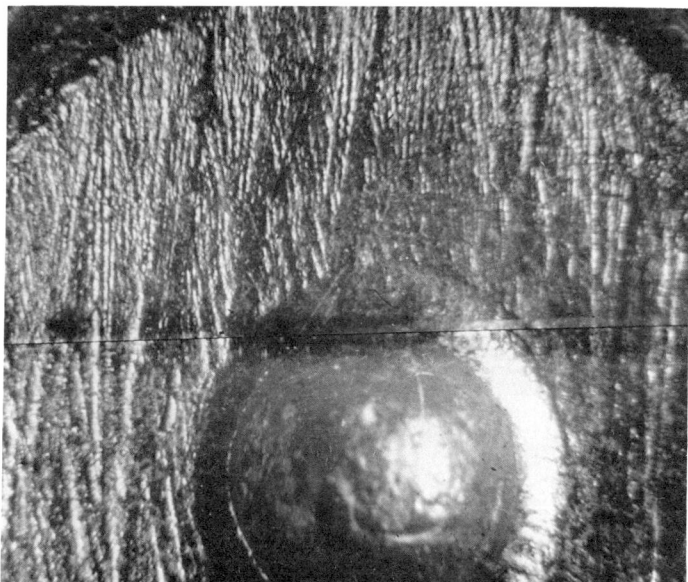

Fig. 25. Matching of breechblock markings (comparison microscope photo). Showing two matchings obtained on fatal shell (below line) and test shell (above line) fired in Sauer Auto Pistol belonging to suspect. See Fig. 41 for photo of breechblock in this gun.

shells be fired and photographed in all cases. If just one shell is fired and photographed one never knows whether successive marks will be repetitive or not, and very erroneous conclusions might be reached. It is most important to know whether the markings are approximately repetitive or not. The binocular microscope is useful in making these tests.

In Appendix No. VIII there will be found several plates illustrating the firing pin impressions made by a number of different makes of .22 cal. arms. Plates Nos. 8 to 14 are made up of reproductions taken from *Firearms Information Service* cards and are used here by permission.*

The reproductions shown in Plates Nos. 15 to 27† are from photographs taken by the author. Because of the hundreds of makes and models of .22 cal. rim fire arms that have been made it is obviously impossible to cover more than a small fraction of them. Those here reproduced are typical and it is hoped that they are sufficiently inclusive to be useful. An examination of the reproductions in this Appendix will disclose the fact that different manufacturers use firing pins which make impressions that are very much alike and also the fact that a manufacturer may make changes from time to time. Sometimes these differences (particularly minor dimensional changes) are due to nonuniformity in shop practice and at other times deliberate major changes are made. In spite of the difficulties and uncertainties involved, a study of firing pin impression types is, nevertheless, often a great aid (1) in determining the type or make of a gun that may have fired an evidence shell and (2) in eliminating a large number of arms that could not have fired that shell. And, finally, it must be remembered that frequently the markings on evidence and test shells may be satisfactorily matched so that the identity of the particular gun that fired a shell can be determined.

Center fire firing pin marks

Firing pins used in center fire guns frequently have a considerable degree of individuality also. The

* *Firearms Information Service* was issued monthly by the H. P. White Laboratory of Belair, Md., in the form of 4×6-inch cards containing a wide variety of information in the firearms field which is particularly useful to the firearms examiner and also of interest to the collector. Unfortunately this service has been discontinued, temporarily we hope.

†In these photographs the orientation of the shells is the same (within close limits) as when they were in the gun at the moment of firing. In some cases a dot of ink was placed on the rim of the shell, to use as a reference point in determining the position of the shell, while in others the shell was oriented with respect to the head stamp.

Fig. 26. Shell heads in Sacco-Vanzetti case. *Left:* Test shell from Sacco's automatic. *Right:* Evidence shell.

Comparison microscope was not used in the investigations. Similarities in the breechblock markings are obvious, however.

ends often have concentric rings made by the cutting tool that formed them and these are impressed in facsimile on the copper at the bottom of the firing pin impression. Inasmuch as these rings are different for all firing pins and since they can often be matched under the comparison microscope with their counterparts on test shells, they are always looked for. Some firing pins have ends that are flat, others are blunt and rounded, while still others are highly tapered, and some are even pointed. Then too, firing pins develop individuality because of wear and chipping. Markings due to these causes, having a high degree of individuality, are frequently encountered. The chance that two firing pins would chip in precisely the same way is very remote indeed. The angle at which a firing pin strikes the primer should be noted. The firing pin in a revolver usually, though not always, strikes at an angle, since the hammer to which it is attached or of which it is an integral part moves through an arc. In some revolvers there is an

independent firing pin which moves forward when struck by the hammer and strikes the primer vertically (to the surface).

Breechblock markings

Breechblock markings are made by the impact of the shell head against the breechblock by the force of the explosion in the cartridge. Inasmuch as these nearly instantaneous pressures amount to a few thousands of pounds per square inch up to as much as 65,000 pounds per square inch (in the case of some rifle ammunition), and since the pressure is exerted equally in all directions, it is obvious that the shell case (at the moment that the bullet leaves it) will strike or be pushed back against the breechblock with considerable force. When the head space is large and the shell head does not lie directly against the breechblock, the shell may acquire a considerable momentum before it strikes the breechblock, and the markings will consequently be more distinct. Soft, uncoated primers give the best impressions. Often several matchings can be found on the same pair of shells (Figs. 24, 25).

It frequently happens that the markings are so well defined and so distinctive that simple enlarged photographs, taken under proper illumination, are sufficient to show that the evidence shell and test shell must have been fired in the same gun. Fig. 26 is a reproduction of Goddard's photographs of the evidence and test shell in the celebrated Sacco-Vanzetti case. The extraordinary similarity of the markings on these shells can lead the experienced firearms examiner to but one conclusion. The comparison microscope was not used in this case as Goddard, the only person using the instrument at that time, was not called into the case until later when the findings were being reviewed by the Governor.

Figs. 27, 28, and 29, taken from the author's files,

Fig. 27. A rather unusual number of markings found on each primer of shells fired in this gun.

Fig. 28. Breechblock markings. *Left:* Test shell fired from suspect's gun. *Right:* Fatal shell found at murder scene.

Fig. 29. Primers on evidence shell (left) and test shell (right) show same breechblock marks and same firing pin drag. All test shells fired showed this.

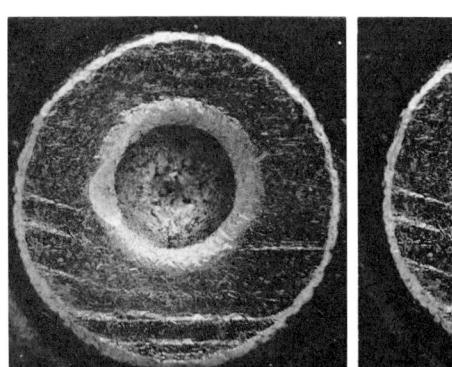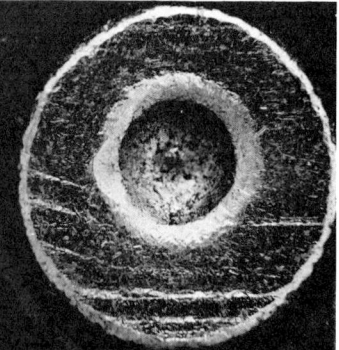

show such an obviously repetitive character of distinctive markings that comparison microscope (or comparison camera) photographs are scarcely necessary. Enlarged photographs (usually 8×10 inches) are better understood by the members of the average jury, to whom a comparison microscope may appear to be a very complicated instrument.

In .22 cal. rim fire ammunition the pressure is ordinarily insufficient to produce breechblock marks of any value, but occasionally repetitive markings are

produced (Fig. 30) and, of course, they should always be searched for. Firing pin impressions, however, can be matched more frequently.

The characteristics of the markings made by the breechblock depend on the processes of manufacture, the particularities or peculiarities of construction, and on what happens to the face of the breechblock subsequent to manufacture. Fortunately for the examiner the possibilities for variation are almost infinite.

Because each manufacturer has a certain procedure for the production of a certain model of arm, which may differ from that used by some or all other manufacturers, and because he follows this procedure fairly consistently, possibly in his different models, it should be possible to classify breechblock faces according to the special characteristics they possess, i.e., certain patterns may be established. Such a classification was attempted by Mezger, Hees, and Hasslacher in Germany and a summary of their findings was published in the *Archiv für Kriminologie*, Vol. 89, pp. 1-32 and 93-116, a translation of which appeared in the *American Journal of Police Science*, Vol. II, pp. 473-499, and Vol. III, pp. 124-145. This work is the most comprehensive of any that has ever been attempted along the line of cartridge classification and identification and is so fundamentally important that we are reproducing the most salient points in Appendix I.

While this classification is interesting it has not

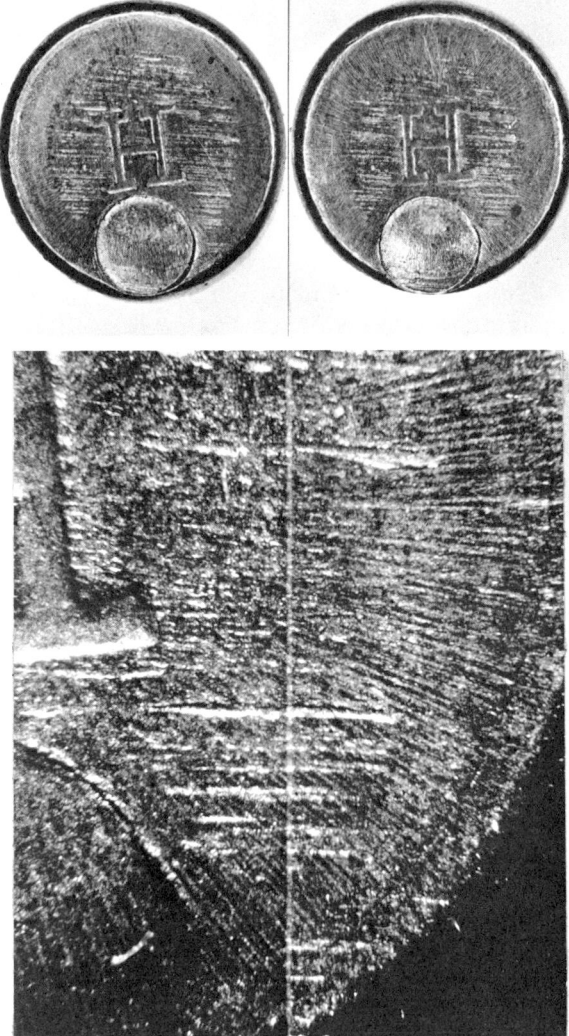

Fig. 30. Matching of breechblock markings on rim fire shells. *Above:* Two shells fired in a Springfield Rifle, Model 4. *Below:* Comparison microscope photo showing good matching of breechblock markings.

come into general use, probably for several reasons, such as inaccessibility of the article, lack of understanding of the system, lack of definiteness in prediction, and, perhaps most important of all, the difficulty of recognizing with certainty the markings to be looked for. Some firearms examiners go as far as to say that any attempt to narrow down the search in such a manner is useless and might even result in missing entirely the gun wanted. And they feel the same way about classifications relating to rifling markings—although here they would recognize that a bullet having, say, four grooves and left hand twist must have been fired from a gun having four lands with left hand twist, and they would so advise those whose duty it is to make the search. Some

examiners take the position that a wise detective will collect everything that might conceivably have anything whatsoever to do with the case and that it is best not to tell him too definitely what he should look for because, in doing so, something not included in specific instructions and information given to him might possibly be overlooked. The author does not subscribe to this point of view because he believes that it underrates the intelligence of the detective, who is entitled to all possible aid.

In center fire cartridges the distinctness of the breechblock impression depends not only on the thickness of the primer, the composition of the primer, the strength of the powder charge, and whether the primer is properly seated, but also on the presence of oil, grease, dirt, or rust on the breech face. It also depends on the amount of head space. Factory stampings often interfere with the making of good impressions on the head of the shell. Formerly, manufacturer's identifying marks (usually a single letter) were placed on primers, but, fortunately, this practice has been largely discontinued if not completely so.

Extractor marks

Extractor marks made by automatic and repeating firearms can frequently be matched and often very effectively, as shown in several of the accompanying photographs (Figs. 31 to 35). In repeating guns, the

Fig. 31. Matching extractor marks (Rifle). *Above line:* Mark on test shell. *Below line:* Mark on fatal shell.

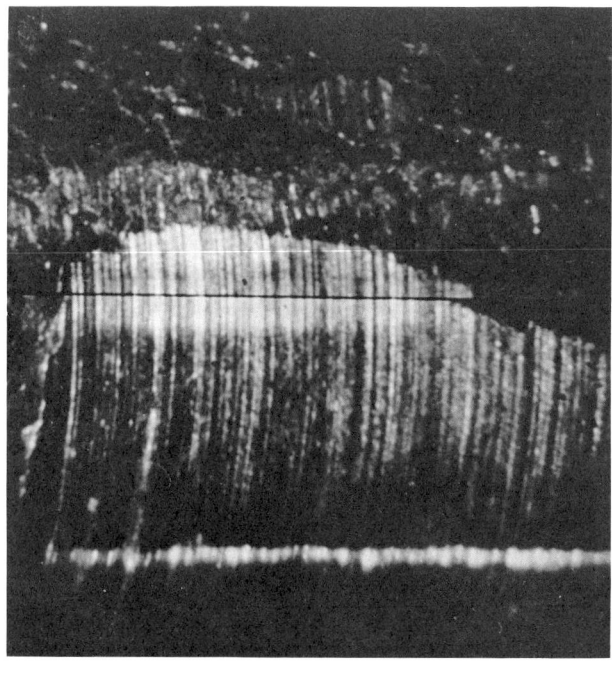

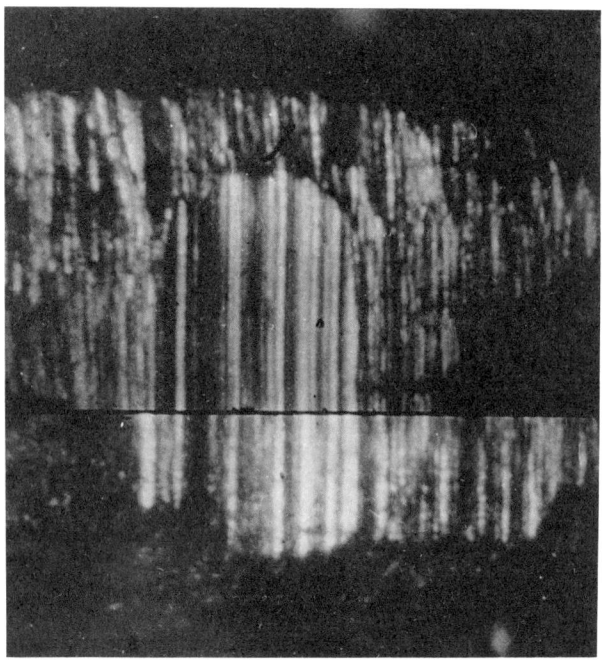

Fig. 32. Matching extractor marks (Pistol). *Above line:* Mark on test shell. *Below line:* Mark on fatal shell.

depth of the impressions will vary considerably, depending on the vigor of the operator. Some guns will give excellent repetitive extractor marks while others will not. A loose extractor will give trouble. Some guns will produce well-defined ejector marks, but they are usually not as useful as extractor marks. The development of these depends even more on the vigor with which the action of the gun is operated. In automatics the force of the action is naturally more uniform and the results are likely to be more uniform also.

Because of the commendable practice of unloading hunting rifles and shotguns at the close of each day's shooting, it is a frequent experience to find several extractor marks and ejector marks on the same evidence shell. Extractor marks may be important in cases where no suspect gun is found or in case the suspect denies ownership of the suspect gun. In a case investigated by the Wisconsin State Crime Laboratory a suspect denied ownership or any knowledge of a gun which laboratory tests showed was the gun which had been used in the commission of a crime. Unfortunately for the suspect, however, he inadvertently dropped two unfired rifle carrtidges while being questioned. When these were examined it was found that they had extractor marks on their rims which matched those on the evidence shell, showing that they had been "worked through" the

rifle in question (Fig. 36). If one finds extractor marks or ejector marks on the same shell that are distinctly different, indicating that they have been worked through different guns, further inquiry into the history of the shell is in order, otherwise an innocent man may be unjustly involved. It must also be remembered that many fired shells have been reloaded and will thus have more than one set of markings when fired again. In the case of shells fired in revolvers, in nonautomatic pistols, and in non-repeating arms in general, extractor marks and ejector marks will rarely be found.

Ejector marks

Ejector marks can sometimes be matched, but less frequently than extractor marks (Fig. 37). They should always be looked for, however, as their total absence might indicate that the shell had been fired from a gun that had no ejector (of which there are several), although this would not necessarily be the case. As already mentioned, the position of the ejector mark in relation to other marks, particularly the extractor mark, is important in helping to identify the make or type of gun.

Other markings

Other marks should always be looked for. Defects in the chamber where the cartridge lies at the moment of explosion will sometimes produce repeti-

Fig. 33. Matching extractor marks (Shotgun). *Above line:* Mark on test shell. *Below line:* Mark on fatal shell.

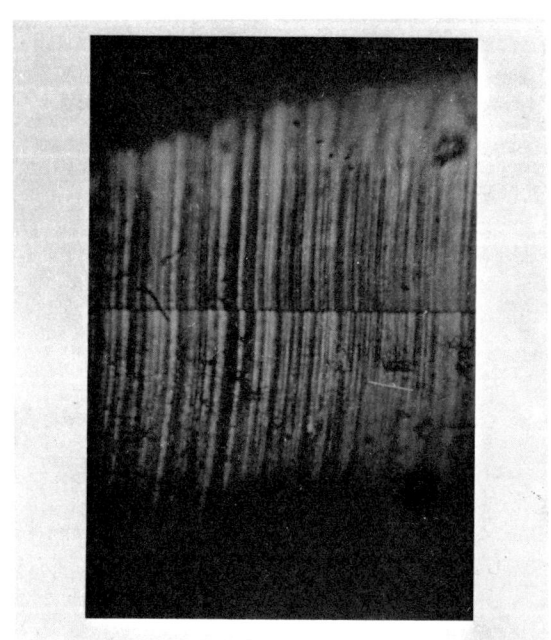

tive marks on the side of a brass shell. Sometimes these marks are only bulges rather than marks that have distinctive character, but they should be looked for. On the other hand, marks which do have a distinct individuality are sometimes found. The imprints made by the lips of magazine clips in auto loading arms may at times be useful. Usually, however, the chief result of examining magazine clip marks is confusion. Occasionally a defect in the loading mechanism will produce a repetitive mark which will be useful in identification. Such a case is illustrated in Fig. 38.

Fig. 34. Matching of extractor marks (Shotgun). *Left:* Above line, extractor mark on fatal shell. Below line, mark made by left hand extractor on test shell. *Right:* Above line, extractor mark on fatal shell. Below line, mark made by right hand extractor on test shell.

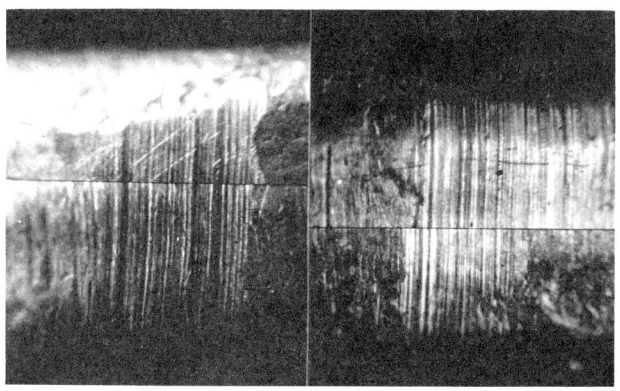

Fig. 36. Matching extractor marks refute statement that suspect did not own rifle. *Above line:* Mark on a cartridge taken from suspect. *Below line:* Mark on evidence shell.

Evidence shell and test shells fired from a Winchester Mod. 94 .32 Spl. rifle showed matching extractor marks, but suspect denied ownership or knowedge of the rifle. Inadvertently he dropped two unfired cartridges while being interviewed. Each of these unfired cartridges had obviously been "worked through" the rifle since each of them had extractor marks on their rims which matched those on the evidence shell, thus refuting the suspect's statement. (Photo by courtesy of Wisconsin State Crime Lab.)

Fig. 35. Matching of extractor marks. (An unusual case.) A .30-30 cartridge was fired in a .32 caliber Marlin Mod. 1893 repeating rifle in a murder case. As would be expected, matching of the fatal bullet with test bullets (of either caliber) could not be obtained. Distinctive breechblock markings were absent. But on the fatal shell there was an excellent extractor mark which could be matched with those produced on test shells.

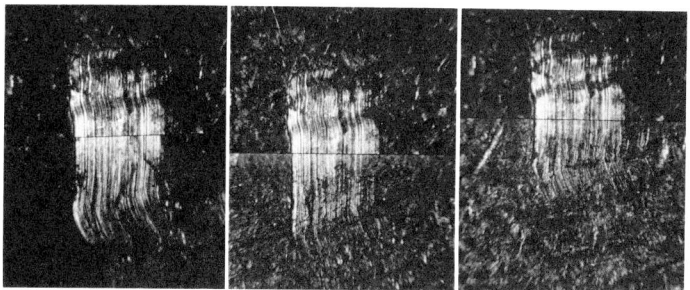

Fig. 37. Matching of ejector marks (Shotgun). *Above line in all three photos:* Ejector mark on fatal shell. *Below line:* Ejector marks made on three different test shells fired in this gun.

In one case in the author's experience, and similar cases have been noted by others, an identification was made by the presence of shear marks on the primer. The primer had been driven partly out of the shell and in the process of ejection had been sheared so as to produce marks which were repetitive

Fig. 38. Matching of loading marks. Comparison microscope photograph showing matching of loading mark on a test shell (above line) with similar mark on evidence shell (below line). Caused by a defect in the loading mechanism of the rifle.

Fig. 39. Scrape marks on primer. *Left:* Scrape mark on primer of shell fired in a .45 cal. Colt automatic pistol. *Right:* Two scrape marks made by same pistol matched under comparison microscope.

on shells fired in this gun. They could be matched nicely (Fig. 39). This type of marking may occur in the dropping-breech type of automatic pistols. Shear marks may sometimes be found on shells fired in a revolver in case the primer is blown back against the breechblock, but such cases are rare. In the case of shear marks which occur on a primer of a shell fired in a revolver, the striations formed may be expected to be curved because the cylinder is being rotated as the mark is being produced, whereas in the case of an automatic pistol the head of the shell moves directly across the breech face producing scratches or serrations which are parallel straight lines.

Another mark produced occasionally but not characteristically by this type of pistol is that caused by firing pin "drag," an example of which is shown in Fig. 29. This was found in a bank robbery case where a Colt .45 had been used. An unusual case of "firing pin drag" is illustrated in Fig. 40. A cheaply-made single barreled shotgun was fired in the author's laboratory to get a test shell. As the cartridge fired the barrel came unlocked, the rear end tipped up, and the shell was ejected violently past the shooter's ear. Quite obviously the firing pin did not have time to get out of the way.

Firing pin "drag marks" are sometimes found in the normal operation of either single or double barreled shotguns—but fortunately under less startling cases than the one described above! Sometimes a firing pin (unless spring loaded) apparently sticks in the indentation made in the primer, and when the breech is opened the pin is pried out and drags across the edge of the indentation it has made.

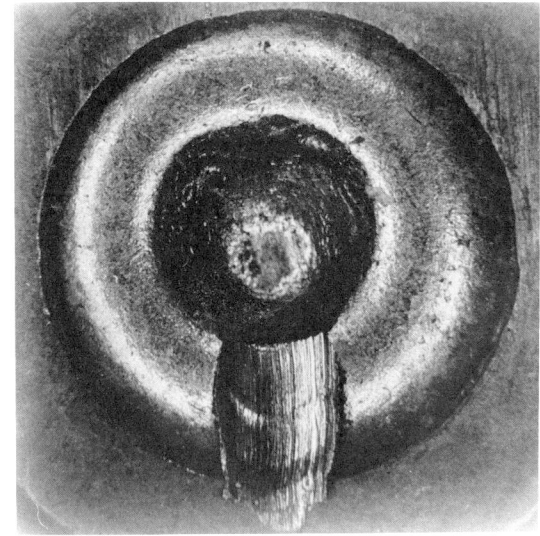

Fig. 40. An unusual case of "firing pin drag," caused by unlocking of the tip-up barrel of a shotgun at moment of explosion.

A "drag" effect may also be produced in the case of a revolver if the point of the hammer after striking the primer does not retract rapidly enough to get out of the way of the rotating cylinder. The side of the impression on the primer may show a gouge caused by dragging the head of the shell over the end of the hammer point (or firing pin, as the case may be). It is also possible that, in a defective gun, the hammer or pin might remain unretracted long enough for the next cartridge head to strike it and even be fired, in case it is a rim fire cartridge.

A slanting mark may be made on the side of a shell by the partial rotation of the barrel during the process of ejection of the shell (in certain automatic pistols). Since the extractor holds the shell during the rotation of the barrel there is a scraping of the shell as it is being withdrawn, thus producing a spiral mark. Since few guns are so constructed, this effect will not be encountered very frequently. This effect is sometimes observed in shells fired in the Savage, Steyr, and similarly constructed automatic pistols. The marks produced by the Savage slant to the right.

Bulges (or marks) in the head of a cartridge are sometimes produced where a portion of the breech block has been cut away to make room for the extractor. Bulges in the tube or body of the shell, just below the rim, are due to the fact that a portion of the chamber has to be cut away to form the ramp up which the cartridge slides from the magazine into the chamber. The presence of this bulge helps to determine the orientation of the shell as it was in the gun, and this together with the position of the extractor (and sometimes the ejector, when such mark is present) may give some information as to the type of automatic to be searched for. Although it does not help in identifying any particular specimen, sometimes a bulge, in itself, will give an important clue as to the type of pistol to be looked for.

Fig. 41. Left: Shell head fired in Sauer Auto Pistol showing cone-shaped mark on primer. *Right:* Breech-block in Sauer Auto Pistol showing cause of mark.

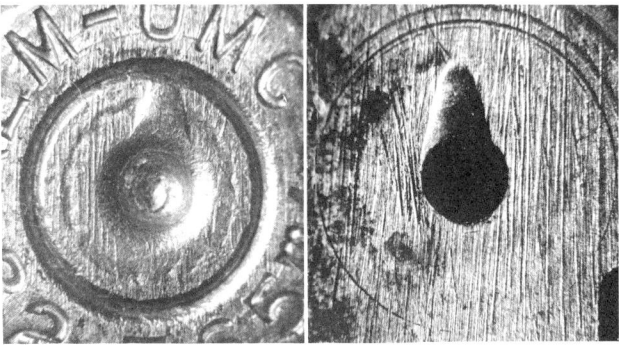

Fig. 42. Marks made by shell striking slide. In the ejection of shells from some makes of automatic pistols the shell often (if not invariably) strikes the edge of the port in the slide and a distinctive mark often results. In some cases these can be matched, in others they cannot. These two photos show marks produced on shells fired in a 7.65 mm. Dreyse. The marks are about half way up the side of the shell directly below the extractor marks and have the appearance of small gashes. Left hand shell is the evidence shell, test shell is at the right. Similar marks were found on all test shells fired. The extractor marks matched very well, positively identifying the murder gun.

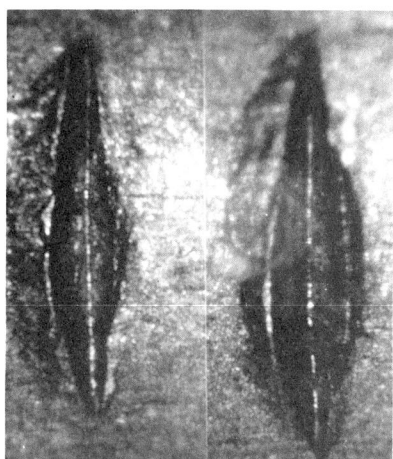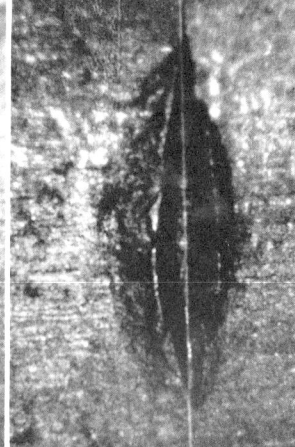

Fig. 43. Enlargement of marks shown in Fig. 42. The photo at the left shows the two gash marks greatly magnified. Mark on evidence shell at the left, test at the right.

The photo at the right shows the two brought together under the comparison microscope in an attempt to get a matching of the marks. The results were not satisfactory, only a general resemblance being shown. 33

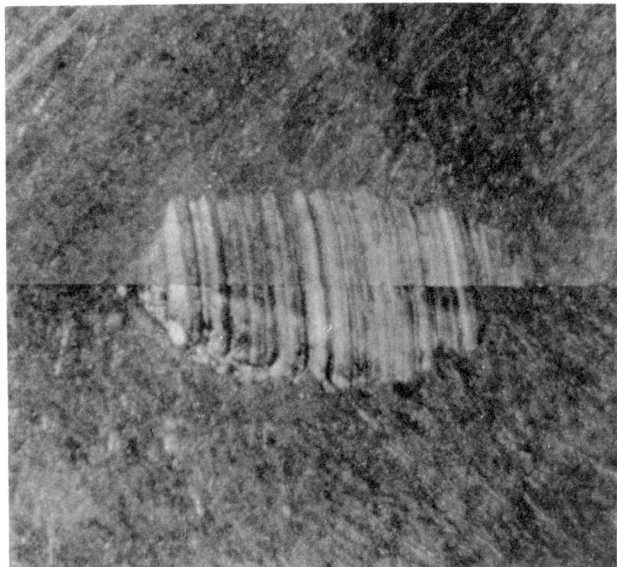

Fig. 44. Identification by markings produced on the side of a fired shell. While this situation seldom occurs, and therefore the procedure is rarely used, such markings may be very useful in making an identification. *Above line:* Mark produced on body of a test shell fired in a Czech M-27 pistol. *Below line:* Mark found on evidence shell. (Courtesy of Wisconsin State Crime Lab.)

The Sauer pistol is a good example, as will be seen in Fig. 41. A cone-shaped bulge will be found in shells fired in Sauer pistols because of the cone-shaped depression just above the firing pin hole in the breech face. This seems peculiar to the Sauer.

In the ejection of fired shells from some automatics the shell may be marked by striking the edge of the port in the slide on its way out. Indeed, this seems to be a characteristic for some makes and the presence of such marks may give a clue as to the make of the gun. Rarely will these marks be sufficiently repetitive to furnish an identification of a particular gun. Such cases have been observed, however, on shells ejected from a post-war commercial Model 1911-A1 Colt. (See Hatcher, Jury, and Weller, p. 323, for an example.*) The flattening of the mouth of a shell ejected from a Colt .45 in the firing operation is quite common, but good repetitive markings are rarely obtained.

The .45 ACP cartridge regularly used in automatic pistols and some U.S. machine guns can also be fired in the 1917 Mod. Colt revolver and the 1917 Mod. S & W revolver, by the use of half-moon clips, each of which holds three cartridges, to hold them in place. If an evidence shell of this type shows no

Firearms Investigation, Identification and Evidence, The Stackpole Co., Harrisburg, Penna.

34

flattening at the mouth it would suggest that it had not been fired in a Mod. 1911 or 1911-A1 automatic, but quite possibly in a Mod. 1917 revolver. The presence or absence of an extractor mark would also be important in this situation.

Some years ago the author had a 7.65 mm. shell, submitted in a murder case, which was positively identified, through a comparison of extractor marks, as having been fired in the suspect's 7.65 mm. Dreyse automatic. In addition to this positive identification an additional feature was noticed. The fatal shell and all test shells fired had a mark like a small gash across the body of the shell at about the midpoint between mouth and head. While these marks could not be successfully matched they were of some significance because they are not customarily found. Their appearance is shown in Figs. 42 and 43. In a case processed at the Wisconsin State Crime Laboratory a splendid matching of such marks on the body of an evidence shell and marks made on test shells fired in a CZ Mod. P-37 pistol was obtained* (Fig. 44).

"No gun" identifications

Positive identifications of firearms that have led to the solution of major crimes have been made in cases where no suspect gun was found. In some instances fired cartridges, either known to have been fired by the suspect on a previous occasion in a gun which belonged to him or found in the possession of a suspect, have been instrumental in solving the case. In other cases a bullet known to have been fired by the suspect from a firearm known to have belonged to him (or to have been in his possession) furnished the necessary evidence. One of these cases is interesting because of its international character. In a murder case which occurred several years ago in Saskatchewan this procedure was used. A former U.S. citizen from Kentucky had moved to Canada to make his home there and became a suspect in a murder case in which no gun could be found. Diligent inquiry in the locality of his former home in Kentucky disclosed that he had owned a rifle of the same caliber as that used in the commission of the murder. An extensive search of the area where he was known to have fired this gun in target practice before moving to Canada revealed bullets that he had fired. When these were compared with the

*Because of the practice of reloading fired cases, fortunately not too common, the firearms examiner must be alert to the possibility that certain marks present on an evidence shell may possibly have been put there by a previous firing in a different weapon. Some markings that are inconsistent (and therefore confusing) may be so explained.

evidence bullet in Canada they were found to match, and he was convicted of the murder.

Determination of the manufacturer of ammunition

The manufacturers of cartridges usually identify their product by a mark placed on the head of the cartridge, and these "head stamps," as they are called, serve to identify the maker of the fired shell case. Since there are many manufacturers there are necessarily a great number and variety of head stamps. A well-equipped firearms identification laboratory should have as large a collection as possible of cartridges and cartridge components for identification purposes. Such extensive collections require much time, patience, and expense in collecting. However, there are compilations of reproductions of head stamps and these are of great value in making identifications.

The determination of the manufacturer of a particular fired bullet is not so easy, particularly if it is of foreign make. The practice of putting an identifying letter on the bullet, formerly quite extensively used, has almost disappeared. Bullets of current U.S. manufacture are not so marked.

The type, shape, and number of serrations in the cannelures are sometimes a clue to the manufacturer. The cannelures are made by knurling them into the formed bullet, or they may be formed as the bullet is swaged. Since different manufacturers use different forms of knurls or swages the cannelures will often be quite distinctive. Known samples in the laboratory "ammunition component parts file" frequently lead to the desired answer. Specifications for cannelures furnished by the manufacturer should not be relied on, as they often do not represent actual production procedures and, therefore, may be misleading. Fortunately, the question of who made the bullet is of little if any importance, but it is important to use bullets of similar size, weight, and dimensions in getting test bullets for comparison purposes.

The problem as to whether two bullets came from the same source and, particularly, out of the same lot of ammunition is an easier one to solve. Formerly, resort was made to chemical analysis and determination of densities, both very time-consuming and tricky operations requiring a considerable degree of skill. Also, a significant amount of the metal of the bullet would be lost because of the size of the sample required for the chemical analysis. These methods need no longer be used since analysis by means of the spectrograph has become so common. Every modern crime laboratory has one of these instruments, but should a police laboratory not have one there are many commercial laboratories who can furnish the service required. A spectrographic test can be made by an expert in a few minutes. The determination of each and every metallic element present is made both qualitatively and quantitatively, and the amount of the specimen required for the analysis is almost microscopic in size, thus no significant amount of the evidence is destroyed.

If the spectrograms of the evidence bullet and a bullet found in the defendant's possession are identical, qualitatively and quantitatively, it is very good evidence that the two bullets not only came from the same manufacturer but in all probability came from the same *batch* of metal! Conversely, if the spectrograms are unlike, it is positive proof that the bullets did *not* come from the *same batch* of metal. Of course, they could have been made by the same manufacturer but at different times. The manufacturer may get his lead from different sources and, consequently, there will be significant differences (as determined spectrographically) in the bullets he makes. Likewise, different manufacturers may get their lead from different sources, and spectrographic differences will show up in their products.

Instrumentation

The comparison microscope

Since the comparison microscope is probably the most important and most widely used scientific instrument in the modern crime laboratory it is fitting that it be discussed first.

The first comparison microscope to be used in the field of criminology was a very crude instrument compared to the highly developed instruments now available. It was designed by Albert S. Osborn for application in the field of document examination and was constructed by the Bausch and Lomb Optical Company. As a matter of fact, Osborn's first idea was to use it for the comparison of the colors (and particularly the ageing) of documents, and it was built to accommodate the filters of the Lovibond Tintometer. But he soon found it to be very useful for other comparisons as well. This instrument is shown in Fig. 45.* There is no hint that it was ever used in the field of firearms identification.

In 1922 C. E. Waite, a special investigator, was assigned by the Governor of New York to a homicide case in which a firearm played a part, and he thus became interested in the possibility of the identification of firearms. But his ideas on the subject were very vague indeed. He gathered much information relative to existing firearms, their specifications and manufacture, but was greatly handicapped by the fact that he had no scientific training nor mechanical background and no particular knowledge of firearms. But he was a promoter and he had an idea. So he formed a group of associates to supply what he himself lacked, and this organization later took the name "The Bureau of Forensic Ballistics." His associates

*A. S. Osborn–*Questioned Documents,* 1st Ed. 1910, page 326.

were Philip O. Gravelle, a photographer and microscopist, John H. Fisher, an expert tool designer and worker with precision instruments, formerly at the Bureau of Standards, and (most important of all) Captain Calvin Goddard who had served in World War I as a Medical Officer, whose hobby was guns of

Fig. 45. Early type comparison microscope. Employed by Albert S. Osborn for document examinations. Constructed by Bausch & Lomb.

all descriptions, and who had a very unusual knowledge of firearms, their construction, manufacture, types and makes, specific models, individual characteristics, and peculiarities. Little did he know at the time that he was destined to become the pioneer and most distinguished worker in the field of firearms identification. Fisher's chief contribution, and the only one of record, was the design of an instrument to which was given the name Helixometer, the purpose of which was to permit observations of the interior of a barrel and measurements of the pitch of the rifling to be made. The instrument was made for a number of years by the Spencer Lens Co., but it was not a success and those in existence are rarely, if ever, used.

To Gravelle must be given the credit for suggesting the use of a comparison microscope in firearms identification. He had been employed in pattern designing for a textile company and was familiar with the use of an instrument of this sort for comparing the fine details of two similar pieces of cloth, and early in 1925 he suggested to the group that a comparison microscope might be useful for making comparisons of fired bullets. Apparently, neither Gravelle nor Goddard knew that Professor E. M. Chamot of Cornell University had used a comparison microscope made by Bausch and Lomb in his studies on primers for the Ordnance Department during World War I. This instrument was a great improvement over that used by Osborn, particularly as it had two mechanical stages for holding the objects being examined. The optical system was also greatly improved.

Fig. 47. Bausch & Lomb comparison microscope. (Early type.) This instrument obtained by author in 1925 on special order. A similar microscope had been made by B & L for Professor Chamot of Cornell University for his study of primers during World War I.

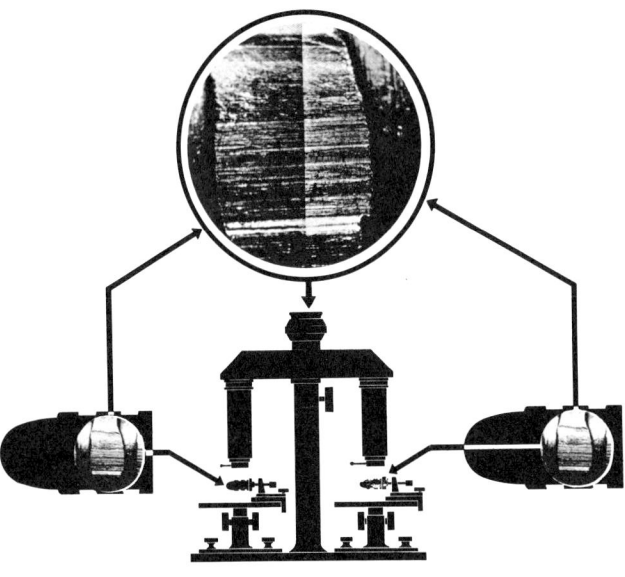

Fig. 46. Diagram illustrating the principle of the comparison microscope. (Schematic illustration by Burton D. Munhall, courtesy of the Institute of Applied Science, Chicago, Ill.)

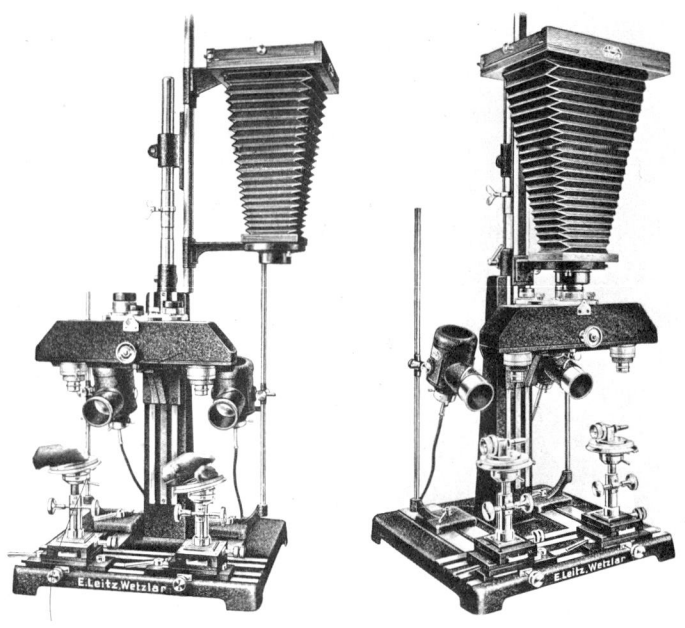

Fig. 48. Leitz comparison microscope made by E. Leitz, Wetzlar, Germany.

As a result of Gravelle's suggestion two compound microscopes, a comparison bridge of foreign manufacture, and a pair of bullet mounts (probably designed by Fisher) built by the Remington Arms Co., were procured and first set up for use in April 1925. It was a great success from the beginning and Goddard published a paper on the subject in the November-December issue of *Army Ordnance*. The instrument soon obtained wide publicity through this and other articles, and to Goddard goes the principal credit for this great advance in firearms identification technique, since Gravelle never actually used the instrument in firearms identifications.

A comparison microscope (Figs. 46 to 52) consists essentially of two compound microscopes, having identical optical systems, so that they give the same magnification, connected by an optical "bridge" containing a combination of prisms such that by viewing two separate objects (one under each microscope) through a single eyepiece the two objects may be compared by bringing the images of parts of each into juxtaposition. The "optical field" seen through the single eyepiece is a circular area divided into two parts by a thin dark line. The object under the left hand microscope (say the evidence bullet) is seen in

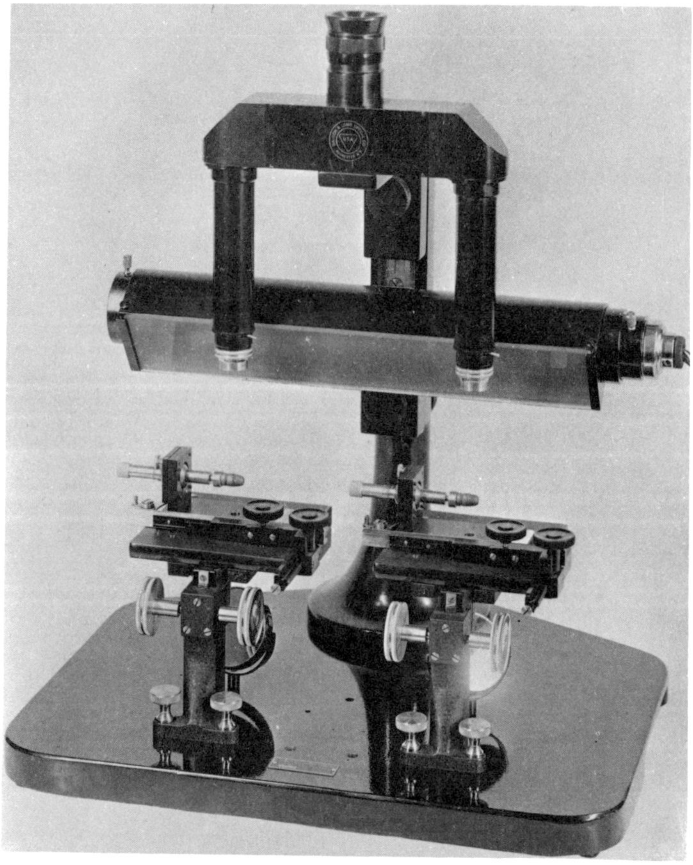

Fig. 49. Bausch & Lomb comparison microscope. A later type. Illumination is from a single lamp rather from individual spot lights whose position and intensity can be adjusted. Such flexibility is desirable.

Fig. 50. Bausch & Lomb microscope and camera. Same microscope as shown in Fig. 49 but with addition of camera.

the left half of this optical field, and the object under the right hand microscope (say a test bullet) is seen only in the right half of the field. Assuming that we have two bullets to be compared, an evidence bullet and a test bullet, the evidence bullet is placed in a "bullet mount" under the left hand microscope and adjusted so that it points directly across (i.e., at right angles to) the central dividing line and in a position such that, say, a third of the rear portion of the bullet is in view. It is now rotated in its mount (by turning the appropriate knob) until a well-defined groove (or land) comes into view and this is brought into the best possible focus by raising or lowering the microscope stage carrying the bullet mount. (All focusing is done by raising or lowering the microscope stages.) Then the test bullet is placed so that about two-thirds of the nose end of the bullet is in view (pointing in the same direction as the evidence bullet, of course) and, after lining up the edges of the test bullet with those of the evidence bullet, the test bullet is slowly rotated to bring successive grooves (and lands) into view until one is found (if any such is present) which not only has the same width, but which also has longitudinal striations or tiny groovelets (scorings) which extend across the boundary line, joining and coinciding with similar markings on the evidence bullet. These markings will be parallel to the edges of the groove. When this condition is attained the bullets are said to be "matched" and, by means of a camera placed above the instrument, a photograph of the matched bullets is taken.

The mounts for the bullets are provided with removable "studs" to the ends of which the bullets are attached by a suitable wax. Several pairs of these studs are provided, usually three. Around the periphery of each pair, indexing numbers are engraved, usually from 1 to 4, 5, or 6, corresponding to the number of lands and grooves most often found. After marking the bullets which have been matched, they are reset on the studs so that each of the marked grooves will be in the No. 1 position. The two bullets are now rotated into the No. 2 position and compared. If these grooves are found to match, the matching is photographed and this process is repeated until all the grooves (and lands) have been compared. Naturally as many matches are obtained as possible, because convincing one's self and convincing a jury "beyond all reasonable doubt" are two quite different matters. The expert must always keep in mind the fact that juries are always unpredictable! If some pairs of grooves (or lands) match and others do not, the expert must be prepared to explain why they do not.

In the majority of cases the best matches of rifling marks are obtained nearer the base end of the bullets, but this is not always the case and actually the identification expert will look for matchings from one end of the "engraved" portion of the bullets to the other to make certain that nothing is overlooked. A high magnification is not necessary and, in fact, is not desirable as it naturally limits the field of observation. The magnification should never be such that the complete width of one groove (or land) cannot be seen clearly. Bullets of different sizes may be examined advantageously with different magnifications. If the grooves are narrow and have very fine striations a higher magnification will be desirable than in the case where a groove is wide and the important striations are fewer and wider. Experiment is the best guide as to the most desirable magnification to use. The author prefers to use matched Micro Tessars as these have diaphragms to control both the depth of focus and the illumination. In examining extractor marks, ejector marks, and the bottoms of firing pin impressions, higher magnifications may be desirable than are used in examining the markings on bullets. Depth of focus is very important here, especially for

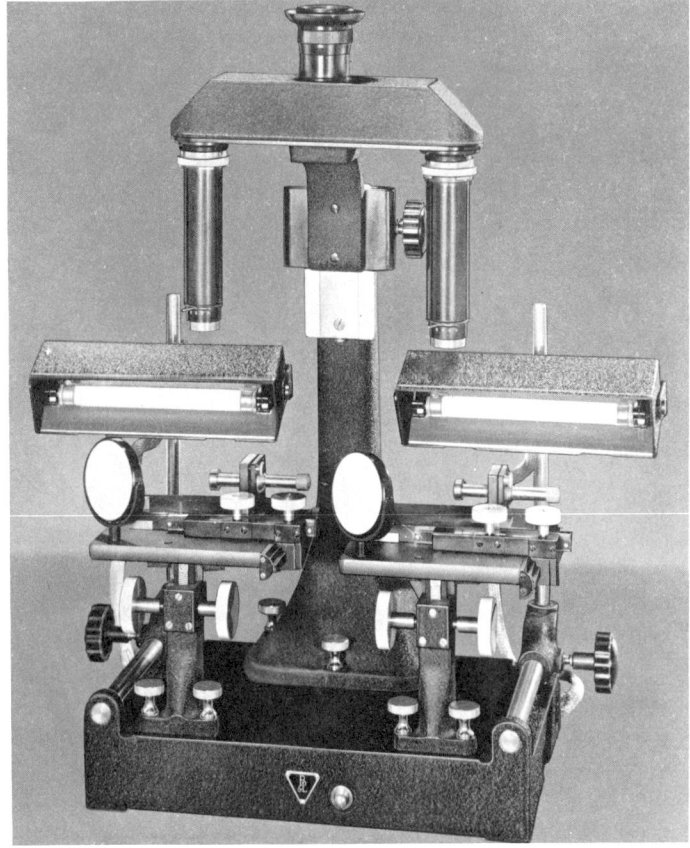

Fig. 51. Bausch & Lomb comparison microscope. Modern type. (Photo by courtesy B & L.)

curved or uneven surfaces, and a small aperture must be used in taking photographs, in order to get the desired depth and clarity in the final picture, since the lens of a camera cannot adjust itself to depth as the eye does.

The comparison microscope is very useful in matching markings on fired shells. It is important in all cases that proper illumination be used. The light must come to each of the two objects being compared at the same angle and, when pictures are taken, must be adjusted so that each object is illuminated evenly and to the same intensity. Oxidized surfaces, be they lead, copper, or brass, have lower reflecting power than clean bright surfaces, hence the importance of having the illumination adjusted properly in order that each half of the negative will have the same density. Bright metal surfaces can be made less reflecting by putting them in an oxidizing atmosphere

for a time, but this procedure is legitimate only on the test bullets and shells and is not often used. The question as to the use of comparison photographs in court will be discussed elsewhere, but the author is firmly convinced that photographs should be taken as a matter of record, if for no other purpose. No man's memory of what he has seen under a microscope is infallible, particularly of such complex systems as those constituting bullet matches, and one photograph is worth hundreds of descriptive words in one's notes! A case may be appealed to a higher court or may be reopened years later. In such cases photographs taken at the time of the original investigation are very valuable indeed.

The accompanying illustrations of comparison microscope matchings (Figs. 53 to 60) show what can be done when conditions are reasonably good. It must not be supposed that convincing matchings can *always* be obtained. Every examiner, no matter how experienced or expert he may be, has had the experience of spending many hours in the futile attempt to get satisfactory and convincing matchings in cases where there was every reason to believe that he had the gun that fired the evidence bullet or shell. There are many causes for such failures. The evidence bullet may have been too small for the bore of the gun, the barrel may have been very rusty or

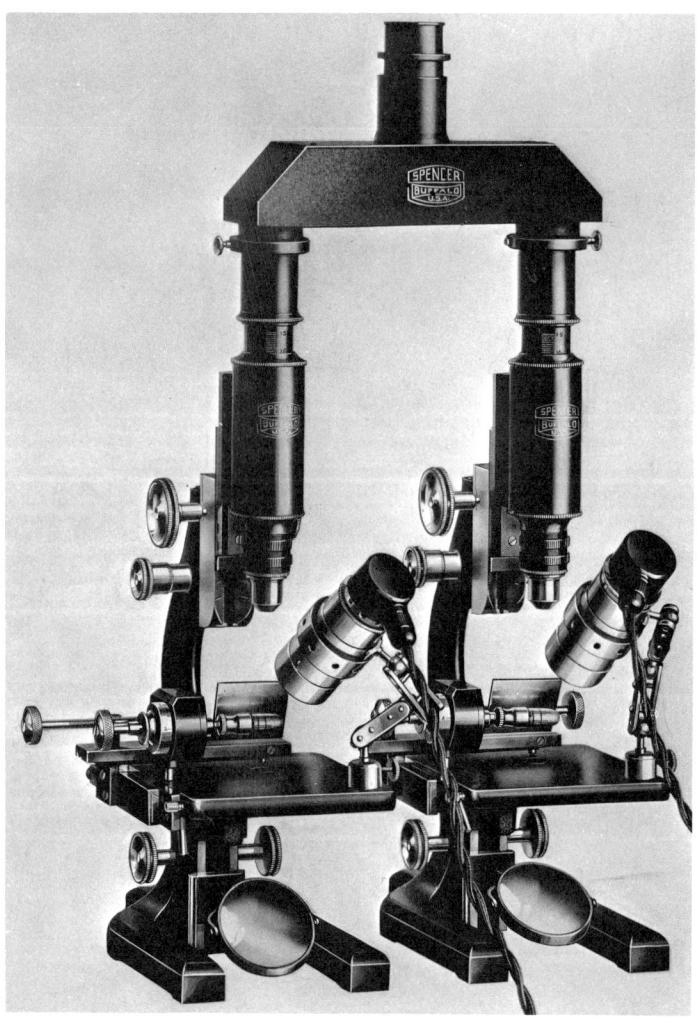

Fig. 52. Spencer comparison microscope. (Photo courtesy American Optical Co.)

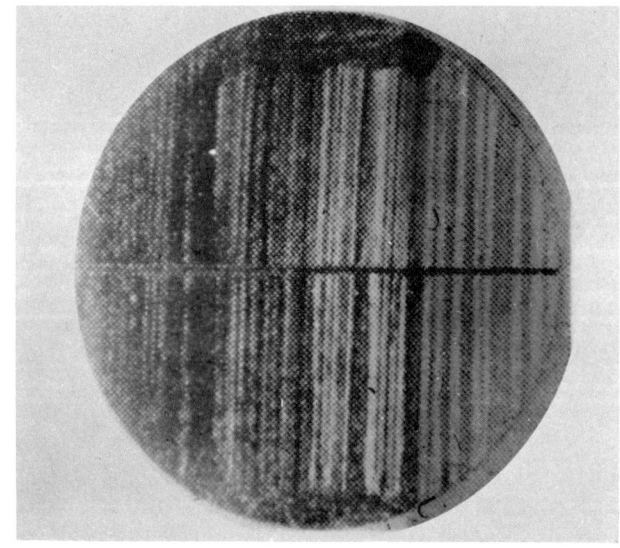

Fig. 53. An early case of matching of rifling marks by means of the comparison microscope. Photograph taken by Goddard subsequent to the trial of Sacco and Vanzetti, while case was being reviewed on order of the Governor. Comparison microscope photographs and comparison microscope testimony not used at the trial. Much of the testimony was very unscientific and irrelevant.

Fig. 54. Comparison microscope matchings. Test bullets above horizontal line, evidence bullets below line. Four different cases.

fouled, the bullet may have been so deformed that no evidence of lands or grooves is present, etc. The author once received a fatal .22 cal. lead bullet that was so crushed and mutilated that it bore no rifling markings whatsoever—it was simply a "misshapen hunk of lead that weighed what a .22 cal. long rifle bullet of a certain make should weigh." (Incidentally, .22 cal. lead bullets, particularly .22 shorts, probably cause more trouble than all other bullets put together.) A spinning bullet fired into plaster may have all identifying marks removed. And primers may sometimes be so hard, or powder pressure may be so low, that no breechblock markings are produced. Many things can happen to produce non-

Fig. 55. Matching of rifling marks.

Left: Matching of marks made by land. *Above line:* Test bullet from suspect gun. *Below line:* Fatal bullet.

Right: Matching of marks made by groove. *Above line:* Test bullet from suspect gun. *Below line:* Fatal bullet.

Note: All six lands and grooves could be matched.   41

Fig. 56. Matching of rifling marks (comparison microscope photos). *Above line:* Rifling mark on test bullet fired from suspect gun. *Below line:* Rifling mark found on evidence bullet.

Fig. 58. Comparison microscope photographs. Showing matchings on two pairs of bullets. Two different guns.

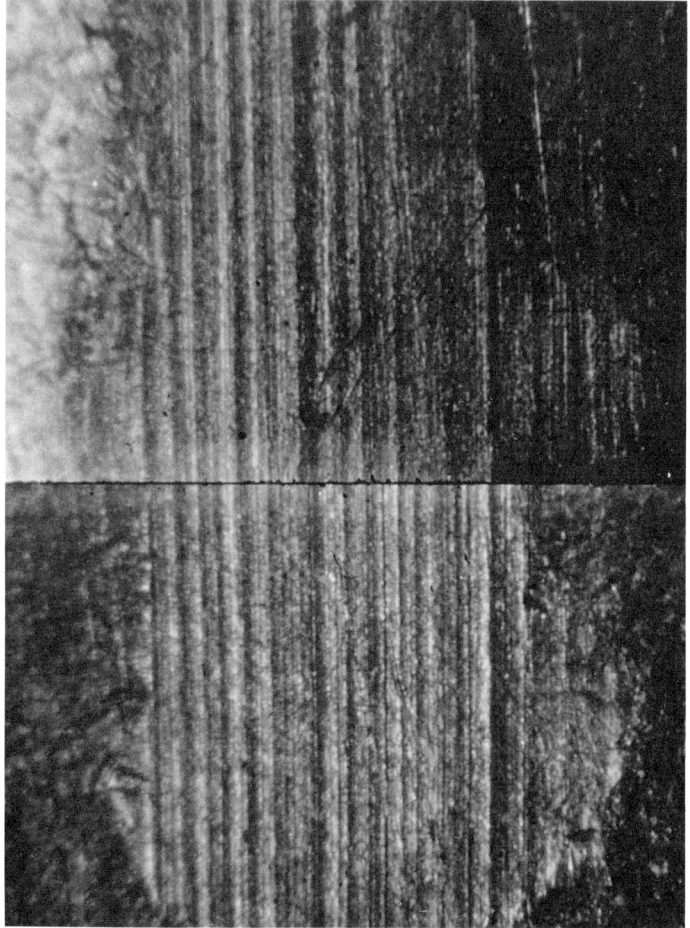

Fig. 57. Comparison microscope photograph. Showing matching of rifling marks on a tiny fragment of bullet jacket taken from victim's kidney by surgeon (upper) with marks produced on a test bullet (lower) fired from suspect's gun. This tiny portion of the copper jacket was all that was found, the remainder having been torn off in passing through the side of an automobile.

Fig. 59. Lines on deformed bullets fail to match. While the matching of the test (upper) bullet with the evidence bullet (lower) is good in each case in the center part of the photos, it will be noted that the lines become farther apart on the evidence bullet, due to its expansion. This is a common occurrence with evidence bullets that are deformed, as they so frequently are. (*Note:* Bullets were fired from different guns.)

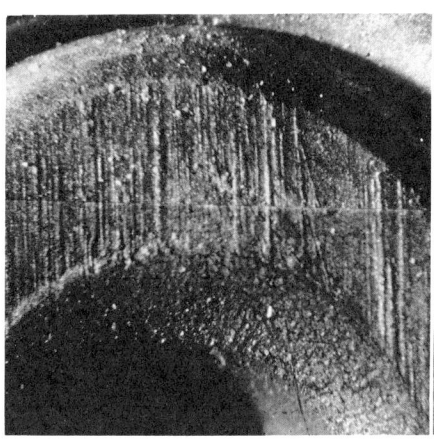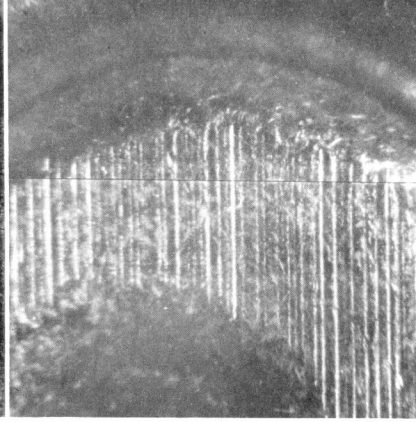

Fig. 60. Matching of breechblock marks (comparison microscope photos). These are matches obtained in three separate cases. In each case, test shell is above line of separation.

matching, but when good matchings *are* obtained no evidence is more convincing!

The comparison camera

Those who for years have had occasion to use a comparison microscope for the examination of bullets and other objects know how very tiring such examinations may become. Not only are they tiring, but they are productive of eyestrain.

Fig. 61. The comparison camera. Used particularly for the examination, comparison, and photographing of fired bullets.

Both of these difficulties disappear with the use of the comparison camera (1)*—the basic idea of which was suggested by May and by Lewis. The operator sits in a comfortable position looking directly ahead at images on a large ground-glass screen. The images are large and clear and are seen by both eyes and are viewed at a normal and comfortable distance, thus materially reducing eyestrain.

A series of knurled control knobs, placed in line a few inches below the ground glass, and one at either side of the ground glass enable the operator to move the specimens in any desired direction and rotate them. After all adjustments of the two juxtaposed images have been made, one sees on the ground glass exactly what he may expect to see in

*Numbers in parentheses refer to Literature Citations given at the end of the chapter.

Fig. 62. Comparison camera. Same as Fig. 63 but from different angle.

Fig. 63. Comparison camera. Showing forward assembly all of which is mounted on a block which slides forward or back to accommodate lenses of different focal length.

the finished photograph. A time switch enables him to expose the plate or film for a predetermined interval.

Both plates and cut films may be used. Eastman Panatomic-X film is very satisfactory because of its lack of grain and its sensitivity to all colors. A "glycin" developer is recommended because it gives very fine grain and the desired contrast.

The complete assembly is shown in Fig. 61. For the sake of clarity in description it is probably best to divide the instrument into several parts and describe each separately.

The carriage

This part of the instrument (Figs. 62, 63, 64) has in its assembly the mechanism for transmitting vertical, horizontal, longitudinal, and circular motion to specimens being compared and photographed. It is so arranged that the image of one object may be juxtaposed above the other exactly. The carriage travels on a pair of ½-inch square tracks, 8 inches in length and secured to the base of the instrument, and it is actuated by a ¼-inch lead screw (G in Fig. 65)

having 28 threads to the inch. All lead screws are of the same diameter and pitch throughout. Rising from the carriage are two supports capable of being moved to the right or left independently of each other by means of two inclined planes and actuated by individual lead screws (H_1 and H_2). Each of these supports carries a bracket to which is attached a small worm and worm gear so arranged that there is virtually no backlash. These worm gear assemblies impart circular motion to the specimens they carry when knobs R_1 and R_2 are turned. The brackets are moved vertically by means of inclined planes built into the supports. The planes are moved by lead screws V_1 and V_2. The shaft in the center of each worm gear is a small split stud to which different types of specimen mounts may be quickly and easily attached. All lead screws are coupled, by means of small Hooke's joints (universal joints, Fig. 64) to the control rods which terminate in the series of control knobs (Fig. 65) at the lower edge of the plate end of the camera; thus the operator may

Fig. 64. Comparison camera. Showing detail of mechanism for rotating bullets.

remain seated while making all adjustments, once the bullets are aligned vertically.

The camera

The camera is not unlike the conventional 8×10-inch view camera. It is "cone-shaped," being about 5 inches square at the lens end and about 12 inches square at the plate end, and is 30 inches long. The small end has two lens rings mounted one above the other. Actually the comparison camera consists of two rigid camera enclosures mounted one above the other with an adjustable horizontal dividing septum to be described later. The lens rings carry a matched pair of Bausch and Lomb lenses. Lenses with various focal lengths are available; a pair of 112 mm. Tessar Ic lenses are used for low magnifications, a pair of 70 mm. focal length Micro Tessars for greater magnification, and even 48 mm. Micro Tessars may be used. The unique feature of the camera body is the fact that it contains an adjustable thin metal partition dividing the camera horizontally into two separate parts, one for each lens. This partition is surfaced with sateen cloth and sprayed with instrument black (a nonglossing lacquer) to prevent halo and ghost images, as the angle of incidence is very low, less than 15° at times. There is no reflection from this metal partition. It is slip-hinged at the lens end and supported at the plate end by two bearing blocks through which run two threaded vertical rods, one at each side of the plate holder but out of line with the light path. A single control knob (D in Fig. 65) at the top of the rear end of the camera permits the adjustment of this dividing partition up or down, the two threaded rods being rotated at the

Fig. 65. Rear end of comparison camera. Bullets may be moved in three dimensions and rotated by turning lettered knobs. Bullet images are necessarily dim in this photo as the lights were on in the room in order to take the picture.

same rate by means of a connecting chain and sprocket drive. The movement of the partition permits the making of comparisons of specimens at any point in their length. The rear of the camera is fitted with a conventional 8×10-inch plate back with ground glass, permitting the use of standard 8×10-inch cut film or plate holders.

The base

The base of the instrument is a 1-inch thick American black walnut board edged with a modified "OG" bead all around. Inset on the under side of this base are two pieces of cold rolled steel, ¼×1 inch, through which are threaded the three adjusting

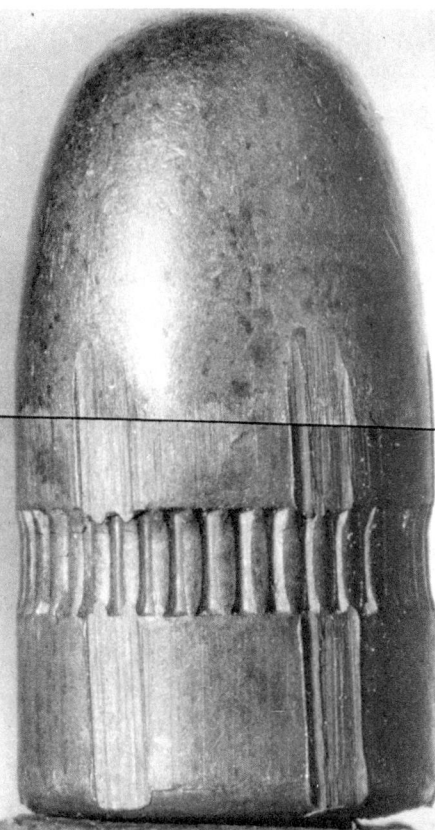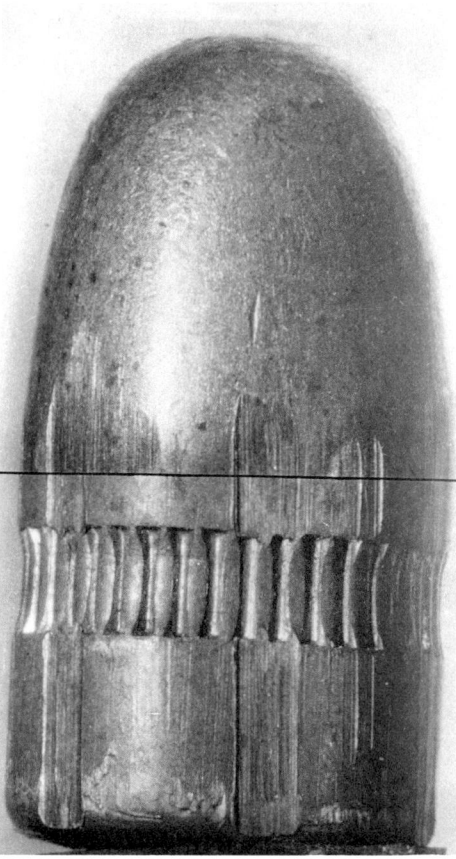

Fig. 66. Comparison camera photographs. Showing the matching of the same pair of bullets in three successive positions. *Above line:* Test bullet. *Below line:* Fatal bullet. (.25 cal. metal-jacketed bullets.)

screws whose ends terminate in knurled knobs, thus giving a three-point support for the instrument. In order that the operator may be seated in a normal position at the instrument, the entire assembly is set on three pyramidal wood blocks of the correct height for the operator's eye level.

Materials used throughout are stainless steel and brass except the inclined planes whose bearing surfaces are faced with cold rolled steel. All exposed brass surfaces are finished with black Hilo crystallizing varnish ("crackle finish"). The camera body is covered with Keratol (simulated leather) and the base is piano finished (several coats of clear Valspar varnish, hand pumiced and polished).

Lighting equipment

At the lens end of the instrument and back of the carriage is a diffusing screen of opal glass illuminated by an ordinary 75-watt light bulb in a desk type reflector, thus providing a white background for the objects being photographed.

There are two adjustable, microscope-type object illuminators (Spencer) which are so positioned that they give oblique lighting to the specimens. These lights are controlled by two rheostats (Fig. 65) so that their intensity can be matched or balanced. This is important, as a test bullet is usually brighter than the evidence bullet.

Another similar pair of lights (not shown in the illustrations) is also used on the opposite side on occasion, or both sets can be used, to get the clarity and definition that are so necessary to good photography. Figure 66 shows a typical example of what can be accomplished with a pair of bullets that show good matching. Below the horizontal dividing line is shown the base end of the evidence bullet, above the line is shown the nose end of a test bullet fired from the suspected gun.* For other examples see Figs. 67 to 74.

Use of photographs of matchings in court

There has been considerable difference of opinion

*This instrument and a number of others were built in collaboration with the author by Mr. Lee K. Henke, Senior Mechanician in the Shop of the Department of Chemistry at the University of Wisconsin.

Fig. 67. Comparison camera photograph. Showing matching of two bullets fired from a .32 cal. Savage automatic pistol. Reproducible markings on lands as well as in the grooves. Jacketed bullets often do not show good markings on lands.

Fig. 68. Comparison camera photograph. Showing matching of two bullets fired from a .38 cal. revolver.

among investigators regarding the use of photographs in court to illustrate the matching of rifling marks, breechblock marks, extractor marks, ejector marks, etc. Some have given up the use of photographs and rely entirely upon a statement that they have examined the evidence bullet or shell and have compared the markings found on same to be identical (or nonidentical, as the case may be) with markings found on test bullets or shells, and upon this statement of their findings in the laboratory they offer an opinion. They argue that since they are qualified as experts to make such examinations it is not necessary that photographic records be made of what their examinations reveal. Furthermore, they state that photographs are likely to be misinterpreted, particularly by defense counsel, and that the jury may be misled more than informed. They point out that photographs (even large enlargements) have to be examined individually by each member of the jury and that this leads to confusion. And, furthermore, in many large police laboratories the work load is so heavy as to preclude the making of photographs in all cases, and if they are used in any cases they must always be used in order to meet questions of the defense counsel. Finally, they state that in many

cases "sufficiently perfect" photographs cannot be produced, although to an experienced examiner the comparisons are of sufficiently good quality to enable *an expert* to form a correct opinion.

All experienced examiners will have much sympathy with these points of view. However, there is another side to be considered. How about the viewpoint of the intelligent and perhaps skeptical juror? Will he be satisfied with the unsupported word of the expert? And what is he to think when the experts

47

Fig. 69. Comparison camera photograph. Shows matching of two bullets fired from a .38 S & W Special revolver.

do not agree? They may have honest differences of opinion. Some of them may be overzealous in their cause and in their opinions. And some are downright dishonest. In the past thirty years the author has met all of these types. As a juror he would want to be shown. And a good photograph accompanied by a full explanation of principles involved and a frank acknowledgement of such limitations as exist will

have a much better effect on the jury than an unsupported statement of an expert who, in the majority of cases, is unknown to the members of the jury. Jurymen often may be uneducated, but few of them are dumb. And the more uneducated they are the more skeptical they are likely to be. It must be admitted that there are two sides to the question of whether photographs should be used in court.

In several cases in the author's experience good photographs of matchings have been a decisive factor. In a very early case which was appealed to the State Supreme Court the justices had photographs of twelve matchings of rifling marks to examine. All six lands and all six grooves on the fatal bullet could be matched against the corresponding lands and grooves on a test bullet. Such visual evidence is incontrovertible and the decision in the lower court was sustained.

In another case, in which a man had been killed by a charge from a shot gun, two experts testified that the fatal shell had been fired from a gun taken from the defendant. Photographs purporting to show identity of marks on the primer with those on test shells were introduced. No comparison microscope photographs of matchings were introduced, however; only enlarged photographs of the head of the shells. When these were examined (during cross-examination, at the request of the State's Attorney) it was discovered that in photographing one shell head the illumination had come from the *right* side while in the other the illumination had come from the *left* side! Since experts on both sides had testified that the illumination must always come from the same side and from the same angle, cross-examination along this line ceased abruptly! In the author's photographs of the fatal shell head and of the heads of several test shells it was very apparent that (1) there were repetitive markings which appeared on the heads of the test shells, and (2) these markings were quite different from the distinctive marking on the head of the fatal shell. In addition, an examination of the firing pin impressions on the fatal and test shells, with the aid of a binocular microscope, showed clearly that one impression had been made by a firing pin having a blunt (or flattened) end while the other had been made by a firing pin with a tapered (more pointed) end. Under visual examination with an ordinary microscope these differences were not observable. They could be seen only with three-dimensional (stereoscopic) vision. The firing pin impression on the fatal shell and the impressions on several test shells were photographed with a stereocamera attached to a binocular microscope and the stereophotomicrographs

Fig. 70. Comparison camera photographs. Four successive matchings on a pair of lead bullets fired from a .38 cal. revolver whose cylinder did not line up properly with the bore of the barrel, causing the shaving of lead. This is a frequent occurrence with poorly-made guns and sometimes with guns of good make which have become badly worn. Test bullet above line. Evidence bullet below line.

Fig. 71. Matching of .22 Short bullets (comparison camera, 60 mm. lenses). The matching of .22 Short bullets is usually a difficult matter and, as in this instance, the results are often inconclusive. Often the bullets will show few if any distinguishing rifling marks and all too frequently they are so deformed that even a comparison of widths of rifling marks may not be satisfactory. This was not the case here.

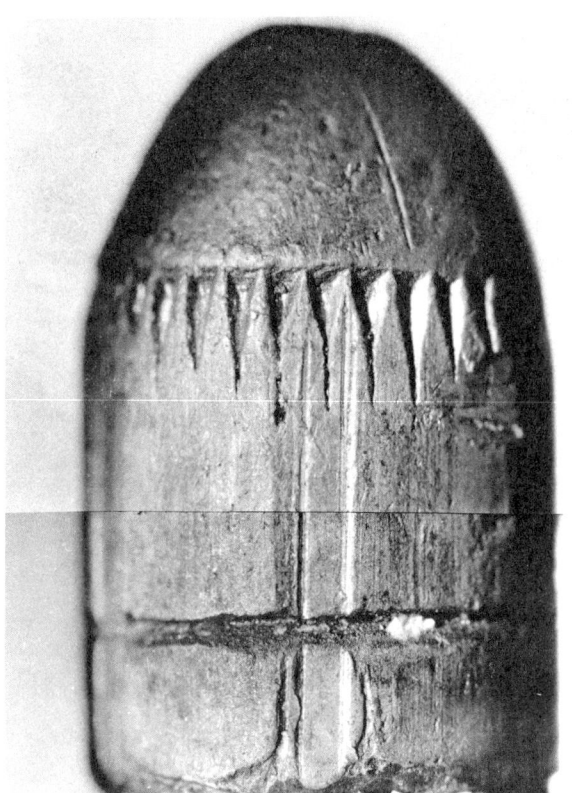

Fig. 72. Comparison camera photograph. Showing four matchings obtained on a pair of .22 cal. lead bullets. *Above line:* Test bullet. *Below line:* Evidence bullet.

Matchings of this quality on .22 cal. lead bullets are rare. This is due to their small size, the softness of lead, the low powder pressures used, and the fact that arms of this caliber are often not cared for properly and are likely to have rifling which is worn, rusty, or leaded.

so obtained were shown to the jury, who acquitted the defendant on the first ballot. Here was a case, certainly, in which the use of photographs, properly taken and of proper type, were the deciding factor in a court case. Without them it would have been the unsupported statement of one expert against two experts.

The author readily admits that if several photographs are being circulated in the jury box while he is testifying about another which he is holding in his hand there is certainly going to be confusion and the members of the jury will be paying little attention to what he is saying, as he will be talking about one photograph while they are looking at another. If each juryman takes time to examine each of several photographs before the next one is shown (as he must if he is to derive any benefit from the photograph) the proceedings will be long drawn out and tedious. To avoid this and to insure that each juror has the best possible opportunity to benefit from visual demonstrations of matchings or similarities found, the author has frequently resorted to the use of lantern slides in *addition* to the enlarged

photographs which are *introduced in evidence* so that they may be examined *later* by the jurymen at their convenience during their deliberations. The slides are left in court so that the jurymen may examine and compare them with the enlargements, as a matter of proper procedure. Each slide is given the same number as the corresponding photograph and it is explained that the slide (which is also a photograph) and the enlarged photograph have been made from the same negative. It is explained that the purpose of showing the slides is to avoid confusion by centering the attention of all of the members of the jury on a single photograph concerning which testimony is being given and to save time. Oftentimes, opposing counsel has asked questions concerning the photographs as they were being shown on the screen and this should be welcomed because it offers the expert additional opportunity to clear up matters for the jury.

If the photographs cannot be defended they should not have been shown in the first place. When a man's life (or future liberty) is at stake he is entitled to a fair and complete trial and the members of the jury are entitled to the best possible presentation of evidence, both pro and con.

The rifling meter

As has already been pointed out, workers in the field of firearms identification often have need of rifling data not presently available to them, either in

Fig. 74. Comparison camera photograph. Showing matching of breechblock markings on primer of a fatal shell (below line) with markings on primer of a test shell (above line) fired from suspect's gun.

Fig. 73. Comparison camera photograph. Evidence bullets are often badly deformed. This makes identification difficult and sometimes impossible. In the case illustrated, however, it was possible to get a quite satisfactory matching of the test bullet (upper) with the fatal bullet (lower).

textbooks, reference books, or from firearms manufacturers. Not infrequently a bullet is brought to the laboratory and the examiner is asked what kind of a gun should be looked for, there being no gun or suspect and perhaps even no known motive for the crime that has been committed. In such a situation it is obvious that the investigation of the case might be much simplified if the authorities could be given some information concerning the type and the probable (or even possible) make of the gun from which the evidence bullet had been fired. Any narrowing down of the search for the gun is clearly of assistance. If it could be said positively that the bullet had been fired from a .32 caliber automatic of a particular

make, the investigators could concentrate their efforts and avoid much loss of time and effort. Unfortunately the usual actual case is not quite so simple, because different manufacturers often have specifications (or at least procedures) which result in "class markings" that are much alike. But, at least, the search can be narrowed down considerably *if proper information is available* to the expert. In the author's experience such information has been very useful to the investigating officers on several occasions, and in one instance it lead directly to the solution of a murder case in which there was no suspect or known motive.

It might appear that the rifling specifications information might be obtained from the manufacturers, and as a matter of fact many manufacturers do have information not only as to present but also past rifling specifications and most of the larger ones will furnish the expert with such data. Also it may be said that these larger, and usually (though not necessarily) responsible, manufacturers do make a sincere effort to follow their own specifications. If each and every manufacturer (past and present) had different specifications and if these specifications were followed at all times, then by making a few observations and measurements on a fired bullet one

51

Fig. 75. The rifling meter. For measuring the pitch of rifling in rifled barrels.

would be able to say with a considerable degree of certainty what make of gun had been used.

But the case is not so simple. In the first place many of the cheaper foreign guns, of which there are probably hundreds of thousands in this country, are "assembled" guns, i.e., the various parts, which may have been made at different shops and under no rigid system of control, were bought up and assembled by a "manufacturer" or dealer who put his own name on the assembled job. In Spain there were a number of shops that devoted themselves exclusively to the rifling of barrels. Some of them had specifications which were followed, more or less, while others seem not to have had any specifications. Another difficulty is that even the reputable manufacturers do make changes in their specifications from time to time, just as typewriter manufacturers change their "fonts," i.e., designs of letters, from time to time. This, however, would be a minor difficulty if the expert had the necessary information as to these changes and when they were made. Actually under certain circumstances these changes may be very useful as they may help to "date" a gun, but this is only so in case the expert does have the information. Often the manufacturers themselves have no record

as to when a change in specifications was made or when it went into effect in their shop practice. One of the world's largest manufacturers has on three occasions had all of its records destroyed, twice by fire and once by flood. In Europe, because of wars and revolutions, valuable records have been destroyed, intentionally in many cases.

In an article published a number of years ago (2) the author stated his intention of making a series of measurements of rifling characteristics of all of the firearms that became available and described in that article the instrument that had been designed and built for the purpose of making accurate measurements of the angle of twist of the rifling in firearms. Because of the enormous number of rifled firearms it has been necessary, as already mentioned, to limit the measurements to hand guns, though it would be of value to have a similar study made on rifles.

The "rifling meter," as we have chosen to call the instrument we have developed for measuring the degree of twist of rifling in a barrel, is shown in Fig. 75. A lead disk, of diameter slightly greater than the bore of the gun, is pushed through the barrel in such manner that it will follow the rifling, and the amount of rotation of the disk is measured at any desired interval by reading the angle on the graduated circle at the interval selected. The lead disk is mounted on the end of a "push rod," the other end of which is inserted into the "hub" carrying the graduated circle and is locked in place. The circle itself is mounted on sturdy ball bearings so that it can rotate freely. After the disk is inserted into the end of the barrel, by turning the hand wheel at the extreme right, a "zero" reading is taken. Then the disk is pushed forward an exact, predetermined amount and the rotation of the disk is determined by taking a reading of angle on the graduated circle and subtracting from this value the original "zero" reading. For example, assume that the "zero" reading (usually made about ¼ to ½ inch from the end of the barrel) was 8.75° and that the reading after the disk had been pushed forward exactly ½ inch was 20.00°, the difference of 11.25° represents the extent of rotation of the rifling in ½ inch of barrel length. Then, for 1 inch it would be 22.50°; and 360/22.50 =16.00 inches, the number of inches required for one complete turn of the rifling. The graduated circle has a vernier which enables one to read to 0.05° (or 3′ of angle). The graduated drum, just to the left of the hand wheel, is graduated into 100 equal divisions, each representing 0.001 inch. So, one rotation of the wheel causes the disk to move forward 0.1 inch. The accuracy of the actuating screw is such that in 10 inches of thrust the error is less than 0.001 inch.

In measuring the rifling of a barrel a series of readings at definite intervals is made in order to see whether the twist is uniform throughout. For a very short barrel the interval chosen would be 0.1 inch, for those 3 to 4 inches in length, 0.2 inch, and for a 6- or 7-inch barrel the interval might well be 0.5 inch. The reproducibility of measurements on barrels that are well rifled and in good condition is very satisfactory. Examples of reproducibility will be given later.

The instrument will now be described in somewhat greater detail especially for the benefit of anyone who cares to have one made. It consists of three essential parts, and for clarity each will be described separately.

Components of the meter

The head—The head is not unlike the tail stock of a modern lathe (Fig. 75). It consists of a lead screw threaded left hand and actuated by a hand wheel. This lead screw is supported by a bronze bearing. Bronze was used because of the pressure that is necessary to start a disc or bullet down the barrel being tested. The lead screw actuates a steel ram, which has a narrow groove milled its entire length. A short spline in the front of the ram housing engages with this groove, thus preventing axial rotation

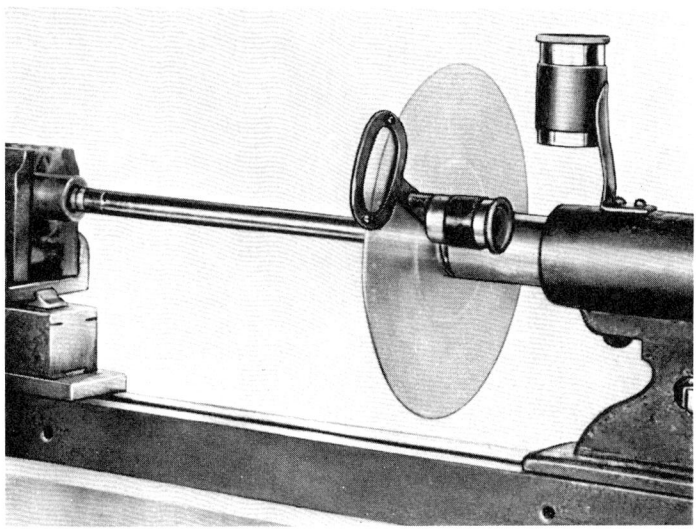

Fig. 76. Dial, vernier, and reading lens. Lens swings on an arc. Dial calibrated 180° right and 180° left.

of the ram when it is moved longitudinally. The threaded bushing in the ram is also of bronze. The steel ram is graduated in sixteenths which are used as a check against the micrometer dial graduations on the sleeve attached to the hand wheel. The lead screw has ten threads to the inch, and the dial is graduated into 100 divisions. Thus every division on the micrometer dial is equal to 0.001 inch. At the opposite end of the ram is mounted, by means of a thrust bearing ("Nice" number 1001), a 5-inch dial divided into 360 divisions, 180° in each direction from zero (Fig. 76). A vernier of twenty divisions is matched to this dial giving readings to .05°. Attached to the thrust bearing is a socket into which the several sizes of push rods fit. This socket has a tapered flat key so that when the push rods are inserted there will be a positive fit with no danger of axial rotation of the push rod in its socket. The free end of each push rod is equipped with two diametrically opposite, pointed piano-wire pins, to prevent axial rotation between the base of the bullet or disc and the push rod face, and a centering pin in the exact center of the face.

Above the ram housing is mounted a magnifier, as can be seen in the figure. Over the vernier is another magnifier on a swivel mounting, so that the vernier can be read in either direction to take care of both right and left hand riflings. The entire head ensemble is held down by two knurled and slotted nuts, so that by loosening them the entire head can be shifted along the bench to any desired position and then firmly clamped to the bed of the bench.

The vise—The vise consists of a pair of parallel jaws faced with Celeron (a fibrous material used for   53

Fig. 77. Auxiliary clamping device for barrels having extreme taper or unusual shape.

making gaskets, etc.), to prevent damaging the barrels clamped in it. Two guide rods are used to keep the jaws in alignment. The jaws are given a bilateral movement through the use of a lead screw threaded both right and left hand from the center. This lead screw terminates in a steel handle having two holes so that a spanner wrench may be used to tighten the barrels in place. Down the center of the "Celeron" facings, whose surfaces are cross-hatched, is cut a fairly deep "V" groove to facilitate the centering of the barrel being measured. The vise body is capable of vertical adjustment by means of a dovetailed inclined plane and actuated by a fine lead screw whose shaft terminates in a knurled knob. After an adjustment is made the vise can be locked permanently in position by means of a V-shaped wedge which is tightened or loosened by means of a thumb screw. The vise parts are enclosed in a heavy steel housing which in turn is fastened permanently in position on the end of the bench.

The bench—In order to eliminate the time necessary for a good iron casting to age and become usable for this purpose, the bench was fabricated from two pieces of channel iron selected for straightness and mounted the desired distance apart by means of spacing blocks held in position by heavy machine screws. The feet were then attached and a light cut was made across the top from end to end. The bench was then checked with a dial indicator, and

the high spots were marked. These were removed by hand scraping until a good surface was presented. Later, when the head assembly was placed in position, this was also filed and hand scraped until by checking with both the indicator and a good straight edge no deviation greater than 0.0005 inch was observed. Because the channels were facing each other they left a space between them which was utilized to help center the head assembly when being moved longitudinally. A spanner wrench was made to fit the vise and another wrench was made to fit the slotted nuts.

The push rods are about 0.010 inch less in diameter than the calibre of the gun with which they are to be used. This diameter is maintained for a distance of about 3/32 inch back from the tip of the rod that holds the bullet or disc, the remainder of the rod has its diameter reduced by about 0.020 inch, so that at no time can there be contact between the gun barrel and the rod.

Because some barrels encountered are frequently tapered to a considerable degree and because some are of odd shapes, they may be difficult to hold securely in the vise. To obviate such difficulties an auxiliary split steel clamp was constructed, having split brass inserts which are interchangeable. These inserts have a hole through them closely approximating the size and shape of the barrel to be held. In use, this clamp is placed around the barrel just back of the front sight, with the back surface of the clamp resting against the front of the vise which takes most of the force of the thrust as the disk (or bullet) is pushed through the barrel. With this device the barrel does not have to be held so securely by the vise, i.e., less pressure has to be applied. This auxiliary clamping device is shown in Fig. 77. Nine sets of brass inserts of various sizes and shapes are available. As most barrels can be held securely in proper position by the vise alone, this auxilliary device is but rarely necessary.

The punch and die set—A necessary accessory to the rifling meter is a punch and die set, such as the one illustrated in Fig. 78. This is used for cutting the lead discs which are to be pushed through the barrel.

Lead bullets were first used, but these became unobtainable because of war restrictions. This turned out to be a fortunate circumstance as the lead discs were found to work much better than lead projectiles. Discs cut by steel dies have accurate, reproducible diameters whereas the diameters of purchased bullets vary considerably. Furthermore, the rifling meter gives the best results when a moderate pressure is required to force the lead object through the barrel. Bullets present a relatively large surface of contact with the walls of the barrel and a slightly over-size bullet requires considerable pressure. This is not desirable. Lead discs cut from ⅟₁₆-inch sheet lead present much less, but sufficient, surface and require only a moderate pressure. Measurements obtained by the use of discs have proven to be much more reproducible and more accurate.

Since there are many calibers it is necessary to have a number of pairs of dies and punches. Indeed, several pairs are desirable for barrels with the caliber known as .38 since these vary all the way from about .35 to .41 inch. For the other calibers the variation is small and usually one pair will suffice for each.

The punch and die set illustrated consists of a

Three degrees clearance, ⅟₁₆ inch below the cutting edge on the dies, and 0.005 inch relief, ⅛ inch back of the cutting edge, are used on the punches. All outside diameters of the shanks of the punches are identical and the same is true for the dies, so that they may be interchanged.

Some of the (inch) sizes of the punches found to be most useful are: 0.228, 0.257, 0.305, 0.309, 0.318, 0.358, 0.379, 0.404, 0.440, and 0.456.

The ⅟₁₆-inch sheet lead used for raw stock for the disks is readily obtainable and causes no appreciable wear on the punches or dies. If wear occurred, the punches and dies could be sharpened easily in any shop equipped with a small, lathe-tool, post grinder, a few thousandths face grind being all that would be

TABLE 3

Reproducibility of rifling meter measurements

(Illustrating the reproducibility of measurements of rifling twist obtainable for a barrel having good rifling and in good condition. Disk pushed into muzzle end of barrel about 0.4″ before first reading was made.)

Gun measured — 7.65 mm. Walther, Mod. PP, Serial No. 757,932

First series of readings			Second series of readings		
Distance disk was moved	Scale reading	Difference for 0.2″	Distance disk was moved	Scale reading	Difference for 0.2″
0.0″	21.50°		0.0″	23.90°	
0.2	27.55	6.05°	0.2	29.95	6.05°
0.4	33.55	6.00	0.4	36.95	6.00
0.6	39.60	6.05	0.6	42.00	6.05
0.8	45.65	6.05	0.8	48.05	6.05
1.0	51.70	6.05	1.0	54.10	6.05
1.2	57.75	6.05	1.2	60.15	6.05
1.4	63.80	6.05	1.4	66.20	6.05
1.6	69.85	6.05	1.6	72.25	6.05
1.8	75.90	6.05	1.8	78.30	6.05
2.0	81.95	6.05	2.0	84.35	6.05
2.2	88.00	6.05	2.2	90.40	6.05

Aver. Diff. = 6.046° for 0.2″, or 30.23° for 1″   Aver. Diff. = 6.046° for 0.2″, or 30.23° for 1″
360° ÷ 30.23° = 11.91″ for 1 turn   360° ÷ 30.23° = 11.91″ for 1 turn.

heavy base plate, semicircular in shape, upon which is mounted a heavy column carrying the punch holder and the operating lever. The dies are set in a secondary heavy steel platform having a series of holes arranged in an arc described by the rotation of the punch holder. The position of each die is such that the punch comes into perfect alignment over each die. Each punch has a tiny pin in the exact center of its face, to produce a centering hole, thus facilitating the exact centering of the disk on the push rod. Exact centering is important.

The punches and dies are made in pairs for any given caliber and are readily interchangeable. The dies are locked in place by headless Allen screws. Both dies and punches are fabricated from high-speed drill rod, hardened, tempered, and ground.

necessary. Two metal drawers, below the dies, catch the disks. The disks are very perfectly formed and have clean-cut edges. They are easily attached to the end of a push rod. After centering the push rod on the disk a light tap with a fiber-faced hammer seats the disk on the pins set into the end of the rod.

Reproducibility of measurements made by the rifling meter

Table No. 3 shows the reproducibility of measurements obtainable by the use of the rifling meter for a rifled barrel that has a uniform twist and is in very good condition. Frequently the twist is not uniform throughout the length of the barrel and in such cases (with exceptions noted below) an average is taken. Occasionally one portion of a barrel will show

Fig. 78. Lead disk-cutter press and dies for cutting lead disks used with the rifling meter.

good, uniform rifling and another portion will show irregularities due to wear, corrosion, or faulty rifling. In such cases the measurements should be limited to that portion of the barrel that shows good rifling. One great advantage of the rifling meter is that measurements can be made at very small intervals of length and any nonuniformity of rifling twist shows up promptly. Since the purpose of the rifling is to cause the bullet to achieve a rapid rotation on its longitudinal axis which will give it stability in flight, it is obvious that a perfectly rifled barrel should have uniform dimensions as to bore, groove and land widths, depth of grooves, and a constant angle of rifling throughout the length of the barrel, and the grooves should be clean cut and all surfaces should be entirely free from any roughness. Of course, such a barrel has not been produced yet and never will be, because absolute perfection is unattainable.

Rifling pitch on fired bullet

The measurement of rifling pitch on a fired bullet is difficult at best, and it is impossible unless the bullet is in very good condition. The chief difficulty is to ascertain precisely the axis of the bullet. If the bullet is mutilated or deformed at all, as lead bullets usually are and jacketed bullets too frequently are, the measurement of rifling angle cannot be made with the precision necessary to be of any value.

For a bullet that is in near perfect condition a satisfactory measurement can be made by using a

Fig. 79. Assembly of apparatus for measuring pitch of rifling on a fired bullet. This is useful only in case the bullet is in near perfect condition.

Gaertner eyepiece protractor on a compound microscope which has a good mechanical stage by means of which the bullet can be moved laterally with precision (i.e., without change of angle). The setup is shown in Fig. 79. If a suitable mechanical stage is not available, the bullet-mount device used on the modern comparison microscope may be used to provide for the lateral movement of the bullet.

The bullet is mounted in firm position on the stage, with the axis of the bullet at right angles to the lateral (horizontal) motion to be used in making the measurement. First, the bullet should be rotated until a groove having good markings is found, preferably one that shows a number of narrow lines parallel to the mark made by the driving edge of the land. The bullet should be in a position such that the groove is centered, i.e., at the top point of its rotation, and in the best possible focus, with side illumination at an angle of about 45°.

The protractor eyepiece is now rotated by the micrometer adjustment with one hand while the bullet is moved laterally on the stage by the other until the vertical cross hair in the eyepiece is lined up perfectly with either the edge of the groove or with a fine bright line parallel to the edge of the groove. There are usually many of these fine bright lines, and by proper adjustment the cross hair can be brought into such position that it either lies in the bright line or obliterates the line selected as the reference line. Several readings (usually five) of the position of the protractor are made and averaged, the readings being made to 3′ of angle by use of the vernier. The operation may be repeated using the edge of the groove to make certain that the line used was, as assumed, parallel to the edge.

To determine the axis of the bullet, light is brought onto the bullet, say from the left side, thus throwing the right edge in shadow against a white background (a white card below). Now this edge of the bullet is brought into sharp focus and the protractor eyepiece is turned until the vertical cross hair is parallel to the edge of the bullet. This is best done by moving the bullet laterally while adjusting the angle of the cross hair until it is lined up exactly with and just touching the edge of the bullet. The position of the cross hair is then read on the protractor. Several settings are made in a similar manner and these are averaged. Now the source of illumination is moved to the opposite side of the microscope, thus throwing the left side of the bullet in shadow, and the operations are repeated and the readings averaged. If the two sides of the bullet are parallel, as they would be in a "perfect" bullet, the averaged values of readings taken on the two sides should agree. Since perfect agreement is rarely found, the mean of the two sets of readings is taken to represent the axis of the bullet. If they do not approximately agree the case is hopeless.

The difference between the axis readings and readings made on the groove represent the angle which the groove makes with the axis of rotation, and from this angle the length of barrel required to produce exactly one turn of the bullet is calculated, using the formula:

$$l = \frac{\pi \times d}{\tan \theta}$$

where l = length of barrel required for one turn
    π = 3.1416
    d = bore diameter
    θ = angle of rifling.

For example, suppose that the bore diameter is 0.3550 inch and that the angle is 4° 0′, then

$$l = \frac{3.1416 \times 0.355}{\tan 4°} = 15.95 \text{ inches}$$

Had the angle been 4° 10′ the calculated length

Fig. 80. Apparatus for measuring angle of rifling pitch from a fired bullet. (An alternate method.)

of the barrel for one turn would have been 15.31 inches—thus demonstrating that the angle of rifling must be determined accurately if the measurements are to have any real value. The majority of "crime bullets" will not be in sufficiently good condition to permit measurement of the rifling angle with the necessary accuracy. For this reason and the additional reasons that the instruments are expensive and that considerable skill in their operation is necessary, the measurement of rifling angle on fired bullets is rarely made.

Alternate methods for measuring rifling angle

Reticle or grid method

While the following method does not have the precision of the method already described it has the advantage that the equipment necessary is more likely to be available. It requires a good compound microscope provided with a well-made mechanical stage which includes a graduated circle and a vernier scale by means of which readings to 3′ of angle may be made. Provision must also be made for holding the bullet firmly in a horizontal position and for rotating it on its axis. The stage is provided with two movements, at right angles to each other, so the bullet can be centered in the field without difficulty. Microscope and stage are shown in Fig. 80.

The eyepiece is provided with a special "reticle" (or grid) which consists of a number of very fine

57

lines which are exactly parallel to each other. The principle may best be described with the aid of a diagram. See Fig. 81. Actually the lines are much narrower than shown and they should be closer together. During the process of measurement the eyepiece containing the reticle remains in fixed position, unlike the Gaertner eyepiece already described.

The procedure is as follows. The bullet is placed in the holder on the mechanical stage and is rotated until a well-defined groove is located—one with sharp edges or with striations (bright lines) parallel to the driving edge on the groove. The bullet is then centered in the field by turning the knobs controlling the vertical and lateral movements of the object on the stage. The circular scale is now rotated until the bright line (or edge of the groove) is lined up exactly with one of the central parallel lines of the reticle and a reading is made, using the vernier to read the angle as accurately as possible. Since the mechanical stage does not (usually) have a micro-adjustment screw, as does the Gaertner protractor, precise settings are more difficult and, consequently, several should be made and averaged.

Fig. 81. Diagram illustrating the principle and technique involved in the determination of the angle of rifling from measurements made on a fired bullet. This reticle (grid of fine parallel lines) is in the eyepiece of the microscope. The angle of rifling is determined by lining up a groove edge with one of the parallel lines and then lining up the sides of the bullet with others of the parallel lines. The amount that the bullet has to be turned to do this represents the angle of the rifling. The lines of the grid are actually much finer than those shown in this illustration.

The microscope tube is now lowered until the edges of the bullet are brought into sharp focus. This does not change the angle, so no error will ensue. The bullet is now turned, by rotating the circular graduated scale, until the sides are parallel to the parallel lines of the reticle through which one sees the bullet. The suggestions made concerning proper illumination of the bullet (by throwing the edges into shadow against a white background) apply here as well as with the protractor eyepiece method. By moving the bullet laterally and at the same time adjusting the angle, it is possible to line up the bullet so that one of the parallel lines of the reticle will just touch the edge of the image of the bullet, thus insuring its being parallel to the same. A reading of angle is now made, and the operation is repeated several times and the results averaged. Now, the opposite edge of the bullet will be parallel with the lines of the reticle *if* the edges of the bullet are parallel. Unfortunately they often are not. To ascertain whether such is the case the bullet is moved laterally until this opposite edge of the bullet is precisely lined up with one of the parallel lines of the reticle. Several readings are taken as before and are averaged. If the average of the readings on the right hand edge of the bullet do not coincide with the average of readings taken on the left hand side, the results of the two series are averaged and this value is taken as the axis of the bullet. The difference in angle between the axis and the edge of the groove now having been determined, a calculation is made as to the length of barrel necessary to produce exactly one turn of the bullet. This calculation has already been explained. As stated previously, the principal difficulty in any method is that of determining the true axis of the fired bullet.

As an example of the application of this method a series of measurements were made on a bullet which had been fired from a .32 cal. Colt automatic pistol. The bullet was placed in a holder such as is used for the earlier forms of the comparison microscope and was centered so that when rotated it did so with a minimum amount of eccentricity. (The parallel lines of the eyepiece grid are helpful in this process of centering, as any eccentric motion is easily detected.) A groove (designated as No. 1) was then brought into proper position—i.e., in the center of the field, and the stage was rotated until one of the parallel lines of the grid coincided with the driving edge of the groove. Five such settings were made and the readings were averaged. Next the stage was rotated until the sides of the bullet were parallel with a pair of the lines of the grid. Five settings were made and the results averaged. This process was repeated for each of the six grooves—a total of 60 settings. The average of all of the angles was 3.36° or 3° 22′. The bore diameter of the gun being 0.305 inch, the length of barrel for one turn of the rifling in the gun would, therefore, be

$$l = \frac{3.1416 \times .305}{\tan 3°22'} = 16.3 \text{ inches.}$$

A second and entirely separate series of measurements on the same bullet gave 16.4 inches for one turn of the rifling.

This illustration shows that when a near perfect bullet is at hand one can make measurements that have some meaning, but such bullets are too rarely encountered in actual cases.

To illustrate what may be done with this method on a fired lead bullet, under near perfect conditions, a .38 Spl. bullet was fired from a .38 cal. Colt Army Special revolver whose rifling was in excellent condition. The bullet was fired into cotton waste. Measurements made with the rifling meter had shown that the rifling in this gun had one turn in 16.0 inches.

Measurements of the angles made between the impressions produced by the driving edges of the lands and the nearly parallel sides of the bullet gave results from which a calculated value of 16.2 inches was obtained for one turn of the rifling. Such excellent values can be obtained under near perfect conditions—i.e., the bullet must be long enough to follow the rifling without slippage or eccentric motion, the impressions made by the driving edges of the lands must be long enough to permit accurate settings, the rifling must be in excellent condition so that clean-cut impressions will be made, and there must be no deformity of the bullet. In actual cases these conditions are rarely met, and the results will be only approximations—but, even so, may be quite useful.

Unless the true axis of the bullet can be determined, the results will be inaccurate. The measurement of angle on a single groove is meaningless. All must be measured and the average value used in the calculation. In the case of short bullets, particularly those that are conical in shape, measurements of rifling angle will have little meaning. The .380 ACP bullet affords a good example. The bullet is quite conical in form, it is relatively short, and the length of bearing surface on the rifling is very short. All attempts to determine the pitch of rifling on such bullets fired through barrels whose rifling pitch was known have been very unsatisfactory. The angles determined are too small and they differ from bullet to bullet fired from the same barrel. With lead bullets, having a larger area of contact with the rifling, much better results are obtained, as has been shown above.

Fig. 82. Measurement of rifling angle on fired bullet. Showing quartz fiber mounted in fixed position directly above the bullet and in exact line with the axis of rotation of the screws that hold the bullet in position.

The bullet is rotated by turning the knob at the extreme right, and the "driving edge" of each land impression is brought directly under the quartz fiber before any settings are made.

After determining the exact position of the quartz fiber, and thus determining the reference axis, measurements of the angle between the land impression and this axis are made for each land impression on the bullet. The average of these values is used in computing the length of barrel required for one turn of the rifling.

Axis of rotation method

Still another method was studied and the results were quite successful. Instead of making settings on the sides of the bullet, in the manner already described, to determine the axis of the bullet, a procedure of determining the "axis of rotation" was devised and the angles that the driving edge of the land impressions made with this "axis of rotation" were measured and averaged.

The bullet is mounted as before and is centered in the same way. Then a fine straight quartz fiber (ca. 0.005 inch in diameter) is fixed in position above the bullet so that it is exactly in line with the axis of the screws which hold the bullet in position. This is used as the "reference axis" and, of course, remains in fixed position. The angles made by the driving edges of the lands with reference to this "axis of rotation" are now measured and averaged on the *theory that if the "axis of rotation" (i.e., the reference axis) and the true axis of the bullet do not exactly coincide the errors will cancel out if measurements are made on all of the grooves on the bullet.* Fig. 82 shows the quartz reference fiber mounted

59

Fig. 83. Leitz instrument for measuring rifling angle. (The author has had no experience with this instrument and therefore is not qualified to pass judgement on it.)

in the axis of the bullet holder.

After centering the bullet in the optical field and bringing the quartz fiber into sharp focus, the mechanical stage, upon which the bullet and holder are mounted, is rotated until the quartz fiber is lined up so that it coincides exactly with one of the parallel lines in the grid in the eyepiece, and a reading is made on the graduated circle of the stage. Several settings (usually five) are made and the average reading is recorded as the "axis of rotation" or reference axis.

The land impression is now brought into sharp focus and the driving edge of the land impression is brought into exact coincidence with one of the parallel lines in the grid in the eyepiece, and a reading is made on the graduated circle of the stage. Several settings (usually five) are made and the readings averaged. The difference between the averaged values of the two sets of readings indicates the angle or slope of that particular land impression with the "axis of rotation." This process is repeated for the driving edge of each land impression on the bullet and the average of all angles is used in the computation of the length of barrel required for one complete turn of the rifling. Readings on less than all of the land impressions present on the bullet will not suffice. A single reading of rifling angle has little

if any value and may be very misleading.

Instead of using fired bullets to test this method it was tried out under more nearly ideal conditions. Three bullets (one Lubaloy coated, the other two of plain lead) were pushed through the barrel of a .38 cal. Colt revolver, using the rifling meter which has already been described. The rifling in this gun was in excellent condition and repeated measurements of the pitch of rifling gave 16.0 inches as the length of barrel required for one turn.

The measurements of pitch of the rifling on the three bullets used in the test gave 15.9, 15.9, and 16.0 inches, thus supporting the theory and showing what can be done with "perfect" bullets.

The accurate measurement of rifling angles on bullets requires not only near perfect conditions, as already indicated, but it also requires equipment not found in the average police laboratory. Furthermore, it requires familiarity with these special instruments and a high degree of skill in their use. Finally it is a time-consuming and tedious procedure. For these various reasons it is not likely that measurements of rifling pitch will ever come into common use in firearms identification laboratories.

Fig. 83 shows an instrument designed and marketed by Leitz for the measurement of rifling angle on fired bullets. The author has had no experience with it.

Visual examination

Some firearms examiners resort to a visual comparison of the slopes of the rifling grooves of the evidence bullet with the slopes on bullets which have been fired from guns whose rifling twist is known. This comparison can be done with the bullets placed under the comparison microscope or, still better, with the comparison camera where the enlarged images of the bullets are viewed on a ground glass.

In either case the two bullets are placed in the usual positions and well-defined grooves are brought into juxtaposition, care being taken to see that the sides of the two bullets are exactly parallel. If, under these conditions, the slopes of the grooves on the two bullets appear to be exactly the same and if the widths of the grooves are alike, the probability that the two bullets were fired from guns having the same rifling characteristics is great.

Obviously this method, in common with the other methods described, can give useful information only in cases where the evidence bullet is in good condition. For deformed bullets no method will work. For the practical use of the method the examiner should have at hand a considerable collection of bullets which have been fired from guns having known rifling twists, and, of course, these bullets also must be in good condition.

Measurement of land impressions

If the measurements of land impressions (grooves) on fired bullets are to have any meaning it is obvious that they must be made by a method that gives both reproducible and reliable results. Preferably it should be a method which does not require the use of prohibitively expensive equipment. If equipment generally available in crime detection laboratories can be modified or added to in order to get a satisfactory means of measurement, so much the better. We believe that this requirement has been attained.

Method of measurement

A number of instruments have been used by various investigators for the measurement of the widths of land and groove impressions on fired bullets, such as the filar micrometer, measuring microscope, traveling microscope (comparator), tool maker's microscope, etc. (3, 4) (Fig. 84). All of these have been tried out in the author's laboratory, and reasonably satisfactory measurements can be made with any of them on bullets fired from new guns, where the edges of the land impression will usually be cleanly cut clear to the bottom of the impression (where the measurement should be made). But they are not entirely satisfactory for measurements made on bullets fired from guns that have seen considerable use and, in consequence, have lands whose edges are slightly rounded. The difficulty is of varying degrees, naturally, depending on the extent of wear on the lands and also on whether metal-jacketed or plain lead bullets are being measured. Lead bullets cause more trouble than jacketed bullets. If the land impressions are not cleanly cut, it is, of course, difficult to see just where the cross hair (reticle) should be set to coincide with the bottom edge of the impression. This difficulty can be largely overcome by the use of a binocular microscope which gives a three-dimensional view of the impressions and thereby reveals details which are not visible (or are confused) when an ordinary microscope is used as the observing instrument.

A method developed by the author was used and the apparatus is shown in Fig. 85. This method involves the use of a Greenough-type binocular microscope (approximate magnification 20) with a

Fig. 84. Leitz instrument for measuring width of lands on fired bullet.

Fig. 85. Complete assembly of apparatus for measuring groove widths on fired bullets. Greenough type binocular microscope on rotatable table, device for holding bullet and measuring groove width, and two-tube fluorescent lamp (Burton).

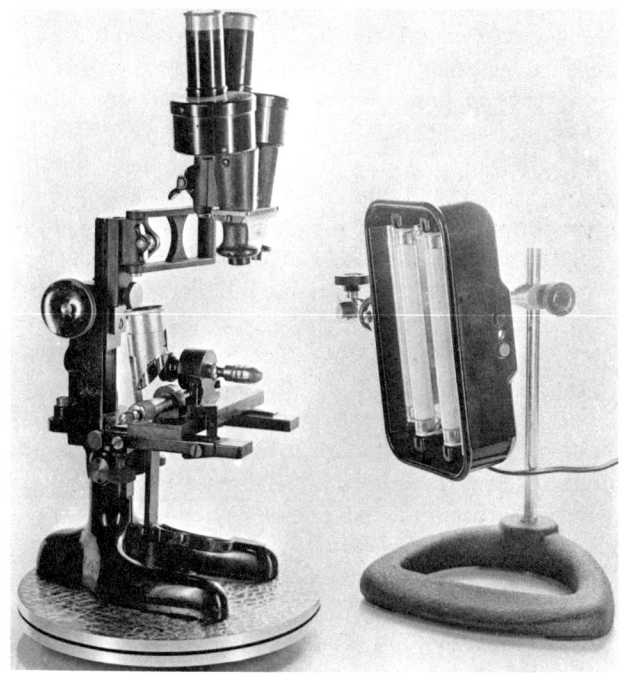

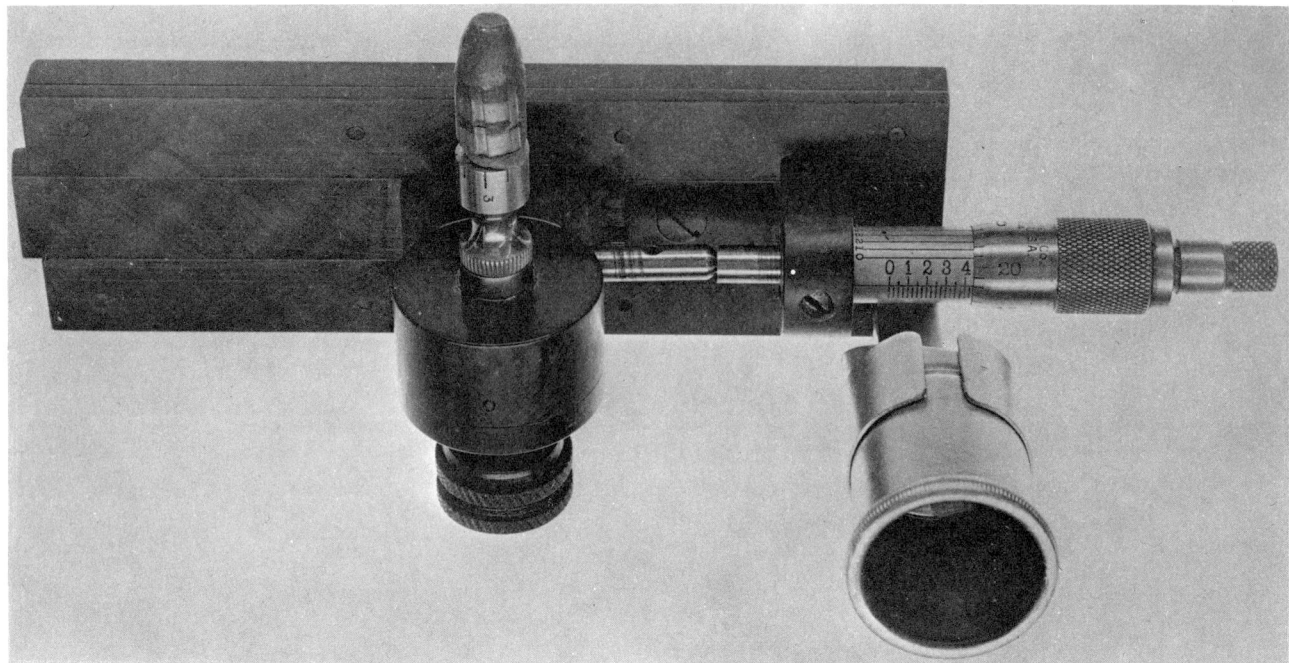

Fig. 86. Device for holding bullet and for measuring width of grooves on a fired bullet. Slide carrying bullet mount moves to right or left as Starrett micrometer spindle is rotated. Lens enables operator to make accurate readings from microscope eyepiece level.

fine cross hair (reticle—consisting of alternating narrow dashes and tiny circles) in one eyepiece and a measuring device (Fig. 86) mounted firmly on the stage. The bullet is caused to move to the right or the left by turning the micrometer spindle. Rotating it clockwise causes the bullet to move to the right (Fig. 85). When it is rotated counterclockwise a coil spring in the base of the device (which presses the bullet mount against the end of the spindle) causes the bullet to move to the left. This permits exact settings of the bullet such that the reticle will coincide with the bottom edge of the land impression.

By taking measurements at the bottom of the land impression one gets reproducible data, irrespective of the depth of the impression. Land impressions may vary in depth from bullet to bullet because of slight differences in their diameters. Naturally, the larger the diameter the deeper the impression will be. And if jacketed bullets are used the depth of the impressions will usually be shallower because of the greater hardness of the jacket. Whether the impression is deep or shallow, the width of the groove at the bottom will be the same if the impression is clean cut, barring other factors. Frequently the lands are narrower at the top than at the base and, consequently, the grooves produced by them will be wider at the top than at the bottom. This is another

reason why the measurements should be made at the bottom of the groove. Occasionally the lands are rounded on the edges, either intentionally (rarely) or because of excessive use. In such cases the measurements will be more difficult and the values obtained less certain.

Several settings on each edge (driving and trailing edges) are made and these are averaged and recorded as the proper setting for that edge. The difference between the averaged right hand and left hand settings represents the width of the land impression.

It will be noted that only one eyepiece is provided with a cross hair. The final setting of the cross hair to coincide with the edge of the groove is made with this half of the optical system. The purpose of the binocular microscope is to furnish a three-dimensional view of the groove and thus enable the operator to study the exact shape of the groove so that he can determine the exact point at which the cross hair should be set.

Before any settings are made the bullet must be carefully positioned (rotated) until each edge of the land impression being measured is in perfect focus at the time the setting is made (otherwise the two edges will not be in the same horizontal plane) and the eyepiece is rotated to line up the reticle with the edges of the impression. Each land impression on the bullet is measured in this manner, and the average of all these measurements represents the average width of the lands in the gun from which the bullet was fired. If one needs to know the width of the grooves in the gun it can be calculated (approximately) from the measured land widths, diameter measurements, and the number of grooves.

When plain lead bullets (or even jacketed bullets) are fired from a revolver, slippage of the bullet frequently occurs when it strikes the rifled part of the barrel. This is because the bullet has already acquired considerable momentum and consequently resists the change in direction required by the twist of the rifling. Slippage does not ordinarily occur when bullets are fired from a pistol or automatic pistol, because here the bullet nose is practically in contact with the rifling at the moment of firing. When slippage does occur one must be very careful in selecting the markings on the bullet which truly represent the width of the land, since the over-all width of the land impression will be different at the two ends, being wider than the land at the nose end of the bullet (Fig. 87).

One side of the land impression (the driving edge) will usually show a clear, distinct edge upon which the reticle is lined up. Then the bullet is moved across the field until the reticle coincides with the other edge of the land impression at the last point of contact of the bullet with the rifling (i.e., at the base end of the bullet). One will then usually observe an impression of the edge of the land which runs toward the nose end of the bullet and which will be parallel with the other edge of the groove upon which the reticle had been set. This impression is often faint (though not necessarily so) and requires proper illumination to bring it out in proper perspective, but with the binocular microscope it can be located and used for a proper setting of the micrometer. Micrometer settings made on land impression edges that are not parallel have no value.

The advantage of using a truly binocular microscope over a microscope with a single optical system is most striking, as it permits one to see the true shape of the edge of the land impression on the bullet. This three-dimensional view is very important as it enables one to see exactly where the reticle should be set, provided proper illumination is used. A two-tube fluorescent lamp (Burton—see Fig. 85) gives very satisfactory illumination and is recommended over the customary small spot lights.

To facilitate what is at best a tedious operation of making a very great number of readings, whose accuracy depends so much on getting exactly the right illumination for the proper setting of the bullet with respect to the eyepiece reticle, the author has devised a simple, rotatable table upon which the microscope is placed. In front of this is the two-tube fluorescent lamp, with the tubes set nearly verti-

Fig. 87. Slippage marks. Bullets fired from revolvers are particularly likely to show slippage marks such as shown here. The bullet, already having attained a high velocity before striking the lands, resists taking a rotational movement because of its inertia. This results in a double impression of the lands. The proper width to measure is indicated by the arrow between the two parallel lines. This represents the width of the land that made the groove.

cally. The table consists of two 8-inch circular plates of aluminum, each ¼ inch thick, between which are ball bearings. The upper plate of the table rotates with a touch of the finger and is quickly turned and adjusted to the position where the light is at the proper angle to reveal clearly the shape of the edge of the groove on the bullet. One who has used this simple device will never return to the practice of trying to get proper illumination by moving the light source about.

A study of the reproducibility of the measurement

The data recorded in Table 4 resulted from a study of the widths of land impressions on a series of lead bullets fired from a group of seventeen .38 Spl. S & W revolvers, all of which had seen extensive

63

TABLE 4
Widths of land impressions on a series of fired bullets

Gun No.	Serial No. on barrel	Serial No. on butt	No. tests fired	No. lands/ No. tests measured	Land impression	
					Average	Largest deviation
2	V-521 282	V-79 702	12	60/12	0.0950″	+0.0006″
						−0.0006
3	V-522 716	V-75 567	11	48/11	0.0972	+0.0006
						−0.0002
4	V-519 202	V-73 721	12	20/4	0.0961	+0.0003
						−0.0002
5	V-523 049	V-81 415	10	20/4	0.0952	+0.0004
						−0.0004
6	V-521 028	V-75 014	12	20/4	0.0938	+0.0004
						−0.0008
7	V-523 053	V-59 873	6	20/4	0.0959	+0.0006
						−0.0006
8	V-525 224	V-81 640	6	19/4	0.0960	+0.0002
						−0.0005
9	V-520 770	V-72 650	6	20/4	0.0957	+0.0005
						−0.0008
				Average.............	0.0956″	
				Largest deviations	+0.0016″	
					−0.0018″	
10	V-524 213	V-81 832	12	20/4	0.0960″	+0.0004″
						−0.0006
11	V-524 185	V-79 257	12	20/4	0.0963	+0.0006
						−0.0007
12	V-520 829	V-79 094	12	20/4	0.0956	+0.0005
						−0.0006
13*	V-520 062	V-78 327	12	0*	—	—
14*	V-527 190	V-82 697	12	0*	—	—
15	V-516 135	V-75 017	6	20/4	0.0976	+0.0006
						−0.0006
16	V-526 624	V-71 565	6	20/4	0.0927	+0.0006
						−0.0006
17*	V-518 596	V-74 798	6	0*	—	—
18	V-519 834	V-74 174	6	20/4	0.0966	+0.0011
						−0.0009
				Average.............	0.0958″	
				Largest deviations....	+0.0018″	
					−0.0021″	

*Bullets not suitable for measurement.
Guns: .38 Spl. S & W, Military and Police, Victory Mod.
Ammunition: 38 Spl. Remington KLEANBORE, Police Service, 158 gr. Lead (5138) Lot No. XO8H25.
Collection Media: Long staple cotton.
Chambers Used: Guns No. 2 to 9 a random chamber was used for each test. Guns No. 10 to 18 a random chamber was chosen and held constant for each series of tests.
Cleaning: Guns cleaned before the first and after the last shot.
Rifling (Mfg. specifications): 5R, 1 turn in 18¾″, bore diam. 0.3555 to 0.3572, groove width 0.114, groove depth 0.005, land width 0.1034. Rifled with hook cutter and lead lapped.

use prior to and after their purchase by the Berkeley, Calif., Police Department.*

The guns are listed as Nos. 2 to 18 in the order in which they were fired. For the details concerning

*These bullets were submitted by Mr. A. A. Biasotti, formerly with the Wisconsin Crime Laboratory and now at the Laboratory of Criminalistics, Office of the District Attorney of Santa Clara Co., San Jose, Calif.

the guns and ammunition used and the conditions under which these tests were fired see Table 4 and supplementary notes. As was expected, since all of these were used guns, some of the bullets were not in suitable condition for measurement. Some of these guns had evidently seen much use—and, possibly, abuse. Measurements were made on those bullets which had at least four measurable land impressions.

Satisfactory measurements could not be made on bullets fired from guns 13, 14, and 17, because the rifling did not leave sufficiently well-defined land impressions.

By reference to the measurements given in Table 4, it is clear that accurate measurements of the widths of land impressions on a fired bullet can be made by the procedure developed, provided the bullets have been fired from guns that are in reasonably good condition and have not been damaged in the process of being collected. It seems fair to conclude that the variation in reproducibility of a series of measurements is not greater than ±0.001 inch, and usually it is less.

Measurements of land widths in new guns of same make and model

It has long seemed desirable to the writer to make a study of the land impressions made on (A) plain lead bullets and (B) metal-cased bullets which had been fired from the *same* guns. It also seemed desirable to make a study of the *variations* in land widths which occur in the same make and model of guns made by a reputable manufacturer. The writer was

furnished sets of bullets, both plain lead and metal cased, which had been fired from the same guns. These guns were the .38 Spl. Smith and Wesson, Military and Police Model, and they had never been fired since leaving the factory. They were the property of the Berkeley Police Department. For the details concerning the guns and ammunition used and the conditions under which these tests were fired see Table 5 and supplementary notes.

Because a new gun has rifling which is not worn, it is to be expected that the imprints of the lands on the fired bullets would be wider and that they would be more cleanly cut than would be the case for a much-used gun. It also is to be expected that a metal-cased bullet would show more cleanly cut land impressions than those made on a lead bullet, because of the softness of lead in comparison to metal-cased bullets. In the case of a new gun, or one having undamaged rifling, it would be expected that the width of the land impressions would be the same on lead and metal-cased bullets if normal powder pressures were used. The first assumption is verified, but the last one seems to be only approximately true.

Table 5 shows that usually the widths of land im-

TABLE 5
Widths of land impressions on lead and metal-coated bullets fired from new guns

Gun No.	Serial No. (Barrel)	No. Tests Lead	No. Tests M.C.	No. lands/ No. tests measured Lead	No. lands/ No. tests measured M.C.	Average width Lead bullets	Average width M.C. bullets	Largest deviation Lead bullets	Largest deviation M.C. bullets	Difference in average width M.C.–Lead
40	C-176 498	6	6	20/4	20/4	0.0987"	0.0991"	+0.0005" −0.0005	+0.0002" −0.0001	−0.0004"
41	C-173 209	6	6	20/4	20/4	0.0983	0.0985	+0.0004 −0.0003	+0.0008 −0.0005	−0.0002
42	C-172 131	6	6	20/4	20/4	0.0995	0.0995	+0.0003 −0.0005	+0.0001 −0.0001	0.0000
43	C-176 826	6	6	20/4	20/4	0.0981	0.0993	+0.0002 −0.0002	+0.0001 −0.0003	−0.0012
44	C-178 156	6	6	20/4	20/4	0.0984	0.0991	+0.0004 −0.0004	+0.0003 −0.0002	−0.0007
45	C-174 010	6	6	20/4	20/4	0.0979	0.0988	+0.0000 −0.0001	+0.0003 −0.0002	−0.0009
46	C-175 000	6	6	20/4	20/4	0.0981	0.0988	+0.0005 −0.0007	+0.0002 −0.0001	−0.0007
47	C-170 859	6	6	20/4	20/4	0.0999	0.1000	+0.0002 −0.0002	+0.0005 −0.0006	−0.0001
	Averages					0.0986"	0.0991"			−0.0005"
	Largest deviations					+0.0013" −0.0007"	+0.0009" −0.0006"	+0.0003" −0.0003"	+0.0003" −0.0003"	

Guns: .38 Spl. S & W, Military and Police (New).

Ammunition: a) Lead: 38 Spl. Remington KLEANBORE, Police Service, 158 gr. Lead (5138) Lot No. X08H25; b) Metal case: 38 Spl. Peters, 158 gr., M.C.

Collecting Media: Long staple cotton

Chamber used: Chamber picked at random and held constant for each series of 6 lead tests followed by 6 M.C. tests.

Cleaning: Guns were cleaned before first and after last shot of each series of lead and M.C. tests.

Rifling Specifications (Mfg. specifications): 5R, 1 turn in 18¾", bore diam. 0.3555 to 0.3572, groove width 0.114, groove depth 0.005, land width 0.1034. Rifled with a *broach cutter* and lead lapped.

pressions on lead bullets are slightly narrower than those found on metal-cased bullets fired from the same gun. In no case were they wider. Since the differences are all in the same direction, it is believed that they are real and are not the result of error in measuring.

Measurements of land widths in a D.W.M. Luger automatic

A series of six bullets which had been fired from a D.W.M. Luger, dated 1916, serial No. 3837-a, were measured to ascertain the reproducibility of land widths. The land impressions on the test bullets were very clean cut, and, consequently, very satisfactory measurements could be made. The average width of the four land impressions on each of the six test bullets was 0.1136 inch, with the largest deviations being +0.0002 and −0.0003 inch. The ammunition used was 7.65 mm. Luger, Remington Kleanbore, 93 gr. M.C. (0730). The gun was cleaned before the first and after the last shot only.

The average land width for this gun had been determined in this laboratory about two years earlier by measuring the widths of the land impressions on lead disks forced through the barrel during the process of measuring the degree of rifling twist by the use of the rifling meter. The gun had not been used in the meantime. The value obtained at that time for the average width of the four lands was 0.1133 inch—a difference of only 0.0003 inch from the average value obtained two years later on six fired bullets.

The land widths for this gun are a little wider than usual for a four-land Luger. Previous measurements on five other Lugers of this type gave 0.108, 0.108, 0.107, 0.102, and 0.110 inch; and a Luger carbine was found to have an average land width of 0.110 inch.

Discussion

Bradford and Brackett (3) have pointed out that when the distance between the two edges of a groove on a bullet is measured by the optical method, one measures a distance on a plane surface and not actually the curved distance (following the contour of the bullet) which they consider to be the true width of the groove. They give a formula whereby the difference can be calculated and a series of curves showing the corrections for various groove widths on bullets from .22 to .45 cal. In the case of the .38 cal. bullets used in this investigation, having a land width of about 0.10 inch, the correction amounts to +0.0014 inch. Surely no fault can be found with their statements—but, actually, in the practice of gun identification it does not matter,

because if one uses the *same* system of measurement on the evidence bullet and on the test bullet he gets his answer as to identity or nonidentity in either case, if a positive identification by such measurements is possible. As a matter of fact, this method is rarely used nowadays to determine identity of a particular gun because the comparison microscope (or, better, the comparison camera) enables one to establish identity or nonidentity more quickly and more strikingly, and photographs of the matches between the evidence and the test bullets can be made and shown to the jury.

A more useful application of a knowledge of groove widths on fired bullets is to assist in the identification of the make (and, sometimes, the model) of gun that fired an evidence bullet when no suspect gun is yet at hand. If one knows the number and widths of the lands in the gun, the direction and pitch of the rifling twist, and the caliber (actual, not nominal)—all of which can be obtained from the evidence bullet if it is in good condition—he is in a position to narrow down the search for the weapon very materially. If his information is sufficiently complete, he may be able to narrow the search down to a single make or at least to two, three, or four makes. This is possible only if one has extensive information concerning rifling characteristics as they actually exist in guns, rather than in manufacturers' tables. The "book values" and the actual values are often quite different—and for many guns even book values are not obtainable. Like typewriter fonts, rifling characteristics are subject to intentional change from time to time as well as to the unintentional errors made during the process of manufacture. Unfortunately, in the case of many of the cheaper foreign guns and particularly those made years ago, little if any attention was paid to the matter of rifling "specifications." This state of affairs is unfortunate for the firearms examiner as it naturally makes his task of identification of make and model of gun more difficult, and sometimes impossible. One American manufacturer (of a very popular gun) very frankly states that his company does not consider that any specification other than bore diameter is of any particular importance in the proper functioning of their guns. It is fortunate for the firearms examiner that all manufacturers are not of this opinion!

The manufacturer's specifications call for a land width of 0.1034 inch for the particular model of S & W revolvers used to fire the bullets whose measurements appear in Tables 4 and 5, but in the many measurements made in the author's laboratory no width as great as this has ever been found for this model of revolver—new or used. It is clear, however, that the lands become narrower as the gun is used. Of course, the edges become worn and this makes a micrometer setting more difficult as the imprint of the land is not as clean cut. The difficulty is greatly reduced, however, by the use of the binocular microscope which reveals the true shape of the groove, when proper lighting is used. This method has been found to be superior to the filar micrometer, the tool maker's microscope, the comparator, or the traveling-stage microscope, in all of which a single eyepiece is used in the observing instrument. A three-dimensional view is necessary to see the true shape of the groove edge.

The measurement of land impressions is a necessary procedure in establishing the rifling characteristics present in a particular arm. The actual widths of the lands may be determined very accurately by measuring the widths of the impressions made by the lands on either a bullet or a lead disk which has been pushed through a barrel under moderate pressure (Fig. 88). In either case the measurements are made with the equipment described in the first part of this section and shown in Fig. 85.

Frequently it is found advantageous to push the disk into the barrel for only a short distance (one-half inch or so) and then remove it for measurement. Clearer impressions are often so obtained. The author makes it a practice to measure all of the land impressions present and to average them. The data recorded in the tables given in a later chapter were so obtained.

In a paper relating to this subject (4), B. D. Munhall concludes that groove widths cannot be measured with a degree of accuracy greater than 0.01 inch. But it would seem from studies made in the author's laboratory that a higher order of accuracy is possible with the apparatus and techniques here described. The reproducibility of the average widths of land impressions on bullets fired from the same gun, as so measured, seems to be of the order of ± 0.001 inch when proper ammunition is used, even in guns that have seen much service. As is well recognized, it is abuse rather than use that is most harmful to the rifling in a gun.

An alternate method for measuring land impressions

A fairly satisfactory measurement of the width of a land impression on a fired bullet may be made by using a stage micrometer, graduated to read to 0.01 mm., in conjunction with a comparison microscope. The stage micrometer is a glass microscope slide, about 1×3 inches, upon which is engraved an

accurate scale, in either the English or metric system, i.e., graduated to 0.001 inch or to 0.01 mm.

The bullet is placed on one stage of the comparison microscope and the micrometer slide is mounted on the other, with a bright white reflector underneath to bring out the lines of the scale clearly. The bullet must be carefully positioned (by rotating) until both of the edges of the groove are in focus. Final adjustment of the position of the micrometer slide is made so as to bring the zero of the scale to coincide with one edge of the groove and then the width of the groove can be read directly on the scale. Experiments were made with steel scales graduated to 0.01 inch but the desired accuracy could not be obtained because of the coarse graduations and the width of the engraved lines.

Fig. 88. Lead disk on end of "thrust rod" after being forced through a rifled barrel, in operation of the rifling meter.

A comparison of this method with the method described above, and regularly used by the author, shows that values obtained by the two methods agree quite closely for bullets which show well-defined, clear-cut grooves. For bullets having less well marked land impressions the method involving stereoscopic vision is much better.

Measurement of bore and groove diameters

In a barrel having an even number of lands and grooves the bore diameter is the distance between the tops of opposite lands. In a barrel having an odd number of lands and grooves the bore diameter is the diameter of a circle which would touch the tops of all of the lands. The groove diameter for a barrel having an even number of grooves is the distance from the bottom of a groove to the bottom of the opposite groove. The groove diameter for a barrel having an odd number of grooves may be defined in two ways. It may be defined as: (A) The

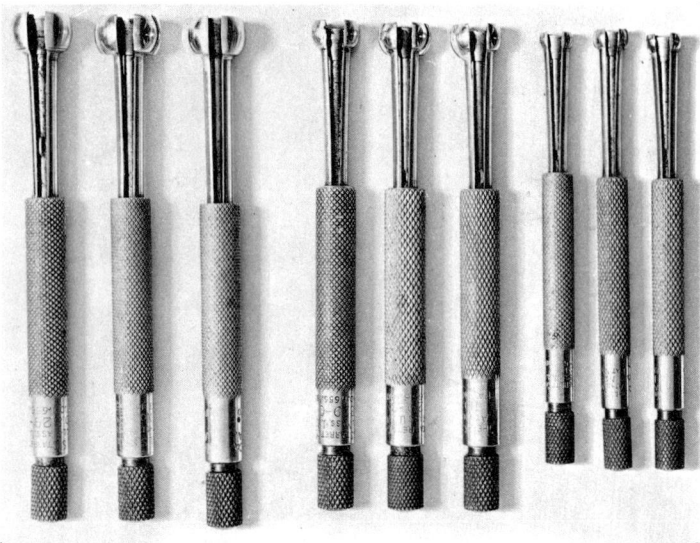

Fig. 89. Set of Starrett Small Hole Gauges, modified as described in the text. Used for measuring bore and groove diameters of rifled barrels.

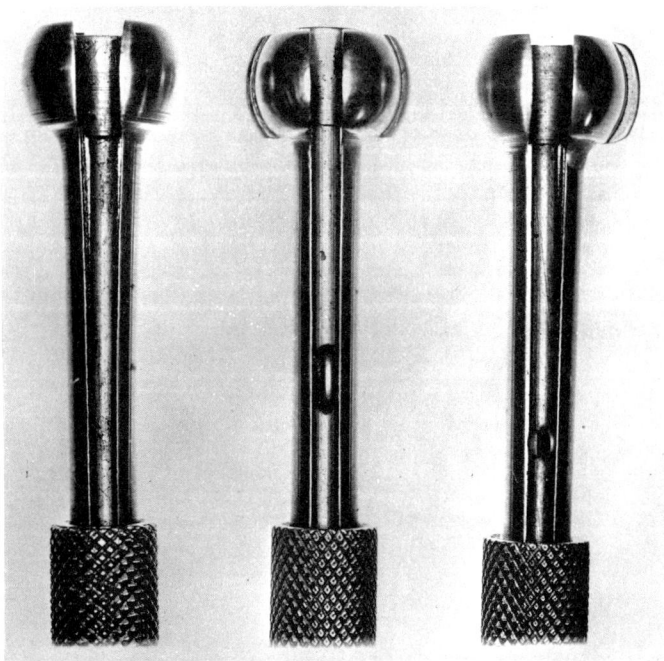

Fig. 90. Enlargement of three gauges shown in Fig. 89. *Left:* Unmodified gauge. *Center:* Two "fins" (for even number of grooves). *Right:* One "fin" (for odd number of grooves).

diameter of a circle which would just touch the bottoms of all of the grooves or (B) The distance from the bottom of a groove to the top of the opposite land. The second definition has been chosen for the measurements recorded in this work because the distance from the bottom of a groove to the top of the opposite land is readily measureable.

The conventional Starrett Small Hole Gauges can be used for measurements of the land-to-land (i.e., bore) diameter for barrels that have an even number of lands, but they cannot be used for the measurement of groove diameters because the gauge will not reach the bottom of the groove. (The "split ball" of the gauge will strike the "shoulders" of the groove, except possibly in some cases of large-caliber barrels having exceptionally wide grooves.) And these gauges cannot be used to measure either groove or bore diameters where the barrel has an uneven number of lands and grooves.

The problem of making satisfactory measurements in all guns was solved in the following way. Three sets of Starrett Small Hole Gauges were procured. One of these sets was used in the conventional manner for measuring land-to-land diameters. A second set was provided with a pair of oppositely placed "fins," as shown in Figs. 89 to 91, and was used to make the measurements of groove diameters for those barrels that had an even number of grooves. The third set (Figs. 89, 90, 92) was modified by providing a single "fin" on each gauge and these gauges were used to measure the "groove diameters" (the distance from the bottom of a groove to the top of the opposite land) in barrels having an odd number of grooves. These "fins" may be soldered on with silver solder, or, as pointed out by B. D. Munhall, they may be made by using a larger gauge and grinding away the unwanted metal until the desired shape is produced. The "fins" made by the second method will probably be more durable, but no particular difficulty has been experienced with the original method.

In the case of barrels having an odd number of lands there remains the problem of measuring the land or bore diameter, which cannot be done with the Starrett gauges. Consequently resort was had to the time-honored method of using tapered steel gauges to make these measurements (Fig. 93). These gauges are made of tempered, high-carbon steel and are accurately ground so that the taper is uniform. The over-all length is 3 inches and the tapered portion is about 2⅜ inches in length. The difference in diameters at the ends of the ground portion is approximately 0.020 inch. This small change in diameter naturally increases the accuracy of the measure-

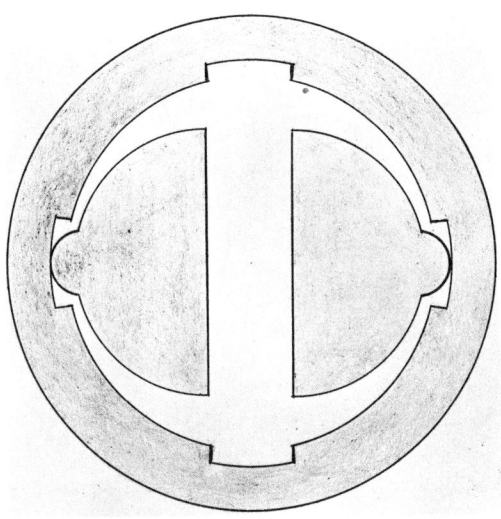

Fig. 91. Diagram of modified Starrett Small Hole Gauge, with two "fins," for measuring groove diameters when number of grooves is even.

Fig. 92. Diagram of modified Starrett Small Hole Gauge, with one "fin," for measuring "groove diameters" when number of grooves is odd.

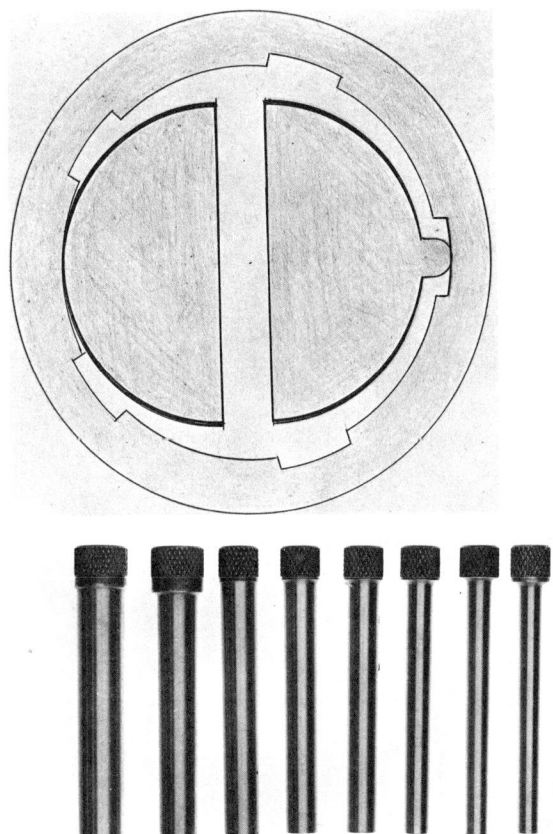

Fig. 93. Set of tapered gauges. Used for measuring bore diameter of guns having an odd number of grooves. Taper is such that there is a difference in diameters of ca. 0.020″ at the two ends of the taper. Complete set consists of 13 gauges.

ments. The entire set consists of 13 such tapered gauges, covering the range from ca. 0.200 inch to 0.465 inch. In using the tapered gauge, a bit of colored vaseline is placed on the gauge at the point where it will make contact; the gauge is then inserted into the barrel and is rotated gently as it makes contact. This leaves a colored ring with a sharp line of demarcation and the diameter of the gauge at this point is measured with a Starrett micrometer having a vernier enabling one to make readings to 0.0001 inch. (This micrometer is also used to measure the other gauges described above.) For convenience the micrometer is mounted on a stand, leaving both hands free to hold the gauge and to operate the micrometer (Fig. 94).

With the tapered gauge the measurement of bore diameter has to be made at the end of the barrel. This is unfortunate because the bore may not be the same at this point due to the "crowning" process, to accidental burring, or to wear. In the case of the barrels with even numbers of lands, the diameter can

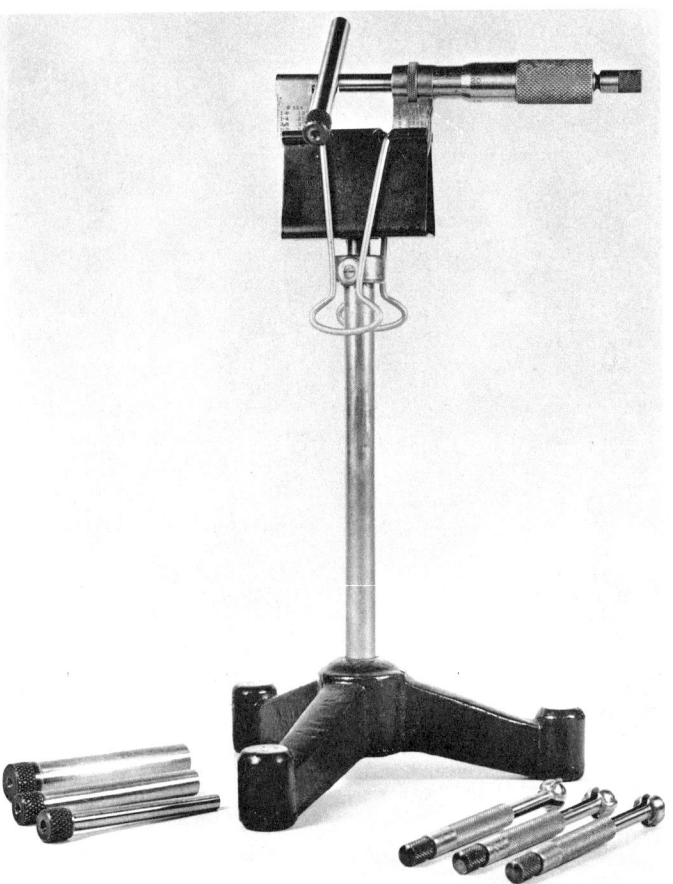

Fig. 94. Micrometer stand, a simple and convenient device for holding the micrometer so that one may have use of both hands for manipulation.

be measured at any portion of the barrel that can be reached by the gauge and the measurements can be made with more confidence. Any nonuniformity (or inequalities) in either the bore diameter or groove diameter can be readily detected (and measured) in such barrels. In this way a very good idea can be obtained as to the perfection of the rifling, or the condition of the rifling if the gun has seen considerable use. This statement applies to the grooves in guns having an odd number of grooves (where the modified Starrett gauge can be used) but not to the land diameter since this has to be measured with the tapered gauge. In general it is good procedure to make measurements at least one inch from the end of the barrel because more uniformity is found there than at the muzzle. As with all such measurements, several settings should be made and the average of the readings taken.

Groove depths

The depths of grooves is, of course, readily determined from the data obtained by the procedure described above. In the case of barrels having an even number of grooves the groove depth will be one half the difference between the groove and bore diameters. For barrels having an odd number of grooves the depth of the grooves will be the difference between the groove diameter (as defined above) and the bore diameter.

Table 6 illustrates the reproducibility that may be obtained by the procedures described above. Reproducibility such as shown in this table can be obtained only in case of barrels that are in good

condition (i.e., free from corrosion or rust) and obviously there must be no damage to the bore at the muzzle where the bore diameter measurement is made. In other words it must not be "out of round" or "burred." This difficulty, of course, does not appear in the case of guns having an even number of grooves because the measurements need not be made right at the muzzle end. Experience in the author's laboratory, and elsewhere, has shown that, in general, it is better to take measurements of bore and groove diameter at a point about one inch from the end of the barrel. This avoids any possible error due to "burring" at the muzzle or to excessive wear at the muzzle. This procedure was followed in the case of all barrels having an even number of grooves. Fortunately most guns have an even number of grooves, though there are notable exceptions.

Actually a knowledge of the depths of grooves in a rifled barrel is not ordinarily of great importance in firearms investigations, for reasons stated in section on depth of grooves in Chapter 2.

Reproducibility of measurements on rifling characteristics

Inadvertently two separate series of measurements were made, well over a year apart, on the same gun—a .32 Savage Auto Pistol, Serial No. 212,696. These are given in Table 7. The excellent agreement of the values obtained, which were discovered only when the data were tabulated some time later, gives added confidence in the reproducibility of the measurements made by the techniques employed.

Measurements of the rifling in different specimens of the same models of three makes of guns are given in Table 8. Since, as already shown, it is possible (in guns whose rifling is in good condition) to measure the widths of lands accurately to ±0.001 inch, length of barrel for one turn of rifling to ±0.1 inch, and bore and groove diameters to ±0.0002 inch, it is clear that the differences between related specimens

TABLE 6

Illustration of reproducibility obtainable in measurements of groove depths for barrels having an odd number of grooves

(Measurements made on .32 cal. Smith & Wesson No. 82,406)

A.	Land-groove diameter, using gauge having one "fin"		
Groove	Series 1	Series 2	Series 3
No. 1	.3082″	.3082″	.3081″
No. 2	.3083	.3083	.3083
No. 3	.3084	.3084	.3084
No. 4	.3084	.3084	.3084
No. 5	.3080	.3080	.3080
Av.	.3083″	.3083″	.3083″

B.	Bore diameter, using tapered gauge and micrometer
	Measurement No. 1 – .3032″
	Measurement No. 2 – .3030″
	Measurement No. 3 – .3030″
	Measurement No. 4 – .3031″
	Measurement No. 5 – .3031″
	Av. .3031″

C. Depth of groove = 0.3083″ − 0.3031″ = 0.0052″

TABLE 7

Separate measurements made on same gun show reproducibility

	Series I (Oct. 5, 1955)	Series II (Feb. 10, 1957)
1 turn of rifling in	12.02 inches	12.00 inches
Duplicate measurements	11.97 inches	12.00 inches
Width of land in gun (i.e., average width of all 6 grooves on disk)	0.041 inch	0.040 inch
Bore diameter	0.3050 inch	0.3050 inch
Groove diameter	0.3158 inch	0.3158 inch
Groove depth	0.0054 inch	0.0054 inch

shown in Table 8 are real and represent either changes in practice or lack of control in shop practice. Data on more specimens of each make and model would be needed in order to draw definite conclusions.

Measurements of rifling data for three specimens of the 6.35 mm. Walther Mod. 5 are given in Table 9. Outwardly these specimens are alike, but there is a curious situation as to the rifling characteristics. It

would appear from these measurements that specifications were changed from time to time. Other specimens would have been very desirable, as additional measurements are clearly needed for this model.

Setup for photographing hand guns

Good photographs of guns should show details clearly so that inscriptions, numbers, proof marks, etc. can be read on the finished prints, assuming that they are clear on the specimen. The most important element in obtaining such photographs is proper illumination. The gun photographs in this book were taken under the illumination and other conditions given in the following paragraphs. Naturally, some of the detail of the photographs was lost in the process of reproduction, either in the engraving or the printing process.

A 4×5 Kodak Master View Camera provided with a Kodak Ektar coated lens, f-4.5 and 152 mm. focus,

TABLE 8

Variation in rifling characteristics in different specimens of the same make and model of gun

I. Data for 3 specimens of 6.35 mm Astra Mod. 200*			
	Serial No. 656280	Serial No. 684149	Serial No. 686019
Number of lands	6	6	6
Direction of twist	left	left	left
Inches for 1 turn	9.63	9.62	10.13
Width of land	0.036″	0.039″	0.043″
Groove diameter	0.2524″	0.2523″	0.2508″
Bore diameter	0.2460″	0.2469″	0.2470″

II. Data for 2 specimens of 6.35 mm. Walther Mod. 8*		
	Serial No. 703782	Serial No. 720440
Number of lands	6	6
Direction of twist	Right	Right
Inches for 1 turn	9.63	7.95
Width of lands	0.032″	0.043″
Groove diameter	0.2523″	0.2520″
Bore diameter	0.2471″	0.2450″

III. Data for 2 specimens of 6.35 mm. Sauer Mod. 28*		
	Serial No. 252171	Serial No. 253211
Number of lands	6	6
Direction of twist	Right	Right
Inches for 1 turn	9.37	9.35
Width of lands	0.023″	0.040″
Groove diameter	0.2550″	0.2538″
Bore diameter	0.2460″	0.2460″

*Rifling was in good to excellent condition in all guns.

TABLE 9

Inconsistencies in rifling characteristics in different specimens of the same make and model of gun.

	Serial No. 91189	Serial No. 92141	Serial No. 94908
Number of lands	4	6	4
Direction of twist	Right	Right	Right
Inches for 1 turn	9.85	9.5	9.6
Width of land	0.065″	0.028″	0.069″
Groove diameter	0.2538″	0.2536″	0.2541″
Bore diameter	0.2452″	0.2446″	0.2473″

Note: An earlier specimen (Serial No. 41526) was found to have 6 lands. Unfortunately the rifling was not in good condition and accurate measurements could not be made.

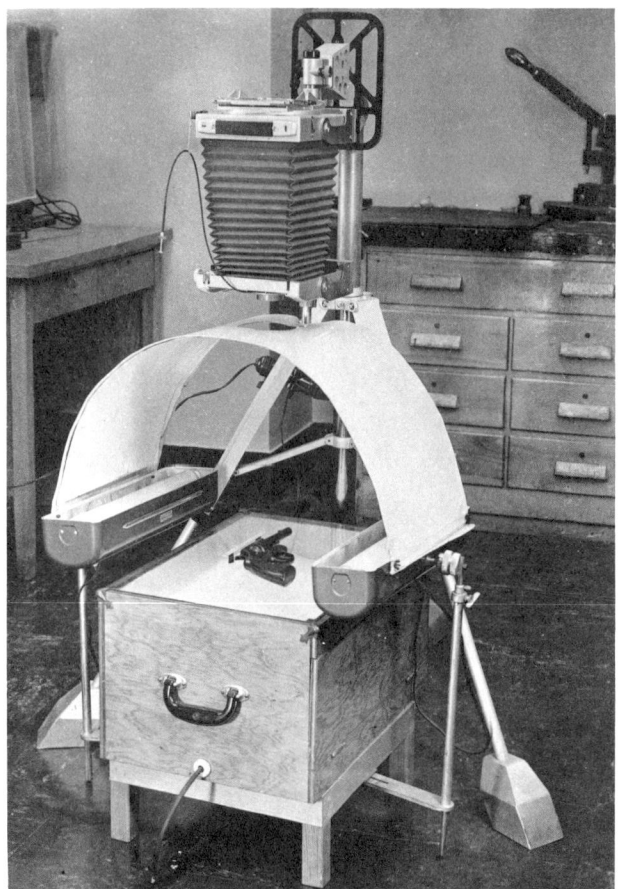

Fig. 95. Photography of hand guns. Equipment used by the author for photographing hand guns. It is described fully in the text.

was used. The camera was mounted on a Bruneau pneumatic tripod which gives firm support. Panatomic-X cut films developed in glycin developer gave satisfying detail, contrast, and grain. The illumination was provided by the equipment shown in Fig. 95. The "light box" is 15½ inches wide, 22 inches long, and 11 inches deep, and is placed on a stand 6 inches high. Near the bottom are five 15-watt G.E. white fluorescent tubes and the interior of the box is painted with aluminum paint. At the top of the box is a plate-glass cover upon which the gun is placed. Three inches below the plate glass is an opal glass, filling the whole cross section of the box. This diffuses the light to give an evenly lighted background. The box has a hinged door on one side for the replacement of tubes when required.

At each side of the box there is a 15-watt fluorescent lamp in a reflector and these are supported by telescoping tubes so that they can be moved up or down as desired. Lateral adjustment is also provided. The lamp reflectors are faced upwards so that no light passes directly from the light source to the object being photographed. Passing from the outer edge of one lamp housing to the outer edge of the other is a 40×16-inch curved reflector lined with glass-beaded screen material ("Dalite"). The reflector has an elliptical 3×6-inch opening at the top to allow the light from the object to pass to the camera lens above. All of the light which reaches the object being photographed is reflected light, part coming from the tubes in the box and part from the tubes at the sides of the box. This arrangement gives a soft, even illumination, free from shadows and free from glare.

A scale is placed alongside the gun being photographed. It is important that this scale be placed at the proper height. If it is laid on the glass it will be farther from the lens than the axis of the barrel and an erroneous effect will be produced. Being farther from the lens, the scale will naturally be reduced in size in the photograph. The accompanying photograph, Fig. 96, of two 6-inch scales, one laid on the plate glass and the other supported at a height of

$^{11}/_{16}$ inch above it, shows this parallax effect clearly. There is an apparent difference of ¼ inch in the length of the two 6 inch scales. Naturally the less the distance between the camera lens and the object being photographed the greater the parallax effect will be. Obviously, to get proper dimensions the scale must be supported at a height coinciding with the axis of the barrel. When the exposure is made the diaphragm is set at f-32 to give the depth of focus necessary to bring out details.

It is desirable that both sides of each gun be photographed. Otherwise details that are important to the expert or the collector will be missed.

Frequently one has occasion to photograph a nickel-plated gun that shows rust spots. These can be eliminated to a considerable degree by careful dusting of the discolored surface with aluminum powder. Fig. 97 shows, for the purpose of illustration, an extreme case. Discolored spots on guns with

Fig. 97. Better photographs of rusted nickel-plated guns can be made by first dusting with aluminum powder.

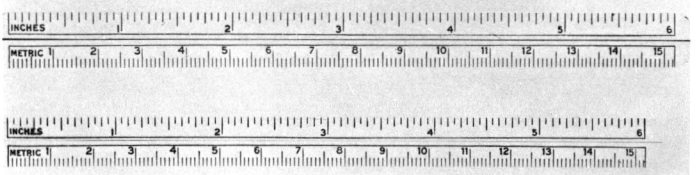

Fig. 96. Illustrating importance of proper placement of scale in gun photography. The upper scale was $^{11}/_{16}''$ closer to the camera. Scale should be supported so that it is at the same level as the bore of the barrel.

blued finish can be greatly improved for photographing by rubbing with steel wool and rebluing the area with one of several rebluing preparations that are on the market. This should not be done on aluminum surfaces, of course.

Three-dimensional photographs

It is well known that to determine the true shape of an object two eyes are better than one. In the examination of such things as firing pin impressions (and many others) it is very important to determine their true shapes and this cannot be done with the ordinary monocular microscope because one sees the object from one viewpoint only. With a binocular microscope (the Greenough type, having two separate optical systems) one uses both eyes and consequently secures two images of the object, from slightly different angles, which blend together to give a true impression of the shape of the object. For this reason all such examinations should be made with a binocular microscope. Two firing pin impressions, which with the ordinary microscope may appear to have the same shape, may be shown to have quite different shapes when viewed under a binocular microscope. One may have been made with a blunt firing pin while the other was made with a more pointed (or tapered) firing pin. Viewed with the ordinary microscope the impressions might appear to be identical, but not with the binocular microscope.

It may be very important to demonstrate such differences in court. The unsupported word of the expert that two firing pin impressions have different shapes (or the same shape, as the case may be) when viewed under a binocular microscope, an instrument about which the members of the jury may not have any knowledge, will certainly not be as convincing as a visual demonstration which each of them can see for himself. Since the average jury member is quite unfamiliar with even an ordinary compound microscope it would serve no good purpose to try to have each jury member look at an object through a binocular microscope, where the pupillary distance has to be adjusted for each individual, and by himself. Stereo photographs, however, are something about which practically everyone has knowledge and experience, and these can be shown to the members of the jury in a short time.

Stereo photomicrographs are not particularly difficult to make if one has suitable equipment. There are cameras on the market which are especially designed for the purpose. Some of these are used in conjunction with the binocular microscope and some are simply stereo cameras with very short-focus lenses which produce the necessary magnification. Some have even used a single camera to secure the two photos from a slightly different angle. This is difficult and is not recommended.

The author uses a camera and binocular microscope, as shown in Fig. 98. The microscope is an older type of Bausch and Lomb instrument having three pairs of objectives and is well adapted for the purpose. The camera consists of a box with a partition down the middle, and a removable back in which are mounted two ground glasses in such position that each will be at right angles to the pathways of light through the optical systems of the microscope. A plate holder, for two 3½ × 3½-inch plates, is provided. When this replaces the ground glasses upon which the images are focused, the plates are in precisely the same positions the ground glasses were in. At the bottom of the camera there are "muffs" to make light-tight connection between the microscope and camera. The camera, as made by Bausch and Lomb, was modified so as to permit lateral movement of each of the "muffs." As received, these were in fixed position on the bottom plate of the camera. This plate was cut in two and the pieces mounted in a slide which permits the lateral motion of each which is necessary to bring the images into proper position on the ground glasses. The images must not only be in focus but must be exactly centered in order that the two pictures will

Fig. 98. Stereocamera on binocular microscope. Shows a rifle shell head being photographed. As set up here the head of the shell is illuminated with a Silverman Illuminator (large size), which gives even illumination from all directions.

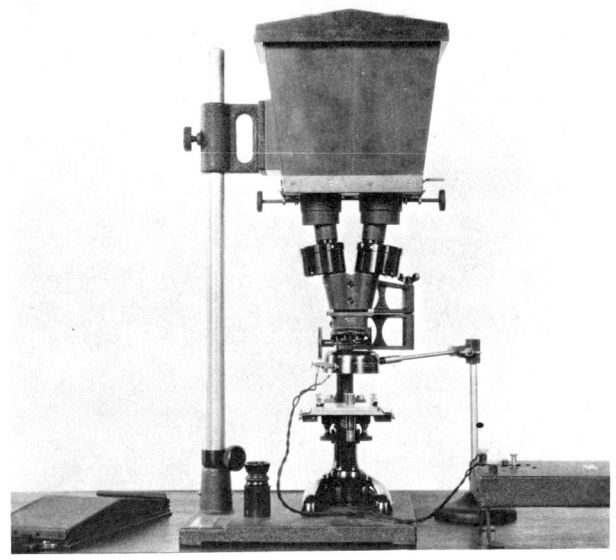

register properly when viewed in a stereoscope.

Panchromatic plates rather than cut films are used because the two photographs, when viewed in the stereoscope, must be in exact register. Since films of the size used do not always lie perfectly flat they are unsuitable. The slightest "buckling" would destroy the register. In printing, the two plates are put into a printing frame in such a manner as to bring them into the same position in relation to each other that they were in when the exposure was made. Obvi-

ously a good stereoscope is also necessary to secure proper register of the two images.

The accompanying stereo photomicrographs, reproduced full size, (Figs. 99, 100) will show, when viewed through a stereoscope, the advantage of this type of photography.

The problem of vibration and its elimination

In laboratories where there is troublesome vibra-

Fig. 99. Stereophotomicrographs. The binocular microscope, which gives a three-dimensional view of an object, is indispensable. To make a permanent record of what the binocular microscope reveals, a three-dimensional photograph is necessary. Above are examples of such photos. To bring out the third dimension they must be viewed with a stereoscope.

tion, special arrangements must be made to meet this situation since relatively slow-speed photography is used in photographing guns. In the processes involving magnification, such as photographing objects under a microscope, vibration is particularly troublesome.

Mounting the photographic equipment on a base which is firmly attached to the floor usually increases the difficulty since vibrations of the floor will be transmitted to the apparatus because of the attachment. The opposite course should be taken—there

will be no vibration of the equipment if it is "floated" quite independently of the vibrating floor.

In the case of the comparison microscope, where the camera and microscope are mounted rigidly on the same base, vibration is less than it would be if they were mounted separately because, under such circumstances, they will vibrate as a unit and the difficulty is thus minimized. In photomicrography at higher magnifications, however, and particularly if there is much vibration in the building, the whole assembly should be supported so that the vibrations

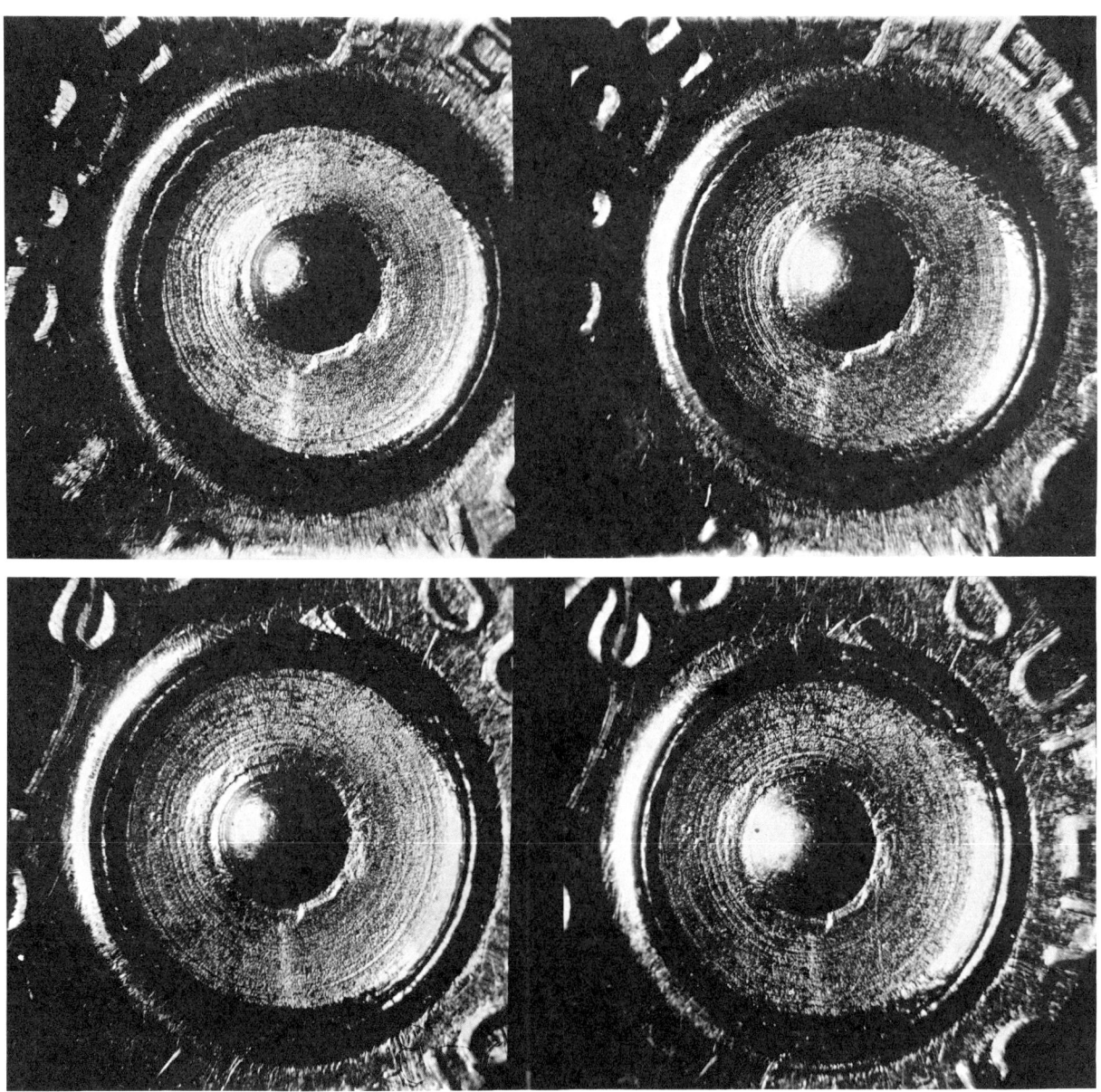

Fig. 100. Stereophotomicrographs. Showing breech-block markings on two shells fired in the same gun. To bring out the third dimension these must be viewed with a stereoscope.

will be completely absorbed. In the case where the microscope and camera are mounted firmly on the same base, the entire assembly may be mounted on a foam-rubber support (or supports). If this does not suffice, a modification of the procedure described below may be used.

In the case where a large assembly is used, such as the one described above for photographing hand guns, the assembly may be too heavy to be supported adequately by the use of foam rubber. In such a case a partially inflated innertube of suitable size placed under a platform carrying the entire photographic setup can be used. A circular platform is recommended, as projecting corners are not desirable, and a 2- or 3-inch rim around the lower edge of the platform not only helps to conceal the innertube but

helps to hold it in place. Obviously this rim must not touch the floor. Such an arrangement will "float" a fairly heavy assembly and all vibration will be damped out. Because of its inertia, a heavy assembly, when so supported, will vibrate less than a lighter one.

References

1 MATHEWS, J. H., and HENKE, LEE K. The Comparison Camera. Jour. Crim. Law and Criminology 37: 247 (1946).
2 MATHEWS, J. H., and HENKE, LEE K. The Rifling Meter. Ibid. 35: 134 (1944).
3 BRADFORD, L. W., and BRACKETT, J. W. R. Identification News. March 1953.
4 MUNHALL, B. D. Proceedings of the I. A. I. 1950 (pp. 166–171).

Restoration of serial numbers

Occasionally guns found at or near the scene of a shooting or taken from a suspect will have had the serial number removed either by filing or, less frequently, by grinding. The serial numbers on stolen guns are also frequently removed. The practice of removing serial numbers is not as popular among criminals as it once was as they have now learned that their efforts are futile.

Fortunately, when occasion demands, there are methods whereby numbers which have been removed can often be restored to such an extent that they can be read and photographed, provided the filing or grinding is not too deep.

The principles involved are as follows: When the numbers are stamped in by a hard steel die, the die is struck a sharp blow to make each digit sink into the metal to the proper depth, or the die may be forced into the metal under pressure. In either case, the stamping of these numbers disturbs the crystals of the metal and puts them under a strain which is permanent. There will thus be a zone of strain immediately surrounding each digit and extending a short distance below the limit of penetration of the die. It is a fact well known to metallurgists and metallographers that metal treated with certain etching reagents will react (dissolve) at a different rate in areas which are under strain than in areas which are not under strain. These unequal rates of solution of strained and unstrained metal make it possible, in many cases, to "bring out" numbers that have been removed by filing or grinding. This is because the act of filing or grinding is usually stopped as soon as the numbers just disappear, thus leaving some of the zone of strained metal. If, however, the removal of surface metal is continued until all the metal in the zone of strain is removed the numbers cannot then be restored.

When a gun is brought to the laboratory for the restoration of a serial number the first thing to do is to examine the gun both inside and out to see whether any such number is present. Often times with suitable illumination and some magnification the number can be discovered and deciphered, particularly if the surface is wetted.

Many cases can be solved quite simply, particularly for some makes of revolvers, by removing the grip plates and examining the frame where the number may be stamped. If this fails, the inside of the grip plates may show a pencilled serial number. Disassembly of the gun may reveal serial numbers in several places, depending on the make of the gun. In automatics of foreign make the last three digits of the serial number are often placed on the barrel, but seldom does the entire number appear there—unless it is a two- or three-digit number. Oftentimes, on the other hand, the number on the barrel may bear no relation to the serial number, so one must not assume that because a number is there it necessarily is a part of a serial number. So, instead of being helpful in interpreting a serial number that comes out faintly upon etching it may add to the confusion. It may or it may not help. One must be familiar with the practice of the manufacturer of that make of gun.

A knowledge of the place where a serial number may usually be found is, of course, of great assistance.* Also, one must not confuse a manufacturer's number with the serial number. As an example, take the "J. C. Higgins" Model 88 revolver. The model number is present on both sides of the grips. The

*For information on the location of serial numbers on various automatic pistols see *The Identification of Pistols by Serial Numbers and Other Markings*, by V. Krcma. Jour. of Forensic Sciences, Vol. 6, p 479 (1961).

manufacturer (High Standard Co.) puts his identification number and the statement of model and caliber on the left side of the barrel. The serial number is on the lower right side of the frame (and only there). The manufacturer's identification number must not be confused with the serial number.

Failing to find any useful information by a careful inspection of the gun, one may then resort to a restoration of the number. The first thing to do is to take a good photograph, preferably enlarged several times, of the area upon which the number should appear, in order to show the exact condition that existed before any treatment was made. This is important as a matter of record and, of course, is routine procedure in most laboratories. Next, if the area is rough, as it is very likely to be, it should be made smooth and then polished. Care must be taken not to remove too much metal—but smoothing and polishing will make the figures more distinct as they appear.

The choice of etching agent depends on the nature of the metal. A rather extensive investigation of this matter was made in the author's laboratory and fifteen different etching solutions were studied. Of the fifteen used, a number were found to be very inferior. On the other hand, it was found that certain solutions might work well on cast steel but not on cold rolled steel or malleable cast steel. Formulas for the nine solutions found to be useful are given in Table 10.

The final conclusions were that solutions Nos. 2, 8, 9, 10, and 11 can be used successfully on cold rolled steel. Solutions 1, 2, 3, and 5 will give good results on cast steel. When No. 3 is used the metal has to be immersed in the solution and the solution boiled

to get good etching. This often cannot be done, so No. 3 is not recommended. Solutions Nos. 2, 3, 4, and 10 can be used successfully on malleable cast steel. No solution found to date is equally good for all of the different kinds of steel encountered in gun manufacture.

In general, the technique used is to swab the filed surface with a cotton swab wet with the reagent, which may or may not be heated. Etching naturally proceeds faster with hot solutions. Sometimes care must be taken not to etch too fast, particularly if the filing has been deep. The numbers may come up and then vanish—and once gone they cannot be restored. Another technique is to build a little "dam" or retaining wall of modeling clay or a suitable wax around the part to be etched and to fill this little "pond" with the reagent (cold) and wait for development of the numbers. As the numbers appear they should be photographed (or at least recorded) promptly for fear that they may disappear—to be forever lost. They are best photographed while wet, as the numbers show up better then. To prevent too-rapid evaporation they may be wetted with glycerine while being photographed. The best results are highly dependent on proper illumination. Some experimentation will be necessary to determine the best angle for this.

Some study was made of "anodic" or "electrolytic" etching. In this process the metal to be etched is made the anode in an electrolytic bath of some dilute acid or etching solution and a current of electricity is then passed through the bath.

While it was found possible to restore numbers in this way, the process seemed to offer no advantages over the use of reagents alone and is more difficult to carry out.

Professor Ralph Turner of the State University of Michigan, who worked with the author on the problem of restoration of serial numbers while a student (and who is largely responsible for the results obtained), has more recently made a study of the electrolytic process, basing his procedure on suggestions made to him in a personal communication from Mr. Shigeo Arai of the Scientific Crime Detection Laboratory of Tokyo. The results of this study were presented at the 5th Annual meeting of the American Academy of Forensic Sciences in 1953 in a paper by Turner and Burgess.

The electric circuit used by Arai and by Turner is shown in the accompanying diagram (Fig. 101). The gun (or other object) is made the anode and the cathode consists of a loop of wire (or a battery clip) which holds a cotton swab kept wet with the solution. The metal surface, which has been smoothed and

TABLE 10

Etching solutions recommended for various kinds of steel

No. 1		No. 5	
HCl (conc.)	40 cc.	Picric acid	
H_2O	30 cc.	(saturated alcoholic solution)	
C_2H_5OH	25 cc.	No. 8	
$CuCl_2$ (crystals)	5 gm.	HNO_3	
No. 2		(4% solution in amyl alcohol)	
HCl (conc.)	120 cc.	No. 9	
H_2O	100 cc.	HNO_3	
$CuCl_2$ (crystals)	90 gm.	(1% solution in water)	
No. 3		No. 10	
$FeCl_3$ (6% solution in water)		Ammonium persulphate	
No. 4		(10% solution in water)	
(Heyn's Solution)		No. 11	
$CuNH_4Cl_2$ (crystals)	1 gm.	CH_3OH	10 cc.
HCl (conc.)	12 cc.	C_2H_5OH	10 cc.
H_2O	12 cc.	$C_5H_{11}OH$	10 cc.
		HNO_3	
		(4% in acet. anhyd.)	30 cc.

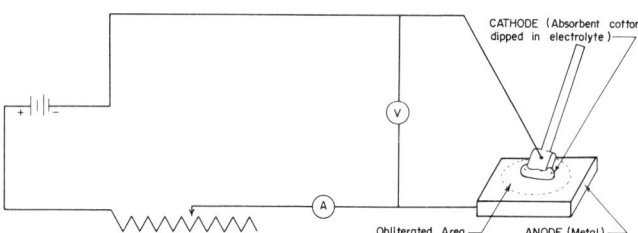

Fig. 101. Restoration of serial numbers. Diagram showing an ideal setup for the electrolytic process of etching to restore obliterated serial numbers.

polished and treated with acetone or other suitable solvent to remove grease or oil, is gently swabbed with the wet cotton cathode over the area to be etched. Then, starting with a value below the decomposition potential of the solution, a voltage is applied across the electrodes and gradually increased until a point is reached at which the current will flow. If the voltage is raised much beyond this point the flow of current will increase rapidly. This threshold value at which the current starts to flow will be different for different solutions. It should not be exceeded more than a few tenths of a volt. (While the purpose of this electrolytic method is to speed up the process of etching it must not be speeded up too much since pitting will then occur, and the procedure may get out of control and the numbers will be irretrievably lost. There will be an optimum voltage (and amperage) which will give the best results. This optimum must be determined by experiment.) After a few minutes the numbers should begin to appear and care must be taken that the etching process does not proceed too far. In but few cases will more than ten minutes be required and it may take as little as three or four. As soon as the numbers can be read the process is stopped and the electrolyte is washed off completely—using a neutralizing solution, followed by water. If the results appear to be satisfactory a photograph should be taken, after removing the water with acetone and applying a thin coating of oil. The author prefers to use glycerine rather than oil to keep the surface wet while photographing.

Turner tried the solution suggested by Arai (H_2O– 500 cc.; conc. H_2SO_4–15 cc.; gelatin–1 gram; and $CuSO_4$–1 gram) but after considerable experimentation found combinations of ingredients that produced better results. The results for eight solutions were reported. Some were based on Arai's suggestions and others on the solutions previously used in the author's laboratory but later modified as to concentrations. The eight solutions had compositions as shown in Table 11.

As was to be expected, the success obtained depended on the nature of the metal being etched and on the ingredients and their concentrations in the electrolyte. Summarizing, it may be said that the best results for various metals were obtained by using the following solutions as given in Table 11: for rolled steel, Nos. 2, 3, 4, and 7; for cast iron, Nos. 3 and 4; for aluminum, Nos. 1, 2, 4, and 7; and for brass, Nos. 1, 3, and 7.

TABLE 11
Etching solutions for electrolytic etching

No. 1		No. 5	
HCl (conc.)	40 cc.	HCl (conc.)	60 cc.
H_2O	30 cc.	H_2O	50 cc.
C_2H_5OH	25 cc.	$CuCl_2$	45 gm.
$CuCl_2$	5 gm.		
No. 2		No. 6	
HCl (conc.)	20 cc.	H_2SO_4 (conc.)	7.5 cc.
H_2O	30 cc.	H_2O	250.0 cc.
C_2H_5OH	25 cc.	Gelatine	0.5 gm.
$CuCl_2$	5 gm.	$CuSO_4$	0.5 gm.
No. 3		No. 7	
HCl (conc.)	40 cc.	(Heyn's)	
H_2O	30 cc.	HCl (conc.)	12 cc.
C_2H_5OH	25 cc.	H_2O	12 cc.
$CuCl_2$	2.5 gm.	$CuNH_4Cl_2$	1 gm.
No. 4		No. 8	
HCl (conc.)	10 cc.	H_2O	100 cc.
H_2O	30 cc.	CrO_3	20 gm.
C_2H_5OH	25 cc.	Na_2SO_4	1.5 gm.
$CuCl_2$	5 gm.		

The advantage of the improved electrolytic process lies in the fact that much time is saved, the end result being obtained in a few minutes whereas in the older process it often took many hours. Since there is the danger of etching too far, so that the numbers disappear forever, it is advantageous to reduce the time of watching for the numbers to appear. The end result is no better, but time is saved. The disadvantages are apparent—the process requires more equipment and somewhat more skill, but neither of these is serious.*

Serial numbers are often removed from objects other than guns and, since it is a matter of common knowledge among police officers that serial numbers can be restored, the firearms examiner is often given the problem of restoration on these other objects. Among such are: automobile engine blocks, typewriters, adding machines, I.B.M. machines of various kinds, tape recorders, microscopes, watches, sewing machines, washing machines, and many other items

*It should be pointed out that while the assembly of apparatus such as has been described is doubtless preferable, quite satisfactory restorations have reportedly been made by the electrolytic method by simply using one, two, or three dry cells with no adjustable resistance or measuring instruments.

of commerce any one of which may have its serial number removed to prevent the tracing of original ownership.

The author has had occasion to restore the number on an automobile engine block. The block was placed in a horizontal position, with the side on which the number is usually found being uppermost, and a "retaining wall" of suitable wax was placed around the area where the number should appear. The little "pond" was then filled with a 5% aqueous solution of ammonium persulphate. The next morning the entire serial number was legible. To bring the number out in a shorter time a 10% solution would be preferable.

Many cases, because of the nature of the metal, require special solutions as already indicated for the different kinds of steels and iron. Brass requires a very different solution. The author once had occasion to restore serial numbers which had been removed from an oxyacetylene welding outfit. This outfit had been used to remove the hinges from a vault door in

a small town bank by melting them. Upon completion of the job the robbers left the welding outfit behind. Knowing that certain brass fittings should show serial numbers, which quite obviously had been removed, the investigating detectives brought these fittings to the laboratory. The job was not difficult. The following solution is an excellent one for brass and consequently was the one used: sodium sulfate (anhydrous), 1.5 gm.; chromic acid (CrO_3), 20 gm.; water (distilled), 100 cc.

In some cases the criminal first removes the serial number, then with a sharp instrument and a hammer he pounds a large number of new marks into the metal and, since these are superposed on the original digit marks, the process of restoration is made more difficult and often impossible.

Nevertheless, despite the difficulties and the frequent failures even in the limited number of cases he may meet, the firearms examiner must be prepared to undertake this process whenever it offers help in the solution of a problem presented to him.

Pitfalls for the unwary

Offhand judgments are nowhere more dangerous than in the field of firearms investigations, where the life or liberty of a person may be at stake, and the old adage that "a little learning is a dangerous thing" is nowhere better exemplified. Even those who have had years of experience frequently run into something new and unexpected. A good philosophy to adopt is "to expect the unexpected." An investigator who knows all the answers is a very dangerous person!

Some, but by no means all, of the situations that may cause trouble are listed and discussed below. A number of these may appear quite obvious, but they, as well as those not so obvious, should be kept in mind. Others, while occurring more rarely, are definite possibilities that the examiner must consider. No single investigator is likely to encounter them all. Doubtless there are many others that might be included in this listing.*

1. Automatic pistol cartridges may be fired in revolvers

The average American-made revolver designed for the .32 S & W cartridge will chamber satisfactorily cartridges of the .32 cal. automatic pistol type, and many revolvers chambered for the .32-20 cartridge will also chamber the .32 cal. automatic cartridge. Tests made at the Northwestern University Crime Laboratory by Goddard's associates on the fitting of different makes of ammunition gave the results shown in Table 12.

Since ammunition of the .32 automatic pistol type is of the so-called "rimless" variety, ejection of the

*Taken to a considerable extent from a compilation made by the late Col. Goddard and his associates, by permission.

empty shells cannot be effected with the extracting mechanism of arms chambered for the .32 S & W ammunition. Employment of this type of ammunition is, however, by no means unusual, in spite of this drawback.

A number of foreign manufacturers, especially in Belgium and Germany, at one time produced revolvers chambered for cartridges of the .25 and .32 caliber automatic pistol type. Most of them were of the solid frame type, but at least one, by Henrion, Dassy, and Heuschen in Liége, had automatic ejection. It was made in a 20-shot model in .25 caliber and a 16-shot model in .32 caliber. Each model had two barrels and the cylinder in each had two concentric rows of chambers which were staggered with respect to each other, the bullets from the outer row passing through the upper barrel and those from the inner row passing through the lower barrel. These are collectors items in this country and cases involving them are not likely to be encountered.

As all firearms men are doubtless aware, both the 1917 Colt and 1917 Smith & Wesson revolvers were specially designed to handle the regular .45 cal. automatic pistol cartridge. Half-moon clips, each holding three cartridges, held the cartridges in proper position and facilitated the loading and the removal of fired cartridges. The finding of a fired .45 bullet or cartridge, therefore, does not necessarily mean that an automatic pistol was used. Many revolvers of the 1917 Army type are in circulation. It must also be remembered that fired .45 caliber bullets may have come from the Thompson, Reising, or M-3 submachine guns.

Ordinarily all bullets above .22 caliber which are designed for automatic pistols are of the jacketed

81

type. At one time Winchester made some .32 automatic pistol cartridges having lead bullets—either for experimental purposes or foreign use. A fired .32 caliber lead bullet having no indication of slippage

TABLE 12
The fit of different makes of ammunition in various guns

S & W Safety Hammerless Model Revolver, Cal. .32 S & W

Satisfactory fit (for .32 ACP cartridge)		Loose fit (for .32 ACP cartridge)	
A.E.P.	Savage	D.C. Co.	Peters
D.W.A.	U.S.	D.W.M.	S.F.M.
F.N.	Western	Hirtenberger	U.M.C.
Nobel	W.R.A.		

Hopkins and Allen Safety Police Model Revolver, Cal. .32 S & W

Satisfactory fit		Loose fit	
D.C. Co.	S.F.M.	A.E.P.	Savage
D.W.A.	U.S.	D.W.M.	U.M.C.
F.N.	Western	Hirtenberger	
Nobel	W.R.A.		
Peters			

Harrington and Richardson Hammerless Revolver, Cal. .32 S & W

Satisfactory fit		Loose fit	
A.E.P.	Peters	None	
D.C. Co.	Savage		
D.W.A.	S.F.M.		
D.W.M.	U.S.		
F.N.	Western		
Hirtenberger	W.R.A.		
Nobel			

Iver Johnson Safety Hammerless "Automatic" Rev., Cal. .32 S & W

Satisfactory fit		Loose fit	
D.C. Co.	Peters	A.E.P.	U.M.C.
D.W.A.	Savage	D.W.M.	Western
F.N.	U.S.	S.F.M.	
Hirtenberger	W.R.A.		
Nobel			

U.S. "Automatic" Hammerless Revolver, Cal. .32 S & W

Satisfactory fit		Loose fit	
D.C. Co.	Nobel	A.E.P.	S.F.M.
D.W.A.	Peters	D.W.M.	Western
F.N.	U.S.	Savage	U.M.C.
Hirtenberger	W.R.A.		

Colt Police Positive Revolver, Cal. .32 S & W

Satisfactory fit		No fit	
A.E.P.	D.W.M.	F.N.	U.M.C.
D.C. Co.		Nobel	Western
		Peters	W.R.A.
		Savage	

Various Spanish-Made Revolvers, Cal. .32–20

Satisfactory fit		No fit	
A.E.P.	D.W.M.	Nobel	U.M.C.
D.C. Co.	F.N.	Peters	Western
D.W.A.		Savage	W.R.A.

S & W Military and Police Revolver, Cal. .32–20

Satisfactory fit		No fit	
A.E.P.	D.W.M.	F.N.	U.M.C.
D.C. Co.	Western	Nobel	W.R.A.
		Savage	

marks could, therefore, have been fired not only from an automatic pistol but from an automatic pistol type of cartridge as well. Because of the rarity of such cartridges in the U.S. cases of this kind will be rare indeed for the U.S. examiner.

2. *The use of adapters*

Ammunition especially designed for use in revolvers or for use in automatic pistols can be fired in rifles (or shotguns) by the use of adapters or supplemental chambers. The principal manufacturers of these in the United States have been the Winchester Repeating Arms Co. and the Marble Arms and Manufacturing Co. They have been produced in great variety, the Marble Co. listing as many as twenty-three.

Table 13 shows a number of cartridges and the various rifles in which they may be fired by the use of adapters.

Examiners to whom fired revolver type and automatic pistol type bullets are submitted should always keep in mind that the evidence bullets may have been fired from rifles. And a .22 caliber fired bullet bearing no rifling marks may have been fired from

TABLE 13
Cartridges that may be fired in various rifles by means of adapters

Cartridges	Rifles
22 cal. L.R.	.22 cal. H.P. Savage
.25 ACP	.25-35 cal. rifle
	.25 cal. Remington
	.250-3000 Savage
	6.5 mm. (.256) Mannlicher-Schönauer Mod. '03
	.25 cal Short Stevens
.32 ACP	.30 U.S. Army
	.30-40
	.300 Savage
	.303 British
	.303 Savage
	.32 Winchester Special
	8 mm. rifles
.32 Short Colt	.30 cal. Remington
	.30-30 rifles
	.32 Winchester Special
	.32-40 rifles
.32 Long Colt	.32 Winchester Special
	.32-40 rifles
.32 S & W	.30 cal. U.S. Army
	.303 British
	.303 Savage
	.30-40 rifles
	.30 Gov't Rimless '03 and '06
	.30 cal. Winchester
.380 ACP	.35 cal. Remington
	.35 cal. Winchester Mod. '95
.35 S & W	8 mm. rifles

a shotgun by using an adapter designed for such use.

3. Pistol or revolver bullets may be fired from rifles after being loaded into rifle cartridge cases

Because so many rifle, revolver, and pistol bullets have so nearly the same diameter the possibilities of such substitutions are so numerous that it would be futile to attempt to list them all. A very few are given in Table 14.

4. Revolver type bullets may be fired from automatic pistols

Probably most firearms examiners have had cases where revolver type bullets have been fired from automatic pistols, and cases where other ammunition has been used in guns not specifically designed for such ammunition. A few, but by no means all, such possibilities are listed in Table 15.

5. Interchange of automatic pistol barrels

Probably most of such interchanges in military type pistols occur unintentionally. In the case of such pistols, particularly those which are used for

training purposes, very few keep their original barrels. Intentional interchange is sometimes practiced by the criminal. Such interchanges have taken place, even during the course of a murder trial. In the Sacco-Vanzetti case it was discovered that such a substitution had been made. Fortunately, a Commonwealth expert had made a photograph of the original barrel which disclosed identifying peculiarities and the judge ordered the original barrel restored. The substitution occurred while the evi-

TABLE 14

Small arms bullets that may be loaded into rifle cartridge cases

Bullets	Diam.	Rifle cartridge cases	Diam.
.30 Luger	.308	.303 Savage and British	
.32 Auto	.308	7.62 mm. Russian	
		.30 Springfield	.308
		.30 Krag	.308
		.30-30 All makes	.308
.32 S & W	.313	.32-40	.319
.32 S & W Long	.313		
.32-44 S & W	.323	.32 Ideal	.323
.38 S & W	.358	.35 Remington Auto	.358
.38 Short Colt	.358	.35 Winchester '86	.358
.38 Long Colt	.358	.35 Newton	.358
.38 Colt Special	.358	.35 Whelen	.358
.38 S & W Special	.358	.35 Magnum	.358
.36 Colt Percussion	.375	.38-55	.375
		.38-56	.375
		.38-70	.375
		.38-72	.375
		.375 Magnum	.375
.400 .38-40	.400	.40 Sharps	.403
		.40 Ballard	.403
		.40 Remington	.403
		.40 Winchester	.403
		.40 Marlin	.403
		.40 Stevens	.403
		.40 Colt	.403
.45 Colt S.A.	.454	.45-60	.456
.45 Auto Rim	.454	.45-70	.456
.450 Webley	.457	.45-90	.456
.455 Webley	.457	.45-125	.456

TABLE 15

Cartridges that may be used in arms of a different chamber

Arms chambered for the following cartridges	Will also accommodate the following cartridges
.32 A.P.	.32 S & W
.32 S & W	.32 A.P.
.32-20	.32 A.P., .32 S & W, .32 S & W Long
.35 S & W A.P.	.32 A.P., .32 S & W
.38 S & W	.380 C.F.
38 Short Colt	.380 C.F.
.38 Long Colt	.380 C.F., .38 Short Colt
.38 Special	.380 C.F., .38 Short Colt, .38 Long Colt
.38-40	.380 C.F.
.41 Short, center fire	.38 S & W, .38 C.F.
.41 Long, center fire	.38 S & W, .380 C.F., .38 Short Colt, .38 Long Colt, .38 Spl., .41 Short C.F.
.44-40	.38-40, .44 Bulldog, .44 Webley, .44 Russian
.44 Russian	.38-40*, .44 Bulldog, .44 Webley, .44-40*, .44 S & W American, .44 Spl.
.44 Special	.44 Bulldog, .44 Webley, .44 Russian, .44 S & W American
.45 Colt	.38-40, .44 Bulldog, .44 Webley, .44 Russian, .44-40, .44 S & W American, .44 Spl.
.45 Rev. Model 1917	.38-40, .44 Bulldog, .44 Webley, .44-40, .44 Russian, .44 S & W American, .45 Auto Pistol, .455 A.P.
.45 A.P.	.44 Bulldog, .44 Webley
.455 A.P.	.38-40, .44 Bulldog, .44 Webley, .44-40, .44 Russian, .44 S & W American, .44 Spl., .45 A.P.
.455 Colt	.38-40, .44 Bulldog, .44 Webley, .44-40, .44 Russian, .44 S & W American, .44 Spl., .45 A.P., .455 A.P., .380 A.P.
.380 A.P.	.380 A.P.
.38 A.P.	9 mm. Browning Long
.45 S & W Scofield	.38-40*, .44 Bulldog, .44 Webley, .44-40*, .44 Russian, .44 S & W American, .44 Spl., .45 S & W
9 mm. Browning Long	.32-20, .38 S & W, .380 C.F., .38 A.P.
7.65 mm. Luger	7.65 mm. Luger
9 mm. Luger	.32-20, 7.65 mm. Luger
.32 S & W Long	.32 A.P., .32 S & W

*Will fire if nose of bullet is shortened.

dence gun and a similar gun had been disassembled and reassembled in court.*

6. *Replacement of a firing pin*

Such replacements are not difficult to make in the case of most automatic pistols, but are more difficult in some other types of arms. The author has had one such case involving a rifle. A game warden who was in a tree making a deer survey was shot by a hunter who mistook him for a bear. Upon discovering his mistake the hunter ran away. No bullet was recovered but a fired rifle shell was found in the vicinity of the shooting. While the firing pin impression was a good one, other markings, such as extractor marks, ejector marks, and breech-face marks, were not. The suspect's rifle was confiscated after considerable time had elapsed and the owner had had the firing pin replaced—a fact brought out by good detective work. Naturally the firing pin impressions on the evidence shell and the test shells fired in the laboratory with the new firing pin did not agree. Usually other markings of sufficiently good quality are present so that such an interchange of firing pins would be of no avail. While such cases of interchange may be rare they must be kept in mind as a possibility.

7. *Refiling of breech face*

Such a procedure, if skillfully done, could cause trouble. Fresh filing would of course be obvious because of the bright appearance of the freshly filed surface—but the surface could be easily oxidized, reblued or renickeled, as the case required, by a person having the necessary skill, so that it would be very difficult to determine whether recent filing had been done. Obviously a much easier and simpler procedure in most cases would be to dispose of the weapon. However, in case it was known that the suspect owned a weapon of the type which had been used in a murder its disposal would cast more suspicion, and it would be to his advantage to produce the weapon—skillfully altered (if possible)—or a similar weapon procured for the purpose.

*One must also keep in mind the possibility that an automatic pistol cartridge may sometimes be fired in an automatic pistol of caliber for which it was not intended. Such a case was reported by Walter Hepner in *Kriminalistik*, Vol. 12, No. 3, pp. 101–104 (March 1958). A young man shot himself in the head (fatally) by using a 9 mm. Short cartridge in a 7.62 mm. Tokarev automatic pistol. A barrel chambered for the 7.62 bottle-necked cartridge will easily take a 9 mm. Short cartridge. Although the bullet is considerably oversized, the force of explosion is sufficient to carry it through the barrel with rather high velocity. Usually the spent cartridge will not be extracted, however.

8. *Refiling or reshaping the firing pin*

Such changes could be made and the possibility should be kept in mind. Many firing pins have definite identifying characteristics which can be removed very easily by filing or by a little work with an emery cloth. Here again a bright surface would be suspicious but the brightness can be very easily removed. If one had to depend wholly on firing pin impressions this might be a useful technique for the criminal, but, fortunately, we usually have other markings on a fired shell which are even better than the firing pin impression.

9. *Replacing a revolver barrel*

In the case of most solid-frame revolvers the barrels are not easily removed, especially by an unskilled person, and such substitutions are not common. In the case of some cheaply made foreign revolvers of the solid-frame type the barrels can be unscrewed without difficulty—some even without tools. In well-made solid-frame revolvers a vise would be required and an unskilled person would probably leave marks of the vise on the gun. In the case of the tip up or break open type revolver only a screwdriver would be necessary to remove the barrel, while the opposite extreme is represented by those guns in which the barrel and frame are integral.

10. *Relining a barrel*

No cases are known to the author where this practice, quite common for legitimate purposes when barrels become badly worn, has been used to conceal a crime. However the possibility exists. The fact that such an operation has been performed is readily revealed by an examination of the muzzle of the gun which will clearly show a ring of demarcation between the metal of the liner and that of the original barrel. Finding barrels which have such liners, however, is not prima facie evidence that they have been relined. The .22 caliber Derringer now being made in Germany and recently introduced into the U.S. has liners or inserts in the barrels.

11. *The use of spherical bullets*

"Round ball" ammunition is available and because of the short area of contact of the ball with the rifling such bullets do not acquire well-defined rifling marks such as are found on the modern elongated projectile. Such bullets would doubtless spell a lot of trouble for firearms examiners if they were commonly used. Lead balls of from .25 to .50 caliber are easily obtained and can be handloaded by anyone familiar with the process. Cartridges provided with lead balls and reduced loads are also purchasable. They are used for gallery practice or for shooting small animals. However, they have sufficient power to be lethal at short range. Fortunately they are seldom used by the criminal.

12. *The use of steel balls as bullets*

It is even more fortunate that this practice is not a common one because it would be impossible to identify such a projectile since it would bear no rifling marks. A person familiar with handloading would have no difficulty in making a lot of trouble for the firearms examiner.

13. *Other metals harder than lead*

Other metals, such as zinc or tin, could be cast as bullets and handloaded. These metals, because of their hardness, would not take identifying rifling marks. No case is known to the author where such bullets have been used by a criminal, but surely such cases will occur sooner or later. A person intent on murder would not be likely to be disturbed as to the effect such hard bullets would have on the rifling in his gun. A spectroscopic analysis of the residue in a barrel in which tin or zinc bullets had been used would doubtless be discomfiting to him, however.

14. *Firing cartridges in oversized chambers*

This is certainly not a common practice but is possible, as was demonstrated in an English murder case many years ago. The assassin wrapped narrow strips of paper around .25 cal. ACP cartridges to make them fit tightly in the larger-caliber murder weapon. The possibility of a recurrence of such a procedure should not be forgotten, since the case was given considerable publicity at the time.

15. *Firing a bullet through a bulged barrel*

Bulges in a barrel frequently occur when there is already some object in the barrel, such as a cleaning rag or a previously fired bullet which did not clear the barrel. Several such barrels have come to the author's laboratory—one with a lodged bullet still in the barrel. Because of the increase in diameter in the region of the bulge, a bullet fired through a bulged barrel will lose firm contact with the rifling and after passing the bulge the lands and grooves already impressed on the bullet will not be in phase with the grooves and lands of the gun beyond the bulge. Consequently, a new set of rifling impressions will be made on the bullet. In looking for the weapon that fired a bullet bearing duplicate rifling marks, particular attention should be paid to weapons having bulged barrels. Duplicate sets of rifling marks can

also be produced by recovering a fired bullet, reloading it in a cartridge and firing it a second time. If the two sets of rifling marks do not agree this is a very probable explanation.

16. *Oversized bore in rifled barrels*

An oversized bore results in slippage of bullets fired through it and since successively fired bullets do not slip in exactly the same manner repetitive markings are not produced. Identifications can not be made on such bullets. The effect is naturally one of varying degree. Sometimes by firing a number of test bullets enough semblance of identity may be found to warrant a conclusion. In other cases no semblance of identity will be found when test bullets are compared either with each other or with the evidence bullet, because, even though the rifling may be in good condition, the bullet does not fill the cross section of the bore sufficiently to produce marks of any value. To get information regarding the true character of the bore an oversized bullet may be fired through it, but this only infrequently gives the examiner any substantial help. Three such revolvers that had been used in a shooting during a bank robbery were once submitted to the author. The guns were obviously of very poor construction and were fired with some trepidation in order to get test bullets. Using the ammunition for which the guns were intended, as indicated by markings on the guns, the test bullets had obviously "slithered" through the barrels without picking up repetitive marks. Though many bullets were fired, no two test bullets showed sufficient identity to enable one to say that they had passed through the same barrel. Needless to say, no better comparisons could be obtained with the evidence bullets. Probably every examiner has had a similar experience—but it is unusual to have three such guns submitted in connection with a single case!

17. *Fired bullets that have no rifling marks*

Several possibilities exist. The bullet may have been fired (1) from one of several smooth bore arms or (2) from a barrel in which the rifling has been worn away so completely as to leave no rifling marks—an occurrence by no means uncommon. The bullet may have been fired (3) from a "zip gun"—a homemade gun having a gas pipe or other tube for a barrel. Many such cases have occurred. It may have been fired (4) in a shotgun by the use of an adapter, of which many have been available. Or the evidence bullet (or bullets) may have been fired (5) from a shotgun shell by simply removing the original charge of shot and replacing it with one or several bullets.

A further "refinement" of this last procedure was thought up by an ingenious criminal in a large midwestern city several years ago, with the evident intent of "pinning" an intended murder against a particular person by making it appear that his gun was used. A shotgun shell was loaded with bullets that had been fired from this person's gun and recovered for the purpose—all without his knowledge of course. Fortunately for the owner of the rifled arm the shooting never came off, as the plans were discovered.

18. Rifled tubes for shotguns

At one time Remington made rifled tubes that could be inserted into shotgun barrels to increase the versatility of the weapon. Unlike adapters these tubes extended through the entire length of the barrel. The possibility of encountering bullets fired through such a device is remote, but it does exist.

19. Rifled tubes for pistols or revolvers of larger caliber

Small-caliber rifled tubes may be inserted in the barrel of larger-caliber (.38 and upward) revolvers or pistols for target shooting or "plinking." As such tubes are of .22 caliber they are not likely to be used to commit a murder as the arm would be much more effective without this device. At close range, however, and in a situation where the noise produced by a larger cartridge would be an important matter, such a device might be chosen. It is a definite possibility.

20. Interchange of cylinders

An example is the firing of a .44-40 type cartridge in a revolver designed for the .44 Spl. cartridge by substituting a cylinder bored for the .44-40 type. Most criminals would not have access to such specially bored cylinders and the possibility of the use of one in a criminal case is remote. Revolvers which have cylinders designed for the use of automatic pistol type of ammunition may have a normal cylinder substituted therefor, or vice versa. Here again the chance of this being done is remote, but possible.

21. Firing pins for either rim or center fire

Some rifles (e.g., the .32 cal. Marlin Mod. 1892) were supplied with two firing pins, one for center fire and the other for rim fire cartridges. The possibility of interchange of firing pins after the commission of a shooting should be kept in mind, particularly in cases where firing pin impressions and other markings on a shell case are inconsistent. Another situation is presented by certain models of

the single-shot Ballard rifles which were supplied with reversible firing pins, one end designed for center fire, the other for rim fire. A reversal might be made after a shooting and the examiner should know of the possibility of such a reversal. As these guns are not widely used and as most felonious shootings are done with hand guns, this situation is not likely to be met.

22. Disintegrating bullets

Some ammunition manufacturers have devised bullets for target shooting that disintegrate upon striking a hard surface. The Remington Co. demonstrated that this breakup into a fine powder does not occur (at least, not with their product—the "Kantsplash' bullet) when the bullet strikes flesh, although it does occur upon striking bones. This being the case, such bullets fired from a rifled arm should be identifiable if recovered from the fleshy part of a body, provided there has been no impact with bone material. This type of bullet is not likely to be used by a person intending to commit a crime, but they could be encountered in accidental shootings, especially in target practice by persons who have not been properly tutored in the handling of firearms.

23. Confusion of serial numbers

In some cases serial numbers may be of considerable importance, such as in tracing ownership of a gun. The subject of restoration of serial numbers has been dealt with elsewhere in this book. Serial numbers should be examined with care so that alterations or additions that may have been made will be detected. Sometimes the digits are not clearly stamped and may be misread if they are not examined closely with a lens. The digits 0, 6, and 8 seem to be the ones that cause most confusion, though 1 and 4 may be confused if the stamping is lightly done. Digits are frequently added to the original number, but usually these are obvious if one examines the number carefully with a lens. The "font," i.e., the shape, or the size may not be consistent with the rest of the digits, or the added digit may not be properly spaced or it may be tilted. Any such irregularities are suspicious and should be noted by the examiner. In the case of some of the cheaper foreign-made guns the numbers are stamped very unevenly—apparently by hand and very inexpertly.

The author has had many instances in which the number actually present on the gun did not agree with the number supplied by the person who delivered the gun. In most cases this was due to careless observation. In a few cases, patent numbers, patent application numbers, or manufacturers' identification numbers (not serial numbers) have been mistaken for serial numbers. The firearms examiner who discovers that a law enforcement officer has made an error in recording the serial number of a found or confiscated gun is well advised to see that the matter is straightened out before the law enforcement officer identifies the gun in court. Much embarrassment, or even more serious consequences, will thus be avoided. Courts do not take kindly to such mixups!

In the case of automatic pistols the numbers on the frame and on the slide may not agree, showing that an interchange has been made. For safety, all the numbers appearing on a gun (and their location) should be recorded. In several makes of guns the serial number may have a letter either before, following, or below the digits of the number. Since this letter is informative it should always be recorded. For some arms it is really an important part of the serial number, for example when found on a German Luger or Mod. P-38.

In some cases the number designates whether the arm is destined for commercial or military use, in others it indicates a model type and the small letters used on certain foreign military arms designate that the gun is one of a particular "block" or "run." The purpose of the use of the letters was to avoid the necessity of using more than four digits in a serial number. Some of the early Lugers did not have these letters but they were used by all German manufacturers later on. The same is true for the P-38.

Letter suffixes do not appear to have been used on the Lugers made at Berne, Switzerland, and in other countries, because of the limited number produced.

While the author has not seen two Lugers or two P-38 models that have the same serial number, including the same suffix letter, it appears that it might be possible because the same suffix letter was used by Mauser and by Walther in one instance at least. The author has personally seen a P-38 No. 1167-d with full Walther markings and a P-38 No. 3272-d with full Mauser markings, both guns dated 1944. If both firms made guns that were in the same "block" designated by the letter d, it would seem very likely that cases of two guns having identical serial and suffix numbers may be found. However, it is not likely that two Lugers made by the same manufacturer will have the same numbering, but it could happen.*

The markings on Lugers and Mod. P-38s are not always consistent. Sometimes a gun produced in the period where letter suffixes were customarily used was not given a suffix letter and some P-38 pistols by Walther have five-digit numbers with no suffix letter.

In some of the better foreign-made, nonmilitary automatics the serial numbers will be found on the barrel as well as on the frame and slide and for such makes, where it is known to be the practice to so number the barrels, a different number on a barrel indicates that a substitution has been made. However, for the cheaper variety of foreign-made automatics, and especially for those in which the barrels have been rifled by firms who specialized in that operation, the number on the barrel is of no significance as far as the rest of the gun is concerned. As has been stated elsewhere, these cheap guns are, for the most part, assembled guns—the parts of which were made by different firms, particularly in Belgium and Spain.

*That such things can happen is attested by the fact that two different Walther Mod. P-38 pistols examined and measured by the author were found to have identical serial numbers (3240-n). While the rifling measurements were very nearly the same, as would be expected, they were measurably different. Both pistols were marked as having been made in 1943.

PART II

Measurements of rifling

Data on hand guns

The role of Class Characteristics of rifling in firearms identification has already been explained and discussed at some length. Because of the paucity of reliable information concerning rifling characteristics as they *actually exist* in guns, rather than in manufacturers' specifications, and because no reliable information was available for guns of many makes and models it seemed worth while to make a comprehensive series of measurements of all the makes and models of hand guns that could be obtained for study.

The results of these measurements are presented here in tabulated form. The methods whereby the data were obtained have already been described in the chapter on Instrumentation. A very large number of the guns that were obtained from various sources had rifling in such poor condition as to make acceptable measurements impossible, and consequently these were not measured. This accounts for the fact that there are many photographs of guns for which there are no reported measurements. In some cases where the condition of the rifling was not as good as desired comment has been made under Remarks.

Since many models were produced over a considerable number of years, during which there may have been changes in rifling practice, and because of the fact that many manufacturers did not follow their own specifications closely, it was clearly desirable that a number of specimens (as many as possible, in fact) be measured to get a more true picture. It will therefore be noted that for some makes and models many measurements were made,

whereas for others measurements for only one specimen appear in the tables. The reason for this difference, of course, is accessibility—for some of the rarer guns one is fortunate to secure even a single specimen in which the rifling is in sufficiently good condition to measure. In cases where data for a single specimen are found in the tables it must not be concluded that *all* of the guns of the same make, model, and caliber would give identical data. All that can safely be said about such guns is that the particular specimen which was measured had the reported measurements. Another specimen, and this is particularly true for the cheaper and less well made guns of Spanish and Belgian origin, might have quite different rifling. Some early American manufacturers, for example, the Forehand Arms Co. and Hopkins and Allen, also changed their practices in a capricious manner. Each of these firms produced revolvers which bore specific model names in which different specimens varied as to direction of twist, number of grooves, and degree of twist. On the other hand, the better modern manufacturers both here and abroad are as a rule more consistent, and though changes are made from time to time they are less frequent and are probably made with what is considered good reason. As has been stated earlier, the quality of workmanship in the guns now made in Spain is much improved, since the number of manufacturers has been reduced to three for automatics and to two for revolvers. And the same can be said for Belgium since the small shops have practically disappeared.

Data on revolvers and automatic pistols arranged by caliber and manufacturer

Measurements made on a large number of hand guns are presented in Tables 16 and 17. An arbitrary separation into the two types of guns has been made. Table 16 includes automatic (or self-loading) pistols; Table 17 includes revolvers and nonautomatic pistols. A few submachine gun barrels were also measured. The guns in each table have been arranged according to caliber and the manufacturers are listed alphabetically under each caliber. In quite a number of cases the name of the manufacturer could not be ascertained.

TABLE 16
Rifling measurements on automatic pistols

Caliber and Manufacturer	Model (or Name)	Serial No.	Dir'n of Twist	Inches for 1 turn	No. of Lands	Land Width (inches)	Bore Diameter (inches)	Groove Diameter* (inches)	Remarks
Caliber: 5 mm.									
Charola y Anitua, Eibar, Spain	Charola-Anitua	137	R	9.7	4	.069	.2005	.2094	Modeled after Bergmann.
Caliber: .22									
Astra Unceta y Cia., Guernica, Spain	Astra—M2000	50478	L	9.3	6	.033	.2124	.2198	Formerly Esperanza y.
	" M2000/2	57121	L	9.5	6	.033	.2122	.2210	Unceta; and Unceta y Cia.
	" M2000	59506	L	9.5	6	.015	.2130	.2194	Unusually narrow lands.
	do.	73555	L	9.4	6	.035	.2130	.2202	
	do.	82730	L	9.5	6	.039	.2123	.2213	
	do.	82736	L	9.5	6	.039	.2122	.2212	
	Astra—M4000	790004	L	9.6	6	.040	.2139	.2185	
Pietro Beretta, Gardone V.T. (Brescia), Italy	Mod. 948	003053N	R	13.9	6	.040	.2138	.2190	
	do.	018631N	R	13.7	6	.029	.2124	.2192	Short bbl. 3 3/8" long.
	do.	018631N	R	13.9	6	.031	.2190	.2250	Long bbl. 5 15/16" long.
	do.	022903N	R	14.0	6	.042	.2132	.2190	
	Mod. 1950	50236CC	R	13.5	6	.041	.2134	.2190	Sold in U.S. as MINX.
	Olympic	7	R	13.8	6	.021	.2124	.2205	Uses .22 short ctge.
	"	955	R	13.8	6	.034	.2140	.2203	Uses .22 long ctge.
Vincenzo Bernardelli, Gardone V.T. (Brescia), Italy	Baby	1136	R	10.0	6	.058	.2135	.2183	Uses .22 short ctge.
	Target Pistol	686	R	17.9	6	.045	.2132	.2214	Uses .22 L.R. ctge., 150 mm. bbl.
Colt's Pt. F.A. Mfg. Co., Hartford, Conn.	.22 Long Rifle	11667	L	16.1	6	.034	.2158	.2230	Pre-Woodsman Model.
	do.	21077	L	14.3	6	.032	.2142	.2166	"Woodsman" not on gun.
	do.	39397	L	14.0	6	.039	.2150	.2222	do.
	Woodsman Mod.	88487	L	14.6	6	.038	.2142	.2167	
	do.	96024	L	14.6	6	.033	.2143	.2167	
	do.	106660	L	14.6	6	.037	.2145	.2230	
	do.	131329	L	14.4	6	.036	.2151	.2177	
	do.	156633	L	14.5	6	.038	.2143	.2224	
	do.	12019-S	L	14.1	6	.042	.2148	.2173	
	do.	68421-S	L	14.0	6	.038	.2137	.2163	
	do.	71712-S	L	14.0	6	.038	.2134	.2212	
	do.	73993-S	L	14.0	6	.038	.2136	.2216	
	Match Target	40530-S	L	14.0	6	.039	.2134	.2160	
	do.	41993-S	L	13.9	6	.041	.2140	.2214	
	do.	43781-S	L	14.0	6	.040	.2131	.2160	
	do.	51133-S	L	14.1	6	.038	.2137	.2157	
	do.	61384-S	L	14.0	6	.039	.2140	.2158	
	do.	78461-S	L	14.1	6	.037	.2132	.2152	
	Officers Model	19694-C	L	14.3	6	.044	.2143	.2222	
	Officers Mod. Target	56040	L	14.1	6	.040	.2132	.2157	
	Challenger	10963-C	L	14.0	6	.049	.2131	.2213	

*Distance from bottom of a groove to the bottom of opposite groove if barrel has an even number of grooves; or the distance from the bottom of a groove to the top of the opposite land if barrel has an odd number of grooves.

Caliber and Manufacturer	Model (or Name)	Serial No.	Dir'n of Twist	Inches for 1 turn	No. of Lands	Land Width (inches)	Bore Diameter (inches)	Groove Diameter* (inches)	Remarks
Colt's Pt. F.A. Mfg. Co.	Challenger	23624-C	L	13.9	6	.037	.2134	.2220	
	Ace	1263	L	14.0	6	.036	.2139	.2233	
	Service Ace	S-M693	L	14.1	6	.034	.2145	.2168	
	Conversion Unit for 38 Super	None	L	11.9	6	.041	.2125	.2215	For Super 38. Ser. No. 57256.
	Junior Colt	1703cc	L	9.6	6	.066	.2150	.2164	Made by Astra Unceta y Cia. for Colt. (Auxiliary barrel)
Bonifacio Echeverria, Eibar, Spain	F-Star Sport	341198	R	12.3	6	.040	.2122	.2194	
	do.	341360	R	12.1	6	.046	.2126	.2190	
	do.	346352	R	12.4	6	.040	.2120	.2194	
	do.	347236	R	12.3	6	.041	.2119	.2141	
	Star Olimpic	383992	R	12.6	6	.040	.2137	.2207	
	Star—Mod. HF	519344	R	12.4	6	.035	.2124	.2183	
Erma Waffenfabrik, Erfurt, Germany	Target Pistol	5752	R	17.4	6	.048	.2125	.2205	4 1/2" bbl. —. 22 L.R.
	do.	6126	R	17.4	6	.046	.2139	.2217	8" bbl. —. 22 L.R.
Fegyvergyar, Budapest, Hungary	Type 29	3258	R	15.6	6	.031	.2126	.2236	Identical in form to Mod. 29; probably on Mod. 29 frame.
Gabilondo y Cia., Elogibar, Spain	Llama Especial	178778	R	15.65	6	.052	.2111	.2173	
	do.	196431	R	15.4	6	.051	.2113	.2185	Mod. XV—"Airlite."
	Llama—Spl.	183225	R	15.5	6	.051	.2109	.2164	Special De Luxe Model.
Armi Galesi, Brescia, Italy	Galesi Mod. 503A	102148	R	8.35	6	.041	.2075	.2114	Dated 1955.
Hämmerli and Co., Lensburg, Switzerland	Olympia Pistole	O-5103	R	17.6	6	.026	.2150	.2230	
Hartford Arms and Equipment Co., Hartford, Conn.	.22 L.R. Auto	3299	R	14.85	6	.052	.2165	.2217	
	do.	4181	R	14.8	6	.043	.2162	.2208	
High Standard Mfg. Co., Hamden, Conn.	HI Stan'd Mod. A	39573	R	14.0	6	.034	.2130	.2190	
	HI Stan'd Mod. B	109833	R	13.8	6	.026	.2123	.2183	
	do.	17009	R	13.8	6	.033	.2122	.2194	
	do.	54055	R	13.9	6	.029	.2125	.2150	
	HI Stan'd Mod. C	63344	R	13.9	6	.032	.2128	.2200	
	HI Stan'd Mod. HB	287037	R	14.0	6	.030	.2130	.2200	
	do.	292330	R	14.0	6	.027	.2140	.2167	
	HI Stan'd Mod. H-D	110587	R	13.7	6	.034	.2123	.2174	
	do.	125762	R	13.8	6	.029	.2129	.2158	
	do.	179213	R	14.0	6	.030	.2130	.2196	
	do.	181039	R	14.0	6	.026	.2131	.2158	
	do.	194570	R	14.0	6	.022	.2137	.2191	
	do.	194570	R	14.0	6	.022	.2137	.2191	
	do.	197522	R	14.0	6	.031	.2133	.2185	
	do.	303779	R	14.0	6	.028	.2134	.2182	
	do.	498335	R	17.0	6	.055	.2163	.2213	
	Duramatic	494815	R	17.3	6	.055	.2168	.2210	
	Sport King	339074	R	14.0	6	.024	.2137	.2158	
	do.	367174	R	13.9	6	.022	.2130	.2192	
	do.	368916	R	13.9	6	.022	.2132	.2192	
	do.	376135	R	14.0	6	.024	.2125	.2195	
	do.	400899	R	16.1	6	.058	.2178	.2200	Note change in rifling.
	do.	510201	R	16.0	6	.058	.2180	.2220	
	"J.C. Higgins" Mod. 80	663886	R	16.2	6	.058	.2178	.2212	Made for Sears, Roebuck and Co.
Hispano Argentina Fabrica de Automoviles Sociedad Anonima, Buenos Aires, Argentina	Hafdasa—Army	54296	L	16.1	6	.031	.2196	.2246	Also known as Ballester-Molina Army Mod. Copied from U.S. M1911.
	Hafdasa—Pocket Mod.	93629	L	15.3	6	.037	.2157	.2225	Only 200 were made.
Mre. D'Armes Automatiques Bayonne, Bayonne, France	Le Chasseur	37	R	12.7	6	.055	.2138	.2210	Sold in U.S. by W.A.C.
	do.	2603	R	12.6	6	.053	.2124	.2184	
	M.A.B.—Mod. F	4706	R	15.8	6	.051	.2136	.2220	
Mre. D'Armes des Pyrénées, Hendaye, France	Pistolet de Tir "UNIQUE"	420594	L	18.3	6	.062	.2108	.2130	Word RANGER on bbl. and grips.
	do.	429402	L	12.0	6	.057	.2117	.2181	do.
	"UNIQUE" Mod. 52	466115	L	12.3	6	.066	.2126	.2174	
	"J.C. Higgins"— Mod. 85	508255	R	12.1	6	.062	.2124	.2140	Made for Sears, Roebuck Co.
	do.	532564	R	12.0	6	.067	.2119	.2131	do.
	Mikros	555078	R	12.3	6	.062	.2128	.2150	Introduced 1958.

Caliber and Manufacturer	Model (or Name)	Serial No.	Dir'n of Twist	Inches for 1 turn	No. of Lands	Land Width (inches)	Bore Diameter (inches)	Groove Diameter* (inches)	Remarks
Mre. de Machines du Haut Rhin, Mulhouse-Bourtzwiller, France	PP Walther	10026B	R	9.9	6	.063	.2150	.2230	Licensed by Walther.
The Reising Arms Co., Hartford, Conn.	Reising	1816	R	15.6	6	.029	.2160	.2268	
	"	1874	R	15.6	6	.030	.2169	.2249	
	"	10967	R	15.0	6	.040	.2151	.2212	Plant moved to New York.
Rigarmi, Brescia, Italy	Rino Galesi	28859	R	8.6	6	.056	.1983	.2020	Dated 1958.
"Rigarmi" (Rino Galesi), Brescia, Italy	HIJO—Militar	10609	R	8.1	6	.052	.2030	.2068	Imitation of Walther Mod. P.P.
Robar et Cie., Liége, Belgium	Melior	L-0077	R	9.55	6	.036	.2091	.2159	Firm had other names: Robar and DeKerkhove; Etablissements Robar; L. Robar and Co.
Römerwerk, A.G., Suhl, Germany	Römerwerk—L.R.	614	R	14.3	6	.035	.2132	.2233	
	do.	1088	R	14.3	6	.031	.2129	.2235	
	do.	1599	R	14.4	6	.034	.2126	.2232	2 3/8" bbl.
	(same gun)	1599	R	14.4	6	.034	.2126	.2230	5 7/8" bbl.
Schall and Co., New Haven, Conn.	Target auto	7156	R	16.4	4	.110	.2171	.2207	10-ctge. mag. 5 3/4" bbl.
Smith and Wesson, Springfield, Mass.	Target Auto M-41	3895	R	15.0	6	.038	.2150	.2234	
		4767	R	15.0	6	.038	.2142	.2233	
Soc. Industrie Suisse, Neuhausen, Switzerland	S.I.G. (S.P. 47/8)"	40032	R	17.7	6	.036	.2138	.2204	Interchangeable bbls. and slides for .22, 7.65 mm., and 9 mm. Par. ctges.
	do.	40379	R	17.7	6	.037	.2145	.2206	Auxiliary barrel.
Franz Stock, Berlin, Germany	Target Auto	289	R	16.1	6	.033	.2164	.2260	
Sturm, Ruger and Co., Southport, Conn.	Ruger—Std. Mod.	7272	R	14.1	6	.027	.2157	.2233	
	do.	7805	R	14.0	6	.029	.2151	.2180	
	do.	7829	R	14.0	6	.027	.2150	.2230	
	do.	14939	R	14.0	6	.026	.2148	.2242	
	do.	32018	R	13.9	6	.055	.2143	.2199	Note change in land width.
	do.	32062	R	13.9	6	.059	.2155	.2193	
	do.	68514	R	13.5	6	.044	.2149	.2213	
	do.	80277	R	13.7	6	.044	.2152	.2206	
	do.	90224	R	14.0	6	.044	.2166	.2218	
Tallares de Armas Livianas Argentinas, Bahia, Argentina	Tala	0222	L	16.0	6	.041	.2159	.2267	
Unceta y Cia., Guernica, Spain	Astra 2000	50478	L	9.3	6	.033	.2124	.2198	Formerly Esperanza y Unceta; Now Astra Unceta y Cia.
	do.	82736	L	9.5	6	.039	.2122	.2212	
	Astra 4000	790004	L	9.6	6	.040	.2139	.2185	
U.S. Armory, Springfield, Mass.	.22 Adapter for U.S. .45	15	R	15.0	6	.046	.2175	.2271	Orig. No. 102547. New No. 15. Exp. Mod. ca. 1917.
Waffenfabrik Walther Zella-Mehlis, Germany	PP Walther	146520P	R	9.5	6	.044	.2104	.2210	
	Target Pistol	1443	R	16.2	6	.040	.2140	.2230	.22 L.R. 11 7/8" bbl.
	(same gun)	1443	R	18.0	6	.035	.2138	.2244	.22 L.R. Reg. bbl. 7 1/2".
	Target Pistol	5256	R	17.9	6	.047	.2138	.2204	
	Olympia Mod.	7922	R	17.9	6	.046	.2152	.2230	
	Exptl. Mod.	None	R	18.0	6	.047	.2130	.2208	.22 bbl. on P-38 frame. ca. 1940.
Whitney Firearms Inc., North Haven, Conn.	Wolverine	100136	R	17.2	6	.052	.2185	.2233	Also called "Lightning Mod."
	"	Bbl. A	R	17.6	6	.052	.2178	.2226	Bbl. only—unused.
	"	Bbl. B	R	17.3	6	.054	.2182	.2228	do.
	"	100781	R	17.0	6	.053	.2199	.2243	
Fabrica de Armas Zaragoza, Mexico Puebla	Modelo Corla	34	R	16.3	8	.026	.2010	.2056	Only 65 were made.

Caliber: .25

Caliber and Manufacturer	Model (or Name)	Serial No.	Dir'n of Twist	Inches for 1 turn	No. of Lands	Land Width (inches)	Bore Diameter (inches)	Groove Diameter* (inches)	Remarks
Colt's Pt. F.A. Mfg. Co., Hartford, Conn.	Pocket Mod.	44222	L	16.4	6	.048	.2458	.2516	
	do.	51796	L	16.3	6	.038	.2436	.2520	
	do.	171895	L	16.4	6	.035	.2439	.2531	
	do.	212895	L	14.2	6	.038	.2463	.2556	Unusual rifling twist.
	do.	233640	L	16.7	6	.037	.2428	.2489	
	do.	270839	L	16.0	6	.035	.2429	.2539	An unused gun.
	do.	276962	L	16.5	6	.035	.2457	.2551	
	do.	295373	L	17.3	6	.038	.2443	.2539	
	do.	337908	L	16.0	6	.033	.2437	.2516	
	do.	348722	L	16.4	6	.034	.2438	.2515	

Caliber and Manufacturer	Model (or Name)	Serial No.	Dir'n of Twist	Inches for 1 turn	No. of Lands	Land Width (inches)	Bore Diameter (inches)	Groove Diameter* (inches)	Remarks
Colt's Pt. F. A. Mfg. Co.	Pocket Mod.	373416	L	16.4	6	.036	.2437	.2517	Apparently unused gun.
	do.	377351	L	16.0	6	.036	.2438	.2536	
	do.	393447	L	16.4	6	.036	.2435	.2521	
	Junior Colt	1703	L	9.6	6	.044	.2453	.2522	Made by Astra Unceta y Cia. for Colt's.
Harrington and Richardson, Worcester, Mass.	Self Loading	513	R	12.0	5	.072	.2460	.2510	
	do.	3435	R	12.2	6	.029	.2455	.2551	
	do.	4894	R	11.8	6	.021	.2475	.2563	
	do.	11711	R	12.6	6	.037	.2451	.2549	
Phoenix Arms Co., Lowell, Mass.	Phoenix	108	L	10.0	7	.038	.2427	.2467	Similar to Old Mod. Melior (and Jieffeco)
Webley and Scott, Ltd., Birmingham, England	Webley V. P.	139534	R	10.1	6	.022	.2459	.2539	
	do.	153249	R	10.0	6	.034	.2472	.2580	

Caliber: 6.35 mm.

Caliber and Manufacturer	Model (or Name)	Serial No.	Dir'n of Twist	Inches for 1 turn	No. of Lands	Land Width (inches)	Bore Diameter (inches)	Groove Diameter* (inches)	Remarks
Domingo Acha, Ermua, Spain	Looking Glass	46204	L	10.6	6	.056	.2443	.2549	
	do.	53227	L	10.7	6	.050	.2454	.2536	
	do.	92527	L	11.1	6	.058	.2480	.2530	
Hijos de Jose Aldazabal, (or Hijos de C. Arrizabalaga) Eibar, Spain	Sharp Shooter	7776	R	11.0	6	.053	.2460	.2510	Maker's name uncertain. Sold by Ojanguren y Vidosa.
Aguirre y Cia., Ermua, Spain	Protector	103015	R	9.7	6	.038	.2454	.2534	
Gaspar Arizaga, Eibar, Spain	Modial	3204	R	10.9	6	.035	.2482	.2554	
	"	11181	L	10.4	6	.024	.2482	.2529	
Francisco Arizmendi, Eibar, Spain	Kaba "Speziall"	18345	R	12.2	6	.047	.2462	.2576	Copy of Kaba "Speziall" made by August Menz, Suhl, Germany.
	Walman	17012	R	10.5	6	.036	.2473	.2592	
Arizmendi y Goenaga, Eibar, Spain	Kaba "Speziall"	5665	R	10.7	6	.039	.2461	.2561	
	Walman	7155	R	12.3	6	.029	.2485	.2547	Bears A and G trade mark.
Azanza y Arrizabalaga, Eibar, Spain	"REIMS" Pat.— Mod. 1914	2625	L	9.5	6	.034	.2450	.2529	
Martin A. Bascaran, Eibar, Spain	Martian—Commercial	6487	L	10.1	6	.051	.2453	.2520	
	Thunder	5516	R	10.9	6	.052	.2464	.2540	
Beistegui Hermanos, Eibar, Spain	Bulwark	34639	R	9.8	6	.063	.2456	.2510	
Pietro Beretta, Gardone V. T. (Brescia), Italy	1919 Type	25430	R	10.1	6	.040	.2467	.2533	
	do.	132490	R	10.3	6	.041	.2467	.2525	
	do.	601287	R	11.7	6	.025	.2450	.2534	Dated 1934.
	Mod. 1934	602456	R	11.95	6	.022	.2465	.2538	Also called Mod. 318. Introduced 1935.
	do.	606460	R	10.0	6	.042	.2467	.2524	Dated 1935.
	Bantam	44689A	R	10.2	6	.036	.2469	.2531	
	"	46446A	R	10.1	6	.036	.2471	.2531	Dated 1950.
	"	68480A	R	10.3	6	.037	.2469	.2517	Dated 1953.
	"	79564A	R	10.0	6	.035	.2467	.2527	Dated 1953.
	Featherweight	32715A	R	10.3	6	.036	.2467	.2531	Dated 1949.
	Mod. 418	08276C	R	10.2	6	.035	.2462	.2522	Dated 1956.
Theodor Bergmann, Suhl, Germany	Bergmann—Mod. II	None	R	9.8	6	.030	.2441	.2524	
	Lignose Mod. 2A	44170	R	9.6	6	.036	.2443	.2517	Sold by Akt. Ges. Lignose, Berlin, Germany.
	Lignose Mod. 3A	47622	R	9.7	6	.033	.2443	.2523	do.
	Lignose Mod. 2	54781	R	9.5	6	.033	.2433	.2501	do.
	Lignose Mod. 3	54882	R	9.7	6	.027	.2409	.2493	do.
	do.	11834	R	9.5	6	.022	.2457	.2521	
Theodor Bergmann (Heirs), Suhl, Germany	Bergmann Erben Mod. II	05613	R	9.9	6	.038	.2482	.2540	Gun made by Aug. Menz.
Vincenzo Bernardelli, Gardone V. T. (Brescia), Italy	Bernadelli	774	R	9.6	6	.041	.2425	.2515	Dated 1946.
	"	11345	R	9.6	6	.038	.2414	.2508	Dated 1947.
	"	34955	R	10.2	6	.055	.2432	.2516	Dated 1950.
	"	42304	R	10.4	6	.052	.2432	.2476	
	"	52083	R	10.1	6	.058	.2425	.2502	
V. Bernedo y Cia., Eibar, Spain	Bernedo	2709	R	11.0	6	.045	.2472	.2539	Pat. No. 69952
Gregorio Bolumburu, Eibar, Spain	Regina	- - -	R	15.5	6	.034	.2420	.2468	
	"	3062	R	14.9	6	.040	.2458	.2532	
	"	3665	R	15.7	6	.045	.2477	.2527	
	"	11639	R	15.0	6	.032	.2468	.2554	

Caliber and Manufacturer	Model (or Name)	Serial No.	Dir'n of Twist	Inches for 1 turn	No. of Lands	Land Width (inches)	Bore Diameter (inches)	Groove Diameter* (inches)	Remarks
Gregorio Bolumburu	Marina	---	L	9.1	6	.054	.2442	.2530	
Česka Zbrojovka, Strakonice, Czechoslovakia	CZ Mod. 1936	23258	R	7.95	6	.025	.2454	.2597	Plants located in several cities.
	do.	26035	R	7.9	6	.027	.2444	.2572	
	do.	26107	R	7.9	6	.032	.2445	.2573	
	CZ Mod. 1945	50118	R	7.95	6	.031	.2459	.2563	Dated 1947.
	do.	51662	R	7.9	6	.035	.2444	.2560	
	do.	54215	R	7.9	6	.037	.2459	.2565	Dated 1947.
	do.	59955	R	7.9	6	.030	.2457	.2570	Dated 1947.
	do.	63976	R	7.9	6	.028	.2460	.2526	
	do.	89281	R	7.9	6	.036	.2456	.2516	Dated 1948.
	do.	110787	R	7.9	6	.034	.2457	.2580	Groove depth unusual.
	"Z" Aut. Pistole	163795	R	10.5	6	.032	.2455	.2564	Formerly the DUO made by F. Dušek in Opotschno C.Z. took over mfg. ca. 1948.
	do.	165790	R	11.1	6	.030	.2453	.2514	Dated 1948.
	do.	185750	R	10.7	6	.046	.2442	.2540	Dated 1951
	do.	200762	R	10.6	6	.031	.2440	.2533	
Charles Ph. Clement, Liége, Belgium	Clement Mod. 1908	16410	R	9.4	6	.050	.2453	.2545	
Fab. D'Armes F. Delu et Cie., Liége, Belgium	Delu	554	L	10.1	6	.047	.2448	.2530	
	"	43420	R	10.0	6	.038	.2448	---	
Deutsche Werke, Akt., Erfurt, Germany	Ortgies	283	R	7.2	6	.036	.2476	.2580	
	"	39410	R	7.1	6	.033	.2438	.2526	
	"	80039	R	7.1	6	.034	.2445	.2517	
	"	83961	R	7.1	6	.035	.2441	.2521	
	"	100779	R	7.2	6	.029	.2445	.2520	
	"	139014	R	7.1	6	.031	.2440	.2540	
	"	140389	R	7.1	6	.029	.2438	.2536	
	"	175393	R	7.1	6	.032	.2439	.2529	
G.C. Dornheim, A.G., Suhl, Germany	"Gecado"	30560	R	7.4	6	.061	.2457	.2540	"Gecado" is Dornheim's trade mark. But gun has Spanish proof marks.
F. Dušek Opotschno, Czechoslovakia	DUO	9071	R	10.5	6	.036	.2447	.2505	
	"	74557	R	10.8	6	.033	.2440	.2530	Dated 1943
	"	89304	R	10.65	6	.042	.2453	.2527	Dated 1944.
	"	117951	R	10.65	6	.044	.2445	.2519	
(Mfr. not known)	EBAC	189038	R	12.2	6	.042	.2453	.2507	EBAC—prob. a dealer.
Echave y Arizmendi, Eibar, Spain	Protector	741	L	10.8	6	.038	.2449	.2519	
	1916 Mod.	1059	R	8.3	4	.080	.2573	.2703	E.A. trade mark on slide.
	Bronco (1918)	38015	L	11.2	6	.051	.2460	.2520	Pat. 66130
	do.	38302	L	11.0	6	.049	.2451	.2523	do.
	"Renard Pat."	7808	L	10.1	6	.040	.2448	.2500	Identical to "Protector." No. 262 on bbl. and frame. No. 7808 on slide.
	"Selecta"—M1918	---	L	10.2	6	.044	.2465	.2523	
Bonifacio Echeverria, Eibar, Spain	Star—Early Mod.	57	R	9.3	6	.026	.2467	.2693	ca. 1906.
	Star—Mod. CO	202493	R	9.7	6	.039	.2461	.2505	Also called Pocket Mod. by mfr.
	do.	351497	R	12.5	6	.035	.2466	.2506	
	do.	387926	R	12.0	6	.046	.2461	.2525	
	Star—Mod. C.U.	524762	R	12.8	6	.037	.2467	.2528	
A. Errasti, Eibar, Spain	Errasti	7672	L	10.9	6	.030	.2450	.2535	
Esperanza y Unceta, Guernica, Spain	Victoria—M1916	229363	L	10.6	6	.057	.2468	.2530	Esp. and Un. markings.
	Astra Mod. 1924	269399	L	9.9	6	.056	.2463	.2513	
	do.	270689	L	9.7	6	.045	.2463	.2527	
	do.	296916	L	9.9	6	.036	.2440	.2495	
	Union I	20493	R	9.8	6	.057	.2468	.2556	Made for E. y U. by firm in Ermua.
"Fab. D'Armes de Guerre de Grande Precision" (Exporters), Eibar, Spain	"Liberty"	108	L	10.1	6	.038	.2455	.2569	No such mfr. existed; name used to delude buyer.
Fabrica de Materiel de Guerra, Santiago, Chile	F.M.E.	9685	R	8.95	6	.034	.2434	.2662	
Fab. Nat'l. D'Armes de Guerre, Herstal, Belgium	Baby Browning	16005	R	11.35	6	.036	.2447	.2516	
	do.	21151	R	9.7	6	.033	.2447	.2527	
	Browning—M1906	47515	R	9.5	6	.024	.2449	.2549	

Caliber and Manufacturer	Model (or Name)	Serial No.	Dir'n of Twist	Inches for 1 turn	No. of Lands	Land Width (inches)	Bore Diameter (inches)	Groove Diameter* (inches)	Remarks
Fab. Nat'l. D'Armes de Guerre	Baby Browning	116472	R	9.8	6	.031	.2437	.2530	Marked "Browning Arms Co., St. Louis. Made in Belgium."
	Browning—M1906	910530	R	9.6	6	.036	.2440	.2525	
	do.	994739	R	9.8	6	.042	.2443	.2530	
Fegyvergyar. Budapest, Hungary	Liliput	408185	R	10.0	4	.060	.2430	.2533	Femaru Fegyver és Gepgyár, R.T.
	"	429691	R	9.9	4	.058	.2429	.2535	
Soc. Francaise D'Armes Automatiques, St. Etienne, France	"Automatique Francaise"	56	R	10.2	6	.029	.2486	.2556	
Mre. Francaise D'Armes et Cycles de St. Etienne, St. Etienne, France	Policeman	10962	R	10.4	6	.033	.2444	.2506	
	"	26356	R	10.4	6	.032	.2454	.2523	
	"	115902	R	10.7	6	.041	.2460	.2528	
	Mod. de Poche	16590	R	10.3	6	.039	.2448	.2530	
	"Franco"	158239	R	10.6	6	.040	.2460	.2522	Same as Policeman Mod.
A. Francotte, Liége, Belgium	Francotte	1441	R	9.9	4	.081	.2428	.2522	
Industria Armi Galesi, Brescia, Italy	Mod. 9	149580	R	8.0	6	.055	.2420	.2538	Dated 1947.
	do.	151903	R	11.8	6	.056	.2498	.2544	Dated 1947.
	do.	163250	R	7.3	6	.065	.2471	.2519	Dated 1952.
	do.	169500	R	8.9	6	.063	.2413	.2513	Dated 1953.
Garate, Anitua y Cia., Eibar, Spain	Tigre	7406	R	9.7	6	.056	.2470	.2546	Bbl. No. 432
C.G. Haenel, Suhl, Germany	Schmeisser Mod.	6941	R	9.7	4	.060	.2442	.2522	Measurements approximate.
	do.	24072	R	9.65	4	.064	.2475	.2563	
	do.	21021	R	10.1	4	.064	.2455	.2521	
	do.	34836	R	10.1	4	.068	.2461	.2541	
J. Jacquemart, Herstal, Belgium	Monobloc	4141	R	9.5	6	.047	.2414	.2473	
A. Krausser Waffenfabrik, Zella-Mehlis, Germany	Helfricht Mod. III	804	R	9.7	6	.035	.2450	.2516	Also sold as the "Helkra."
	do.	---	R	9.6	6	.027	.2446	.2518	Serial No. removed.
	Helfricht Mod. IV	2578	R	9.8	6	.024	.---*	.---*	*Meas. not reliable.
Fr. Langenhan, Zella-Mehlis, Germany	F.L. Mod. II	15274	R	9.5	4	.067	.2399	.2527	
Fritz Mann, Suhl, Germany	Mann—W.T.	8998	R	9.8	6	.031	.2450	.2540	Dated 1921.
	do.	15427	R	9.6	6	.032	.2457	.2545	do.
Mre. D'Armes Le Page, Liége, Belgium	Pistolet Aut.—Le Page	6423	R	9.9	6	.035	.2455	.2580	
Mre. Liégeoise D'Armes á Feu, Liége, Belgium	"Liége"	41765	R	9.6	6	.039	.2448	.2540	Identical to New Mod. Melior made by Robar.
Mre. D'Armes Automatiques Bayonne, Bayonne, France	M.A.B. Type A	h28	R	11.2	6	.046	.2456	.2566	Model not designated at beginning of manufacture.
	M.A.B. Mod. A	79354	R	12.4	6	.046	.2452	.2518	Sold in U.S. by W.A.C.
	M.A.B. Mod. E	8576	R	12.2	6	.044	.2447	.2536	do.
Man. de Armas de Fuego, Guernica, Spain	Alkar	75056	R	10.6	6	.038	.2445	.2536	Same trade mark as on Alkartasuna.
Waffenfabrik Mauser, Oberndorf, a/N, Germany	Pocket Type—1910	14676	R	7.2	6	.040	.2470	.2520	Mod. designations not used until 1934.
	do.	35753	R	7.1	6	.040	.2450	.2520	
	do.	223138	R	7.1	6	.047	.2457	.2517	
	do.	276655	R	7.3	6	.038	.2455	.2526	
	Pocket Type—1914	365496	R	7.1	6	.047	.2463	.2513	Made ca. 1930-33.
	W.T.P. Mod. I	14527	R	7.15	6	.046	.2461	.2511	Made in 1930.
	W.T.P. Mod. II	61873	R	7.0	6	.046	.2445	.2525	
	do.	73769	R	7.1	6	.047	.2452	.2520	
	do.	58077	R	7.0	6	.044	.2453	.2515	
Francois Mayor, Lausanne, Switzerland	Mayor	510	R	26.6	4	.045	.2457	.2517	Swiss Pat. No. 86863 issued to E. Rochat.
August Menz, Suhl, Germany	Menta	4863	R	9.6	6	.025	.2465	.2547	
	Liliput	5708	R	8.45	6	.035	.2483	---	Rifling worn.
Oesterr. Waffenfabriks Ges., Steyr, Austria	Steyr Mod. 1909	80622-A	R	12.45	6	.048	.2461	.2555	N. Pieper Patent.
	do.	99955-A	R	8.65	6	.043	.2460	.2552	N. Pieper Pats. No. 9379 ('05) and 25025 ('06)
	do.	104188-A	R	8.75	6	.046	.2457	.2569	do.
	do.	87860-A	R	8.85	6	.045	.2465	.2552	

Caliber and Manufacturer	Model (or Name)	Serial No.	Dir'n of Twist	Inches for 1 turn	No. of Lands	Land Width (inches)	Bore Diameter (inches)	Groove Diameter* (inches)	Remarks
Oesterr. Werke gws Anstalt, Vienna, Austria	O.W.A.	18315	R	10.0	6	.046	.2473	.2568	Inscrip. on slide: Pat. I.A. Kulturstaaten.
Ojanguren y Vidosa, Eibar, Spain	"Salvaje"	7423	L	11.1	6	.043	.2500	.2532	Patented 1918.
D.F. Ortega de Seija, Madrid, Spain	Benemerita	---	R	10.8	6	.026	.2451	.2517	de Seija may have been a dealer.
"Phoenix Arms," Location unknown	Phoenix	2046	R	9.85	6	.030	.2439	.2599	Inscrip. on slide: Phoenix Arms Pat. No proof marks. Prob. Spanish.
	"	3028	R	9.6	6	.027	.2424	.2626	do. Unusually deep grooves.
Anc. Etablissements Pieper, Herstal, Belgium	Bayard 1908	12576	L	9.4	6	.032	.2425	.2526	ca. 1908 or 1909.
	do.	36049	L	9.9	6	.022	.2395	.2475	
	Bayard—Mod. 1930	11463	L	9.6	6	.021	.2419	.2539	
Zbrojovka Praha, Prague, Czechoslovakia	Praha	3724	R	10.0	4	.084	.2435	.2545	Condition of rifling not good.
Mre. D'Armes des Pyrenées, Hendaye, France	"UNIQUE"	312597	L	13.1	6	.039	.2466	.2528	
	Pistolet Mikros	3570	R	12.0	6	.043	.2458	.2516	Mag. cap. 6 ctges.
	"Le Sans Pareil"	345282	R	12.7	6	.040	.2468	.2522	
Retolaza Hermanos, Eibar, Spain	Titan	50786	R	10.9	6	.050	.2462	.2523	
	Stosel No. 1	324	L	9.7	6	.052	.2467	.2509	
	Liberty	4757	R	9.65	6	.045	.2469	.2511	
Rhein. Metallwaren u. Masch. Fab., Sömmerda, Germany	Dreyse	1641	R	10.1	4	.035	.2445	.2541	Early model. Two extractors.
	"	2817	R	10.3	4	.047	.2452	.2540	One extractor.
	"	74204	R	10.0	4	.059	.2451	.2553	do.
Robar et Cie., Liége, Belgium	Melior—Old Mod.	13690	R	9.6	6	.033	.2434	.2542	
	Melior—New Mod.	112470	R	9.45	6	.031	.2434	.2544	
	do.	112507	R	9.5	6	.031	.2418	.2520	
	do.	102971	R	9.6	6	.033	.2426	.2540	
	do.	43873	R	9.6	6	.023	.2435	.2527	
	Jieffeco	11378	R	9.8	6	.030	.2432	.2532	Sold by Jannsen Fils and Co.
	"	30758	R	9.4	6	.023	.2422	.2562	do.
Russian Arsenal Tula (Tulski Oruzheinyi Zavod), Tula, Russia	"Tula-Korovin"	53706	R	7.3	6	.033	.2448	.2542	Also known as "Pistolet Korovin."
	do.	200614	R	7.6	6	.030	.2454	.2554	do.
	"TOZ"	328117	R	7.0	6	.036	.2459	.2539	Identical to Korovin.
Santigo Salaberrin, Ermua, Spain	Tisan	28573	R	9.7	6	.052	.2450	.2497	
	"Aut. Pistole 6.35"	D-3711	R	9.5	6	.044	.2451	.2521	Identical to Tisan.
Modesto Santos, Eibar, Spain	Action—Mod. 1920	30552	R	10.4	6	.043	.2456	.2526	
	MS	4578	R	7.85	6	.057	.2471	.2531	
	"	52271	R	10.9	6	.069	.2460	.2503	
	"	54406	L	10.7	6	.048	.2435	.2545	Only mark is MS on grip.
J.P. Sauer u. Sohn, Suhl, Germany	Old Mod.	38433	R	14.3	6	.043	.2460	.2525	Made ca. 1921-23.
	do.	44407	R	14.6	6	.039	.2456	.2524	
	V.P.—First Form	6063	R	14.2	6	.038	.2448	.2526	
	V.P.—Mod. 1928	252171	R	9.4	6	.023	.2460	.2550	
	do.	253211	R	9.4	6	.040	.2460	.2538	
	do.	11158	R	9.5	6	.029	.2451	.2545	Top ejection.
Fab. de Armas S.E.A.M., Eibar, Spain	S.E.A.M.	63137	R	8.2	6	.064	.2492	.2538	Soc. Española de Armas y Municiones, Eibar.
Seytres "Fabrique á St. Etienne," St. Etienne, France	Pistolet Aut. Francais— "UNION"	1924	R	11.0	6	.053	.2421	.2575	
N. Simson and Co., Suhl, Germany	Simson Selbstlader	24581	R	9.3	6	.052	.2444	.2578	Marked N. Simson and Co.
	do.	24061	R	9.8	6	.051	.2445	.2561	Marked Waffenfabriken Simson and Co.
	do.	27718	R	9.6	6	.048	.2443	.2540	do.
Soc. Industrielle Suisse, Neuhausen, Switzerland	Chylewski	592	R	9.0	6	.033	.2440	.2538	
Franz Stock, Berlin, Germany	Stock	466	R	9.6	4	.048	.2503	.2610	
	"	9319	R	9.2	4	.044	.2500	.2600	
Tanfoglio and Sabotti Brescia, Italy	Sata	0721	R	9.9	6	.043	.2455	.2545	Pat. 1955, dated 1958.
Unceta y Cia., (Formerly Esp. y Unceta) Guernica, Spain	Astra—Mod. 200	656280	L	9.6	6	.036	.2460	.2524	A new gun.
	Astra—Mod. 202	684149	L	9.6	6	.039	.2469	.2523	New gun.
	do.	686019	L	10.1	6	.043	.2470	.2508	do.
Tomas de Urizar y Cia., Eibar, Spain	"Allies"	69	R	15.4	6	.043	.2483	.2681	Made for Berasaluze Areitio-Aurtena y Cia.

Caliber and Manufacturer	Model (or Name)	Serial No.	Dir'n of Twist	Inches for 1 turn	No. of Lands	Land Width (inches)	Bore Diameter (inches)	Groove Diameter* (inches)	Remarks
Tomas de Urizar y Cia.	"Express"	10075	R	11.4	6	.043	.2453	.2515	Sold by Garate, Anitua y Cia.
	"Princeps" Pat.	463	R	4.3	6	.029	.2456	.2534	Prob. made for Thieme y Edeler (dealers), Eibar.
	do.	3294	R	4.7	6	.034	.2468	.2549	Export. by Fab. d'Armes de Guerre de Grande Precision.
	do.	13378	R	5.75	6	.045	.2490	.2552	
A. Vilímec, Kdyně, Czechoslovakia	Slavia	70510	R	11.8	6	.027	.2440	.2526	
Carl Walther Waffenfabrik, Zella-Mehlis, Germany	Mod. 1	Removed	R	9.9	6	.038	.2470	.2530	
	Mod. 2	56974	R	9.6	6	.028	.2491	.2567	
	Mod. 5	91189	R	9.85	4	.065	.2452	.2538	
	do.	94908	R	9.6	4	.069	.2473	.2541	
	do.	92141	R	9.5	6	.028	.2426	.2536	Other 6-groove specimens found.
	Mod. 7	32272	R	10.2	4	.069	.2430	.2493	
	Mod. 8	397675	R	9.8	6	.020	.2490	.2558	
	do.	703782	R	9.6	6	.032	.2471	.2523	
	do.	720440	R	7.95	6	.043	.2450	.2520	Unusual twist.
	Mod. 9	509084	R	9.4	6	.011	.2503	.2583	
	do.	558728	R	9.55	6	.017	.2480	.2554	
Wiener Waffenfabrik, Vienna, Austria	Little Tom	26668	R	15.4	6	.054	.2458	.2576	
E. Zehner, Suhl, Germany	Zehna	14722	R	7.2	4	.060	.2450	.2538	
A. Zoli, Gardone V.T. (Brescia), Italy	Zoli	2592	R	9.9	6	.040	.2450	.2544	Dated 1957.
Manufacturer unknown	Kobra	4	R	9.6	4	.066	.2454	.2521	Made in Germany.
	"	137	R	9.6	4	.080	.2445	.2497	do.
Manufacturer unknown	Merke	3654	R	7.7	6	.060	.2503	.2585	Made in Spain.
Caliber: 7 mm.									
Adlerwaffenwerke, Zella St. Blasii, Germany	Adler	1231	R	8.5	6	.029	.2772	.2830	Rifling in poor condition.
	"	1245	R	8.6	6	.024	.2780	.2857	Rifling worn. (Less than 500 made.)
Japanese Arsenal	"Baby" Mod.	3919	R	11.1	6	.029	.2711	.2809	Also called "Officers Model."
Caliber: 7.62 mm.									
Russian Arsenals, Tula, Russia	Tokarev—M1933	45311	R	9.6	4	.097	.3023	.3139	Dated 1935.
	do.	YK 168	R	9.55	4	.080	.3012	.3123	Dated 1939.
	do.	YH 367	R	9.4	4	.078	.3020	.3144	Dated 1939.
	do.	B16437	R	10.1	4	.082	.3015	.3137	Dated 1941.
	do.	TB 392	R	10.5	4	.077	.3024	.3144	Dated 1941.
	do.	Л 798	R	9.6	4	.074	.3016	.3136	Dated 1941.
	do.	НА 2760	R	9.7	4	.078	.3017	.3143	Dated 1942.
	do.	ИЯ 2412	R	9.7	4	.082	.3022	.3150	Dated 1943.
	do.	A-5-5203	R	10.2	4	.073	.3021	.3136	Dated 1943.
	Tokarev—M-1951	19696	R	9.6	4	.074	.3017	.3137	Dated 1952. (Chinese)
	Tokarev—M-1933	БК-1396	R	9.45	4	.086	.3020	.3134	Dated 1949.
	do.	ЛУ 1706	R	9.6	4	.080	.3030	.3145	Dated 1947.
Caliber: 7.63 mm.									
Eulogio Arostegui, Eibar, Spain	Super Azul	28848	R	13.65	6	.057	.3020	.3078	MM31 on frame. Copy of Mauser Mod. 712.
Bonifacio Echeverria, Eibar, Spain	Star Mod. A	A-5597	R	14.7	6	.037	.3014	.3084	Similar to Colt .45; no grip safety; 7.63 mm. Mauser ctge.
	do.	A-6473	R	14.9	6	.037	.3017	.3109	
Waffenfabrik Mauser, Oberndorf, a/N, Germany	M.P.—Mod. 1896	411	R	9.85	4	.117	.3013	.3113	Special lot made for troop training.
	M.P.—Ca. 1900	29575	R	9.9	4	.112	.3012	.3110	5-ctge. mag., 4" bbl., fixed sights.
	do.	29604	R	9.95	4	.112	.3024	.3114	
	M.P.—Ca. 1907	34090	R	9.85	4	.115	.3007	.3117	Comm. Mod., 5 1/2" bbl., Sights adj. to 1000 m.
	M.P.—Mod. 712	93669	R	7.9	6	.040	.3022	.3106	Full or semi-automatic.
	M.P.—Ca. 1910	99789	R	9.9	4	.113	.3013	.3111	Commercial model.
	M.P.—1912	202183	R	7.85	6	.043	.3013	.3122	Std., 10-shot mag., 5 1/2" bbl.

Caliber and Manufacturer	Model (or Name)	Serial No.	Dir'n of Twist	Inches for 1 turn	No. of Lands	Land Width (inches)	Bore Diameter (inches)	Groove Diameter* (inches)	Remarks
Waffenfabrik Mauser	M.P.—1912	251851	R	7.85	6	.041	.3016	.3116	Std., 10-shot mag., 5 1/2" bbl.
	do.	284669	R	7.85	6	.044	.3023	.3040	Dated 1920. 5 1/2" bbl. Sights adj. to 1000 m.
	M.P.—Variant	314591	R	7.9	6	.045	.3017	.3117	Nonstandard. Hand stamped 1920. Prob. made in 1918.
	M.P.—Ca. 1916-17	359612	R	7.9	6	.040	.3008	.3110	Standard commercial type.
	M.P.—"Police Style"	433900	R	7.8	6	.041	.3009	.3105	Mfd. ca. 1924-26, std.
	do.	446956	R	7.9	6	.044	.3022	.3104	Std. Mod. Mfd. ca. 1924-26. 3 3/4" bbl.; sights adj. to 500 m.
	do.	452783	R	7.9	6	.045	.3034	.3120	do.
	M.P.	853525	R	7.85	6	.044	.3021	---	
	"	891516	R	7.9	6	.039	.3007	.3109	
	"	918280	R	7.9	6	.042	.3200	.3272	May be a re-rifled bbl. Sights adj. to 1000 m.
A.W. Schwarzlose, G.m.b.H., Berlin, Germany	Mod. 1898-"Standart"	421	R	9.0	4	.085	.3000	.3112	Sights adj. to 500 m.; 10-ctge.
Waffenfabrik Steyr, Steyr, Austria	Mannlicher—M1903	406	R	10.55	4	.107	.3020	.3132	
	Mannlicher—M1905	6956	R	9.85	4	.100	.3029	.3159	
Unceta y Cia., Guernica, Spain	Astra Mod. 900	5273	R	10.1	6	.056	.3030	.3100	Mod. after Mauser; Mauser ctge.
	Astra Mod. 902	9705	R	10.1	6	.064	.3037	.3097	Same except extra large mag.
Zulaica y Cia., Eibar, Spain	Royal	3370	R	13.7	6	.042	.3018	.3100	Copy of Mauser Mil. Pistol. Sights adj. to 1000 m.
	"	B-22530	R	13.7	6	.060	.3010	.3098	Similar to Mauser No. 712.

Caliber: .32

Caliber and Manufacturer	Model (or Name)	Serial No.	Dir'n of Twist	Inches for 1 turn	No. of Lands	Land Width (inches)	Bore Diameter (inches)	Groove Diameter* (inches)	Remarks
Colt's Pt. F.A. Mfg. Co., Hartford, Conn.	Pocket Mod.—Browning Pat.	8664	L	15.5	6	.038	.3055	.3185	Only pat. Apr. 20, 1897.
	Pocket Mod. 1903	290675	L	16.1	6	.046	.3036	.3155	
	do.	327335	L	16.3	6	.046	.3047	---	
	do.	336899	L	16.2	6	.046	.3048	---	
	do.	356813	L	16.4	6	.050	.3053	.3103	
	do.	371041	L	16.0	6	.046	.3043	.3061	
	do.	393330	L	16.0	6	.045	.3050	.3130	
	do.	475252	L	16.2	6	.048	.3049	.3122	
	do.	484602	L	16.1	6	.047	.3041	.3112	
Davis-Warner Corpn., Assonet, Mass.	Infallible	3672	R	11.2	6	.059	.3023	.3169	
	"	Removed	R	11.5	6	.053	.3016	.3130	
Harrington and Richardson, Worcester, Mass.	Self Loading	10030	R	12.0	6	.030	.3033	.3143	
	do.	33459	R	12.1	6	.026	.3035	.3109	
	do.	25701	R	12.1	6	.027	.3039	.3119	
Remington—UMC, Ilion, N.Y.	P.A.—M51	PA66970	R	15.8	7	.036	.3038	.3088	
	do.	PA69850	R	16.0	7	.037	.3040	.3094	
	do.	PA90601	R	16.0	7	.047	.3050	.3089	
	do.	PA64349	R	15.9	7	.033	.3040	.3080	
Savage Arms Co. (Later Savage Arms Corpn.), Utica, N.Y.	1907 Mod.	4527	R	16.4	6	.045	.3092	.3150	Early production.
	do.	38652	R	16.0	6	.039	.3057	.3121	
	do.	57151	R	16.0	6	.034	.3031	.3124	
	do.	72146	R	12.0	6	.039	.3050	.3110	
	do.	80029	R	12.1	6	.050	.3061	.3124	
	do.	92611	R	12.0	6	.039	.3047	---	
	do.	115314	R	12.2	6	.051	.3062	.3121	
	do.	117847	R	12.1	6	.051	.3062	.3110	
	1915 Mod.	130200	R	12.1	6	.040	.3046	.3108	Hammerless, 10-ctge.
	1907 Mod.	174655	R	12.1	6	.044	.3058	.3150	
	do.	179594	R	12.0	6	.044	.3052	.3121	
	do.	200665	R	12.1	6	.040	.3048	.3114	
	do.	205601	R	12.0	6	.037	.3045	.3125	1917 Type hammer.
	do.	203379	R	12.1	6	.037	.3045	.3117	
	do.	210732	R	12.1	6	.042	.3046	.3122	
	do.	212696	R	12.0	6	.040	.3050	.3158	
	do.	222785	R	12.0	6	.039	.3049	.3129	
	Mod. 1917	244838	R	12.1	6	.038	.3055	.3129	
	do.	250661	R	12.0	6	.039	.3043	.3119	
	do.	236805	R	12.0	6	.042	.3055	.3127	

Caliber and Manufacturer	Model (or Name)	Serial No.	Dir'n of Twist	Inches for 1 turn	No. of Lands	Land Width (inches)	Bore Diameter (inches)	Groove Diameter* (inches)	Remarks
Webley and Scott, Ltd., Birmingham, England	Met. Police Mod.	29449	R	10.1	6	.048	.3060	.3246	Insc. on slide: 7.65 and .32 Automatic Pistol.
	do.	47074	R	10.1	6	.036	.3034	.3188	do.
	M-1906	72482	R	10.1	6	.032	.3032	.3212	do.

Caliber: 7.65 mm.

Caliber and Manufacturer	Model (or Name)	Serial No.	Dir'n of Twist	Inches for 1 turn	No. of Lands	Land Width (inches)	Bore Diameter (inches)	Groove Diameter* (inches)	Remarks
A. Aldazabal Manufactura de Armas, Eibar, Spain	"A.A.A."	408	L	10.4	6	.050	.3010	.3100	
Acha Hermanos, Ermua, Spain	None stated	210	L	10.4	6	.043	.3008	.3091	Probably made in World War I.
S.A. Alkartasuna Fab. de Armas, Guernica, Spain	Alkartasuna	44384	L	10.3	6	.050	.3005	.3109	No. on bbl. 873.
	"	77325	L	10.3	6	.047	.3010	.3110	No. on bbl. 232.
	"	77683	L	10.6	6	.040	.3002	.3087	No. on bbl. 432.
	"	77689	L	10.4	6	.042	.3011	.3113	No. on bbl. 436.
	"	78238	L	10.4	6	.045	.3036	.3118	
	Alkar	79896	L	10.4	6	.048	.3009	.3110	Small pocket model.
Francisco Arizmendi, Eibar, Spain	Roland	7952	R	10.4	6	.051	.3055	.3115	Arizmendi trade mark.
	Walman	19091	R	11.1	6	.055	.3012	.3096	Dated 1926.
	"	19094	R	10.9	6	.041	.3012	.3122	
	Ydeal	853	R	10.9	6	.057	.3010	.3110	
Arizmendi y Goenaga, Eibar, Spain	Singer	5477	R	12.5	6	.036	.3030	.3110	Has Arizmendi y Goenaga trade mark.
	"	9905	R	10.8	6	.041	.3037	.3164	
	"Teuf-Teuf"	16463	R	11.4	6	.035	.3008	.3087	A "Teuf-Teuf" in name only.
Arizmendi y Zulaica, Eibar, Spain	Cebra	59421	L	10.8	6	.057	.3041	.3116	
Hijos de Arrizabalaga, Eibar, Spain	"Pistola Automatica"	49667	R	14.85	6	.052	.3026	.3104	Hijos de Arrizabalaga on bbl.
	Sharp Shooter	11142	R	10.9	6	.052	.3041	.3119	Possibly by Hijos de J.J. Aldazabal. Sold by Ojanguren y Vidosa.
Azanza y Arrizabalaga, Eibar, Spain	1914 "Reims" Pat.	967	L	11.1	6	.047	.3010	.3114	Sold by Aldazabal, Eibar.
	Mod. 1916	29474	L	11.0	6	.057	.3019	.3107	
	do.	910	L	10.8	6	.053	.3015	.3121	
Fab. de Martin A. Bascaran, Eibar, Spain	"Martian"	40349	L	12.5	6	.058	.3019	.3129	Mfr.'s name on slide. No. on bbl. 595.
	"	11532	L	10.2	6	.039	.3011	.3103	Mfr.'s name on slide. No. on bbl. 38.
	Martian	Removed	R	10.4	6	.036	.3021	.3180	No name on gun. Name MARTIAN on slide. Not like Nos. 11532 and 40349.
Becker and Holländer, Suhl, Germany	Beholla	2012	R	8.5	6	.029	.3012	.3126	Beholla Selbstlade Pistole.
	"	503	R	8.5	6	.037	.3017	.3113	
Beistegui Hermanos, Eibar, Spain	1914 Aut. Pistol	42300	L	12.2	6	.045	.3015	.3088	
Pietro Beretta, Gardone V.T. (Brescia), Italy	1915 Type	63514	R	10.3	6	.046	.3037	.3133	
	Mod. 1935	416944	R	10.2	6	.046	.3021	.3124	Dated 1936; Redesigned and called Mod. 1934.
	Mod. 1934	418009	R	10.3	6	.048	.3022	.3114	Dated 1936.
	do.	468964	R	10.5	6	.044	.3036	.3106	Dated 1941.
	do.	497011	R	9.85	6	.053	.3027	.3113	Dated 1943.
	do.	526309	R	9.9	6	.047	.3023	---	Dated 1944.
	do.	536692	R	9.9	6	.045	.3024	.3116	Dated 1944.
	do.	555005	R	9.9	6	.054	.3031	.3111	Dated 1944.
	do.	570694	R	9.9	6	.040	.3015	---	Dated 1944.
	do.	573499	R	9.9	6	.044	.3022	.3110	Dated 1944.
	do.	768414	R	10.25	6	.045	.3023	.3117	Dated 1951.
	do.	802635	R	10.1	6	.046	.3024	.3110	
	do.	824439	R	10.1	6	.045	.3022	.3106	Sold in U.S. as PUMA. Dated 1954.
	do.	876250	R	10.1	6	.047	.3026	.3116	Sold as PUMA. Dated 1955.
Waffenfabrik Bern, Bern, Switzerland	Luger M 1924	19792	R	9.8	4	.110	.3006	.3098	First Swiss Mod. at Bern.
	Luger M 06/29	56634	R	9.9	4	.112	.3006	.3100	Last Swiss Mod. at Bern.
Vincenzo Bernardelli, Gardone V.T. (Brescia), Italy	Target Mod.	24656	R	10.0	6	.054	.2990	.3113	Dated 1956. 9 7/8" bbl.
	Mod. 60	40108	R	17.5	6	.060	.3013	.3103	Dated 1959.
Gustav Bittner, Weipert, Austria	Bittner	1702	R	12.0	8	.082	.2938	.3036	Nominally 7.7 mm. but has same bore as 7.65. Ejects shell but does not reload.

Caliber and Manufacturer	Model (or Name)	Serial No.	Dir'n of Twist	Inches for 1 turn	No. of Lands	Land Width (inches)	Bore Diameter (inches)	Groove Diameter* (inches)	Remarks
Böhmische Waffenfabrik, A. B., Prag Werk, and Strakonice, Czechoslovakia	Czech—Mod. 27	74639	R	9.9	6	.050	.3021	.3095	Germans changed name from Česka Zbrojovka.
	do.	99860	R	9.85	6	.050	.3017	.3087	
	do.	110205	R	9.9	6	.050	.3016	.3092	
	do.	113396	R	9.8	6	.043	.3020	.3090	
	do.	128586	R	9.9	6	.055	.3018	.3100	
	do.	133010	R	9.85	6	.053	.3014	.3098	
	do.	211235	R	10.0	6	.056	.3022	.3090	
	do.	224846	R	9.9	6	.051	.3022	.3105	
	do.	292905	R	9.9	6	.049	.3020	.3092	
	do.	328235	R	9.85	6	.050	.3022	.3087	
	do.	373237	R	9.85	6	.051	.3020	.3094	
	do.	379004	R	9.9	6	.046	.3020	.3096	
	do.	401496	R	9.85	6	.051	.3025	.3097	
	do.	445398	R	9.8	6	.060	.3025	.3097	
	do.	462298	R	9.85	6	.051	.3021	.3085	
	do.	472024	R	9.9	6	.053	.3017	.3089	
	do.	473056	R	9.85	6	.044	.3019	---	
Gregorio Bolumburu, Eibar, Spain	Regina	50104	L	10.4	6	.048	.3044	.3108	
	Bristol	113	L	10.3	6	.040	.3009	.3091	
Česka Zbrojovka, A. S., V. Praze, Czechoslovakia	Praha	6877	R	9.5	4	.075	.3007	.3108	
	Mod. 27	481894	R	9.9	6	.052	.3020	.3094	Dated 1945.
	do.	486328	R	9.85	6	.051	.3021	.3095	Made after liberation from Germans (1945).
Česka Zbrojovka Národní Podnik, Strakonice, Czechoslovakia	Mod. 27 (Commercial)	568519	R	9.85	6	.054	.3016	.3092	Dated 1947. New name adopted under Communist rule.
Chinese Unknown	Imit. Browning M1900	26063	R	5.7	5	.091	.2966	.3038	Several guns may have same number.
Chas. Ph. Clement, Liége, Belgium	Clement—M1907	5894	R	9.8	6	.027	.3030	.3158	
Deutsche Waffen u Munitionsfabrik, Berlin, Germany	Luger—M1900	513	L	9.7	4	.089	.3014	.3120	Swiss Cross on top of barrel. German proof marks.
	do.	2648	R	9.8	4	.108	.3016	.3115	
	1900/06	50193	R	9.9	4	.103	.3014	.3124	
	Luger M1908	9338	R	10.0	4	.107	.3011	---	
	do.	86391	R	9.8	4	.108	.3009	.3109	
	do.	3837a	R	9.6	4	.113	.3007	.3105	1908 Frame. Bbl. No. 3837a. Date 1916.
	do.	4073i	R	9.8	4	.111	.3014	.3114	
	do.	6272-i	R	10.0	4	.110	.3014	.3116	Bbl. No. 6272-i. No number on frame.
	do.	8781-i	R	9.9	4	.112	.3010	.3095	Bbl. No. 8781-i.
	do.	9314-i	R	9.9	4	.109	.3013	.3126	Bbl. and frame No. 9314-i.
	do.	6851-k	R	9.8	4	.102	.3013	.3111	"Commercial" stamped on frame. No. 51 on all major parts.
	do.	8191-1	R	9.9	4	.102	.3022	---	
	do.	1380-p	R	9.9	4	.104	.3010	.3128	Bbl. No. 1380-p.
	do.	81745	R	9.8	4	.108	.3010	.3114	Bbl. and frame No. 81745. 45 on all major parts. No letter suffix.
	Luger Carbine	24268	R	17.8	4	.115	.3010	.3112	
	do.	50016	R	17.9	4	.110	.3010	.3112	11 3/4" bbl., No. 1276a.
	D. W. M. (Browning)	1276a	R	9.9	6	.040	.3021	.3097	
	do.	4647	R	9.9	6	.037	.3014	.3108	D. W. M. a copy of Browning Mod. 1910.
Deutsche Werke, A. G., Erfurt, Germany (See also Ortgies and Co.)	Ortgies	43368	R	8.0	6	.040	.3029	.3123	
	"	52979	R	7.9	6	.033	.3031	.3137	
	"	54362	R	8.0	6	.030	.3029	.3179	
	"	55943	R	7.9	6	.028	.3023	.3140	
	"	114849	R	7.9	6	.031	.3020	.3146	
	"	131320	R	7.85	6	.027	.3029	.3133	
	"	134940	R	7.95	6	.026	.3017	.3129	
	"	148194	R	7.9	6	.029	.3022	---	
	"	154819	R	7.9	6	.033	.3017	.3143	
	"	158378	R	7.85	6	.027	.3019	.3125	
	"	162293	R	8.0	6	.034	.3025	.3133	
	"	199186	R	8.0	6	.030	.3019	.3140	
	"	201433	R	7.8	6	.030	.3029	.3129	
	"	224995	R	7.9	6	.032	.3035	.3124	
	"	227576	R	7.95	6	.032	.3020	.3116	

Caliber and Manufacturer	Model (or Name)	Serial No.	Dir'n of Twist	Inches for 1 turn	No. of Lands	Land Width (inches)	Bore Diameter (inches)	Groove Diameter* (inches)	Remarks
Echave y Arizmendi, Eibar, Spain	E. A. Mod. 1916	1399	L	10.0	6	.048	.3011	.3092	
	Bronco Mod. 1918	10571	L	10.2	6	.057	.3001	.3150	"Bronco" Pat. No. 66130.
	do.	26792	L	11.1	6	.064	.3025	.3079	Rifling considerably worn.
Hijos de A. Echeverria, Eibar, Spain	Vesta	110670	L	10.2	6	.055	.3015	.3105	
	"	113576	L	10.3	6	.049	.3050	.3116	Grooves deeper on driving edge.
	"	142394-P	L	10.3	6	.038	.3017	.3081	
	"	110870	L	10.3	6	.052	.3015	.3105	
Erquiaga y Cia., Eibar, Spain	Fiel	13225	L	10.7	6	.055	.3012	.3087	
Bonifacio Echeverria, Eibar, Spain	"STAR" (Copy)	20873	R	12.3	6	.046	.3033	.3102	Copy of 1919 type, or prototype of same.
	STAR 1919 Type	37364	R	12.1	6	.040	.3020	.3105	
	do.	37799	R	12.0	6	.035	.3020	.3095	
	Star Mod. S. I.	380748	R	12.4	6	.044	.3017	.3130	
	do.	390734	R	12.6	6	.043	.3020	.3120	
	"Izarra"	7733	L	10.3	6	.051	.3009	.3099	B. Echeverria's name on slide.
	"	3591	L	10.3	6	.049	.3014	.3094	do.
Esperanza y Unceta Cia., Guernica, Spain (See also Unceta y Cia. for Astras)	Astra—Mod. 1911	1727	R	9.8	6	.036	.3030	.2143	No. 1727 on bbl. "HOPE" bbl. Note direction of twist.
	do.	6586	R	12.0	6	.026	.3021	.3150	No. 6586 on bbl. "HOPE" bbl.
	do.	9685	R	9.7	6	.048	.3025	.3143	No. 9685 on bbl. "HOPE" bbl.
	Astra—Mod. 1915	Removed	L	9.5	6	.059	.3016	.3100	No. 4169 on bbl. "HOPE" bbl.
	do.	72889	L	9.5	6	.057	.3008	.3090	No. 7442 on bbl. "HOPE" bbl.
	Astra—Mod. 1916	70211	L	9.6	6	.046	.3014	.3098	No. 5857 on bbl. "HOPE" bbl.
	do.	75140	L	9.4	6	.055	.3014	.3106	No. 1618 on bbl. "HOPE" bbl.
	1916 Mod. Brunswig	84006	L	9.5	6	.044	.3016	.3110	Esperanza and Unceta markings. No. 6206 on bbl. "HOPE" bbl.
	do.	84070	L	9.4	6	.032	.3019	.3111	Same except bbl. No. 1798.
Fab. Nat'l. D'Armes de Guerre, Herstal, Belgium	Browning Mod. 1900	7742	R	7.4	5	.039	.3001	.3059	
	do.	94106	R	7.45	5	.033	.3023	.3068	
	do.	194285	R	9.5	5	.033	.3016	.3040	Rifling considerably worn.
	do.	416485	R	9.8	6	.031	.3020	.3100	No. of lands changed.
	do.	437308	R	9.3	6	.031	.3016	- - -	
	do.	623086	R	9.6	6	.031	.3013	.3096	
	do.	630389	R	9.5	6	.030	.3034	.3114	
	do.	703712	R	9.5	6	.037	.3034	.3115	
	Browning Mod. 1910	61556	R	9.65	6	.032	.3010	.3113	
	do.	62969	R	9.6	6	.040	.3027	.3117	
	do.	88785a	R	9.7	6	.033	.3020	.3110	
	do.	95970	R	9.6	6	.026	.3013	- - -	95970 on bbl; 38303 on frame.
	do.	140071	R	9.4	6	.021	.3016	- - -	
	do.	213940	R	9.6	6	.039	.3053	.3127	Sold in Austria by Alcock and Pierce.
	do.	320461	R	9.55	6	.041	.3006	.3096	
	do.	387336	R	9.55	6	.024	.3020	- - -	
	do.	419755	R	9.7	6	.027	.3023	- - -	
	do.	437145	R	9.8	6	.040	.3028	.3100	
	Browning Mod. 1922	56041	R	9.6	6	.026	.3020	.3098	
	do.	140192	R	9.8	6	.022	.3020	.3100	Has German accept. marks. Made during Occupation.
	do.	156295	R	9.6	6	.023	.3017	.3101	Has German accept. marks.
	do.	193386	R	9.7	6	.026	.3017	.3100	do.
	do.	59285-a	R	9.7	6	.027	.3015	.3096	do.
	do.	7708-b	R	9.8	6	.026	.3018	.3098	do.
	do.	8792-c	R	9.6	6	.029	.3016	.3102	do.
	do.	20044	R	9.7	6	.031	.3014	.3102	do.
"Fab. D'Armes de Guerre," Eibar, Spain	Paramount	130	R	10.9	6	.056	.3019	.3155	Name assumed for sales purposes.
	"	4038	L	11.0	6	.032	.2994	.3113	
	"	5653	R	15.8	6	.057	.3047	.3087	
	No model name	7045	L	10.3	6	.044	.3002	.3130	Similar to No. 5653.

Caliber and Manufacturer	Model (or Name)	Serial No.	Dir'n of Twist	Inches for 1 turn	No. of Lands	Land Width (inches)	Bore Diameter (inches)	Groove Diameter* (inches)	Remarks
"Fab. D'Armes de Guerre"	No model name	11090	L	11.3	6	.052	.3007	.3312	Letters L.C. on rear of frame.
	do.	11826	L	11.4	6	.049	.3024	.3142	do.
Fegyvergyar, Budapest, Hungary	Frommer Stop	76573	R	10.2	4	.106	.3019	.3129	
	do.	79394	R	9.9	4	.110	.3027	.3139	
	do.	88328	R	9.4	4	.116	.3017	.3133	
	do.	221363	R	9.9	4	.104	.3021	.3179	
	do.	334561	R	9.75	4	.112	.3016	.3150	
	do.	338353	R	10.0	4	.113	.3023	.3124	
	do.	358543	R	9.8	4	.108	.3018	.3158	
Gabilondo y Cia., Elgoibar, Spain	Bufalo	2937	R	10.4	6	.049	.3010	.3100	Rifling considerably worn.
	"	7553	R	9.6	6	.040	.2102	.3012	
	Plus Ultra	16139	R	12.0	6	.055	.3023	.3091	20-ctge. Discontinued 1932.
	Llama—Mod. X	68833	R	11.8	6	.040	.3025	.3125	
	do.	73214	R	11.9	6	.043	.3020	.3134	
	do.	109428	R	12.0	6	.044	.3016	.3100	
	Llama—Mod. X-A	143254	R	12.0	6	.043	.3025	.3091	
	do.	143884	R	11.9	6	.042	.3026	.3118	
	do.	143926	R	12.0	6	.040	.3030	---	
	do.	148686	R	11.9	6	.044	.3024	.3104	
	do.	164138	R	12.5	6	.051	.3035	.3095	
Gabilondo y Urresti, Eibar, Spain	Ruby—1915 Mod.	61026	R	10.3	6	.048	.3011	.3096	
	do.	27105E	R	10.4	6	.051	.3012	.3076	
Garate, Anitua y Cia., Eibar, Spain	None stated	23969	L	10.45	6	.054	.3031	.3112	Marked: "Pistola Automatica."
Industria Armi Galesi, Brescia, Italy	Galesi Mod. 6	145233	R	10.8	6	.056	.2982	.3052	
	Galesi Mod. 9	201524	R	10.2	6	.052	.2918	.3038	Sold in U.S. as Mod. 515A. Dated 1956.
Fab. D'Armes de Guerre, Haute Precision Armand Gavage, Liége, Belgium	Gavage	2514	R	9.6	6	.052	.3011	.3081	
Isidro Gaztañaga, Eibar, Spain	Destroyer	26756	L	12.25	6	.037	.3007	.3095	
	"	46723	L	12.0	6	.048	.3025	.3097	
H.M. Gering and Co., Arnstadt, Germany	Leonhardt	20660	R	10.0	6	.049	.3061	.3139	Rifling worn.
	"	37963	R	9.5	6	.059	.3014	.3100	Rifling in good condition.
	"	29681	R	9.6	6	.044	.3045	.3145	
Jäger and Co., Suhl, Germany	Jäger	3889	R	14.5	4	.057	.3018	.3126	
	"	5833	R	8.9	4	.053	.3024	.3154	
	"	6766	R	17.7	4	.068	.3036	.3121	
	"	8343	R	14.7	4	.052	.3043	.3169	
	"	9102	R	14.8	4	.054	.3023	.3123	
Kohout and Spol., Kdyně, Czechoslovakia	"MARS"	8457	R	10.7	6	.052	.3026	.3100	8457 on frame, 8387 on slide.
	"	9341	R	10.5	6	.046	.3012	.3090	9341 on frame, 5905 on slide.
Fr. Langenhan, Zella-Mehlis, Germany	F.L. Selbstlader	2477	R	9.55	4	.088	.3040	.3167	
	do.	18351	R	9.55	4	.059	.3034	.3150	
	do.	18845	R	9.6	4	.072	.3036	.3134	
	do.	20995	R	9.6	4	.066	.3028	.3162	
	do.	36228	R	9.4	4	.066	.3024	.3140	
	do.	63886	R	9.5	4	.077	.3022	.3168	
	do.	508	R	9.5	4	.065	.3003	.3148	
Mann Werke, Suhl, Germany	Mann-Pocket Mod.	42013	R	9.7	4	.043	.3053	.3135	
Mre. D'Armes Le Page, Liége, Belgium	Le Page	14624	L	9.5	6	.042	.3089	.3157	Poor job of rifling.
Mre. D'Armes Automatiques Bayonne, Bayonne, France	M.A.B.—Mod. C	12369	R	12.1	5	.087	.2999	.3041	
	M.A.B.—Mod. D	62334	R	12.3	6	.043	.3012	.3096	
	do.	92964	R	12.0	6	.036	.3013	.3105	
	do.	66775	R	12.3	6	.044	.3007	.3099	
	do.	69878	R	12.3	6	.026	.3010	.3090	
	M.A.B.—Mod. R	916	R	12.5	6	.044	.3010	.3100	Sold in U.S. by W.A.C.
Mre. D'Armes St. Etienne, St. Etienne, France	M.A.S.—Mod. 1925 No. 1	None	R	10.0	4	.062	.3023	.3125	
	M.A.S.—Mod. 1935-S	F-986	R	9.9	4	.064	.3017	.3115	
Waffenfabrik Mauser, Oberndorf, a/N, Germany	Pocket 1910 Type	19456	R	7.95	6	.047	.3020	.3090	
	Pocket 1914 Type	76754	R	7.85	6	.043	.3020	.3106	First form. Mfd. ca. 1915-20.
	do.	86297	R	7.8	6	.042	.3020	.3110	do.

Caliber and Manufacturer	Model (or Name)	Serial No.	Dir'n of Twist	Inches for 1 turn	No. of Lands	Land Width (inches)	Bore Diameter (inches)	Groove Diameter* (inches)	Remarks
Waffenfabrik Mauser	Pocket 1914 Type	152586	R	8.0	6	.058	.3025	.3104	
	do.	157201	R	7.95	6	.042	.3026	---	
	do.	188242	R	7.95	6	.030	.3018	.3090	
	do.	280714	R	7.9	6	.045	.3019	.3083	
	do.	297308	R	7.8	6	.042	.3028	---	
	do.	310833	R	7.9	6	.043	.3030	.3081	Mfd. ca. 1930-33.
	do.	331443	R	7.9	6	.034	.3012	.3096	
	do.	338192	R	8.0	6	.043	.3024	.3075	
	do.	385242	R	8.0	6	.046	.3024	.3087	
	do.	493254	R	8.0	6	.042	.3015	.3087	
	do.	496407	R	8.0	6	.043	.3022	.3092	
	New Mod. 1934	537463	R	7.8	6	.036	.3020	.3100	
	do.	562416	R	7.7	6	.039	.3034	---	
	do.	574126	R	8.0	6	.032	.3019	.3105	
	do.	586969	R	7.9	6	.039	.3022	---	
	do.	589565	R	7.85	6	.040	.3020	.3083	
	do.	617615	R	7.85	6	.042	.3018	---	
	do.	619487	R	7.90	6	.044	.3023	.3096	Mfd. ca. 1938-39.
	do.	622833	R	7.8	6	.040	.3020	.3092	
	Mod. H Sc	729247	R	7.9	6	.043	.3030	.3104	
	do.	739940	R	7.75	6	.042	.3023	---	
	do.	745703	R	7.8	6	.043	.3018	---	
	do.	818884	R	7.7	6	.041	.3028	.3092	
	do.	846319	R	7.9	6	.038	.3026	---	
	do.	866002	R	7.9	6	.050	.3026	.3088	
	do.	871370	R	7.8	6	.052	.3021	.3085	
	do.	902322	R	9.85	6	.047	.3029	.3090	Unusual twist.
	do.	Removed	R	9.9	6	.052	.3026	.3086	do.
August Menz, Suhl, Germany	Menz—Mod. II	787	R	8.6	6	.059	.3014	.3132	
	Menta	8915	R	9.5	6	.050	.3037	.3151	
	Menz	72322	R	15.0	6	.028	.3032	.3128	Model not known.
	Menz—PB Spl.	3073	R	9.4	6	.043	.3000	.3100	
Metallwaren Waffen u. Maschinenfabrik, A.G., Budapest, Hungary	Mod. 37	5152	R	8.0	6	.041	.3017	.3103	Dated 1941.
	do.	6415	R	7.9	6	.047	.3021	.3097	Dated 1941.
	do.	14496	R	7.85	6	.040	.3020	.3107	Dated 1941.
	do.	27694	R	7.95	6	.041	.3025	.3093	Dated 1941.
	do.	37468	R	7.9	6	.045	.3022	.3100	Dated 1941.
	do.	52236	R	7.9	6	.037	.3023	.3101	Date not noted.
	do.	52613	R	7.9	6	.041	.3019	.3101	Dated 1943.
	do.	65271	R	7.9	6	.041	.3030	.3094	Dated 1943.
	do.	68200	R	7.9	6	.042	.3024	.3100	Dated 1943.
	do.	69909	R	7.9	6	.039	.3020	.3100	Dated 1943.
Cooperativa Obrera, Eibar, Spain	Longines	89198	L	10.3	6	.062	.2993	.3133	
R.S. Industria Obrera Armera, Eibar, Spain	Omega	A-166	R	10.6	6	.054	.3050	.3114	Bbl. mkd. T.U. Prob. made by T. Urizar y Cia.
Ortgies and Co., Erfurt, Germany (See also Deutsche Werke)	Ortgies	195	R	7.9	6	.034	.3023	.3118	
	"	9575	R	7.9	6	.037	.3017	.3135	
	"	10614	R	7.9	6	.033	.3025	.3155	
Anc. Etablissements Pieper, Herstal, Belgium	Bayard Mod. 1909	2860	L	10.7	6	.042	.3041	.3112	Frequently called Mod. 1908.
	do.	177512	L	10.9	6	.032	.3043	.3127	do.
	do.	198523	L	9.85	6	.031	.3040	.3102	do.
	do.	265890	L	12.6	6	.034	.3042	.3102	do.
Zbrojovka Praha, Prague, Czechoslovakia	Praha	1921	R	9.9	4	.101	.3041	.3154	Marked Praha 5-20.
	Praha—Mod. 1921	3995	R	10.6	4	.126	.3029	.3049	
Mre. D'Armes des Pyrenées, Hendaye, France	"UNIQUE"	32007	L	12.35	6	.043	.3020	.3106	
	"	40313	L	12.4	6	.058	.3017	.3093	Has German accept. marks.
	"	42227	L	12.1	6	.059	.3008	.3109	do.
	"	45885	L	12.3	6	.065	.3012	.3112	
	"	55898	L	12.2	6	.043	.3026	.3092	do.
	"	59376	L	12.2	6	.045	.3021	---	
	"	61416	L	12.1	6	.047	.3026	.3095	do.
	"	72100	L	10.5	6	.059	.3011	.3141	Marked: Le Veritable Pistolet "UNIQUE." Also "55 UNIS FRANCE 96." No name of maker.
	"	72154	L	10.5	6	.053	.3037	.3104	do.
Retolaza Hermanos, Eibar, Spain	Paramount	7751	L	12.3	6	.037	.2990	.3090	Sold in U.S. by Paramount Trading Co., N.Y.
	"	8462	R	8.8	6	.051	.3045	.3137	Possibly not made by R.H.

Caliber and Manufacturer	Model (or Name)	Serial No.	Dir'n of Twist	Inches for 1 turn	No. of Lands	Land Width (inches)	Bore Diameter (inches)	Groove Diameter* (inches)	Remarks
Retolaza Hermanos	Retolaza—1914	103	L	12.5	6	.035	.3008	.3108	
	do.	19975	L	11.8	6	.038	.3020	.3094	
	do.	39499	L	10.4	6	.056	.3011	.3093	
	Stosel No. 1	29235	L	12.0	6	.050	.3010	.3100	Mkd. Automatic Pistol "Stosel"—No. 1 Patent.
	do.	30335	L	12.6	6	.039	.3016	.3120	do.
	Titanic—M1914	2820	R	13.9	6	.038	.3020	.3098	
Rhein. Metallwaren u. Masch. Fab., Sömmerda, Germany	Dreyse	170(?)	R	16.6	4	.042	.3023	.3139	No. 170 in several places. Marked K. S. GEND.
	"	40293	R	17.3	4	.054	.3012	.3106	
	"	53522	R	16.6	4	.040	.3024	.3118	
	"	65920	R	16.6	4	.049	.3021	.3095	
	"	158925	R	16.1	4	.040	.3009	.3107	
	"	232435	R	17.35	4	.050	.3022	.3140	
	"	233746	R	16.5	4	.055	.3016	.3112	
	"	233916	R	16.5	4	.061	.3018	.3134	
	"	234546	R	16.15	4	.059	.3015	.3108	
	"	241002	R	16.7	4	.059	.3010	.3112	
	"	245626	R	17.35	4	.053	.3017	.3101	
	"	248246	R	15.8	4	.055	.3014	.3092	
	"	248422	R	15.9	4	.051	.3007	.3102	
	Rheinmetall	255290	R	16.6	4	.053	.3020	.3080	
	"	264659	R	16.7	4	.047	.3025	.3111	
Robar et Cie., Liége, Belgium	Melior—Old Mod.	22287	R	9.6	5	.058	.3021	.3074	S. G. D. G. Pat. 24875—1908.
	do.	26899	R	9.5	5	.049	.3011	.3073	
	Melior—New Mod.	54894	R	9.6	5	.069	.3022	.3062	New Mod. numbering began at 27351.
	Jieffeco	20164	R	9.6	5	.044	.3025	.3058	Made for Jannsen Fils and Co.
Iraola Salaverria, Eibar, Spain	Salaverria	8554	L	10.5	6	.050	.3021	.3109	
	Destructor	4609	R	10.7	6	.052	.3000	.3100	
Soc. Alsacienne de Construction Mecanique, Cholet, France	S. A. C. M.—1935A	4904-A	R	9.85	4	.083	.3012	.3125	
	do.	5487-A	R	9.9	4	.089	.3021	.3131	
	do.	6330-A	R	9.85	4	.083	.3019	.3131	German accept. marks.
	do.	B1599-A	R	9.9	4	.088	.3012	---	
	do.	C2039-A	R	9.9	4	.083	.3012	.3141	German accept. marks.
J. P. Sauer and Sohn, Suhl, Germany	Sauer I	17849	R	16.6	6	.029	.3024	.3104	Commonly called 1914 Mod. or old model.
	do.	99281	R	14.3	6	.030	.3024	.3104	do.
	do.	121051	R	14.2	6	.038	.3029	.3107	do.
	do.	132720	R	14.2	6	.030	.3006	.3094	do.
	do.	138561	R	14.5	6	.030	.3022	.3106	do.
	Behorden Mod.	190913	R	14.2	6	.050	.3016	.3110	Also called 1930 Mod.
	do.	208969	R	14.2	6	.048	.3015	.3115	do.
	Mod. 38(H)	277180	R	9.4	4	.057	.3019	.3103	First called "Sauer Selbstlade Pistole Mod. H Kal. 7.65." Soon renamed "Mod. 38 (Behorden Mod.)." Commonly called Mod. 38 (H).
	do.	309010	R	9.55	4	.062	.3025	.3099	
	do.	311285	R	9.5	4	.064	.3020	.3107	
	do.	350192	R	9.45	4	.057	.3019	.3095	
	do.	404058	R	9.4	4	.058	.3021	.3099	
	do.	436474	R	9.5	4	.061	.3018	.3094	
	do.	458521	R	9.4	4	.069	.3011	.3085	
	do.	460423	R	9.5	4	.061	.3024	.3094	
	do.	460555	R	9.5	4	.061	.3014	.3098	
	do.	480971	R	9.4	4	.064	.3020	.3098	
	do.	485938	R	9.4	4	.066	.3019	.3097	
	do.	504519	R	9.5	4	.059	.3020	.3100	
A. W. Schwarzlose, G. m. b. H., Berlin, Germany	Schwarzlose—M1908	345	R	8.2	4	.095	.2967	.3053	Sold by Warner Arms Corp., Brooklyn.
	do.	1518	R	8.2	4	.093	.2960	.3052	do.
	do.	5710	R	8.0	4	.088	.2960	.3044	do.
Schweizerische Ind. Ges.	SIG SP 47/8	P53477	R	9.8	4	.104	.3015	.3101	Extra bbl. for Target Mod. SIG.
Stenda Werke Waffenfabrik, Suhl, Germany	Stenda	60676	R	9.45	6	.041	.3028	.3098	
	"	61747	R	9.6	6	.046	.3020	.3122	
	"	61907	R	9.7	6	.045	.3027	.3111	
	"Beholla"	49781	R	9.6	6	.037	.3015	.3095	Marked Stenda-Werke.

Caliber and Manufacturer	Model (or Name)	Serial No.	Dir'n of Twist	Inches for 1 turn	No. of Lands	Land Width (inches)	Bore Diameter (inches)	Groove Diameter* (inches)	Remarks
Oesterreichische	Steyr—Mod. 1909	25084	R	9.9	6	.041	.3021	.3141	N. Pieper Pat.
Waffenfabrik	Steyr	55528-P	R	9.8	6	.034	.3021	.3176	Pat. 9379 (1905);
Steyr,									25025(1906).
Steyr, Austria									
Steyr-Daimler-Puch,	Mod. SP	87	R	9.9	6	.038	.3019	.3107	Dated 1959.
Steyr, Austria									
Franz Stock,	Stock	6742	R	9.4	4	.052	.3017	.3101	
Berlin, Germany	"	9851	R	9.7	4	.066	.3016	.3100	
Unceta y Cia.,	Astra—Mod. 300	595199	R	9.4	6	.039	.3024	.3109	Discontinued 1948.
Guernica, Spain	Astra—Mod. 3000	664586	R	9.5	6	.045	.3026	.3112	In current production.
(See Esperanza y	Astra—Mod. 3003	665809	R	9.6	6	.044	.3027	.3113	do.
Unceta)									
Tomas de Urizar y	"Express"	4493	R	15.1	6	.051	.3027	.3110	Made by Urizar and Co.
Cia.,									for Garate, Anitua and
Eibar, Spain									Co. Bbl. may not be
									original.
	Venus	2679	R	6.5	6	.036	.3023	.3137	
	LeSecours	6758	R	9.4	6	.051	.3000	.3076	Rifling worn, fair condition.
	Princeps	859	R	6.15	6	.040	.3039	.3150	
Urrejola y Cia.,	None stated	4246	L	11.0	6	.045	.3010	.3104	Prob. made in World War I.
Eibar, Spain									
Carl Walther	Mod. 4	81756	R	9.7	4	.065	.3013	---	Walther Selbstlade Pistole
Waffenfabrik,									Mod. 4. Introduced 1910.
Zella-Mehlis,	do.	103361	R	9.9	4	.073	.3020	.3134	do.
Germany	do.	253782	R	10.0	4	.077	.3014	.3104	do.
	do.	267431	R	9.8	6	.071	.3020	.3142	Change in rifling.
	do.	Removed	R	9.5	6	.040	.3036	.3180	
	Mod. PP	235084-P	R	9.9	6	.056	.3021	.3100	Introduced 1929.
	do.	242094-P	R	10.0	6	.053	.3021	---	
	do.	300849-P	R	10.0	6	.055	.3023	.3117	
	do.	315066-P	R	9.9	6	.056	.3023	.3111	
	do.	752505	R	9.4	6	.055	.3015	.3109	
	do.	757932	R	11.9	6	.064	.3018	.3110	Unusual twist.
	do.	906670	R	9.35	6	.056	.3023	.3108	
	do.	932248	R	9.3	6	.052	.3021	.3104	
	do.	961555	R	9.5	6	.053	.3020	.3110	
	Mod. PPK	212884-K	R	9.8	6	.054	.3025	.3110	Introduced 1931.
	do.	266679-K	R	9.65	6	.054	.3020	.3094	
	do.	321506-K	R	10.0	6	.060	.3018	.3113	
	do.	356608-K	R	9.9	6	.055	.3023	.3107	
	do.	396021-K	R	10.0	6	.053	.3020	.3110	
	do.	429376-K	R	10.0	6	.056	.3022	---	
	do.	793277	R	9.4	6	.054	.3021	.3107	
	do.	850599	R	9.3	6	.051	.3023	.3111	
Zulaica y Cia.,	"Ruby" Type	5129	L	10.9	6	.036	.3025	.3106	Also bears name Beistegui
Eibar, Spain									Hermanos. Letters
									Z.C. on frame.
	Royal	10886	L	13.2	6	.041	.3026	.3165	Bbl. No. 216. Frame Nos.
									10886 and 55149.
									Sold by Beistegui
									Hermanos.
	"	44127	R	12.0	6	.075	.3032	.3120	
	"	70273	R	9.5	6	.074	.3030	.3098	
Manufacturer	"Astra"	62211	R	9.6	6	.052	.3020	.3084	"Military Automatic" on
unknown (Spanish)									slide. Not made by
									Esp. and Unceta.
									Mark I.S. on frame
									(Iraola Salaverria?)
Manufacturer	"Demon"	3153	R	9.6	6	.061	.3028	.3122	"Aut. Pistol "Demon" Cal.
unknown (Spanish)									7.65, .32 cal. Metal-
									covered bullet. "
Manufacturer	"Republic"	39898	R	9.7	6	.062	.3023	.3098	Common Eibar Type.
unknown (Spanish)									

Caliber: ".35"

Caliber and Manufacturer	Model (or Name)	Serial No.	Dir'n of Twist	Inches for 1 turn	No. of Lands	Land Width (inches)	Bore Diameter (inches)	Groove Diameter* (inches)	Remarks
Smith and Wesson,	S & W .35 Auto-	3553	R	11.9	6	.066	.3110	.3224	Actually .32 cal. Used
Springfield, Mass.	matic								special S & W ctge.
	do.	6459	R	12.0	6	.060	.3113	.3221	do.
	do.	8153	R	12.1	6	.062	.3102	.3220	do.

Caliber: 8 mm.

Caliber and Manufacturer	Model (or Name)	Serial No.	Dir'n of Twist	Inches for 1 turn	No. of Lands	Land Width (inches)	Bore Diameter (inches)	Groove Diameter* (inches)	Remarks
Th. Bergmann,	Simplex	2153	R	8.2	4	.062	.3084	.3150	German proof marks.
Suhl, Germany									

Caliber and Manufacturer	Model (or Name)	Serial No.	Dir'n of Twist	Inches for 1 turn	No. of Lands	Land Width (inches)	Bore Diameter (inches)	Groove Diameter* (inches)	Remarks
Fegyvergyar, Budapest, Hungary	Roth-Steyr	2535	R	10.0	4	.104	.3135	.3325	See A.G. Steyr Waffenfabrik
	do.	4893	R	10.0	4	.101	.3132	.3312	
	do.	22466	R	9.9	4	.098	.3128	.3306	
	do.	23325	R	9.9	4	.105	.3175	.3325	23325 on right side. 7883.27 on left side.
Japanese Arsenals	Nambu M14 (1925)	8249	R	11.0	6	.042	.3162	.3265	Dated Aug. 1942.
	do.	13586	R	11.0	6	.042	.3167	.3263	Dated Nov. 1944.
	do.	14162	R	11.0	6	.043	.3160	.3274	
	do.	17459	R	10.95	6	.034	.3159	.3301	Dated Nov. 1943.
	do.	32968	R	11.0	6	.038	.3156	.3260	
	do.	48354	R	11.0	6	.040	.3160	---	
	do.	67900	R	11.0	6	.044	.3166	.3260	Dated Mar. 1943.
	do.	70826	R	11.0	6	.039	.3157	.3269	Dated Apr. 1943.
	do.	71391	R	11.1	6	.048	.3159	.3279	
	do.	94795	R	11.1	6	.041	.3162	---	
	do.	95751	R	11.0	6	.042	.3161	.3261	Dated Oct. 1943.
	Mod. 94 (1934)	8384	R	10.9	6	.038	.3164	.3284	
	do.	10338	R	11.1	6	.038	.3162	.3276	Rifling worn.
	do.	18554	R	11.0	6	.032	.3152	---	
	do.	58825	R	11.0	6	.041	.3161	.3295	
	do.	65020	R	10.9	6	.043	.3157	.3281	
	do.	66186	R	11.15	6	.040	.3159	.3275	
	do.	68274	R	11.4	6	.043	.3160	.3280	
Waffenfabrik Steyr, Vienna, Austria	Roth-Steyr	34047	R	9.9	4	.101	.3138	.3305	See also Fegyvergyar.
	do.	49670	R	9.9	4	.102	.3132	.3302	
	do.	51403	R	9.9	4	.100	.3143	.3305	Army markings: 30 FK 268.

Caliber: 7.92 mm.

Caliber and Manufacturer	Model (or Name)	Serial No.	Dir'n of Twist	Inches for 1 turn	No. of Lands	Land Width (inches)	Bore Diameter (inches)	Groove Diameter* (inches)	Remarks
Erma P. Geipel, G.m.b.H., Waffenfabrik, Erfurt, Germany	M.G.—42	None	R	9.5	4	.061	.3114	.3244	German light machine gun.

Caliber: .38 and .380

Caliber and Manufacturer	Model (or Name)	Serial No.	Dir'n of Twist	Inches for 1 turn	No. of Lands	Land Width (inches)	Bore Diameter (inches)	Groove Diameter* (inches)	Remarks
Colt's Pt. F.A. Mfg. Co., Hartford, Conn.	1900 Type	98	L	14.7	6	.028	.3490	.3557	Comm. type purch. by Ord. Dept. Gov't. accept. mks. (J.T.T.)
	Navy Contract— 1902	1002	L	17.2	6	.029	.3487	.3549	Marked: U.S.N. 2 on slide. Only 200 made for trial.
	Army Contract 1900	1700	L	17.4	6	.033	.3489	.3577	Late 1900. Ord. Insp. Mark R.A.C.
	Military Mod. 38	15664	L	17.3	6	.032	.3489	.3575	Prob. 1902. Ord. Insp. Marks J.T.T. and R.A.C.
	Pocket Mod. 1903	19739	L	15.6	6	.033	.3499	.3579	Early issue.
	Type of 1902	37125	L	15.9	6	.052	.3488	.3550	1902 Comm. type; 1908 type spur hammer.
	Military Mod. 1902	31561	L	16.5	6	.045	.3493	.3547	
	Pocket Mod. 1903	22241	L	16.5	6	.040	.3497	.3569	
	do.	35723	L	16.0	6	.057	.3487	.3555	
	do.	46728	L	16.2	6	.056	.3487	.3581	
	do.	66179	L	16.5	6	.057	.3487	.3545	
	do.	134567	L	15.8	6	.054	.3480	.3556	
	do.	137783	L	16.1	6	.057	.3476	.3572	
	.380 Hammerless	26560	L	16.6	6	.060	.3500	.3592	
	do.	29069	L	16.8	6	.064	.3486	.3574	
	do.	56605	L	16.3	6	.054	.3486	.3567	
	do.	57028	L	15.9	6	.059	.3500	.3566	
	do.	58644	L	16.4	6	.059	.3485	.3535	
	do.	74527	L	16.2	6	.058	.3492	.3568	
	do.	94783	L	16.9	6	.057	.3486	.3554	
	do.	89123	L	16.5	6	.052	.3482	.3551	
	Super 38	1704	L	16.0	6	.053	.3484	.3560	
	do.	10316	L	16.2	6	.054	.3480	.3566	
	do.	19757	L	16.0	6	.054	.3486	.3566	
	do	15477-W	L	15.9	6	.056	.3488	.3564	Commander Model.
	do.	50121	L	15.9	6	.054	.3489	.3585	
	do.	57256	L	16.1	6	.056	.3490	.3590	
	do.	33536LW	L	16.0	6	.055	.3482	.3564	Commander Model.
High Standard Corp., Hamden, Conn.	Mod. G-380	2084	R	15.2	6	.050	.3434	.3524	
Remington—U.M.C. Ilion, N.Y.	P.A.—M51	PA-9800	R	16.3	7	.046	.3490	.3544	
	do.	PA-17131	R	16.1	7	.038	.3485	.3526	

Caliber and Manufacturer	Model (or Name)	Serial No.	Dir'n of Twist	Inches for 1 turn	No. of Lands	Land Width (inches)	Bore Diameter (inches)	Groove Diameter* (inches)	Remarks
Remington—U. M. C.	P. A.—M51	PA-20356	R	16.0	7	.046	.3487	.3533	
	do.	PA-26905	R	16.5	7	.038	.3477	.3529	
Savage Arms Co., Utica, N. Y.	Mod. 1913	B-2163	R	12.0	6	.046	.3491	.3557	
	do.	B-13470	R	12.0	6	.043	.3554	.3737	Unusual bore diam.
	Mod. 1917	B-21950	R	16.2	6	.059	.3483	.3549	Change in twist.
	do.	B-27860	R	16.1	6	.055	.3488	.3565	
Caliber: 9 mm.									
Astra-Unceta y Cia., Guernica, Spain	Condor (Mod. 800)	8-22144	R	9.6	6	.080	.3506	.3580	
Pietro Beretta, Gardone V. T. (Brescia), Italy	1915 Type	5096	R	10.4	6	.049	.3509	.3607	
	1923 Type	623002	R	10.0	6	.050	.3496	.3584	1915 Mod. improved in 1919 and 1923.
	Mod. 1934	535012	R	9.9	6	.051	.3487	.3593	Dated 1936.
	do.	595602	R	9.9	6	.049	.3490	.3586	Dated 1937.
	do.	640800	R	9.9	6	.046	.3492	.3584	Dated 1937.
	do.	641640	R	9.9	6	.052	.3497	.3580	Dated 1937.
	do.	720734	R	10.0	6	.045	.3486	.3580	Dated 1938.
	do.	821456	R	9.8	6	.050	.3491	.3591	Dated 1940.
	do.	891842	R	9.95	6	.051	.3490	.3600	Dated 1941.
	do.	930630	R	9.95	6	.045	.3490	.3602	Dated 1941.
	do.	20830	R	10.2	6	.064	.3491	.3560	Has Rumanian markings; 1941.
	do.	02147	R	10.4	6	.053	.3489	.3578	Probably special order; 1941.
	do.	08991	R	9.9	6	.052	.3500	.3592	Has Rumanian markings; 1941.
	do.	953386	R	9.8	6	.052	.3488	.3570	Dated 1942.
	do.	979567	R	9.8	6	.053	.3489	.3613	Dated 1942.
	do.	F-63599	R	9.8	6	.050	.3494	.3591	Probably special order. Dated 1942.
	do.	3662AA	R	9.9	6	.045	.3492	.3600	Gun dated 1943.
	do.	4996BB	R	9.85	6	.049	.3489	.3583	No. 9667 on bbl.; dated 1944.
	M. P.—38-42	4575	R	9.8	6	.049	.3477	.3581	Made under German supervision.
	do.	7316	R	9.9	6	.049	.3475	.3568	do.
	Mod. 1951	03010	R	10.0	6	.051	.3492	.3568	Dated 1957.
Vincenzo Bernardelli, Gardone V. T. (Brescia), Italy	Bernardelli (Exptl. Mod.)	21	R	9.8	6	.046	.3454	.3602	For 9 mm. Long ctge. Only a few made.
	do.	024	R	17.6	6	.058	.3450	.3619	do.
	Bernardelli	47	R	9.8	6	.050	.3456	.3590	Mkd. "Lungo" E Parabellum
Ceska Zbrojovka, Brno, Prague, and Stakonice, Czechoslovakia	Mod. 1922	17590	R	9.9	6	.057	.3466	.3560	Inscr. on slide: 9 mm. N Cs. St. Zbrojovka, A. S., Praze. Designed by Nickl. Made 1930 at Czech State Arsenal.
	Mod. 1924	21086	R	10.0	6	.051	.3450	.3558	1926 accept. mark.
	do.	36537	R	9.9	6	.051	.3450	.3574	do.
	do.	46316	R	9.9	6	.050	.3445	.3567	1927 accept. mark.
	do.	51860	R	9.8	6	.062	.3443	.3560	do
	do.	57399	R	10.1	6	.054	.3457	.3563	do.
	do.	80092	R	9.9	6	.047	.3453	.3587	1928 accept. mark.
	do.	83266	R	9.9	6	.062	.3464	.3554	
	do.	---	R	9.9	6	.057	.3446	.3536	Inscr. on top of slide: Česka Zbrojovka A. S. Praze 1903. Has 1930 accept. mk.
	do.	128382	R	10.0	6	.059	.3450	.3549	1937 accept. mark.
	do.	134758	R	10.0	6	.052	.3464	.3530	do.
	do.	163641	R	10.45	6	.055	.3465	.3573	Inscr. on top of slide: Česka Zbrojovka, A. S. Praze.
	do.	Removed	R	9.9	6	.053	.3453	.3575	No marking. Ca. 1938.
	Mod. 1938	262337	R	9.9	6	.064	.3501	.3581	Inscr. on 1938 Mods.: Česka Zbrojovka A. K. C., Spol V, Praze.
	do.	268181	R	10.0	6	.056	.3515	.3613	
	do.	269206	R	9.8	6	.054	.3510	.3604	1939 accept. mark.
	do.	273013	R	9.8	6	.062	.3506	.3594	do.
	do.	276466	R	10.0	6	.058	.3500	.3584	do.
	do.	278907	R	10.0	6	.060	.3506	.3590	do.
	do.	284178	R	9.8	6	.058	.3500	.3590	do.
	do.	286976	R	9.9	6	.056	.3506	.3566	

Caliber and Manufacturer	Model (or Name)	Serial No.	Dir'n of Twist	Inches for 1 turn	No. of Lands	Land Width (inches)	Bore Diameter (inches)	Groove Diameter* (inches)	Remarks
Česka Zbrojovka	Mod. 1938	287282	R	9.8	6	.052	.3505	.3589	
Deutsche Waffen u.	Luger—M 1904/06	6254	R	9.85	6	.079	.3482	.3580	Navy model.
Munitionsfab.,	Luger 1908	246	R	9.9	6	.083	.3480	.3578	1917 on bbl. 7 7/8" bbl.
Berlin, Germany	do.	2777	R	9.9	6	.087	.3484	---	do.
	do.	3854	R	9.9	6	.077	.3487	.3585	Dated 1914.
	do.	6878	R	10.0	6	.085	.3492	.3552	
	do.	8608-a	R	9.6	6	.073	.3483	.3585	
	do.	5617-c	R	9.8	6	.084	.3482	.3578	
	do.	7698-d	R	10.0	6	.083	.3480	.3584	
	do.	6933-h	R	9.85	6	.079	.3479	.3591	Dated 1916.
	do.	8629-h	R	9.9	6	.080	.3484	.3578	Luger Lang Mod.; 7 7/8" bbl.; Dated 1917.
	do.	8756-l	R	9.8	6	.079	.3482	.3588	Dated 1915.
For other Lugers see Berne; Erfurt; Krieghoff; and Mauser.									
Deutsche Werke, A.K.T., Erfurt, Germany	Ortgies	28417	R	9.8	6	.040	.3522	.3605	Rifling in fair condition
Bonifacio Echeverria, Eibar, Spain	Star 1919 Type	66012	R	10.3	6	.036	.3505	.3601	Discontinued in 1921.
	Star Mod. D	D-209217	R	9.6	6	.043	.3485	.3537	
	Star Type A	24000	R	9.15	6	.060	.3492	.3562	Pre. Mod. A. Similar to U.S. 45, but no grip safety.
	Star Mod. MD	312418	R	12.2	6	.063	.3491	.3580	Like U.S. M1911, but no grip safety. Takes long ctge.
	Star Super Mod. A	314434	R	12.65	6	.070	.3490	.3585	
	Star Mod. S	345506	R	12.1	6	.065	.3482	.3572	Uses short ctge (.380).
	do.	425693	R	12.6	6	.065	.3482	.3572	do.
	do.	S-335361	R	12.0	6	.065	.3482	.3578	
Name changed to Star—A.S. (Star—Sociedad Anonima)	Star Mod. B	218465	R	10.7	6	.059	.3492	.3549	Like U.S. M1911, but no grip safety. 9 mm. Par.
	do.	220118	R	10.8	6	.060	.3488	.3550	do.
	Star—Super B	484427	R	12.55	6	.059	.3490	.3560	Parabellum.
	Star—Mod. DK	526744	R	12.3	6	.057	.3487	.3576	
Erfurt Arsenal, Erfurt, Germany	Luger—1908	639	R	9.8	6	.073	.3485	.3534	
	do.	3883	R	10.0	6	.072	.3494	.3589	Bbl. dated 1918 and 1920.
	do.	5739	R	9.8	6	.079	.3489	.3593	Dated 1916.
	do.	59-K	R	9.9	6	.080	.3483	.3583	Dated 1917.
(For other Lugers see Berne; D.W.M.; Krieghoff; and Mauser)									
Esperanza y Unceta, Guernica, Spain	Campo Giro M1913	60	R	10.2	6	.052	.3495	.3609	On bbl. 1904-1913. On frame Mod. 1913. Uses Bergmann-Bayard ctge.
	Campo Giro Mod. 1913-16	5496	R	9.6	6	.062	.3487	.3601	
	do.	11337	R	9.5	6	.065	.3495	.3575	
Fab. Nat'l. D'Armes de Guerre, Herstal, Belgium	Browning Long Model 1903	3531	R	16.0	6	.038	.3537	.3635	
	do.	9219	R	17.9	6	.031	.3525	.3631	Unusual twist.
	Browning Mod. 1910	285495	R	9.5	6	.030	.3519	.3597	Rifling worn.
	Browning Mod. 1922	11954	R	9.5	6	.031	.3514	.3614	Has Jugoslav markings.
	do.	15976	R	9.5	6	.036	.3503	.3581	
	do.	56182	R	9.65	6	.032	.3512	.3620	
	do.	60040	R	9.7	6	.029	.3501	.3598	
	do.	227048	R	9.5	6	.037	.3520	.3618	
	Browning H.P.	29179	R	9.9	6	.076	.3481	.3583	
	do.	38096	R	9.8	6	.075	.3481	.3585	
	do.	61915	R	9.9	6	.075	.3479	.3585	
	do.	90691	R	9.9	6	.083	.3488	.3596	
	do.	91952	R	9.85	6	.084	.3491	.3584	
	do.	42255-a	R	9.8	6	.074	.3503	.3595	German accept. marks. Made under German supervision.
	do.	60401-a	R	9.8	6	.082	.3497	.3587	German accept. marks.
	do.	11084-b	R	9.85	6	.077	.3482	.3592	do.
	do.	11564-b	R	9.8	6	.085	.3502	.3604	do.
	do.	15063-b	R	9.7	6	.078	.3480	.3596	do.

Caliber and Manufacturer	Model (or Name)	Serial No.	Dir'n of Twist	Inches for 1 turn	No. of Lands	Land Width (inches)	Bore Diameter (inches)	Groove Diameter* (inches)	Remarks
Fab. Nat'l. D'Armes de Guerre	Browning H.P.	16577-b	R	9.9	6	.090	.3495	.3585	German accept. marks.
	do.	36030-b	R	9.9	6	.080	.3483	.3591	do.
Fegyvergyar, Budapest, Hungary	Frommer Baby	Removed	R	9.55	4	.130	.3467	.3596	Marked "7.65 mm. Frommer Baby," but has 9 mm. bbl.
	Frommer Stop	112294	R	10.15	4	.127	.3454	.3609	
	Fegyvergyar M29	23742	R	9.8	4	.126	.3445	.3587	
	do.	23836	R	9.8	4	.124	.3444	.3576	
	Fegyvergyar M37	59733	R	10.0	4	.117	.3444	.3604	
	do.	141404	R	9.9	4	.122	.3453	.3578	
	do.	234495	R	9.8	4	.116	.3435	.3581	
Mre. Francaise D'Armes et Cycles de St. Etienne, St. Etienne, France	Le Francais "Army Model"	8863	R	14.6	6	.058	.3550	.3620	Marked "Type Armee."
Gabilondo y Cia., Elgoibar, Spain	Llama Mod. XI(Par)	114142	R	12.1	6	.062	.3475	.3549	Marked "Llama Especial."
	Llama Mod. III-A	137243	R	12.0	6	.063	.3487	---	do.
	do.	146372	R	11.9	6	.053	.3481	.3555	do.
	do.	151588	R	12.0	6	.065	.3475	.3523	De Luxe Mod. (Engraved).
	Tauler—Mark P	13146	R	12.35	6	.057	.3480	.3568	Marked: Mod. Military and Police; Mfr. disc. 1933.
Societa Siderurgica Glisenti, Turin, Italy	Glisenti Mod. 1910	1158-B	R	9.9	6	.077	.3483	.3587	
	do.	F-1644	R	10.0	6	.085	.3495	.3590	
	do.	M-946	R	9.8	6	.080	.3493	.3595	
	do.	0-409	R	9.9	6	.083	.3484	.3584	
Guide Lamp Division, Gen. Motors Corp., Anderson, Ind.	U.S. M3	C-153424	R	10.0	4	.112	.3492	.3596	U.S. Submachine gun 9 mm. Par., also in .45 cal.
C.G. Haenel Waffen u. Fahrrad-Fabrik, Suhl, Germany	M.P.—40	980-a	R	9.9	6	.081	.3480	.3580	German machine pistol.
Haerens Rustkammer (Royal Arsenal Factory), Copenhagen, Denmark	Bayard Mod. 1920/21	5808	L	10.0	6	.036	.3471	.3581	Marked: Haerens Rustkammer.
	do.	4858	L	9.9	6	.038	.3471	.3591	Marked: Haerens Tøjhus.
Husqvarna Vapenfabriks, A.B., Husqvarna, Sweden	Lahti—M40	B-8436	R	9.5	6	.055	.3456	.3540	Parabellum ctge.
	do.	D-13054	R	9.5	6	.054	.3454	.3554	do.
	do.	H-740	R	9.4	6	.053	.3458	.3553	do.
	Browning M-07	100723	R	15.8	6	.027	.3517	.3613	Mfr. stopped 1942.
John Inglis Co., Ltd., Toronto, Canada	Browning—Mk. I	3T8681	R	10.0	6	.070	.3479	.3577	World War II production.
Kirikkale Tüfek Fabrikular, Kirikkale, Turkey	Kirikkale	10028	R	9.6	6	.062	.3487	.3589	Dated 1948. Same as Walther Mod. PP.
	"	14125	R	9.8	6	.048	.3491	.3635	Dated 1949. Same as Walther Mod. PP.
Heinrich Krieghoff Waffenfabrik, Suhl, Germany	Luger—1908	1740	R	9.8	6	.076	.3479	.3587	Has Krieghoff trade mark.
Mre. D'Armes Automatiques Bayonne, Bayonne, France	M.A.B.—Mod. R	1020	R	12.3	6	.041	.3480	.3564	Sold in U.S. by W.A.C.
Mre. de Machines du Haut Rhin, Mulhouse-Bourtzwiller, France	Walther Mod. PP	10188-A	R	10.2	6	.071	.3517	.3599	Made under Walther license.
Fritz Mann, Suhl, Germany	Mann	42012	R	11.8	4	.086	.3500	.3622	
Waffenfabrik Mauser, Oberndorf, a/N., Germany	Mil. Pistol	43273	R	9.9	6	.076	.3486	.3582	Fig. 9 on grips, 9 mm. Par.
	do.	73432	R	9.9	6	.080	.3490	.3582	do.
	do.	78598	R	9.9	6	.077	.3485	.3582	do.
	do.	84405	R	13.8	4	.131	.3496	.3606	Unusual rifling twist, 10 ctge., ca. 1908.
	do.	136702	R	9.8	6	.073	.3486	.3590	Weimar Republic Police Type. From surplus parts. Non-std., 1920.
	do.	139173	R	9.9	6	.081	.3499	.3595	
	Luger—1908	3964	R	9.9	6	.091	.3483	.3583	Marked byf and 42.
	do.	5148	R	9.8	6	.081	.3485	---	Marked 42.
	do.	5252	R	9.9	6	.074	.3479	.3526	Marked S/42. Dated 1936.

Caliber and Manufacturer	Model (or Name)	Serial No.	Dir'n of Twist	Inches for 1 turn	No. of Lands	Land Width (inches)	Bore Diameter (inches)	Groove Diameter* (inches)	Remarks
Waffenfabrik Mauser	Luger—1908	8621	R	9.8	6	.074	.3477	.3522	Marked S/42. Dated 1936.
	do.	2320	R	9.8	6	.076	.3480	.3518	Marked S/42. Dated 1938.
	do.	3109	R	9.9	6	.081	.3483	.3583	Marked 42. Dated 1939.
	do.	5988	R	10.0	6	.094	.3481	.3541	Marked S/42.
	do.	9915(?)	R	9.8	6	.080	.3483	---	Marked S/42. Dated 1939.
	do.	7591a	R	9.9	6	.082	.3483	.3540	Marked S/42.
	do.	2896h	R	10.0	6	.089	.3476	.3584	
	do.	6350i	R	9.85	6	.082	.3475	.3580	
	do.	6438t	R	9.85	6	.084	.3484	.3588	D.W.M. parts assembled by Mauser.
	do.	6481t	R	9.90	6	.084	.3477	.3587	do.
	do.	5800u	R	9.85	6	.083	.3532	.3580	Marked 42. Dated 1939.
	do.	2811y	R	9.8	6	.082	.3482	.3574	Marked S/42. Dated 1942.
	do.	3540y	R	9.8	6	.082	.3483	.3563	Marked S/42. Dated 1937.
	do.	7445y	R	9.9	6	.080	.3477	.3581	Marked S/42. Dated 1939.
	Mod. P-38	9638	R	9.9	6	.090	.3476	.3586	Marked byf 42. No suffix.
	do.	3272d	R	9.8	6	.084	.3477	.3577	Marked byf 44.
	do.	4473d	R	9.8	6	.083	.3480	.3532	Marked byf 43.
	do.	5136d	R	9.8	6	.078	.3477	.3579	Marked byf 43.
	do.	4750g	R	9.8	6	.080	.3482	.3590	Marked byf 44.
	do.	1021v	R	9.8	6	.085	.3481	.3581	do.
	do.	6010(?)	R	9.8	6	.083	.3477	.3585	do.
	do.	3382w	R	9.9	6	.083	.3476	.3578	do.
	do.	518f	R	9.8	6	.081	.3480	.3517	Marked: $\frac{SVW}{45}$ (Mauser 1945).
Metallurgica Bresciana, Brescia, Italy	Brixia	909	R	10.0	6	.090	.3512	.3626	
	"	D-653	R	9.9	6	.078	.3483	.3573	
José Cruz Mugica (dealer), Eibar, Spain	"Mugica" Mod. 120	114896	R	11.95	6	.063	.3473	.3581	Made by Gabilondo for Mugica.
Anc. Etablissements Pieper, Herstal, Belgium	Bayard M.P. M1908	14242	L	10.15	6	.043	.3475	.3579	Also known as Bayard-Bergmann.
	do.	15996	L	10.25	4	.047	.3486	.3580	do.
	Bayard Pocket Mod.	70440	L	9.9	6	.051	.3482	.3616	1908 Type.
	do.	216923	L	10.1	6	.051	.3502	.3630	do.
Fabryka Bronn Radom, Radom, Poland	Radom Vis 35	B-0250	R	9.9	6	.081	.3488	---	
	do.	D-1967	R	9.8	6	.084	.3479	.3591	
	do.	D-5478	R	9.8	6	.085	.3481	.3585	
	do.	E-5536	R	9.9	6	.080	.3477	.3583	
	do.	F-2763	R	9.8	6	.094	.3480	.3496	
	do.	F-5575	R	9.9	6	.087	.3483	.3609	
	do.	G-5489	R	10.0	6	.085	.3472	.3587	
	do.	L-7004	R	9.9	6	.081	.3486	.3596	
	do.	P-8177	R	9.9	6	.085	.3479	.3583	
	do.	U-7180	R	9.9	6	.080	.3484	.3590	
	do.	W-1331	R	9.9	6	.082	.3480	---	
Republic Espanola	"R.E." 9 mm. Largo	5262	R	9.95	6	.052	.3472	.3560	Copy of Astra 400, made by Spanish Repub. Army at Valencia, later at Tarassa.
Schmeisser Werke, Suhl, Germany	M.P.—40	1286	R	9.9	6	.081	.3485	.3583	Machine pistol. 9 mm. Par. ctge.
	do.	3109-e	R	9.9	6	.088	.3482	.3588	do.
Smith and Wesson, Springfield, Mass.	S & W Pocket Mod.	1321	R	10.1	6	.065	.3470	.3550	9 mm. Par. ctge. Introd. 1955.
	do.	2488	R	10.1	6	.061	.3466	.3548	do.
Soc. Industrie Suisse, Neuhausen, Switzerland	SIG (S.P. 47/48)	P-50114	R	9.85	6	.077	.3486	.3570	Interchangeable bbls. and slides. .22 cal., 7.65 mm., and 9 mm. (Par.).
	do.	P-53477	R	9.8	6	.070	.3489	.3581	Target model.
Spreewerk, G.m.b.H. Metallwaren Fab., Berlin-Spandau, Germany	Mod. P-38	5850a	R	9.8	6	.076	.3488	.3617	
	do.	526d	R	9.9	6	.081	.3486	.3594	
	do.	4296h	R	9.7	6	.078	.3484	.3596	
	do.	8990-1	R	9.9	6	.084	.3484	.3600	
	do.	578s	R	9.9	6	.085	.3489	---	
	do.	3527s	R	9.8	6	.084	.3489	.3595	
	do.	1407u	R	9.9	6	.087	.3482	.3600	
	do.	286v	R	9.9	6	.082	.3482	.3590	
	do.	5207w	R	9.9	6	.087	.3482	.3571	
Steyr-Daimler-Puch A.G., Steyr, Austria	M-P 40	894a	R	9.9	6	.082	.3494	.3590	Machine pistol. Dated 1941.

Caliber and Manufacturer	Model (or Name)	Serial No.	Dir'n of Twist	Inches for 1 turn	No. of Lands	Land Width (inches)	Bore Diameter (inches)	Groove Diameter* (inches)	Remarks
Osterreichische	Repetier Pist.	310	R	8.0	4	.154	.3487	.3621	Mod. 1911, or Steyr Hahn.
Waffenfabrik	M.12 Selbstlade Pistole—Steyr	4070j	R	7.9	4	.124	.3483	.3600	M.1912. Dated 1912.
Steyr,	do.	6876d	R	7.9	4	.128	.3494	.3620	M.1912. Dated 1914.
Vienna, Austria	do.	4203f	R	7.9	4	.126	.3488	.3626	do.
	do.	3257j	R	7.9	4	.131	.3495	.3605	M.1912. Dated 1915.
	do.	707u	R	7.9	4	.134	.3499	.3603	M.1912. Dated 1917.
	do.	8529v	R	7.9	4	.120	.3498	.3620	do.
	do.	562r	R	7.8	4	.131	.3496	.3610	do.
	do.	2655x	R	7.9	4	.128	.3518	.3650	M.1912. Dated 1918.
	do.	1348g	R	7.9	4	.130	.3502	.3614	do.
Tikkakoski o/y, Sakara, Finland	Suomi M.G.	9207	R	9.5	6	.058	.3444	.3561	Suomi Submachine gun. 9 mm. Par.
Unceta y Cia., Guernica, Spain	Astra M 300	562882	R	9.5	6	.059	.3505	.3605	Uses Brng. Short (.380) ctge.
(See also Astra-	do.	574729	R	9.5	6	.056	.3504	.3598	
Unceta y Cia.)	do.	575971	R	9.4	6	.052	.3504	.3600	
	do.	590845	R	9.4	6	.051	.3504	.3594	
	Astra M 400	1163	R	9.4	6	.044	.3479	.3593	Also known as Mod. 1921. Some used 9 mm. Brng. Long; some used Bayard ctge.
	do.	7659	R	9.55	6	.047	.3499	.3609	9 mm. Long
	do.	23360	R	9.55	6	.061	.3498	.3594	9 mm. Bayard ctge. Dated 1924.
	do.	97749	R	9.4	6	.048	.3479	.3583	9 mm. Long.
	do.	98631	R	9.4	6	.049	.3488	.3598	do.
	Astra M 600	2522	R	9.4	6	.055	.3478	.3591	Uses 9 mm. Par. ctge.
	do.	3054	R	9.4	6	.051	.3490	.3614	do.
Valtion Kivääri	Lahti (L-35)	2308	R	9.45	6	.060	.3464	.3544	Designed by A.J. Lahti.
Tehdas (State	do.	3356	R	9.55	6	.072	.3472	.3550	Adopted Finland 1935.
Rifle Factory), Jyväskyla, Finland	do.	9100	R	9.45	6	.063	.3462	.3550	Uses 9 mm. Par. ctge.
Voino Tekhnichki Zavod, Yugoslavia	Yovanovitch Mod. 1913	3344	R	9.4	6	.045	.3508	.3590	Mkd: L. Yovanovitch Pat. Mod. 1931
Carl Walther Waffenfabrik, Zella-Mehlis	Mod. 6	710	R	9.9	4	.090	.3476	.3609	Mod. of 1915. Mkd: Carl Walther Waffenfabrik, Zella St. Blasii.
(Thür), Germany	Mod. PP	154880-P	R	9.8	6	.046	.3489	.3571	
	do.	159745-P	R	9.5	6	.052	.3493	.3577	
	do.	952229-P	R	9.35	6	.058	.3478	.3562	
	Mod. P-38	8668f	R	9.8	6	.076	.3481	.3581	Dated 1941.
	do.	466	R	9.8	6	.078	.3486	.3604	Dated 1942.
	do.	3764	R	9.8	6	.076	.3483	.3594	do.
	do.	1823a	R	9.9	6	.082	.3480	---	do.
	do.	9552b	R	9.85	6	.086	.3482	.3594	do.
	do.	7641h	R	9.9	6	.087	.3484	.3598	do.
	do.	4810f	R	9.85	6	.079	.3480	.3576	Dated 1943.
	do.	1009g	R	9.9	6	.077	.3478	---	do.
	do.	8768-1	R	9.9	6	.083	.3480	.3586	do.
	do.	1443m	R	9.9	6	.084	.3474	.3582	do.
	do.	3240n	R	9.9	6	.085	.3480	---	do.
	do.	3240n	R	9.9	6	.081	.3586	.3730	Same no. and date as above, but not same gun.
	do.	1167d	R	9.8	6	.083	.3484	---	Dated 1944.
	do.	4926f	R	9.9	6	.082	.3479	.3592	do.
	do.	5063f	R	9.9	6	.079	.3480	.3585	do.
	do.	5013	R	9.85	6	.081	.3480	.3590	Dated 1945.
	do.	3822g	R	9.9	6	.086	.3487	---	Date not noted.
	do.	6762	R	9.9	6	.081	.3478	---	do.
	do.	92731	R	9.9	6	.082	.3480	.3586	do.
	Armee Mod.	034	R	9.9	6	.075	.3487	.3575	Presentation pieces. Hammerless.
	do.	050	R	9.9	6	.075	.3473	.3577	do.
	Mod. Heeres Pistole	23013	R	9.9	6	.075	.3480	.3580	
	Prototype of M. P-38	None	R	9.9	6	.075	.3474	.3566	Only one specimen made.
Manufacturer unknown (Spanish)	Handy—M 1917	95	R	15.2	6	.060	.3507	.3567	
	do.	139	R	15.3	6	.057	.3518	.3586	

Caliber and Manufacturer	Model (or Name)	Serial No.	Dir'n of Twist	Inches for 1 turn	No. of Lands	Land Width (inches)	Bore Diameter (inches)	Groove Diameter* (inches)	Remarks
Caliber: .45									
Chinese Gov't. Arsenal Shansei, China	Mauser M. P. Type	5343	R	11.0	6	.070	.4448	.4578	Copy Mauser M. P. Marked 1st Mod., 18 Year Pattern. .45 ACP Made 1930.
Colt's Pt. F. A. Mfg. Co., Hartford, Conn.	"Contract 1907"	3	L	18.85	6	.079	.4450	.4542	U.S. Gov't. Contract 1907. First 100 Type.
	Mil. Mod. 1905	598	L	15.5	6	.035	.4447	.4535	
	do.	5063	L	18.9	6	.054	.4445	.4543	1908 Variation.
	Mod. 1909	12	L	15.45	6	.066	.4452	.4524	Only 15 made.
	U. S.—Mod. 1911	89878	L	15.65	6	.096	.4445	.4540	
	do.	C-113697	L	15.8	6	.068	.4441	.4529	
	do.	C-126228	L	16.3	6	.064	.4447	.4500	
	do.	137061	L	16.0	6	.067	.4445	.4533	
	do.	149564	L	15.9	6	.069	.4436	.4488	
	do.	166600	L	15.6	6	.074	.4445	.4514	
	do.	171927	L	16.6	6	.083	.4451	.4541	
	do.	290343	L	16.0	6	.075	.4442	.4528	
	do.	304318	L	16.3	6	.081	.4451	.4541	
	do.	322289	L	16.2	6	.076	.4461	.4525	
	do.	481603	L	16.4	6	.069	.4445	.4519	
	do.	433860	L	16.1	6	.069	.4435	.4517	
	do.	452877	L	16.6	6	.082	.4443	.4544	
	do.	563271	L	16.2	6	.069	.4435	---	
	U. S. Mod. 1911A1	278079	L	16.0	6	.068	.4436	.4516	
	National Match	1971-NM	L	16.0	6	.070	.4422	.4516	
	do.	C164055	L	16.1	6	.067	.4430	.4526	
	Commander	3953-LW	L	16.0	6	.070	.4436	.4510	
	"	20770-LW	L	16.0	6	.070	.4438	.4517	
	National Match	None	L	16.0	6	.070	.4429	.4523	Un-numbered pre-production pilot model. Tool room sample.
Colt's Pt. F. A. Mfg. Co. (For Auto-Ordnance Corp., N.Y.)	Thompson M 1928	None	R	16.0	6	.074	.4449	.4531	Thompson submachine gun. Barrels only, hence no serial numbers.
	do	None	R	16.1	6	.074	.4438	.4530	
	do.	None	R	16.5	6	.074	.4433	.4529	
Bonifacio Echeverria, Eibar, Spain	Star—Mod. MD	3956	R	11.65	6	.070	.4440	.4510	Inscr.: Guardia Nacionale de Nicaragua
Gabilondo y Cia., Elgoibar, Spain	Llama Mod. IX-A	152809	R	14.5	6	.077	.4447	.4539	Marked: Llama Especial
	Ruby	437	L	10.4	6	.090	.4416	.4490	Inscription: G.C.— Elgoibar 1924. No. on bbl. is 372
	"	550	L	10.5	6	.085	.4420	.4488	
Hispano Argentina Fabrica de Auto-moviles Sociedad Anonima, Buenos Aires, Argentina	Hafdasa	12956	L	16.0	6	.072	.4440	.4510	Like U.S. M1911, but no grip safety.
	"	B-4842	L	16.15	6	.071	.4447	.4513	do.
Ithaca Gun Co., Inc., Ithaca, N.Y.	U. S. Mod. 1911A1	1247367	L	16.75	6	.067	.4448	.4532	
Kongsberg Vapen-fabrik, Kongsberg, Norway	Mod. 1914	2589	L	16.1	6	.068	.4427	.4519	Norwegian Colt. Dated 1922.
	do.	3806	L	15.3	6	.070	.4436	.4538	Norwegian Colt. Dated 1923.
Mexican Gov't. Arsenal, Mexico City, Mexico	Obregon	A-90	L	16.35	6	.062	.4417	.4499	Marked 11.43 mm. cal.
Reising Arms Co., New York, N.Y.	Reising M55	None	R	16.2	6	.068	.4416	.4503	Submachine gun.
Remington Arms U.M.C. Co., Inc., Ilion, N.Y.	U. S. Mod. 1911	6387	L	16.0	6	.100	.4453	.4525	
Remington Rand, Syracuse, N.Y.	U. S. Mod. 1911A1	1798076	L	16.3	6	.076	.4456	.4518	
Savage Arms Co., Utica, N.Y.	Type 1906	196	R	16.0	6	.040	.4458	.4524	Made for U. S. 1907 Army Trials.
Union Switch and Signal Co., Swissvale, Pa.	U. S. Mod. 1911A1	998306	L	16.0	6	.071	.4432	.4502	
Caliber: 11.35 mm.									
Dansk Rekyriffel Syndikat, Copen-hagen, Denmark	Schouboe Mod. 1907	300	R	18.6	6	.115	.4398	.4530	Made for 1907 U. S. Army Trials.

Caliber and Manufacturer	Model (or Name)	Serial No.	Dir'n of Twist	Inches for 1 turn	No. of Lands	Land Width (inches)	Bore Diameter (inches)	Groove Diameter* (inches)	Remarks
Caliber: .455									
Colt's Pt. F.A. Mfg. Corp., Hartford, Conn.	M1911 R.A.F.	W-106434	L	16.2	6	.076	.4509	.4573	Made for R.A.F.
P. Webley and Son, Birmingham, Eng.	Webley-Fosbery	320	R	20.1	7	.040	.4399	.4511	Automatic revolver.
Webley and Scott, Ltd., Birmingham England	Mark I	60	R	10.0	6	.038	.4472	.4576	Dated 1913.
	do.	368	R	10.2	6	.058	.4470	.4576	do.
	do.	138882	R	10.0	6	.045	.4474	.4600	Not dated.

TABLE 17
Rifling measurements on revolvers and nonautomatic pistols

Caliber and Manufacturer	Model (or Name)	Serial No.	Dir'n of Twist	Inches for 1 turn	No. of Lands	Land Width (inches)	Bore Diameter (inches)	Groove Diameter* (inches)	Remarks
Caliber: .22									
American Standard Tool Co., Newark, N.J.	S.A., Rim Fire	23295	R	31.0	3	.141	.2096	---	Revolver.
Vincenzo Bernardelli, Gardone V.T. (Brescia), Italy	Pocket Rev.	1371	R	9.9	6	.050	.2137	.2183	S & W type.
Colt's Pt. F.A. Mfg. Co., Hartford, Conn.	Camp Perry Mod.	2125	L	14.0	6	.036	.2152	.2241	
	Frontier "Scout"	6647-Q	L	14.1	6	.039	.2138	.2218	
Derringer Corp., Germany	Derringer (Upper bbl.)	7377	R	15.6	6	.053	.2160	.2230	Copy of Remington Derringer. Barrels are inserts.
	(Lower bbl.)	"	R	15.7	6	.053	.2178	.2223	
Eig Corporation (Dealer), Miami, Fla.	Eig	16430	R	16.7	8	.037	.2160	.2194	Made in Germany.
Fiala Arms and Equipment Co., New Haven, Conn.	Fiala Mod. 20	2459	R	16.0	4	.103	.2185	.2213	Repeating pistol 7 1/2" bbl.
	(same gun)	"	R	16.0	4	.100	.2183	.2223	Extra bbl. 3".
Great Western Arms Co., Los Angeles, Calif.	"Frontier"	G.W. 8082	R	14.1	6	.050	.2189	.2254	Copy of Colt Frontier Mod.
Harrington and Richardson, Worcester, Mass.	S.S. Pistol	---	R	16.0	6	.028	.2131	.2176	
	Rim Fire Rev.	509066	R	24.00	6	.023	.2120	.2177	
	do.	376935	R	12.0	5	.059	.2120	.2186	
	Mod. 1906	98683	R	12.3	5	.067	.2142	---	
	Premier	4994	R	12.0	5	.054	.2117	---	
	"	111220	R	12.0	5	.061	.2117	.2139	
	Trapper	55457	R	12.0	6	.043	.2130	.2208	
	"	122559	R	12.0	5	.059	.2120	.2162	
	"	180404	R	12.0	6	.028	.2124	.2190	
	Hammerless	12782	R	12.05	5	.083	.2143	---	
	Victor	85466	R	12.2	6	.040	.2093	.2189	
	Young America	6-308	R	12.0	5	.062	.2120	---	
	do.	481720	R	12.1	5	.063	.2110	.2216	
	Mod. 922	127125	R	12.0	6	.029	.2133	.2205	
	do.	137390	R	12.15	6	.029	.2120	.2198	
	do.	G-2293	R	16.0	6	.044	.2170	---	
	do.	J-33280	R	16.1	6	.044	.2159	---	
	do.	K-18998	R	16.05	6	.040	.2160	.2247	
	do.	L-53987	R	16.2	6	.045	.2162	---	
	do.	M-4689	R	16.0	6	.043	.2161	.2242	

*Distance from bottom of a groove to the bottom of opposite groove if barrel has an even number of grooves; or the distance from the bottom of a groove to the top of the opposite land if barrel has an odd number of grooves.

Caliber and Manufacturer	Model (or Name)	Serial No.	Dir'n of Twist	Inches for 1 turn	No. of Lands	Land Width (inches)	Bore Diameter (inches)	Groove Diameter* (inches)	Remarks
Harrington and Richardson	Mod. 922	M-31159	R	16.0	6	.043	.2161	.2241	
	do.	M-42375	R	16.05	6	.047	.2169	.2237	
	do.	M-78016	R	15.9	6	.045	.2160	.2246	
	do.	M-82951	R	16.0	6	.048	.2159	.2241	Unused gun.
	do.	N-17344	R	16.0	6	.044	.2160	.2241	do.
	do.	P-3658	R	16.0	6	.045	.2166	.2236	
	do.	P-4919	R	16.0	6	.044	.2160	.2237	
	Mod. 923	K-10093	R	16.0	6	.052	.2166	.2247	
	do.	L-42038	R	16.0	6	.045	.2158	.2246	
	do.	L-65245	R	16.0	6	.051	.2160	.2240	
	do.	L-74311	R	16.1	6	.046	.2161	.2246	
	Sportsman	30021	R	16.2	6	.027	.2135	.2191	
	do.	30024	R	16.3	6	.025	.2135	.2197	
	do.	67959	R	16.0	6	.045	.2123	.2173	
	do.	M-8361	R	16.0	6	.044	.2157	.2249	
	do.	N-7162	R	16.1	6	.042	.2163	.2250	
	do.	S-14799	R	12.0	6	.031	.2134	---	
	22 Special	497655	R	12.0	6	.044	.2120	---	
	do.	500511	R	12.0	6	.042	.2120	.2208	
	do.	512880	R	12.0	6	.044	.2126	.2228	
	do.	622974	R	12.0	6	.028	.2111	.2203	
Hartford Arms and Equip. Co., Hartford, Conn.	Target Pistol	1272	R	14.8	6	.036	.2134	.2188	.22 L.R., Single-shot pistol.
High Standard Mfg. Corp., Hamden, Conn.	Sentinel	18928	R	16.1	6	.053	.2211	.2253	
	"	638055	R	16.0	6	.056	.2197	.2252	
	Higgins Mod. 88	660697	R	14.9	6	.054	.2196	.2252	
	do.	764097	R	15.0	6	.054	.2200	.2258	
	do.	777269	R	14.9	6	.055	.2199	.2249	
	Double Nine	844684	R	15.8	6	.058	.2202	.2240	Introduced 1958.
Hopkins and Allen, Norwich, Conn.	Mod. XL No. 1	587	L	24.5	5	.076	.2075	.2108	
	Mod. XL—D.A.	1762	R	19.2	6	.049	.2190	.2307	
	Tramps Terror	1769	L	24.05	3	.137	.2104	.2150	Rifling worn.
	Range Model	9834	R	18.7	6	.058	.2184	.2250	
	Safety Police	G-4784	R	19.0	6	.055	.2203	.2247	
	do.	H-4274	R	16.7	6	.048	.2117	.2227	Single-shot pistol.
Iver Johnson Arms and Cycle Works, Fitchburg, Mass.	Favorite No. 1	113	R	37.3	5	.064	.2097	.2131	Supposedly made by I.J.
	Target Mod. 1900	98305	R	23.1	5	.057	.2120	---	
	Supershot Sealed 8	8920	R	14.0	5	.066	.2191	.2236	
	do.	11015	R	13.8	5	.067	.2196	---	
	do.	15800	R	14.05	5	.070	.2191	---	
	do.	21059	R	14.2	5	.066	.2188	.2243	
	do.	L-22257	R	14.0	5	.071	.2206	.2244	
	do.	M-54678	R	16.3	5	.072	.2179	.2215	
	do.	N-13909	R	16.1	5	.066	.2182	.2221	
	do.	N-20698	R	16.2	5	.069	.2186	.2216	
	United States Rev.	7331	R	11.4	5	.062	.2182	.2249	"United States Revolver Co." Dealer. Revolvers made by I.J.
	do.	9162	R	11.6	5	.066	.2203	.2265	
	do.	28798	R	22.2	5	.064	.2187	.2236	
	Target Mod. 55	C-1205	R	16.1	5	.067	.2178	.2213	
	Target Mod. 57	D-1611	R	16.5	5	.068	.2179	.2219	
Mre. Liégeoise, Liége, Belgium	No name	3793	R	21.5	5	.038	.2166	.2220	Rifling considerably worn.
John P. Lower, Philadelphia, Pa.	"W.L. Grant"	1445	R	16.4	6	.052	.2153	.2321	6-shot, 3" bbl., S.A. sheathed trigger.
J.M. Marlin, New Haven, Conn.	XX Standard 1873	4023	R	30.8	6	.045	.2092	.2284	7-shot, S.A., 3" rd. bbl., hinged frame, latch at bottom.
Sheridan Products, Inc., Racine, Wis.	Sheridan	01107	R	12.0	6	.037	.2142	.2190	Self ejecting—S.S. pistol.
	"	02479	R	12.1	6	.043	.2147	.2193	do.
	"	05072	R	12.0	6	.044	.2140	.2185	do.
	"	05104	R	12.0	6	.043	.2147	.2187	do.
	"	08314	R	11.9	6	.043	.2145	.2192	do.
S-M Corporation, Alexandria, Va.	Sporter	1	R	13.8	6	.043	.2147	.2217	Ejects shell but does not reload.
Smith and Wesson, Springfield, Mass.	Mod. No. 1	16101	R	22.4	5	.067	.2125	.2170	2nd modification of Mod. No. 1
	do.	78988	R	21.3	5	.060	.2135	---	do.
	H.E. 1st Mod.	2759	R	10.0	6	.062	.2196	.2268	Hand ejector, 1st Mod.
	Mod. K-22	K-27432	R	15.0	6	.039	.2143	---	
	do.	K-150667	R	15.0	6	.042	.2150	.2238	
	K-22 Masterpiece	K-5200	R	14.9	6	.038	.2144	.2246	
	do.	K-188564	R	15.1	6	.039	.2147	.2255	
	do.	K-258136	R	15.05	6	.041	.2142	.2238	

Caliber and Manufacturer	Model (or Name)	Serial No.	Dir'n of Twist	Inches for 1 turn	No. of Lands	Land Width (inches)	Bore Diameter (inches)	Groove Diameter* (inches)	Remarks
Smith and Wesson	Mod. 48 Magnum	K-369102	R	10.05	6	.043	.2199	.2259	.22 Magnum ctge.
	Combat Master-piece.	54386	R	15.0	6	.039	.2147	.2247	Unused gun.
	do.	315036	R	15.5	6	.037	.2147	.2200	
S.R.L. Ind. Argentina, Buenos Aires, Argentina	Ttibar	1112	L	21.6	6	.045			Single shot pistol. Ejects shell but does not reload.
J. Stevens Arms and Tool Co., Chicopee Falls, Mass.	Target Pistol	1218	R	15.7	6	.023	.2187	.2202	S.S., S.A., sheathed trigger.
	do.	43219	R	15.9	6	.024	.2191	.2225	"Off Hand" Mod., S.A., S.S.
	do.	47591	R	15.6	6	.025	.2186	.2240	S.S., S.A., trigger guard.
	do.	82699	R	16.4	6	.026	.2179	.2252	S.S., S.A., sheathed trigger.
	do.	1377A	R	16.4	6	.023	.2185	.2220	do.
	"Target" Model	7162	R	15.8	6	.026	.2173	.2203	S.S., S.A., 8" bbl., Pat. Apr. 27, 1920.
Sturm, Ruger and Co., Southport, Conn.	Single Six	8238	R	13.8	6	.044	.2153	.2217	
	do.	21235	R	14.1	6	.042	.2170	.2220	
Whitneyville Armory, Whitneyville, Conn.	Whitneyville	23493	R	29.7	7	.049	.2105	---	7-shot, 3" oct. bbl., S.A., sheathed trigger.

Caliber: 5.5 mm.

Caliber and Manufacturer	Model (or Name)	Serial No.	Dir'n of Twist	Inches for 1 turn	No. of Lands	Land Width (inches)	Bore Diameter (inches)	Groove Diameter* (inches)	Remarks
J. Ancion—Marx, Liége, Belgium	Velo Dog	None	R	21.2	4	.080	.2226	.2296	Marked 5.5 mm.
Arizmendi y Goenaga, Eibar, Spain	Velo Dog	97	R	3.25	5	.073	.2230	.2262	Marked 6 mm.
Mre. Francaise D'Armes et Cycles de St. Etienne, St. Etienne, France	Velo Dog	1791	R	13.1	4	.079	.2222	---	
	do.	5494	R	13.4	6	.052	.2236	.2344	
	do.	8199	R	8.2	5	.078	.2236	.2282	
D.D. Oury, Liége(?), Belgium	Velo Dog	6376	L	25.4	5	.070	.2238	---	Belgian Proof Marks.

Caliber: 6.5 mm.

Caliber and Manufacturer	Model (or Name)	Serial No.	Dir'n of Twist	Inches for 1 turn	No. of Lands	Land Width (inches)	Bore Diameter (inches)	Groove Diameter* (inches)	Remarks
August Schüler, Suhl, Germany	Reform—R.P. Bbl. No. 1	4147	R	8.4	4	.077	.2476	---	Repeating pistol. Measurements approx.
	" " 2	"	R	8.4	4	.077	.2476	---	
	" " 3	"	R	8.4	4	.077	.2476	---	
	" " 4	"	R	8.4	4	.077	.2476	---	

Caliber: 7 mm.

Caliber and Manufacturer	Model (or Name)	Serial No.	Dir'n of Twist	Inches for 1 turn	No. of Lands	Land Width (inches)	Bore Diameter (inches)	Groove Diameter* (inches)	Remarks
L. Ancion-Marx, Liége, Belgium	Lefaucheux	77	R	18.9	4	.131	.2907	.3129	
	Lefaucheux	39	L	22.0	4	.105	.2864	.2950	No name or identification mark. May not have been made by A-M.
J.P. Sauer and Sohn, Suhl, Germany	Bar Pistol	3978	R	8.0	4	.065	.2563	.2665	4 bbls. in line. Only one meas'd.

Caliber: .30 cal.

Caliber and Manufacturer	Model (or Name)	Serial No.	Dir'n of Twist	Inches for 1 turn	No. of Lands	Land Width (inches)	Bore Diameter (inches)	Groove Diameter* (inches)	Remarks
John Calvert, Leeds, England	Pocket Rev.	731	R	10.3	5	.049	.2907	.2951	6-shot, S.A., bbl. hinged at top, latch at bottom, sheathed trigger. Rifling in poor condition.
Colt's Pt. F.A. Mfg. Co., Hartford, Conn.	Colt New 30	7786	L	16.00	6	.075	.2758	.2872	
J.M. Marlin, New Haven, Conn.	XXX Standard 1872	3628	R	30.5	6	.086	.2830	.3030	
	do.	4418	R	31.4	6	.089	.2827	.2879	
Moore's Pat. Fire Arms Co., Brooklyn, N.Y.	Pocket Rev.	2893	L	24.9	5	.090	.3016	.3049	
	Belt Mod.	6654	L	23.9	5	.089	.3017	.3084	
National Arms Co., Brooklyn, N.Y.	Pocket Rev.	28904	L	24.1	5	.094	.3013	.3100	
E. Remington and Sons, Ilion, N.Y.	Smoot Pat. Rev.	1355	L	10.2	5	.102	.3014	.3070	Pat. Oct. 21, 1873.

Caliber: .31

Caliber and Manufacturer	Model (or Name)	Serial No.	Dir'n of Twist	Inches for 1 turn	No. of Lands	Land Width (inches)	Bore Diameter (inches)	Groove Diameter* (inches)	Remarks
Allen and Wheelock, Worcester, Mass.	Pocket Rev.	693	L	15.4	6	.080	.2957	.3077	Bar hammer, percussion.
Colt's Pt. F.A. Mfg. Co., Hartford, Conn.	Mod. of 1848	11573	R	ca. 120	7	.068	.3100	.3173	

Caliber and Manufacturer	Model (or Name)	Serial No.	Dir'n of Twist	Inches for 1 turn	No. of Lands	Land Width (inches)	Bore Diameter (inches)	Groove Diameter* (inches)	Remarks
Manhattan Fire Arms Mfg. Co., New York, N.Y.	Belt Type	274	L	48.0	7	.062	.3047	.3145	
Massachusetts Arms Co., Chicopee Falls, Mass.	Side Hammer Rev.	973	R	83.1	7	.060	.3081	.3176	Wesson and Leavitt's Pat.
Walch Fire Arms Co., New York, N.Y.	10-Shot	1269	R	36.0	6	.085	.3189	.3295	5 chambers, 2 hammers, 2 trig.'s (one sheathed), each chamber 2 charges, Perc. type.
Frank Wesson, Worcester, Mass.	S.S. Pistol	13	L	49.3	5	.097	.3080	.3156	Pat. May 31, 1870.
Whitneyville Armory, Whitneyville, Conn.	S.A. Rev.	12506	R	27.2	7	.060	.3021	---	Pat. May 23, 1871.
Caliber: .32									
Aetna Arms Co., New York, N.Y.	Aetna No. 2	921	R	12.2	5	.093	.3030	.3068	5-shot, S.A., R.F., solid frame, sheathed trigger, Pat. May 23, '76.
E. Allen, Worcester, Mass.	V.P. Pistol	4748	R	20.4	6	.077	.3090	.3162	Pat. March 17, '65.
Armero Especialiatas Reunidas, Eibar, Spain	Alfa	51006	R	15.1	5	.088	.3035	.3095	
Arana y Cia., Eibar, Spain	"El Cano"	2455	R	12.1	5	.088	.3068	.3108	Dated 1924.
Joseph Brazier, Wolverhampton, Eng.	Brazier Rev.	9758	R	31.8	3	.128	.3172	.3200	Brazier Pat. No. 906 (on gun) Meas. approximate.
Brooklyn Arms Co., Brooklyn, N.Y.	Slocum	2348	L	13.2	6	.055	.3010	.3140	Slocum Pat. Apr. 14, 1863.
Chicago Fire Arms Co., Chicago, Ill.	Protector	6196	R	36.3	5	.102	.2979	.3028	7-shot "Palm Pistols," Pat. Mar. 6, 1883; Aug. 9, 1893. No. 6196 poor cond.; No. 8424 excellent cond.
	"	8424	R	38.2	5	.099	.2948	.2990	
Colt's Pt. F.A. Mfg. Co., Hartford, Conn.	Frontier Mod.	303484	L	16.5	6	.039	.3048	.3130	
	do.	329762	L	13.7	6	.053	.3045	.3139	
	do.	341796	L	16.1	6	.046	.3056	.3142	
	New Pocket	15244	L	15.5	6	.031	.3073	.3130	
	Pocket Positive	43077	L	15.3	6	.038	.3053	.3196	
	do.	47451	L	16.1	6	.056	.3050	.3126	
	do.	66201	L	16.4	6	.056	.3051	.3125	
	New Police	13437	L	15.9	6	.043	.3036	.3152	
	do.	19752	L	14.75	6	.031	.3050	.3132	
	do.	25174	L	14.9	6	.033	.3042	.3140	
	do.	26936	L	14.9	6	.032	.3046		
	do.	27530	L	16.4	6	.041	.3052	.3177	
	Bisley Mod.	295675	L	16.3	6	.040	.3053	.3165	
	do.	295722	L	15.3	6	.038	.3058	.3134	Rifling worn.
	Police Positive	318083	L	15.4	6	.050	.3056	.3140	
	do.	153532	L	16.2	6	.043	.3055	.3133	
	do.	161099	L	17.1	6	.050	.3051	.3138	
	Police Pos. Spl.	93444	L	16.7	6	.061	.3049	.3137	Unused gun.
	do.	142362	L	18.7	6	.058	.3058	.3177	Unusual twist.
	do.	302659	L	16.3	6	.046	.3049	.3135	
	do.	321370	L	16.0	6	.044	.3044	.3134	
	do.	365672	L	15.95	6	.046	.3047	.3142	
	do.	426686	L	16.1	6	.045	.3041	.3125	
	Army Special	502594	L	16.0	6	.046	.3045	.3062	New gun.
Manuel Escodin, Eibar, Spain	Mod. of 1926	M289004	R	19.85	5	.086	.3055	---	Copy S & W Mil. and Pol. Mod. For .32 long ctge.
	do.	M293324	R	19.9	5	.082	.3044	.3094	do.
	Mod. 31	M347331	R	20.5	6	.056	.3061	.3135	Copy S & W Mil. and Pol. Mod. For .32 Winchester ctge.
Fab. Mat. de Guerra del Ejercito, Santiago, Chile	"Famae"	1243	R	17.2	6	.051	.3025	.3169	Copy Colt Mil. and Pol. Mod. For .32 long ctge.
Forehand Arms Co., Worcester, Mass.	Hammerless	7268	R	17.1	6	.094	.3085	.3207	Last Pat. Jan. 8, 1888.
	"	15901	L	18.2	6	.081	.3032	---	do.
	"	365831	R	16.65	6	.065	.3036	---	

Caliber and Manufacturer	Model (or Name)	Serial No.	Dir'n of Twist	Inches for 1 turn	No. of Lands	Land Width (inches)	Bore Diameter (inches)	Groove Diameter* (inches)	Remarks
Forehand and Wadsworth, Worcester, Mass.	Pocket Rev.	7682	R	18.7	6	.087	.3108	.3148	
	do.	232097	R	17.2	6	.100	.3091	.3171	
	British Bull Dog	47826	R	15.7	5	.118	.3071	---	Considerably worn.
Andrew Fyrberg and Co., Hopkinton, Mass.	D.A. Pocket Rev.	13004	R	12.0	5	.092	.3046	---	
Garate Anitua y Cia., Eibar, Spain	Detective No. 26	7709	L	14.0	6	.061	.3172	.3262	Copy Colt Mil. and Pol. Mod.
	Mod. 333	71643	L	17.5	6	.053	.3041	.3125	Ident. to Trocaola. Marked G.A.C. Arms Co.
Guisasola Hermanos y Cia., Eibar, Spain	"Smith Eibar"	33979	R	14.0	5	.086	.3095	.3128	Copy S & W Mil. and Pol. Mod.
Harrington and Richardson, Worcester, Mass.	Old Mod.	131	R	12.05	5	.094	.3033	.3104	6-shot, C.F., Hammer type, D.A.
	do.	599	R	12.2	5	.128	.3032	---	do.
	Vest Pocket	1476	R	12.1	5	.093	.3034	.3061	5-shot, 1 1/8" bbl.
	The American	14	R	24.9	5	.088	.3047	---	
	do.	147	R	22.1	5	.093	.3041	.3093	D.A., solid frame.
	do.	445	R	12.1	5	.089	.3040	.3082	do.
	do.	501	R	12.3	5	.095	.3044	---	do.
	do.	541	R	12.1	5	.093	.3036	.3090	do.
	do.	574	R	12.1	5	.092	.3043	---	do.
	do.	1522	R	12.1	5	.097	---	---	do.
	do.	1606	R	12.0	5	.091	.3032	.3080	do.
	do.	5255	R	12.1	5	.089	.3033	.3087	do.
	do.	74147	R	12.0	5	.090	.3030	.3074	do.
	do.	204968	R	12.05	5	.092	.3039	.3094	do.
	Victor	36536	R	12.1	5	.091	.3045	---	do.
	"	39380	R	12.1	5	.093	.3026	.3079	do.
	"	47333	R	12.1	5	.085	.3030	.3070	do.
	"	56743	R	12.0	5	.059	.3026	.3172	do.
	"	92919	R	12.5	5	.086	.3034	.3092	Small Mod. takes a .32 short ctge.
	Safety Hammer D.A.	688	R	12.1	5	.092	.3036	.3084	Pat. April 5, 1887.
	do.	752	R	12.1	5	.093	.3040	.3123	
	do.	8861	R	12.1	5	.091	.3035	.3080	
	Young America D.A.	320	R	12.4	5	.102	.3033	.3081	Solid frame.
	do.	425	R	12.1	5	.097	.3044	.3071	do.
	do.	842	R	23.5	5	.089	.3045	.3085	do.
	do.	9626	R	12.2	5	.094	.3052	.3091	Safety Hammer Model.
	Y.A. Bull Dog	514277	R	12.0	6	.062	.3037	.3171	Young America Bull Dog.
	Premier	124509	R	12.1	5	.088	.3054	---	Rifling worn.
	"	500220	R	12.0	6	.059	.3042	.3140	
	Auto Ejecting	1972	R	12.2	5	.097	.3043	---	
	do.	3481	R	12.4	5	.093	.3049	.3102	
	do.	4450	R	12.1	5	.105	.3073	.3157	
	do.	D-44991	R	12.2	5	.094	.3044	.3091	
	do.	H-56113	R	12.3	5	.106	.3062	.3094	
	do.	G-92141	R	12.1	5	.088	.3058	.3103	
	do.	134070	R	12.1	5	.103	.3068	---	
	do.	151910	R	12.2	5	.084	.3047	---	
	do.	158935	R	12.0	5	.092	.3057	.3088	
	do.	202779	R	12.1	5	.091	.3030	---	
	do.	303960	R	12.0	5	.089	.3032	.3098	
	do.	334525	R	12.0	5	.093	.3040	.3073	
	do.	341682	R	12.0	5	.091	.3020	.3098	
	do.	386711	R	12.1	5	.097	.3032	.3089	
	do.	432993	R	12.0	5	.093	.3037	.3103	
	do.	442241	R	12.0	6	.060	.3037	.3165	
	do.	461532	R	12.1	5	.086	.3036	.3097	
	do.	469748	R	12.1	5	.092	.3050	.3103	
	Hammerless	2172	R	12.2	5	.107	.3065	---	
	"	28800	R	12.2	5	.097	.3048	---	
	"	69014	R	12.0	5	.086	.3049	.3086	
	"	84051	R	12.2	5	.088	.3048	---	
	"	147068	R	12.0	5	.091	.3050	.3097	
	"	229649	R	12.2	5	.091	.3056	.3103	
	"	239198	R	12.2	5	.100	.3037	.3090	
	"	253982	R	12.2	5	.093	.3052	---	
	"	262896	R	12.1	5	.089	.3050	.3110	
	Mod. '04	54206	R	12.0	5	.096	.3060	---	Mod. 04-32-; 6-Shot.
	do.	68148	R	12.05	5	.089	.3047	---	

Caliber and Manufacturer	Model (or Name)	Serial No.	Dir'n of Twist	Inches for 1 turn	No. of Lands	Land Width (inches)	Bore Diameter (inches)	Groove Diameter* (inches)	Remarks
Harrington and Richardson	Mod. 1905 D.A.	19991	R	12.0	5	.093	.3038	.3077	
	do.	85883	R	12.1	6	.060	.3042	.3216	
	Mod. 632	N-3183	R	12.0	6	.058	.3030	.3135	Solid frame, D.A.
	do.	R-53400	R	16.0	6	.058	.3030	.3140	Note change in twist.
	H & R "Automatic"	532357	R	12.0	6	.060	.3040	.3164	This is a revolver.
Hopkins and Allen, Norwich, Conn.	Dictator	2912	R	22.7	6	.056	.3030	---	Pat. May 27, 1879. Rifling much worn.
	Blue Jacket No. 2	4711	L	23.3	6	.062	.2986	.3186	Pat. March 28, 1871.
	do.	7424	L	25.0	5	.107	.3033	.3084	Pat. March 28, 1871; May 27, 1879. Rifling somewhat pitted.
	Ranger No. 2	9462	R	24.6	6	.073	.3015	.3094	Pat. March 28, 1871. Rifling much worn.
	XL Double Action	1294	R	19.7	6	.062	.3023	.3065	
	do.	2413	L	28.9	5	.102	.3050	---	Pat. Jan. 5, 1886. Rifling worn.
	do.	7403	R	19.2	6	.055	.3029	.3105	
	do.	6147	R	19.0	6	.056	.3030	---	
	XL 3 Double Action	1942	R	22.7	6	.062	.3040	---	
	Universal D.A.	704	L	27.2	5	.093	.3032	.3080	Pat. Mar. 28, 1871; Jan. 5, 1886. Has H and A grips. "Thames Arms Co." on gun.
	Bull Dog	1980	L	24.6	5	.085	.2989	---	
	Forehand D.A.	3359	R	19.2	5	.066	.2960	---	F and W on grips.
	Forehand Mod. 1901	1838	R	18.7	6	.069	.3034	.3090	
	do.	2278	R	20.1	6	.066	.3032	---	
	Double Action No. 6	2028	R	18.7	6	.077	.3023	.3089	
	do.	5190	R	19.4	6	.065	.3020	---	
	do.	8196	R	18.9	6	.044	.3017	.3177	Unusually deep grooves.
	No designation	3258	R	18.8	6	.069	.3046	.3106	Hinged frame, D.A.
	Hammerless	03681	R	19.3	6	.057	.3043	.3120	Pat. Dec. 6, 1898.
	Safety Police	1159	R	18.9	6	.051	.3036	.3118	
	do.	3476	R	19.1	6	.068	.3020	.3097	Hammerless.
	do.	D-4129	R	19.3	6	.061	.3050	.3112	Hammerless.
	do.	E-1740	R	19.3	6	.067	.3040	---	Hammer type. Pat. 1906.
	do.	G-9168	R	19.1	6	.068	.3048	.3154	
	Merwin Hulbert	7524	R	17.0	5	.079	.3020	.3221	Made for M-H Co. by H and A. 5 shots, folding hammer spur.
	do.	9210	R	17.1	5	.083	---	---	As above but 7 shots.
Thos. Horsley and Son, Doncaster, England	Horsley	321	R	21.9	4	.109	.2293	---	Solid frame, D.A.
La Industrial Orbea, Eibar, Spain	S and W Type	141219	R	10.0	4	.084	.3152	.3266	Copy Smith and Wesson.
	do.	180458	R	10.1	4	.076	.3161	.3267	do.
Iver Johnson Arms and Cycle Works, Fitchburg, Mass.	Hammer Mod.	1382	R	25.2	5	.092	.3103	.3155	For long ctge.
	do.	1624	R	24.8	5	.096	.3063	.3106	For short ctge.
	do.	28686	R	23.5	5	.092	.3062	.3125	For short ctge.
	do.	20764	R	23.6	5	.106	.3057	---	
	do.	46415	R	24.9	5	.095	.3098	.3134	For short ctge.
	do.	49254	R	24.0	5	.101	.3047	.3129	do.
	do.	58565	R	24.0	5	.105	.3043	.3084	I.J. on frame. U.S. on grips.
	do.	70839	R	23.9	5	.092	.3049	.3129	For short ctge.
	do.	74100	R	24.3	5	.079	.3048	.3166	Unusually deep grooves.
	do.	82266	R	24.4	5	.094	.3053	.3115	For long ctge.
	Hammerless	102	R	23.2	5	.091	.3046	.3104	For short ctge.
	"	13855	R	24.3	5	.107	.3048	.3101	do.
	"	30881	R	24.3	5	.089	.3050	.3124	
	"	36343	R	23.2	5	.089	.3044	---	
	"	45590	R	24.8	5	.107	.3048	---	
	"	55201	R	24.4	5	.111	.3055	.3084	
	"	55468	R	25.7	5	.100	.3036	.3121	Unusually deep grooves.
	"	99343	R	23.8	5	.087	.3056	.3110	
	"	H-20027	R	23.5	5	.091	.3043	.3150	
	"	U-13541	R	24.0	5	.092	.3053	.3115	For short ctge.
	Mod. 1900	6936	R	37.9	5	.106	.3060	---	Solid frame.
	do.	8275	R	39.7	5	.101	.3038	.3069	
	do.	23139	R	37.7	5	.101	.3043	---	
	Safety Hammer	6594	R	23.7	5	.091	.3054	.3107	Hinged frame.
	do.	6776	R	24.8	5	.088	.3050	.3131	For short ctge.
	do.	8229	R	23.5	5	.094	.3036	---	
	do.	E-19537	R	24.8	5	.108	.3063	---	

Caliber and Manufacturer	Model (or Name)	Serial No.	Dir'n of Twist	Inches for 1 turn	No. of Lands	Land Width (inches)	Bore Diameter (inches)	Groove Diameter* (inches)	Remarks
Iver Johnson Arms and Cycle Works	Safety Hammer	F-12064	R	24.3	5	.089	.3057	---	
	do.	F-31247	R	24.0	5	.095	.3031	---	
	do.	S-48126	R	23.2	5	.090	.3033	---	
	do.	A-95383	R	25.3	5	.110	.3042	---	
	U.S. Rev.	11224	R	23.65	5	.090	.3037	.3100	"United States Revolvers" made by I.J. for U.S. Revolver Co.
	do.	23758	R	23.3	5	.096	.3020	.3093	Solid frame type.
	do.	48858	R	22.9	5	.089	.3025	.3098	do.
	do.	50972	R	24.0	5	.091	.2998	.3080	do.
	do.	6875	R	24.0	5	.094	.3067	.3121	Hinged frame type.
	do.	30699	R	24.4	5	.091	.3051	---	do.
	do.	35713	R	24.4	5	.088	.3043	---	do.
	do.	50356	R	22.6	5	.089	.3039	.3090	do.
	do.	72764	R	21.8	5	.099	.3040	---	do.
	do.	75554	R	23.8	5	.088	.3049	.3119	do.
	do.	76776	R	23.2	5	.090	.3057	.3117	do.
	Hammerless	28139	R	23.5	5	.090	.3054	.3123	do.
	"	64097	R	25.0	5	.089	.3041	---	do.
	"	74417	R	24.0	5	.090	.3059	.3110	do.
Lee Arms Co., Wilkesbarre, Pa.	Red Jacket No. 3	29497	L	28.8	6	.077	.3068	.3191	
J. Lloyd Lewis, England	Lewis	570	R	22.5	5	.131	.2920	.3013	"C.F. 320 bore, with self-acting safety, Pat. Dec. 11, 1873."
"Maltby, Henley and Co." Prob. actually made at Columbia Armory, Tenn.	Columbian	16100	R	19.6	5	.122	.3100	---	"Columbian New Safety Hammerless" Pat. by J.T. Smith, Rock Falls, Conn. Pat. Jan. 24, '88, Oct. 29, '89. Sold by Maltby, Henley and Co., New York. Rifling much worn.
	"	5663	R	15.65	5	.092	.3115	.3170	Pract. no twist. Rifling in excellent cond.
J.M. Marlin, New Haven, Conn.	No. 32 St'd. 1873	3356	R	30.0	6	.099	.3048	.3148	Hinged at top, bbl. tips up. 6-shot, S.S., sheathed trigger, R.F., Pat. July 1, '78.
	No. 32 St'd. 1875	9291	R	12.0	6	.036	.3035	.3139	do.
Meriden Fire Arms Co., Meriden, Conn.	Meriden Rev.	194733	R	12.0	5	.090	.3064	.3129	Hinged frame type, 5-shot, C.F.
	"Empire State"	252221	R	12.1	5	.080	.3040	.3098	Sold by Empire State Arms Co.
	"Eastern Arms Co."	1059	R	12.1	5	.100	.3047	---	Hinged frame, hammer type, 5-shot. Sold by Eastern Arms Co.
	do.	10819	R	12.0	5	.103	.3062	.3121	Hinged frame, hammerless. Sold by Eastern Arms Co.
	Secret Service Spl.	120860	R	12.1	5	.094	.3050	---	Sold by Howard Arms Co., Chicago.
Moore's Pat. Fire Arms Co., Brooklyn, N.Y.	The National	706	L	24.9	5	.089	.3020	.3087	D. Williamson's Pat. June 5, May 17, 1864. Uses "teat" ctge.
Orbea Hermanos, Eibar, Spain	S & W Type	22171	R	10.1	6	.040	.3175	.3295	Copy of S & W Mil. and Pol. Mod.
Lucius W. Pond, Worcester, Mass.	Pond's Sep. Chamber	374	L	24.6	5	.112	.2986	.3061	Pond's "Separate Chamber Rev." 6-shot, front loading, removable steel chambers.
	Pocket Rev.	2367	L	23.9	5	.106	.3043	.3130	Bbl. hinged at top, tips up on release of catch. Pat. July 10, '60. Marked "Made for S & W." Infringement, 6-shot, R.F., S.A., sheathed trigger.
E.A. Prescott, Worcester, Mass.	Belt Mod.	53	R	36.0	5	.114	.3040	.3088	Brass frame, 6-shot, R.F., S.A., sheathed trigger, Pat. Oct. 2, '60. Infringement of S & W patent.

Caliber and Manufacturer	Model (or Name)	Serial No.	Dir'n of Twist	Inches for 1 turn	No. of Lands	Land Width (inches)	Bore Diameter (inches)	Groove Diameter* (inches)	Remarks
E. Remington and Sons, Illion, N.Y.	Rider's Pat. Pistol	191	L	14.4	5	.101	.3002	.3058	"Rider's Magazine Pistol" Pat. Aug. 15, '71.
Otis A. Smith, Rock Falls, Conn.	Smith Pat. Rev.	2172	L	28.8	5	.100	.3005	.3079	Marked:"Smith's Pat. Apr. 15, '73." 5-shot, S.A., R.F., 3" rd. bbl.
	Mod. of 1883	879	R	16.2	5	.079	.3115	.3175	Marked: "Smith's Pat. Mod. 1883. Shell ejector—Pat. Dec. 20, 1881."
Smith and Wesson, Springfield, Mass.	Mod. 1 1/2, S.A.	6020	R	22.0	5	.096	.3025	.3107	First form of Mod. 1 1/2.
	do.	15919	R	21.8	5	.094	.3017	.3064	do.
	do.	34492	R	23.3	5	.102	.3003	.3064	"New Mod." of Mod. 1 1/2.
	do.	50434	R	16.2	5	.102	.3005	---	do.
	do.	63047	R	23.1	5	.108	.3005	.3022	do.
	do.	96248	R	22.8	5	.096	.3028	.3067	do.
	do.	49208	R	12.0	5	.088	.3031	.3089	Unused gun. Last Pat. Apr. 20, '75; Dec. 18, '77.
	do.	80812	R	18.85	5	.087	.3023	---	
	do.	92302	R	18.9	5	.087	.3048	---	
	No. 2 (Old Mod.)	5237	R	20.3	5	.104	.3010	.3042	First mod. for .32 long ctge. Pat.: Apr. 3, '85; July 5, '59; Dec. 18, '60.
	do.	30585	R	21.3	5	.101	.3055	---	do.
	do.	33226	R	21.3	5	.100	.3010	---	do.
	do.	50960	R	23.0	5	.094	.3012	.3080	do.
	.32 D.A. 2nd Mod.	34974	R	12.1	5	.089	.3040	.3079	For .32 short ctge. Last Pat.: May 11, '80; Jan. 5, '82.
	.32 D.A. 3rd Mod.	51479	R	18.7	5	.088	.3037	.3083	do.
	do.	96577	R	18.8	5	.087	.3035	.3091	do.
	do.	110924	R	18.5	5	.087	.3046	.3099	do.
	New Departure	34724	R	18.8	5	.092	.3032	.3088	1st Model. Also called "Safety Hammerless."
	do.	47660	R	18.9	5	.090	.3030	.3091	do.
	do.	66487	R	18.9	5	.089	.3038	.3130	do.
	do.	68888	R	19.2	5	.098	.3043	---	do.
	do.	77958	R	19.3	5	.090	.3034	.3078	do.
	do.	82406	R	18.6	5	.084	.3030	---	do.
	do.	134307	R	18.6	5	.088	.3031	.3075	2nd Mod. of New Departure.
	Mod. I—H.E.	2713	R	18.75	5	.091	.3038	.3090	1st form of Mod. I Hand Ejector. Last Pat. July 16, 1895.
	do.	11357	R	18.9	5	.089	.3033	.3083	do.
	do.	264413	R	18.3	5	.089	.3040	.3080	Mod. of 1903, 5th change.
	do.	333017	R	18.4	5	.086	.3034	.3078	Mod. I Hand Ejector, 3rd Model. Also called "Regulation Police."
	do.	393734	R	18.8	5	.082	.3035	.3086	do.
	do.	627170	R	18.7	5	.089	.3035	.3081	do.
	32-20 Winchester	48888	R	12.1	5	.098	.3046	.3080	Mod. of 1905, 3rd change.
	do.	68877	R	11.8	5	.095	.3037	.3087	Mod. of 1905, 4th change.
Thames Arms Co., Norwich, Conn.	Thames	8328	R	12.1	6	.072	.3049	.3121	Hinged frame, D.A., C.F. Pat. Jan. 5, Oct. 5, '86.
	"	9703	R	17.3	5	.076	.3050	.3129	
Trocaola, Aranzabal y Cia., Eibar, Spain	T.A.C. Mod. 1924	403	R	10.9	6	.048	.3050	.3122	6-shot, D.A., for long ctge.
	S & W Type	120148	R	10.4	6	.037	.3166	.3274	Copy S & W Mil. and Pol. Mod.
Union Arms Co., New York, N.Y.	Belt Mod.	150	R	23.9	5	.125	.3011	.3094	.32 short ctge., 6-shot, S.A., R.F., sheathed trigger.
Wesson and Harrington, Worcester, Mass.	Pocket Rev.	1259	R	22.6	5	.101	.3043	.3078	5-shot, S.A., R.F., 2 1/4" bbl., sheathed trigger, .32 short ctge.
Whitneyville Armory, Whitneyville, Conn.	Pocket Rev.	13432	R	30.2	5	.104	.3017	.3074	5-shot, S.A., R.F., 3 1/4" bbl., sheathed trigger, Pat. May 25, '71.
Manufacturer unknown (Spanish)	"Crucero"	10	R	14.5	6	.045	.3077	.3155	Military and Police Type.
	"Rural"	16350	R	15.2	5	.071	.3079	.3115	Inscription: Guaranteed 1925 "Rural Model." Copy of Colt.

Caliber and Manufacturer	Model (or Name)	Serial No.	Dir'n of Twist	Inches for 1 turn	No. of Lands	Land Width (inches)	Bore Diameter (inches)	Groove Diameter* (inches)	Remarks
Caliber: 7.65 mm.									
Francisco Arizmendi, Eibar, Spain	"F.A." Pocket	807	R	10.3	6	.095	.3189	.3277	Solid frame, sheathed trigger. For long ctge., 5-shot.
Mre. D'Armes Le Page, Liége, Belgium	Le Page	None	R	9.4	4	.086	.3036	.3127	9-shot, D.A., solid frame.
Caliber: 8 mm.									
Acier Forge St. Etienne, St. Etienne, France	Fr. Ord. M1892	H-25225	L	9.7	4	.068	.3162	.3270	Also known as the "Lebel."
Garate Anitua y Cia., Eibar, Spain	None	19623	L	12.3	6	.033	.3154	.3188	May have been made for Garate, Anitua to sell.
Orbea Hermanos, Eibar, Spain	"Orbea"	115882	R	10.05	4	.085	.3153	.3273	Prob. made for French ctge., 1892.
Rast and Gasser, Vienna, Austria	Army Rev.	23422	R	5.95	4	.112	.3151	.3239	5-shot, D.A.
	do.	106684	R	6.00	4	.101	.3154	.3324	8-shot, D.A.
	do.	86336	L	10.1	5	.094	.3014	.3065	8-shot, D.A., dated 1916.
Mre. D'Armes St. Etienne, St. Etienne, France	French Ord. M1892	F-22171	L	9.4	4	.078	.3151	.3272	Modele D'Ordonnance 1892.
	do.	G-34020	L	9.5	4	.070	.3152	.3270	do.
	do.	I-1459	L	9.45	4	.084	.3162	.3288	do.
	do.	I-4241	L	9.5	4	.075	.3153	---	do.
Mre. Francaise D'Armes et Cycles, St. Etienne, France	Gaulois No. 3	11369	R	16.8	4	.045	.2960	.3024	Uses special Gaulois C.F. ctge.
Caliber: .36									
Manhattan Fire Arms Co., Newark, N.J.	Navy Type	31975	R	31.5	5	.114	.3707	.3766	Similar to Colt Navy Mod. 1851.
Volcanic Repeating Arms Co., New Haven, Conn.	Volcanic	1119	R	37.1	6	.130	.3867	.4009	7-shot rep. pistol, tubular mag. Propellant in base of bullet. Pat. Feb. 14, 1854.
	"	2520	R	37.5	6	.130	.3820	.4030	do.
American Arms Co., Boston, Mass.	Pocket Rev.	11890	R	12.1	5	.116	.3518	.3542	5-shot, hinged frame, S.A., sheathed trigger. No extractor.
	do.	17280	R	12.2	5	.103	.3506	---	Hinged frame, ring extractor (full diam. of cyl.), S.A. Pat. Dec. 5, '82; Mar. 27, '83.
Arriola Hermanos, Eibar, Spain	"Eibar 1927"	117110	R	14.0	5	.108	.3465	.3553	Copy Colt Mil. type. Arriola Bros. may have been dealers.
Beistegui Hermanos, Eibar, Spain	"B.H." Rev.	06012	R	12.0	5	.109	.3471	.3534	Copy S and W Mil. type, 6-shot. For .38 long ctge. 5 3/4" bbl.
Blissett and Sons, England	R and G Type Rev.	8509	R	12.1	4	.128	.3546	.3713	Appears ident. to Rast and Gasser and may only have been sold by Blissett and Sons. Belgian Proof Mks.
Caliber: .38									
Colt's Pt. F.A. Mfg. Co., Hartford, Conn.	New Line 38	384	L	16.5	6	.102	.3727	.3917	Bears name: "Pet Colt," name used by Kittredge and Co.
	do.	7457	L	48.3	7	.076	.3707	.3792	5-shot, R.F.
	S.A. Army Mod.	217637	L	16.4	6	.043	.3949	.4087	.38 W.C.F. ctge.
	do.	331735	L	15.4	6	.058	.3950	.4030	Frontier "Target Mod." Pat.: Sept. 19, '71; July 2, '72; Jan. 19, '75.
	do.	340592	L	15.9	6	.070	.3953	.4017	.38 W.C.F. ctge.
	D.A. Army Mod.	50230	L	16.2	6	.044	.3960	.4060	First Colt D.A.
	Lightning Mod.	8738	L	16.0	6	.041	.3647	---	No ejector. Pat.: Sept. 19, '71; Sept. 15, '74; Jan. 19, '75. Has U.S. Express No. 8738 USX.
	do.	15285	L	15.6	6	.026	.3655	.3716	Has ejector. Pats. as above.
	do.	60614	L	16.4	6	.031	.3627	.3733	do.

Caliber and Manufacturer	Model (or Name)	Serial No.	Dir'n of Twist	Inches for 1 turn	No. of Lands	Land Width (inches)	Bore Diameter (inches)	Groove Diameter* (inches)	Remarks
Colt's Pt. F.A. Mfg. Co.	Lightning Mod.	Removed	L	17.1	6	.026	.3634	.3702	U.S. Exp. No. 93748 USX. Has ejector. Pat. as above.
	New Service	113916	L	15.6	6	.061	.3953	.4031	.38 W.C.F.
	do.	F-14277	L	16.8	6	.047	.3946	.4037	do.
	D.A. Colt	595	L	14.9	6	.027	.3636	.3697	Marked: D.A. 38 on frame. No. 595 on frame. Last Pat. Mar. 5, '95.
	do.	818	L	14.9	6	.031	.3623	.3724	Marked D.A. 38. No. 818 on crane.
	do.	2860	L	17.1	6	.025	.3573	.3667	U.S. Army Mod. 1896, No. 142860 on butt. No. 2860 on crane.
	D.A. Army 1901	4165	L	16.2	6	.035	.3619	.3723	U.S. Army No. 174165 on butt. Dated 1902. No. 4165 on crane.
	do.	138481	L	16.1	6	.025	.3639	.3697	U.S. Army Mod. 1901 on butt.
	do.	8609	L	16.1	6	.031	.3623	.3692	Dated 1902. U.S. Army No. 178609 on butt.
	do.	1428-K	L	16.4	6	.039	.3643	.3727	No. 1428k on crane. No. on butt filed off.
	do.	7196-K	L	13.9	6	.073	.3573	.3662	U.S. Army No. 107106 on butt.
	do.	7618-K	L	14.2	6	.061	.3570	.3671	U.S. Army No. 157618 on butt.
	Army Special	512060	L	16.0	6	.049	.3466	.3542	
	Official Police	536808	L	16.0	6	.056	.3467	.3537	
	do.	555487	L	16.2	6	.053	.3470	.3525	
	do.	733590	L	14.0	6	.057	.3479	.3529	
	Police Positive	15705	L	17.8	6	.033	.3505	.3614	Pat. July 4, 1905.
	do.	40944	L	15.8	6	.060	.3473	.3523	
	do.	140085	L	16.55	6	.054	.3467	.3545	
	do.	393237	L	16.0	6	.055	.3470	.3550	
	Officers Mod.	412586	L	15.6	6	.059	.3470	.3521	
	do.	412898	L	16.3	6	.062	.3474	.3558	
	do.	423506	L	18.5	6	.057	.3470	.3550	
	do.	784746	L	16.0	6	.055	.3465	.3547	New gun.
	Detective Spl.	427424	L	16.0	6	.057	.3478	.3538	
	Cobra	5403-LW	L	16.0	6	.058	.3470	.3546	
Forehand Arms Co., Worcester, Mass.	D.A. Rev.	10585	L	18.0	6	.096	.3510	---	Solid frame. F & W on grip plates.
	do.	36634	L	17.9	6	.100	.3500	.3562	Solid frame. F & W on grip plates. Pat. June 2, '91.
	do.	78731	L	17.1	6	.102	.3510	.3582	Hinged frame. F & W on grip plates. Pat. Dec. 7, '86; Jan. 11, '87.
	do.	123098	L	17.5	6	.091	.3514	---	Marked Pat. Jan. 11, 1887.
	do.	74344	L	18.0	6	.100	.3517	.3671	Hinged frame, F & W on grip plates. Pat. Dec. 7, '86; Jan. 11, '87.
	do.	214436	L	18.0	6	.093	.3511	.3606	do.
Forehand and Wadsworth, Worcester, Mass.	Bull Dog	432	R	15.9	5	.105	.3574	.3687	S.A., sheathed trigger, Pat. Sept. 24, Oct. 22, '81; Jan. 27, '71 Bird's eye grips.
	Mod. of 1901	3314	R	19.7	6	.087	.3499	.3541	
	Forehand "Automatic"	11507	L	17.0	6	.087	.3530	.3730	"Automatic Ejecting" Pat. Dec. 7, '86; Jan. 11, '87.
	D.A. Rev.	50323	R	17.8	6	.099	.3500	.3592	Pat. Dec. 7, '86; Jan. 11, '87.
Andrew Fyrberg and Co., Hopkinton, Mass.	Pocket Rev.	24236	R	12.6	5	.144	.3523	---	Hinged frame. Pat. Aug. 4, '03.
Fabrica De Armas Garantazadas, Eibar, Spain	Apache	59865	R	15.0	5	.086	.3480	.3536	Mil. and Pol. Type. 1925 Model.
	"	59915	R	15.0	5	.085	.3483	---	do.
"Garantazado," Eibar, Spain	Pocket Mod. 1A	8864	R	12.3	5	.107	.3500	---	Name TANKE on grip plates.
Garate, Anitua y Cia., Eibar, Spain	S & W Type	32471	L	11.4	6	.083	.3468	.3560	

Caliber and Manufacturer	Model (or Name)	Serial No.	Dir'n of Twist	Inches for 1 turn	No. of Lands	Land Width (inches)	Bore Diameter (inches)	Groove Diameter* (inches)	Remarks
Great Western Arms Co., Los Angeles, Cal.	Derringer	112	R	18.0	6	.065	.3498	.3582	Upper bbl. Copy of Remington Derringer.
			R	18.0	6	.065	.3498	.3582	Lower bbl.
Harrington and Richardson, Worcester, Mass.	Safety Hammer D.A.	197	R	12.1	5	.108	.3519	.3582	
	Defender	1378	R	12.0	6	.070	.3503	.3618	
	"	2694	R	12.0	6	.069	.3507	.3557	
	"	A-588	R	12.0	6	.066	.3486	.3616	
	H & R D.A.	2022	R	12.1	5	.119	.3510	---	Hinged frame. Double action. Nonautomatic; ejecting.
	do.	2051	R	12.1	5	.099	.3518	---	Hinged frame. D.A., Pat. Oct. 4, '87. "Auto. Ejecting".
	do.	6631	R	12.1	5	.123	.3542	---	"H and R Police" Pat. Oct. 4, '87.
	do.	8026	R	12.1	5	.102	.3517	---	do.
	do.	18948	R	12.1	5	.107	.3521	.3554	Hinged frame. D.A. Pat. Oct. 4, '87. "Auto. Ejecting".
	do.	40417	R	12.0	5	.099	.3523	.3583	do.
	do.	63448	R	12.2	5	.102	.3536	---	do.
	do.	73288	R	12.4	5	.102	.3530	---	do.
	do.	E-78972	R	12.2	5	.107	.3517	---	do.
	do.	G-84686	R	12.3	5	.103	.3535	.3571	do.
	do.	351458	R	12.0	5	.105	.3512	.3560	do.
	do.	400981	R	12.2	6	.074	.3522	.3623	do.
	do.	491683	R	12.0	5	.102	.3523	.3569	do.
	Victor	3261	R	12.15	5	.108	.3506	---	Solid frame. D.A.
	"	5694	R	12.2	5	.102	.3508	---	do.
	"	11315	R	12.15	5	.110	.3495	---	do.
	"	12019	R	12.15	5	.111	.3513	---	do.
	"	18381	R	12.0	5	.103	.3519	.3587	do.
	The American D.A.	47	R	12.0	5	.114	.3519	.3569	Solid frame.
	do.	48	R	12.0	5	.113	.3502	---	do.
	do.	127	R	12.0	5	.104	.3515	.3572	do.
	do.	130	R	12.1	5	.112	.3499	.3557	do.
	do.	198	R	12.1	5	.110	.3500	---	do.
	do.	145311	R	12.0	5	.103	.3516	---	do.
	do.	156896	R	12.0	5	.109	.3503	---	do.
	Mod. of 1904	12405	R	12.15	5	.098	.3505	---	Solid frame. D.A.
	do.	34741	R	12.2	5	.102	.3509	---	do.
	do.	115786	R	12.05	5	.103	.3502	.3561	do.
	Hammerless	18784	R	12.15	5	.101	.3515	---	
	"	28337	R	12.2	5	.101	.3523	.3563	
	"	42362	R	11.9	5	.100	.3516	.3557	
	"	92405	R	12.25	5	.102	.3523	---	
	"	153724	R	12.1	5	.105	.3507	---	
	"	156751	R	12.0	5	.102	.3489	.3574	
	"	189677	R	12.0	6	.075	.3515	.3631	
Hopkins and Allen, Norwich, Conn.	XL—Double Action	1192	R	22.3	6	.080	.3498	---	Solid frame.
	do.	4914	R	24.5	6	.091	.3506	.3659	do.
	XL—Navy	1154	R	24.0	5	.133	.3593	---	6-shot, solid frame, S.A., R.F., Pat. Mar. 28, '71; Apr. 27, '75.
	XL—No. 4	294	R	24.0	6	.090	.3576	.3696	5-shot, S.A., R.F., Pat. Mar. 28, '71.
	XL—Bull Dog	1753	R	23.1	6	.071	.3500	.3623	5-shot, D.A., C.F., Fold. hammer. Pat. Mar. 28, '71; Jan. 27, '85. Sheathed trigger.
	do.	5318	R	24.0	6	.081	.3520	---	do.
	D.A. Rev.	2477	R	21.4	5	.091	.3512	---	Hinged frame. Fold. hammer. Pat. Jan. 5, Oct. 5, '86.
	do.	2803	R	20.3	5	.100	.3515	.3576	do.
	D.A. No. 6	787	R	19.3	6	.089	.3516	---	Solid frame.
	do.	1235	R	19.1	6	.080	.3500	.3587	Marked "Forehand Model" but identical to Mod. No. 6.
	do.	2028	R	18.8	6	.083	.3498	---	
	do.	3782	R	19.2	6	.086	.3508	.3588	
	do.	Removed	R	18.6	6	.089	.3508	---	
	D.A.—1893	2231	R	20.6	5	.102	.3510	---	5-shot, hinged frame, Pat. Jan. 5, Oct. 5, '86; Sept. 26, 1893.

Caliber and Manufacturer	Model (or Name)	Serial No.	Dir'n of Twist	Inches for 1 turn	No. of Lands	Land Width (inches)	Bore Diameter (inches)	Groove Diameter* (inches)	Remarks
Hopkins and Allen	Safety Police	583	R	18.9	6	.078	.3506	.3568	Hinged frame. Pat. Aug. 21, 1906.
	do.	C-744	R	18.6	6	.085	.3510	.3566	do.
	do.	7009	R	18.9	6	.079	.3517	.3585	do.
	"Imp. Arms Co."	49	R	18.3	6	.090	.3505	---	Revolvers marked "Imperial Arms Co." reputed to have been made by H and A.
	Merwin Hulbert— S.A.	6970	R	21.8	5	.108	---	---	Made for Merwin, Hulbert and Co. Pats. Jan. 24, Apr. 21, Dec. 15, '74; Aug. 3, '75; July 11, '76; Mar. 6, '77; Apr. 17, '77.
	do.	1121	R	21.2	5	.102	.3510	.3554	do.
	do.	4565	R	20.4	5	.110	.3510	.3580	do.
	Merwin Hulbert— D.A.	3949	R	20.5	5	.102	.3513	---	Made for Merwin, Hulbert and Co., Pat. Apr. 17, '77; June 15, '80; Mar. 14, '82; Jan. 9, '83.
	do.	17062	R	20.0	5	.115	.3509	.3588	do.
Iver Johnson Arms and Cycle Works, Fitchburg, Mass.	Smoker	23	R	29.0	5	.115	.3503	.3540	
	"Shattuck Pat"	409	R	32.6	5	.118	.3594	.3625	Pat. Nov. 4, '79; Mar. 6, '83.
	do.	5268	R	33.6	5	.116	.3593	---	do.
	do.	7896	R	32.7	5	.110	.3598	.3646	do.
	American Bull Dog	4	R	40.9	5	.138	.3496	---	
	do.	1787	R	38.0	5	.137	.3512	---	
	do.	3411	R	23.8	5	.103	---	---	
	do.	4997	R	24.8	5	.107	.3542	.3595	
	do.	6103	R	25.1	5	.109	.3516	.3581	
	Boston Bull Dog	2704	R	35.1	5	.114	.3497	.3601	Made for sale by J.P. Lovell Arms Co., Boston.
	Lightning Express	3996	R	31.7	5	.119	.3550	.3640	
	Safety Hammer	277	R	23.8	5	.110	.3504	---	Hinged frame, D.A., 5-shot.
	do.	7430	R	24.0	5	.109	.3546	---	
	do.	56006	R	24.3	5	.107	.3533	.3589	
	do.	57399	R	24.2	5	.106	.3529	.3614	
	do.	62772	R	24.8	5	.125	.3500	.3550	
	do.	66671	R	24.5	5	.130	.3502	---	
	do.	69839	R	24.9	5	.114	.3526	---	
	Hammerless	26874	R	24.1	5	.105	.3509	.3559	Hinged frame, D.A., 5-shot.
	"	38541	R	24.1	5	.124	.3516	---	
	"	39730	R	24.1	5	.111	.3517	.3601	
	"	44900	R	25.2	5	.117	.3526	---	
	"	64698	R	23.9	5	.111	.3507	---	
	"	72051	R	24.2	5	.109	.3494	.3580	
	"	79430	R	25.3	5	.124	.3523	.3568	
	"	87337	R	24.8	5	.104	.3515	---	
	"	94282	R	24.6	5	.124	.3516	.3565	
	"	D-12459	R	24.4	5	.123	.3525	.3578	
	U.S. Rev.	19206	R	22.9	5	.110	.3496	---	Made for U.S. Rev. Co. by I.J. Solid frame. Hammer type.
	do.	6800	R	24.3	5	.113	.3538	.3606	Hinged frame. Hammer type.
	do.	12896	R	24.7	5	.126	.3535	---	do.
	do.	32754	R	24.6	5	.110	.3543	.3626	do.
	do.	33608	R	24.3	5	.109	.3480	---	do.
	do.	49074	R	25.0	5	.107	.3530	.3589	do.
	do.	87970	R	23.6	5	.110	.3520	.3600	do.
	do.	90706	R	24.0	5	.108	.3528	.3594	do.
	Hammerless	5280	R	24.2	5	.125	.3554	---	
	"	7971	R	24.2	5	.112	.3522	.3587	
	"	12252	R	24.5	5	.110	.3525	.3603	
	"	19576	R	24.1	5	.115	.3512	.3581	
Fabrique d'Armes Reunies (Liége United Arms Co.), Liége, Belgium	Texas Ranger	66	R	ca. 10.7	4	.154	.3444	---	Rifling much worn.
J.M. Marlin, New Haven, Conn.	Standard 1878	2970	R	12.0	6	.048	.3508	.3610	Patented July 1, 1873.
	do.	3494	R	12.4	6	.056	.3500	.3606	Pat. July 1878. Bbl. hinged at top. S.A., R.F.

Caliber and Manufacturer	Model (or Name)	Serial No.	Dir'n of Twist	Inches for 1 turn	No. of Lands	Land Width (inches)	Bore Diameter (inches)	Groove Diameter* (inches)	Remarks
Meriden Fire Arms Co., Meriden, Conn.	Secret Service	7475	R	12.1	5	.103	.3497	.3584	
	Secret Service Spl.	266067	R	12.0	5	.113	.3528	.3582	
	Hammerless	310638	R	12.2	5	.100	.3488	.3550	
	"Eastern Arms Co."	10430	R	12.0	5	.132	.3515	.3577	Sold by Eastern Arms Co.
	do.	115868	R	12.2	5	.101	.3525	---	do.
	"Empire State"	44673	R	12.3	5	.108	.3502	---	Sold by Empire State Arms Co.
	"Howard Arms Co."	10616	R	12.0	5	.117	.3503	---	Sold by Howard Arms Co., Chicago.
	do.	32195	R	12.2	5	.129	.3524	---	
	do.	40244	R	12.3	5	.106	.3527	---	Same No. under grip.
	do.	42430	R	12.7	5	.140	.3512	---	do.
	do.	101224	R	12.3	5	.098	.3533	---	No. under grip 75423.
	Secret Service Spl.	51395	R	12.2	5	.117	.3515	---	Marked "Secret Service Special Howard Arms Co., Chicago."
Orbea Hermanos, Eibar, Spain	"O.H. Rev."	181	R	19.7	5	.119	.3470	---	Copy S & W Mil. and Pol. Mod. 38 Spl. ctge.
	do.	122217	R	19.8	5	.119	.3470	.3530	do.
	do.	E-14053	R	20.1	5	.128	.3490	.3547	do.
E. Remington and Sons, Ilion, N.Y.	Smoot Pat. Rev.	Removed	L	14.3	5	.107	.3632	.3666	5-shot, S.A., sheathed trigger. Pat. W.S. Smoot Oct. 21, '73.
Royal Small Arms Factory, Enfield, England	No. 2—Mark I	A-8941	R	15.0	7	.029	.3535	.3599	Dated 1932.
	No. 2—Mark I*	A-8771	R	15.1	7	.027	---	---	Dated 1942.
	do.	Z-5359	R	14.9	7	.027	.3539	.3592	Not dated.
	do.	J-9010	R	15.1	7	.035	.3546	.3585	Dated 1940.
	do.	3266	R	15.2	7	.029	.3540	.3590	Dated '44.
	do.	Z-5635	R	15.4	7	.030	.3540	---	Dated 1943.
	do.	696-ZB	R	15.3	7	.026	.3537	.3591	
Smith and Wesson, Springfield, Mass.	No. 2—1st Mod.	22528	R	12.1	5	.100	.3502	.3555	Last Pat. Jan. 19, '75.
	No. 2—2nd Mod.	74349	R	12.3	5	.101	.3505	.3554	Last Pat. May 11, '80.
	do.	82663	R	12.0	5	.100	.3500	.3555	Last Pat. May 11, '80. Perfect condition.
	Mod. 2 1/2—1st Issue	751	R	12.0	5	.101	.3505	---	Pats. Jan. 17, 24, '65; July 11, '65; Aug. 24, '69; Jan. 19, '75; Reissue July 25, '71.
	do.	6962	R	11.9	5	.098	.3515	---	do.
	D.A.—2nd Mod.	117286	R	18.7	5	.102	.3513	---	Pat. May 11 and 25, '80.
	D.A.—3rd Mod.	153209	R	18.9	5	.099	.2510	.3560	Last Pat. Jan. 3, '82.
	do.	170538	R	18.9	5	.096	.3505	---	do.
	do.	216608	R	19.4	5	.093	.3530	.3567	do.
	do.	241785	R	18.75	5	.096	.3510	.3556	do.
	do.	320740	R	18.7	5	.103	.3510	---	do.
	D.A.—4th Mod.	398221	R	19.0	5	.101	.3510	---	Last Pat. Apr. 9, '89.
	do.	470570	R	18.85	5	.098	.3505	---	do.
	38 Hand Ejector	6980	R	18.1	5	.095	.3465	---	Mil. and Pol. First Model.
	do.	13808	R	18.8	5	.091	.3465	.3528	do. (1899)
	do.	34857	R	20.0	5	.088	.3498	.3539	Mil. and Pol. Mod. 1902.
	do.	86858	R	19.3	5	.092	.3493	.3527	Mil. and Pol. Mod. 1905.
	do.	143452	R	18.6	5	.088	.3480	.3519	do.
	do.	148097	R	18.5	5	.094	.3462	.3519	do.
	do.	332357	R	18.75	5	.095	.3476	.3512	do.
	do.	313085	R	18.9	5	.103	.3470	.3574	do.
	Mil. and Police	224363	R	18.9	5	.101	.3473	.3530	"Airweight." Pract. unused.
	do.	43235	R	18.95	5	.099	.3468	.3520	"Airweight."
	S & W Special	445138	R	18.8	5	.091	.3463	.3519	
	do.	490351	R	18.95	5	.091	.3473	.3524	
	do.	V-560962	R	18.85	5	.099	.3468	.3528	
	do.	S-934701	R	18.8	5	.094	.3463	---	
	do.	V-266988	R	18.45	5	.102	.3470	.3528	
	Combat Master-piece	K-167590	R	18.75	5	.100	.3470	.3521	
	Detective Spl.	V-177370	R	18.6	5	.102	.3480	.3522	
	38/44 H.D.	S-77305	R	18.8	5	.100	.3469	---	Not fired since leaving factory.
	do.	S-77324	R	18.9	5	.100	.3465	---	do.
	do.	S-77329	R	18.9	5	.101	.3464	---	do.
	do.	S-77382	R	18.9	5	.101	.3464	---	do.
	do.	S-77391	R	18.85	5	.100	.3467	---	do.
	do.	S-77394	R	18.85	5	.100	.3470	---	do.
	do.	S-77472	R	18.85	5	.101	.3472	---	do.
	do.	S-79780	R	18.85	5	.099	.3466	---	

Caliber and Manufacturer	Model (or Name)	Serial No.	Dir'n of Twist	Inches for 1 turn	No. of Lands	Land Width (inches)	Bore Diameter (inches)	Groove Diameter* (inches)	Remarks
Smith and Wesson	Safety Hammerless	43556	R	18.75	5	.095	.3505	.3560	"New Departure" 3rd Model.
	do.	100011	R	18.75	5	.095	.3511	.3563	do.
	do.	111615	R	18.75	5	.100	.3500	.3550	do.
	do.	125685	R	19.0	5	.096	.3510	.3554	"New Departure" 4th Model.
	do.	163662	R	18.9	5	.094	.3508	.3554	do.
	do.	174331	R	18.1	5	.096	.3514	.3558	do.
	do.	219527	R	18.75	5	.099	.3511	.3561	"New Departure" 5th Model.
	do.	229359	R	18.1	5	.097	.3504	.3624	do.
Sociedad Alfa (Eibar Worker's Guild), Eibar, Spain	Alfa	225	R	13.8	5	.099	.3471	- - -	"Armero Especialistas Reunidas" apparently the same mfr.
	"	18901	R	14.1	5	.095	.3480	.3530	
	"	23721	R	14.0	5	.093	.3476	- - -	
	"	50138	R	15.45	5	.110	.3472	.3534	
	"	52783	R	14.45	5	.115	.3472	.3520	
Thames Arms Co., Norwich, Conn.	Thames	253	R	12.0	6	.091	.3541	.3589	Hinged frame. Pat. Sept. 2 and 10, '02.
Fab. de Trocaola Aranzabal y Cia., Eibar, Spain	S & W Type	191704	R	10.6	6	.060	.3494	.3566	Copy S & W Mil. and Pol.
	do.	195806	R	10.6	6	.059	.3487	.3571	do.
	T.A.C.	253955	R	10.9	6	.060	.3472	.3555	
Manufacturer unknown (Spanish)	Alamo Ranger	34	R	15.1	5	.084	.3476	.3536	Inscr.: "Made in Spain. 38 Spl. S & W ctge." 6-shot, D.A., 5 3/8" bbl.
Webley and Scott, Ltd., Birmingham England	Mark IV	85881	R	15.0	7	.041	.3540	.3573	War production.
	do.	124965	R	15.75	7	.034	.3526	- -	do.
Whitneyville Armory, Whitneyville, Conn.	Belt Mod.	1019	R	23.7	5	.149	.3669	.3761	Solid frame, brass, 5-shot, S.A., R.F., sheathed trigger.

Caliber: 9 mm. Rev.

Caliber and Manufacturer	Model (or Name)	Serial No.	Dir'n of Twist	Inches for 1 turn	No. of Lands	Land Width (inches)	Bore Diameter (inches)	Groove Diameter* (inches)	Remarks
Japanese Arsenal	Mod. 1926	15616	R	22.2	4	.098	.3548	.3664	"26 Year Style."
	do.	25074	R	22.3	4	.097	.3550	.3708	do.
	do.	34158	R	22.0	4	.101	.3549	.3743	do.
	do.	47012	R	22.3	4	.109	.3553	.3681	do.
	do.	Removed	R	22.35	4	.099	.3545	.3672	do.
Manufacturer unknown (German)	Bull Dog Type	27	R	14.5	4	.118	.3494	.3595	"Union Sales Co., Germany" on frame.
Manufacturer unknown	Lefaucheux	- - -	R	18.3	4	.149	.3545	.3659	Made in Liége.

Caliber: 9.4 mm.

Caliber and Manufacturer	Model (or Name)	Serial No.	Dir'n of Twist	Inches for 1 turn	No. of Lands	Land Width (inches)	Bore Diameter (inches)	Groove Diameter* (inches)	Remarks
J.H. Damm, St. Elberfeld, Germany	Pin Fire Rev.	None	R	18.75	8	.063	.3678	.3854	6-shot, D.A., pin fire, side gate, rod ejector, folding trigger.
Ned. Wapenmagaziji, Haarlem—S'Hage, Holland	Army Rev.	35	R	21.4	4	.165	.3732	.3884	Maybe made in Belgium. Has Belgian Proof Marks

Caliber: .41

Caliber and Manufacturer	Model (or Name)	Serial No.	Dir'n of Twist	Inches for 1 turn	No. of Lands	Land Width (inches)	Bore Diameter (inches)	Groove Diameter* (inches)	Remarks
Colt's Pt. F.A. Mfg. Co., Hartford, Conn.	S.A. Frontier	159241	L	16.5	6	.047	.3960	.4039	
	do.	262055	L	17.4	6	.047	.3938	.4036	
	Lightning	11947	L	15.9	6	.022	.3959	.4000	Pat. Sept. 19, 1871, Sept. 15, 1874, and Jan. 19, 1875.
	Thunderer	2248	L	16.0	6	.028	.3957	.4127	
	"	57427	L	15.5	6	.031	.3969	.4051	
	D.A.—41	6421	L	16.4	6	.039	.3931	.4068	
	do.	83435	L	16.0	6	.038	.3955	.4046	
	do.	185590	L	15.3	6	.037	.3942	.4024	
	do.	220518	L	15.5	6	.048	.3954	.4096	Pat.: Aug. 5, 1884; Nov. 6, 1888; Mar. 5, 1895.
	do.	366188	L	13.7	6	.056	.3947	.4023	D.A. Army Special 41.
Moore's Pat. F.A. Co., Brooklyn, N.Y.	S.S. Pistol	20174	R	19.3	3	.202	.3725	- - -	Williamson's Pat. Oct. 2, 1866.
National Arms Co., Brooklyn, N.Y.	S.S. Pistol— "National Deringer"	2195	L	25.0	5	.119	.3715	.3858	Moore's Pat. Feb. 24, 1863.
E. Remington and Sons, Ilion, N.Y.	Derringer	212	L	10.65	5	.081	.3945	- - -	Only measured upper bbl.
	"	497	L	10.3	5	.105	.3848	.4003	Upper bbl.
	"	497	L	10.3	5	.107	.3842	.3998	Lower bbl.
	"	L-75380	L	11.0	5	.087	.3934	.3990	Upper bbl.

Caliber and Manufacturer	Model (or Name)	Serial No.	Dir'n of Twist	Inches for 1 turn	No. of Lands	Land Width (inches)	Bore Diameter (inches)	Groove Diameter* (inches)	Remarks
E. Remington and Sons	Derringer	L-75380	L	11.0	5	.087	.3932	.3996	Lower bbl.
	"	L-98953	L	10.7	5	.087	.3938		Upper bbl.
	"	L-98953	L	10.7	5	.087	.3942		Lower bbl.

Caliber: .42

Alexandre Le Mat, Paris, France	Le Mat Pat. Rev.	1106	R	56.0	5	.100	.4008	.4120	No. 1106 on frame and barrel. No. 1125 on cylinder.

Caliber: 10.35 mm.

R. Fabb. D'Armi, Brescia, Italy	Ital. Ord. Rev.	615	R	9.7	4	.149	.4081	.4299	Dated 1888.
Castelli, Brescia, Italy	Ital. Ord. Rev.	3997	R	10.0	4	.165	.4095	.4297	Dated 1914. Marked 10.35 cal.
	do.	7240	R	10.0	4	.160	.4088	.4300	Dated 1917.
	do.	F-3457	R	10.0	4	.156	.4026	.4090	Dated 1922.

Caliber: 10.4 mm.

Siderurgica Glisenti, Brescia, Italy	Ital. Ord. Rev.	B-577	R	9.85	4	.149	.4081	.4223	
	do.	9436	R	9.9	4	.150	.4096	.4298	
Metallurgica Bresciana, Via Tempini, Brescia, Italy	Ital. Ord. Rev.	C-9489	R	9.9	4	.148	.4085	.4213	Dated 1922
F. Tettoni, Brescia, Italy	Mod. 1916	C-96	R	15.7	4	.154	.4105	.4339	F. Tettoni, Brescia, on frame. Manufacturer not verified.

Caliber: 10.55 mm.

Erfurt Arsenal, Erfurt, Germany	German Ord. Rev.	1523-b	R	22.5	4	.154	.4160	.4325	Mod. 1893. 6-shot, S.A.
V. Chas. Schilling— C. G. Haenel, Suhl, Germany	German Ord. Rev.	3429	R	22.8	4	.154	.4180	.4365	6-shot, S.A., solid frame.
	do.	6957	R	22.9	4	.150	.4163	---	do.

Caliber: 10.6 mm.

Gebrüder Mauser, Oberndorf, a/N., Germany	German Ord. Rev.	479	R	22.8	4	.153	.4206	.4387	Mod. 1880. Dated 1881.
	do.	1701	R	22.9	4	.146	.4207	.4409	do.
Rhein. Metallwaren u. Masch. Fab., Sömmerda, Germany	German Ord. Rev.	2477	R	22.9	4	.150	.4166	.4336	Marked "Dreyse."
Sauer and Söhn; V.C. Schilling; and C.G. Haenel, Suhl, Germany	German Ord. — Model 1879	---	R	22.5	4	.149	.4168	.4356	All parts bear No.18, but no ser. no. on gun.

Caliber: 11 mm.

Auguste Francotte ct Cic., Liége, Belgium	Lefaucheux	89797	R	17.6	7	.091	.4328	---	Pin Fire
L. Gasser, Vienna, Austria	Austrian Ord. Rev.	14278	R	10.9	6	.086	.4278	.4496	Ottakring Pat.
Perrin et Cie., Paris, France	Army Rev.	673	R	19.1	6	.072	.4327	.4615	Imported into U.S. during Civil War.
Mre. D'Armes St. Etienne, St. Etienne, France	French Ord. Rev.	F-46862	R	16.2	4	.202	.4425	.4510	Mod. 1873. Dated 1875.
	do.	G-17207	R	14.2	4	.125	.4408	.4512	do.
	do.	H-23845	R	13.8	4	.176	.4367	.4417	do.
	do.	J-25850	R	13.9	4	.163	.4341	.4487	Mod. 1873. Dated 1886.

Caliber: .44

Colt's Pt. F.A. Mfg. Co., Hartford, Conn.	S.A. Army	61	L	16.55	6	.037	.4213	.4267	"Frontier Six Shooter"— Mod. 1878
	do.	65955	L	16.0	6	.037	.4216	.4300	do.
	do.	74254	L	15.9	6	.041	.4241	.4373	
	S.A. Army 44 Spl.	74917	L	16.1	6	.064	.4199	.4300	Pat. Sept. 19, 1871, July 2, 1872, and Jan. 19, 1875.
	Bisley-Frontier	200828	L	17.6	6	.058	.4202	.4322	"Frontier Six Shooter"— 44/40"
	do.	276415	L	15.5	6	.050	.4197	.4267	do.
	do.	296761	L	16.4	6	.049	.4191	.4289	do.
Connecticut Arms and Mfg. Co., Naubuc, Conn.	Hammond Bull Dog	659	R	21.45	5	.140	.4265	.4329	"Bulldozer." Pat. Oct. 25, '64. S.A., R.F., Single shot pistol.

Caliber and Manufacturer	Model (or Name)	Serial No.	Dir'n of Twist	Inches for 1 turn	No. of Lands	Land Width (inches)	Bore Diameter (inches)	Groove Diameter* (inches)	Remarks
Esprin Hermanos, Eibar, Spain	Euskaro	25371	R	10.6	5	.124	.4092	---	Hinged frame, D.A., has safety.
Hopkins and Allen, Norwich, Conn.	Mod. 1873	2031	R	20.1	5	.136	.4225	---	
	M-H Army Type	1588	R	17.0	5	.031	.4415		Made by H and A for Merwin, Hulbert and Co., 6-shot, S.A.
Iver Johnson Arms and Cycle Works, Fitchburg, Mass.	American Bull Dog	4424	R	31.8	5	.141	.4177	---	
Rogers and Spencer, Willowdale, N.Y.	Army Type	3571	R	36.1	5	.129	.4399	.4513	6-shot, S.A., Perc.
Smith and Wesson, Springfield, Mass.	No. 3 S.A. (Russ)	7183	R	23.0	5	.127	.4135	.4251	No. 3 S.A. Russian, First mod.
	do.	57923	R	20.1	5	.124	.4197	---	do.
	No. 3 S.A. (New Mod.)	3125	R	20.1	5	.128	.4188	---	Pat. Jan. 17, 24, '65; July 11, '65; Aug. 24, '69; Jan. 19, '75; Re. July 25, '71. Dated 1874.
	do.	11329	R	20.0	5	.127	.4185	.4259	Pat. Jan. 17, 24, '65; July 11, '65; Aug. 24, '69; Jan. 19, '75; Re. July 25, '71. Not dated.
	do.	34644	R	18.7	5	.129	.4178	.4241	do.
	44 Special	60742	R	20.1	5	.118	.4178	---	
	Heavy Duty	1252	R	20.0	5	.124	.4196	.4251	Pat. Mar. 27, '94; May 21, '95; Aug. 4, '96; Dec. 22, '96; Oct. 8, '01; Feb. 6, '06.
	1950 Mod.	34095	R	18.9	5	.126	.4181	.4249	

Caliber: 11.5 mm.

Caliber and Manufacturer	Model (or Name)	Serial No.	Dir'n of Twist	Inches for 1 turn	No. of Lands	Land Width (inches)	Bore Diameter (inches)	Groove Diameter* (inches)	Remarks
Werder, Germany	Lightning Mod. 1869	1123	R	31.3	4	.172	.4349	.4555	Single-shot pistol.

Caliber: .45

Caliber and Manufacturer	Model (or Name)	Serial No.	Dir'n of Twist	Inches for 1 turn	No. of Lands	Land Width (inches)	Bore Diameter (inches)	Groove Diameter* (inches)	Remarks
Colt's Pt. F.A. Mfg. Co., Hartford, Conn.	S.A. Army	61900	L	15.9	6	.019	.4473	.4557	"Frontier" Mod. Pat. Sept. 19, '71; July 2, '72; Jan. 19, '75.
	do.	106437	L	15.6	6	.033	.4455	.4567	do.
	do.	122562	L	17.1	6	.031	.4458	.4532	do.
	do.	137672	L	16.0	6	.017	.4473	.4573	do.
	do.	353415	L	16.0	6	.026	.4460	.4534	do.
	Bisley-Frontier	23969	L	15.9	6	.027	.4480	.4550	
	do.	214264	L	16.2	6	.031	.4449	.4563	
	Special Target	317012	L	16.3	6	.071	.4451	.4505	Sometimes called "Bisley Flat Top Mod."
	New Service	75129	L	15.3	6	.062	.4456	.4546	
	do.	321228	L	15.9	6	.070	.4442	.4542	
	D.A. .45 Army	36080-E	L	17.9	6	.065	.4452	.4545	
	do.	197231-H	L	14.8	6	.071	.4451	.4511	
	do.	293595-H	L	16.2	6	.067	.4444	.4523	
	do.	208866	L	16.2	6	.075	.4452	.4519	1917 U.S. Army Type
	S.A. Army	16419 SA	L	16.0	6	.070	.4442	.4522	
Deane, Adams, and Deane, London, England	D.A. Rev.	None	R	18.6	6	.123	.4340	.4524	5-shot, D.A., Solid frame, perc.
Great Western Arms Co., Los Angeles, Calif.	"Frontier"	G.W. 2701	R	16.1	6	.064	.4434	.4534	Copy Colt Frontier Model.
Smith and Wesson, Springfield, Mass.	Schofield	4331	R	20.0	5	.132	.4382	---	Last Pat. July 25, '71.
	"	976	R	22.8	5	.130	.4372	.4425	2nd Mod. Pat. Apr. 22, '73.
	U.S. Army M1917	13878	R	14.7	6	.071	.4447	.4509	
	Mil. and Police	S-85636	R	15.1	6	.061	.4450	.4500	1950 Model.
Starr Arms Co., New York, N.Y.	Starr Pat. Rev.	2217	L	35.5	6	.118	.4500	.4698	Starr's Pat. Jan. 15, '56. 6-shot, D.A., percussion.

Caliber: .455

Caliber and Manufacturer	Model (or Name)	Serial No.	Dir'n of Twist	Inches for 1 turn	No. of Lands	Land Width (inches)	Bore Diameter (inches)	Groove Diameter* (inches)	Remarks
Smith and Wesson, Springfield, Mass.	Mod. 455 Mark II	24025	R	18.75	5	.140	.4415	.4527	Pat. Oct. 8, '01; Dec. 17, '01; Feb. 6, '06
	do.	27683	R	18.7	5	.135	.4470	.4528	do.
	English Service	70155	R	20.0	5	.131	.4480	---	Has English Proof Marks. Marked "Not English made."

Caliber and Manufacturer	Model (or Name)	Serial No.	Dir'n of Twist	Inches for 1 turn	No. of Lands	Land Width (inches)	Bore Diameter (inches)	Groove Diameter* (inches)	Remarks
Smith and Wesson	English Service	7916	R	20.0	5	.130	.4477	---	Has English Proof Marks. Marked: "Not English made."
Webley and Scott, Ltd., Birmingham, England	Mark I	19520	R	20.0	7	.035	.4421	---	
	Mark VI	5048	R	20.2	7	.038	.4442	---	
	do.	212739	R	20.1	7	.040	.4463	---	Dated 1916.
	do.	265390	R	20.1	7	.030	.4425		Dated 1917.
	do.	350361	R	20.2	7	.036	.4425	.4470	
	do.	388521	R	20.0	7	.044	.4433	---	
Caliber: 12 mm.									
Mre. Liegéoise D'Armes a Feu., Liége, Belgium	Galand	515	R	19.3	12				C.F. Galand Pat. Lands semicylindrical in shape.
Caliber: .50									
E. Remington and Sons, Ilion, N.Y.	Navy Mod. 1867	2839	R	30.0	3	.235	.5003	.5062	S.S. Pistol. Pat. May 3, Nov. 18, '64; Apr. 17 '68.

Section II

Data on automatic pistols arranged by number of grooves and direction of twist

Introductory statement

To assist the investigator who wishes to ascertain the possible make of an automatic pistol from which an evidence bullet has been fired, from measurements and observations he has made on that bullet, the data contained in Tables 16 and 17 have been re-arranged according to the number of grooves and direction of twist for each of the calibers from .22 to .455. These are given in Table 18.

As a knowledge of the groove diameter is of little importance, for reasons explained in a previous chapter, the values for these have been omitted. As has also been pointed out, measurements on a single specimen must not be considered as necessarily representing the established rifling characteristics (i.e., "book values") of pistols of that make, model, and caliber, or even of normal production of the same. Other specimens may differ markedly and often do. It will be noted that for each caliber, make, and model the number of specimens that were measured is stated.

It is obvious that there is a considerable variation in the values for the land widths, particularly; and

this is unfortunate because this is the determination that is most easily made. Vice versa, the degree of rifling twist is a characteristic which does not vary much (proportionately), but, again unfortunately, this is the characteristic most difficult to determine from measurements on the evidence bullet.

Even for the pistols made by manufacturers of arms of high quality there are variations in rifling characteristics which are greater than were expected; and this is naturally disappointing because it had been hoped that established specifications would be followed much more closely than they actually are. Had such been the case the information obtained in this extensive series of measurements would have been more useful. However, from both a scientific and a practical point of view, it is important to know what the facts really are, whether the results are helpful or not.

From the statements made above, the author hopes that he has not left the impression that the data in these tables are of no value and that rifling characteristics are not helpful in giving information as to the make of weapon which may have fired an evidence bullet. In some cases they will be useful and in others they will not, which was the situation before this study was made. The difference is that now we have a much better knowledge of what the facts actually are.

TABLE 18
Automatic pistols arranged by number of grooves and direction of twist

Class (No.- Twist)	Gun Name and/or Model	Manufacturer	Inches for 1 turn	Width of Land (inches)	Bore Diameter (inches)	No. Meas'd	Remarks
.22 Caliber							
4-R	Charola-Anitua	Charola, Anitua y Cia.	9.7	.069	.2005	1	
"	Fiala Repeating Pistol	Fiala Arms and Equipment Co.	16.0	.100-.103	.2183-.2185	2	
4-L	None encountered						
5-R	None encountered						
5-L	None encountered						
6-R	Beretta—Mod. 948	Pietro Beretta	13.7-14.0	.029-.042	.2124-.2190	4	
"	" Mod. 1950	do.	13.5	.041	.2134	1	
"	" Olympic	do.	13.5-13.8	.021-.034	.2124-.2140	2	
"	Bernardelli—Baby	V. Bernardelli	10.0	.058	.2135	1	
"	" Target Pistol	do.	17.9	.045	.2132	1	
"	Erma Target Pistol	Erma Waffenfabrik	17.4	.046-.048	.2125-.2139	2	
"	Galesi—Mod. 503A	Industria Armi Galesi	8.35	.041	.2075	1	
"	Hämmerli—Olympia	Hämmerli and Co.	17.6	.026	.2150	1	
"	Hartford—.22 L.R.	Hartford Arms and Equipment Co.	14.8-14.85	.043-.052	.2162-.2165	2	
"	"J.C. Higgins"—Mod. 80	High Standard Mfg. Co.	16.2	.058	.2178	1	
"	"J.C. Higgins"—Mod. 85	Mre. d'Armes des Pyrénées	12.0-12.1	.062-.067	.2119-.2124	2	
"	HI Stan'd—Mod. A	High Standard Mfg. Co.	14.0	.034	.2130	1	
"	do. Mod. B	do.	13.8-13.9	.026-.033	.2122-.2125	3	
"	do. Mod. C	do.	13.9	.032	.2128	1	
"	do. Mod. HB	do.	14.0	.027-.030	.2130-.2140	2	
"	do. Mod. HD	do.	13.7-14.0	.022-.034	.2123-.2137	8	
"	do. Duramatic	do.	17.0 17.3	.055	.2163-.2168	?	
"	do. Sport King	do.	13.9-14.0	.022-.024	.2125-.2137	4	
"	do. do.	do.	16.0-16.1	.058	.2178-.2180	2	Note change in rifling.
"	Hungarian—Type 29	Fegyvergyar	15.6	.031	.2126	1	
"	Llama—Mod. XV	Gabilondo y Cia.	15.4-15.6	.051-.052	.2109-.2113	3	
"	M.A.B.—Mod. F	Mre. d'Armes Automatiques Bayonne	15.8	.051	.2136	1	
"	" Le Chasseur Mod.	do.	12.7-12.6	.053-.055	.2124-.2138	2	
"	Melior	Robar et Cie.	9.55	.036	.2091	1	
"	Reising	Reising Arms Co.	15.0-15.6	.029-.040	.2151-.2169	3	
"	Rino Galesi	Rigarmi	8.6	.056	.1983	1	Dated 1958
"	Römerwerk	Römerwerk Akt. Ges.	14.3-14.4	.031-.035	.2126-.2132	4	
"	Ruger—Standard Mod.	Sturm, Ruger and Co.	14.0-14.1	.026-.029	.2148-.2157	4	
"	do.	do.	13.9-14.0	.044-.059	.2143-.2166	5	Note change in land width.
"	S.I.G.—SP 47/48	Soc. Industrie Suisse	17.7	.036-.037	.2138-.2145	2	
"	S and W Target Auto— Mod. 41	Smith and Wesson	15.0	.038	.2142-.2150	2	
"	Mod. F—Star Sport	Bonifacio Echeverria	12.1-12.4	.040-.046	.2119-.2126	4	
"	Star—Olimpic Mod.	do.	12.6	.040	.2137	1	
"	Star—Mod. HF	do.	12.4	.035	.2124	1	
"	Walther—Mod. PP	Mre de Machines du Haut Rhin	9.9	.063	.2150	1	
"	" Mod. PP	Waffenfabrik Walther	9.5	.044	.2104	1	
"	" Target Pistol	do.	16.2-18.0	.035-.047	.2138-.2140	3	

Class (No.-Twist)	Gun Name and/or Model	Manufacturer	Inches for 1 turn	Width of Land (inches)	Bore Diameter (inches)	No. Meas'd	Remarks
6-R	Walther—Olympia Mod.	Waffenfabrik Walther	17.9	.046	.2152	1	
"	Whitney	Whitney Firearms Inc.	17.0-17.6	.052-.054	.2178-.2199	4	Formerly called Wolverine and Lightning.
6-L	Astra—Mod. 2000	Astra Unceta y Cia.	9.3-9.6	.033-.040	.2122-.2139	7	One specimen had groove width of 0.015".
"	Colt—.22 L.R.	Colt's Pt. F.A. Mfg. Co.	16.1	.034	.2158	1	Pre-Woodsman Model.
"	do.	do.	14.0-14.3	.032-.039	.2142-.2150	2	Note change of twist.
"	Colt—Woodsman	do.	14.0-14.6	.033-.042	.2134-.2167	9	
"	" Match Target	do.	13.9-14.1	.037-.041	.2131-.2140	6	
"	" Officers Mod.	do.	14.1-14.3	.040-.044	.2132-.2143	2	
"	" Challenger	do.	13.9-14.0	.037-.049	.2131-.2134	2	
"	" Ace	do.	14.0	.036	.2139	1	
"	" Service Ace	do.	14.1	.034	.2145	1	
"	" Conversion Unit	do.	11.9	.041	.2125	1	
"	Hafdasa—Army Mod.	Hispano Argentina Fab. de Automoviles, Soc. Anon.	16.1	.031	.2196	1	
"	" Pocket Mod.	do.	15.3	.037	.2157	1	
"	Tala	Tallares de Armas Livianas Argentinas	16.0	.041	.2159	1	
"	Ttibar	S.R.L. Ind. Argentina	21.6	.045		1	Single shot pistol. Ejects fired shell.
"	Pistolet de Tir "UNIQUE"	Mre. d'Armes des Pyrénées	18.3	.062	.2108	1	
"	do.	do.	12.0	.057	.2117	1	Obviously a change in specifications.
"	"UNIQUE"—Mod. 52	do.	12.3	.066	.2126	1	
7-R	None encountered						
7-L	None encountered						
8-R	Modelo Corla	Fab. de Armas Zaragoza	16.3	.026	.2010	1	Only about 100 made.
8-L	None encountered						

6.35 mm. (.25) Caliber

Class (No.-Twist)	Gun Name and/or Model	Manufacturer	Inches for 1 turn	Width of Land (inches)	Bore Diameter (inches)	No. Meas'd	Remarks
4-R	Dreyse	Rheinische Metallwaren u. Maschinenfabrik	10.0-10.3	.035-.059	.2445-.2452	3	
"	E.A.—1916 Mod.	Eschave y Arizmendi	8.3	.080	.2573	1	
"	Francotte	A. Francotte	9.9	.081	.2428	1	
"	Kobra	Unknown (German)	9.6	.066-.080	.2445-.2454	2	
"	Kommer—Mod. II	Th. Kommer Waffenfabrik	9.8-10.0	.065-.089	.2457-.2463	3	
"	Langenhan—Mod. II	Fr. Langenhan	9.5	.067	.2399	1	
"	Liliput	Fegyvergyar	9.9-10.0	.058-.060	.2429-.2430	2	
"	Mayor	Francois Mayor	26.6	.045	.2457	1	Pat. by E. Rochat.
"	Merke	Unknown (Spanish)	7.7	.060	.2503	1	
"	Praha	Zbrojovka Praha	10.0	.084	.2435	1	
"	Schmeisser—Mod. I	C.G. Haenel	9.65-10.2	.060-.068	.2442-.2475	4	
"	Stock	Franz Stock	9.2-9.6	.044-.048	.2500-.2503	2	
"	Walther—Mod. 5	Waffenfabrik Walther	9.6-9.85	.065-.069	.2452-.2473	2	Also made with 6-R.
"	" Mod. 7	do.	10.2	.069	.2430	1	
"	Zehna	E. Zehner	7.2	.060	.2450	1	
4-L	None encountered						
5-R	H and R Self Loading	Harrington and Richardson	12.0	.072	.2460	1	Very early production. Soon changed to 6-R.
"	"Protector" Patent	Prob. Echave y Arizmendi	9.3	.100	.2466	1	Possibly made by Santigo Salaberrin.
5-L	None encountered						
6-R	Action	Modesto Santos	10.4	.043	.2456	1	
"	Alkar	Man. de Armas de Fuego	10.6	.038	.2445	1	
"	"Allies"	Berasaluze Areitio-Aurtena y Cia.	15.4	.043	.2483	1	
"	"Automatique Francaise"	Soc. Francaise d'Armes Automatique	10.2	.029	.2486	1	
"	Beretta—1919 Type	Pietro Beretta	10.1-10.3	.040-.041	.2467	2	Earlier production.
"	do.	do.	11.7	.025	.2450	1	Late production.
"	Beretta—Mod. 1934	do.	10.0-11.95	.022-.042	.2465-.2467	2	Also called Mod. 318.
"	" Bantam	do.	10.0-10.3	.035-.037	.2462-.2471	5	
"	" Featherweight	do.	10.3	.035	.2467	1	
"	Bergmann Mod. II	Th. Bergmann Waffenfabrik	9.8	.030	.2441	1	
"	" Erben Mod. II	August Menz	9.9	.038	.2482	1	
"	Bernardelli	Vincenzo Bernardelli	9.6-10.4	.038-.058	.2414-.2432	5	
"	Bernedo	V. Bernedo y Cia.	11.0	.045	.2472	1	
"	Browning—Baby	Fab. Nat'l. de Armes de Guerre	9.7-11.35	.031-.036	.2437-.2447	3	
"	Browning—Mod. 1906	do.	9.5-9.8	.024-.042	.2440-.2449	3	
"	Bulwark	Beistegui Hermanos	9.8	.063	.2456	1	
"	CZ—Mod. 1936	Ceska Zbrojovka	7.9-7.95	.025-.032	.2444-.2454	3	

Class (No.-Twist)	Gun Name and/or Model	Manufacturer	Inches for 1 turn	Width of Land (inches)	Bore Diameter (inches)	No. Meas'd	Remarks
6-R	CZ—Mod. 1945	Česka Zbrojovka	7.9-7.95	.030-.037	.2444-.2460	8	
"	Chylewski	Soc. Industrielle Suisse	9.0	.033	.2440	1	
"	Clement—Mod. 1908	Charles Ph. Clement	9.4	.050	.2453	1	
"	Delu	Fab. d'Armes F. Delu et Cia.	10.0	.038	.2448	1	Also made with 6-L.
"	DUO	F. Dušek	10.5-10.65	.033-.044	.2440-.2453	4	
"	E. B. A. C.	Unknown (Prob. Spanish)	12.2	.042	.2453	1	
"	Express	Tomas de Urizar y Cia.	11.4	.043	.2453	1	
"	F. M. E. (or FAMAE)	Fab. de Material de Guerra	8.95	.034	.2434	1	
"	"Le Francais"—Policeman	Mre. Francaise d'Armes et Cycles de St. Etienne	10.4-10.7	.032-.041	.2444-.2460	3	
"	"Le Francais"—Pocket Mod.	do.	10.3-10.6	.039-.040	.2448-.2460	2	
"	Galesi—Mod. 9	Industria Armi Galesi	7.3-11.8	.055-.065	.2413-.2498	4	
"	Gecado	Trade mark of G. C. Dornheim	7.4	.061	.2457	1	Has Spanish Proof Marks.
"	H & R Self Loading	Harrington and Richardson	11.8-12.6	.021-.037	.2451-.2475	3	Earliest production was with 5-R.
"	Helfricht—Mod. III	A. Krausser Waffenfabrik	9.6-9.7	.027-.035	.2446-.2450	2	
"	Jieffeco	Robar et Dekerkhove	9.4-9.8	.023-.030	.2422-.2432	1	
"	"Kaba Spezial"	Francisco Arizmendi	10.7-12.2	.039-.047	.2461-.2462	2	Spanish version of Kaba made by Menz.
"	Liberty	Retolaza Hermanos	9.65	.045	.2469	1	
"	"Liége"	Mre. Liégeoise d'Armes a Feu	9.6	.039	.2448	1	Identical to New Mod. Melior.
"	Lignose—Mod. 2	Theodore Bergmann	9.5	.033	.2433	1	
"	" Mod. 2A	do.	9.6	.036	.2433	1	
"	" Mod. 3	do.	9.5-9.7	.022-.027	.2409-.2457	2	
"	" Mod. 3A	do.	9.7	.033	.2443	1	
"	Liliput	August Menz	8.45	.035	.2483	1	
"	Little Tom	Wiener Waffenfabrik	15.4	.054	.2458	1	
"	M. A. B. —Type A	Mre. d'Armes Aut. Bayonne	11.2	.046	.2456	1	Model designations had not yet been adopted.
"	" Mod. A	do.	12.4	.046	.2452	1	
"	" Mod. E	do.	12.2	.044	.2447	1	
"	Mann—W. T. Mod.	Fritz Mann	9.6-9.8	.031-.032	.2450-.2457	2	
"	Mauser—Type 1910	Waffenfabrik Mauser	7.1-7.3	.038-.047	.2450-.2470	4	
"	" Type 1914	do.	7.1	.047	.2463	1	
"	" W. T. P. Mod. I	do.	7.15	.046	.2461	1	
"	" " Mod. II	do.	7.0-7.1	.044-.047	.2445-.2453	3	
"	Melior—Old Mod.	Robar and Dekerkhove	9.6	.033	.2434	1	Later Robar et Cie.
"	" New Mod.	do.	9.45-9.6	.023-.033	.2418-.2434	4	
"	Menta	August Menz	9.6	.025	.2465	1	
"	Merke	Unknown (Spanish)	7.7	.060	.2503	1	
"	Mikros	Mre. d'Armes des Pyrénées	12.0	.043	.2458	1	
"	Mondial	Gaspar Arizaga	10.9	.035	.2482	1	Also made with 6-L.
"	Monobloc	J. Jacquemart	9.5	.047	.2414	1	
"	M. S.	Modesto Santos	10.9	.069	.2460	1	
"	Ortgies	Deutsche Werke	7.1-7.2	.029-.036	.2438-.2476	8	
"	O. W. A.	Oesterr, Werke gws Anstalt	10.0	.046	.2473	1	
"	Pistolet Aut. LePage	Mre. d'Armes LePage	9.9	.035	.2455	1	
"	Phoenix	Pheonix Arms	9.85	.030	.2439	1	Prob. Spanish.
"	"Princeps" Pat.	Tomas de Urizar y Cia.	4.3-4.7	.029-.034	.2456-.2468	2	For Thieme y Edeler.
"	Regina	Gregorio Bolumburu	14.9-15.7	.032-.045	.2468-.2477	3	
"	Salaberrin "Aut. Pist. 6.35"	Santigo Salaberrin	9.5	.044	.2451	1	
"	Le Sans Pareil	Mre. d'Armes des Pyrénées	12.7	.040	.2468	1	
"	Sata	Tanfoglio and Sabotti	9.9	.043	.2455	1	
"	Sauer—Old Mod.	J. P. Sauer u. Sohn	14.3-14.6	.039-.043	.2456-.2460	2	
"	" V. P.—First Form	do.	14.2	.038	.2448	1	
"	" V. P. —Mod. 28	do.	9.4-9.5	.029-.040	.2451-.2460	2	
"	S. E. A. M.	Soc. Española de Armas y Municiones	8.2	.064	.2492	1	
"	Sharp Shooter	Hijos de José Aldazabal	11.0	.053	.2460	1	
"	Simson	Waffenfabriken Simson and Co.	9.6	.048	.2443	1	
"	Slavia	A. Vilimec	11.8	.027	.2440	1	
"	Star—ca. 1906	Bonifacio Echeverria	9.3	.026	.2467	1	
"	" Mod. CO	do.	9.7	.039	.2461	1	
"	" Mod. CO	do.	12.0-12.5	.035-.046	.2461-.2466	2	Note change in twist.
"	" Mod. CU	do.	12.8	.037	.2467	1	
"	Steyr—Mod. 1909	Oesterr. Waffenfabrik Ges.	12.45	.048	.2461	1	
"	do.	do.	8.65-9.0	.043-.046	.2457-.2465	3	Note change in twist.
"	Thunder	Martin A. Bascaran	10.9	.052	.2464	1	
"	Tigre	Garate, Anitua y Cia.	9.7	.056	.2470	1	
"	Tisan	Santigo Salaberrin	9.7	.052	.2450	1	
"	Titan	Retolaza Hermanos	10.9	.050	.2462	1	

Class (No.-Twist)	Gun Name and/or Model	Manufacturer	Inches for 1 turn	Width of Land (inches)	Bore Diameter (inches)	No. Meas'd	Remarks
6-R	"TOZ"	Tulski Oruzheinyi Zavod	7.0	.036	.2459	1	"TOZ" same as Korovin.
"	Tula-Korovin	do.	7.3-7.6	.030-.033	.2448-.2454	2	
"	Pist. Aut. Francais "UNION"	Seytres Fabrique à St. Etienne	11.0	.053	.2421	1	
"	Walman	Francisco Arizmendi	10.5	.036	.2473	1	
"	"	Arizmendi y Goenage	12.3	.029	.2485	1	
"	Walther—Mod. 1	Carl Walther Waffenfabrik	9.9	.038	.2470	1	
"	" Mod. 2	do.	9.6	.028	.2491	1	
"	" Mod. 5	do.	9.5	.028	.2426	1	Also made with 4-R.
"	" Mod. 8	do.	9.6-9.8	.020-.032	.2471-.2490	1	
"	" Mod. 8	do.	7.95	.043	.2450	1	Note change in rifling.
"	" Mod. 9	do.	9.4-9.55	.011-.017	.2480-.2503	2	
"	Webley—V.P.	Webley and Scott, Ltd.	10.0-10.1	.022-.034	.2459-.2472	2	
"	Zoli	A. Zoli	9.9	.040	.2450	1	
6-L	Astra—Mod. 200	Astra Unceta y Cia.	9.6	.036	.2460	1	
"	" Mod. 202	do.	9.6-10.1	.039-.043	.2469-.2470	2	
"	Bayard—Mod. 1908	Anc. Etablissements Pieper	9.4-9.9	.022-.032	.2395-.2425	2	
"	" Mod. 1930	do.	9.6	.021	.2419	1	
"	Bronco—1918	Echave y Arizmendi	11.0-11.2	.049-.051	.2451-.2460	2	
"	Colt—Pocket Mod.	Colt's Pt. F.A. Mfg. Co.	14.2-17.3	.033-.048	.2428-.2458	13	Values of 14.2 and 17.3 very exceptional. 11 of 13 meas'd. showed twist 16.0 to 16.5". Av. = 16.2".
"	"Junior Colt"	Astra Unceta y Cia.	9.6	.044	.2453	1	Made for Colt Co.
"	Delu	Fab. d'Armes F. Delu et Cie.	10.1	.047	.2448	1	Also made with 6-R.
"	Errasti	A. Errasti	10.9	.030	.2450	1	
"	"Liberty"	Unknown (Spanish)	10.1	.038	.2455	1	
"	Looking Glass	Domingo Acha	10.6-10.7	.050-.056	.2443-.2454	2	
"	Marina	Gregorio Bolumburu	9.1	.054	.2442	1	
"	Martian (Com'l)	Martin A. Bascaran	10.1	.051	.2453	1	
"	Mondial	Gaspar Arizaga	10.4	.024	.2482	1	Also made with 6-R.
"	MS	Modesto Santos	10.7	.048	.2435	1	
"	Protector	Echave y Arizmendi	10.8	.038	.2449	1	
"	"Reims" Pat. Mod. 1914	Azanza y Arrizabalaga	9.5	.034	.2450	1	
"	"Renard Pat."	Echave y Arizmendi	10.1	.040	.2448	1	
"	Stosel—No. 1	Retolaza Hermanos	9.7	.052	.2467	1	
"	"UNIQUE"	Mre. d'Armes des Pyrénées	13.1	.039	.2466	1	
"	Victoria—Mod. 1916	Esperanza y Unceta	10.6	.057	.2468	1	Now Astra Unceta y Cia.

7.62 mm. Caliber

Class (No.-Twist)	Gun Name and/or Model	Manufacturer	Inches for 1 turn	Width of Land (inches)	Bore Diameter (inches)	No. Meas'd	Remarks
4-R	Tokarev	U.S.S.R. Arsenals	9.4-10.5	.073-.097	.3020-.3150	12	
4-L	None encountered						

7.63 mm. Caliber

Class (No.-Twist)	Gun Name and/or Model	Manufacturer	Inches for 1 turn	Width of Land (inches)	Bore Diameter (inches)	No. Meas'd	Remarks
4-R	Mannlicher—Mod. 1903	Waffenfabrik Steyr	10.55	.107	.3020	1	
"	" Mod. 1905	do.	9.85	.100	.3029	1	
"	Mauser Mil. Pistol	Waffenfabrik Mauser	9.85-9.95	.112-.117	.3007-.3024	5	
"	Schwarzlose—Mod. 1908 "Standart" Mod.	A.W. Schwarzlose	9.0	.085	.3000	1	
4-L	None encountered						
5-R	None encountered						
5-L	None encountered						
6-R	Astra—Mod. 900	Unceta y Cia.	10.1	.056	.3030	1	
"	" Mod. 902	do.	10.1	.064	.3037	1	
"	Mauser—Mil. Pistol	Waffenfabrik Mauser	7.8-7.9	.039-.045	.3013-.3034	10	
"	do M-712	do.	7.9	.040	.3022	1	
"	Star—Mod. A	Bonifacio Echeverria	14.7-14.9	.037	.3014-.3017	2	
"	Super Azul	Eulogio Arostegui	13.65	.057	.3020	1	
"	Royal	Zulaica y Cia.	13.7	.060	.3010	1	
6-L	None encountered						

7.65 mm. (.32) Caliber

Class (No.-Twist)	Gun Name and/or Model	Manufacturer	Inches for 1 turn	Width of Land (inches)	Bore Diameter (inches)	No. Meas'd	Remarks
4-R	Dreyse	Rhein. Metallwaren u. Maschinenfabrik	15.8-17.35	.040-.061	.3007-.3024	13	
"	Frommer Stop	Fegyvergyar	9.4-10.2	.104-.116	.3016-.3027	6	
"	Jäger	Jäger and Co.	8.9-17.7	.052-.068	.3018-.3043	5	Av. twist—14.1".
"	Langenhan	Fr. Langenhan	9.4-9.6	.059-.088	.3003-.3040	7	
"	Luger—Mod. 1924	Waffenfabrik Bern	9.8	.110	.3006	1	
"	" Mod. 06/29	do.	9.9	.112	.3006	1	
"	" Mod. 1900	Deutsche Waffen u. Munitions Fab.	9.8	.108	.3016	1	

Class (No.- Twist)	Gun Name and/or Model	Manufacturer	Inches for 1 turn	Width of Land (inches)	Bore Diameter (inches)	No. Meas'd	Remarks
4-R	Luger—Mod. 1908	Deutsche Waffen u. Munitions Fab.	9.6-10.0	.102-.113	.3007-.3022	11	Av. twist—9.85".
"	" Carbine	do.	17.8-17.9	.110-.115	.3010	2	
"	Mann—Pocket Mod.	Mann Werke	9.7	.043	.3053	1	
"	M.A.S.—Mod. 1925—No. 1	Mre. d'Armes St. Etienne	10.0	.062	.3023	1	
"	" Mod. 1935S	Mre. d'Armes St. Etienne	9.9	.064	.3017	1	
"	Praha	Česka Zbrojovka	9.5	.075	.3007	1	
"	"	Zbrojovka Praha	9.9	.101	.3041	1	
"	S.A.C.M.—1935A	Soc. Alsacienne de Construction Mecanique	9.85-9.9	.083-.089	.3012-.3021	5	
"	Sauer—Mod. 38(H)	J. P. Sauer u. Sohn	9.4-9.55	.057-.066	.3011-.3024	12	
"	Schwarzlose—Mod. 1908	A.W. Schwarzlose	8.0-8.2	.088-.095	.2960-.2967	2	
"	Stock	Franz Stock	9.4-9.7	.052-.066	.3016-.3017	2	
"	Walther—Mod. 4	Carl Walther Waffenfabrik	9.7-10.0	.065-.077	.3013-.3020	4	Also made with 6-R.
4-L	None encountered						
5-R	Browning—Mod. 1900	Fab. Nat'l. d'Armes de Guerre	7.4-7.45	.033-.039	.3001-.3023	2	Later production had 6-R.
"	Jieffeco	Robar and Dekerkhove	9.6	.044	.3025	1	Later Robar et Cie.
"	M.A.B.—Mod. C.	Mre. d'Armes Aut. Bayonne	12.1	.087	.2999	1	
"	Melior—Old Mod.	Robar and Dekerkhove	9.5-9.6	.049-.058	.3011-.3021	2	Later Robar et Cie.
"	" New Mod.	do.	9.6	.069	.3022	1	
5-L	None encountered						
6-R	Astra—Mod. 1911	Esperanza y Unceta	9.7-9.8	.036-.048	.3025-.3030	2	
"	Astra—Mod. 300	Astra Unceta y Cia.	9.4	.039	.3024	1	
"	" Mod. 3000	do.	9.5-9.6	.044-.045	.3026-.3027	2	
"	Beholla	Becker and Holländer	8.5	.029-.037	.3012-.3017	2	
"	"	Stenda Werke	9.6	.037	.3015	1	
"	Beretta—1915 Type	Pietro Beretta	10.3	.046	.3037	1	
"	Beretta—"Mod. 1935"	do.	10.2	.046	.3021	1	Later designated as Mod. 1934.
"	" Mod. 1934	do.	9.85-10.5	.040-.054	.3015-.3036	12	
"	Bernardelli—Target	V. Bernardelli	10.0	.054	.2990	1	
"	Browning—Mod. 1900	Fab. Nat'l. Armes de Guerre	9.3-9.8	.030-.037	.3013-.3034	5	Earlier production had 5 lands.
"	" Mod. 1910	do.	9.4-9.8	.021-.041	.3006-.3053	10	
"	" Mod. 1922	do.	9.6-9.8	.022-.031	.3014-.3020	8	
"	Bufalo	Gabilondo y Cia.	10.4	.049	.3010	1	
"	Clement—Mod. 1907	Charles Ph. Clement	9.8	.027	.3030	1	
"	Czech—Mod. 27	Böhmische Waffenfabrik	9.8-10.0	.043-.060	.3014-.3025	18	Germans changed name from Česka Zbrojovka.
"	" Mod. 27	Česka Zbrojovka (in Prague)	9.85	.051	.3021	1	Made after liberation by Germans.
"	" Mod. 27	Česka Zbrojovka Narodní Podnik	9.85	.054	.3016	1	
"	Demon	Unknown (Spanish)	9.6	.061	.3028	1	
"	Destructor	Iraola Salaverria	10.7	.052	.3000	1	
"	D.W.M.	Deutsche Waffen u. Munitions Fab.	9.9	.037-.040	.3014-.3021	2	
"	Express	Tomas de Urizar y Cia.	15.1	.051	.3027	1	
"	Galesi—Mod. 6	Industria Armi Galesi	10.8	.056	.2982	1	
"	" Mod. 9	do.	10.2	.052	.2918	1	
"	Gavage	Fab. d'Armes de Guerre, Haute Precision Armand Gavage	9.6	.052	.3011	1	
"	Hungarian—Mod. 37	Metallwaren Waffen u. Maschinen Fabrik	7.9-8.0	.037-.045	.3017-.3025	10	
"	Infallible	Davis-Warner Corp.	11.2-11.5	.053-.059	.3016-.3023	2	
"	Leonhardt	H. M. Gering and Co.	9.5-10.0	.044-.059	.3014-.3061	2	
"	Llama—Mod. X	Gabilondo y Cia.	11.8-12.0	.040-.044	.3016-.3025	3	
"	" Mod. XA	do.	11.9-12.5	.040-.051	.3024-.3035	5	
"	M.A.B.—Mod. D	Mre. d'Armes Aut. Bayonne	12.3	.026-.044	.3007-.3012	3	
"	" Mod. R	do.	12.5	.044	.3010	1	
"	Mars	Kohout and Spol	10.5-10.7	.046-.052	.3012-.3026	2	
"	Martian	Martin A. Bascaran	10.4	.036	.3021	1	Also made with 6-L.
"	Mauser—1910 Type	Waffenfabrik Mauser	7.95	.047	.3020	1	
"	" 1914 Type	do.	7.8-8.0	.032-.058	.3012-.3030	12	
"	" New Mod. 1934	do.	7.7-8.0	.032-.044	.3018-.3034	8	
"	" Mod. H Sc	do.	7.7-7.9	.038-.052	.3018-.3030	7	
"	" do.	do.	9.85-9.9	.047-.052	.3026-.3029	2	Apparently a change in twist.
"	Menta	August Menz	9.5	.050	.3037	1	
"	Menz—Mod. II	do.	8.6	.059	.3014	1	
"	" Mod. (?)	do.	15.0	.028	.3032	1	
"	" PB Special	do.	9.4	.043	.3000	1	
"	Omega	R. S. Industria Obrera Armera	10.6	.054	.3050	1	

Class (No.-Twist)	Gun Name and/or Model	Manufacturer	Inches for 1 turn	Width of Land (inches)	Bore Diameter (inches)	No. Meas'd	Remarks
6-R	Ortgies	Ortgies and Co.	7.9	.033-.037	.3017-.3025	3	
"	"	Deutsche Werke, A.G.	7.8-8.0	.026-.040	.3017-.3035	15	
"	Paramount	Unknown (Spanish)	8.8	.051	.3045	1	Possibly made by Retolaza Hermanos.
"	"Pistola Automatica"	Hijos de Arrizabalaga	14.85	.052	.3026	1	
"	Plus Ultra	Gabilondo y Cia.	12.0	.055	.3023	1	
"	"Princeps" Pat.	Tomas de Urizar y Cia.	6.15	.040	.3039	1	
"	Roland	Francisco Arizmendi	10.4	.051	.3055	1	
"	Royal	Zulaica y Cia.	9.5	.074	.3030	1	
"	Ruby—1915 Mod.	Gabilondo y Urresti	10.3-10.4	.048-.051	.3011-.3012	2	
"	Sauer—Model of 1913	J.P. Sauer u. Sohn	16.6	.029	.3024	1	
"	do.	do.	14.2-14.5	.030-.038	.3006-.3029	5	Note change in twist.
"	Sauer—Behorden Mod.	do.	14.2	.048-.050	.3015-.3016	2	
"	Savage—Mod. 1907	Savage Arms Co.	16.0-16.4	.034-.045	.3051-.3092	3	Early production.
"	" Mod. 1907	do.	12.0-12.2	.039-.051	.3045-.3062	13	Note change in twist.
"	" Mod. 1915	do.	12.1	.040	.3046	1	
"	" Mod. 1917	do.	12.0-12.1	.038-.042	.3043-.3055	3	
"	Le Secours	Tomas de Urizar y Cia.	9.4	.051	.3000	1	
"	Sharp Shooter	Hijos de José Aldazabal	10.9	.052	.3041	1	
"	Singer	Arizmendi y Goenaga	10.8-12.5	.036-.041	.3030-.3037	2	
"	Star—1919 Type	Bonifacio Echeverria	12.0-12.3	.035-.046	.3020-.3033	3	
"	" Mod. S.I.	do.	12.4-12.6	.043-.044	.3017-.3020	2	
"	Stenda	Stenda Werke Waffenfabrik	9.5-9.7	.041-.046	.3020-.3028	3	
"	Steyr—Mod. 1909	Oesterr. Waffenfabrik Steyr	9.8-9.9	.034-.041	.3021	2	
"	Venus	Tomas de Urizar y Cia.	6.5	.036	.3023	1	
"	Walman	Francisco Arizmendi	10.9	.041	.3012	1	
"	Walther—Mod. 4	Carl Walther Waffenfabrik	9.5	.040	.3036	1	Also made with 4-R.
"	" Mod. PP	do.	9.3-10.0	.052-.056	.3015-.3025	8	
"	" Mod. PPK	do.	9.3-10.0	.051-.060	.3018-.3025	8	
"	Webley—Met. Police Mod.	Webley and Scott, Ltd.	10.1	.036-.048	.3034-.3060	2	
"	" Mod. 1906	do.	10.1	.032	.3032	1	
"	Ydeal	Francisco Arizmendi	10.9	.057	.3010	1	
6-L	Alkar—Pocket Mod.	Alkartasuna Fab. de Armas	10.4	.048	.3009	1	
"	Alkartasuna	do.	10.3-10.6	.040-.050	.3005-.3036	5	
"	Bayard—Mod. 1909	Anc. Etablissements Pieper	9.85-12.6	.031-.042	.3040-.3043	4	
"	B.H.—1914 Aut. Pistol	Beistegui Hermanos	12.2	.045	.3015	1	
"	Bristol	Gregorio Bolumburu	10.3	.040	.3009	1	
"	Bronco—Mod. 1918	Echave y Arizmendi	10.2-11.1	.057-.064	.3001-.3025	2	
"	Brunswig—1916 Mod.	Esperanza y Unceta Cia.	9.5	.044	.3016	1	
"	Cebra	Arizmendi y Zulaica	10.8	.057	.3041	1	
"	Colt—1903 Mod.	Colt's Pt. F.A. Mfg. Co.	15.5-16.4	.038-.050	.3036-.3055	9	
"	Destroyer	Isidro Gaztañaga	12.0-12.25	.037-.048	.3007-.3025	2	
"	E.A.—Mod. 1916	Echave y Arizmendi	10.0	.048	.3011	1	
"	Izarra	Bonifacio Echeverria	10.3	.049-.051	.3009-.3014	2	
"	Longines	Cooperativa Obrera	10.3	.062	.2993	1	
"	Martian	Martin A. Bascaran	10.2-12.5	.039-.058	.3011-.3019	2	Also made with 6-R.
"	Le Page	Mre. d'Armes Le Page	9.5	.042	.3089	1	
"	Paramount	Retolaza Hermanos	12.3	.037	.2990	1	
"	"	Unknown (Prob. Retolaza)	11.0	.032	.2994	1	Marked "Fab. de Armes de Guerre" (Sales organization)
"	Regina	Gregorio Bolumburu	10.4	.048	.3044	1	
"	"Reims" Pat. Mod. 1914	Azanza y Arrizabalaga	11.1	.047	.3010	1	
"	"Reims" Pat. Mod. 1916	do.	10.8-11.0	.053-.057	.3015-.3019	1	
"	Retolaza—Mod. 1914	Retolaza Hermanos	10.4-12.5	.035-.056	.3008-.3020	3	
"	Royal	M. Zulaica y Cia.	13.2	.041	.3026	1	
"	Salaverria	Iraola Salaverria	10.5	.050	.3021	1	
"	Stosel—No. 1	Retolaza Hermanos	12.0-12.6	.039-.050	.3010-.3016	2	
"	"UNIQUE"	Mre. d'Armes des Pyrénées	12.1-12.4	.043-.065	.3008-.3026	7	All war production—German supervision.
"	"UNIS" Mod.	do.	10.5	.053-.059	.3011-.3037	2	Made for a dealer.
"	Vesta	Hijos de A. Echeverria	10.2-10.3	.038-.055	.3015-.3017	3	
"	"	do.	10.3	.049	.3050	1	This specimen had "ratchet grooves".
7-R	Remington P.A.—M51	Remington—U.M.C.	15.8-16.0	.033-.047	.3038-.3050	4	
7-L	None encountered						

".35" Caliber

Class (No.-Twist)	Gun Name and/or Model	Manufacturer	Inches for 1 turn	Width of Land (inches)	Bore Diameter (inches)	No. Meas'd	Remarks
6-R	S & W - ".35" Auto	Smith and Wesson	11.9-12.1	.060-.066	.3102-.3113	3	Actually .32 cal.
6-L	None encountered						

8 mm. Caliber

Class (No.-Twist)	Gun Name and/or Model	Manufacturer	Inches for 1 turn	Width of Land (inches)	Bore Diameter (inches)	No. Meas'd	Remarks
4-R	Roth-Steyr	Fegyvergyar	9.9-10.0	.098-.105	.3128-.3175	4	

Class (No.- Twist)	Gun Name and/or Model	Manufacturer	Inches for 1 turn	Width of Land (inches)	Bore Diameter (inches)	No. Meas'd	Remarks
4-R	Roth-Steyr	Waffenfabrik Steyr	9.9	.100-.101	.3132-.3143	3	
"	Simplex	Th. Bergmann	8.2	.062	.3084	1	
4-L	None encountered						
6-R	Nambu—M14 (1925)	Japanese Arsenals	10.95-11.1	.034-.048	.3156-.3167	11	
"	" Mod. 94 (1934)	do.	10.9-11.4	.032-.043	.3152-.3164	7	
6-L	None encountered						

9 mm. (.38 and .380) Caliber

Class (No.- Twist)	Gun Name and/or Model	Manufacturer	Inches for 1 turn	Width of Land (inches)	Bore Diameter (inches)	No. Meas'd	Remarks
4-R	Frommer—Baby	Fegyvergyar	9.55	.130	.3467	1	
"	" Stop	"	10.15	.127	.3454	1	
"	Hungarian—M29	"	9.8	.124-.126	.3444-.3445	2	
"	" M37	"	9.8-10.0	.116-.122	.3435-.3453	3	
"	Mann	Fritz Mann	11.8	.086	.3500	1	
"	Mauser Mil. Pistol	Waffenfabrik Mauser	13.8	.131	.3496	1	Also made with 6-R.
"	Steyr—Mod. 1911	Oesterr. Waffenfabrik Steyr	8.0	.154	.3487	1	
"	" Mod. 1912	do.	7.8-7.9	.120-.134	.3483-.3518	9	
"	U.S.—Sub. Mach. M3	Guide Lamp Div., Gen. Motors	10.0	.112	.3492	1	
"	Walther—Mod. 6	Carl Walther Waffenfabrik	9.9	.090	.3476	1	
4-L	Bayard-Bergmann	Anc. Etablissements Pieper	10.25	.047	.3486	1	Also made with 6-L.
5-R	None encountered						
5-L	None encountered						
6-R	Astra Mod. 300	Unceta y Cia.	9.4-9.5	.051-.059	.3479-.3605	4	
"	" Mod. 400	do.	9.4-9.55	.044-.061	.3478-.3499	5	
"	" Mod. 600	do.	9.4	.051-.055	.3478-.3490	2	
"	Beretta—1915 Type	Pietro Beretta	10.4	.049	.3509	1	
"	" 1923 Type	do.	10.0	.050	.3496	1	
"	" Mod. 1934	do.	9.8-10.0	.045-.052	.3475-.3494	13	
"	" Mod. 1934	do.	9.9-10.4	.052-.064	.3491-.3500	3	Made for Rumania
"	" Mod. 1951	do.	10.0	.051	.3492	1	
"	" Mach. Pist.—M38-42	do.	9.8-9.9	.049	.3475-.3477	2	Made under German supervision.
"	Bernardelli	Vincenzo Bernardelli	9.8	.050	.3456	1	
"	Brixia	Metallurgica Bresciana	9.9-10.0	.078-.090	.3483-.3512	2	
"	Browning—Mod. 1903	Fab. Nat'l. d'Armes de Guerre	16.0-17.9	.031-.038	.3525-.3537	2	Also called Browning Long
"	" Mod. 1910	do.	9.5	.030	.3519	1	
"	" Mod. 1922	do.	9.5-9.7	.029-.037	.3501-.3520	5	
"	" H.P.	do.	9.7-9.9	.074-.090	.3479-.3503	12	
"	" M 07	Husqvarna Vapenfabriks	15.8	.027	.3517	1	
"	" Mk. I	John Inglis Co., Ltd.	10.0	.070	.3479	1	
"	Campo Giro—Mod. 1913	Esperanza y Unceta	10.2	.052	.3495	1	
"	do. 1913/16	do.	9.5	.065	.3495	1	
"	CZ—Mod. 1922	Česka Zbrojovka	9.9	.057	.3466	1	Marked: 9 mm. N Cs-Prague
"	CZ—Mod. 1924	do.	9.8-10.45	.047-.062	.3443-.3465	12	10.45" twist very unusual.
"	CZ—Mod. 1938	do.	9.8-10.0	.052-.056	.3505-.3506	2	
"	LeFrancais—Mil. Mod.	Mre. Francaise d'Armes et Cycles de St. Etienne	14.6	.058	.3550	1	Marked: Type Armee
"	German Mach. Pist. M40	C.G. Haenel Waffen u. Fahrrad Fab.	9.9	.081	.3480	1	
"	do.	Schmeisser Werke	9.9	.081-.088	.3482-.3485	2	
"	German—Mod. P-38	Mauser Werke	9.8-9.9	.078-.090	.3476-.3482	8	
"	do.	Spreewerk, G.m.b.H. Metallwaren	9.7-9.9	.076-.087	.3482-.3489	9	
"	do.	Carl Walther Waffenfabrik	9.8-9.9	.076-.087	.3478-.3487	18	
"	Glisenti—Mod. 1910	Soc. Siderurgica Glisenti	9.8-10.0	.077-.085	.3483-.3495	4	
"	Handy—Mod. 1917	Unknown (Spanish)	15.2-15.3	.057-.060	.3507-.3518	2	
"	HI Standard—Mod. G-380	High Standard Corporation	15.2	.050	.3434	1	
"	Kirikkale	Kirikkale Tüfek Fabrikular	9.6-9.8	.048-.062	.3487-.3491	2	Identical to Walther Mod. PP
"	Lahti—M40	Husqvarna Vapenfabriks	9.4-9.5	.053-.055	.3454-.3458	3	
"	" L35	Valtion Kivääri Tehdas	9.45-9.55	.060-.072	.3462-.3472	3	
"	Llama—Mod. IIIA	Gabilondo y Cia.	11.9-12.00	.053-.065	.3475-.3487	3	
"	" Mod. XI	do.	12.1	.062	.3475	1	
"	Luger—Mod. 1908	Deutsche Waffen. u. Mun. Fab.	9.6-10.0	.073-.087	.3479-.3492	10	
"	do.	Erfurt Arsenal	9.8-10.0	.072-.080	.3483-.3494	4	
"	do.	Heinrich Krieghoff Waffenfabrik	9.8	.076	.3479	1	
"	do.	Mauser Werke	9.8-10.0	.074-.094	.3475-.3485	17	
"	M.A.B.—Mod. R	Mre. d'Armes Aut. Bayonne	12.3	.041	.3480	1	
"	Mauser—Mil. Pistol	Waffenfabrik Mauser	9.8-9.9	.073-.081	.3485-.3490	5	
"	"Mugica"—Mod. 120	Gabilondo y Cia.	11.95	.063	.3473	1	This is a Llama Mod. XI
"	Ortgies	Deutsche Werke	9.8	.040	.3522	1	
"	Radom—Vis 35	Fabryka Bronn Radom	9.8-10.0	.080-.087	.3479-.3488	10	

139

Class (No.-Twist)	Gun Name and/or Model	Manufacturer	Inches for 1 turn	Width of Land (inches)	Bore Diameter (inches)	No. Meas'd	Remarks
6-R	Savage—Mod. 1913	Savage Arms Co.	12.0	.043-.046	.3491-.3554	2	
"	" Mod. 1917	do.	16.1-16.2	.055-.059	.3483-.3488	2	
"	SIG (SP 47/48)	Soc. Industrie Suisse	9.85	.077	.3486	1	
"	Smith and Wesson	Smith and Wesson	10.0	.061-.065	.3466-.3470	2	
"	Star—1919 Type	Bonifacio Echeverria	10.3	.036	.3505	1	
"	" Type A	do.	9.15	.060	.3492	1	
"	" Mod. B	do.	10.7-10.8	.059-.060	.3488-.3492	2	
"	" Mod. D	do.	9.6	.043	.3485	1	
"	" Mod. MD	do.	12.2	.063	.3491	1	A machine pistol.
"	" Super Mod. A	do.	12.65	.070	.3490	1	
"	" Mod. S	do.	12.0-12.6	.065	.3482	3	
"	" Mod. Super B	do.	12.55	.059	.3490	1	
"	" Mod. DK	do.	12.3	.057	.3487	1	
"	Suomi—M.G.	Tikkakoski o/y	9.5	.058	.3444	1	
"	Tauler—Mark P	Gabilondo y Cia.	12.35	.057	.3480	1	
"	Walther—Mod. PP	Carl Walther Waffenfabrik	9.35-9.8	.046-.058	.3478-.3493	3	
6-L	Bayard M.P.—Mod. 1908	Anc. Etablissements Pieper	10.15	.043	.3475	1	Also known as the Bayard-Bergmann.
"	" " Mod. 1920/21	Haerens Rustkammer	10.0	.036	.3471	1	
"	do.	Haerens Tøjhus	9.9	.038	.3471	1	
"	Bayard Pocket Mod. 1908		9.9-10.0	.051	.3482-.3486	2	
"	Colt—1900 Type	Colt's Pt. F.A. Mfg. Co.	14.7	.028	.3490	1	
"	" Army contract 1900	do.	17.4	.033	.3489	1	
"	" Navy contract 1902	do.	17.2	.029	.3487	1	
"	" Mil. Mod. 38	do.	17.3	.032	.3489	1	Made ca. 1902.
"	" Type of 1902	do.	15.9	.052	.3488	1	
"	" Mil. Mod. 1902	do.	16.5	.045	.3493	1	
"	" Pocket Mod. 1903	do.	15.6	.033	.3499	1	Early issue.
"	" do.	do.	15.8-16.5	.040-.057	.3476-.3497	6	
"	" 380 Hammerless	do.	16.0-16.8	.052-.064	.3482-.3500	8	
"	" Super 38	do.	15.9-16.2	.053-.056	.3480-.3490	7	
7-R	Remington P.A.—M51	Remington—U.M.C.	16.0-16.5	.038-.046	.3477-.3490	4	
7-L	None encountered						

.45 Caliber

Class (No.-Twist)	Gun Name and/or Model	Manufacturer	Inches for 1 turn	Width of Land (inches)	Bore Diameter (inches)	No. Meas'd	Remarks
6-R	Llama—Mod. IX-A	Gabilondo y Cia.	14.5	.077	.447	1	
"	Reising—Mod. 55	Reising Arms Co.	16.2	.068	.4416	1	Submachine gun.
"	Savage—Type 1906	Savage Arms Co.	16.0	.040	.4458	1	
"	Star—Mod. MD	Bonifacio Echeverria	11.65	.070	.4440	1	
"	Thompson—M1928	Colt's Pt. F.A. Mfg. Co.	16.0-16.5	.075	.443-.4449	3	Submachine gun.
6-L	Colt—U.S. Contract 1907	Colt's Pt. F.A. Mfg. Co.	18.85	.079	.4450	1	
"	" Mil. Mod. 1905	do.	15.5	.035	.4447	1	
"	" do.	do.	18.9	.054	.4445	1	1908 variation.
"	" Mod. 1909	do.	15.45	.066	.4452	1	Only 15 made.
"	" National Match	do.	16.1	.067	.4430	1	
"	" Commander	do.	16.0	.070	.4436	2	
"	Colt 45—See U.S. Army Mods. 1911 and 1911Al						
"	Hafdasa	Hispano Argentina Fabrica de Automoviles Sociedad Anonima	16.0-16.15	.071-.072	.4440-.4447	2	
"	Norwegian Army—Mod. 1914	Kongsberg Vapenfabrik	15.3-16.1	.068-.070	.4427-.4436	2	
"	Obregon	Mexican Gov't. Arsenal	16.35	.062	.4417	1	Marked—11.43 mm.
"	Ruby	Gabilondo y Cia.	10.4-10.5	.085-.090	.4416-.4420	2	
"	U.S. Army—Mod. 1911	Colt's Pt. F.A. Mfg. Co.	15.6-16.6	.064-.096	.4435-.4451	14	
"	do.	Remington Arms—U.M.C. Co.	16.0	.100	.4453	1	
"	U.S. Army—1911-Al	Colt's Pt. F.A. Mfg. Co.	16.0	.068	.4436	1	
"	do.	Ithaca Gun Co., Inc.	16.75	.067	.4448	1	
"	do.	Remington-Rand	16.3	.076	.4456	1	
"	do.	Union Switch and Signal Co.	16.0	.071	.4432	1	

.455 Caliber

Class (No.-Twist)	Gun Name and/or Model	Manufacturer	Inches for 1 turn	Width of Land (inches)	Bore Diameter (inches)	No. Meas'd	Remarks
6-R	Webley—Mk. I	Webley and Scott, Ltd.	10.0-10.2	.038-.058	.4470-.4474	3	
6-L	Colt—Mod. 1911 R.A.F.	Colt's Pt. F.A. Mfg. Co.	16.2	.076	.4509	1	Made for Royal Air Force.
7-R	Webley-Fosbery	P. Webley and Son	20.1	.040	.4399	1	An automatic revolver.
7-L	None encountered						

Data for some old revolvers with "gain" rifling

In the course of this study of rifling characteristics, in which over 2500 handguns (revolvers, pistols, and automatics) have been measured, a number of revolvers have been found that have "gain" rifling, i.e., the rate of turn increases from breech to muzzle.

Although such rifling has been known for a long time, it does not appear to have been used in handguns except for a few models of fairly early Colts and Remingtons. Its use was soon given up, but there are in existence today, in museums and in private collections, many guns having this type of rifling.

The guns that have gain rifling are of the percussion type, though some of them have been converted to rim fire or center fire. Percussion-type guns are not likely to be used by the criminal today because it is so much easier to use cartridges. However, these older guns do have interest for the collector or specialist.

The guns were, for the most part, obtained from the Rosebush Collection in the museum of the Wisconsin State Historical Society at Madison, Wis. A few came from the Nunnemacher Collection in the Milwaukee Public Museum and some from private collectors. Many of the guns examined had rifling which was too corroded to allow reliable measurements to be made and consequently were not measured.

The twist of the rifling was measured by means of the "Rifling Meter"—an instrument designed and built at the University of Wisconsin and described in the chapter on Instrumentation.

In using this instrument, a lead disk about ¹⁄₁₆ inch thick and of suitable size (slightly larger than the bore) is forced through the barrel to be measured and readings of angular rotation of the disk (which follows the rifling) are made at equally spaced intervals—the length of interval depending on the length of the barrel and upon whether the barrel has gain rifling or not. The disk is mounted on the end of a "thrust rod" which in turn is held in the center (or hub) of a graduated circle which is mounted on ball bearings so that friction is reduced practically to zero.

In the case of gain rifling it has been found desirable to make measurements at short intervals, usually 0.2 inch, and to plot the successive readings of rotation against the length of barrel traversed. Measurements can be made from either end (if the barrel can be removed), and wherever possible they were made from both ends and the readings were plotted on the same graph. If the two plots coincide where they overlap it serves as a good check on the accuracy of the measurements.

Inasmuch as the rifling is more likely to have defects near the ends of the barrel, the readings near the end may be in slight error, and an extrapolation of the curve will give more accurate results for values in these regions. In a number of cases it was found desirable to use the extrapolated value—as indicated in the accompanying plots of data. In a few cases the condition of the barrel, at one end or the other, necessitated more extrapolation than is desirable, but the error certainly is not great. In the case of guns having barrels longer than the thrust rod, measurements were made from each end, wherever possible, and the two plots combined in case they overlapped in the center section. The methods used to measure bore diameters, groove diameters, and land widths are described elsewhere in this book. (See chapter on Instrumentation.)

Principles and theory

The accuracy of flight of a fired bullet depends to a considerable degree on its velocity, rate of spin, shape, and the perfection of that shape. If anything happens to deform the bullet or to make it at all imperfect in shape its flight will not be true.

When a cartridge is fired in a revolver the bullet jumps forward and acquires a very considerable velocity before it encounters the rifling which, presenting a curved contour, produces a change in direction. When the bullet strikes the rifling it has to follow the curve of the lands of the rifling because it fits closely. But because of its high velocity at the moment of impact it resists changing its direction, and there is always a tendency for the bullet to slip before it settles down to follow the rifling.

The result is that lead bullets fired from a revolver almost invariably show "skid marks" due to this slippage. Jacketed bullets usually show it, but naturally the slippage is not so marked. This slippage produces a surface that is not perfectly symmetrical, as it should be for perfect flight of the bullet.

In a rifle or in an automatic pistol, on the other hand, we have a different situation since in guns of these types the forward end of the bullet is practically in contact with the beginning of the rifling and engages the rifling before it has acquired much velocity and momentum. Consequently slippage is usually absent.

The purpose of gain rifling, in which there is little or no angle of twist of the rifling at the breech but rather a gradual increase in angle of twist toward the muzzle, is to help the bullet to follow the rifling without slippage, as there is no *sudden* change in its direction after it has acquired considerable velocity.

The theory seems to be sound, and gain rifling was used in some of the revolvers made around the middle of the last century. But it was given up after a few years, perhaps partly because it was not easy to do a good job of rifling of this kind. It seems more likely, however, that it was not found to be effective in such short barrels.

There seems to be a great deal of variation from gun to gun and little standardization, in the cases studied at least. Also the shapes of the plots of the data indicate that there often was not a uniform change in the rifling pitch from breech to muzzle, as one would naturally expect. Furthermore, it was quite evident during the measurements that the rifling was not as "perfect" as in contemporary guns which do not have the gain rifling.

At any rate, this method of rifling did not survive, and in making measurements of over 2500 guns from 23 countries no modern guns were found to have this type of rifling. Gain rifling, therefore, as far as handguns are concerned, is only of historic interest and is not very likely to be encountered in criminal investigations—although the possibility exists, since many early Colts and Remingtons have been converted to take rim fire or center fire cartridges. An informed criminal might take advantage of this situation.

As already mentioned, the idea of gain rifling has long been known, but little regarding it is to be found in the literature. It has been used principally in heavy ordnance where it has been shown to be of considerable advantage in reducing the wear on the rifling, thus increasing the life of the barrels. In the case of a rifle barrel, or any barrel of considerable length, having a constant rifling pitch, the maximum wear occurs at the breech end of the barrel—say the first third of its length.

In this zone the temperature is highest and the gas pressures are greatest. If the rifling pitch is constant, as is the usual case, the rotational forces against the driving edges of the lands will be greatest in this region of high pressures, and consequently the wear of the lands will be the greatest in this zone. Continual wear on the lands eventually will result in slippage of the bullet, and it will not acquire the desired velocity nor the rotational spin necessary to produce stable flight.

Another point to be considered is the fact that bullets used in automatics (and many bullets for rifles) are jacketed with copper or an alloy which, being harder than lead, does not have as great a tendency to slip and to strip. There will be less fouling, but the wear on the rifling will be greater because of the greater hardness of the bullet metal. It would therefore appear to be advantageous to have the bullet achieve the desired rate of spin gradually rather than abruptly.

By using gain rifling, where the pitch of the rifling is zero or near zero at the breech and gradually increases toward the muzzle, it was thought that slippage and wear on the rifling might be reduced. The bullet, entering the rifling with high momentum, would be well "engraved" by the lands before it was subjected to a gradually increasing rotational torque required to give it the desired spin as it leaves the barrel. Thus gain rifling should do two things: (1) reduce slippage and (2) reduce the wear on the lands thus prolonging the life of the barrel.

Extensive experiments have been made in Germany and in this country on various types of gain rifling in the case of the larger-bore machine gun barrels and others where driving bands are used.

While in such cases there may be a decided advantage in the use of gain or "progressive" rifling, it seems most unlikely that it can ever be shown to be of any advantage in the case of revolver barrels. The changing angle would produce a broadening of the grooves made by the lands on the bullet and would tend to lead to inaccuracy and gas leakage. The shortness of the barrel would also be a deterrent factor.

The results of investigations on Colt and Remington revolvers, here reported, seem to indicate that these manufacturers had some of the above-mentioned ideas about the possible advantages of gain rifling and did some experimenting along different lines.

Discussion of results

By making measurements of the rifling angle at intervals of 0.2 inch throughout the entire length of a barrel, data were obtained which made it possible to make graphs or plots which show the rate of change of the rifling angle. This was done for all the barrels that were in sufficiently good condition to measure, and it was found that the plots fell into six general types, as shown in the graphs.

In Type I the rifling angle increases regularly from breech to muzzle. This was the type most often encountered.

In Type II the angle increases fairly regularly at first then more rapidly toward the muzzle.

TABLE 19
Data for revolvers having "gain" rifling

Cal.	Make	Model	Serial No.	Barrel Length (in.)	Dir'n. of Twist	Inches for one turn at breech	Inches for one turn at muzzle	No. of lands	Avg. Width of land (in.)	Bore Diam. (in.)	"Groove Diam." (in.)	Type of Rifling
.28	Colt	Root Pat. Side Hammer	5377	3.5	L	85	21.8	7	0.050	0.2576	0.2663	II
.31	Colt	Old Pocket Mod. 1849	230871	4.0	L	∞	41.1	7	0.061	0.3083	0.3167	I
.31	Colt	Old Pocket Mod. 1849	241072	4.0	L	ca. 240	38.9	7	0.061	0.3070	0.3151	III
.31	Colt	Old Pocket Mod. 1850	141184	6.0	R	55.5	20.0	7	0.060	0.3070	0.3170	II
.31	Colt	Old Pocket Mod. 1850	194967	6.0	L	∞	26.2	7	0.065	0.3112	0.3169	I
.31	Colt	Old Pocket Mod. 1850	197108	6.0	L	ca. 240	27.2	7	0.058	0.3095	0.3193	I
.31	Colt	Old Pocket Mod. 1850	203885	6.0	L	∞	26.7	7	0.061	0.3097	0.3182	I
.31	Colt	Old Pocket Mod. 1850	250855	6.0	L	∞	36.0	7	0.062	0.3117	0.3176	I or IV
.31	Colt	Old Pocket Mod. 1850	301121	6.0	L	ca. 180	28.2	7	0.069	0.3141	0.3229	IV
.36	Colt	New Mod. Pocket	3459	4.5	L	90	30.0	7	0.090	0.3713	0.3795	I
.36	Colt	New Mod. Police 1862	9878	5.5	L	ca. 180	29.4	7	0.067	0.3723	0.3806	I
.36	Colt	New Mod. Police 1862	39351	5.0	L	90	29.8	7	0.082	0.3706	0.3824	I
.36	Colt	Old Mod. Navy 1851	7211	7.5	R	> 360	18.5	7	0.076	0.3698	0.3801	I
.36	Colt	Old Mod. Navy 1851	8258	7.5	R	> 360	18.0	7	0.075	0.3605	0.3715	I
.36	Colt	Old Mod. Navy 1851	9288	7.5	R	ca. 110	21.2	7	0.071	0.3615	0.3733	I
.36	Colt	Old Mod. Navy 1851	11871	7.5	R	ca. 240	20.9	7	0.075	0.3599	0.3714	I
.36	Colt	Old Mod. Navy 1851	113540	7.5	L	ca. 300	19.5	7	0.083	0.3700	0.3808	I
.36	Colt	Old Mod. Navy 1851	127531	7.5	L	ca. 120	19.7	7	0.071	0.3704	0.3814	VI
.36	Colt	New Mod. Navy 1861	7283	7.5	L	> 360	21.2	7	0.070	0.3671	0.3800	I
.38	Colt	New Mod. Navy Conversion	11236(2)	7.5	L	72	22.9	7	0.072	0.3743	0.3850	III
.38	Colt	New Mod. Pocket Conversion	306773	3.5	L	72	18.7	7	0.097	0.3707	0.3790	I
.44	Colt	Dragoon No. 2	13580	7.5	R	ca. 240	19.5	7	0.097			I
.44	Colt	Dragoon No. 3	19247	7.5	R		19.2	7	0.100	0.4438	0.4506	I
.44	Colt	New Mod. Army 1860	8951	8.0	R	> 360	20.9	7	0.077	0.4425	0.4541	I
.44	Colt	New Mod. Army 1860	37503	7-7/8	L	ca. 140	18.0	7	0.092	0.4360	0.4514	I
.44	Colt	New Mod. Army 1860	111473	8.0	R	> 360	19.5	7	0.089	0.4411	0.4505	I
.44	Colt	New Mod. Army 1860	131557	8.0	L	ca. 240	19.0	7	0.081	0.4412	0.4508	I
.44	Colt	New Mod. Army 1860	158793	8.0	L	> 360	18.5	7	0.099	0.4437		IV
.31	Remington	New Model Pocket	1033	3.0	L	34.3	19.5	5	0.095	0.3107	0.3172	I or II
.36	Remington	New Model Belt	27092	7.5	L	ca. 110	21.8	5	0.100	0.3600	0.3650	II
.44	Remington	New Model Army	101118	8.0	L	ca. 120	21.2	5	0.130	0.4380	0.4481	I
.44	Remington	New Model Army	115319	8.0	L	ca. 110	21.8	5	0.126	0.4360		IV
.44	Remington	New Model Army	117012	8.0	L	ca. 103	21.8	5	0.119	0.4382	0.4510	V
.31	E. Whitney	Officers' Model	8484	6.0	R	ca. 200	40.9	7	0.065	0.3100	0.3235	I

Note: For guns having an odd number of grooves the difference between the bore diameter and the "groove diameter" represents the depth of the groove. The term "groove diameter", as here used, represents the distance from the bottom of a groove to the top of the opposite land.

In Type III the angle remains constant for a time, then increases at a regular rate for about two-thirds of the barrel length, then increases at a diminishing rate.

In Type IV the angle increases linearly for about two-thirds of the barrel length, then at a diminishing rate to the muzzle.

In Types V and VI we have plots that may be and probably are the results of mechanical difficulties. When these guns were made, about a hundred years ago, the art of rifling had not reached its present state of perfection. Inasmuch as no apparent useful purpose could be served by such rifling, it is pre-

sumed that the result achieved was unintentional. The author's guess is that these barrels were intended to be rifled similarly to those of Type I.

The accompanying tabulations show the results of the measurements made, and the type of plot is indicated. While Type I predominates, it is believed that Types II, III, and IV also were intentional. Unfortunately we have no records which show what any of these types of rifling accomplished, if anything.

It seems from a study of these plots that the American manufacturers must have had in mind some of the considerations and claims found in the fairly recent German work. However, it is probable

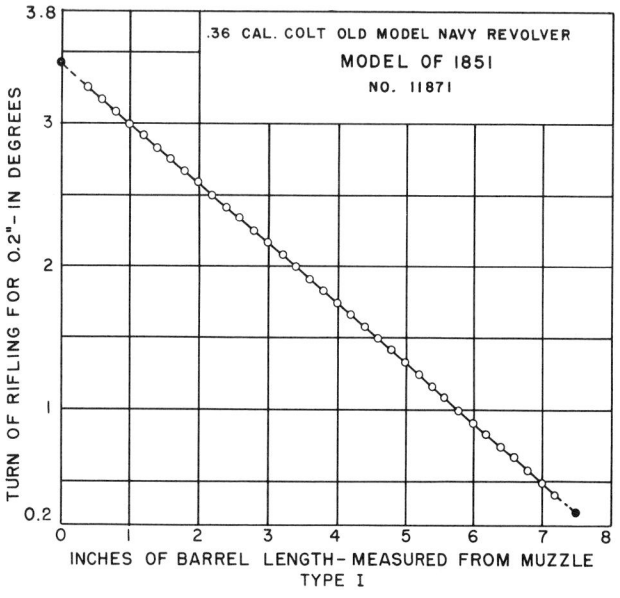

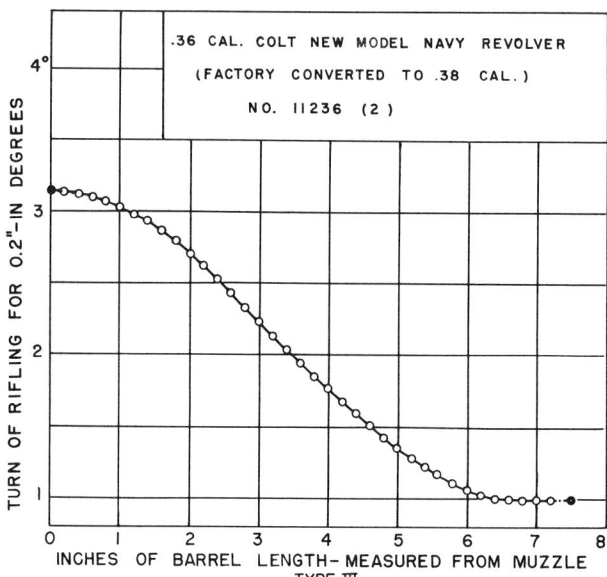

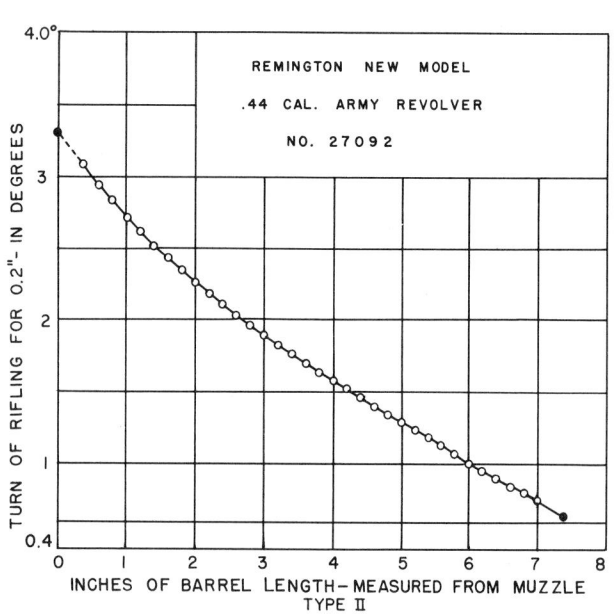

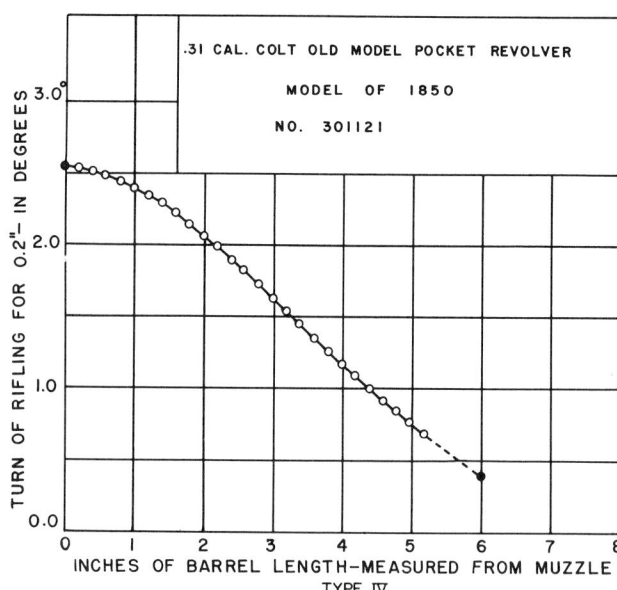

that the principal concern was the prevention of slippage due to the sudden encounter of the bullet with the rifling rather than the prevention of wear on the lands. The impression is that the first four types are definitely different experimental attempts to improve the ballistic performance of the gun. Whether they were based on sound theory or were just cut-and-try attempts one cannot know unless some records of the experimentation are found. The author realizes that it is not safe to generalize too much from the data obtained on such a relatively

small number of barrels as were measured. One should have a very large number to measure to enable him to draw conclusions with certainty, but unfortunately they were not available.

The use of gain rifling in hand guns in the United States was of very short duration. Whether it was given up because of its ineffectiveness or because of the difficulties encountered in producing good rifling of this sort is not known, but one seems justified in concluding that both of these were contributing factors.

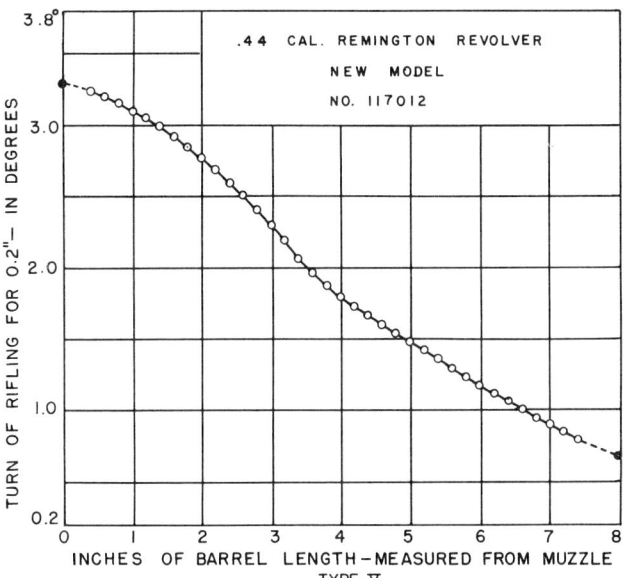

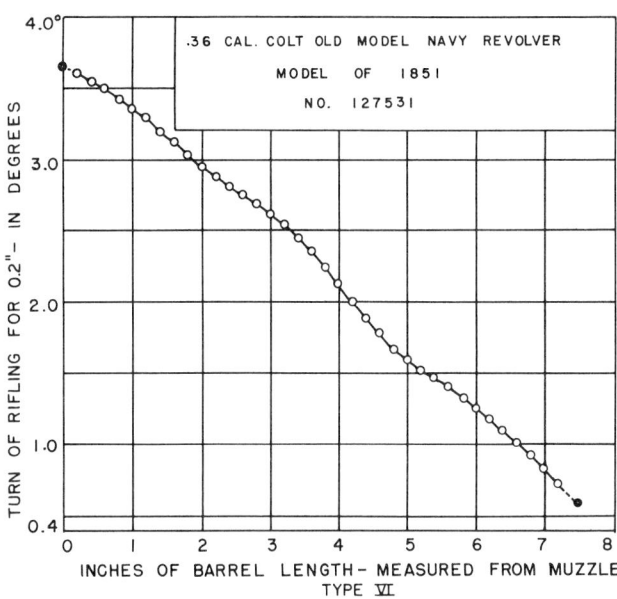

Miscellaneous notes on automatic pistols

Miscellaneous notes on automatic pistols

The title of this Part quite correctly describes its contents. The material represents an accumulation of results of several years work and is of such a nature that it is not well adapted to a set format or pattern of presentation.

For obvious reasons no claim of complete coverage of automatic pistols is made. The multiplicity of makes and models, together with the paucity and unreliability of information concerning many which are known to exist, makes such coverage impossible. Fortunately many of these are of lesser importance, from the standpoint of law enforcement, but information concerning them would surely be of interest to advanced collectors. Little information will be found here concerning some of the better-known makes, such as the Colts which have been competently described at length by Donald Bady in his *Colt Automatics* (Fadco Publishing Co. 1956).

Nor is infallibility claimed. No doubt there are errors, but it is hoped that there are not too many. As has been pointed out previously, the information which is available from different supposedly reliable sources often differs, and to make matters even more confusing the information obtained from some manufacturers at different dates concerning their own product and past performance sometimes is not consistent. In such instances all that an author can do is to make the best of the situation, making the best evaluation he can with such material as is available, or else omit all subject matter concerning which there is conflicting information. The author has used both alternatives in the preparation of material for this chapter.

For additional photographs and illustrations of guns mentioned in this chapter see Part IV and Part V.

Adler pistol

The Adler pistol is of the blow backtype and was manufactured ca. 1904 to 1906. It had a fully exposed, fixed, and tapered barrel, an internal bolt with recoil spring and guide enclosed in a large and clumsy housing, a pivoted frame closure, and a somewhat streamlined grip frame. It had a mechanical thumb safety, located on the left side of the bolt housing.

The name Adler was derived from the name Adlerwaffenwerke which was used by Max Hermsdorf for patent and trade purposes. It is quite likely that the name had some rather direct connection with the Adler Fahrrad Werke, a large manufacturer of bicycles of that period. Presumably the original patent was issued to a Herr Haeussler, whose name not only always appears on the pistol but is also associated with other patents in the period 1903–1905. A German Patent No. 176909, issued August 22, 1905, to Max Hermsdorf "trading as the Adlerwaffenwerke" at 12 Hammerweg, Zella St. Blasii, contains many details of the Adler pistol. Prior to 1905, Hermsdorf's name is to be found on patents which he assigned to Krupp. From this it would appear that Haeussler obtained the original patent and that Hermsdorf made and patented certain improvements in the design and arranged for its manufacture.

Adler pistols are marked (on the right side)

PATENT HAEUSSLER

ADLERWAFFENWERKE

ENGELBRECHT AND WOLFF

The specimens examined (Nos. 1231 and 1245) both bear the same monogram on the grip pieces. This shows an eagle with outstretched wings, a banner, two concentric circles beneath the banner in which appear the letters MHZ (presumably for Max Hermsdorf, Zella), below which are the words FABRIK ZEICHEN (Factory Mark). While it is not confirmed, it is believed that the pistol was actually made by Engelbrecht and Wolff for Max Hermsdorf, owner of the Adlerwaffenwerke, the contemplated distributor.

The matter is one of historic interest only, as the pistol was made for a very short time and apparently in limited number. It seems likely that the numbering started at 1000 (or some such figure) rather than at No. 1, because of the scarcity of specimens, all of which are collectors' items.

That an Adler pistol will ever figure in a shooting case is unlikely, not only on account of the rarity of the item but also on account of the obsolescence and practically complete disappearance of the special cartridge which was designed and made for this gun. While this has been described as a 7.25 mm. cartridge it would seem more appropriate to class it as 7 mm. (as has been done for the specimen in the Liége Museum) or as a 7.1 mm. because, according to measurements made and reported by White and Munhall, the diameter of the bullet was 0.280 inch (7.1 mm.). Moreover, the bore measurements made in the author's laboratory on the two pistol specimens available show values of 0.2772 and 0.2800 inch.

The two pistols examined show only slight differences in machining, in the size and shape of the front sight, and in the size and location of the pins and screws. Such differences would be expected in handmade specimens. While these pistols both had molded hard rubber grip pieces, carrying the monogram described, others have reported specimens that have checkered wood grip pieces.

Alkartasuna (Alkar) pistols

S. A. Alkartasuna Fabrica de Armas was one of the Spanish pistol manufacturers of lesser importance, but they did play a part in World War I and many specimens of their product are to be found in this country, having been brought back by returning soldiers. This firm was organized during World War I, in 1917, to manufacture (under license) the Ruby automatic pistol originated by Gabilondo y Urresti in 1914.

Information supplied by Gabilondo y Cia. states that the Alkartasuna firm was founded by some workmen of the Esperanza y Unceta factory. The demands made by the French for this pistol, which was used by them as a secondary standard service

pistol, were so heavy that Gabilondo y Urresti could not meet them. Consequently a number of other Spanish firms eventually participated in their production. Some, like Alkartasuna, were new companies and manufactured under license. Others were already established firms, some of which were licensed while apparently others were not. Many of these firms ceased to exist after the war.

From specimens examined, and also from those reported by others, it appears that there were several types of Alkartasuna (or Alkar) pistols. Presumably, some of these were made after the close of the war, as production apparently continued until some time in 1920 when the Alkartasuna factory burned down. Whether the factory was rebuilt and operated under the same name, or some other, is not known with certainty. Gabilondo y Cia. state that the Alkartasuna Company was completely dissolved in 1922.

From the limited number of specimens examined, some conclusions can be drawn and some conjectures made that may be of interest.

Specimens Nos. 44,384, 77,325, 77,683, 77,689, and 78,238 are all 9-shot copies of the Ruby and are essentially alike, although they do not appear to have been made with the same tools. All four specimens are marked S. A. ALKARTASUNA and all bear the conventional trade mark. This mark may be described as an "angular" letter S, above which is the word ALKAR and below it the abbreviation Mca. Regisda. (for Marca Registrada, i.e., Mark Registered). (See Photos of Trade Marks.) The dimensions of various parts of these four pistols are not always the same. For example, the length varies as much as four mm. Curves, angles, and slopes are obviously not all the same. They are close, but not exact, copies of the Ruby.

Specimen No. 79,896 is a 7-shot pistol, only 127 mm. in length and 100 mm. in height, whereas the 9-shot models are over 160 mm. in length and 120 mm. in height. Like the others, it has the name S. A. ALKARTASUNA on the left side of the slide and has hard rubber grip plates, on each of which there is a monogram containing the word ALKAR and a large angular letter S, similar to the one in the trade mark. The grip pieces on the 9-shot specimens bore no such markings and were usually of wood.

Specimen No. 83,172 is also a 7-shot pistol, but it is different from the preceding one in that it is 150 mm. in length and 100 mm. in height and has slightly curved instead of straight, vertical serrations in the finger grips on the rear of the slide. It has the hard rubber grips with the same monogram as that on No. 79,896. The trade mark stamped on the barrel, however, has a form which is different from that on the other pistols. It consists of the angular letter S with the word TRADE above and the word MARK below. The principal difference in the two specimens is in the length of the barrel and slide. In addition to the variant trade mark, the slide on this specimen bears the inscription: STANDARD AUTOMATIC PISTOL "ALKAR" PATENT 62,277. Obviously this pistol was made for sale in English-speaking countries.

Specimen No. 75,056 is of 6.35 mm. caliber and represents quite a different type of pistol in several respects. The most prominent feature is a cartridge indicator built into the left hand grip piece, so that the number of cartridges in the magazine can be seen at a glance. This pistol is 112 mm. in length and 85 mm. in height, and the magazine holds 7 cartridges.

This pistol bears the Alkartasuna conventional trade mark on the slide, but the Alkartasuna name does not appear anywhere on the gun. Instead, the inscription on the slide reads: MANUFACTURA DE ARMAS DE FUEGO - GUERNICA (ESPAÑA). The safety is of the push-through type and is located back of the grip frame instead of in front, as in the other models. The grip frame is much wider at the bottom than at the top, furnishing a much better grip. The name ALKAR appears on both grip pieces, along with the caliber designation (CAL 6.35), the monogram being quite different in design from that present on the 7.65 mm. specimens. The gun has the appearance of being well made.

The numbering system used is not known, nor is it obvious from the limited number of specimens that have been examined. The lowest-numbered specimens of the Alkartasuna reported are Nos. 11,037 and 12,465, both of which are the 7-shot model. Higher-numbered specimens (No. 44,384 and those in the 70,000 range) are of the 9-shot variety. Nos. 11,037 and 12,465 are both marked: S. A. ALKARTASUNA FABRICA DE ARMAS - GUERNICA; and they have the conventional trade mark. Details concerning them are lacking, however. If a continous numbering system was used for all the Alkartasuna copies of the Ruby, it would appear that the first ones made were of the 7-shot variety and that a change to the larger-capacity magazine was made somewhere along the line.

It seems unlikely that the 7-shot specimens Nos. 79,896 and 83,172 were made during the war. The pistols are of a different type and both have hard rubber grips, not used on the known wartime pistols, and an embossed monogram on the grips. These are distinctly not military type weapons. Since the factory continued to operate after the close of the war, until 1920 when it burned, it seems reasonable to suppose that these pistols were made for the commercial trade, particularly in other countries, in that period.

Reportedly the S. A. Alkartasuna firm went out of business in 1922. The 6.35 mm. pistol No. 75,056, though it bears the Alkartasuna trade mark and bears the name ALKAR, does not fit into the picture as a product of the wartime firm. It not only does not bear the Alkartasuna name but does bear the name: MANUFACTURA DE ARMAS DE FUEGO - GUERNICA (ESPAÑA). This suggests that this pistol was made by a different firm or a reorganized firm to which was given a new name. The latter conjecture seems more likely.

Arizmendi pistols

The name Arizmendi has long been known in the Spanish arms industry, the firm Arizmendi y Goenaga having been established in 1886. Up to 1913–14, twenty-seven catalogs had been issued. While the earlier years had been devoted to the manufacture of revolvers it appears that early in this century the firm began to take interest in the rapidly developing popularity of the automatic pistol. The Walman pistols originated around 1907–09 and were based on patents issued to the firm.

Some time around 1914, or shortly thereafter, the firm name was changed to Francisco Arizmendi. The 1913–14 catalog (No. 27) has the name "Francisco Arizmendi (Sucesor)" printed below the name F. Arizmendi y Goenaga and in different ink.

The principal automatics for which this firm is known are the Walman, Victor, Ydeal, and Singer. The name Victor was, for some unknown reason, dropped and the name Singer substituted therefor. Later a new model of the Singer was brought out, in which were incorporated improvements made in the Walman and Ideal models. This improvement consisted particularly in a chamber cartridge indicator which enabled one to ascertain, by sight or touch, whether there was a cartridge in the chamber. This device is shown in Fig. 102. The new Singers were considerably heavier than their predecessor, the Victor. The weights of the 6.35 and 7.65 mm. Victors were 265 and 530 grams, respectively, whereas the weights of the corresponding Singers were 320 and 630 grams, without magazines. The Ydeal was the lightest of the series. As originally made, the Ydeal (then made in 6.35 mm. only) weighed 240 grams as compared to 270 grams for the 6.35 mm. Walman and 265 grams for the 6.35 mm. Victor.

All of these pistols were of a simple blowback   151

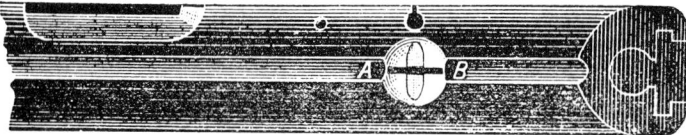

1

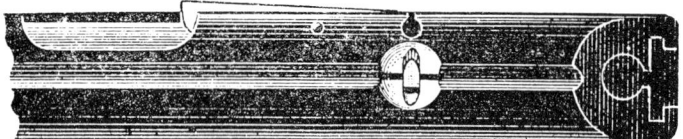

2

Fig. 102. Francisco Arizmendi cartridge indicator used on Singer, Walman, and Ideal automatic pistols.

Fig. 1. shows the mechanism when there is no cartridge in the barrel. The extractor is level, without any rise from the side of the slide, and the groove A-B on the slide forms a straight line with the groove of the indicator.

Fig. 2. shows that the barrel contains a cartridge: (1) by the unlevel sides of the slide, the extractor stands out of the barrel; and (2) by the broken line of the barrel and the indicator.

type, based on the Browning. They had thumb safeties, located at the rear of the frame in each case, and they had magazine safeties which prevented accidental discharge when the magazine was removed. None were provided with grip safeties.

Both Arizmendi y Goenaga and successor, Francisco Arizmendi, produced pistols under the name "Kaba Spezial." The original Kaba Spezial was made by August Menz in Suhl, Germany, and sold by Karl Bauer of Berlin, from whose name the name Kaba was derived. The Kaba Spezials as made by Arizmendi y Goenaga and by Francisco Arizmendi were not copies of the German pistol. The latter had the forward part of the slide cut away, exposing the entire length of the barrel, which was not the case in the Spanish-made Kabas. The two Spanish pistols were not alike in some respects and appear not to have been made with the same tools. The monogram on the grip plates of the specimen made by Francisco Arizmendi, bearing the words KABA SPEZIAL, is almost an exact copy of the monogram on the original German pistol.

During World War I a pistol of the Ruby type was made by this firm for the French Army. Both names, Arizmendi y Goenaga and (later) Francisco Arizmendi, are listed as manufacturers of such pistols. Whether such production was under license from Gabilondos y Urresti, to whom the Ruby patent had

been issued in 1914, is not known. (See Gabilondo Pistols for a discussion of the Ruby pistols.)

This firm is no longer producing revolvers or pistols, as they were among the many firms denied permission to do so after the Spanish revolution.

Astra (and related) pistols

These pistols have a long and important history in Spanish firearms manufacture as they are among the best that have been produced in Spain; furthermore, the company is one of three that are permitted by the present government to make automatic pistols. Astra pistols are not only popular in Spain but also have a wide sale in other countries, including the U.S.

The firm of Esperanza y Unceta was founded by Don Juan Esperanza and Don Pedro Unceta on July 17, 1908. Esperanza was a native of Aragon who had come to Eibar some years earlier to learn to become a mechanician and had become a very good one, having received many awards for his skill. Unceta, a highly born native of Eibar, had learned the mechanician's trade in a little shop owned by one of his uncles. He had become a manufacturer, dealer, and exporter of arms. In addition he had engaged in other activities, such as hardware merchant and "banking correspondent." Obviously he had more experience and presumably took the lead in establishing the new enterprise. The original notarized agreement stated that: "The parties hereto constitute a regular collective mercantile Sociedad, domiciled in this town, which will trade under the name of Pedro Unceta y Juan Esperanza; which will be devoted to mechanical fabrication of different articles or manufactures of iron and steel."

Señor Esperanza was to have charge of the shop, while the general direction and administration was to be in the hands of Señor Unceta, and the agreement was specified to be binding for 10 years. At just what date the names were reversed to Esperanza y Unceta is not known, but the firm operated under this new name until 1926, at which time the name was changed to Unceta y Cia., as Esperanza left the firm at that time. The firm was now under the management of a "double directorate" which included Don Canuto Unceta as well as Don Rufino Unceta. Since the name Astra had long been used on arms made by the firm, the firm name was again changed, in 1953, to capitalize on this name, and became Astra-Unceta y Cia., under which name it still operates. While continuing the manufacture of arms, the firm has other interests, such as the manufacture of pneumatic tools, pumps, etc.

Returning to 1908—the first activities of the partnership were restricted to the manufacture of parts for other pistol manufacturers, but it was soon decided to undertake the manufacture of a complete automatic pistol of their own. This resulted in a pistol which they named the Victoria. The success attained with this pistol soon made it evident that more space and added facilities were desirable, and a search for such space began in Eibar but met with no success. The need for more space became still more acute when, in 1912, the Spanish Army adopted a military type of pistol which the company was asked to manufacture.

Don Venancio Lopez de Ceballos y Aguirre, Count of Campo Giro, was a military officer (and engineer) who started designing automatic pistols for military use as early as 1900. His first patents date from 1904 and further patents were obtained in 1910, 1912, and 1913, following further improvements and simplifications in manufacture. Upon adoption of his 1910 Model by the Army, Campo Giro gave an order to Esperanza y Unceta for the manufacture of 1000 pieces. This made additional space and facilities imperative and, having secured the necessary space and additional financial encouragement in the city of Guernica, a new plant was built in that city in 1913. By the time the plant was completed Campo Giro had made still further improvements and the pistol now became the Model 1913. Still later improvements resulted in the Mod. 1913/16. For further details on these arms see the separate section on Campo Giro pistols.

From 1913 on, Don Rufino Unceta, son of Don Pedro, became the dominant force in the firm as his father had left the firm at the time the move to Guernica was made. The manufacture of the Campo Giro pistols was only an incident in the life of this firm, but it was a most important one. It not only gave the firm a new location, more financial backing, and a profitable contract with the Army but also ideas for new designs for pistols which they later manufactured.

Victoria—Manufacture of the pocket pistol Victoria, of which over 50,000 had been made at Eibar, was continued at Guernica, along with the newly developed military type Campo Giro. The Victoria was a simple blowback of the early Browning type and was made in two calibers, 6.35 and 7.65 mm., both of similar design. The 7.65 mm. model was the first to be produced, the 6.35 mm. version not appearing until approximately 40,000 of the larger caliber had been made. Unfortunately they were numbered in the same numbering series. The lowest number seen for a 6.35 mm. specimen, marked VICTORIA - MODEL 1911, is No. 54,170 (obviously made at Eibar), and

the highest number observed is 229,170, on a specimen marked VICTORIA - MODEL 1916, made at Guernica. These two pistols are identical in design but do not appear to have been made on the same set of tools.

The first Victorias, according to recent correspondence, were made with external hammers "until No. 62,000, approximately," but no such specimens have been encountered. As specimen Serial No. 1 is in the Astra-Unceta museum, the first part of the statement cannot be doubted, but specimen No. 54,170 is a "hammerless." A puzzling statement from the present firm is that in November 1914 they began marking the Victoria pistols with the name Astra "from serial No. 82,000 up." This is confusing in that Astra - Mod. 1911 (7.65 mm.) specimens have been examined and photographed by the author; and it has already been noted that a 6.35 mm. 1916 Victoria bears the number 229,363.

Pistols identical to the Victoria were furnished to Thieme and Edeler of Liége with the marking "BTE PATENT - SPAIN." They were also sold in Belgium under the names The Automatic Leston, Museum, Salso, Sat, and others.

6.35 mm. Astras

As indicated above it is not clear as to when the name Victoria was changed to Astra on the 6.35 mm. pistols, and it may well be that both names were used for some time. Specimen No. 251,141 which is identical to the pistol marked Victoria No. 229,363 bears the name Astra, as do those of this design produced subsequently. This Astra specimen is marked "1924 Model." Actually there was no 1924 Model, the designation simply indicates the year in which it was made. When the Banco de Pruebas (Proof House) began to function it required that completed pistols be stamped with the year of manufacture. Pistols which were unblued were stamped with the Spanish proof marks, without the year.

The name Astra had previously been used on the 7.65 mm. pistol (No. 925, for example) which bears the inscription

7.65 mm. 1911 MODEL AUTOMATIC PISTOL - ASTRA PATENT

The brand name Astra was not actually registered until November 25, 1914, hence it appears that the name was used prior to official registration, a practice not uncommon. Many Spanish pistols bear the word PATENT though no patent was issued. In passing, it may be remarked that at least one other Spanish manufacturer pirated the name Astra, and this may have been the reason for the registration, i.e., pro-

153

tection. The author owns a 7.65 mm. pistol bearing the name Astra which obviously is not an Esperanza y Unceta product (though similar in design), as it is very inferior in workmanship and does not have the word HOPE on the barrel—a distinguishing feature of the early production of this firm.

The early 1911 Victoria and the 1911 Astra pistols did not have a grip safety. The grip safety is reported, in recent correspondence with the firm, to have been introduced at Serial No. 233,460 (year not stated). Presumably the pistol was made in both forms, with and without this additional safety device, as the 6.35 mm. specimens No. 251,141 and No. 269,399 (the latter owned by the author) do not have the grip safety. No. 296,446 in the same caliber does have a grip safety.

Model 200—Recent correspondence from the firm also states that the Mod. 200 (a "new model" having a grip safety) includes the 6.35 mm. pistols numbered in the following serial number blocks: 233,460–

317,350; 500,001–506,000; 648,601–663,300; 678,001–710,000; 722,001–759,500; and 780,001–785,300 (Figs. 103, 104).

The statement is made that with the introduction of this new model (in May 1920) the use of the word HOPE on the barrel was discontinued. This statement does not seem to correspond to some facts, however, as specimens with serial numbers as high as 269,399 (specimen owned by the author) have the word HOPE on the barrel and are of the earlier design. Evidently both the earlier and the 200 design were made simultaneously.

Pistols in the 200 Series appeared with several finishes, and to distinguish between them they were designated as Models 200, 200/1, 200/2, 200/3, etc., depending on the kind and extent of engraving. Specimens of Mod. 200 with serial numbers approaching 900,000 have been examined and measured, so production of this model did not cease at No. 785,300 as might be inferred from the statement above concerning numbering blocks. This model is sold in the U.S. under the names Astra Fire Cat and Astra Fire Cat CE (engraved).

7.65 mm. Astras

The early 7.65 mm. Astra was identical to the Victoria of the same caliber. Just when the name Astra was introduced for this model is not known but a specimen bearing the Serial No. 925 and marked "Model 1911" seems to indicate that the new name and numbering were adopted at about that time. Specimen No. 1727 is also marked 1911, No. 4169 is marked Mod. 1915 and Nos. 70,211 and 75,140 are marked Mod. 1916. The date 1911 and the absence of the word GUERNICA indicate manufacture in Eibar, as the word Guernica appears on pistols made after the factory was moved to that city. From the facts cited, it is concluded that the name Astra was actually used before 1914.

Soon after World War I broke out, a shortage of pistols developed in France and several manufacturers in Spain, including Esperanza y Unceta, were given orders for pistols of 7.65 mm. caliber. Specimens marked 7.65 mm. 1915 MODEL AUTOMATIC PISTOL - ASTRA PATENT (Serial No. 4169) and two others marked 7.65 mm. 1916 MODEL AUTOMATIC PISTOL - ASTRA PATENT (Serial Nos. 70,211 and 75,140) have been measured and photographed. These are all of the same type and general appearance as the 1911 specimen but have different dimensions and clearly were not made on the same set of tools. For example, the 1911 Astra is 145 mm. long and 98 mm. high, whereas the 1915 version is 160 mm. long and 125 mm. high, with an increased magazine capacity

Fig. 103. 6.35 mm. Astra Mod. 200, Esperanza y Unceta, Guernica, Spain.

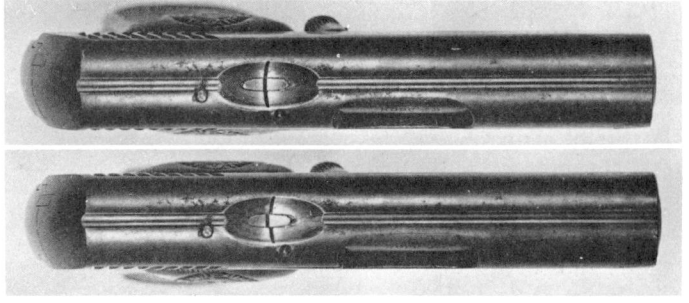

Fig. 104. 6.35 mm. Astra Mod. 200, Esperanza y Unceta, Guernica, Spain (Showing cartridge indicator).

of 8 rounds. The 1916 Model has about the same dimensions. All of these are in the same numbering series.

The manufacturer states that these pistols were furnished not only to France but also to Italy (after the latter came into the war on the allied side) and that the total production of the wartime type was about 150,000 pieces. Manufacture of this model was discontinued at the close of the war as it was superseded by Model 400, which became the official weapon.

Model 100—This seems to have been a factory designation for the 7.65 mm. pistol that started out as the Victoria, but when this particular designation first came into use is not known. The manufacturer says that it applies to the pistols of the Victoria type

made up to the year 1915 when the war type, with enlarged magazine capacity, was introduced. This wartime model appears to have been given the nomenclature "Mod. 100 Special" at a later date, as it is so designated in factory literature of ca. 1925. No figures as to total production are extant, as all of the Eibar and many of the early Guernica records have been destroyed. Furthermore the 7.65 and 6.35 mm. pistols were in the same numbering series, and the ratio in which they were produced is not known.

The tabulation of calibers, serial numbers, and remarks in Table 20 may be of value to those interested in the relationships of the early models of pistols of 6.35 and 7.65 mm. caliber made by Esperanza y Unceta.

Tubular types

Astra pistols Models 300 (and 300/1, 2, 3, 4), 400, 600, and the 3000 series are of the tubular cross section Browning modification type and date from 1921 to 1948 in inception. The Campo Giro influence is evident. The 300 and 400 models were pre-World War II models, the 600 a war model, and the 3000 and 4000 series are of post-World War II origin.

Model 400—Also known as the 1921 Military Model. This preceded Mod. 300. Several forms and modifications exist. Usually it will be found in 9 mm. Largo (Bergmann) and much less frequently in 7.65 mm. caliber. While chambered nominally for the 9 mm. Largo, other cartridges may be used in it, such as: .38, .380 ACP, 9 mm. Parabellum, 9 mm. Steyr, and 9 mm. Browning Long. The shorter cartridge must be fed through the magazine in order that the rim may be caught and held against the breech face, otherwise the firing pin will not strike the primer.

TABLE 20
Data on early pistols made by Esperanza y Unceta

Cali-ber mm.	Model	Serial No.	Remarks
6.35	1911 Mod. Victoria Pat.	54,170	Browning 1906 type, has no grip safety.
6.35	1916 Mod. Victoria Pat.	229,363	Practically identical.
6 35	Marked 1924 Mod. Astra	251,141	Identical to 1911 Mod. Victoria.
6.35	Model not stated on gun	269,399	do.
6.35	do.	270,689	do.
6.35	do.	296,446	Identical to above, except grip safety added.
7.65	1911 Mod. Victoria Pat.	71,020	Identical to 1911 Mod. Victoria, but lanyard loop added.
7.65	1911 Mod. Astra Pat.	925	Identical to above.
7.65	do.	1,727	do.
7.65	do.	21,020	do.
7.65	1915 Mod. Astra Pat.	4,169	Similar to Mod. 1911 but increased magazine cap. Made on different set of tools.
7.65	1916 Mod. Astra Pat.	70,211	Similar to Mod. 1915. Some variation in dimensions.
7.65	do.	75,140	Identical to above.
7.65	1916 Mod. Brunswig	45,940 (on frame) 80,006 (on slide)	Very similar if not identical to 1916 Astra.
7.65	do.	46,404 (on frame) 84,070 (on slide)	Same as above.

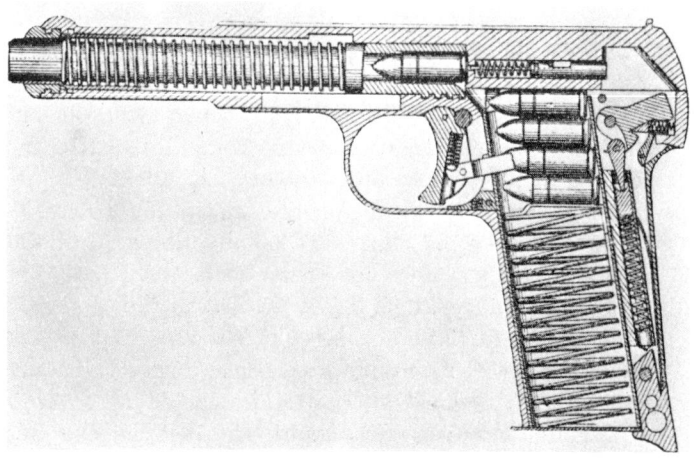

Fig. 105. 9 mm. Astra Mod. 400. Sectional view.

This model was sold commercially from 1921 on and was adopted into Spanish military service in October 1921 without special markings, the commercial form being used. The earliest specimens produced had a spring buffer beneath the barrel at the chamber, but this feature was soon dropped. Sometime in the 1930's this model was supplied to the French service, without special markings, but with plain serrated grip pieces instead of molded rubber. In about 1940 the position of the magazine release was changed from directly below the grip frame to the left side, near the bottom. This feature appears in later models. After World War II the Spanish Army replaced this pistol with the Star (Super) made by Echeverria.

According to factory information, 105,275 units of the Mod. 400 had been made up to 1946. Presumably production stopped at that time.

During the Spanish Revolution the Mod. 400 (or Spanish Army pistol of 1921) appeared in two forms very closely resembling the pistol as made by Astra-Unceta y Cia. In fact these pistols are so like the pistols as made by Astra-Unceta as to tooling and machining that appear to be genuine, however Astra-Unceta disclaims the manufacture of either of them.

One specimen examined (Serial No. 5262) has fluted hard rubber grip pieces each bearing a monogram consisting of the letters RE (for Republic Española) intertwined, in a circle. Another specimen (Serial No. 727) has pebbled hard rubber grip pieces each bearing a monogram consisting of a circle with the name F. ASCASO inscribed therein. On the top of the barrel there is stamped an elliptical monogram containing the words F. ASCASO TARRASA CATALUNA (in three lines).

The disclaimer of manufacture by Astra-Unceta is supported by the rifling. Like the genuine Astra 400 these two pistols have six grooves with right hand twist, but the angle is different in each. Genuine Astra 400 pistols have been found to have one turn of the rifling in 9.4 to 9.55 inches, whereas the rifling in the "RE" specimen has one turn in 10.0 and that in the Ascaso one turn in 12.0 inches.

Models 300 and 3000—(Also called *Baby Astra*)—In both 9 mm. and 7.65 mm. calibers, this was simply a shorter version of the Mod. 400. It was first brought out in 9 mm. caliber in 1922 as the Mod. 300. It was adopted into the Spanish Navy and Police Service in 1922, without special markings or numbers. In the 7.65 mm. cal. it was designated Mod. 3000. Manufacture was discontinued in 1948, in the 7.65 mm. cal., at least, according to factory information. Serial numbering blocks for this model are as follows:

350,001–378,700; 506,001–648,000; 663,301–678,000; 710,001–722,000; 779,851–780,000; and 790,001–809,300.

Model 600—This is the same as Mod. 400, except that it was made in 9 mm. Parabellum caliber. Some 8000 were delivered to the Germans in 1942. Production was continued after the war until 1946, according to factory information, but they were offered for sale as late as 1948. A limited number were produced in 7.65 mm. caliber sometime after the war. Serial numbers are stated by the manufacturer to have extended from 1 to 59,546. Presumably this includes both calibers.

The 900 series (military pistols)

These are copies, for the most part, of the Mauser Military Pistols. While they appear to be much the same, there are in fact a number of changes. Commercial manufacture and sale date from ca. 1928 and were discontinued in the late 1930's.

Model 900—Box magazine, 10 rounds, charger loaded, 7.63 mm. Mauser caliber.

Model 902—Integral box magazine, 20 rounds, charger loaded, 7.63 mm. Mauser caliber.

Model 903—10- or 20-round insert magazines, 7.63 mm. Mauser caliber.

Model "F"—Similar to Mod. 903 except that the caliber was 9 mm. "Largo" (Bergmann).

Other older models

Astra 700 Special—This pistol was produced around 1925. It was simpler in construction than the preceding models and had no grip safety. Some 4000 of these were made and sold as an "economy pistol."

Astra 700—In more recent years (exact date not known) a new 700 Model was designed but was made only in prototype form. Only a few specimens were made.

Astra 1000—This 7.65 mm. pistol was made for Astra-Unceta y Cia. by a firm in Ermua. It had an 11-round magazine. No figures as to production are available, but the number was probably small.

Factory literature gives the data for the Mod. 100 Special, Mod. 700 Special, and Mod. 1000 shown in Table 21. No description of the Mod. 100 Special

TABLE 21
Data on three older models of Astra pistols

Model	Caliber, mm.	Length, mm.	Height, mm.	Bbl. length, mm.	Mag. cap.	Weight, gm.
100 Special	7.65	155	120	85	8	825
700 Special	7.65	160	125	95	8	725
1000	7.65	200	140	130	11	1050

has been seen, but from the photograph it appears to be like the pistol produced in wartime and probably is the same.

Brunswig—Pistols made by Esperanza y Unceta have been sold under the name Brunswig. Two have been examined and measured. Both are "mongrels" in that the serial numbers on the frames do not agree with those on the slides. One has a frame No. 45,940 and slide No. 84,006 while the other has frame No. 46,404 and slide No. 84,070. Nor do their dimensions agree, the former being 150 mm. in length and 130 mm. in height, while the latter is 145 mm. in length and 127 mm. in height. Both bear Esperanza y Unceta markings on the frames, indicating that they were made before 1926 (the date of change of the name of the firm) and the serial numbers on the slides indicate that these were made during World War I. Both have Esperanza y Unceta barrels, with the familiar mark HOPE.

These pistols were assembled from stores of parts, some perhaps only partially finished, left over from the war production period, for some particular dealer who wished to use the brand name Brunswig. No advertisements for a pistol of this name have been seen by the author. This is but one of many cases where, at the close of a war, left-over pistols and parts have been sold under various brand names.

Union—This was a cheap line of pistols which were sold by Esperanza y Unceta but which were made by a firm in Ermua according to designs and specifications furnished them. They were manufactured especially for the foreign trade and were advertised in circulars printed in several foreign languages but not in Spanish. They were made and sold in approximately the period 1924 to 1931. Data for these pistols, as found in descriptive circulars, are given in Table 22. Recent correspondence states that there was a Mod. V. also, differing from Mod. I in that it had a triple safety rather than a single safety. It is also stated that Mod. IV has three safety devices, including a grip safety. Neither of these statements is confirmed by the literature issued at the time these pistols were being sold.

While there is much similarity between the Union and the Victoria or Astra series, they are not identical. Apart from differences in dimensions there is

TABLE 22
Data for Union pistols

	Mod. I	Mod. II	Mod. III	Mod. IV
Length, mm.	115	115	145	130
Height, mm.	75	100	95	125
Thickness, mm.	20	20	30	20
Weight, gm.	385	445	700	570
Mag. cap. ctges.	6	8	6	11

also a difference in the method of attachment of the grip plates. In the case of the 7.65 mm. 1911 Victorias and the 7.65 mm. 1911 Astras there is but one grip plate screw and this is located near the center of the plate. One Mod. 1911 Astra (No. 923, the lowest number seen) has one screw in the center of the grip plate and another at the bottom, on each plate. Later specimens have but one screw, located near the center of the plate. In the 1915 and 1916 7.65 mm. Astras there are two screws in the grip plates, one at the top and one at the bottom. The same is true for the Brunswig. In the case of the Union 7.65 mm. Mod. III there is only one screw, but (unlike the 1911 models) this screw is located at the rear edge of the grip plate.

The illustration of the Mod. I Union shows a single grip-plate screw, located at the rear edge of the plate, while the plates for the 6.35 mm. Mod. II have two screws each (doubtless because of the greater length of the plates), one at the top of the plate and one at the bottom. All of the 6.35 mm. Victorias and the 6.35 mm. Astras have only one screw for each grip plate, and these are always centrally located.

Current models 1959

Model 200—This 6.35 mm. model has had a long life. It was introduced in 1920 and is still being made. It has three safety features: thumb, magazine, and grip safeties. In this country it is sold as the Fire Cat (Fig. 106).

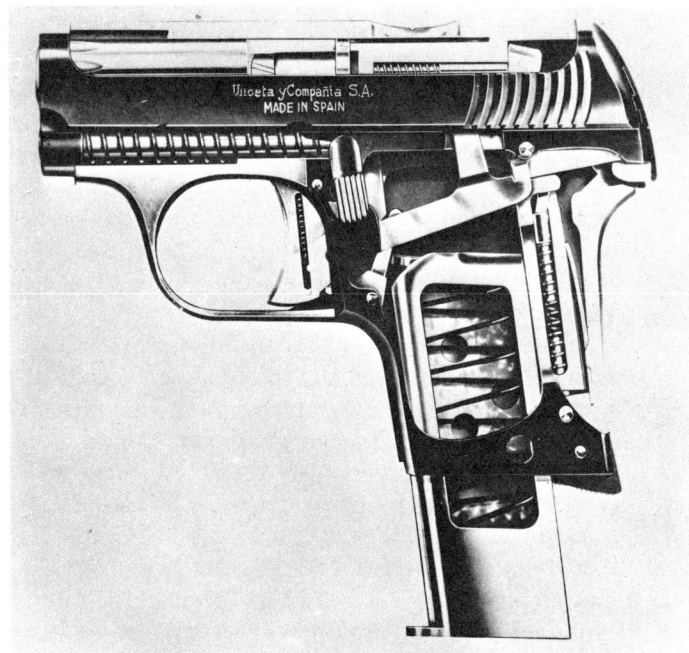

Fig. 106. 6.35 mm. Astra. Sectional view.

Model 2000—This pistol is patterned after the Mod. 200 but has an external hammer. It has only two safety devices, the grip safety having been omitted. The external hammer, however, does add to the safety of this arm. It is made in both .22 Short and 6.35 mm. (.25) calibers and is sold in the U.S. as the Cub. More recently the .22 Short has been provided with a 4-inch barrel, which protrudes 1½ inches from the forward end of the slide. This increases the line of sight materially and no doubt improves accuracy in aiming. The rear sight is adjustable laterally. In this form the pistol is now called the Camper model.

A simple four-piece conversion unit is available for the 6.35 mm. Cub, by means of which .22 Short cartridges may be used instead of the more expensive cartridges.

Model 800 (Condor Model)—This 9 mm. Parabellum (Luger) cartridge pistol is of the tubular type, originally brought out in 1921 as the Mod. 400. It

in the two larger calibers but not in the .22. The safety features are the same as in the Condor model.

A conversion unit may also be had for this model, by means of which either the .32 and .380 may be converted to use .22 L.R. cartridges. The units consists of a complete slide and a special magazine.

All of the current models may be obtained in a variety of finishes: blue; heavy chrome plate; hand-engraved silver plate with "ivory" plastic grips; and even a gold plate with either "pearl" or engraved grip pieces.

Astra-Unceta y Cia. are currently making a small automatic pistol for the Colt Co., which is designated the Junior Colt. It is of .25 caliber but has a conversion unit, similar to that furnished for the Cub, which permits the use of .22 Short cartridges. The design seems identical to that of the Cub, and the dimensions are very nearly the same. On the

TABLE 23
Factory data for the current Astra models

Model and Name	Caliber	Over-all length, inches	Barrel length, inches	Height, inches	Weight without mag., ounces	Mag. cap., ctges.
Mod. 200 (Fire Cat)	.25	4⅛	2⅖	3	11⅘	6
Mod. 2000 (Cub)	.25	4⁷⁄₁₆	2¼	3¼	12	6
Mod. 2000 (Cub)	.22 Sht.	4⁷⁄₁₆	2¼	3¼	11	6
Mod. 2000 (Camper)	.22 Sht.	6³⁄₁₆	4	3¼	11½	6
Mod. 800 (Condor)	9 mm. Par.	8¼	5⁵⁄₁₆	5⅛	32½	8
Mod. 4000 (Falcon)	.22 L.R.	6½	3⅔	4⅓	20	10
Mod. 4000 (Falcon)	.32	6½	3⅔	4⅓	24¾	8
Mod. 4000 (Falcon)	.380	6½	3⅔	4⅓	24¾	7

bears considerable resemblance to the Mod. 600. However, this 1958 version has an external hammer and the thumb safety is located at the rear of the frame instead of just back of the trigger guard. The pistol has been streamlined to give a better grip and a more attractive appearance. As in the case of the earlier tubular models it does not have the grip safety.

When a cartridge is in the chamber and the hammer is in the cocked position a "signal pin" protrudes from the rear of the frame enabling the shooter to ascertain by touch or sight whether or not the pistol is in condition to fire. This model is intended for police, military, and other protection uses.

Model 4000—This model, also known as the Falcon, is made in three calibers: .22 L.R., 7.65 mm. (.32) and 9 mm. Short (.380). It also is a tubular type and resembles the Mod. 300. However, it has an external hammer and has been highly stream-

lined. Like the Condor it has the "signal pin" device

left side of the slide is the inscription "JUNIOR COLT - CAL. .25" and on the right the inscription "COLT'S PT. F. A. MFG. CO., U.S.A." On the right side of the frame appear the words "MADE IN SPAIN FOR COLT'S." Specimens seen are not of the quality of workmanship that one expects to find on a product bearing the name of the Colt company.

Bayard M.P. Mod. 1908 (Bergmann Patent)

This recoil-operated weapon originated as the Bergmann Marspistole* in 1903, being the last of a series of military pistols designed by Theodor Bergmann, and was made from 1903 to 1906 at the Bergmann Industriewerke at Gaggenau, Germany.

*This "Mars" is not to be confused with automatics produced under the same name in Czechoslovakia, England, and France, all of which were different from each other.

In 1907 the firm Anciens Etablissements Pieper (A.E.P.) of Herstal, Belgium, purchased the manufacturing rights, both for military and commercial purposes, and apparently took over all existing stores of component parts and also agreed to accept all contract obligations made by Bergmann prior to 1907. It had been the intention of Bergmann that this arm should be produced in 7.63, 9, 10, and 11 mm. calibers, but up to the time of sale the 9 mm. appears to have been the only one in production.

The measurements on this arm were as follows: length, 25 cm. (9¾ inches); height, 145 mm. (5¾ inches); width, 32 mm. (1¼ inches); length of barrel, 102 mm. (4 inches); number of grooves, 6; direction of twist, left.

Two other varieties of the 1903 Mars pistol series were made. The first was a special 11 mm. caliber made for the British Ordnance Board tests of 1904. The other was made for the early .45 cal. U.S. service automatic pistol, the Bergmann designation for this arm being 11.6 mm. Still another 10 mm. model (probably experimental only) has been reported. None of these are likely to be encountered.

The Pieper firm changed the nomenclature to Bayard Mod. 1908 and continued to supply the Spanish Government, which had adopted it in 1905. The Pieper version of the pistol differed from the German type in that the barrel was slightly longer, the grip frame wider, an integral barrel extension was used, and the rifling was changed to six grooves, with left hand twist. Since German component parts were taken over (and apparently used up) variations will be found—such as a four-groove barrel on a gun bearing the A.E.P. name. One such gun has been measured by the author.

The 9 mm. cartridge used was a rimless type developed by Bergmann in 1898 for use in an earlier weapon, the Bergmann No. 6 Military Pistol. While somewhat similar to the American .38 ACP cartridge, it is not identical, being rimless and tapered. The cartridge is even more similar to, but not identical with, the 9 mm. Steyr.

At the time of acquisition of the Bergmann license, the Mars was used both by the Spanish and Greek armies. Sometime between 1908 and 1914 the Greek Government purchased a number of these Bayard pistols. On September 22, 1911, the Danish Government adopted the Bayard Mod. 1908, after competitive tests. The Danes adopted their own nomenclature, designating it as Pistol Pattern 1910 (or Model 1910), and the pistols made for them by A.E.P. are so marked on the left side of the barrel extension. From 1908 to 1910 the pistol was fitted with molded rubber grips bearing the Bayard crest and was made with solid, smooth walls of the cartridge magazine well. From 1911 on, the crest was omitted from the grip pieces, and finger tabs were introduced to the magazine well. This was the form adopted by the Danes.

Upon delivery, each of the 4840 pistols purchased was given a Danish inventory number, ranging from 1 to 4840, and these numbers were stamped into the right side of the barrel extension in front of the hammer. They should not be confused with the A.E.P. serial number which appears on the under side of the receiver on a flat ahead of the magazine housing. Production of the Bayard M.P. Mod. 1908 (or Bayard-Bergmann, as it is often called) ceased during or directly after World War I and was never resumed.

In 1922 the Danish Ordnance Department decided to manufacture the Bayard M.P. since they no longer could get them from Pieper. Under Royal Army Order of February 11, 1922, the Bayard design, renamed the Model 1910, was modified to have extra-large grip pieces of a plastic material (Trolit) covering the dismounting button and to have a screw retention of the right side frame cover plate instead of a spring-loaded latch. This was the design of pistol to be manufactured in the Royal Arsenal Factory at Copenhagen and to it was assigned the nomenclature Model 1910/21. The pistols were marked HAERENS TØJHUS (for Royal Army) or HAERENS RUSTKAMMER (for Army Storage Arsenal). Only the pistols made by the Danes will bear either of these markings, and they will also be marked M. 1910/21 and carry their own serial number series, starting at No. 1. Since existing stores of the older Mod. 1910 were modified to the new design, pistols with Belgian markings will be found which have been provided with the larger grip pieces and also the marking M. 1910/21, really a misnomer. From specimens examined and measured by the author it appears that the Danes adopted essentially the same rifling specifications as were used by A.E.P.

From 1911 to 1922 all Bayards in Danish service were made by A.E.P.; from 1922 to 1935 the Danes made their own Mod. 1910/21 Bayard or modified the Mod. 1910 they had purchased to conform with the M. 1910/21. In 1940 the Danes replaced the Bayard with the Belgian F.N. Browning High Power, to which they later gave the designation Mod. 1946. In 1948 this pistol was replaced with the 9 mm. Neuhausen pistol—S.I.G. (47/8)—and was given the designation Mod. 1949. The Brownings on hand were classified as "substitute standard" and are still in use. 159

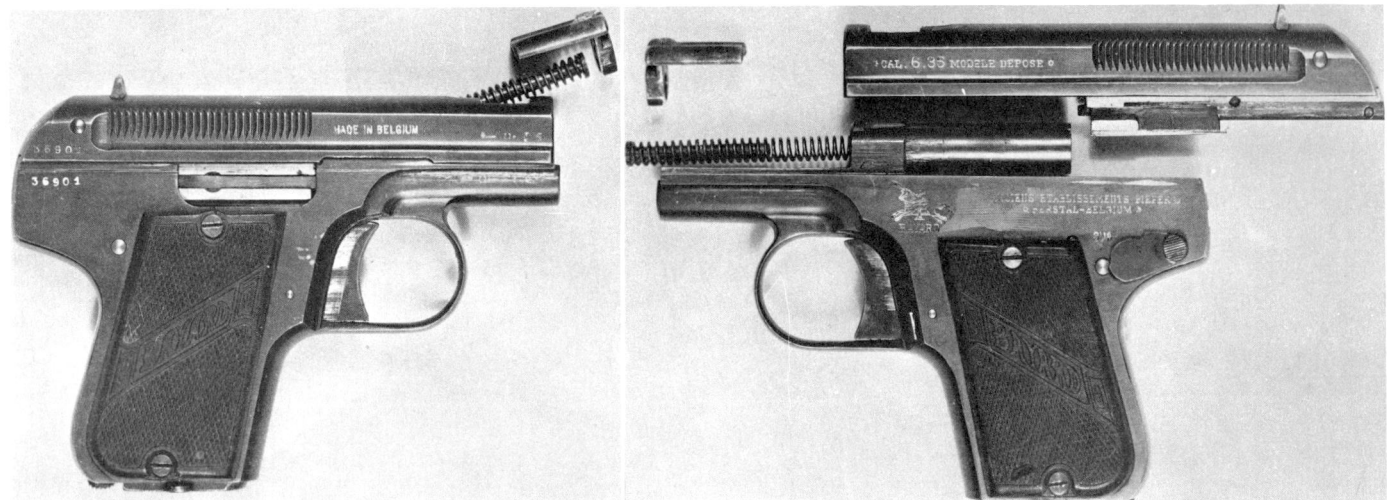

Fig. 107. 6.35 mm. Bayard Mod. 1908, Anc. Etablissements Pieper, Herstal, Belgium.

Fig. 108. 6.35 mm. Bayard Mod. 1908, Anc. Etablissements Pieper, Herstal, Belgium.

Bayard pocket models

The Bayard pocket models were made by Anciens Etablissements Pieper (A.E.P.) and were produced in three calibers: 6.35, 7.65, and 9 mm. The first to be produced was the so called Model of 1908 which appeared in late 1909 or early 1910. The first advertisement of this pistol appeared in the April 1, 1910, issue of *Schuss und Waffe*. The design was based on patents taken out by B. Clarus from 1905 to 1907 and purchased by A.E.P. in 1907 or early in 1908.

In 1911 the 9 mm. model appeared and was advertised in the May 1 issue of *Schuss und Waffe* in that year, and the 6.35 mm. model was introduced to the public in the August 1912 issue of the same publication. The proper model designations would therefore be: 6.35 mm., Model 1912; 7.65 mm., Model 1910; and 9 mm., Model 1911.

These pistols are characterized by their small size. The 7.65 mm. and 9 mm. models are no larger than the ordinary 6.35 mm. pistol. The three models have the same dimensions (Figs. 107, 108).

The Model 1923 Bayard was made in the same three calibers: 6.35, 7.65, and 9 mm. They bear a very close resemblance to the F.N. Brownings, and operate the same way. Catalog information indicates that the 6.35 mm. guns had a magazine capacity of 6 cartridges, a weight of ca. 12 ounces, and dimensions of ca. 4 1/16 × 3 1/8 × 3/4 inch. The 7.65 and 9 mm. guns also had magazine capacities of 6 cartridges, but the weight was ca. 20 ounces, and dimensions were ca. 5 3/4 × 3 1/4 × 1 inch.

According to the manufacturers, the distinctive feature of the 1923 Model is a shock absorbing device which permits the use of 7.65 and 9 mm. ammunition in a very small, light pistol. "This device receives the locking mechanism as it is thrown back and weakens the recoil to such an extent that it becomes almost imperceptible. It consists of a special spring which is located behind the recoil spring in a cylinder case and which works only after the previous stretching of the locking spring, thanks to the pin in the interior of the latter." Another feature is in the omission of the automatic safety, present in many other automatic pistols, whose purpose is to prevent discharge after the magazine has been removed. This omission was adopted after a number of Mod. 1923 pistols had been made and the stated reason for the change is that since this automatic safety device may be broken or rendered inoperative its presence is more dangerous than its omission. They consider that full reliance should be placed on the main safety which, being on the outside, can be seen. If a cartridge has inadvertently been left in the chamber and the magazine is reinserted the automatic device is unlocked thereby and the pistol can be discharged should the main safety be off. Hence the automatic safety device is dangerous and should not be used, in their opinion.

The 1930 Model is of the same type as the Model 1923, the principal point of difference appears to be in the magazine release. On the 1923 Model this is a pivoting affair, similar to that used on the 1910 and 1922 F.N. Brownings, whereas on the Model 1930 Bayard this has been changed to a two-pointed sliding design that does not project so much.

Beholla group

During and after World War I, four pistols, said to have been made from the same set of drawings, were produced in Germany by four separate firms. The original pistol was the Selbstlade Pistole "Beholla" and was made by Becker and Holländer Waffenbau at Suhl. Apparently, this pistol was intended for military use and many of them, including those bearing very low serial numbers, are found to bear the German War Office stamp, indicating that they were accepted for military service. The other three (Leonhardt, Menta, and Stenda) evidently were not made for military use but were exclusively for commercial sale and do not bear the stamp of acceptance.

These pistols are of a simple blowback type, in which the firing pin acts as an ejector. The barrel is secured by a pin passing through an enlargement in the receiver, below the chamber. This pin can be

D.R.P. (Deutsches Reich Patent), but the later ones do, and it is believed that this mark may have been added at the time that permission was given to the other three firms to manufacture the same design pistol. The mark is not found on the other three makes.

Just when Becker and Holländer stopped making the Beholla is not known. But pistol No. 49,781 bears the legend SELBSTLADE PISTOLE "BEHOLLA" CAL. 7.65 D.R.P. (on the left side) and STENDA–WERKE, G.m.b.H. WAFFENBAU, SUHL (on the right side) and has the authentic Beholla grip pieces. These markings, and the fact that all of the pistols so far encountered with Stenda markings have serial numbers higher than the number on this "maverick," suggest that the Stenda Company may have taken over completely from the Becker and Holländer firm at this period of production. This might well have been about 1920.

Stenda–German Patent D.R.P. 342,190 shows that Stenda Werke developed a new type of barrel fasten-

TABLE 24
Measurements and rifling data for Beholla series
(Compiled from data in the *Pistolen Atlas*, by Mezger, Hees, and Haslacher)

	Beholla	Leonhardt	Menta	Stenda
Total length, mm.	140	141	142	141
Barrel length, mm.	74	74	74	80
Weight (empty), gm.	628	614	621	630
Number of grooves	6	6	6	5*
Width of grooves, mm.	.81–.87	1.09–1.20	.87–.95	2.72-2.88
Dir. of twist	R	R	R	R
Rifling angle	5.85°	5.7°	6.7°	2.9°
Mag. cap., ctges.	7	7	7	5

*Most Stendas seen by the author have 6 grooves.

tapped out through holes in the breech slide, when in the closed position. All four of these pistols are of 7.65 mm. ACP caliber. Data on all four are given in Table 24.

Beholla–Early Beholla pistols seem to be of a commercial form but the entire production is reported to have been taken into military service. The pistol originated about 1915. The early specimens have hard rubber grips with a monogram consisting of the letters BH, intertwined. Specimens made later have serrated wood grip pieces. Pistols made by Becker and Holländer are marked SELBSTLADE PISTOLE "BEHOLLA" Cal. 7.65 (on left side) and BECKER AND HOLLÄNDER, WAFFENBAU, SUHL (on right side).

Specimens Nos. 503, 774, 2012, 27,463, and 30,0003 are known, the last being of the military variety. All five of these have six grooves and right hand twist with one turn in from 8.5 to 9.6 inches.

The earliest Beholla pistols do not bear the mark

ing sometime in the autumn of 1920. Pistols of the Beholla type having the Stenda type of barrel fastening are found to be marked ST. W. or STENDA. Advertising material of the summer of 1920 fails to mention the Stenda and refers only to the Beholla. All this suggests that sometime prior to the autumn of 1920 the manufacture of Beholla pistols was transferred from Becker and Holländer to Stenda Werke, but that sales continued under the name Beholla. And it is also considered very likely that shortly thereafter manufacture of the pistol was modified to incorporate the newly patented barrel fastening feature and that from then on the pistol was marketed with full Stenda markings, the Beholla name having been dropped.

Specimens of pistols having "pure" Stenda marking, carrying the Serial Nos. 61,747, 61,907, and 68,959, suggest that the Stenda serial numbers may be a continuation of the Beholla series of numbering. The first two of these pistols have six grooves, right hand twist with one turn in 9.6 and 9.75 inches, respectively, which is practically in line with the Becker and Holländer-made Beholla. However, specimen No. 68,959 and another whose serial number has been removed have variant rifling characteristics: five grooves, right hand twist with one turn in 18.7 and 18.8 inches, respectively. These latter two specimens suggest that the rifling was changed to meet Stenda ideas. How many Stendas were produced is not known, but production is thought to have stopped in the mid-1920's.

Leonhardt—The Leonhardt, made by H. M. Gering of Arnstadt, is practically identical to the Beholla, as made by Becker and Holländer.

Specimen No. 29,681 is identical, with the exception that the hard rubber grip pieces, while similar in design, were not formed by the same die which formed those found on the Menta (another of the Beholla group). The inscription on the left side reads SELBSTLADE PISTOLE "Leonhardt" (the last word in script) and that on the right side reads GERING & CO. ARNSTADT.

A second specimen, No. 37,963, differs from the Beholla in the shape, style, and dimensions of the grip pieces, which are of wood and bear no monogram, and in the shape of the safety release lever. The inscription on the left side of the slide reads SELBSTLADE PISTOLE "LEONHARDT." With the exception of the serial number this is the only marking that appears. Not even the caliber is stated.

The two specimens have six rifling grooves, right hand twist, with one turn in 9.6 and 9.7 inches, respectively. This conforms to measurements of the original Beholla.

Specimen No. 24,281, shown in the Pistol Atlas, is identical to No. 37,963 except that it has grip pieces like those on the Menta and the safety lever is like that on the Stenda.

Menta—The Menta was made by August Menz of Suhl. The specimen examined, Serial No. 8915, was identical externally to the Beholla in practically all respects. The only apparent differences are in the grip pieces, which are also of hard rubber but entirely different in design (with no name or letter monogram),* and in the location of the magazine release. This protrudes from the rear of the lower end of the grip frame instead of from underneath.

The only markings, in addition to the serial number, read MENTA "KAL." 7.65. The rifling has six

grooves, right hand twist with one turn in 9.5 inches. This degree of twist is in line with that found in the Beholla.

Specimen No. 6574, reported in the Pistol Atlas, appears to be identical to No. 8915.

August Menz also produced a Menta in 6.35 mm. caliber, which is identical in design to the 7.65 mm. pistol. The only differences in manufacture are the number of serrations in the finger grip at the rear end of the slide (5 instead of 7) and the reduction in size. Specimen No. 4863 has been examined and No. 5347 has been reported. They are identical.

Beistegui Hermanos

Beistegui Hnos. not only manufactured revolvers and automatic pistols but they also marketed arms made by others. Both the Bulwark and the Libia were definitely made by them. Pistols marked simply B.H. have been reported in both 6.35 and 7.65 mm. calibers but have not been seen and their existence or genuineness cannot presently be verified.

Bulwark (and Libia)—The Libia pistol is identical to the Bulwark and was given a special name for export sale by Fab. d'Armes de Guerre de Grande Precision, an exporting house located in Eibar (not a manufacturer, as the name would imply). Both of these pistols show the same design and details of manufacture and both carry the inscription "PATENT DEPOSE NO. 67,259." The pistol was made in both 6.35 and 7.65 mm. calibers (ACP) and was made in hammerless and hammer models. The hammerless type, at least, had three safety devices, including a grip safety. In design it is a simple blowback type and specimens examined appear to have been reasonably well made. The 6.35 mm. model was 112 mm. long, 76 mm. high, and 13 mm. thick, weighed about 400 gm., and had a magazine capacity of 6 cartridges. The 7.65 mm. model was 138 mm. long, 90.5 mm. high, and 16 mm. thick, weighed about 600 gm., and had a capacity of 7 cartridges. The hammer type has not been encountered and details are not available.

A 6.35 mm. specimen, photographed by the author, has markings identical to those normally found on Bulwark pistols except for the Fab. d'Armes de Guerre de Grande Precision inscription, but it differs sufficiently in details of manufacture to warrant the conclusion that it must have been made with a different set of tools. The workmanship appears inferior. The grip pieces bear a monogram consisting of the letters B.H., but with the important difference that on this pistol the letter H is on top of the B whereas in the genuine Beistegui monogram the letter B is

---

*When comparing pistols which are as similar as those in the Beholla group it must be remembered that grip pieces are interchangeable and that those found on a pistol may not be the originals. Therefore, differences which depend mainly on grip piece patterns are not necessarily significant.

uppermost. It is not likely that this pistol was made by Beistegui.

Advertising literature issued by Beistegui shows two models of 7.65 mm. Bulwark pistols. One model is identical in design to the regular 6.35 mm. model and has the three safety devices. The other model is considerably larger and does not have the grip safety. It fires 9 rounds instead of 6 and is 175 mm. in length. The weights are given as 850 gm. and 550 gm., respectively. The barrels in all Beistegui pistols and revolvers were rifled by Teodoro Elcoro, according to contemporary records.

A specimen marked

7.65 1914 MODEL AUTOMATIC PISTOL

BEISTEGUI HERMANOS - EIBAR (ESPANA)

with serial No. 42,300 is of the "Ruby" type, and very likely this was made by Beistegui, with or without license from Gabilondo y Urresti, for the French military forces. Many Spanish firms were so engaged during World War I. Beistegui Hnos. is one of the firms listed by Gabilondo as having made the Ruby type pistol under their own name.

Other pistols marketed by Beistegui Hnos. include the Royal line, a 6.35 mm. Paramount, and the Mauser 7.63 mm. M.P. Whether this Paramount (there were several of them) was actually made by them is not known. As advertised, this was a 6.35 mm. pistol with or without the grip safety device. The length was stated to be 110 mm. and weight 310 gm. Since it could be had with the grip safety device it might appear that it may have been made by Beistegui. The pistol is, however, unlike the Bulwark (though it has the same dimensions) in that the slide safety lever is in front of the grip frame instead of back of it. The grip pieces carry the name Paramount rather than the B.H. monogram. No patent number is given nor does the Beistegui name appear.

Since the trade name "Royal" was granted to M. Zulaica in 1909 for use on automatic pistols it seems likely that the Royal pistols marketed by Beistegui were probably not made by them.

Two quite dissimilar 7.65 mm. models are shown in Beistegui literature. One had an exposed hammer, fired 12 rounds, was 205 mm. in length, and weighed 920 gm. The other was hammerless, fired 9 rounds, was 150 mm. in length, and weighed 800 gm. The hammer model shows the Zulaica monogram while the other has no monogram on the grip pieces. This latter model appears quite similar to the Ruby type originated by Gabilondo y Urresti and made by many manufacturers in Spain for the French during World War I. It is most unlikely that it was made by Beistegui Hermanos.

The Royal 7.63 mm. imitation of the Mauser M.P. is a Spanish product, presumably made by Zulaica y Cia., and is quite similar to the Astra imitation made by Unceta y Cia. Beistegui advertising shows the 10-cartridge magazine and the shoulder stock.

Beretta

This large group of pistols was and is manufactured by Fabrica d'Armi Pietro Beretta, Gardone Val Trompia (Brescia), Italy. This is certainly one of the oldest firearms manufacturing firms in existence, as it was founded in 1680. It is still very active. For nearly three centuries it has enjoyed an excellent reputation for the arms it has produced. Previous to 1915 their chief product was shotguns, but in that year they turned their attention to automatic pistols and, to date, well over two million have been made.

The early pistols, and most of the later ones, are of a simple blowback design with a highly functional firing system. Since their introduction they have constantly been improved. In 1950 it was realized that there was need for a powerful, compact, and effective 9 mm. caliber pistol for military use and this led to the development of a fully locked, recoil-operated design which has since become known as the 1951 Model (or M951). The 1956 catalog states that it was available to foreign countries for military use. The pistol had, at that time, been adopted by the Egyptian Army. Though it was reserved solely for military use up to 1956, this restriction seems now to have been removed.

1915 Type–7.65 mm. (Brng.) This was a blowback with internal hammer, Mauser pocket pistol type of barrel mounting, and a firing pin which acted as ejector. It had straight grip frame, wood grips, magazine capacity of 7 cartridges, and 6-R rifling. It was made for Italian army and police use only and was marked PS (Pubblica Sicurezza, public security) for police use or RE (Regio Esercito) for army use. It was covered by 1915 patents and discontinued in 1919.

1915 Type–9 mm. Parabellum (or M910 ctge.) This was a slightly modified version of the 7.65 mm. type, but somewhat larger and provided with an ejector. It was for military and police purchase only and had either RE or PS markings. It was discontinued in 1919 (Figs. 109, 110).

1915, 1919 Type–7.65 mm. (Brng.) This was a greatly modified version of the 1915 Type, with an original barrel mounting, changed safety lever, inter-

163

nal hammer, straight grip frame, metal grip plates, magazine capacity of 8 ctges., and 6-R rifling. Specimens were marked PS and some also were sold commercially from about 1920 to 1930.

1919 Type—6.35 mm. (Brng.) This. was a somewhat modified and improved version of the 7.65 mm. 1915, 1919 Type. A grip safety device which blocked the sear motion was added. Molded plastic grips were later changed to sheathed grip pieces of the 1935 form. It had a magazine capacity of 7 ctges., and an internal hammer. It was introduced in the early 1920's and one specimen dated 1935, with Serial No. 606,460, has been noted.

Model 1923—9 mm. Parabellum (or M910 ctge.)

This was a further modification of the 1915 design, greatly enlarged and, for the first time, with external hammer. It had RE markings but was also sold commercially from 1923 to ca. 1936 or 1937. It could be had with a combination shoulder stock-holster. It had a magazine capacity of 8 ctges. and 6-R rifling. It was the first Beretta to have an official model designation (Modello 1923).

Model 1931—7.65 mm. (Brng.) This model, often called the Navy Model, returned to the 1915, 1919 Type in size, but was greatly streamlined and had an improved firing system and a closed bridge slide. Known specimens have wood grip pieces and show the RM crest, indicating that they were for Navy

Fig. 109. 9 mm. Beretta Mod. 1915, Pietro Beretta, Gardone V. T. (Brescia), Italy.

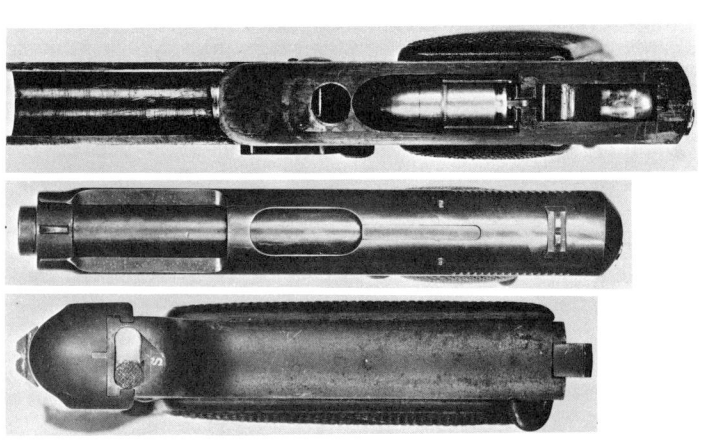

Fig. 110. 9 mm. Beretta Mod. 1915. Pietro Beretta, Gardone V. T. (Brescia), Italy. Note the top ejection of fired shell and the very unusual position of safety lever.

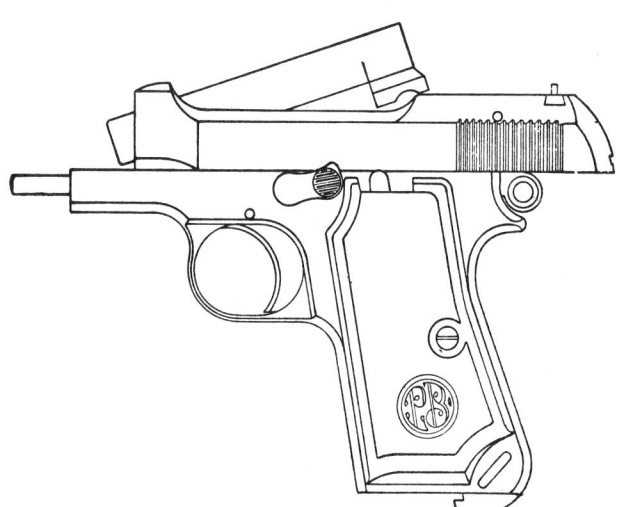

Fig. 111. Beretta Mod. 1934. Showing method of disassembly.

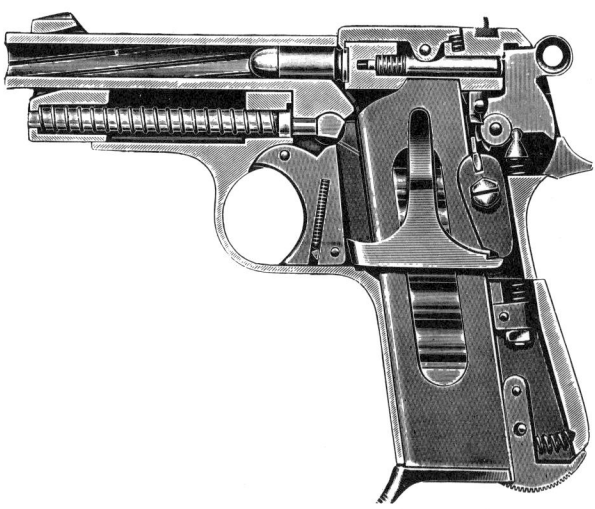

Fig. 112. Beretta Mod. 1934. Sectional view.

use. It is believed that they were not sold commercially.

Model 1934–9 mm. (.380) This is a further streamlined version of the 1931 model, with sheathed plastic grip pieces (Figs. 111, 112). It was designed for and adopted by the Italian military service. Specimens show the RE mark. It was also sold commercially in large quantities. (Mag. cap. 7 ctges., rifling 6-R.) This pistol is currently known as Mod. 934 (Corto). It appears to be identical to the pre-war Mod. 1934.

Model 1935–7.65 mm. (Brng.) There seems to be some confusion concerning the proper nomenclature for this model. It is stated that though it was first issued as the Modello 1935 (and was so marked) it was later given the designation Modello 1934 and that specimens were so marked. The 1956 Beretta catalog designates it as Mod. 935. This pistol is identical in design to the 9 mm. Modello 1934, though smaller in size. (Mag. cap. 8 ctges.) It is currently advertised as an Ordnance pistol for the Italian Navy, Air Force, and Police.* It is sold commercially and is obtainable in extra finishes as "Mod. 935 bis" and "Mod. 935 D.D.," both de luxe types.

Model 318–6.35 mm. In the mid-1930's the 6.35 mm. Mod. 1919 was improved by addition of the newest modifications. The new model had the same shaped grip safety but the grip frame was more streamlined. Serial numbers for the Mod. 318 are continued from the 1919 Type, starting around 610,000. This model was generally known as Mod. 1934. When the change of name to Modello 318 was made is not known, but the pistol seems to date from 1935. (Mag. cap. 8 ctges., rifling 6-R.) Presumably, production of this pistol was stopped at the start of World War II. The highest serial number noted is 622,297, found on a pistol marked as made in 1939.

Following World War II, in 1946 or soon thereafter, some changes in the design of the Beretta pistols were made. Production of the 7.65 and 9 mm. pistols had been continued during the war, under German supervision.

Model 418–6.35 mm. (Brng.) Model 318 was redesigned, but not greatly changed in appearance, and given the designation Mod. 418. The more obvious changes are in the shape of the grip safety, a better design, and the use of slanting rather than vertical serrations on the rear of the slide. In the current production the Beretta design on the grips

*Pistols intended for the Air Force may be marked AM (Aeronautica Militare) or RA (Regio Aeronautica). Those for Navy use may be marked RM (Regio Marina). Those for Army use are marked RE (Regio Esercito, i.e., Royal Army).

has been changed. High quality chromium-nickel forged and hammered steel is used, according to catalog statements. This pistol is obtainable in three degrees of finish—standard (Mod. 418), chromium plated and engraved (Mod. 420), and the de luxe type (Mod. 421). The last is richly engraved and gold plated and has "turtle shell" grip pieces. (Mag. cap. 8 ctges. Rifling 6-R.) For the Mod. 418, serial numbering started at No. 1-A and by 1957 it had

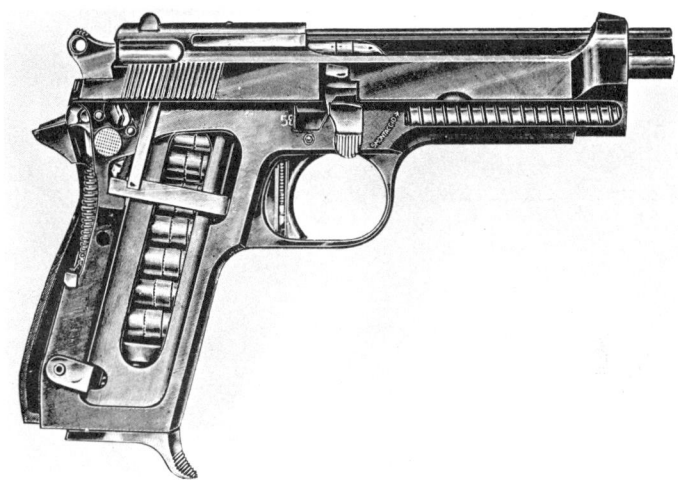

Fig. 113. 9 mm. Beretta Mod. 1951. Sectional view.

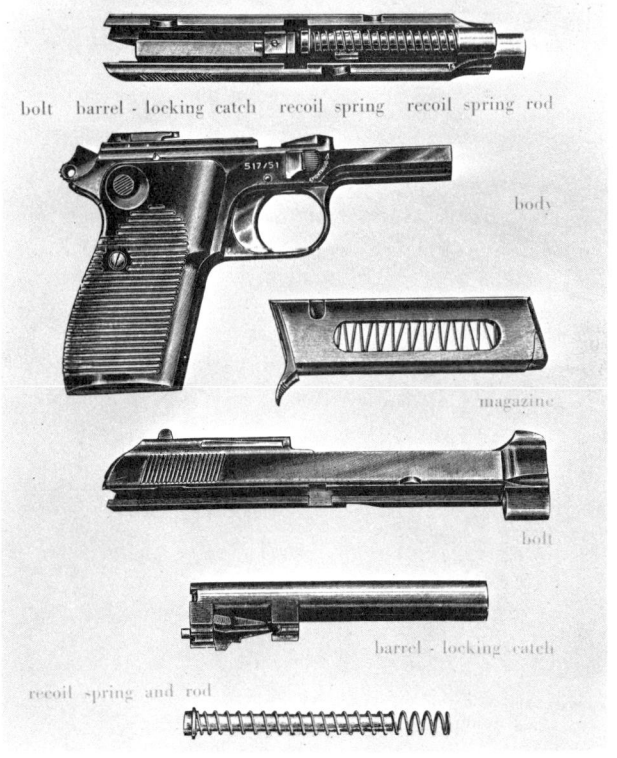

Fig. 114. 9 mm. Beretta Mod. 1951. Disassembled.

passed 100,000. This and other Beretta models have appeared with aluminum alloy frames, with a resulting decrease in weight.

Model 951—9 mm. Parabellum ("Lungo Parabellum"). This pistol was designed and produced in 1951 especially for the Italian Navy and Air Forces, for special detachments. It has a recoil-operated barrel locked by a special vertically sliding catch, standard magazine capacity of 8 and a special magazine capacity of 10 ctges. The body is of light alloy ("Ergal") and the shape of the grip is quite similar to the German P-38 (Figs. 113, 114, 115).

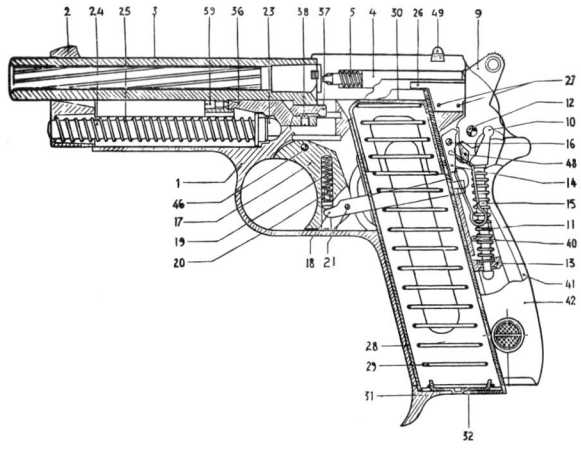

Fig. 115. 9 mm. Beretta Mod. 1951. Schematic view.

Fig. 116. .22 cal. L. R. Beretta Olympic Mod. Disassembled.

Model 948—.22 cal. L.R. This is a comparatively new member of the Beretta family, with factory designation Mod. 47. Known as the "Featherweight," it is made of duraluminum alloy and weighs 480 grams (less than 17 ounces). (Barrel length, 3$\frac{5}{16}$ inches; over-all length, 5$\frac{7}{8}$ inches; mag. cap., 8 ctges.) It is similar in appearance to Mod. 935. A special 150-mm. barrel, interchangeable with the standard barrel, is obtainable for target shooting. Mod. 948 is sold in the U.S. as the "Plinker."

Model 950 c.c.—.22 cal. Corto (short). This is a new pistol of quite different construction from previously made Berettas. The barrel is hinged at the front end, in front of the trigger guard, and tips up from the rear. It has an exposed hammer, double safety catch, and a duraluminum frame. (Mag. cap., 7 ctges.; barrel length, 2$\frac{3}{8}$ inches; over-all length, 4$\frac{11}{16}$ inches.) It is sold in the U.S. as the "Minx."

Model 950 c.c. Special—Same as above except that it has a 100-mm. (about 4 inches) barrel.

Model 949 Corto—This is a .22 caliber target pistol known as the "Tipo Olimpionico"—specially designed for Olympic target shooting. It has a muzzle deflector, adjustable weights, and a hand-lapped barrel. (Length of barrel, 8¾ inches; length over-all, 12½ inches; weight, 38 oz.) It has a trigger pull of 1½ pounds (Fig. 116).

Model 949 L.R.—This is the same as Model 949 except for the cartridge used.

The Roman numerals appearing on Beretta pistols which were made during the Fascist regime represent the year of that regime and probably were required by government order.

The 9 mm. Mod. 1934 Berettas made in 1941 and 1942 are normally in the 800,000 to 900,000 range of serial numbers. Variant serial numbers are frequently found, however. Some of these are definitely pistols made for (or sold to) some foreign country, such as Nos. 02,147, 08,991, and 20,830, all of which are dated 1941 and bear evidence of being sold to Rumania. These are marked P. BERETTA - CAL. 9 SCURT - MO. 1934 - BREVET. Some of these have the Roman numerals, while others do not. Other variant markings have been found, such as No. F-63,599 (dated 1942), 3662-AA (dated 1943), and 4996-BB (dated 1944). Presumably these also were made on some special order.

For rifling specifications for currently made Berettas see Appendix II.

Bergmann—Early types

Theodor Bergmann was one of the first to produce a practical automatic pistol, the actual inventor of which was Louis Schmeisser, however. In the period 1892 to 1905 many designs were produced and the pistols were manufactured at Bergmann's Industrie-werke at Gaggenau (Baden), Germany. These early Bergmann pistols are now collectors' items of very considerable value because only a few guns were made in many of the designs produced (some even being practically prototypes) and because by 1907 the firm had either discontinued manufacture of all of these or had licensed their manufacture to others.

There are two classes of designs for this period: (1) the blowback type which originated in 1892 and (2) the recoil-operated type which originated in 1896. The activities for this period are, concisely, as follows:

1892, 1893, 1894—Three distinct, experimental blowback designs were evolved. The designs were characterized by the frontal magazine packet loading and the "enclosed" trigger guard. It would seem that all three pistols fired a necked, grooveless, 8 mm. cartridge; later reduced in all proportions to the 6.5

mm. grooveless type, and still later to a grooved type.

1896-2, 1896-2*, 1896-2's—A total of five different forms of the 5 mm. commercial blowback exist. All are known as the 1896-2 with suffix designations. The figure 2 represents the 5 mm. cartridge. Variants are distinguished by absence of extractor (earliest type for the grooveless cartridge), addition of extractor, increased barrel length, hair trigger, etc. This was the first commercial Bergmann pistol (Figs. 117, 118).

1896-3, 1896-3's—This is the commercial blowback design in 6.5 mm. Bergmann caliber. Many variants of this exist, including the extractorless early type, long-barrel type, etc.

1896-4—A military-size blowback, this follows the same pattern as the other 1896 commercial pistols. It is chambered for an 8 mm. cartridge with straight case. Only one form is known.

1897-5—This was the first recoil-operated, locked-bolt design. Mod. 1896 had a removable barrel and no rigid bolting; the closure cylinder of the 1897 model is bolted rigidly into a movable barrel while discharging the pistol, and directly afterwards the barrel retracts with the cylinder a few (6) millimeters until the unbolting takes place. It had been found that the loose bolting in the 1896 model was unsatisfactory for the higher velocities desired. The 1897 Mod. was a military size, chambering a 7.65 mm. necked cartridge of the Mauser style (Figs. 119 to 122). The designation "7.8 mm. Bergmann" sometimes seen is a misnomer, being merely a nomenclature given by the ammunition manufacturer (D.W.M.) for this cartridge. At least three variant forms are known for the 1897 model, differing principally in grip contour, grip piece style, pressure venting, etc. While they enjoyed a fairly wide commercial sale, they were not adopted for military

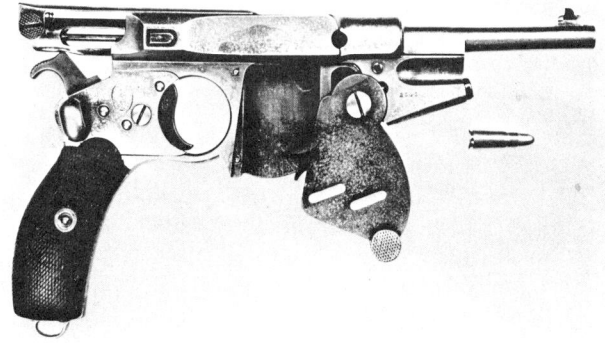

Fig. 117. Bergmann Mod. 1896. Bergmann's Industrie Werke, Gaggenau (Baden), Germany. Commercial type. One of several variations.

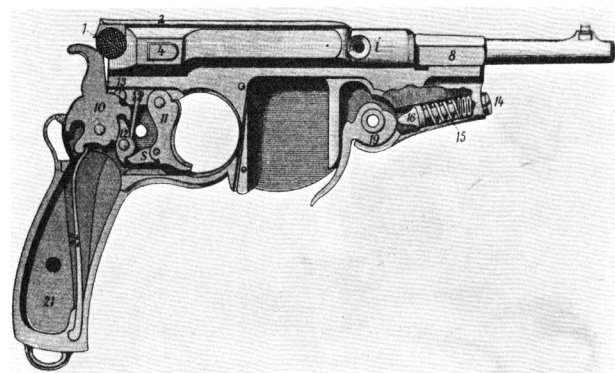

Fig. 118. Bergmann Mod. 1896. Commercial type. Sectional view.

Fig. 119. Bergmann Military type (1897). 167

use. An 1897-5 "Karabiner" existed. This was merely a longer-barrel version with an accompanying wooden butt-stock. The holster could be attached for carbine use. The figure 5 following the date of the

Fig. 120. Bergmann Military type (1897).

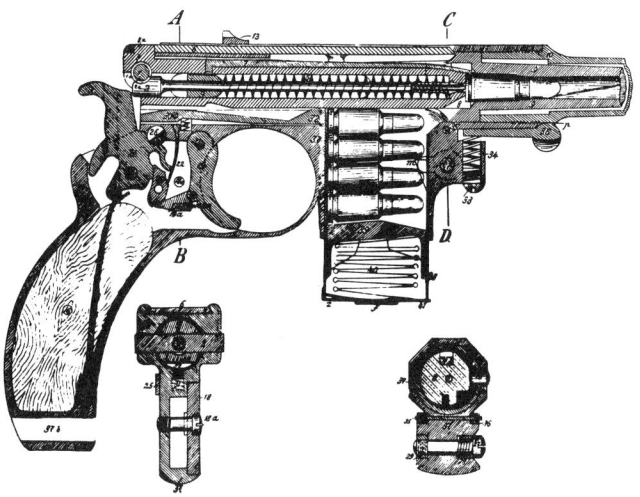

Fig. 121. Bergmann Military type (1897). Action closed. (Part of barrel cut away).

model (Mod. 1897-5) refers to the cartridge, as do all other such figure suffixes to the date nomenclatures designating the models of these Bergmann pistols. The rifling specifications for the 7.65 mm. Bergmann Mod. 1897-5, as shown by original Bergmann records, are as follows: bore diameter, 0.301 inch; groove diameter, 0.309 inch; depth of grooves, 0.0045 inch; number of grooves, 6; direction of twist, Right; width of grooves, 0.158 inch; width of lands, 0.079 inch; and one turn of rifling in 9.45 inches. Rifling specifications for the other models are not available.

99/203, 99/507—These are two experimental, locked-bolt, recoil-operated types that marked the transition from the 1897-5 design to the 1903 Mars design. They may have chambered the 9 mm. cartridge, later known as the 9 mm. Bergmann. A discrepancy exists within the cartridge numbers in that No. 6 became the 9 mm. Bergmann cartridge, whereas it was originally assigned to a 7.5 mm. cartridge.

1903—This series is officially known as "Die Bergmann Selbstlade Pistole Mars Modell 1903." This is the locked-bolt, recoil-operated weapon ultimately sold by license to the Belgian firm of A.E.P. (Pieper) (Figs. 123, 124). The Mars pistol was evolved over a period of five years, beginning in 1899. It was commercially manufactured in 7.63 mm. Mauser and 9 mm. Bergmann from about 1903 to the end of 1906. Two other cartridges were offered commercially but not widely sold. A 10 mm. type has never even been seen but is listed in Bergmann literature. An 11 mm. type was originally specially developed for trial by the British Government in 1903 and was later offered commercially, but was not popular. A very few (possibly less than ten) samples were made

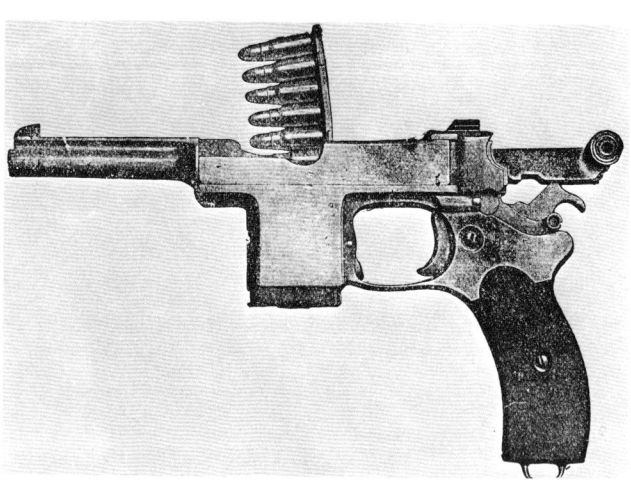

Fig. 123. Mars Military Pistol Mod. 1903. Bergmann's Industrie Werke, Gaggenau (Baden), Germany.

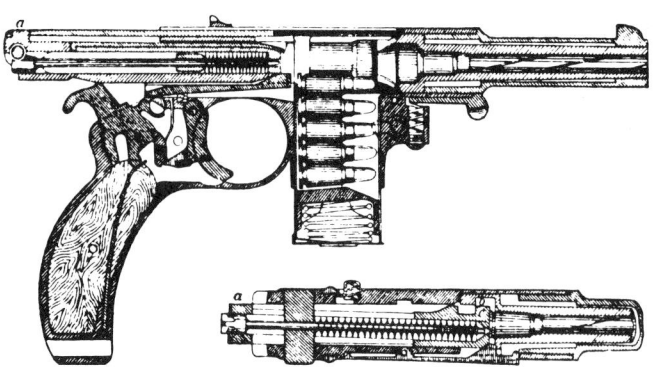

Fig. 122. Bergmann Military type (1897). Action open.

in .45 caliber for the experimental U.S. auto pistol cartridge of 1906. In this .45 caliber, the weapon was tested in the U.S. in 1907. This last pistol was never offered commercially. Its factory designation was "11.6 mm." The 7.63 mm. and 9 mm. Mars types were available in 6-round, as well as the popular 10-round, type. The 9 mm. Mars type was adopted into Spanish service in September 1905. It was advertised for sale as late as 1911 (ALFA Catalog, published by Adolf Frank, Hamburg, Germany).

Bergmann literature shows that the 1896-2, 3, 4, and 1900-5 were being marketed as late as 1901. The 1900-5 was replaced by the Mars 1903, but the 1896-2, 3, and 4 types were undoubtedly sold as late as 1906. The 1897 and 1899 types do not appear in sales literature after 1900.

Bergmann Pocket Models

Production of the 5 and 6.5 mm. Bergmann blowback pistols of earlier type ceased about 1904. Inasmuch as it is reliably reported that the firm of V. Charles Schilling, long associated with Bergmann, actually made these pistols for Bergmann in the period 1896 to 1904, at which time the Schilling firm was taken over by H. Krieghoff, it seems a safe conclusion that these circumstances account for the cessation of production. Pistols of this type and vintage, bearing the name of Bergmann, are found to carry the V.C.S. mark of Schilling.

Some years later, prior to World War I but probably not earlier than 1910, a very different type of pocket pistol made by Theodor Bergmann Maschinen u. Waffenfabrik of Gaggenau (Baden) and Suhl (Thuringia) appeared. Presumably, production was stopped by World War I. In 1920 several pre-war firms, including the Lignose powder company, combined to form the firm Aktien Gesellschaft Lignose-Berlin, which appears to have been primarily a sales organization. This firm marketed several but not all

of these newer models of Bergmann pistols under the name Akt. Gesellschaft Lignose - Abt. Suhl, i.e., the Suhl Division of the parent firm in Berlin. The pistols sold by them have the word LIGNOSE on the grips. The Bergmann model nomenclature was not changed. Commercial sale was continued through the 1920's, apparently under both the Bergmann and Lignose names, and later under the name of Lignose. Production seems to have stopped somewhere in the 1930's.

There were two series of these new Bergmann pistols, the "Taschen" (pocket) and the "Einhand" (one hand). Both were pocket pistols, so "Einhand Taschen" would have been a more accurate designation for the second series. Whereas the earlier types of Bergmann pistols had been made at Gaggenau, either by Bergmann's Industriewerke or by V. Charles Schilling, these newer pistols were made at Suhl.

The "Taschen" series were a full-slide blowback type, with a mechanical safety. They follow closely the pattern established by the F.N. 6.35 mm. Browning model of 1906—a pistol that has probably had more imitation as to principles of construction and operation than all other systems combined.

Models Nos. 2 and 3 - 6.35 mm.—These are alike except that the grip frame in No. 3 is longer in order to take a magazine holding 9 rounds, whereas the No. 2 magazine holds only 6 (Fig. 125).

Model No. 4/5. - 7.65 and 9 mm.—The No. 4/5 model follows the same general design, except that

Fig. 124. Mars Military Pistol. With shoulder stock-case.

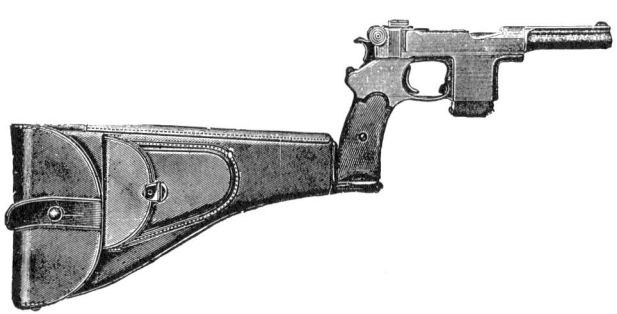

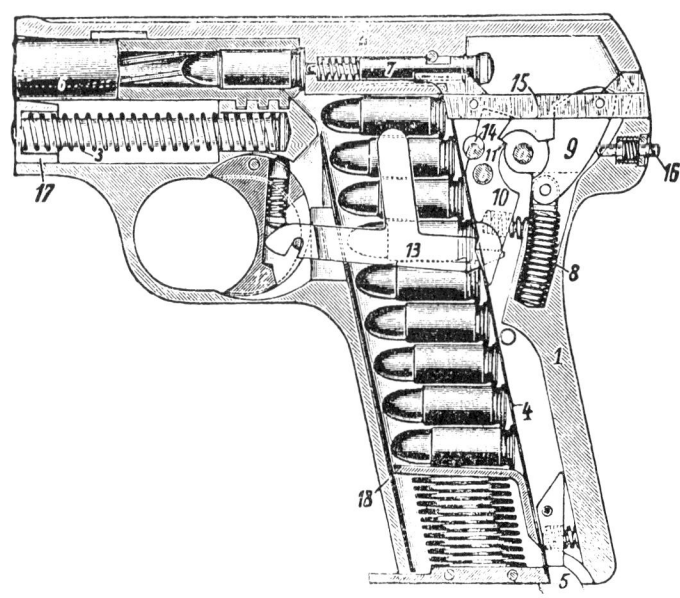

Fig. 125. Lignose Mod. 3. Theodor Bergmann, Suhl, Germany.

it has larger components. The pistol is made for either of two barrels. Provided with a 7.65 mm. barrel it becomes Mod. 4, and with a 9 mm. (Short) barrel its nomenclature is Mod. 5.

The Mod. 4/5 seems not to have been made in considerable numbers. This is probably due, in part at least, to the fact that it appeared only shortly before or at about the time that Lignose took over the other models. For some reason this model was not marketed by them.

The "Einhand" pocket models are characterized by a cocking device which permits cocking and firing with one hand, a feature which Bergmann stressed as being an important feature in a gun used for self defense. The forward edge of the trigger guard is curved, like the trigger, and by pulling it back with the trigger finger the whole guard moves backward and cocks the pistol. This feature was the invention of Witwold Chylewski, an Austrian, and was used in a 6.35 mm. (Browning cartridge) pistol which he designed in the period 1910–1913. Aside from prototype manufacture prior to 1914, no production of the pistol was undertaken until about 1918 or 1919, at which time Chylewski made a contract with the Sociéte Industrielle Suisse (S.I.G., Neuhausen) for the production of a few hundred pieces. Apparently this was not intended as a production program but mainly for the purpose of getting samples to aid him in interesting some manufacturer. At any rate, Chylewski succeeded in interesting the Bergmann firm and from 1920 on this "one hand" feature was used on the "Einhand" pistols produced by them. The Chylewski pistol bears only a general resemblance to the Bergmann-made pistol. (See section on Chylewski pistol.)

Models Nos. 2A and 3A "Einhand"—These are similar to the Taschen Models Nos. 2 and 3 except for the "Einhand" feature which makes them slightly heavier.

All models in all variations may be found with either wood grips (uncommon) or hard rubber grips (common), the latter bearing either the name BERGMANN or LIGNOSE on the grips. Some of the Bergmann-marked pistols (Mods. 2 and 3) have a single large letter B on a metal plate set into plain wood grip pieces. These are early post-World War I specimens.

More recently a new and different pistol appeared under the name Theodor Bergmann-Erben (Theodor Bergmann Heirs), quite evidently a sales organization.

The 7.65 mm. Theodor Bergmann-Erben Special (No. 3797, at least) is practically identical to the August Menz 7.65 mm. P.B. Special, the only apparent difference (shown in illustrations) is the shape of the notch on the lower edge of the slide on the left side. Another specimen of the 7.65 mm. Bergmann-Erben Special, marked Mod. II on the slide, is slightly different, having no notch on the slide and having a somewhat different magazine release. Both pistols do have the characteristic Menz features and doubtless were made by Menz, in Suhl. The Menz P.B. Special was advertised as being made in three calibers: 5.6 mm. (.22 cal. Long Rifle, C.F.), 7.65 mm., and 9 mm. Short. Whether the Bergmann-Erben appears in all of these calibers is not known.

The 6.35 mm. Theodor Bergmann-Erben pistol bears no resemblance to the Menz pistols, except that it is constructed and operates on the Browning principle. Cartridge ejection is at the top rather than at the right side, the safety is at the rear of the frame, it does not have the exposed hammer, and

TABLE 25
Data for "Taschen" and "Einhand" Bergmann pistols (from Bergmann Manual)

Measurement	6.35 mm. "Taschen" and "Einhand" series				"Taschen" Models 4/5 7.65 mm. and 9 mm.	
Model No.	2	2A	3	3A	4	5
Over-all length, mm.	118	118	118	118	126	126
Height, mm.	75	75	100	100	103	103
Thickness, mm.	23	23	23	23	25	25
Distance btw. sights, mm.	110	110	110	110	116	116
Barrel length, mm.	54.5	54.5	54.5	54.5	60	60
Magazine cap., ctges.	6	6*	9	9	8	7
Grooves and dir. of twist	6-R	6-R	6-R	6-R	6-R	6-R
Weight, empty, gm.	375	385	415	425	535	535

*No. 2A could be provided with a special, protruding magazine holding 9 cartridges.

the disassembly is entirely different. It does have the crossed pistols emblem of Bergmann which was used on many but not all of the Bergmann-made pistols.

Bergmann-Simplex

According to the best recent information, the pistol that later became known as the 8 mm. Bergmann-Simplex was first issued as the Bergmann Selbstlade Pistole Modell 1901 and was introduced sometime in the winter of that year. In its original form it had a longer barrel than the Simplex and the grip frame shape was like the earlier 1897 Bergmann. By 1901–1902 the Mod. 1901 was reduced to a pocket type, with shorter barrel and a rounded grip frame characteristic of the final Simplex pistol. It has been conjectured that this pistol may have been made for Bergmann by V. Charles Schilling, but this has not been verified.

After 1902 the Bergmann-Simplex was made in Belgium, with or without license, by some unknown manufacturer. This gun bore the name SIMPLEX on the grip plates, but not elsewhere, and no manufacturer's name appears on the gun. It was 7¾ inches in length—rather large for a "pocket pistol," as it purported to be. The cartridge was that known as the 8 mm. Bergmann-Simplex, manufacture of which ceased many years ago. It was originally developed for the 1895 Mod. Bergmann pistol.

It has been rumored that there was also a Spanish version of the Simplex. This may be due to the fact that there seems to have been a great variation in the quality of workmanship evident in the specimens which have been examined. Some authorities state (and others infer) that although the pistol was developed in Germany it was not made in that country and that it was produced in Belgium in 1897. It is believed that this date is too early.

Only two specimens of the Simplex pistol have been seen by the author. One of them, Serial No. 351, bears the inscription

PATENT

BREVETE

S.G.D.G.

which stands for Brevete Sans Garantie du Gouvernment (Patented without Guarantee of the Government). There is little doubt but that this gun was made in Belgium.

The second one, Serial No. 2153, which appears to be of better workmanship, bears the inscription

PAT.

BREVETE

D.R.G.M.

The letters D.R.G.M. stand for Deutsche Reich Gebrauch Muster (i.e., the German Reich License for Use). The presence of the French word "Brevete" does not necessarily mean that the gun was not made in Germany as it does appear on pistols definitely known to have been made there—some early Bergmanns for example. The conclusion is that both may have been made in Belgium, and this is further borne out by the identity of all details in the grip monogram which consists of the word SIMPLEX. Admittedly, grips can be transferred from one gun to another—which naturally sometimes leads to confusion.

Bernardelli

The firm of Vincenzo Bernardelli, located at Gardone V.T., Italy, is one of the oldest manufacturers of Europe still in operation. It was founded in 1865 and has long enjoyed a reputation for fine workmanship.

Bernardelli learned the art of firearms manufacture as an employee of the Franzini Arms Factory located in Gardone Val Trompia. This was one of the important factories of its day, and Bernardelli had become chief of the Damascus barrel division. In 1865 he had decided to set up his own small factory for the making of barrels in the little village of San Carlo. In the course of a decade his work had developed to the point where he was making entire guns, although in limited numbers. In this he was aided by his four sons, Pietro, Lodovico, Antonio, and Giulio, each of whom was responsible for some particular manufacturing process or detail. The firm soon outgrew its original quarters and began a search for better facilities and room for expansion.

In 1899 Vincenzo Bernardelli died and the management was taken over completely by his capable sons. In 1908 a large factory, formerly a textile establishment, and a large surrounding area for future development became available and were secured. Adequate water power for current operations was included in the purchase.

Following World War I the factory was modernized. Special new machinery was installed and power facilities were increased. Following World War II the plant was again expanded and newer machinery and manufacturing methods were installed. New types of weapons were added, such as automatic pistols and automatic rifles. During the period 1928 to 1933 the firm had manufactured the 10.4 mm. Italian Service revolver, known as the Ordinanza Mod. 89, but no modern type of revolver had been made until after World War II. Now one is being produced in both .22 and .32 calibers.

A new model of the Bernardelli automatic pistol appeared in 1959 and was designated the Model 60. This model is made in .22 L.R., 7.65 mm., and 9 mm. Short calibers. As with the previous models, the system has the fixed barrel, a magazine disconnector safety as well as the thumb operated safety, twin buffer springs in the frame, and the usual good quality of finish and workmanship. In addition, this model has an external hammer which may be carried at half-cock with safety. The sear group assembly is newly designed to give a better trigger pull. The take-down has been simplified. The slide is drawn back 1.5 cm. (ca. ⅗ inch) then, after the slide release button is pushed, the slide is raised at the rear end and removed by sliding it over the front end of the barrel. On the .22 L.R. type, if provided with the 200-mm. barrel, it is necessary to unscrew and remove the front sight ramp to permit the slide to pass over it.

The automatic pistols are:

.22 cal. L.R. or Short. "Baby" Model. Mag. cap. 5 ctges. Introduced in 1949.

.22 cal. L.R. Standard Model. 90-mm. barrel. Mag. cap. 8 ctges. Introduced in 1949 (Fig. 126).

.22 cal. L.R. Standard Model with 150-, 220-, or 250-mm. barrel.

6.35 mm. (Browning) V.P. Model. Two magazines. Standard mag. holds 5 ctges., long mag. holds 8 ctges. Introduced in 1945.

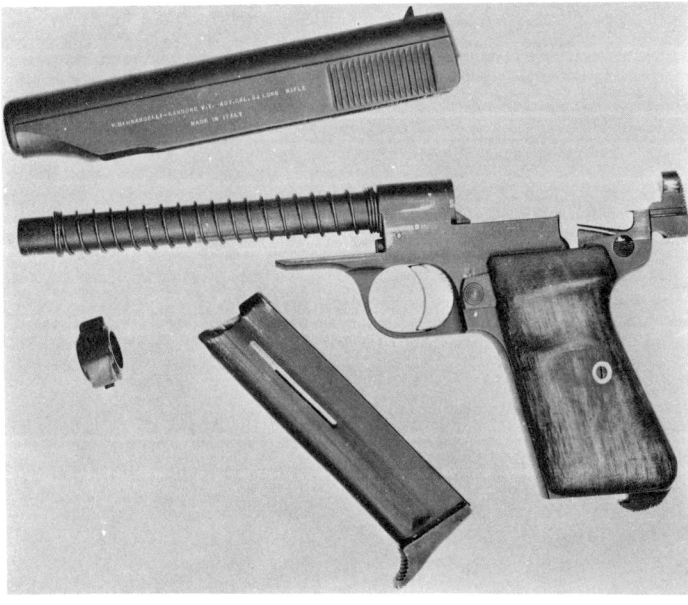

Fig. 126. .22 cal. Bernardelli Standard Mod. Standard Model has 90 mm. barrel. 150, 200, and 250 mm. barrels also available.

7.65 mm./9 mm. (Brng.) Pocket Model. Same model takes either 7.65 or 9 mm. barrels, interchangeably. Special 7.65 mm. barrels can be supplied in lengths of 150, 200, and 250 mm. on order. Special mag. with cap. of 17 ctges. also available. Introduced in 1947.

9 mm. Long or 9 mm. Parabellum. Model U.B. Large Pocket Model. Mag. cap. 8 ctges. Introduced in 1950.

Factory data for the various models are given in Table 26.

Brixia

The Glisenti pistol, known as the Pistola Automatica M910, used for a time by the Italian Army and Navy, did not prove to be sufficiently successful. In 1910 and 1911 the firm of Metallurgica Bresciana, Gia Tempini (Brescia), Italy, patented several modifications and simplifications of the Glisenti. By 1911 this firm had put this new version of the pistol into production as the Pistola Automatica Brixia. It was offered commercially and for service use. Apparently it was not adopted for service use and there is no evidence that it proved to be commercially popular. It was not long in production.

There is some evidence to support the belief that the firm Societa Siderurgica Glisenti underwent a reorganization and became the Metallurgica Bresciana Tempini, which accounts for the monogram MBT which appears on the right hand grip piece of the Brixia pistols. It is also reported that manufacture of the M910 (Glisenti) was continued by MBT, for the Italian service. Production was probably stopped with the advent of World War I.

At least one 6.35 mm. blowback vestpocket pistol was devised by this firm ca. 1912, but it apparently was not commercially successful.

Browning (Fabrique Nationale) Blowback Series—1898 to 1900

The Browning automatic pistol was patented in the U.S. on April 20, 1897, by John M. Browning, several patents being issued to him on that date. Soon thereafter the Fabrique Nationale D'Armes de Guerre in Herstal, Belgium, secured a license to use the patents and to conduct its own development of a pistol based on the features covered by these patents. At the same time development work was proceeding at the Colt factory in the U.S.

By 1898, F.N. had achieved an original design based on the Browning patents. The members of this first series of F.N. pistols are characterized by hav-

TABLE 26
Data for Bernadelli pistols as manufactured in 1959

Measurement	All models except No. 60					Model 60		
	6.35 mm.	7.65 and 9 mm. Short	.22 Long or Short	.22 L.R.	9 mm. Long or Par.	7.65 mm.	9 mm. Short	.22 L.R.
Over-all length, mm.	105	158	105	158	175	165	165	166
Barrel length, mm.	53	120	53	90*	100	90	90	90**
Height, mm.	68†	90‡	68	120	135	123	123	123
Weight, gm.	262	725	262	710	920	670	660	690
Mag. cap., ctges.	5 or 8	8§	5	8	8¶	8	7	8

*Special barrels available: 150, 200, or 250 mm. in length. Each has detachable front sight.

†Height with 8-cartridge magazine is 80 mm.

‡Special barrels available: 150, 200 or 250 mm. in length.

§Cartridge capacity for 9 mm. Short–7 ctges. Extra-long magazines holding 17 cartridges are available for the 7.65 mm. model.

¶Manufacturer recommends the 9 mm. Parabellum cartridge, though the others can be used.

**A 200-mm. barrel is also available, equipped with adjustable rear sight and a front sight ramp held by a counterplane to the top of the muzzle. Before disassembly is possible the front sight ramp must be removed in order that the slide may slip over it.

ing the recoil spring mounted above the barrel and a firing pin which is loaded by a link arrangement housed in an extended projection on the top of the slide at the rear. The 1898 Type was chambered for a 7.65 mm. cartridge which Browning himself had designed with the help of Winchester engineers. This pistol was presented to the Swiss Government for trial at Berne in the summer of 1898. The exact details of this first prototype pistol are not known.

By 1899 a distinct commercial form had been developed and was offered as the Modele 1899. This 1899 commercial pistol is characterized by checkered, molded hard rubber grip pieces and by having a smooth frame and receiver, with a straight grip frame. A number of transitional 1898–1899 Browning F.N. types have been observed to have the Mauser insignia. Though produced in some quantity, they were not offered commercially but were used for sales and promotional purposes in Germany in the hope of stimulating enough interest to justify their possible production at the Mauser plant. This hope was not realized.

In March 1900 the 1899 pistol was adopted into the Belgian service and full production began. This 1900 Model, as it is now called, appeared with F.N. crests or trade marks on the grip pieces (Figs. 127, 128).

A few of the 1900 type were manufactured in the 9 mm. Short caliber sometime after 1905. None were offered commercially.

When major production began in the spring of 1900, the basic serial number series was started. Numbers from 1 to about 10,000 may be found with letter prefixes or suffixes. At 10,000 a lanyard loop was added, together with several other external modifications. The design on the grip pieces was also changed at that point. Early in the 100,000

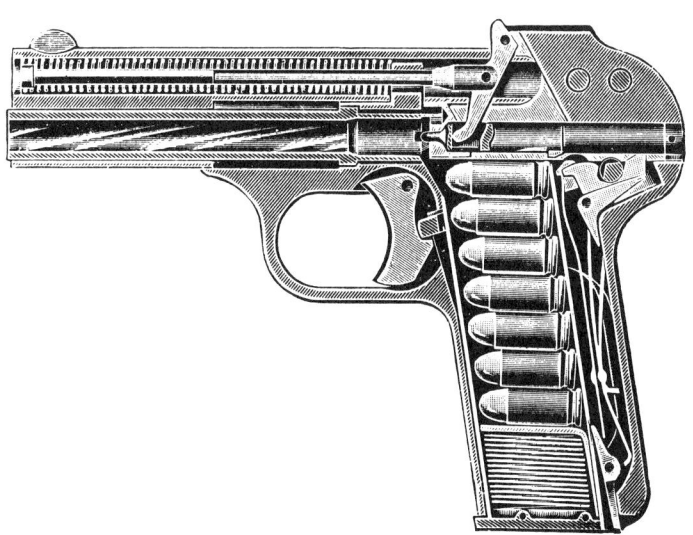

Fig. 127. Browning Mod. 1900. Sectional view.

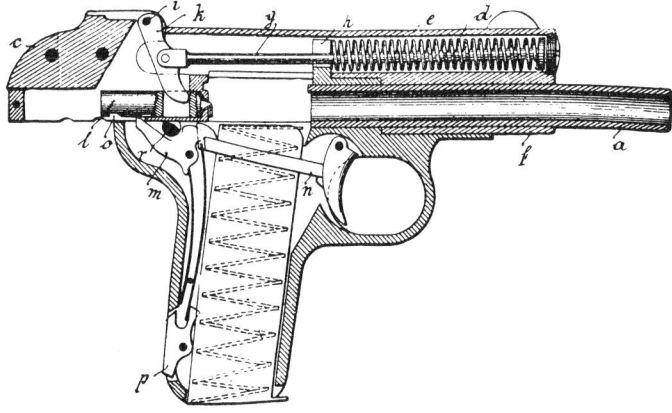

Fig. 128. Browning Mod. 1900. Schematic view.

173

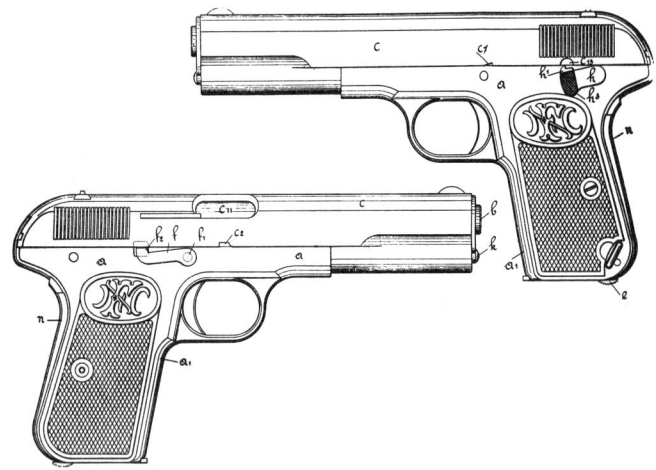

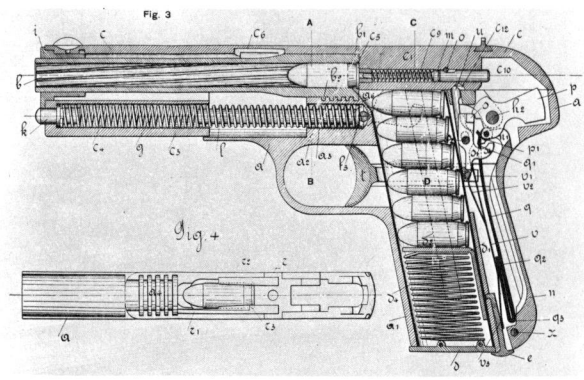

Fig. 130. Browning Mod. 1903. Factory drawing.

Fig. 129. 9 mm. Browning Mod. 1903. Sketches showing both sides. Factory drawing.

series the pistol reached its common form. The head of the safety lever was serrated, and the F.N. script insignia was introduced on the grip pieces. It is stated that 250,000 were made in the first six years. Production of the 1900 type ceased sometime around 1911–1913.

The 1900 type has been extensively copied in oriental countries. Most of these pistols have markings which are imitations of the F.N. markings, often coupled with Mauser markings on the same specimen. These imitations need never be confused with the genuine F.N. product as the markings are never exactly as they should be and, furthermore, the workmanship is obviously very inferior. The author has examined many specimens, many having the same serial number, incidentally, and none has ever been found to have even fairly good rifling.

These oriental copies, generally considered to be mostly Chinese, are to be found in both 7.65 mm. and 7.63 mm. Mauser caliber. Occasionally one is found in 9 mm. Parabellum. The 1898 and 1899 types have also been copied, but apparently not so frequently. Some authorities are of the opinion that many automatic pistol imitations generally accredited to the Chinese were probably made in India.

Browning (Fabrique Nationale) Post–1900 Models

Mod. 1903—9 mm. Long "Modele de Guerre." The basic design of this pistol dates from 1901–1902. It is a blowback type, with concealed hammer and with spring below the barrel (Figs. 129 to 131). Production began in 1903 under the nomenclature

"Pistolet Automatique Browning Grande Modele," and by the summer of that year it was in full production. It was offered to the Swedish Government as the Modele 1903, and at the trials conducted in 1903 and 1904 it was so successful that it was adopted by that country and given the nomenclature Pistol m/07. Specimens of this pistol with full Swedish markings (Husqvarna Vapenfabriks Aktiebolag - System Browning) and with the conventional Husqvarna monogram on the grip pieces have been encountered. This would seem to indicate that these specimens, at least, were made in Sweden. This is confirmed by a personal letter from this manufacturer stating that the m/07, which they describe as "similar to the Browning," was made by them and was discontinued in 1942. This would seem a little late, unless it was made for commercial sale, since the Swedish Government adopted the Walther H.P. pistol in 1939 as the Pistol m/39, and since Husqvarna also states that they produced the Lahti m/40 from 1939 to 1944. Just when the Swedes began production of the m/07 Browning is not known, but it may well have been in 1923 (or thereabouts) since F.N. discontinued the manufacture of this model at that time, and it certainly would not be obtainable thereafter. The Belgian Government adopted the 1903 Browning for military use shortly after it appeared.

This pistol is chambered for the 9 mm. Long Browning cartridge, specially developed for it by F.N. in 1902–03. A very limited number of these pistols were manufactured during World War I, in the 9 mm. Short Browning size, supposedly under German supervision during the occupation.

Many of these pistols in the 9 mm. Browning Long cartridge were purchased by Denmark (for police use only), by Turkey (for service use), by Czechoslovakia (in 1919 and 1920), by Holland, and,

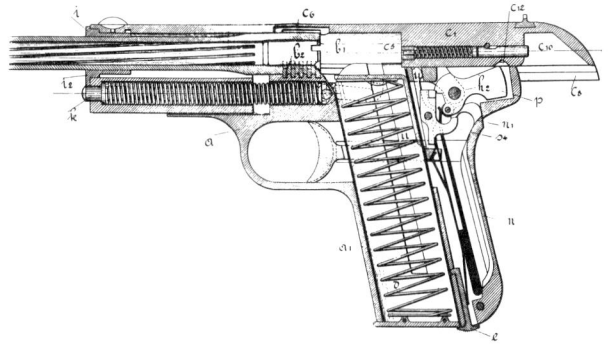

Fig. 131. 9 mm. Browning Mod. 1903. Action open. Factory drawing.

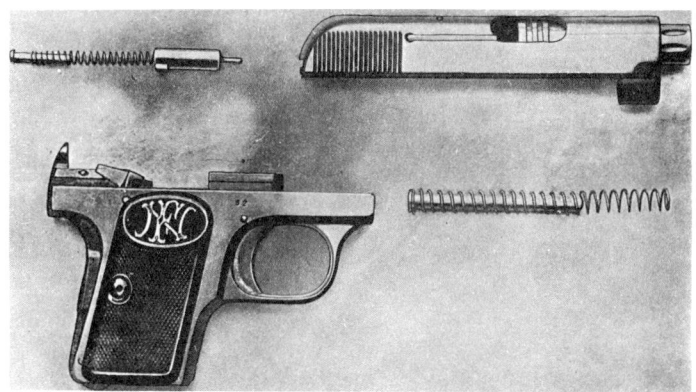

Fig. 132. "Pistolet Browning 6.35 mm." Partially disassembled.

reportedly, by Russia (prior to 1917). It has been stated that the pistol could be had with special markings on order.

The pistol was available in three "De Luxe" models in addition to the standard model. Data for the standard model are as follows: over-all length, 205 mm.; height, 116 mm.; length of barrel, 128 mm.; thickness, 31 mm.; weight, empty, 930 gm.; and magazine capacity, 7 ctges.

A wood holster-stock was available, allowing the pistol to be fired like an automatic rifle. Magazines with a capacity of 10 cartridges were available for such use.

This pistol was still in production in 1923 but was discontinued at about that time or very shortly thereafter.

Mod. 1906—6.35 mm. ACP Pistolet Browning Cal. 6.35 is the proper designation for this pistol, although an early manual refers to it as the "Browning Baby Pistol." Later, however, an entirely new and smaller "vestpocket" 6.35 cal. pistol was produced and this new pistol was officially named the Baby Browning. The designation "Mod. 1906" for the pistol introduced in 1906 is not an official designation but is the one most commonly in use (Fig. 132).

As first issued this pistol did not have a mechanical safety. This addition may have been made in the 100,000 series, but this is not known with certainty. Pistols with this additional safety were advertised as the "Triple Surete" model. Later editions of the F.N. catalogs mention both the Triple Surete model and the Baby model, the latter referring to the newly introduced smaller (vestpocket) model.

The Triple Surete model was obtainable with the "Standard" finish and in six additional "De Luxe" models. Data for the standard model are: over-all length, 113.5 mm.; height, 76 mm.; length of barrel,

53.6 mm.; thickness, 23.5 mm.; weight, empty, 350 gm.; and magazine capacity, 6 ctges. This pistol was supplied with a special barrel, ca. 112 mm. in length, for the Czechoslovakian market.

Mod. 1910 (*Mod. 1910/22*)—7.65 mm. and 9 mm. Short. The 1910 pistol (including the 1922 variation) was based largely on patents issued to John M. Browning in Europe from 1905 through 1925. The basic design is characterized by a recoil spring surrounding the barrel, a full slide, and three to four underlugs on the barrel, below the chamber, for holding the assembly to the frame. Other features are the grip safety, magazine safety, and mechanical safety ("triple surete") (Fig. 133).

When first brought out commercially, in 1910, the pistol was known as the "Nouveau Modele" to distinguish it from the 7.65 mm. 1900 Mod., as the latter was still in production at that time. Though the 7.65 mm. size was the only one produced at first,

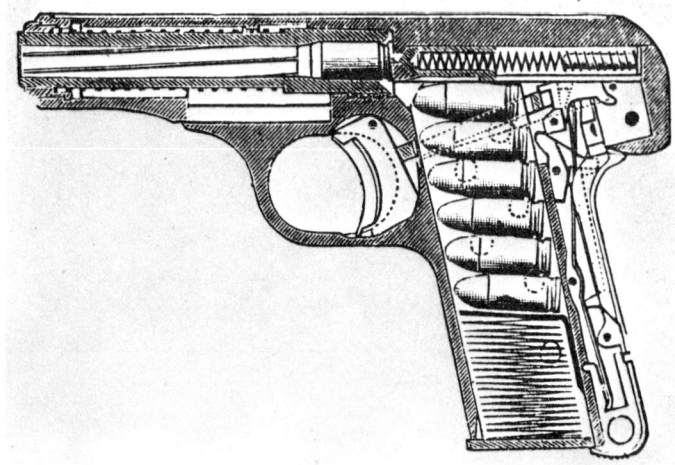

Fig. 133. 7.65 mm. Browning Mod. 1910. Sectional view.

a 9 mm. Short version was introduced in 1922, after certain design changes had been made. At that time the official nomenclature for the pistol was changed to Pistolet Automatique Browning Modele 1910 - Cal. 7.65 m/m or 9 m/m. It is frequently called Mod. 1910/22. Data on these pistols are given in Table 27.

The 1910 model, in either caliber, seems not to have been adopted for military service by any nation, but it was used widely by police forces, including those of Denmark, Sweden, and Japan. It was sold commercially in large numbers and by ca. 1912 it had so superseded the Mod. 1900 that that model was dropped. Manufacture of the 1910 type, in both calibers, was continued through the 1930's, along with the 1922 Model described below. During World War II the Germans, who took over the F.N. plant, made the newer 1922 Mod. only, but production of the 1910 models was resumed after the war.

The 1910 type of Browning has been extensively copied by Spanish manufacturers. In some cases they made direct copies, while in others only certain features of design were used. The Czech Praga pistol dating from 1910 is a copy of the Mod. 1910 Browning. Certain design features of the latter are present in the Czech M 27 and in the Hungarian Frommers M 29 and M 37.

Mod. 1922—7.65 mm. and 9 mm. Short. The Browning 1922 is similar in principle to the 1910 Mod. but is considerably larger and has some modifications. The barrel length was increased about one inch, necessitating an addition of a barrel extension unit for the slide. This particular means of extension was introduced in order to make it possible to continue using the basic forging and machine setups of the 1910 slide and frame. Almost immediately after introduction, the magazine capacity was increased, necessitating an increase in length of the grip frame. Very few specimens having the shorter grip frame are to be found (Fig. 134).

Other changes include a simple bolting device that makes removal of the barrel easy, and the slide is fitted with fore and rear sights. The pistol was specifically designed for military and police use.

TABLE 27
Data for 7.65 and 9 mm. Mod. 1910 Browning F.N. pistols

Measurement	7.65 mm.	9 mm.
Over-all length, mm.	152	152
Height, mm.	99	99
Length of barrel, mm.	87	87
Thickness, mm.	27	27
Weight (empty), gm.	570	560
Magazine cap., ctges.	7	6
Rifling	6-R	6-R

Types and models of the Browning Mod. 1922 pistol that have appeared are as follows:

Pistolet Automatique Browning Modele 1922 Cal. 7.65 m/m.—This was offered for commercial sale and was also adopted for Belgian military service in 1922, thus making obsolete the Mod. 1903 which was dropped from production in 1923. French service issue prior to 1935 has also been reported. It was also used by the Danish police.

Pistole 626(b)—The 7.65 mm. pistol was made under German supervision during the occupation, from November 1940 on, and was given this nomenclature. As thus made, it had checkered wood grip pieces and the lanyard loop was omitted. More than 350,000 were made.

Pistool M 25 No. 1—7.65 mm. Dutch service issue from 1925 through World War II. These pistols are identified by having a brass plate brazed to the slide. They were possibly made by the Dutch, but this is not confirmed.

Pistolet Automatique Browning Modele 1922 Cal. 9 m/m.—This pistol was offered for commercial sale as well as for the military and police use, in Belgium, France, Sweden, Czechoslovakia, and perhaps other countries.*

Mod. 1935 H.P.—The 1935 Browning High Power, or "Pistolet Automatique Browning Modele de Guerre Grande Puissance," resulted from basic design and principles originated by J. M. Browning in 1925 and 1926. The design was undertaken at the request of Fabrique Nationale. Numerous prototype forms appeared between 1926 and 1935. Early in 1935 two forms of the pistol were offered for sale

*A number of these pistols were obtained from F.N. by the Yugoslav Government before World War II and were used in the Mikhailovich army that fought against the forces of Tito. Those seen bear interesting inscriptions. The inscription on the right side is a hyphenated Serbian word, meaning "Army-State" (i.e., Army-State property), and this is followed immediately by the F.N. serial number. This number is probably in a special series. The inscription on the left side is that regularly used by F.N. The coat of arms, which appears on the top of the slide, is that of the Kingdom of the Serbs, Croats, and Slovenes (i.e., Yugoslavia). This coat of arms was frequently used on the grips as well as on the holster and also appeared as a shoulder patch on the uniforms of the Mikhailovich army. Tito's army used the hammer and sickle in the same manner. The inside shield of the coat of arms has the Yugoslav double-headed eagle bearing the symbols of Serbia (upper right), Croatia (upper left), and Slovenia (bottom). These symbols are: the Croatian "checkerboard" signifying union, the Serbian Cross with the Cyrillic letters CCCC (SSSS in English) meaning "Unity Alone Saves Serbia," and the Slovenian sword at the bottom. The outside shield with the crown surmounted by a cross indicates the union of the three nations into the Kingdom of the Serbs, Croats, and Slovenes.

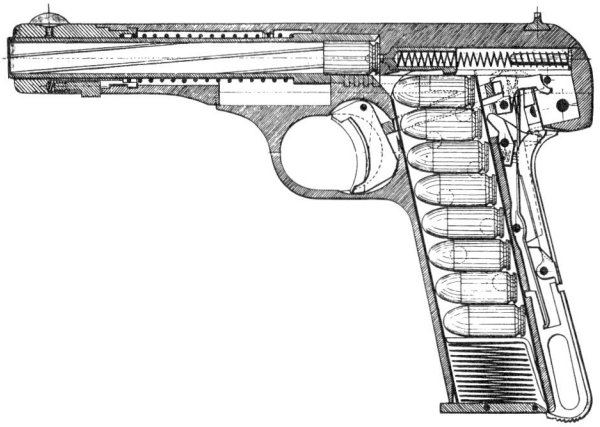

Fig. 134. 9 mm. Browning Mod. 1922. Sectional view.

rounds and seems to have been produced in several calibers, including 7.65 mm. Parabellum, and 7.65 mm. French Long. It is presumed that both were intended for offer in service tests in France and Switzerland. This reduced capacity version does not seem to have been manufactured for commercial use. A variant Adjustable Sight type was produced in small numbers with a 1000-meter sight instead of the regular 500-meter sight.

During World War II the John Inglis Co., of Toronto, Canada, secured a license to manufacture the pistol in several forms for Canadian, British, Chinese, Greek, and Austrialian use. Both radial-sight and the ordinary-sight types were supplied with Chinese markings. Inglis also made a special

throughout the world and, at the same time, were offered to many countries for possible adoption as service weapons (Fig. 135, 136).

The first type was called the "Ordinary Model" and it featured a conventional rear sight. The second was the "Adjustable Rear Sight Model" which featured a radial leaf rear sight and also provision for a shoulder stock-holster. Both pistols were made in 9 mm. Parabellum caliber and had 13-round magazine capacity. The Ordinary model was quickly adopted into the Belgian military service, without special markings, and by the Latvian army (with special serial numbering series and with a crest engraved on the top of the slide). The Adjustable Sight Model was reportedly purchased by the French service in large numbers, but it was not adopted officially nor were the pistols specially marked. The Rumanian Government is reported to have adopted the Ordinary type in 1938 or 1939. It was adopted by the Danish Government in 1939, but the advent of war prohibited delivery. However, the Danish order was completed after the war, in 1946, and the pistol was called by them the "m/46." It had special markings and a lanyard loop on the left side of the grip frame.

It is reported that about 6000 Browning H.P. pistols were supplied to the Lithuanian Government in about 1937. Other adoptions of this splendid pistol are reported to be: Belgian Congo, Ethiopia, Holland, Indonesia (one crest for the air force, another for the army), Paraguay, El Salvador, Syria, Siam, and Venezuela. Each of these was in a special numbering series, and many had special markings, such as crests, etc. on the slides.

A special reduced magazine capacity type of the Ordinary model was made in 1936. It contained 9

Fig. 135. 9 mm. Browning High Power Mod. Partially disassembled.

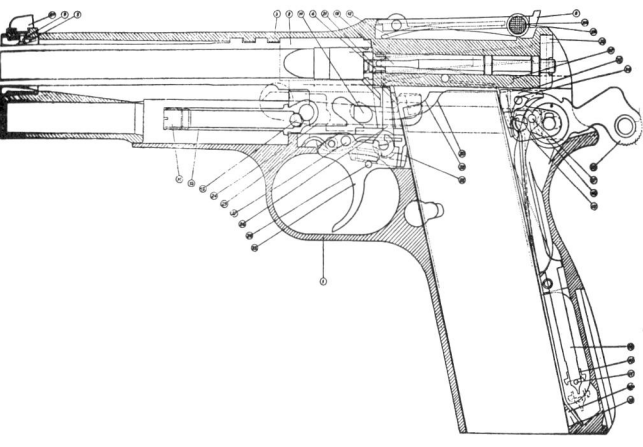

Fig. 136. 9 mm. Browning High Power Mod. Schematic view.

variant form with radial sight but without the shoulder-stock attachment in limited numbers. This firm also experimented with "duraluminum" frames to produce "lightweight" types. The Belgians also experimented with such "lightweight" types after the war. Production in Canada ceased at the close of the war. Manufacture of the Ordinary model was resumed by F.N. as the Model 1946 (for military use) and as the High Power (for commercial use), at the close of the war.

The following is a tabulation showing other forms and nomenclatures for this pistol:

Pistole 640(B)—This was the ordinary-sight model as produced during the war under German supervision. Specimens are characterized by the presence of the German Waffenamt marks, which also appear on other models made under German supervision.

Modele M.P.—This is a reported selective-fire type originally developed by F.N. prior to World War II, with change lever.

Pistol No. 1 Mark I (Browning F.N. 9 mm. H.P.)—This is British nomenclature for the Canadian-produced pistol with radial sight.

Pistol No. 2 Mark I (Browning F.N. 9 mm. H.P.)—Same as above, but for the Canadian-produced pistol with ordinary sight.

S. L. Pistol No. 2 Mark I—The British service version of the pistol purchased from F.N. after World War II.

S. L. Pistol No. 2 Mark I*—The Canadian firm originated a modification of the ejector, and pistols so provided were given the Mark I* nomenclature. The British have continued this in the post-war period.

Campo Giro pistols

The count of Campo Giro (Don Venancio Lopez de Ceballos y Aguirre) was a widely known army officer and firearms designer at the turn of the century. The automatic pistols which bear his name originated around 1900. The earliest form, dating from 1904 to 1905 (often referred to as Modelo 1904), was a recoil-operated arm with an oblique-travel locking wedge housed below the barrel at the chamber. This 1904 Type (or prototype) was reportedly made at the Oviedo Arsenal (Fab. de Armas Portatiles de Oviedo). The only available data are: over-all length, 10.7 inches; barrel length, 6.7 inches; number of grooves, 4.

1904 Type—Three distinct forms of the 1904 Type are known. Only the external differences between them are reported. The first, or standard type, featured a spur hammer and had a sharp, angular

grip frame contour with a straight rear edge. The second form introduced large radius edges on the grip frame and gave a very generous radius to the rear edge. The third type had a round-head hammer and a rounded-edge grip frame. All three forms accepted a stock formed from heavy wire which could be screwed into the base of the grip frame. The caliber of these early types is very probably the 9 mm. Bergmann. A blowback version in 7.65 mm. caliber has been reported, but this has not been confirmed. Some of these may have been made by Esperanza y Unceta; all must be classed as experimental.

1910 Type—The 1910 type had even larger radius curves on the grip frame and featured very small wood grip pieces rather than the molded hard rubber pieces of the earlier type. The caliber of the 1910 type is known to be 9 mm. Bergmann. The first order received was for the production of 1000 specimens. The pistol had created a very favorable impression in the army because of its rapidity of fire, easy loading, and accuracy. Campo Giro and the manufacturers, however, were not entirely satisfied and, after certain defects had been eliminated and improvements made, a new model was submitted to the Commission of Artillery Testing in 1913 and was accepted. In this new type a muffling system reduced to a minimum the violence of the return of the bolt and increased the accuracy of the weapon; a simple alteration in the mechanism made it easier to handle and some devices of "safety and double safety" were added, thus increasing the safety of the shooter greatly. This new model displaced the older one and 13,200 of the improved model were made.

In one of its reports the Testing Commission made the following comments, after testing the new model:

"The Count of Campo Giro has done the State and the Army a great service with his intelligence, perseverence, and ability, not only with the creation of the new type of pistol now declared official, but with the continuation of his labors and creation of a new type of weapon, even better perfected than the former."

Unfortunately the Count did not have the opportunity to see the full fruition of his labors, for he died soon after the delivery of the first lot of the new pistols and before they were in full scale production.

Mod. 1913—The Modelo 1913 of the Campo Giro was made by Esperanza y Unceta, and specimens are so marked. Its caliber was 9 mm. Bergmann (or 9 mm. "Largo" in Spanish terminology). This new pattern differed radically from the earlier types in that it became a blowback system. The locking wedge was eliminated and a spring buffer was used. As first produced, the Modelo 1913 was based on patents taken out by Aguirre in 1912. It was the first commercial model, the serial numbers starting at 1 (Fig. 137, 138).

Mod. 1913/16:—A further modification and external simplification of the safety system took place in 1915 and led to the new model designation Modelo 1913/16. In 1921 the model designation was again changed to become Modelo 1921, as part of a plan to standardize the nomenclature of Spanish service weapons. Production was discontinued, however, in 1921 and was never resumed.

Measurements made in the author's laboratory on Campo Giros Serial No. 60 (marked Pista. Auta. Mod. 1913) and Serial No. 11337 (marked Pista. Auta. Mod. 1913/16) gave the data shown in Table 28.

Charola y Anitua pistols

The Charola-Anitua pistol is only of historic interest, being one of the very early automatics whose

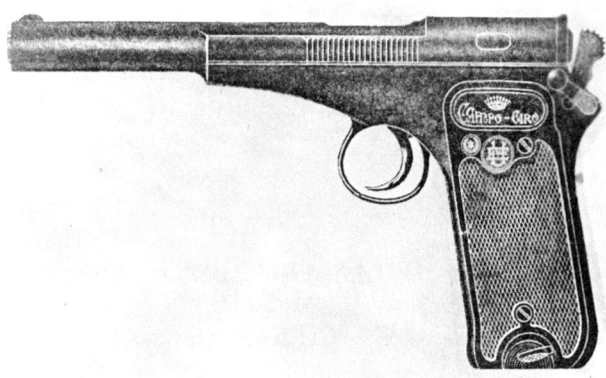

Fig. 137. 9 mm. Campo Giro 1913 Mod.

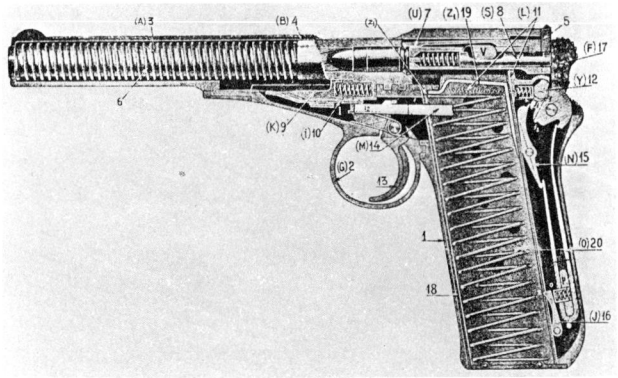

Fig. 138. 9 mm. Campo Giro 1913 Mod. Sectional view.

manufacture covered but a short period of time, and is now known only as a collector's item.

It was originally made in 5 mm. caliber by Garate y Anitua, Fabricantes de Armas de Fuego in Eibar, Spain. Production started in 1907. Somewhat later, at a date unknown, a 7 mm. model appeared, but specimens of this are very rare indeed and descriptions of this model have not been seen.

Specifications for the 7 mm. Charola cartridge have been published, however, originally by the Soc. Francaise des Munitions (June 1903) and reproduced by White and Munhall. Like the more familiar 5 mm. Charola cartridge (generally known as the 5 mm. Clement) it is of the rimless, bottle-neck type.

The existence of a 6.5 mm. model has also been reported, but is not mentioned in any known literature. This latter specimen is said to be similar to the 7 mm. type except that it has an integral magazine instead of one that is detachable and that the frame and other dimensions (excluding barrel length) are somewhat less. The barrel is longer, thus making the total length greater. It may be remarked at this point that barrel lengths never appeared to be fixed quantities on the Charolas.

Some authorities consider that the Charola-Anitua is a copy or modification of one of the Bergmanns, but actually it bears more resemblance to the Mod. 96 Mauser. No doubt the design may have been influenced by both the Bergmann and the Mauser, but certainly it is not a copy of either, the actual construction being quite different. Like the Mauser it is a recoil-operated, locked-bolt type, but while the principle is the same the method of accomplishment is not.

The pistol was also made in Belgium, whether under license or not is not known, and apparently in larger numbers than in Spain. It seems to have had considerable sale in Russia. The Belgian copies, particularly, show considerable variation in details from specimen to specimen, and the workmanship and materials used were of very inferior quality compared to those made in Eibar. Although many of the Belgian-made pistols were marked STANDART, that word seems to have been a misnomer.

TABLE 28
Data on two Campo Giro pistols

Measurement	Modelo 1913 Ser. No. 60	Modelo 1913/16 Ser. No. 11337
Length over-all	9.5 inches	9.5 inches
No. of grooves and dir.	6-R	6-R
1 turn of rifling in	9.5 inches	10.2 inches
Bore diameter	0.3495 inch	0.3495 inch
Width of land	0.052 "	0.065 "

179

Data for the 5 mm. Charola-Anitua, as they appeared in *Armas Automaticas* (Barcelona, 1903), are as follows: total length, 230 mm. (9¹⁄₁₆ inches); barrel length, 104 mm. (4⅛ inches); weight, empty, 572 grams (ca. 20 oz.); magazine capacity, 6 ctges.; muzzle velocity, 300 m./sec.; and maximum range, 800 meters. No specifications for rifling were given.

For the 7 mm. model the following rifling specifications, taken from a drawing dated July 1903, are the only ones available: bore diameter, 7.075 mm. (0.2785 inch); groove diameter, 7.400 mm. (.2913 inch); groove width, 3.1 mm. (.122 inch); land width, 2.7 mm. (.106 inch); and number of grooves, 4.

The above data were taken from a pistol with serial No. 10,349. This number gives no real clue to the total number made as it is not known whether the different calibered models were numbered in the same or different numbering series, nor is it known at what figure serial numbering started. It is also not known whether this specimen was made in Belgium or in Spain.

Chylewski pistol

The 6.35 mm. Chylewski automatic pistol is of interest particularly because it was the forerunner of the Einhand Lignose made for Akt. Gesellschaft Lignose by Bergmann. The pistol was designed by Witold Chylewski, an Austrian, around 1910–13. He contracted with the Soc. Industrielle Suisse (later S.I.G.) to produce a few hundred guns, apparently to be used principally as promotion specimens. By 1919 he had succeeded in interesting Theodor Bergmann, who took over the rights to manufacture the arm. (See Bergmann Pocket Pistols.)

The only real contribution made by Chylewski was the provision whereby the pistol could be cocked and fired with one hand. The forward end of the trigger guard was shaped like a trigger and by pulling back the guard with the trigger finger the gun was loaded and cocked, ready for firing. The idea was that the gun would be used for personal protection and could be carried safely in the pocket in unloaded condition until an emergency arose. The "one hand" feature made it possible to load, cock, and fire with one hand, without even taking the pistol out of the pocket. This system was not sufficiently popular to warrant its continued use and has long since been succeeded by other safety features.

Clement pistols

The Clement pistols were produced by Charles Ph. Clement of Liége, Belgium. Although their

manufacture has long since ceased and covered only a short period of time (1903 to ca. 1914), they are nevertheless of interest historically because they represent an original and unique design which was produced at a relatively early date in the development of pocket automatics and also because specimens are still frequently encountered.

Modele 1903—The first Clement pistol to be produced actually had no model designation at the time it appeared. Later on, when a new model was produced (1907), the designation Modele 1903 was applied to distinguish it from the new model.

This first pistol was designed to take a 5 mm. cartridge which had been developed in Spain for the Charola-Anitua automatic. The Charola was also made for a time in Belgium, as was also the cartridge. The pistol was of poor design and did not long survive, but the cartridge survived because of the relatively greater success of the Clement and became more generally known throughout Europe as the Clement cartridge. In fact, the distribution of the 5 mm. Clement pistol must have been considerable, because the cartridge was still available as late as 1932—25 years after production of the pistol had ceased.

The 1903 Clement was very much like the models which succeeded it, and which will be described briefly later, but it differed in some features. Like the models of 1907, 1908, and 1909, it was a simple blowback type, with fixed barrel and sliding "bolt" (or breechblock unit). The short barrel housing and the long housing for the mainspring and spring guide were an integral unit. The shorter barrel housing was below the spring housing, which extended the entire length of the pistol. This whole unit could be removed by removing screws at the rear end, where it was attached to the frame, then the breechblock could be removed. In this earliest model the breechblock did not extend all the way from the barrel to the rear end of the frame, as it did in the later models. The magazine release was unique, in that it consisted of a small rectangular button located centrally on the back strap of the frame at a point about one inch from the bottom. Pressure on this button released the magazine.

The monogram on the grip pieces consisted of two interlocking capital letters C, one of which faced to the right and the other to the left. This monogram was used on later models, but with an important difference. In the later models the letters are placed so that they read crosswise of the grip whereas in this first model they read lengthwise (i.e., they are turned 90°).

The serial numbering began with No. 1 and was

180

evidently limited to this model. Figures as to total production are not available.

Modele 1907—In 1907 a new model was introduced. The principal change was that the bolt assembly, while operating in the same manner, had a vertical slot at the rear end extended all the way around the pillar at the back of the frame, to which pillar the barrel and spring housing section was attached by a single screw. The bolt section was 70 mm. (2¾ inches) in length, and about 65 mm. of it was covered with vertical serrations to provide finger grips. The serrations for the finger grips on the 1903 model covered a length of only 10 mm. and did not provide a satisfactory hold. The peculiarly situated magazine release of the earlier model was continued, as was the method of disassembly (Figs. 139, 140).

The 1907 model was made in both 7.65 and 6.35 mm. calibers, the 7.65 appearing first. Evidently a new numbering series was started for this model, but whether both calibers were numbered in the same series is not known, although it seems unlikely. The highest observed number (on a 7.65 mm. specimen) is 7263, but there may have been many more. Production of this model continued well into 1908, at which time certain modifications were made and a new model designation assigned.

Catalog data for the 6.35 mm. Mod. 1907 are as follows: total length, 115 mm.; barrel length, 50 mm.; weight, 350 gm.; and mag. cap., 6 ctges. Data for the 7.65 mm. gun are as follows: total length, 150 mm.; barrel length, 70 mm.; weight, 600 gm.; and mag. cap., 6 ctges.

Modele 1908—In the 1908 model the magazine release formerly used was discarded and a new form consisting of a push button located at the bottom of the grip frame, near the rear edge, was substituted. Pushing this button in releases the magazine. Specimen No. 6168, which in all other respects is a Mod. 1907, shows this change and represents a transitional type. Evidently this specimen was one from the later production of the 1907 model which, as already stated, continued well into 1908. The most notable change which characterized the 1908 model was the change in the shape of the grip. Instead of being stubby with sloping sides, the sides were squared up, with parallel sides, which not only improved the appearance but also furnished a much better hold.

Specimen No. 10,414 is typical of the Mod. 1908 and is shown partially disassembled in the photograph, Fig. 141. The upper section shows the hous-

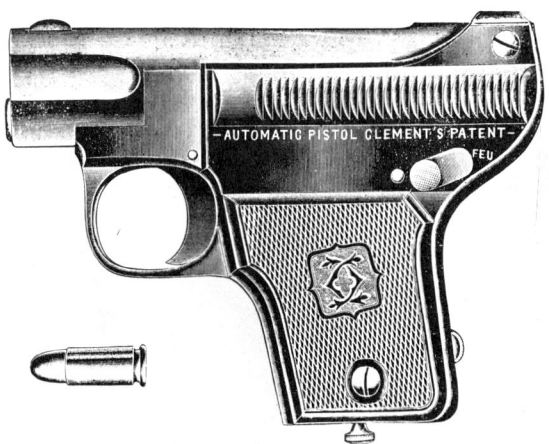

Fig. 139. 6.35 mm. Clement Mod. 1907.

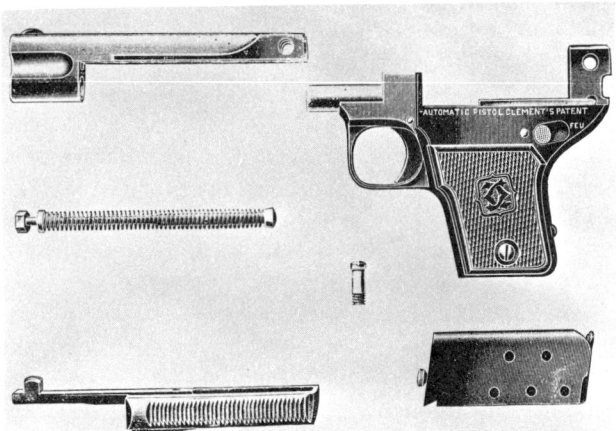

Fig. 140. 6.35 mm. Clement. Disassembled.

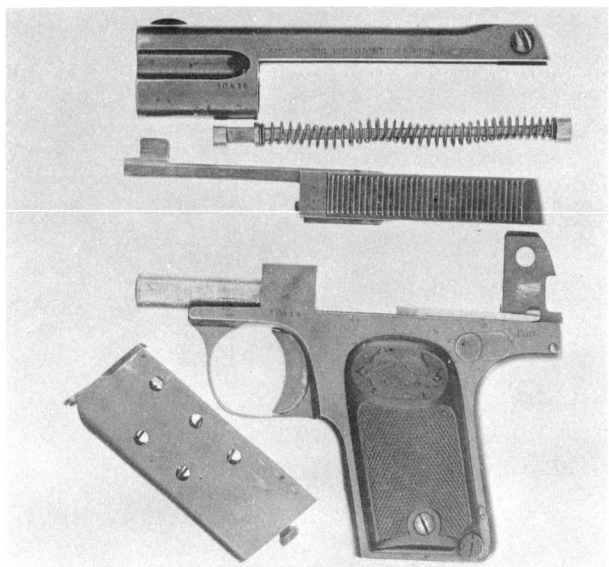

Fig. 141. Clement Mod. 1908. Disassembled.

181

ings for the barrel and spring and guide. The spring and spring guide have been removed and are shown below. The bolt, or breechblock section, has a long vertical slot back of the breech face to permit the bolt to slide back past the post to which the housing section is pivoted. The narrow bar extending to the left of the bolt has a slotted pillar into which the forward end of the spring guide fits. When the gun is fired the bolt moves back and pulls the spring back, thus compressing it.

The extractor is located in the customary position, alongside the breechblock. An ejector on the left side ejects the shell to the right. A spring-loaded firing pin, 30 mm. in length, is mounted in the rear of the breechblock and the point of the pin is held out of contact with the cartridge until it is struck by the hammer which is mounted in the lower section. This hammer is actuated by a flat spring. A thumb safety is located near the rear end of the frame, on the left side. The location is the same for all models. Unlike most modern pistols, removal of the magazine does not prevent firing. All of the foregoing models have a knob on the lower end of the magazine to assist in its withdrawal.

The serial numbers on specimens examined suggest that they are a continuation of the numbering series used on the 1907 model. No specimens of the 1908 model in 7.65 mm. have been seen, nor have known advertisements of this model suggested that it was available in this caliber.

Modele 1909—This model represents more of a change in design, particularly in the method of disassembly. Instead of being disassembled by the removal of a screw at the rear end, as in previous models, this pistol has a trigger guard which is

pinioned at the front end. By springing the rear end out of its socket and pushing it down, the section containing the barrel, spring, and guide is unlocked and the forward end can be tipped up. The breechblock assembly can then be removed. To disengage the barrel and spring section completely (rarely necessary) the screw at the rear end has to be removed; otherwise, no tools are necessary except for the removal of the single screw in each grip piece (Fig. 142).

The thumb safety lever and the magazine release button are like those in the 1908 model. Unlike the preceding models, however, observed specimens do not have the knob on the bottom of the magazine.

Catalog data for the Mod. 1909 6.35 mm. are as follows: total length, 115 mm.; weight, 350 gm.; and magazine capacity, 6 ctges. (The barrel length, measured by the author, is 51 mm.) Data given for the 7.65 mm. gun are as follows: total length, 150 mm.; weight, 600 gm.; and magazine capacity, 6 ctges.

The data above are for the standard production model. Experience has shown that the above data are subject to some variations from specimen to specimen. One specimen (No. 36,571) having a barrel length of 115 mm. and a total length of ca. 185 mm. has been measured. Whether other specimens with long barrels were made is not known.

The serial numbering is presumably a continuation of that used on the 1907 and 1908 models. Production of the 7.65 mm. model is said to have continued well into the year 1913, while that of the 6.35 mm. model may have continued into 1914, as the pistol was still advertised for sale in that year.

Specimen No. 33,353 (as shown in the *Pistolen Atlas*), in 6.35 mm. caliber, is exactly like measured specimen No. 16,410. Specimen No. 7601 (as shown in the *Pistolen Atlas*), in 7.65 mm. caliber, is similar to the 6.35 mm. model in all respects with the important exception that it does not have the little lever under the left grip piece for disassembly of the rear end. It does, however, have the pivoted trigger guard. This specimen seems to be a transition type between the 7.65 mm. Mod. 1907 and the 7.65 mm. Mod. 1909. Its serial number suggests that it was probably a specimen of the late Mod. 1907 production, actually manufactured in 1908, and that there was no 7.65 mm. pistol with the (official) designation of Mod. 1908.

Patents on Clement pistols were taken out in the U.S. on April 3, 1903, and June 24, 1907, (both by Charles Ph. Clement), and on June 9, 1909, (by R. Wiles).

Fig. 142. Clement Mod. 1909. Specimen has unusually long barrel.

Colonial pistols

Pistols bearing the name COLONIAL and the trade mark EC (letters intertwined) in a circle, with the words TRADE above and MARK below, and sometimes (but not always) bearing the inscription FABRIQUE DE ARMES DE GRANDE PRECISION PATENT DEPOSE 39391 are frequently encountered. Manufacture of these pistols is often attributed to this firm. As a matter of fact, according to information received from the Spanish Ministry of Munitions and from the Eibar Proof House, no such manufacturing firm ever existed. The name was simply one coined by a clever dealer and exporter of firearms. To make the name still more impressive it often appeared in the form FABRIQUE DE ARMES DE GUERRE DE GRANDE PRECISION.

The patent referred to is a Marca (trade mark) patent, rather than a patent on a firearm design. The patent, which covers the name Colonial, was issued in November 1920 to the firm Etxezarraga y Abaitua of Eibar. Presumably this firm actually manufactured the pistol for the dealer whose name appears on the gun. The EC trade mark, described above, is present on other pistols which do not carry the name Colonial, some of which were made at least as late as 1928. The name Colonial will also be found on pistols made in France by Mre. d'Armes des Pyrénées, in Hendaye, according to information from that firm. These were made to be sold by a certain dealer who wished to use that name.

The Spanish Colonial pistols appear in both 6.35 and 7.65 mm. calibers. Both are simple blowbacks in type—copies of the Browning system and not distinguished in any particular feature. The 6.35 mm. model has a monogram on the grip pieces showing a front view of an ape-like face under which appears the name Colonial. The 7.65 mm. model has a quite different monogram, consisting of a medallion center with the raised letters EC in a circle, above which stands an eagle with outstretched wings. Below the circle is the name COLONIAL.

As the 7.65 mm. pistol weighs about two pounds and has a swiveled lanyard ring it appears to have been intended for military use. Very likely it was developed during World War I, despite the patent date. It greatly resembles the Browning 1910 in appearance, though it is by no means as well made, and, like most of the Eibar copies of the Browning, has the thumb safety in front of the left grip piece instead of behind it.

The over-all length is 7 inches, barrel length 4 inches. The rifling has 6 grooves with right hand twist. Magazine capacity is 9 rounds. The front sight is integral with the slide and semicircular in shape. The rear sight is simply a notch milled out of the slide.

Czech pistols

Historical

The history of the manufacture of automatic pistols in Czechoslovakia dates back to 1918–1919, at which time three factories started producing such arms. These three were:

1. Československé závody na výrobu zbraní, Brno (Czechoslovak weapon factories, Brno). This name was changed later to Československá Zbrojovka, akc. spol. under which name the plant operated until the German occupation when it was changed to Brünner Waffenfabrik, A.G., Brünn.

2. Jihočeská Zbrojovka, s.s r.o., located in Pilsen (Plzeň in Czech). The name of this firm was later changed to Jihočeská Zbrojovka, a.s. and still later, when the firm was joined with "Hubertus," the name was again changed to Česká Zbrojovka, a.s. Plants for the manufacture of pistols were established in Prague and in Strakonice.

3. Zbrojovka Praga, located in Prague. This firm went out of business in 1926.

The development and operations of these firms will now be considered in some detail.

On March 1, 1919, the original Czech Government arsenal for the production of small arms was established in what had been an artillery production plant, at Brno (Moravia), Czechoslovakia. This arsenal was given the name Československé závody na výrobu zbraní, Brno. First produced was the Mannlicher Model 95 short rifle, followed soon thereafter by their initial production of hand grenades of which some 300,000 had been produced by 1922. In 1922, or shortly thereafter, Engineer Josef Nickl from the Mauser Werke at Oberndorf directed the installation of machinery in the Brno factory for the production of the Mauser Mod. 24 rifle, for which arm drawings and specifications were also supplied. Not long thereafter the VZ 26 (i.e., Mod. 26) light machine gun went into production. A large part of the machine gun production was delivered under contract to Persia, Turkey, and Mexico. In 1930 some 20,000 Model 26 machine guns were delivered to the Rumanian Government; and technicians and engineers were sent from Brno to set up a plant in Rumania to manufacture this arm. This gun has been used in 24 different countries.

The first automatic pistol made specifically for

military use was developed at Brno from a pistol originating at the Mauser plant. This pistol, which became known as Pistole 9 mm. N, was designed by the Mauser engineer Nickl in 1916. The story is that the Mauser firm was not greatly impressed with this design but had to give it more attention than they felt it deserved because of the influence of the designer. The system was basically a rotating barrel scheme placed on the existing Mauser pocket pistol design of frame and firing system, but with the addition of an external hammer and a different method of assembly. Very few specimens were actually made at the Mauser plant, but a few do exist, having been made experimentally from 1916 on. They will be found to be marked MAUSER WERKE A. G. OBERNDORF, A.N. PIST. KAL 9 M/M. It is stated that the Mauser firm licensed the Nickl design to the Czech army, through an Austrian dummy corporation, in about 1921. The pistol was first made at Brno for service use. These pistols will be found to be marked "9 mm. N Čs. st. zbrojovka, Brno."

In 1923 the production of pistols was moved to Česká Zbrojovka in Prague, and by 1932 economic and other factors caused a partial shut down of the Brno factory. Activities were revived, however, by taking on heavy industry as well as small arms manufacture, and it became necessary to change the factory from its status as a Government owned arsenal to a stock company under the name Československá Zbrojovka, akc. spol. The Government, however, retained a controlling interest; the balance of the stock being spread among the subsidiary companies, with an arrangement whereby employees could purchase a share after five years of service.

In the period 1934–35 England expressed an interest in the Bren and Besa machine guns. An order was placed for 200 Bren guns and arrangements were made for Czech technicians to go to England with working drawings for both the Bren and Besa machine guns. These men and the drawings left Czechoslovakia just before Hitler invaded that country on March 15, 1939. The Brno plant was seized by the Germans and was operated by them throughout the period of occupation under the name Brünner Waffenfabrik, A.G. Brünn, and was given the code designation "bh." Many types of small arms were produced in these years.

At the close of World War II when the Germans left Czechoslovakia, the old name Československá Zbrojovka, akc. spol. was restored; but when the country was nationalized by the Communists in 1948 the name was again changed to Českaslovenská Zbrojovka-Národní Podnik (Národní Podnik means

National Enterprize).

In 1919 a second large plant for the manufacture of automatic pistols came into being. Architect Karel Bubla persuaded some financially able people, most of whom were also interested in the Skoda Works in Pilsen, to raise the necessary capital to start the production of small arms in order to eliminate (or reduce) the imports of such weapons from Austria, Belgium, and Germany. The newly formed company "of limited liability" (as the name suggests) was called Jihočeská Zbrojovka, s.s r.o., and was supervised by the "Agriculturel Industrial Bank."

First to be produced was the 6.35 mm. Fox semiautomatic pistol, designed by Alois Tomiška. This first pistol was essentially a hand-produced item until 1923 when standardized mass production methods were adopted.

In 1922 the Czech Ministry of National Defense (Ministerstvo národní obrany) appointed a commission to study the ability of this firm to mass produce weapons with interchangeable parts. In 1923 this commission reported favorably and the Government moved the production of the official service pistol to Česká Zbrojovka, a.s., the new name for this firm after it was combined with the Hubertus firm. Pistols were made at both Prague and Strakonice. Thus this firm, ČZ as it became generally known, became the largest maker of pistols in Czechoslovakia.

In 1923 ČZ absorbed another company and entered the field of bicycle production, and in 1924 the manufacture of motor cycles began. Still later the firm produced a Czech version of the Lewis and Vickers machine gun, a new Czech aircraft machine gun (Models 28 and 30), flare pistols, and air rifles. In 1938 this plant started the first Czech submachine gun production. During World War II large quantities of the Czech Pistole Mod. 27 were made, also parts for the German MG 34 and 42 and parts for Walther P-38 pistols, cannons, etc.

Pistols made at Prague will have various markings such as: ČESKÁ ZBROJOVKÁ A.S. V PRAZE, ČESKÁ ZBROJOVKÁ AS V PRAZE, ČESKÁ ZBROJOVKÁ AKC. SPOL PRAZE, all of which mean the same, the abbreviations "A.S.," "AS," and "AKC" all standing for "Akciová spolecnost," which is roughly equivalent to the German "A.G.," the Swedish "A.B.," the Spanish "S.A.," and the English "Ltd." The letter V in Czech means "in;" V PRAZE therefore means "in Prague."

From 1939 to 1941, pistols made at Prague under German supervision were marked BÖHMISCHE WAFFENFABRIK A.G. IN PRAG on the top of the slide, and from 1941 to 1945, when the German occupation ended, the pistols were marked with the letters "fnh," the German code letters for this plant.

The firm known as Zbrojovka Praga (Arsenal Praga) dates back to 1918, when construction of a factory was started by A. Nowotńy, who had previously owned and run a gun shop. By the end of 1918 machinery had been installed. Nowotńy had been able to interest some very able designers, said to have included the Holek brothers, František Myška, and K. Krnka. Some of these men were engaged in the design of machine guns, and prototypes of such were made. The automatic pistols made by this firm will be discussed a bit later.

Unfortunately this firm did not prosper and it was taken over by the Průmyslová Banka (Industrial Bank) in 1926, and the factory was closed down.

Czech service pistols

Praga—The first service pistol made in Czechoslovakia was the Praga, a 7.65 mm. pistol made by Zbrojovka Praga. Just when production was started is not known, but very likely in 1919. All of the specimens seen by the author were marked as made in 1920 and 1921, the highest serial number being 6409 (date on barrel, 22-12-21). Production ceased by 1926 as the firm went out of business in that year.

This pistol was a modification of the F.N. Browning Mod. 1910. The barrel had three lugs, and the barrel bushing was different. The position of the ejection port on the top of the slide was changed. The inscription on the left side of the slide has always been found to read ZBROJOVKA PRAGA PRAHA. This pistol was adopted for use by the Czechoslovakian Police in 1921, and these were supplied with serrated or plain wooden grip pieces, which is a common practice for military arms. Pistols sold for commercial use were supplied with very attractive hard rubber grip pieces, with the word Praga (in script) embossed thereon. Some specimens sold commercially had somewhat longer barrels than the standard model.

VZ 1922—Actually this is unofficial nomenclature for the 9 mm. short (.380) Nickl pistol, the design for which was acquired from Mauser. As made by the Czechs, the original German design was followed very closely. How many of these were made is not known, but a specimen examined by the author, marked as having been made in 1923, bears the Serial No. 17,590. Since specimens of the next model (Mod. 24), which superseded this model, bear numbers at least as low as 21,086, it would appear that the production of this short-lived model was not very great.

VZ 1924—The 1924 model follows closely the design of the preceding model. The design was changed slightly with respect to the barrel locking arrangement, and a number of other minor changes were made. The "hooding" of the trigger is the only important externally-observable difference between the original and the Mod. 1924, as first produced. Later it became more streamlined in appearance.

No figures as to total production by the Czechs are available, but a specimen examined by the author bore the Serial No. 134,738, and was marked as having been made in 1937. A variant of Mod. 24 having an extra-large magazine capacity appeared in about 1930. These reportedly were made on a special contract and not for use by the Czech army. A specimen examined by the author bore the Serial No. 1903 and was dated 1930.

VZ 1927—In 1926 František Myška redesigned the Model 24, eliminating the rotating barrel lock and converting it to a blowback design. This 7.65 mm. pistol went into production as the VZ 27 (Mod. 27) and was the standard Czech Police pistol until 1951. Like the Mod. 24, it was made in Prague.

By the time the Germans took over in 1939 a considerable number of these pistols had been made. Specimen No. 30,020 bears the inscription BÖHMISCHE WAFFENFABRIK A.G. IN PRAG on the top of the slide and is thought to have been made soon after the Germans took over the factory. The highest serial number observed bearing the code "fnh" (Böhmische Waffenfabrik A.G.) is 473,056 (made in 1945) and the lowest serial number bearing the immediate postwar inscription ČESKÁ ZBROJOVKA A.S. V PRAZE on the top of the slide (also made in 1945) is 481,894. It would seem from this that at least 443,000 pistols of this model were made during the German occupation.

A special silencer was devised and made for the Mod. 27 pistol, for use by the German army. The length of this device was 205 mm. and pistols equipped with it had slightly larger barrels with a groove on the end for the attachment (Fig. 143).

Fig. 143. 7.65 mm. Czech Mod. 27. Provided with silencer.

A specimen, Serial No. 8363 (dated 1930), with smooth wood grip pieces and without commercial markings has been reported. This may very well be a special contract piece for some police or military use, and production was probably limited. Possibly other specimens will be found with full commercial markings, thus refuting this hypothesis.

During the German occupation, an experimental Mod. 27 in .22 caliber rim fire was produced. This pistol bears the inscription KAL. .22 LANG FÜR BÜCHSEN and obviously was intended for target practice. With the exception of the caliber this pistol was identical to the regular Mod. 27. Apparently not many were made.

While the Mod. 27 pistol was intended for police and civilian use when made by the Czechs, the Germans found it suited to the needs of the Luftwaffe, and by 1942 all production was diverted to such use. All specimens so used bear the "fnh" code mark and German acceptance marks; and commercial markings are absent.

Toward the end of the war the Germans were hard pressed for time and pistols made in that period were poorly finished and more crudely made. Czech workmen were probably not cooperating very enthusiastically!

Immediately following the end of the war in 1945 the Czechs resumed the manufacture of pistols and changed the inscriptions back to the prewar name of Česká Zbrojovka A.S. V. Praze, but in 1948, following the Communist *coup d'etat,* the name was

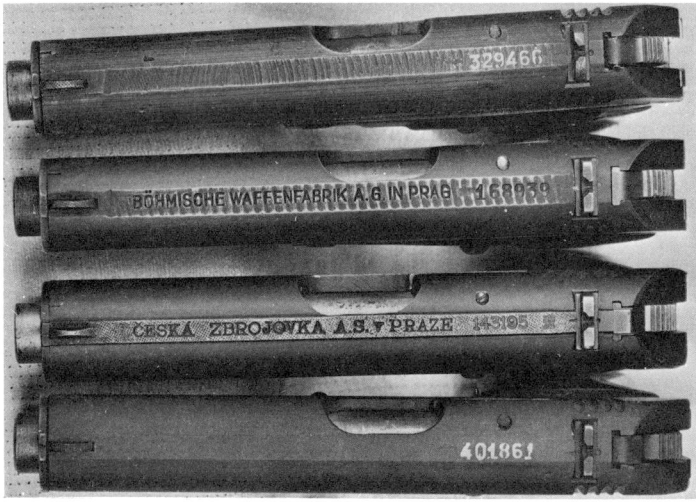

Fig. 144. Czech and German markings on Czech Pistole Modell 27.
No. 1 (Top): Late in World War II, during German occupation.
No. 2: Early World War II, during occupation.
No. 3: Original Czech markings, to 1939.
No. 4: Same as No. 1, except dull finish was used.

changed to Česká Zbrojovka Národní Podnik and this name appears on pistols made since that time. For various markings to be found on Mod. 27 pistols see Fig. 144.

Production of Mod. 27 is thought to have ceased in 1951, at the time of the introduction of a new model (Mod. 50). The highest serial number seen by the author for a Mod. 27 is 568,519, and though marked as having been made in 1947 it bears the Communist form of the firm name, indicating that it was one of the last made before the Communists took control or that it was assembled from parts made before that time.

VZ 1938—In 1937 a 9 mm. pistol of entirely new design was developed by František Myška and production was started in 1938; hence this model was designated Mod. 1938. By 1939 it was being supplied, in limited quantities, to the Czech army. The Mod. 1938 (or Mod. 38) is characterized by having a double-action firing system, and hinged forward-pivoted barrel assembly. To lift the barrel for inspection or cleaning, all that is necessary is to push to the left the catch on the left side of the slide. Because of the double-action feature and the impossibility of cocking the arm by hand (the hammer being set so low), the use of a safety lever seemed superfluous and it is rarely found. Numerous early variants and modifications of this pistol exist; one rare modification does have a mechanical safety lever on the left side of the slide (Figs. 145 and 146). Mod. 38 pistols are marked simply ČESKÁ ZBROJOVKA AKC. SPOL. V PRAZE. Serial numbers are on both slide and frame on the left side, and the inspector's mark and date are on the right side of the frame.

The German occupation, beginning March 15, 1939, took place just about the time the production of this new model was getting well under way. All stores of pistols and parts were immediately taken over, the nomenclature was changed to Pistole 39(t), and production was discontinued.

All of the many specimens of the Mod. 1938 pistol seen by the author have serial numbers falling in the range 250,000 to 290,000, which suggests that the numbering may have been started arbitrarily at 250,000. None have been observed to have German acceptance marks, but all bear Czech markings and the year of manufacture. It seems that the manufacture of this pistol was not resumed after the war.

VZ 50—This pistol, officially designated Pistole VZ 50, is a 7.65 mm. blowback Walther PP type and was designed by Jan and Jaroslav Kratchovíl. It was developed in 1947-48. In 1951 it was supplied on a trial basis to the Czech police as VZ NB 50 (the letters NB standing for Národní Bezpečnost, i.e., National Police) and was sold commercially both in Czechoslovakia and in the export trade.

This pistol has a push button release of the magazine (just back of the trigger) and a finger rest. The thumb-operated safety is located on the left side of the frame (below the finger grip serrations on the left side of the slide) rather than at the rear on the left side of the slide as on the Walther. The loading indicator has been changed from the Walther pin protruding to the rear (over the hammer) to a button which protrudes (when loaded) through the left side of the slide just over the serrations. The right side of the grip (which resembles that on the P-38) bears the customary CZ monogram, whereas the left grip piece is moulded for a large safety lever and bears no monogram. The take-down lever

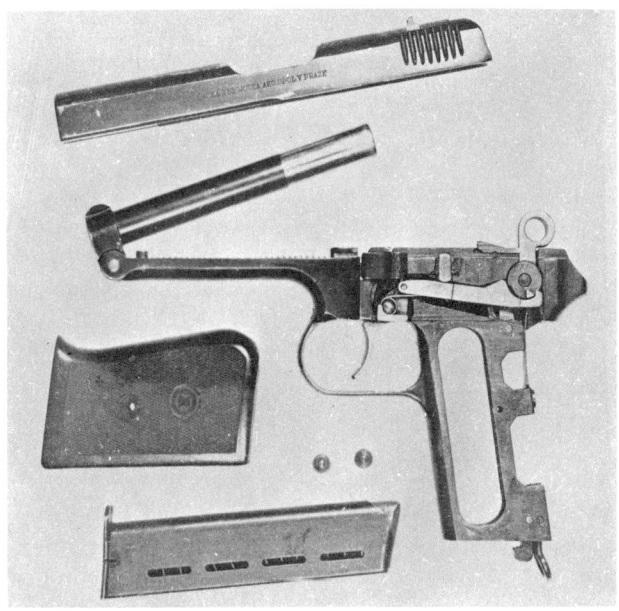

Fig. 145. Czech Mod. 1938. Disassembled.

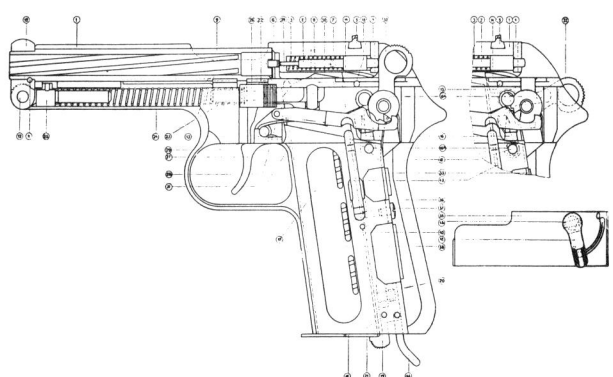

Fig. 146. Czech Mod. 1938. Schematic view.

is on the right side just above the front part of the trigger guard and the trigger guard is solid (not hinged as on the Walther). The hammer is modified slightly, the perforated ring spur being replaced by a solid elliptical spur. Like the Walther, this pistol has an automatic safety block to prevent discharge by a blow or fall, if dropped in a loaded condition. The pistol has a very attractive appearance and seems to be well made.

VZ 52—Pistole Model 52 is a more recent military pistol, replacing the Russian Tokarev. It is chambered for the new Czech cartridge Model 48 in 7.62 mm. caliber. This new cartridge is interchangeable with the Russian 7.62 and the 7.63 Mauser cartridges. It is loaded about 20% heavier than the Russian. This recoil-operated Mod. 52 pistol has a locking system similar to the German MG 42 machine gun.

Czech commercial pistols

The Praga—Known as Praga Mod. 1921, this 6.35 mm. pistol is of the vestpocket type and was designed by Václav Holek for A. Nowotný who built the factory known as "Zbrojovka Praga" in 1918. Advertisements printed in 1922 state that the pistol was made in Vršovice, a suburb of Prague. The pistols will be found to be marked ZBROJOVKA PRAGA/ PRAHA/PATENT CAL. 6.35.

Specimen No. 2599 (the earliest seen by the author) bears the date (on the barrel) 13–10–21, Specimen No. 3724 bears the date 18–10–21 and No. 6409 is dated 22–12–21. Specimen No. 1910 has been reported by Wandrus[*] but no date is shown.

The Praga is a curious gun in shape, particularly as to the forward end of the slide, which gives the gun the appearance of "an oversized can opener." The pistol was designed for one-hand operation, which was accomplished by the provision of a cocking groove located on the top of the slide near the muzzle. Retraction of the slide with the index finger in this groove loads and cocks the weapon and also brings the folded trigger into proper position for shooting. Obviously the arm has no trigger guard. The pistol is of the blowback type and the fired shells are ejected through a port in the right side of the slide. Although specimens of this freak gun are not uncommon it is safe to say that the production was not large, particularly as the plant closed down in 1926.

The Fox—This was a small pocket pistol of 6.35 mm. caliber, designed by Alois Tomiška in Pilsen,

[*]*Czech Automatic Pistols* by Harry Wandrus and John Griebl (privately printed).

Czechoslovakia. In the years 1919–1921 it was hand made by Jihočeská Zbrojovka s.s. r.o. (South Bohemian Arsenal). Specimens so made will bear the monogram ZJ on hard rubber grips. The arm had a folding trigger and, of course, no trigger guard.

CZ Mod. 1922—Jihočeská Zbrojovka was joined by the Hubertus firm and became Česká Zbrojovka, A.S. This firm introduced more modern methods and produced machine-made pistols with interchangeable parts. The Fox pistol was subjected to considerable alteration and emerged as the 6.35 mm. CZ Mod. 1922; production continued until 1936. The front and rear sights of the Fox were replaced by an aiming groove and the folding trigger gave way to the conventional type of trigger and guard. As in the Fox, the rear end of the slide, carrying the finger grip serrations, is smaller in diameter than the rest of the slide. Both pistols have a thumb-operated safety lever at the rear end of the frame, below the serrations. The pistol was attractive in appearance, had good balance and a mechanical safety but no grip safety.

Specimen No. 2140, examined by the author, is marked ČESKÁ ZBROJOVKA AKC. SPOL. V PRAZE, indicating that it was made at the Prague factory. It has wood grip pieces, rather than the more common hard rubber grip pieces shown in factory advertising, and these carry the familiar CZ monogram. This pistol is dated "8.23" (presumably indicating manufacture in August 1923) and bears the official markings of the Prague Proof House. Literature printed in English indicates that this pistol was intended for export trade as well as sale in Czechoslovakia.

CZ Mod. 1936—This 6.35 mm. pistol, also intended for the commercial trade, was designed by František Myška and it replaced the Mod. 1922. As it was introduced at an inauspicious time, shortly before World War II, it is not likely that the production was large. Specimens seen by the author are all numbered in the 20,000 to 27,000 range.

This is a double-action pistol with some good features. When the magazine is withdrawn (by releasing it with the catch at the bottom of the grip) both the trigger and hammer are disconnected, making it impossible to fire the arm. In addition, there is a thumb-operated slide safety (mounted on the frame) which locks the slide to prevent firing and, by placing the catch in another notch, the slide is held back in position for disassembly. Retracting and releasing the slide puts a cartridge in the chamber but does not cock the arm because of the double-action feature. Pulling the trigger both cocks and discharges the pistol. The barrel has two lugs and

these serve to distinguish it from some of the other Czech pistols; and it is the only 6.35 mm. Czech pistol to have a safety lever on the left side of the body, just above the trigger (Fig. 147).

Model 1936 pistols are marked, on the left side of the slide, ČESKÁ ZBROJOVKA AKC. SPOL. V PRAZE, and carry the usual CZ monogram on the hard rubber grip pieces.

CZ Mod. 1945—The 6.35 mm. Mod. 1936, originally designed by František Myská, was redesigned and simplified by Jan Kratchovíl. It retains many of the features of the previous model including much the same appearance. The mechanical safety on the slide was omitted, as it was not considered necessary because of the double-action system. The safety on the 1936 model served another purpose, however, as it was used to lock the slide in position for disassembly; a feature unfortunately missing in the 1945 version. The barrel has only one lug, whereas Mod. 36 has two. A magazine disconnector prevents accidental discharge when the magazine is out and a cartridge is in the chamber.

All Mod. 1945 pistols bear the inscription (on the left side of the slide), ČESKÁ ZBROJOVKA-NÁRODNÍ PODNIK STRAKONICE, and on the frame below will be found the words MADE IN CZECHOSLOVAKIA, below which will be a proof mark and the date of manufacture. Numerous specimens examined by the author range in serial numbers from 50,118 (dated 47) to 110,787 (dated 1949).

The DUO—The DUO is a 6.35 mm. pistol originally made by František Dušek, Opočno (Bohemia), Czechoslovakia, about 1926. It is striker fired; the barrel has three lugs, a thumb operated safety mounted on the rear of the frame by means of which the slide can be locked, and also a magazine safety.

Pistols made before the German occupation in

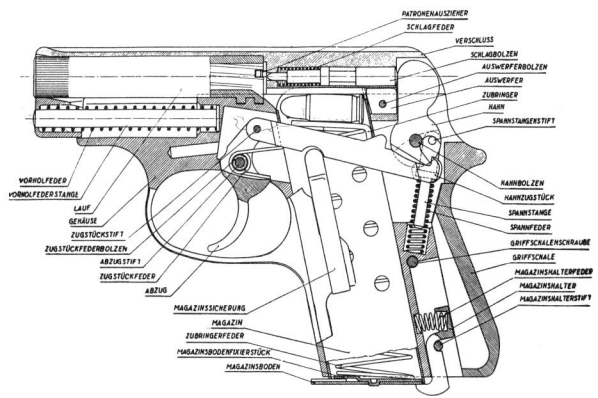

Fig. 147. Czech Mod. 1936. Schematic view.

1939 were marked AUTOMAT PISTOLE "DUO" CAL. 6.35 F. DUŠEK, OPOČNO, while pistols made during the German occupation were marked AUTOMAT PISTOLE "DUO" CAL. 6.35 F. DUŠEK, OPOTSCHNO. Dusek was allowed to operate under his own name in that period, the only change being the use of German spelling for the name of the town in which the plant was located.

At the close of the war, apparently prior to 1950, the manufacture of this pistol was taken over by Česká Zbrojovka-Národní Podnik (the factory having been "nationalized"), and pistols dated 1950 will be found to carry the inscription Z AUT. PISTOLE R 6.35 mm. MADE IN CZECHOSLOVAKIA on the slide. The letter "R" in this inscription stands for the Czech word "ráže," which means caliber. The date and proof mark will also be on the left side of the slide and the serial number will be found on the right side of the slide, both as usual for the DUO type pistols. Because of the presence of the letter Z on the slide and the presence of a new monogram on the grips containing the letter Z, these pistols are sometimes referred to as the "Z" pistols.

No data as to the total production of these pistols are available. Specimens with serial numbers as low as 9071 (a pre-war pistol) have been seen, indicating that probably the serial numbering started at 1. At what point in numbering the Germans took over is not known, however specimens 74,557 to 117,951 are known (from their markings) to have been made during the occupation. Specimens Nos. 163,795 and 165,795 (dated 1948) and bearing Czech markings seem to indicate that resumption of the manufacture of this pistol actually started in 1948 (the year of "nationalization") rather than the usually accepted date of 1950. As far as is known this pistol is still in production.

The Mars—The name Mars has been used by pistol manufacturers in several countries, for arms which bear no resemblance to each other. The Mars pistols made in Czechoslovakia were made by Kohout & Spol. (i.e., Kohout and Co.), in Kdyně, and usually are so marked.

The 6.35 mm. Mars was copied from the 1906 Mod. of the Browning and does not have much to distinguish it. It was made without a grip safety, without notches in the slide for engagement of the thumb operated safety which is located on the frame behind the left grip piece, and with a grip that was much narrower at the bottom than at the top. Such a grip is undesirable as it does not furnish a good hold.

The left side of this pistol will be found to be marked MARS 6.35 KOHOUT & SPOL. KDYNĚ.

No information as to when this pistol originated or how many were made is at hand. Known specimens bear serial numbers up to ca. 20,000, but the 7.65 Mars may have been numbered in the same series. Manufacture ceased in 1945.

The 7.65 mm. Mars, also a low-priced pistol, is a striker-fired copy of the F.N. Browning Mod. 1910 and was made without grip safety and without notches in the lower edge of the left slide to hold the slide in open position for take-down.

The markings on the slides were not uniform. On specimen Serial No. 8457 (dated 1939) the inscription on the left side of the slide reads "Automat. pistole MARS cal. 7.65," whereas on specimen Serial No. 9341 (dated 1941) the inscription reads "MARS 7.65 KOHOUT & SPOL. KDYNĚ." The two specimens are alike in all respects, except that No. 8457 has plain wood grip pieces while No. 9341 has fluted wood grip pieces. Since a 1942 specimen has the number 10,356, and as production is known to have ceased in 1945, the total production could not have been great.

Slavia—This 6.35 mm. pistol, of the Browning type with no unusual features, was made by Antonín Vilímec of Kdyně (Bohemia), Czechoslovakia. Specimens Nos. 1440, 2031, and 15,028 show grip pieces which have parallel sides whereas those on specimen No. 70,510 are broader at the top and cover more of the grip frame. Otherwise the specimens appear to be alike. These pistols no doubt date from some time in the 1920's, as No. 70,510 is dated 1931. Specimens of this pistol are uncommon in this country.

The left side of the slide bears the simple inscription „SLAVIA" together with the date and the Prague proof mark. The serial number is also on the left side, at the forward end of the frame.

Production of this pistol ceased in 1939, at the time of the German occupation, and has not been resumed.

The Niva—Little is known about this 6.35 mm. modification of the F.N. Browning Mod. 1906. It is said to have been made by Posumavská Zbrojovka (owned by Kohout & Spol. of Kdyně).

The PZK—This is also a pocket pistol of the 1906 Browning type. This pistol, like the Niva, was made in very limited quantity by Kohout & Spol.

Czech target pistols

Mod. "P"—This is a single shot pistol, chambered for .22 Short, Long, Long Rifle, or 6 mm. Flobert cartridges and available with barrel lengths of 200, 250, and 300 mm. It is of the break open (tip up) type, the barrel being pinioned at the forward end of the frame. The sights are nonadjustable, with a line of sight almost as long as the pistol. An extractor

189

partially removes the fired case so that it can be grasped by the fingers.

The factory producing this pistol, originally owned by František Pavlíček, is located in the city of Litomyšl (Bohemia), Czechoslovakia. In 1948, along with most Czech plants, it was "nationalized" by the Communists.

This arm came on the market in about 1930, was made during the German occupation, and is still in production.

The Drulov—This is a more pretentious single shot pistol than the Mod. "P." Technical data given are as follows: length, 360 mm. (14.2 inches); barrel length, 250 mm. (9.3 inches); length of aiming line, 300 mm. (11.8 inches); and weight, 1.3 kg. (2.8 lb.).

The foresight is adjustable vertically and the rear sight adjusts laterally. In the literature describing this pistol, it is stated that the pistol "has a simple

hammer mechanism was changed so that retraction of the slide produced cocking to facilitate timed or rapid fire, and a safety of the Colt Mod. 1911A1 type was added to meet range requirements. Also the sights and grips were modified for target use. The take-down is nearly the same as on the Mod. 38.

No information is at hand as to whether this pistol actually went into production or the date at which the design was completed.

D.W.M. pocket pistol

The D.W.M. pocket pistol was brought out by the Deutsche Waffen u. Munitionsfabrik of Berlin late in 1921 and was given the official nomenclature Pistole D.W.M. Modell 22, but the following year the name was changed to Pistole D.W.M. Modell 23, although the only apparent change was in the introduction of

TABLE 29
Data for Czech automatic pistols

Model	Over-all length, inches	Height, inches	Weight, ounces	Mag. cap., ctges.	Barrel length, inches	No. of lands	Inches for 1 turn	Twist	No. of bbl. lugs
Duo	4½	3	15	6	2⅛	6	8	Right	3
Mod. 1922	4⅝	2⅞	....	6	2⅛	....	....	....	....
Mod. 1936	4⅘	3⅜	13¾	8	2½	6	7.87	Right	2
Mod. 1945	5	3⅜	15	8	2½	6	6	Right	1
Slavia Mod. 1921	4½	3⅜	16	8	2⅛	6	8	Right	3
Praga	4⅕	3⅕	12¼	6	2	4	10.6	Right	2

Czech Automatic Pistols, published privately by Harry Wandrus and John Griebl. (Used by permission.)

trigger mechanism with double resistance, the cylindrical breech with lock and rectilinear striker travel. The operation of the striking mechanism is therefore free from any shock and the weapon is perfectly locked when firing." The literature does not state what ammunition the gun takes, but presumably it is chambered for the .22 Long Rifle cartridge. The name of the maker of this pistol is not known, but it is marketed by OMNIPOL.

CZ Mod. 448—Little is known by the author about this pistol other than that it is manufactured by Česká Zbrojovka, is chambered for .22 L.R. cartridges, has a magazine capacity of 10 rounds, and was designed by František Myška and Rudolf Lacina.

ZKP–501–II—This .22 cal. L.R. target pistol is said to have been designed by Joseph and Francis Koucký. It resembles the Czech Mod. 38, but a number of modifications were made to suit it for competitive target shooting. The angle of the grip was increased to give more natural pointing, the

hard rubber grip pieces instead of plain wood pieces. Despite the official nomenclature the pistol is generally known, more simply, as the D.W.M. Pocket Pistol.

Since the manufacture of military types or types suitable for military use was forbidden by the conditions of the peace treaty, the D.W.M. firm naturally looked for something that could be made within the provisions of the treaty. Evidently they were much impressed by the F.N. Browning Model 1910, with which they no doubt had become thoroughly familiar, as the F.N. plant was operated under the supervision of the Germans during the occupation of Belgium in World War I. The D.W.M. pistol is almost an exact copy of the F.N. Browning, the only changes being minor ones. The grip was streamlined somewhat to give a more attractive appearance and better hold, the extractor shape was changed a bit, the magazine catch was made smaller and separate, and, of course, the pistol bore the familiar script insignia D.W.M. that was used on Luger pistols of their manufacture.

Serial numbering started at No. 1 and continued up to 10,000, at which point the military system of serial numbering was adopted and used for each subsequent block of 10,000. In this system the first 10,000 were numbered from 1 to 10,000, then each subsequent block of 10,000 was distinguished by having a different suffix letter added to the serial number—a, b, c, and d. No specimens have been seen having such high numbers, indicating a production of 50,000, but there seems to be some ground for belief that this represents approximately the entire production. Manufacture seems to have ceased in 1928 (or thereabouts) and sales stopped in 1930 or 1931. It may well be that production was discontinued because this pistol was quite obviously an infringement of F.N. patents.

Data for this pistol are as follows: over-all length, 6 inches; height, 4 inches; thickness, 1.5 inches; weight, empty, 20 ounces; and magazine capacity, 7 ctges.

Dreyse pistols

The Dreyse pistols were designed by Louis Schmeisser, a designer-engineer in the employ of the Sömmerda Division of the Rheinische Metallwaren u. Maschinenfabrik. This firm, originally bearing the name Nikolaus von Dreyse, was organized to manufacture a breech-loading arm invented by von Dreyse and adopted for German military use in 1841. Von Dreyse, the son of a master locksmith, was born in Sömmerda in 1787 and died in 1867. For his distinguished services to his country he was made a "Geheimrat," a much prized German honor in the last century.

In 1889 Heinrich Ehrhardt bought into the company and by 1901 had acquired complete control. The name of Waffen u. Munitionsfabrik von Dreyse was dropped and the firm operated under the name Rheinische Metallwaren u. Maschinenfabrik. Presumably because of the length of this name, the firm was often referred to merely as "Rheinmetall" and, after about 1913, pistols bore the inscription RHEIN-METALL ABT. SÖMMERDA in place of the full name of the firm. In 1935 this firm combined with A. Borsig, G.m.b.H. (Berlin) to form a firm known as Rheinmetall-Borsig, A.G. which was very active during the second World War.

7.65 mm. Dreyse—Schmeisser's first design was for a pistol using the Browning cartridge. The pistol dates from 1906, but appears to have been put into production in 1907, hence has become known as the

Modell 1907. It was produced commercially from 1907 to 1914 (or 1915). Serial numbers started at No. 1 and went as high as about 250,000. Over this range of numbers the design was quite stable, the variations being only minor ones, such as the pattern of the serrations for the finger grips. These serrations are placed at the forward end of the slide, which makes it more difficult to pull back the slide. This difficulty is increased by the use of an unusually stiff recoil spring (Figs. 148 to 151).

Some of the early illustrations used to advertise this arm, such as that which appears in the 1911 ALFA Catalog, appear to be of a prototype form rather than of one actually produced commercially.

Fig. 148. 7.65 mm. Dreyse Mod. 1907. Early form.

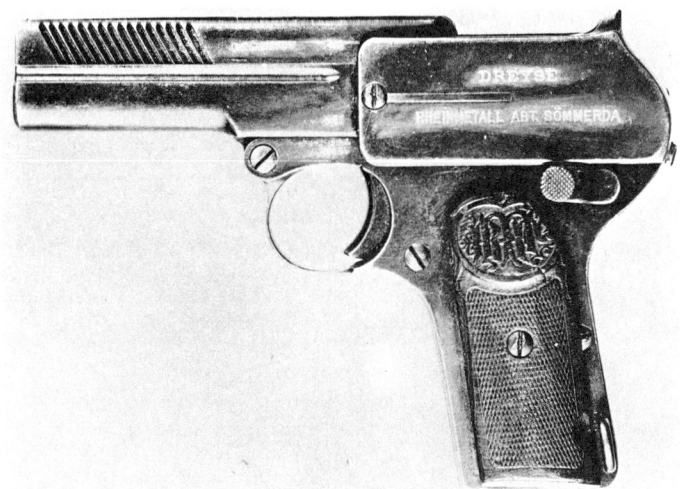

Fig. 149. 7.65 mm. Dreyse Mod. 1907. Specimen has variant serrations on finger grips.

The illustration may be based on an early (1906) drawing. Whether any pistols of this exact form were ever produced is not known.

The Dreyse pistol was advertised as a Police Pistol. Whether it was actually so used to any considerable extent is not known definitely, but one specimen examined was marked K.S. GEND 170 and bore no other number. The number 170 also appeared on the trigger as well as in the customary places for serial numbers. The name Dreyse does not appear. The fact that the full name of the firm appears indicates that it was probably made before 1913. The pistol shows no unusual features of construction, other than having much higher sights than were ordinarily used. It would appear that this

specimen was used for police work, if the word (or abbreviation) GEND is correctly interpreted.

6.35 mm. Dreyse—The 6.35 mm. Dreyse, also using the Browning cartridge, was designed by Schmeisser in 1908 and probably was not offered commercially until 1909 (or possibly 1910), as the patent situation was not cleared up until 1910. The serial numbering is stated to have started at No. 1, and while it is not known how many were made it is reported that production stopped with the beginning of World War I. It seems logical to assume that the total number produced did not exceed 100,000 and was probably less (Fig. 152).

This pistol is of the Browning 1906 type, but without a grip safety. It bears little resemblance to the more complicated and awkward 7.65 mm. model. The early 6.35 mm. pistols had two extractors, one on each side of the slide, but this practice was soon changed. Just when the change was made is not known, but the factory file of 1912 shows the single extractor type whereas advertisements of 1911 show the double type. From this it would appear that the change was made late in 1911 or early in 1912.

It is stated that manufacture of the 6.35 mm. model was resumed for a time in the 1920's by Rheinmetall, but no proof of this has been seen. It is true that both the 6.35 and the 7.65 mm. models were available for purchase at that time because both are advertised in the June 15, 1922, issue of the AKAH Catalog put out by Albrecht Kind, Hunstig bei Dieringhausen (Rheinland), Germany. Both illustrations used show the name Dreyse (rather than Rheinmetall) and the one for the 7.65 states that the model is that of 1907. The illustration of the 6.35 mm. model shows the double extractor. If these

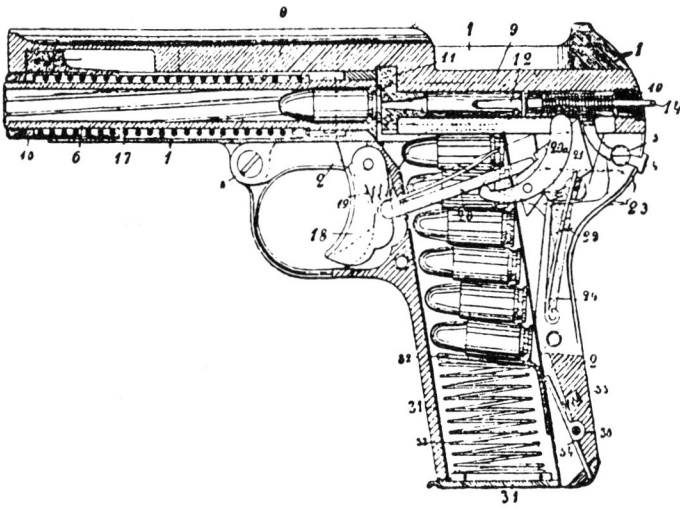

Fig. 150. 7.65 mm. Dreyse Mod. 1907. Schematic view A—Loaded, safety off, and bolt locked.

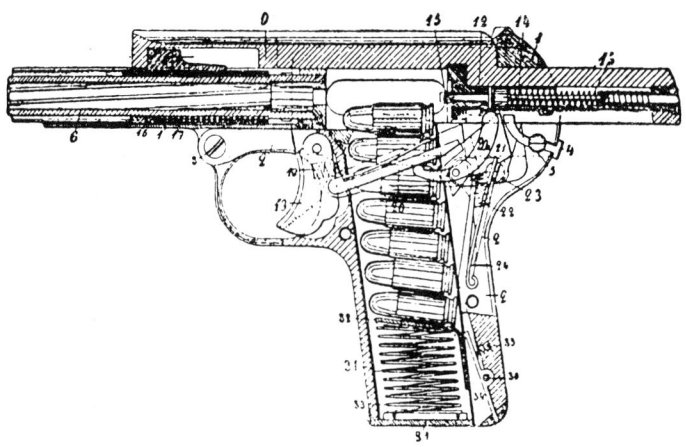

Fig. 151. 7.65 mm. Dreyse Mod. 1907. Schematic view B—Gun fired and bolt at end of its rearward travel.

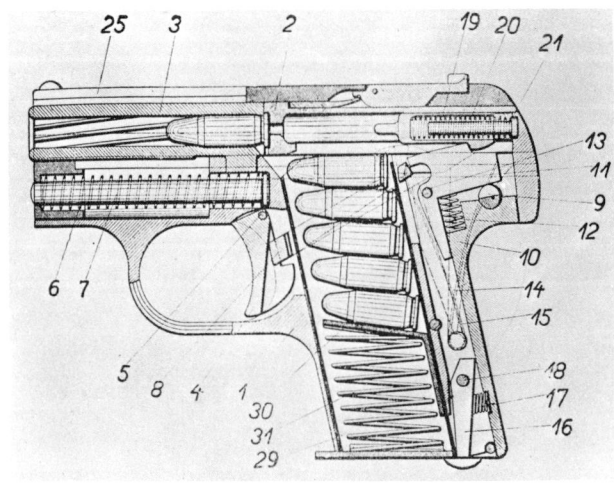

Fig. 152. 6.35 mm. Dreyse. Schematic view.

illustrations have any significance, it appears that the pistols offered for sale by AKAH in 1922 had been made prior to 1913 and were left-over stock.

9 mm. Parabellum Dreyse—The Parabellum Dreyse, also designed by Schmeisser, dates from 1909 or 1910 and seems to have originated more as a commercial venture than a military one. Only the very early (pre-1912) specimens have the full Dreyse markings. The later forms (1912 to 1915) vary in several minor points. There appear to have been at least three variant forms. Very few were made and the 9 mm. Dreyse is now a collector's item (Fig. 153).

Since the Parabellum cartridge is a powerful one for a blowback type pistol and since the original 7.65 mm. Dreyse had an unpleasantly stiff recoil spring, it was necessary to use a still stiffer spring, so stiff, in fact, that the slide could not be pulled back by one hand. The difficulty was solved in an ingenious manner which permitted "bypassing" the recoil spring. In other words, the pistol was so designed that the slide could be disengaged, tilted up, and moved back without the necessity of compressing the recoil spring. Only the main spring was compressed and this required little effort. Once this had been compressed, the slide was moved back and re-engaged. While the solution was an ingenious one, practically it was not good. Construction was too complicated and insufficiently rugged.

7.65 mm. Rheinmetall—The Rheinmetall 7.65 mm. caliber pistol was copied after the Browning Model 1910, which it resembles, but does not have the grip safety. In appearance it bears no resemblance to the earlier 7.65 mm. Dreyse. Apparently the development of this model was still under way in 1921, as Bock states in the 1923 edition of his "*Moderne Faustfeuerwaffen*" that he had been permitted to fire a hand-made specimen in 1921. The pistol and

a cross sectional diagram are shown in the 1923 edition of Bock. The illustration differs in some respects from a specimen examined (No. 255,290). The illustration shows a matted rib running the entire length of the barrel and fairly high sights, both of which are missing in the specimen examined. Both, however, are marked RHEINMETALL ABT. SÖMMERDA (Figs. 154, 155).

Presumably, the serial numbering began at 250,000, where the numbering of the 7.65 mm. Dreyse left off (approximately at least). No information is at hand concerning the total number made, but since it

Fig. 154. 7.65 mm. Rheinmetall.

Fig. 153. 9 mm. (Par.) Dreyse Mod. 1910.

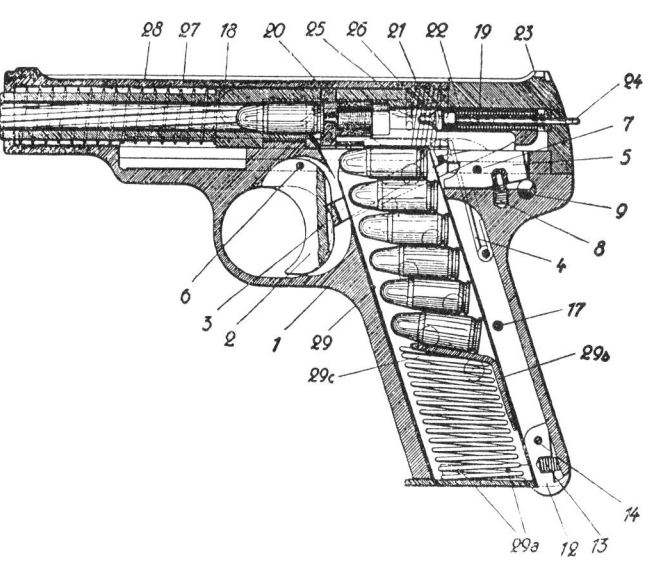

Fig. 155. 7.65 mm. Rheinmetall. Schematic view.

was apparently made for only a short time the total production must have been small. The scarcity of specimens bears this out. Neither the Dreyse (in any caliber) nor the Rheinmetall is mentioned in the 1941 edition of Bock.

An experimental 9 mm. Parabellum blowback (of the 7.65 mm. Rheinmetall type) marked with the Rheinmetall-Borsig emblem has been reliably reported. This indicates that it was made after 1935. It is very probable that it is only an experimental prototype made for possible military adoption and that it went no further.

It has been rumored that an experimental 9 mm. Browning Short was also made, but this report has not been confirmed.

Erma pistols

The ERMA pistols were made by the firm Erfurter Maschinen u. Werkzeugfabrik, B. Geipel, G.m.b.H., Abetilung Waffenfabrik. The name ERMA was derived from this name and came into common use for the firm itself as well as for its products. This firm made at least four different models of small-caliber (.22) rifles, as well as the ERMA pistols.

Two types of .22 cal. L.R. pistols were made, at different times. They are referred to as the "Alte Modell" and the "Neues Modell." Both are of the fixed-barrel, blowback type, with full-length slide, the forward end of which is cut away, exposing the barrel. As the breechblock (which is in the slide) moves back upon firing, the extractor (which is mounted in the breechblock) pulls out the fired shell and ejects it on the right side. Both pistols have exposed hammers and safety devices whereby the hammer may be locked in the cocked position. The trigger pull is said to be about 800 grams (ca. 1¾ pounds), the arm being designed particularly for target shooting. The sights are set as far apart as possible so as to give the longest possible sighting radius.

The Alte Modell, which was introduced in about 1936, has been seen in two barrel lengths, but there may well have been others. Barrels of the ones seen were 110 and 200 mm. long (giving total lengths of 230 and 320 mm.). The pistol can be disassembled quickly by pulling back the slide, locking it in position, and then turning the assembly latch on the left side of the slide, in front of the trigger guard.

The grip is of good length, is well shaped (partially streamlined), set at a good angle to absorb shock and to afford a comfortable hold.

The Neues Modell, brought out in about 1939, embodies much the same design but is different in some respects. Three nomenclatures were assigned, depending on the length of the barrel supplied. Actually, the three barrels are interchangeable and one may have all three of them for the same pistol. Each barrel is threaded so that it can be removed and replaced quickly. Despite this interchangeability, the following names were used:

1. ERMA "Meisterschaftmodell"—300 mm. barrel, total length about 390 mm.

2. ERMA "Sportsmodell"—210 mm. barrel, total length about 300 mm., and weight 1 kg. (2.2 lb.).

3. ERMA "Jägersschaftmodell"—100 mm. barrel, total length about 210 mm.

These "model" designations were probably used for the purpose of specifying the barrel length desired, in case a customer wished only one barrel.

This new model was supplied with a more streamlined grip, set at a smaller angle (i.e., less vertical, by 15°). Whether this was an improvement or not depends on the individual shooter. The magazine release was moved from its position on the frame back of the trigger guard to the base of the grip frame, and the "buttons" on the bottom of the magazine (to assist in its withdrawal), a feature borrowed from the Luger, were omitted. The thumb safety, formerly located at the top of the frame, back of the grip plate, was moved to the slide, directly above its former position. One change that might well have been made but was not, probably because of the cost, would have been the substitution of adjustable rear sights. The problem was solved more simply by using as a front sight one whose "bead" could be adjusted vertically and whose base could be adjusted laterally

Balancing weights, somewhat similar to those used on the Olympia Model Target Pistol, made by several manufacturers, were available. The principal one weighed 250 grams and a supplementary one weighing 100 grams could be added, if desired. These were attached in front of the trigger guard, giving the arm a very awkward appearance, but probably improving accuracy in target shooting.

No figures are available for the total production of either the old or the newer model, but because of the short time intervening between their introduction and the advent of World War II, at which time production was necessarily stopped, the total number produced must have been small. This of course is particularly true for the newer model.

Another ERMA product which should be mentioned is the auxiliary conversion unit developed for the Luger Parabellum pistol, for target practice. The date of its introduction is not known, but it is thought to have been a World War II development as it was not advertised in 1939 catalogs which did advertise ERMA conversion units for military and other larger-bore rifles. These conversion units were made for .22 cal. L. R. ammunition and were available for both the 7.65 and 9 mm. Lugers. The special magazines supplied had capacities of 10 cartridges.

Fiala magazine pistol

While the .22 cal. Fiala is a magazine pistol rather than an automatic, it closely resembles several of the .22 cal. automatics, including the early Colt, and it has some features found on automatics. Consequently, it seems worth while to include it in this chapter.

The pistol was made by the Blakslee Forging Co. of New Haven, Conn., for the Fiala Arms and Equipment Co. of New Haven. It was introduced in 1920 and a total of 4044 pieces were made up to 1923, at which time manufacture ceased. The gun was sold, however, up to ca. 1928. Forty of these pistols were stamped with the name "Botwinik Bros.," presently machinery dealers in Bridgeport, Conn. Contemporary records state that the Blakslee Forging Co. made pistols for the Columbia Arms Co. and that the specifications were identical to those for the Fiala.

The Fiala could be used as a regular target pistol or as either a pocket pistol or a combination rifle-pistol. With the regular 7½-inch barrel the total length was 11¼ inches, with a sighting radius of 9¾ inches. The weight with this barrel was 31 ounces. By substituting a 2¾-inch barrel for the regular barrel one could have a pocket pistol with a total length of 6½ inches, and the weight of this combination was 27 ounces. Or, if one desired the rifle combination, a 20½-inch barrel could be had, together with an easily attached shoulder stock. The total length of this combination was 35 inches and the weight was 3½ pounds. The interchange of barrels was very simple, as they were held in place by an easily removable thumbscrew located on the right side.

The pistol was chambered for the .22 L.R. cartridge. Specified data are as follows: bore diameter, 0.217 inch; number of grooves, 4; right hand twist; one turn in 16 inches; depth of grooves, 0.002 to 0.0025 inch; land width, 0.1024 inch; and magazine capacity, 10 cartridges.

The magazine is inserted in the "handle," a bolt lock is pushed in to release the breechblock slide which is drawn to the rear as far as it will go, permitting the magazine spring to push a cartridge up into position so that when the block moves forward the cartridge will be picked off and chambered. There being no recoil spring, the block is pushed forward by hand. When the action is fully closed the block is locked in position, so there is no danger of premature firing. After the shot is fired the block must again be unlocked and drawn back manually to extract the fired shell and pushed forward to insert the next cartridge.

This pistol was claimed to have an advantage over the single shot pistols, formerly popular for target shooting, in that both extraction and loading are easier and the arm is much safer than an automatic because a manual operation is required to load and unload it. It was also claimed that there was less distortion or damage to the lead bullet because the chambering of the bullet in an automatic pistol is violent compared to the hand chambering operation. Another important claim was that a higher velocity was imparted to the bullet because none of the energy provided by the explosion was used in the compression of a recoil spring and in the moving of mechanical parts.

The pistol was well balanced and performed well. Specimens examined had a good appearance and seemed to be well made. The shooting public, however, evidently preferred the faster-shooting automatic.

French service pistols

Up to World War I the revolver was the side arm used by the French military forces. In that war there was a shortage of revolvers but in nearby Spain there were many manufacturers who could supply automatic pistols, and many hundreds of thousands were so obtained. These pistols were of the modified Browning type so common in Spain. These are sometimes known as the "Ruby" type, because in 1914 Gabilondo y Urresti of Eibar obtained a patent on the pistol which covered this name also and because the first orders of pistols from Spanish manufacturers were obtained by this firm. As the demands from the French far exceeded the ability of this firm to produce, other firms were soon engaged in supplying the same type of pistol.

Soon after the war the Le Francais automatic pistol was produced by Manufacture Francais d'Armes et Cycles, at St. Etienne, but it was not until 1928 that a "military model" (9 mm. Browning Long) was produced. This is described elsewhere, with the other Le Francais pistols. It was never adopted for army use.

Following World War I the French military service began the development of an automatic pistol that would be acceptable for military use. By 1925 they had produced at St. Etienne a blowback type of

195

pistol bearing the inscription "M.A.S. 1925 M NO. 1." The serial number of the specimen examined (Figs. 156, 157) was 0510, which indicates that it was probably an experimental model. By 1932 several changes had evidently been made because specimens then bore the inscription "SE-M.A.S. 1932 Type A No. 4." (Fig. 158).

Modele 1935-A—It was not until 1935 that a suitable model came into being. This pistol, officially desig-nated the "Pistolet Automatique Modele 1935 A," was based on a Petter modification of the Browning system (Figs. 159 to 161). It was put into produc-tion by the firm Sociéte Alsacienne de Constructions Mécaniques (generally known more simply as S.A.C.M.) at Cholet, following government tests made in 1935 and 1936 which led to its adoption. Manufacture was continued until 1942 at which time the Germans took possession. Operations were con-tinued under German supervision, the pistol being used by them as a substitute standard. Production was resumed by the French at the close of the war, but by the present time it has no doubt been discon-tinued in favor of later models. In 1937, S.A.C.M. sold the rights to manufacture a pistol of the Petter design to the Swiss firm S.I.G. in Neuhausen and, in 1938, S.I.G. purchased manufacturing rights for all countries other than France. For an account of these pistols see the section on S.I.G.

The Mod. 1935-A pistol is recoil operated and has the basic Browning locked slide. The barrel is attached through a link arrangement (one on each side of the lug) just ahead of the chamber on the under side. Two lugs on the upper surface of the barrel, ahead of the chamber, lock into corresponding grooves in the under surface of the slide. After ⅛ inch of travel, the barrel is swung downward and out of engagement, permitting full rearward motion of the slide. A spiral recoil spring is located under-neath the barrel.

The pistol has an exposed hammer, which can be placed either at half or full cock. It has a discon-nector safety, operated by the withdrawal of the magazine, a thumb safety located at the rear end of the slide on the left side, and a chamber cartridge

Fig. 156. M.A.S. 1925 Mod. No. 1. One of several experimental models.

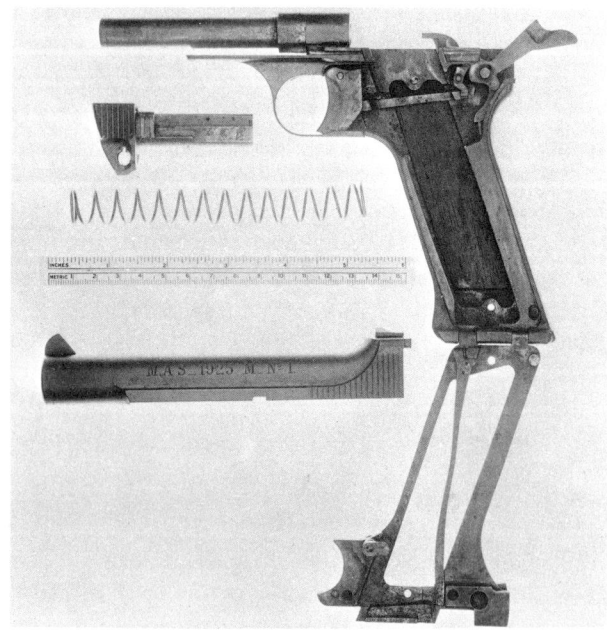

Fig. 157. M.A.S. 1925 Mod. No. 1. Disassembled.

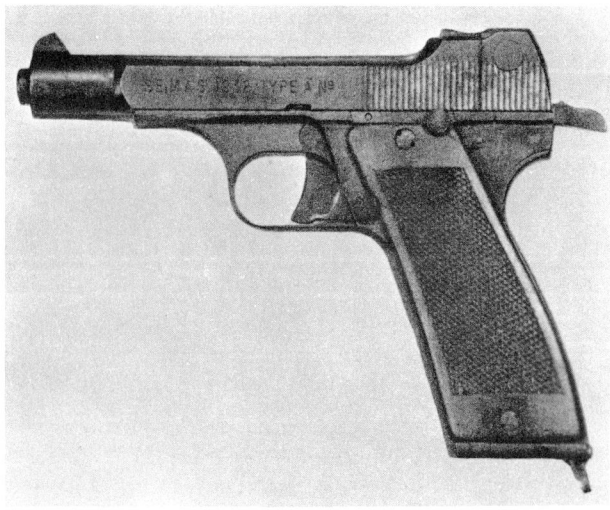

Fig. 158. 7.65 mm. French Service Pistol Type A No. 4.

indicator. The firing pin is spring loaded to prevent accidental firing through jarring. The magazine capacity is 8 rounds and the cartridge is the 7.65 mm. Long. This cartridge is almost identical to both of the very slightly different forms of the cartridge that was developed by the U.S. Government in 1918 for the Pedersen device—a device which permitted the use of .30 caliber pistol cartridges in the military rifle. It is thought that the 7.65 mm. French Long cartridge, used in the French service pistols, is a copy of this U.S. cartridge. It appears that the Pedersen device was so well thought of in Europe, when the well-kept secret of its existence was out, that the Fabrique Nationale and others became greatly interested in its use not only in shoulder arms but as a possibility for military pistols. Though this did not work out, the French considered the cartridge a good one and used it both for their automatic pistol and for the French submachine gun, Model of 1938.

Modele 1935-S—This model, officially designated as the Pistolet Automatique Modele 1935-S, was designed at the Government arsenal, Manufacture d'Armes de St.Etienne, at Saint Etienne. Adoption and manufacture at M.A.S. appears to date from 1939 and the pistol may still be in production. Both the 1935-A and the 1935-S models are fully described in Government manuals dated 1952, with special emphasis, however, on the latter model (Figs. 162 to 165).

The Mod. 1935-S was made at several arsenals, although those marked M.A.S. on the left side of the slide are more common. Others will be found to be marked M.A.T. (Manufacture d'Armes de Tuile) and still others have the marking S.A.C.M. The latter mark may indicate that manufacture of the 1935-S model may have superseded the 1935-A at that plant. A variant of the Mod. 1935-S type, manufactured by two other firms, has the nomenclature Pistolet Automatique Modele 35 S.M.-I. The main difference between this and the regular model is in the design of the mechanical safety. The Mod. 35 S.M.-I. will be found marked either M.A.C. (Manufacture d'Armes de Chatellerault) or S.A.G.E.M. (Sociéte d'Applications Générales Électriques et Mécaniques).

Like the Mod. 1935-A, this is also a Petter modification of the original locked-breech system. The locking arrangement is somewhat different, in that locking lugs are not present on the upper surface of the barrel at the chamber. In place of lugs, a step has been machined at a point slightly ahead of the chamber, and this step engages a cutout in the inner top surface of the slide, thus providing the locking action. Slide and barrel recoil together in the locked position for about ³⁄₁₆ inch at which point the barrel swings down and the slide continues to travel. Apart from

Fig. 159. French Service Pistol M1935-A. Partially disassembled.

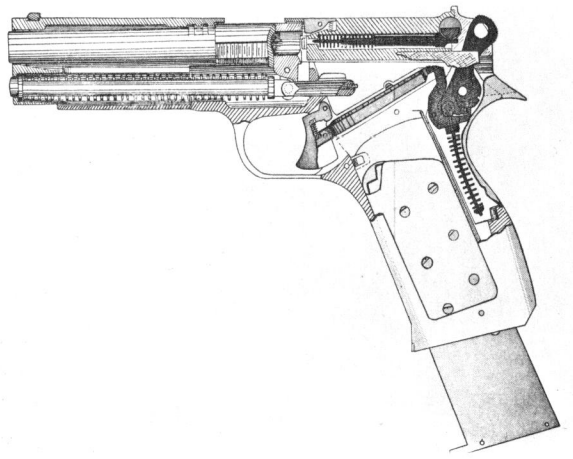

Fig. 160. French Service Pistol M1935-A. Sectional view.

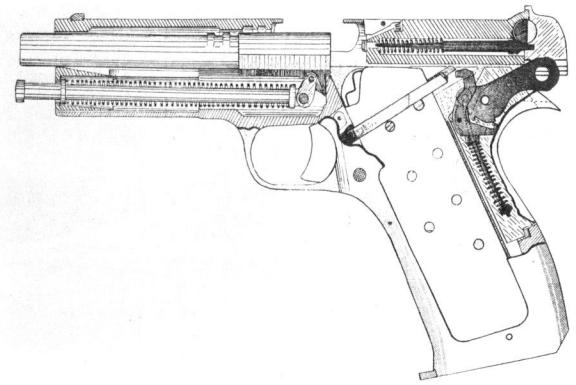

Fig. 161. French Service Pistol M1935-A. Sectional view.

197

this difference, the two models are very much alike in design.

Modele 1948—In this year M.A.S. developed experimentally a 9 mm. Parabellum pistol based on the design of the Mod. 1935-S and gave it the designation Pistolet Automatique Type SE M.A.S. 1948. This change in caliber was made to conform to the NATO standardization of cartridges for pistols and machine guns.

Modele 1950—By 1950 several minor changes in the 1948 model had been made and the nomencla-

ture was changed to Pistolet Automatique Type SE M.A.S. 1950. Conflicting statements as to its official adoption have been made—one to the effect that it was officially adopted in 1952, another that in 1954 it was still in the prototype stage. Requests for information from the French Government have been denied, as such information is "classified." It is very likely that the pistol has been officially adopted (Fig. 166).

In this pistol a conventional Browning rear-link-mounted barrel is used. Two locking ribs are present on the upper surface of the barrel, above and ahead of the chamber. This design differs from the 1935-S type in that lugs are used instead of a cammed shoulder for locking. In fact, the use of lugs in this 1950 type follows the design of the 1935-A model.

The rear sight is a broad U-shaped slot, machined

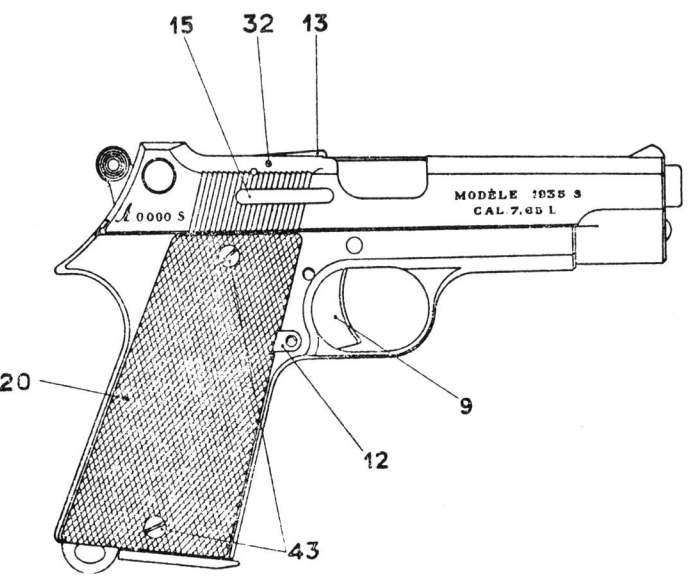

Fig. 162. 7.65 mm. Long. French Service Pistol Mod. 1935-S. Factory sketch.

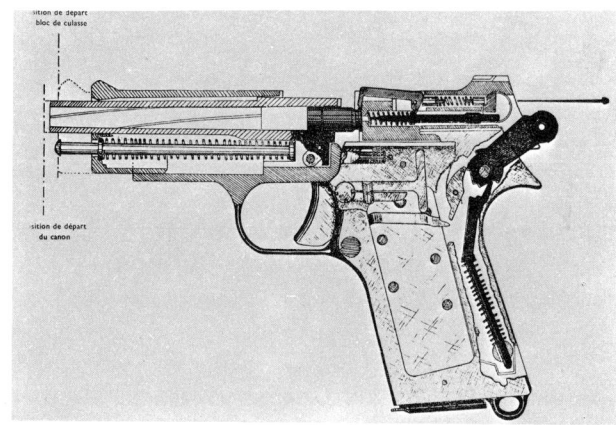

Fig. 164. 7.65 mm. Long. French Service Pistol Mod. 1935-S. Sectional view, showing fired case being withdrawn.

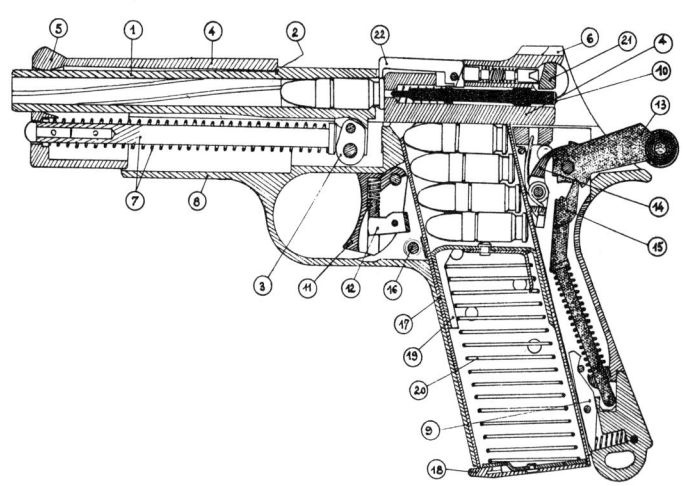

Fig. 163. 7.65 mm. Long. French Service Pistol Mod. 1935-S. Sectional view, showing pistol loaded and cocked.

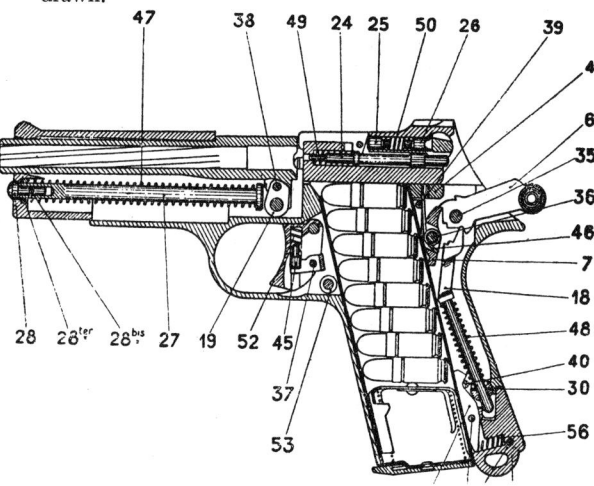

Fig. 165. 7.65 mm. Long. French Service Pistol Mod. 1935-S. Schematic view.

198

Fig. 166. 7.65 mm. Long. French Service Pistol Type SE-M.A.S. 1950.

into a heavy base (or block) on the slide top at the rear end. The fore sight is a tapered, and matted, parallel-sided blade attached to the top of the slide at the muzzle. The pistol has the chamber cartridge indicator (indicating the presence or absence of a cartridge therein) at the rear of the shell ejection port. It has a slot lanyard loop in the rear grip frame. The floor plate of the magazine is removable. The thumb safety is located on the left side of the slide and blocks the hammer just ahead of the firing pin when in the "safe" position. In most respects this pistol has the features of the Mod. 1935-A or the Mod. 1935-S or both.

Frommer (Hungarian) series

Rudolph Frommer of Budapest, Hungary, made important contributions in firearms inventions, some of them very ingenious. In the period 1899 to 1912 he originated two basic designs, both of which, in a number of variant forms, were made by Fegyver és Gépgyár Részvénytársaság (The Small Arms and Machine Factory, Ltd.) of Budapest.

Mod. 1901—The first pistol, design patents for which were obtained in the period 1899–1901, is characterized by having a small-diameter, tubular jacket with recoil spring mounted around the barrel. The pistol is often referred to as the Mod. 1901, though there seems to be no such official designation. Very likely it had none. It seems to have been offered commercially in 1903 and it appeared at the Swedish trials of 1903 and 1904 and at U.S. trials in 1905. It was not adopted as it seemed too complicated. The pistol had the turning head, recoil-operated system and used an 8 mm. cartridge of Roth design. This particular round was later known as the Roth-Steyr

cartridge and was used in the Austrian M7 service pistol. The 1903 Frommer pistols were charger loaded from above into a butt well magazine of 10-round capacity. The rifling characteristics were stated to be as follows: diameter of bore, 0.314 inch; number of grooves, 4; direction of twist, right; one turn of rifling in 10 inches; depth of grooves, 0.008 inch; width of grooves, 0.155 inch; and width of lands, 0.09 inch.

In addition to the army trials already mentioned, it was submitted for trials in the United Kingdom, Austria, and Spain, in all of which it was rejected.

Mod. 1906—In 1906 a smaller and simplified version was introduced and became known as the Mod. 1906. In its original form, the pistol could be had either as a top-charging pistol with fixed butt well magazine (as in the earlier style) or with an insertable sheet-metal box magazine of the later conventional pattern, such as used by the Brownings. The first 1906 pistol was chambered for a small, underpowered 7.65 mm. cartridge, first designed by Roth for a vestpocket pistol ca. 1899. This little cartridge was later given over to J. P. Sauer u. Sohn (German agents for Roth) who adopted it for a small Roth-style pistol known as the Roth-Sauer, and it became known as the Roth-Sauer cartridge. Frommer adopted it at the same time that Sauer did and the cartridge became known also as the Roth-Frommer and, curiously, the Frommer pistol became known as the "Roth-Frommer," an appelation which is quite incorrect.

By 1910 the pistol was further modified, with the hope of increasing its sales appeal (Figs. 167, 168). A grip safety was added and the chambering was adapted to the more popular 7.65 mm. Browning cartridge. These changes improved the popularity of the pistol. The rifling characteristics of this improved model were stated to be: diameter of bore, 0.301 inch; number of grooves, 4; direction of twist, right; one turn of rifling in 10 inches; depth of grooves, 0.0055 inch; width of grooves, 0.120 inch; and width of lands, 0.110 inch.

This 1910 version of the Mod. 1906 Frommer did

TABLE 30

Data for French service models

Measurement	Mod. 1935-A	Mod. 1935-S	Mod. 1950 SE M.A.S.
Caliber	7.65 mm. Long	7.65 mm. Long	9 mm. Par.
Total length	7.6 inches	7.4 inches	7.6 inches
Barrel length	4.3 "	4.1 "	4.4 "
Weight, empty	26 ounces	28 ounces	33 ounces
Mag. capacity	8 ctges.	8 ctges.	9 ctges.
No. of grooves	4	4	4
Direction of twist	Right	Right	Left

not have a very long period of production because of World War I and the necessary diversion of all manufacturing facilities to the production of military items.

Stop Pat.—A second type of Frommer pistol, quite different in design, originated in 1911. This was the Stop Patent system, and is frequently called Mod. 1912. The system is characterized by the two-way recoil spring guide and spring system assembled in a tunnel above the barrel. The operating system is a complex rotating bolt head scheme with internal sleeves (Figs. 169 to 171). The Stop system Frommers were made in both 7.65 and 9 mm. (ACP) calibers. They were used in great numbers in World War I by the Austro-Hungarian armies. The 7.65 mm. Stop was given the nomenclature 19M (19 Minta Pisztoly). In the 1920's, production of the Stop design

gave way to the Browning system, as patented by Frommer. The Stop pistols seem to have been very popular in Austria; just why is a mystery. Like the other early Frommers, they were unnecessarily complicated and easily damaged, and malfunctions were frequent. Construction was too light, especially for a military weapon.

Baby—The Frommer Baby is a smaller version of the Stop and was made in both 7.65 mm. and 9 mm. calibers. The same objections apply to this model, which appears to have been designed as a vestpocket model for civilian use. One specimen examined, marked 7.65 mm., has a 9 mm. barrel.

Liliput—The Frommer 6.35 mm. Liliput, while somewhat similar in appearance to the Stop and Baby models, is different in design, having a blowback operated system. This is apparently the first Browning adaptation made by Frommer. Just when this model was first made is not known but it appeared

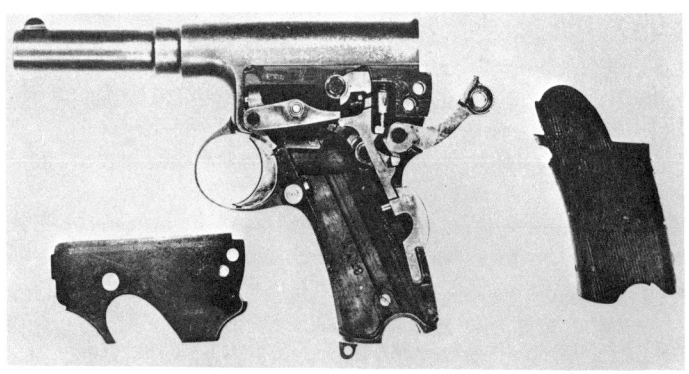

Fig. 167. 7.65 mm. (Brng.) Frommer Mod. 1910. Partially disassembled.

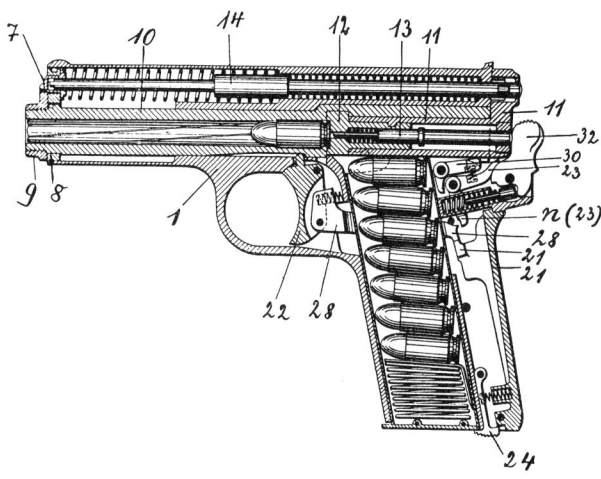

Fig. 169. 7.65 mm. Frommer Stop Mod. Sectional view.

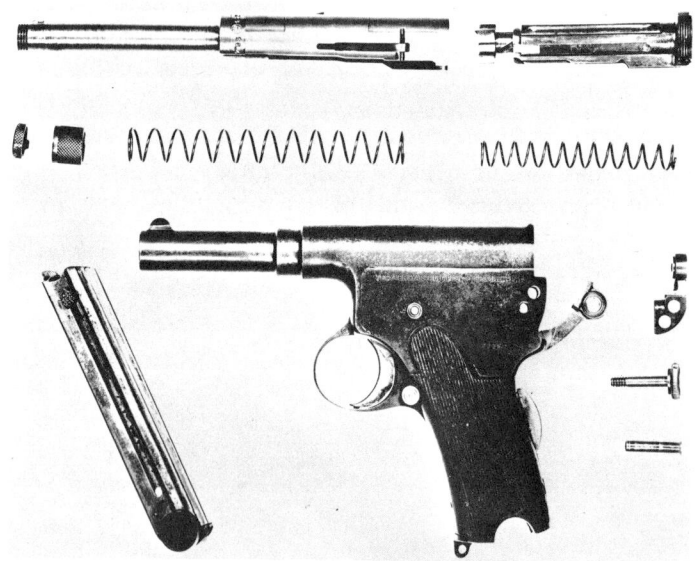

Fig. 168. 7.65 mm. (Brng.) Frommer Mod. 1910. Partially disassembled.

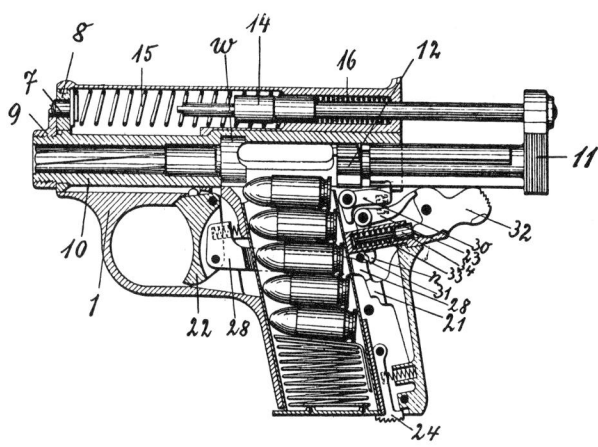

Fig. 170. 6.35 mm. Frommer Baby Mod. Sectional view.

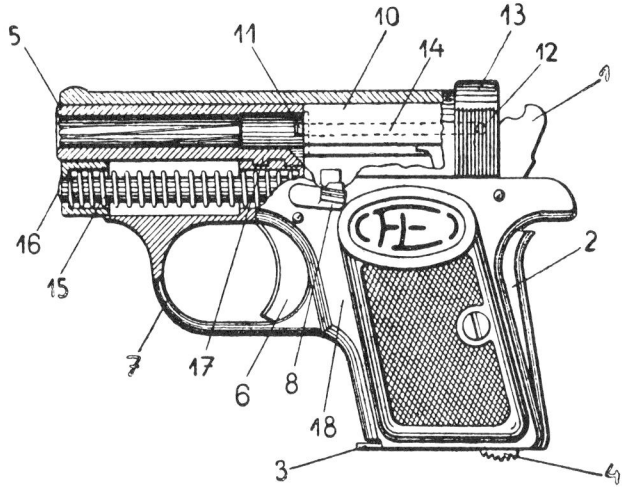

Fig. 171. 6.35 mm. Frommer Liliput Mod. Sectional view.

in 1923 advertisements, so it originated prior to that date. Gerhard Bock discusses this pistol in some detail in the 1923 edition of his *Moderne Faustfeuerwaffen*, but does not give the date of origin. How many were produced is not known. Since observed specimens have serial numbers in the 400,000 range it is suspected that their numbering either followed the Stop numbering or started at some arbitrary high number, perhaps 400,000, as it is not likely that 400,000 guns of this model were made.

Factory data for the Liliput as produced in 1923 are as follows: total length, 110 mm. (4.33″); barrel length, 54.5 mm. (2.14″); height, 75 mm. (2.95″); thickness, 18.5 mm. (0.73″); weight, ca. 300 gm. (10.5 oz); and magazine capacity, 6 ctges.

Mod. 29—The blowback type, patented by Rudolf von Frommer (or his estate), was adopted by the Hungarian military service under the designation Pisztoly 29M (the letter M stands for the word "Minta" meaning Model). The 29M was chambered for the 9 mm. Browning Short cartridge, the Hungarian nomenclature for which was "9 mm. 29M Eles Pisztoly Tolteny." The pistol was manufactured by the Fémáru Fegyver és Gépgyár R.T. (Metalwares, Small Arms and Machine Works, Ltd.) of Budapest. This firm was the post-World War I successor to the Fegyver és Gépgyár Részvénytársaság which had made the earlier Frommers. The earlier firm frequently had used the single word "Fegyvergyar" in marking their weapons and the later firm also frequently used the same designation.

The production of the 29M pistol took place between 1929 and 1935, starting with Serial No. 1 and continuing until about 50,000. When this model was

replaced by the 37M, the serial numbering continued from 50,000.

Sometime around 1932 or 1933, a .22 caliber version of the 29M was developed for gallery practice. The principal difference between the 9 mm. and the .22 models is the slide. The .22 caliber series was numbered from C-10,000, but it seems that only a few dozen were made. Other .22 variants have been reported. The author has examined a specimen Serial No. 3258 (on the frame) which is probably a .22 slide assembled on a regular M29 frame. This modification of the 29M came from the Colt Ace, which was patented in Hungary by Frommer in June 1932. All of this suggests that prototypes or converted forms (such as No. 3258) may date from 1929–1932 and that the complete new specimens (in the C-10,000 series) probably date from somewhere between 1932 and 1935. Because of their rarity not many of these will be encountered.

Mod. 37—In 1936 the M29 was simplified and certain elements eliminated. This redesigned version, also taking the 9 mm. Short cartridge, was adopted by the Hungarian military service as the Pisztoly 37M. Production of this 9 mm. pistol by Fegyvergyar seems to have stopped in 1942.

Early in 1941 the German Ordnance Department (Heereswaffenamt) gave the Hungarians an order for 50,000 pistols of the 37M to be provided with a 7.65 mm. caliber barrel instead of the 9 mm., for exclusive use of the Luftwaffe. While it is not officially confirmed, it appears that the earliest deliveries consisted of pistols having the conventional Hungarian markings, but in 7.65 mm. caliber. Such specimens of the "commercial" 7.65 mm. 37M are said to be found with serial numbers above 200,000, thus indicating that routine production of the 9 mm. 37M was diverted to the 7.65 mm. caliber. Ten specimens with serial numbers ranging from 5152 to 69,909, examined by the author, were all marked "*jhv*" (German code for Metallwaren, Waffen u. Maschinenfabrik, Budapest) and were made in the period 1941 to 1943. They bore German acceptance marks (Figs. 172, 173).

By mid-1941 a change was made in the 7.65 mm. type. A mechanical safety device was added to the frame, on the left side, the form of markings was changed to read Pistole M.37 Cal 7.65, and later in the year this was again changed to read P. Mod. 37. Kal. 7.65. The German three-letter code "jhv" was assigned to the firm, and this code together with the last two digits of the year of manufacture were added to the left side of the slide. The initial order of 50,000, given by the Germans, was filled by the second month of 1942. A second order was placed in

201

mid-1943 calling for delivery of 60,000 pistols, and work on this second contract continued until toward the end of 1944. By this time combat conditions, bombings, etc. became so serious that the program had to be stopped. The serial numbers for the first order ran, naturally, from 1 to 50,000; those for the second order began at 50,001 and continued to about 90,000.

Mod. 1939—A form of the Frommer STOP pistol in 9 mm. Short caliber has appeared with the marking M1939 and a spade-shaped device (meaning unknown) on the top frame housing. The origin and use of this pistol is unknown. It was made by the

Fig. 172. 7.65 mm. Hungarian Pistole M 37. World War II production.

Fig. 173. 7.65 mm. Hungarian Pistole M 37. Disassembled to show main features of construction.

Hungarian firm but apparently not for Hungarian service issue. Those seen do not follow either the nomenclature pattern or the marking style of the Hungarian service. They may have been made to fill some foreign order.

None of the pre-World War II Hungarian pistols were restored to production after 1945. In fact, the firm "Fegyvergyar" is no longer cited as a supplier of pistols. Current Hungarian service pistols are reportedly produced by two Budapest firms, Femaru es Szerszamgepgyar N.V. and Tomegyarto N.V. Details of pistols of current Hungarian make are not available. Lugs, in his *Rucni Palne Zbrane,* shows a photograph of a pistol which he captions a "Madarska pistole vz 48" (Hungarian pistol Mod. 48). From the photograph, this appears to be quite an exact copy of the Mod. PP Walther.

This reportedly unauthorized and but slightly modified Walther was manufactured by the first of the two plants mentioned above, a nationalized arms manufacturing plant. It seems to have been issued to the Hungarian police and special services but not used by the military nor sold commercially (for very good reasons!). A similar arm in 6.35 mm. caliber is reported to have been made and issued for police use.

Like the original Walther Mod. PP it is a blowback, double-action pistol, using the regular Browning type cartridges. The modifications made by the Hungarians consist of the lightening of the trigger guard unit and cutout and added mechanical safety in the form of a firing pin lock which prevents firing until the slide is fully closed, obviously a good feature. The chamber indicator is forced up instead of backward, as in the original Walther.

For the 7.65 mm. model the over-all length is 7 inches; barrel length, $3^{15}\!/_{16}$ inches; weight (empty), 1.65 pounds; and magazine capacity, 8 rounds. The military forces are probably equipped with the Russian Tokarev.

Gabilondo pistols

The name Gabilondo has been connected with the manufacture of firearms for over half a century and is well known the world over. It is one of three companies now permitted to make automatic pistols in Spain. It is also permitted to make revolvers.

The original firm was founded in 1904 under the name of Gabilondos y Urresti—the plural being used because two families of cousins were involved. In 1909 the cousins separated and the name was changed to Gabilondo y Urresti, under which name the company operated until July 1919, at which time the name was changed to its present form of Gabilondo y Cia., of Elgoibar.

Up to 1914 only revolvers were manufactured, such as the Velo Dog, Puppy, Nagant, etc. They also made the "Radium" pistol, sometimes called the "cigarette pistol" because of its appearance, the cartridges being stored inside the butt under a hinged grip. In 1914 they began the manufacture of automatic pistols, a venture which has brought them much success. These first pistols, discussed below, were produced under the name Ruby.

Ruby class (or "Eibar type")

Around 1910 the Spanish firearms industry began the manufacture of a style of automatic pistol patterned after the blowback, internal-hammer design used by Fabrique Nationale in their Modele 1903 (Browning) and by the Colt Co. in the manufacture of their Hammerless Pocket Model of 1903. The Spanish imitations differed in minor points from model to model, but all of them preserved the characteristics which easily marked them as Browning imitations. The common design was a 5- or 7-round type, in 7.65 mm. Browning pistol cartridge caliber. These arms are commonly referred to as the "Eibar Type."

In 1914 the firm of Gabilondo y Urresti, revolver manufacturers, of Elgoibar, introduced an Eibar Type pistol in 7.65 mm. caliber having a nine-round capacity, a feature considered new at the time. The trade name for this pistol was the "Ruby," for which name Gabilondo y Urresti received a Spanish "patent" in 1914, i.e., a copyright giving them exclusive use of the name for use on firearms (both pistols and revolvers). At the present time it is used only on revolvers, but has been used on automatic pistols of their make other than the ones now under discussion. This new pistol was evidently first introduced for commercial sale in the U.S. and in South America.

Soon after the outbreak of World War I the pistol was offered for use in the French Army, and after several tests and trials it was adopted as a subsidiary standard military pistol. The initial French order was placed in May 1915 and called for sustained delivery at the rate of 10,000 pistols a month. In August of 1915 the French increased their demand to a rate of 30,000 a month, but even this rate proved to be too small and further demands were made.

As Gabilondo y Urresti could not meet these constantly increasing demands, special arrangements were made with four other firms in Eibar. These firms were given contracts to produce not less than 5,000 pistols a month. Each firm was to manufacture the pistol under the trade name "Ruby" and to sup-

ply the pistols, together with spare magazines, to Gabilondo y Urresti for delivery to the French. It was provided that if these firms failed to make their quota of 5,000 per month they must pay a penalty for the difference; and, on the other hand, the parent firm was required to purchase all pistols produced in excess of the monthly quota. These first four firms were: Bruno Salaverria y Cia., Eibar; Eceolaza y Vicinai y Cia., Eibar; Hijos de Angel Echeverria y Cia., Eibar; Armera Elgoibaressa y Cia., Elgoibar.

A fifth firm, S. A. Alkartasuna, was organized in Guernica by employees of the Esperanza y Unceta company of that city, for the express purpose of manufacturing the pistol, to which, however, was given the name Alkar or Alkartasuna. (See Alkartasuna) This operation was authorized by Gabilondo y Urresti, so they state.

The combined production of these firms was still not sufficient to supply the demands of the French and still other firms took up the production of this pistol (or a similar one) under their own trade names. These firms were: Esperanza y Unceta, Guernica; S. A. Royal Vincitor, Eibar; Retolaza Hermanos y Cia., Eibar; Beistegui Hermanos, Eibar; Francisco Arizmendi y Goenaga, Eibar.

Although these firms produced independently, there was (it is claimed) an agreement with Gabilondo y Urresti which enabled them to control the prices of pistols delivered to the French. As the war progressed more firms took up the manufacture of this type of pistol but not under the Ruby name. Some bear no names, others are marked Model 1916 (or other year). The following additional firms are reported to have participated:

Azanza y Arrizabalaga, Eibar	Marked "Model 1916," etc.
Arizmendi, Zulaica y Cia., Eibar	Marked "Cebra"
Izidro Gaztañaga, Eibar	Marked "Destroyer"
Erquiaga y Cia., Eibar	Marked "Fiel"
Urrejola y Cia., Eibar	Marked "U. C."
M. Zulaica y Cia., Eibar	Marked "Model 1914," etc.

The total number manufactured and supplied directly by Gabilondo to the French Army is reported to have been somewhere between 150,000 and 200,000. No such large serial numbers have been seen by the author, however. How many were made by other manufacturers for the French will very likely never be known. During World War I a few were reportedly sold to the Italian Government.

At the close of World War I, production of this "military" type of Ruby pistol by Gabilondo was discontinued and a new type, patterned after the Mod. 1910 Browning by F.N., was introduced under the trade names Ruby, Bufalo, and Danton. But the production of the Eibar Type of pistol by other firms was by no means discontinued and was even taken up by firms not participating in the war production.

Other Spanish 7.65 mm. pistols of the Eibar Type, a number of which very closely resembled the Ruby in appearance, came on the market after the end of World War I and production seems to have continued for a number of years. Mail order houses in the U.S. contributed materially to their distribution. Some manufacturers of these Eibar Type pistols are the following: Hijos de C. Arrizabalaga, Eibar; Martin A. Bascaran, Eibar; Echave y Arizmendi, Eibar; Bonifacio Echeverria, Eibar; Iraola Salaverria y Cia., Eibar.

Still other guns of this type, whose makers are not known, have been encountered—such as one marked "L.C." on the frame (sold by Fab. d'Armes de Guerre); one marked "B.G." on the frame (possibly Gregorio Bolumburu); one having no markings except a serial number and a figure 9 in a circle on each grip; one marked "Vilar" and "Model 1924;" one marked "Demon" with a large star weakly impressed on rear of frame; and one marked "32 C. 1924 Automatic Pistol." Undoubtedly there were many more.

Most of the manufacturers whose names have appeared above made pistols other than the Eibar Type, some of which are quite well known.

Plus Ultra—The 7.65 mm. Plus Ultra, made by Gabilondo y Cia., appears to be of the general Eibar Type pistol, but it has a very long grip frame capable of taking a 20-round magazine. The factory reports that its manufacture was discontinued in 1932, which would be at the time that the Llama series was about to begin.

Ruby (Post-W. W. I. type) and Bufalo—As already stated, Gabilondo dropped the Eibar Type of pistol at the close of World War I. In its place they introduced an imitation of the F.N. Browning Mod. 1910, with screw-in muzzle bushing. This pistol was given the name Ruby. Soon thereafter (1919) a contract was made with Armeria Beristain y Cia., a sales organization in Barcelona, whereby the 7.65 and 9 mm. Browning Short pistols of this pattern were to be furnished exclusively to Beristain and sold by them under the name Bufalo. This meant that the name Ruby was dropped from the line of 1910 Browning imitations, but the name soon reappeared. The Beristain contract called for 100 pistols a day, to be sold in America and Spain.

In 1920 a 6.35 mm. vestpocket pistol, copied from the 1906 Browning, appeared under the name Ruby and was sold under this name from 1920 to 1925. It was also sold by Beristain under the name Bufalo.

The alliance between Gabilondo and Beristain apparently was based on the fact that the latter held

patents on a grip safety device and certain other features that Gabilondo desired to use. These patents date from 1916 and 1917. This is borne out by the fact that the original Ruby imitation of the 1910 Browning did not have a grip safety, but the Bufalo did throughout its period of production. Then, when the Bufalo name was dropped (due to cancellation of the contract with Beristain) and the Ruby reintroduced, the grip safety was eliminated. Cancellation of the contract was apparently due to the falling off of sales, particularly in the U.S., due to restrictive legislation on the sale of firearms that had been passed. The grip safety was reintroduced in about 1929 (on the Danton for example), by which time the patents on this device may have expired. The first Dantons (1925) did not have this safety.

In the case of the 6.35 mm. vestpocket type, which had been sold under both names (Ruby and Bufalo), the cancellation on the contract meant only the dropping of the name Bufalo, the production being continued under the name Ruby. An interesting point is that Ruby pistols, in all calibers, were now marked

MANUFACTURED IN SPAIN BY "RUBY" ARMS CO.
PATENT 70724 CAL. 7.65 (32)

for those of the 7.65 mm. caliber and similarly for the other calibers. The use of this fictitious firm name undoubtedly had some relation to the cancellation of the Beristain contract, perhaps only to draw attention back to the name Ruby and away from Beristain (Fig. 174).

Resumption of the production of the 7.65 mm. and 9 mm. Short (1910 Browning imitation) Ruby pistols meant that the pistols that had been produced under that name previous to the Beristain

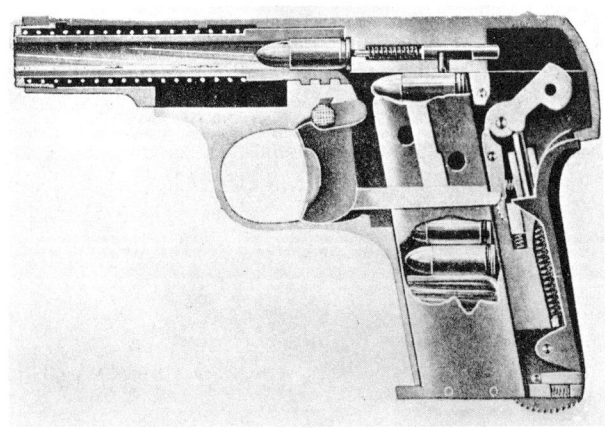

Fig. 174. 7.65 mm. Ruby marked "Ruby Arms Co." Sectional view.

contractual arrangement were now again being produced under the Ruby name. This production of the original model continued from approximately 1923 to 1926.

In 1925 several changes, including a better safety system (but not including a grip safety), were incorporated and the pistol was rechristened the Danton. It has been stated that both the Ruby and Danton were manufactured simultaneously from 1926 to 1929. Communications from Gabilondo y Cia. state that the 6.35 mm. vestpocket model was discontinued in 1925. Literature (undated but probably ca. 1930) describing the "Ruby Arms Co." pistols of 6.35, 7.65, and 9 mm. caliber shows that all three were provided with the grip safety, thus providing three safety devices. The grip safety was added about 1929 and was used until the discontinuance of manufacture.

Literature of the Ruby Arms Co. gives the data for the Ruby pistols as shown in Table 31.

Danton class

The Danton pistols were based on the Gabilondo imitations of the three Browning models of 1906, 1910, and 1922, appearing first under the names of Ruby and Bufalo, and are the last of the early Browning imitations produced. The first Danton pistols were made in 1925 and they went into full production in 1926. Between 1926 and 1932 several variant styles and types were made under the Danton name. Actually, some of these were identical to the Ruby and Bufalo models previously made. Production of the Danton model may have stopped in 1932, as reported, but they were being assembled and sold well into 1933, at which time they were replaced by the presently manufactured Llama series. The specific models of the Danton are given below.

6.35 mm. Mod.—The vestpocket model pistols are merely a carry-over from the vestpocket Ruby design, although they do show some mechanical improvements over the Ruby. There are two styles. The first type, dating from about 1929, has a mechanical safety mounted at the rear of the receiver and loaded by an external spring above the left grip

TABLE 31
Data for Ruby pistols

Measurement	6.35 mm. (6 shots)	7.65 mm. (7 shots) 9 mm. (6 shots)
Total length	115 mm.	150 mm.
Height	75 "	95 "
Maximum width	24 "	30 "
Weight, mag. empty	400 gm.	650 gm.

piece—a modernization of the Ruby mechanical safety which was located above the trigger. The second type, dating from about 1930, is identical to the first except that it has a grip safety not present on the first type.

7.65 mm. Mod.—These medium-size pistols are merely variant forms of the 1910/22 forms of the F.N. Browning. There are two basic frame styles and six forms of the pistol in this caliber: (a) The first style, dating from 1926, has a 7-round capacity, with a mechanical safety of the Eibar pattern (above the trigger) and a magazine release on the underside of the grip frame. (b) The second style also dates from 1926 and is identical to the first style, except that it has a 12-round capacity and a longer grip frame. Both of the 1926 styles have a ring lanyard loop on the left side of the grip frame, near the base. (c) The third style introduced a newer and more streamlined grip frame, with a modernized mechanical safety which is moved to the rear of the receiver, on the left, and is loaded by an external spring. It has a 7-round capacity and the lanyard loop is eliminated. (d) The fourth style is the same as the third, dating from about 1929, but has a 9-round capacity. (e) The fifth style dates from about 1930 and is identical to the third style but has the addition of a grip safety. (f) The sixth style is identical to the fourth except that it also has the grip safety.

9 mm. Browning Short—This was introduced in about 1929 and embodies the improved grip frame. There are two styles: (a) identical to the third style of the 7.65 mm. (above) but having an 8-round capacity; and (b) identical to the first 7.65 mm. style but having the grip safety.

The last Danton pistols made, in 6.35, 7.65, and 9 mm. calibers, were produced in two forms, with and without the grip safety. As stated above, all production of the Dantons had ceased by 1933.

Llama series

Automatic pistols made by Gabilondo from 1914 to 1933 were based on Browning F.N. models of 1903, 1906, 1910, and 1922. In 1931 it was decided to modernize their line by undertaking the manufacture of the external hammer, recoil-operated system originally designed by Browning and used by Colt and the Fabrique Nationale. Work on a new design began in 1931 and culminated in 1932 with a Spanish patent issued on April 12th of that year. The first pistol produced was an exact copy of the Colt Mod. 1911A1, but without the grip safety, and in 9 mm. Largo (Bergmann) and .38 ACP calibers. To this weapon was given the trade name "Llama" which is the name for currently made Gabilondo pistols. For some reason this first model produced later was designated Model IV.

Shortly after the production of this first model, a blowback style based upon the external shape of the Colt-Browning was introduced. A further improvement of the blowback pattern was undertaken and this second blowback style was issued from 1935 on. Somewhat later a variant pattern in 9 mm. Parabellum caliber was produced. After the close of World War II certain models were dropped, grip safeties were added to the remaining models, and a .22 caliber pistol was introduced.

Some details concerning the various Llama models are as given below.

Mod. I.—This was a 7.65 mm. Browning caliber, original blowback style, dating from about 1933-1934, first issued without model designation, with factory catalog designation No. 529. It was an imitation of Colt Mod. 1911.

Mod. II.—This 9 mm. Short version of the Mod. I was identical to Mod. I except for magazine capacity.

Mod. III.—This was a 9 mm. Short, second blowback pattern and more closely approached the external shape of the Mod. 1911A1 Colt. It dates from about 1935 and is believed to have replaced the first two models in distribution and to have been dropped from production in 1954.

Mod. III-A.—This post-World War II version of Mod. III is distinguished by the addition of the grip safety but otherwise is the same as Mod. III. Several styles of grip pieces and markings have been noted.

Mod. IV.—This was the original Llama pistol, dating from 1931–32, in 9 mm. Largo (Bergmann) caliber. It is a full-size reproduction of the Colt-Browning recoil-operated pistol Mod. 1911. When first issued no model number was assigned but the factory catalog designation was No. 528. It has been suggested that the name Modello IV may have been reserved for the Tauler pistol which is identical to it. Both are identical to the Llama Mod. VII.

Mod. V.—Made in 9 mm. Largo (Bergmann) and .38 ACP calibers this appears to be the export version of Mod. IV. It is marked .38 caliber rather than 9 mm. It was made prior to World War II only.

Mod. VI.—This has been reported to be in 9 mm. Browning Short caliber, heavier than Mod. III, but this has not been confirmed. Fully recoil-operated Llama pistols of the Mod. VII (or IV) style are known to have been made in the 7.63 Mauser caliber, expressly for the German trade, and it is possible that the designation of Mod. VI may have been given to these pistols. This is purely a conjecture.

Mod. VII.—This pistol in 9 mm. Largo/.38 ACP is identical to Mod. IV and is, therefore, the original

Llama pistol, manufacture of which dates from 1932. This model was produced until about 1954.

Mod. VIII.—This is identical to the Mod. VII, but with the addition of a grip safety. This addition seems to have been the first application of a grip safety to a Llama pistol and was introduced prior to World War II. This pistol is still made.

Mod. IX.—First described as a recoil-operated style of the Mod. VII, but in three calibers: 7.65 mm. Parabellum, 9 mm. Largo, and .45 ACP. However, factory literature of 1936–39 shows this model in .45 cal. ACP only. It was manufactured from about 1936 to 1954.

Mod. IX-A.—This is the .45 ACP caliber, to which a grip safety was added immediately following World War II. This pistol is still in production.

Mod. X.—This pistol, in 7.65 mm. caliber, was issued along with Mod. III and is merely a smaller version of that model (Fig. 175). It appears to be identical to Mod. I, to which no model number was originally assigned. This dates from about 1935 and was produced until about 1954. A Model X-1 has been noted, but details are unknown. It may be a special variant of the Mod. X.

Mod. X-A.—This is identical to Mod. X, with the addition of a grip safety, which was added immediately following World War II. It is still in production.

Mod. XI.—This is a 9 mm. Parabellum caliber with a variant style of grip frame and hammer and has no grip safety. Earlier issues had a lanyard ring at bottom of left side of the grip frame, but this ring was omitted in later issues and the grip pieces were redesigned. It was produced from 1936 and was still made in 1953 but does not appear in 1955 factory literature.

There are no Llama pistols designated as Models XII, XIII, and XIV as these designations have been reserved for and are used on the Llama revolvers.

Mod. XV.—This is a .22 caliber (Long Rifle) pis-

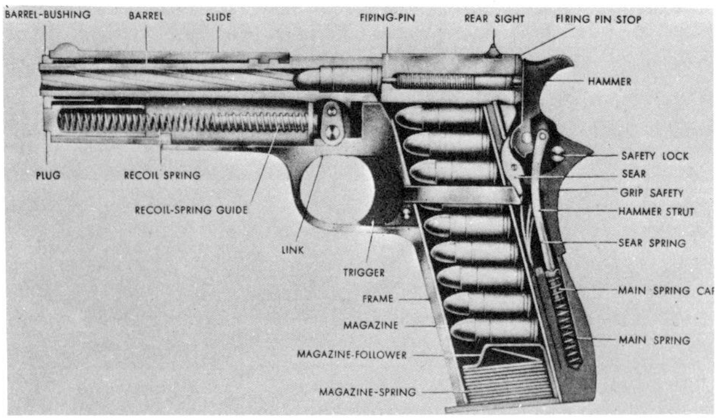

Fig. 175. Cross section of typical Llama pistols.

tol which follows the same general design as the other recent Llama models. It has a double grip safety. This is a post-World War II production.

Mugica pistols

The Mugica automatic pistols are a product of Gabilondo y Cia., sold by José Cruz Mugica, a manufacturer of shotguns in Eibar. A 1958 communication from the former states that the Mugica is the same as the Llama "produced specially for Mr. Mugica to fill an order from Siam." In 1951, however, the Mugica firm issued a four-page pamphlet describing in some detail several models of the Mugica pistol he was offering for sale. The three models illustrated all bear Mugica's markings, including his trade mark on the grips. A typical slide marking is josé cruz mugica – eibar (españa) cal – 7.65 (32) "mugica".

The pistols sold by Mugica and the similar Llama models are given in Table 32.

Tauler pistols

The Tauler automatic pistols were identical to certain models of the Llama series produced by Gabilondo y Cia. and were given special markings for sale by Senor Tauler of Madrid. Tauler was a gunsmith and in addition was an Olympic champion and at one time Captain of the Secret Police.

Gabilondo agreed to supply pistols marked with the Tauler trade mark for those contracts and sales made by Senor Tauler to Spanish police departments and other government departments. The Tauler name (or trade mark) was patented (or registered) on December 13, 1933. Llama pistols were produced and sold under this name from 1933 until 1935, according to information supplied by the Gabilondo firm.

The Tauler pistols and their identical Llama counterparts, sold under this arrangement, were as follows: Tauler Mod. I, 7.65 mm., and Llama Mod. I; Tauler Mod. II, 9 mm., and Llama Mod. II; Tauler

TABLE 32

Pistols sold by Mugica and similar Llama models

Mugica model	Description	Llama model
101-G	7.65 mm. Has grip safety.	X-A
101	Same as Mod. 101-G, without grip safety.	X
105-G	9 mm. Short (.380). Has grip safety.	III-A
105	Same as Mod. 105-G, without grip safety.	III
110-G	9 mm. Long (.38). Has grip safety.	VIII
110	Same as Mod. 110-G, without grip safety.	VII
120	9 mm. Parabellum	XI

Mod. III, 9 mm. Short, and Llama Mod. III; Tauler Mod. IV, 9 mm. Largo (Bergmann), and Llama Mod. VII; and Tauler Mod. V, .38 Super (ACP), and Llama Mod. VII.

Tauler pistols may be encountered with several forms of trade marks; the earliest type coincides with the first Llama trade mark (that of a heart within a circle), the second type shows a dog's head within a circle, and the last showed a kneeling Indian with bow and arrows. This last mark appears on a Tauler pistol marked "tauler mark p - cal. 9 mm." This specimen appears identical to the Llama Mod. VIII, a model which was provided with a grip safety prior to World War II.

Galesi pistols

These pistols are manufactured by the Industria Armi Galesi, located in Collebeato (Brescia), Italy. The firm was founded in 1910 by Nicola Galesi, the father of Giuseppe Galesi who is the present proprietor. The first pistol was made in 1914 and production continued until 1923. In 1923 (or soon thereafter) production of the second model began. This model was based on Pat. No. 219,408 issued to Nicola Galesi on March 30, 1923. Just when production was started is not known, nor is it known how many were manufactured before it gave way to the Mod. 1930. Specimens known to have been made in 1928 bear serial numbers in the 130,000 range. This pistol was of the blowback type with no particularly distinctive or outstanding features. It was produced in both 6.35 and 7.65 mm. calibers.

In 1930 a new model appeared, based on Pat. No. 297,441 issued to Nicola Galesi on June 7, 1930, and it became known as the 1930 Model. This was also made in both 6.35 and 7.65 mm. calibers until 1936, when it was also issued in 9 mm. caliber. This change did not involve any change in model nomenclature. Specimen No. 138,827 in 6.35 mm. caliber dated 1937 shows the sliding floor plate and probably is one of the last to have this feature.

The 9 mm. version of this model was made for war service and is so marked. Following the Italian surrender, possibly as early as 1944, production of the Mod. 1930 in 7.65 mm. caliber was resumed. Speciman No. 145,233 (though undated) is probably of this vintage. It has an extension of the magazine floor plate which forms a rest for the little finger, thus producing a somewhat better grip.

Following World War II (in 1950) the designation of the pistol was again changed, becoming the Mod. 9, but with no important basic changes. Specimens of the 6.35 Mod. 1930 pistols dated 1937 appear to be identical to 6.35 mm. Mod. 9 which are dated 1947, with the exception of the design of the grip plates, the use of finer serrations in the finger grips on the slide, and the slightly more streamlined grip frames on the 1947 Mod. Observed specimens of the Mod. 1930 did not have raised front and rear sights, but such are provided on some (but not all) of the 7.65 mm. Mod. 9 pistols.

The Mod. 9 is produced in .22 Short, .22 Long, .22 L.R., 6.35 mm., and 7.65 mm. calibers and in different sized models for the same caliber. Also, they are available in a profusion of finishes and grip materials for each caliber and size. In fact no less than 54 quotations appear in the price list. All Galesi pistols are numbered consecutively, each caliber having a separate numbering series irrespective of model. Up to June 1959 over 300,000 pieces had been made, including all calibers and models.

The Galesi pistols are widely advertised and apparently well known in this country and, no doubt, will continue to be so, for they are very attractive in appearance. and their stainless steel barrels should render them less likely to corrode and less subject to wearing away of the rifling.

Gaztañaga pistols

The pistol known as the Destroyer was made at Eibar, Spain, by Isidro Gaztañaga. While it is one of the less important pistols, it, nevertheless, is frequently encountered in this country and therefore deserves some comment.

It appears in both 6.35 and 7.65 mm. calibers and is of the Eibar Type, i.e., a copy of the 1906 Browning. The earlier pistols produced, e.g., No. 1699 (marked Model 1913) in 6.35 mm. caliber and No. 1878 (marked Model 1914) in 7.65 mm. caliber, have the thumb safety located back of the left grip plate, whereas later pistols in both calibers have it located in front of the grip plate.

Some specimens, in each caliber, will be found with plain white plastic grip plates while others have checkered hard rubber plates. Some specimens have plain checkered grip plates, while others have a monogram containing the letters I.G. with the word DESTROYER below. Usually the name I. Gaztañaga appears on the slide, or the initials I.G. may appear enclosed in an ellipse at the rear end of the slide, on the left side. The wording of the slide inscription varies. Some, particularly those of early production, bear a model date. Presumably this "model date" simply refers to the year in which the pistol was made.

No information is available as to the total produc-

tion. Known specimens range from No. 1699 to 81,741 for the 6.35 mm. and from No. 1878 to 46,723 for the 7.65 mm. Of course there may have been many more, and it is not known whether the two calibers were numbered in the same or in separate numbering series.

No factory data have been found, but the 1914 catalog of the Union des Fabricants d'Armes de Eibar states that the 6.35 model fired 6 shots and weighed 310 grams, while the 7.65 mm. pistol fired 7 shots and weighed 590 grams. Data from the *Pistolen Atlas* give the magazine capacities as 6 and 7 cartridges, respectively, but give the weights (including empty magazine) as 326 grams for the 6.35 mm. and 633 grams for the 7.65. As to dimensions, measured specimens of the 6.35 had an over-all length of 100 mm. (4″) and height of 75 mm. (3″), while the 7.65 pistol was 150 mm. (5⅞″) in length and 122 mm. (4¾″) high. Barrel lengths are 51 mm. (2″) and 83 mm. (3¼″), respectively.

Isidro Gaztañaga was one of the many Spanish manufacturers who made pistols for the French Army during World War I. Whether the pistols he supplied were his regular 7-round magazine type or the 9-round magazine (Ruby) type is not known.

Indian Model—This appears to be identical to a 7.65 mm. Destroyer that was called the Army Model. Both had longer grips than the regular pistol of this caliber, in order to use a 9-cartridge magazine.

Super Destroyer—This pistol is described as being similar to the Walther Mod. PP and presumably is a copy thereof. It was made by the firm Gaztañaga, Trocaola e Ibarzabal of Eibar, and was sold by José Cruz Mugica, a dealer in Eibar. The manufacturing firm ceased making pistols in July 1936.

Glisenti pistols

The original Glisenti pistol was patented in Italy on June 30, 1905, by the Societa Siderurgica Glisenti, Carcina (Brescia), Italy. It was manufactured by this firm from 1906 on and was originally called the Pistola Automatica Glisenti. The pistol was adopted by the Italian Army in 1906, as the Pistola Automatica M906, and at the time was chambered for the 7.65 mm. Parabellum cartridge. In 1909, however, it was decided to increase the caliber to 9 mm. and to use a weakly loaded Parabellum cartridge. This new-caliber pistol was actually adopted in 1910 and the name was changed to Pistola Automatica M910. Some are marked as having been made in 1909 (Fig. 176).

Despite statements that the Naval issue was distinguished from the Army issue by the presence of an eagle crest on the grips, no evidence supporting this claim exists. In fact, the official Italian War Ministry publication describing the Army issue shows such an eagle crest on the grip pieces. The M906 also shows this eagle crest, and it also appears on the Brixia, developed from the Glisenti.

It appears that the manufacture of this Glisenti pistol did not continue for very long, perhaps because it was difficult for it to displace the well established Mod. 89 Service revolver.

For changes in the Glisenti, made in the hope of increasing its popularity, see the section on the Brixia pistol.

Helfricht pistols

These German pistols, which were also sold under the name Helkra, were reportedly patented by Hugo Helfricht of Zella-Mehlis, and were manufactured by Alfred Krausser of that city. The name Helkra no doubt was derived by combing the first three letters from the names Helfricht and Krausser.

These pistols seem to have originated sometime around 1920. There appear to have been four models (or, more properly, types, as no model designations seem to have been made before the appearance of Mod. 4, which is definitely so-marked). In the first types there is an external safety lever, covered in part by the left grip plate, having (at the left) a knurled head operated by the thumb and extending back of the grip plate to the rear of the frame where the end (hook-like in shape) can be engaged in a notch in the lower edge of the slide. By pushing down on the knurled head in front of the left grip plate the slide is securely locked and the gun cannot be fired.

In the type shown in the Max Leppner Catalog

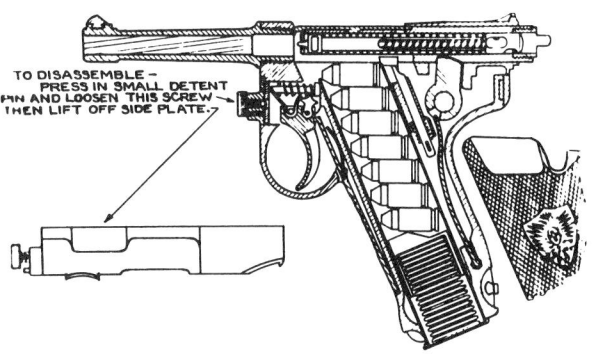

Fig. 176. 9 mm. Glisenti Mod. 1910. Sectional view.

(Zella-Mehlis, Germany) of ca.1921–1922, which is thought to be Type 3, the safety lever is completely covered, with the exception of the exposed head to the left of the grip plate. The specimen bearing serial No. 335 (shown in the Pistol Atlas) and a specimen examined by the author, from which the serial number had been removed, have the long, exposed safety lever.

In the types preceding Mod. 4 the slide does not extend the full length of the pistol but stops about 3/4 inch from the muzzle end, thus giving the pistol a peculiar and unsightly appearance. Mod. 4, however, has a full-length slide and also has the concealed safety lever. Rifling in all known specimens consists of six grooves with right hand twist. Other than the features mentioned above, there is nothing noteworthy about these pistols. It is reported that a 7.65 mm. version of the Helfricht was made, but none have been encountered, nor have descriptions of any been seen.

These pistols are frequently referred to as the Karl Helfricht or K. Helfricht pistols. No pistols with either of these names have been seen, and what authority there may be for the use of either of them is not known. The pistols bear the inscription HEL-FRICHT PATENT, and the monogram on the grip plates consists of the letters KH, overlapping. These letters may come from the names Krausser and Helfricht, or there may have been a Karl Helfricht connected in some way with them.

High Standard pistols

The presently named High Standard Manufacturing Corporation, of Hamden, Conn., started out in 1926 as the High Standard Manufacturing Company, in New Haven, Conn., when C. G. Swebilius and three other men began the manufacture of gun barrel drills. At that time the firm had three employees. In 1932 the firm acquired the Hartford Arms and Equipment Co., of Hartford, Conn. This firm had developed and produced a single-shot pistol, a repeating pistol, and an automatic pistol. Although this firm was in operation for only about two years it appears that they made a few thousand pistols, judging from observed serial numbers. There were at least two models of the automatic pistol, differing, however, only in the weights of their barrels and in the types of grip plates used. The failure of this firm enabled the High Standard company to buy their tools, equipment, etc. at a bankruptcy sale.

The first HI-Standard pistols produced naturally bore a close resemblance to the Hartford. The early Model A, however, was provided with an adjustable

209

rear sight and some dimensions were changed slightly. The early Model B was a replica of the Hartford. In 1940, Model B was redesigned, a slide take-down lever being incorporated on the right side of the frame in place of the old style lever located on the left, just back of the safety. This model was chambered for the .22 L.R. cartridge, and a similar model, Model C, was chambered for the .22 Short. As is the case with most subsequent models, these were obtainable in two barrel lengths, 4½ or 6¾ inches. They had fixed sights and hard rubber grip pieces. Numerous other models followed.

In addition to the original Mod. A (essentially the Hartford) it appears that another Mod. A was introduced in 1936, and one quite similar but having an external hammer and no thumb safety was also produced as Mod. H-A. The external hammer versions are designated by the use of the letter H before the model letter used for the hammerless model.

A variation of the Mod. B was produced in smooth bore, especially designed for .22 Short shot cartridges. This was designated Mod. S-B and was obtainable with 4½-inch barrel only. Mod. B was also produced in an external hammer version, without the thumb safety, and this was designated Mod. H-B. Mod. D was like Mod. A except that it had a heavier barrel, which increased the weight from 36 to 40 ounces. Mod. H-D was the same as Mod. D but with an external hammer and no thumb safety. Mod. H-DM was the same as Mod. H-D but with thumb safety. This model was the outcome of a war-developed model which will be mentioned later. Under the designation H-DM or H-D Military Model it was made from 1946 to 1951.

Mod. E was derived from Mod. A by using an extra-heavy barrel and grips provided with a thumb rest. With the 6¾-inch barrel the total weight was 42 ounces as against 36 ounces for Mod. A. Mod. H-E was the same as Mod. E except that it had an external hammer and no thumb safety.

All of the above-mentioned (except Mod. H-DM) are pre-World War II models and all were discontinued in 1942 because of the advent of that war.

During the first part of World War II the company was engaged in the manufacture of machine gun barrels for the British and later for the U.S. Ordnance Department. This led to a separation of the commercial part of the business from the military, and in 1941 the High Standard Manufacturing Corporation was formed to manufacture pistols, gun barrels, etc. This new corporation acquired new space and increased its personnel and facilities for producing gun barrel drills, .30 caliber Browning machine gun barrels, .45 caliber pistol barrels, rifle barrels, and component parts of artillery and bomb fuses.

In 1943 the firm developed and produced a .22 caliber automatic pistol for military training, and this was given the designation Mod. U.S.A.–H-D, and following the war (in 1946) this became Mod. H-DM (or H-D Military Model). As noted above, its manufacture ceased in 1951.

In 1947 High Standard produced the first of a new series of pistols, known as the G series. The first to be produced represented quite an innovation as it was in .380 caliber, whereas all prior pistol manufacture had been confined to .22 caliber. This pistol was designated Mod. G. It had an external hammer, a thumb safety, 6-cartridge magazine (instead of the customary 10), 5-inch barrel, fixed sights, and checkered plastic stocks. It weighed 40 ounces and was made until 1950. The G series marked the introduction of a new type of disassembly. To remove the barrel and slide, a small latch located in front of the trigger guard is pushed down, whereupon both the barrel and slide can be removed by pushing them forward off the frame.

The .22 caliber members of the G series, produced from 1949 to 1951, consisted of the following:

Mod. G-B—A hammerless model with interchangeable barrels, 4½ and 6¾ inches in length. With the longer barrel it weighed 36 ounces and was 10¾ inches in length. It had fixed sights and the customary 10-round magazine.

Mod. G-D—This was similar to Mod. G-B, in general, but was slightly longer. It had a heavier barrel, bringing the weight up to 41 ounces with the 6¾-inch barrel. It was provided with target sights.

Mod. G-E—This model had the same general specifications as the Mod. G-D but had an extra-heavy barrel, increasing the weight to 44 ounces with the 6¾-inch barrel.

The G series was followed by the .22 caliber Olympic model, of which there were three variations which appeared in 1950, 1951, and 1954, respectively. In this series the disassembly latch in front of the trigger guard was replaced by a push button (or rod) which accomplished the same purpose, i.e., releasing the barrel and slide.

Olympic (First model)—This model had no official designation as Mod. I, nor were the following models given any specific model designation. The first model was made in 1950 and 1951. It had the same general specifications as the Mod. G-E but had a light alloy slide and was chambered for the .22 Short cartridge instead of the L.R.

Olympic (Second type)—The second type, made from 1951 to 1954, was of the same general design as the Supermatic (introduced in the same year) but was chambered for the .22 Short cartridge, had a light alloy slide, and weighed 39 ounces with the 6¾-inch barrel. An interchangeable 4½-inch barrel could be had.

Olympic (Third type)—This type was introduced in 1954. It had a new positive-lock safety, new assembly slide lock, adjustable target rear sight, ramp-type front sight, front and back straps grooved to improve the grip, molded grips (checkered and with thumb rest), raised serrated rib on top of barrel, hooded breech, and adjustable (2- and 3-ounce) weights.

Supermatic model—This model and the Olympic (third type) are alike except that this is chambered for the .22 L.R. cartridge. Like the Olympic it had a built-in stabilizer (muzzle brake) and adjustable balancing weights. It also had the same type of target sights, with click adjustments for windage and elevation. In each model the slide locks automatically in the open position after the last shot has been fired. Both the Olympic and Supermatic were especially designed for expert target shooting.

In 1959 there was a radical change made in the Supermatics. Three models were offered. The Supermatic Trophy and the Supermatic Citation are basically alike, but the former is a de luxe model and far more expensive. The Supermatic Citation Olympic is the same as the .22 L.R. model but takes the .22 Short cartridge. These new Supermatics are characterized particularly by having a new type of barrel. Instead of the heavy, weighted barrel formerly used, the new barrel is slender for the greater part of its length and has longitudinal grooves on its outer surface for the purpose of damping vibrations. At the muzzle end the barrel is large in diameter and is not fluted. This gives more weight at that point and more stability. In addition there is an easily detachable stabilizer firmly installed in concentric alignment with the bore. Improvement in the sights, trigger, and arrangement of hammer and sear are also claimed.

Sport King model—This model was introduced as a general purpose, low-cost model. It was originally produced in 1950. It uses the .22 L.R. cartridge, has a magazine capacity of 10, checkered plastic thumb rest grip and fixed sights. Like the other recent models, interchangeable barrels, 4½ and 6¾ inches, were available. By 1954 it was provided with a new positive lock safety and could be had with either a steel or a forged aluminum frame. With the steel frame and 6¾-inch barrel the weight is 40 ounces, whereas with the aluminum frame and the same length barrel the weight is 30 ounces.

Field King model—This .22 L.R. caliber model was introduced in 1950. As first produced, this pistol was practically identical to the Sport King, except that it had a heavier barrel and was provided with an adjustable rear target sight. It evidently was designed as a less expensive target pistol, compared to the Olympic and Supermatic. This model is not described in the 1958 factory literature and presumably has been discontinued.

Flite King model—This model, greatly resembling the Sport King in appearance, was introduced in 1953. It is chambered for the .22 Short cartridge. It has a light alloy slide and is the lightest of all the models, weighing only 26 ounces with the 6¾-inch barrel.

Duramatic model—This is a lower-priced model, intended for general use, which was introduced in 1954. Several changes in design are incorporated. Instead of the push-button device for unlocking barrel and slide, a circular unlocking nut set into a slot in the slide just in front of the trigger guard is used. Also, different types of thumb safety and magazine release are used and the grip pattern is new. Interchangeable barrels, 4½ and 6½ inches in length, may be used. This appears to be the first time a 6½-inch barrel has been used on any model. This model is not in the 1958 advertising and presumably has been dropped.

Conversion unit—A "quick change" conversion unit, enabling one to use both L.R. or Short cartridges in the Supermatic, Olympic, Field King, and some of the earlier High Standard models, is available.

The High Standard products have an excellent reputation, and among the expert target shooters the Olympic and Supermatic models are preferred above all others.

Japanese pistols

Military types

The three standard military pistols used by the Japanese, all of which were of 8 mm. caliber, were the Nambu (designed in 1904), the Nambu Type 14 (1925), and the Nambu Type 94 (1934). A 7 mm. nonstandard type, to be discussed later, was also used to some extent by officers.

Japanese pistols naturally are marked in Japanese, either in words or symbols (the latter being used to designate arsenals). The Japanese characters appearing on the right side of the receiver on the Nambu (1904), reading from left to right, stand for the words Nambu Shiki (meaning Nambu Type or

211

Style). Those appearing on the left side of the receiver on the Nambu Type 14 (1925), reading from left to right, stand for Juyonen Shiki (meaning 14 Year Type), while those on the Nambu Type 94 (1934), reading from right to left, stand for Kyuyon Shiki (meaning 94 Type). No type (or model) designation was given to the first Nambu, but, as it was designed in 1904, it seems proper to refer to it as the Nambu (1904) to distinguish it from the later types. These later types were given designations that need some explanation.

The reign of the Japanese Emperor preceding the present Emperor Hirohito was known as "Taisho." He took the throne in 1911, so Type 14 (1925) means the "Type of the 14th Year of the Taisho reign" (i.e., 1911 + 14 = 1925).

Hirohito became Emperor in 1925, his reign being known as "Showa." Thus guns bearing the date (right hand side) 18.11 were made in the 11th month of the 18th year of Showa, or November of the year 1925 + 18 (= 1943).

The entire name of the original Nambu pistol is (from the Japanese characters) RIKU SHIKI NAMBU KENJU (meaning, Army Type Nambu Pistol).

The characters for the Nambu Type 14 (1925) stand for KENJU SHIKI 14(1925) or Pistol Type 14 (1925).

The Nambu Type 94 (1934) is named according to a different system. Previous to 1926 the Type (or Model) number of weapons and other equipment was indicated by the year of the reign in which the model was adopted, as explained above. From 1926 to 1940, however, a model was given a number derived from the assumed date of the founding of the Japanese Empire. The last two digits were used to designate the model. Since this particular model was adopted in the Japanese year 2594 (our year 1934), the designation Nambu Type 94 (1934) was assigned as official nomenclature.

Nambu (1904)—The first self-loading pistol used by the Japanese was designed by General (then Major) Kijiro Nambu in 1904. This pistol is frequently referred to as the Model 14 Nambu; but this is erroneous as there was never any such official designation. In its original form it had the designation Riku Shiki Nambu Kenju and was usually referred to simply as the Nambu. Just when production began is not known, but it appears to have been around 1906. It was manufactured by a firm directed by Major Nambu. Officers of the army were allowed to purchase and carry it, though noncommissioned officers were required to carry the Mod. 26 9 mm. revolver. This original manufacturing company continued operations and by the time of World War II

was called the Kokura Rikugun Zoheisho, of Tokyo. It was also known as the Kayoba Factory. The Nambu was also made by the Tokio Gas and Electric Co. about the time of World War I. As made by this firm there were some minor variations of construction and this firm used its own numbering system, starting with No. 1. These pistols can be identified by the presence of the symbol used by the Tokyo Gas and Electric Co.

This original model had a grip safety (omitted in the later model) but no mechanical safety (present on the later model). It had a safety device which prevented firing until the breech is fully locked in position, i.e., an automatic disconnector. It also had adjustable rear sights, which were omitted on the later model. As originally made the pistol was provided with a leather or wood case-shoulder stock which could be attached to the grip frame to convert the pistol into a carbine, a feature copied from Mauser. As the case was in itself too short there was present a telescopic extension which could be pulled out to give the necessary length. Not all of the original Nambu models had this feature and it was given up when the later model was produced. In both models the bolt remains in the open position after the last shot is fired.

Nambu Type 14 (1925)—In 1925 the Japanese Army adopted a modified and improved version of the earlier pistol, and this was designated the Kenju Shiki 14 (Pistol Type 14), to which (1925) was added for the benefit of those not understanding the peculiar system of numbering used by the Japanese.

Manufacture of this pistol was carried out by several government arsenals other than those mentioned, among which were Nagoya Rikugun Zoheisho; Nambu Seisakusho; and Matsu Zoheisho, of Tokio.

The Type 14 (1925) will be found with both Army and Navy markings. A variant form incorporated a spring-holding device for the magazine and a considerably enlarged trigger guard to facilitate the introduction of a gloved finger. The original, rather small, trigger guard had been found to be too small for winter operations. This improvement was made sometime in the late 1930's.

Nambu Type 94 (1934)—The Type 94 pistol was designed by Nambu in 1934 and was intended for commercial sale, particularly in South America and other countries having many Japanese residents. It was first designated as the Automatic Pistol Type B and was made at the Nambu factory. When World War II began it was adopted for military use and production was taken over by Government arsenals (Fig. 177).

The pistol is poorly designed and not well made.

In addition it is a very dangerous weapon as the sear is exposed and a slight pressure on this, when the pistol is cocked, will cause the weapon to discharge. This same feature is present in the Baby Nambu as well. Weapons which have features such as this are very dangerous indeed in the hands of persons who do not know the hazards involved in handling them. Fortunately, ammunition for the 8 mm. Japanese pistols is difficult to get, and for the 7 mm. it is impossible.

7 mm. types

A 7 mm. version of the original Nambu pistol was produced in the early 1920's. Essentially it is a smaller model of the original Nambu, though it differs in some minor features. It is 6¾ inches long as compared to about 9 inches, weighs 23 ounces as compared to 29 ounces, and has a magazine capacity of 7 cartridges whereas the 8 mm. type accommodates 8 cartridges. The cartridge is one especially designed for this gun. The grip safety was retained.

These small pistols were apparently favored by army officers because they were easy to carry, hence the pistol became known as the Officers' Model. Because of its size it is also known, in this country, as the Baby Nambu. The pistol was not produced in great numbers. Official reports indicate that the total production was about 3000, but this figure is not consistent with the serial number range on known specimens, which indicates a larger quantity. It may be that the serial numbers used on pistols intended for commercial sale were different from those used on pistols destined to be sold to officers. It is noted that those having lower serial numbers (e.g., No. 2712) bear the military form of Kayoba arsenal marking, while those having higher numbers (e.g., No. 5919) have the commercial form. One specimen has been reported as having the markings of the Tokyo Gas and Electric Co. If this is correct, it seems likely that the total production was probably larger than is generally assumed. Because of the rarity of this model some authorities were for a time inclined to believe that it did not actually exist.

7 mm. Sword Type—A very unusual and curious form of the 7 mm. pistol was produced, in very small quantity, perhaps as an experiment. Perhaps the designer had a Samurai ancestor who fought with the sword! This type, which has no known designation, has an extra-large grip frame, with higher magazine capacity, which forms the handle and guard on a rather long sword. When the sword is held upright, with the blade in the air, the pistol can be aimed and fired in the normal manner. Such a contraption would certainly not be conducive to

accuracy. A known specimen of one of these oddities bears the serial No. 6328. Whether this is a continuation of the serial numbering of the 7 mm. pistols described above is not known.

Experimental types

A pistol about which very little seems to be known is that developed by Tomisiro Komuro, of Tokyo, in the period 1905–06. These were supposedly chambered for the 7.65 mm. Browning cartridge. A few hundred specimens were made, presumably in the period 1906–1910. The fact that specimens vary in construction details from specimen to specimen suggests that they were never made on a production basis, but probably were handmade. None of these seem to have appeared in this country before World War I and very few since then. No figures as to total production are available.

Two other pistols of Japanese origin are those whose only known designations are Kenju Shiki I and Kenju Shiki II. Very little information is available on either of these models. Shiki I (i.e., Type I) appears to be a 7.65 mm. Browning type, judging from a sketch.

The pistol known as Shiki II (apparently of the Browning type) is said to date from 1940–1944 and apparently was made in some quantity, as specimens in the 2800 serial number range have been

Fig. 177. 8 mm. Nambu Type 94 (1934). (Disassembled. Marked as made at the Nagoya Arsenal).

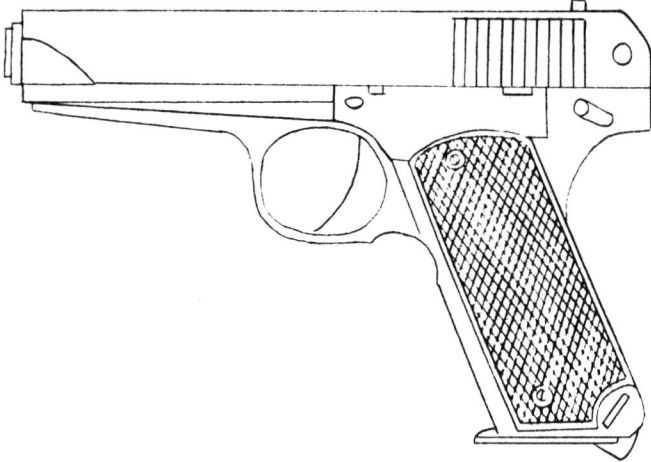

Fig. 178. Kenju Shiki II (i.e., Pistol Type II).

reported (Fig. 178). This assumes, of course, that numbering started at No. 1, which may not have been the case. Two separate experimental "batches," of unknown size, are reported to have been made at the Hamada Arms Shops, after which 500 pieces were made at the Nagoya Arsenal. This may or may not have been the total production. The pistol apparently was to have been adopted by the Japanese military forces, but the end of the war stopped those plans. Some of the experimental models have very large magazines. These pistols are very rarely seen and, naturally, are collectors' items.*

Kimball carbine auto

In 1955 John W. Kimball of Detroit, Michigan, designed and produced a few prototype models of an automatic pistol to take the powerful .30 cal. U.S. carbine cartridge. The gun was of the blowback type with a free-floating barrel which, it was claimed, made the gun more accurate and reduced

*Production of pistols in Japan was stopped in 1945 and all machinery used in their production was destroyed. The production of small arms is now being resumed by the Shin Chuo Kogyo K.K. of Tokio, this firm having received government orders for a limited number of pieces of two models of automatics and one of a revolver. Curiously enough, all three have been designated as "New Model Nambus," though they bear no resemblance to the original Nambu arms. Model 57, in 9 mm. Par. caliber, is essentially a copy of the Colt Mod. 1911. Model 57B, in .32 ACP caliber, seems to have been derived from the 1910 Mod. F.N. Browning but has an exposed hammer and no grip safety. The Model 58 revolver is a copy of the .38 Spl. S & W, apparently with the addition of a thumb-operated safety. As these arms (as of November 1961) are hand produced, production is necessarily slow. All of the above are shown in Volume II.

the kick. The inventor stated that "the barrel recoils straight back 3/16 inch eliminating a great deal of the recoil, thereby keeping the gun on target for faster shooting in an emergency."

A unique feature was the shallow grooving or scoring which was put into the chamber for the purpose of holding the case back at the moment of firing. To prevent the cartridge from being retarded in the act of chambering, the scoring was polished away at the top of the chamber where the nose end of the bullet came in contact with this surface. The scoring, if present at this point, would also be likely to scratch or damage the bullet. How effective this scoring of the chamber was in accomplishing its stated purpose is not known. As the case of this powerful cartridge undoubtedly expanded and pressed tightly against the chamber walls at the moment of firing, the increased friction caused by the scoring should have had some retarding action.

Another feature stressed by the inventor was the smoothness of the trigger pull, which he claimed was attained by a "camming" action. Those who have used the pistol agree on this point and state that the pistol performs remarkably well considering the power of the cartridge.

In 1956 the firm J. Kimball Arms Co., then located in Wayne, Michigan, was formed for the production of the pistol. Factory literature stated that while current demand was for the .30 caliber model it was the intention to produce it in .22 Hornet, .357 Magnum, and .38 Special calibers, as well.

Specifications for the standard .30 caliber model are given in Table 33. Two other models, of the same general construction, were available. The Combat model differed principally in that it had fixed sights and weighed 34 ounces. The Air Crew model was again of the same basic design as the regular model, but had fixed sights, a 3½-inch barrel, a total length of 8 inches, and weighed 29 ounces.

This firm is no longer in operation.

TABLE 33

Specifications for the standard .30 cal. Kimball Carbine pistols

Total length	9.5 inches	No. of grooves	8
Barrel length	5.0 "	Dir. of twist	Right
Bore diameter	0.308 inch	One turn in	12 inches
Groove diameter	0.330 "	Width of lands	0.030 inch
Weight	40 oz.	Width of grooves	0.078 "
Magazine cap.	7 ctges.	Frame — 4140 chrome-molyb. steel	
Muzzle velocity	1524 ft./sec.	Barrel — 4150 chrome-molyb. steel (heat treated)	
Muzzle energy	567 ft-lbs.		

Kommer pistols

Four types or models of Kommer pistols made by the Theodor Kommer Waffenfabrik in Zella-Mehlis, Germany, are known. The dates at which these various models appeared are not known and no production figures are available. It does not seem likely, however, from such data as are at hand that the total production could have been very large.

The first type, to which no model number was assigned, is shown in the AKAH (A. Kind) Catalog of 1922 and presumably appeared around 1920 or 1921. It is a 6.35 mm. pistol of the Browning 1906 type having a somewhat curved rather than the straight grip, however, and a magazine capacity of 8 rounds. Specimen No. 3, examined by the author, had a length of 110 mm. and height of 87 mm. The barrel length is 53 mm. and weight ca. 360 grams with empty magazine.

The next model is referred to as Mod. II as described in the 1932 issue of the AKAH Catalog. It also is of 6.35 Brng. caliber with a magazine capacity of 6 instead of 8 rounds. The grip is not curved and it more nearly resembles the 1906 Browning pistol than does its predecessor. It is 110 mm. in length, 77 mm. in height, has a barrel length of 52 mm., and weighs ca. 350 grams.

No Mod. III is mentioned in the 1932 AKAH Catalog, but an undated Genschow Catalog (No. 82), which from the context appears to be a 1926 or 1927 issue, definitely lists the Mod. III and indicates that it is the same as the Mod. II except for the increased magazine capacity. The length (110 mm.) and the thickness (24 mm.) are the same. The height of Mod. III is given as 92 mm. whereas that for Mod. II is 77 mm., as stated. Both models have four-groove rifling, with right hand twist.

A Mod. IV Kommer pistol of 7.65 mm. caliber is shown in the 1941 edition of Bock. As this is not mentioned in earlier catalogs it may be safe to assume that it came out in ca. 1940. This pistol is different from the preceding models and is definitely of the 1910 Browning type and appears to be quite an exact copy of the same. No specimen of this model has been encountered, however, and presumably not many were made because World War II seems to have ended the pistol making activities of this firm.

Korovin pistols

This is a 6.35 mm. pistol designed by S. Korovin and manufactured at one of the Tula arsenals in the U.S.S.R. This particular aresenal (armory or factory) is the Tulski Oruzheiny Zavod (Tula Weapons Factory) and guns made there are frequently found to be marked with the letters TOZ. It is believed that all of the Korovin pistols were made at this one factory and that they were intended for nonmilitary use, as attested by the fact that specimens are marked with a triangle having the letter T inscribed therein. Arms intended for military use were marked otherwise.

The official nomenclature for the pistol is Pistolet Korovin, but it is quite commonly known as the Pistol T-K, for Tulski Korovin. Many bear no inscription of name of manufacturer, while others are marked TOZ. This name, if it can be considered one, is derived from the name of the arsenal. How long the manufacture took place (supposedly in the 1930's and 1940's) is not known, but it must have continued for some time as serial numbers have been found as high as No. 328,117, yet some are in the 18,000 range, which indicates that the numbering did not start at a high level.

There are a number of variant forms, but basically the pistols are the same. Some notations follow:

1. A reported specimen in the 18,000 serial number range has black, hard rubber grip pieces with the letters TOZ in the form of a monogram. The grip screw (only one is used) is located near the rear edge of the frame, and the front sight is beveled on the front edge.

2. An observed specimen with serial number 53,706 has checkered wood grip pieces and bears no name or initials. Otherwise it is like No. 1.

3. Confirmed specimens in the 40,000 to 60,000 serial number range have checkered wood grip pieces in two styles: (1) short, exposing a serial number directly above (on the frame) as well as a serial number above this (on the slide); and (2) long, fitting clear up to the slide so that the lower of the two serial numbers is covered. The grip piece screw is near the rear edge, and the front edge of the foresight is beveled, as in the earlier specimens.

4. Confirmed specimens in the 200,000 to 230,000 serial number range have either checkered wood grip pieces or black, hard rubber grip pieces bearing the TOZ monogram. The wood grip pieces, in the low 200,000 range, have the grip screw near the rear edge of the frame, but in the case of the hard rubber grip pieces the grip holding screw is located near the center, and these specimens have a half-round fore sight instead of one that is beveled.

5. Serial No. 328,117 shows the characteristics mentioned for the higher numbered specimens in No. 4, having hard rubber grip pieces with the TOZ monogram. It is listed separately here only because

of the large gap between No. 230,000 and No. 328,117, about which we have no information as to variant markings, etc.

Lahti pistols

Lahti (Finnish)—The original 9 mm. Parabellum Lahti military pistol was designed by Aimo Johannes Lahti, who for some time was Chief of the Government Arsenal of Finland. He was an arms designer of note, having previously designed rifles and the Finnish machine gun. The pistol was designed shortly before 1935 and, since it was adopted as the Finnish service hand arm in 1935, it was given the nomenclature L-35. It was manufactured by Valtion Kivääri Tehdas (State Rifle Factory) at Jyväskyla. The pistol is frequently referred to as the VKT-L35 (Fig. 179).

This arm embodies a rather complex recoil-operated system with a yoke locking device and a bolt-accelerator closing device. After some 5000 or 6000 were made the system was simplified somewhat. The yoke lock retaining spring was eliminated, thus simplifying the machining of the receiver and lock. Thus modified, the official nomenclature became L-35SA. Several other variations are said to have been made, each involving a change in official designation, but details are lacking.

How many Lahtis were made in Finland is not known, but specimens with serial numbers up to 9200 are known. Some of the changes reported seem to appear in specimen No. 9100. The shoulder stock attaching ridge (with slot) is missing, as is also the cartridge indicator (chamber indicator) previously present on the top of the receiver.

Lahti (Swedish)—The Lahti design was adopted by Sweden for its military forces in 1940, and was given the nomenclature Pistole m/40. Popularly it is known as the Lahti m/40. In 1907 Sweden adopted the F.N. Browning Mod. 1903 as its official side arm and gave it the designation Pistole m/07. In 1939 they decided to change to the Walther HP (or P-38 in German military nomenclature) and contracted with Walther to furnish this pistol, to which they gave the designation Pistole m/39.

The outbreak of war, however, stopped deliveries about as soon as they began and the Swedish Government immediately turned to the Finnish Lahti, for whose manufacture they obtained a license. The production of this pistol was turned over to the experienced firm Husqvarna Vapenfabriks, Aktiebolag, of Husqvarna. This firm had made the Browning type m/07 pistol from the time that it was no longer obtainable from Fabrique Nationale in Belgium. Although it had been planned to drop the m/07 in 1939, the inability to get delivery of the Walther and the usual delays in the production of a new model (the Lahti) changed these plans and necessitated the continuance of production of the m/07 for some time. A communication from the firm states that production of the m/07 ceased in 1942 and that production of the m/40 was discontinued in 1944 (Figs. 180, 181).

How many were produced is not known, but it is reported that during World War II the pistol was issued to the Danish Free Troops stationed in Sweden, under the nomenclature 9 mm. Pistol m/40s. At the close of the war the Danes took these pistols back with them to Denmark, where they were issued to the police.

Langenhan pistols

The Langenhan (or "F.L.") pistols were made by Langenhan Gewehre und Fahrradfabrik at Zella-Mehlis (Thür.), Germany. This firm was founded in 1842 and possession was lost by the Langenhan family in 1945. Before World War I the firm made quite a variety of small-caliber arms, air pistols, etc. Early in the war a shortage of side arms developed and the Langenhan firm was commissioned to make a 7.65 mm. automatic pistol designed by Fr. Langenhan. The first mention of this pistol appears to have been made in the June 1915 issue of the German firearms publication *Schuss und Waffe*.

7.65 mm. "F.L."—Production of the Langenhan 7.65 mm. self-loading pistol for the German military forces appears to have begun in 1915. No model designation was assigned to the pistol at that time,

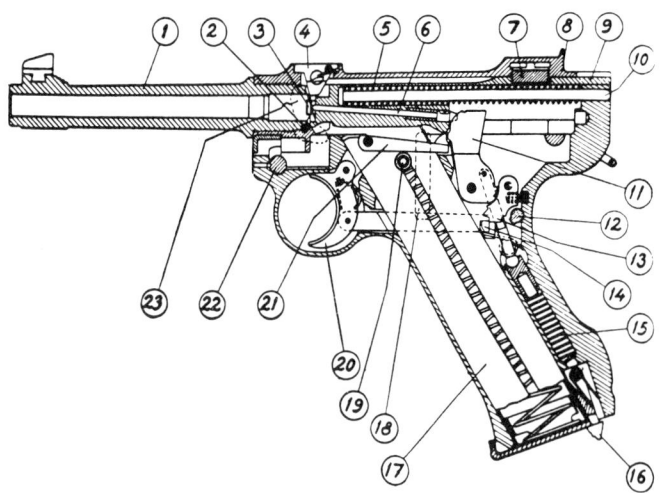

Fig. 179. 9 mm. Lahti Mod. L-35. Sectional view.

but later it became known as the Modell I because of the fact that two other Langenhan pistols were put on the market and these were eventually designated as Mod. II and Mod. III. It is said that the entire production of the 7.65 mm. pistol was taken by the German armed forces and that none were offered for commercial sale. The absence of advertisements in contemporary catalogs bears out this statement. Also, most (but not all) specimens will be found to carry the German military acceptance mark, a capital D with a crown above. It may be that some were offered for sale after the war. No information is available as to the total production, but the fact that, although many have been examined, no specimens have been found with serial numbers higher than ca. 64,000 would seem to indicate that the total production could not have been large (Fig. 182).

The action of this pistol is of the blowback type, with no external hammer. The arm is unique in that the slide and breechblock are separate units which are locked together by means of a stirrup located near the rear end of the slide. This stirrup is held in place by a screw having a large head. Loosening

this screw a few turns allows one to lift up the stirrup whereupon the slide and breechblock are separated and may be removed. While this arrangement makes this pistol one of the easiest to disassemble, it also introduces an element of considerable danger, as the screw is likely to work loose thus permitting the breechblock to be blown back into the shooter's face. Although, judging from the size of the screw head, it was the intention of the manufacturer that the screw be tightened by the fingers only, it has been shown by experience that this is not sufficient for safety.

As first issued the pistol had a cartridge ejection port on the right side of the slide, directly above the magazine. Just when this was eliminated is not known, but Serial No. 2477 shows this feature while No. 6347 does not. Specimen No. 2477 bears the inscription D.R.G. ANGEW (Pat. applied for), and No. 6347 bears the inscription, on the right side of the frame, F. L. SELBSTLADER - D.R.G.M. 625263 - 633251, indicating that two "design patents" had been issued at some time prior to the manufacture of No. 6347. Apparently the only patent that could be obtained was a design patent. These patent numbers appear on all specimens examined which have higher serial numbers.

The first pistols issued had checkered wood grip

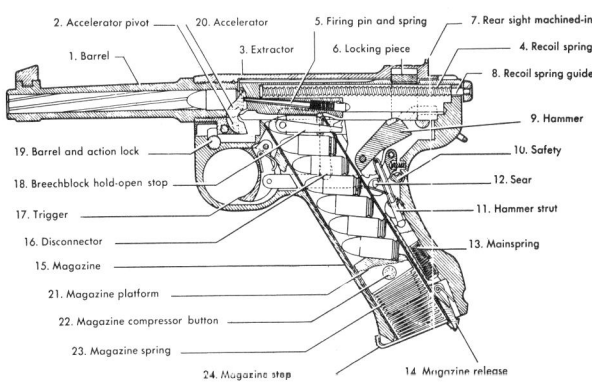

Fig. 180. 9 mm. Lahti Mod. 40. Sectional view.

2. Accelerator pivot
1. Barrel
19. Barrel and action lock
18. Breechblock hold-open stop
17. Trigger
16. Disconnector
15. Magazine
21. Magazine platform
22. Magazine compressor button
23. Magazine spring
24. Magazine stop
20. Accelerator
3. Extractor
5. Firing pin and spring
6. Locking piece
7. Rear sight machined-in
4. Recoil spring
8. Recoil spring guide
9. Hammer
10. Safety
12. Sear
11. Hammer strut
13. Mainspring
14. Magazine release

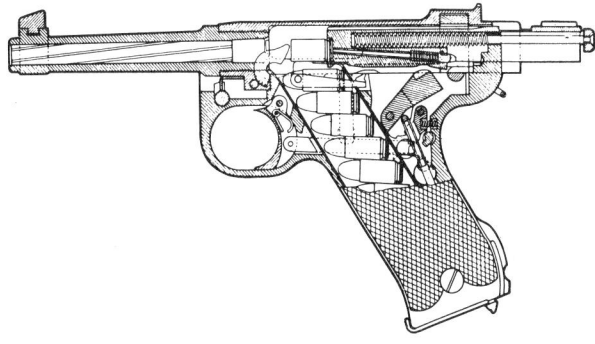

Fig. 181. 9 mm. Lahti Mod. 40. Sectional view, with action open and fired shell about to be ejected.

Fig. 182. 7.65 mm. Langenhan. To disassemble, the large screw head at the rear end of the slide is loosened, the yoke is raised, and the barrel removed.

pieces without any monogram or decoration of any kind. Later these were replaced with molded hard rubber plates bearing the letters F.L. on a semi-elliptical field.

One specimen, bearing the serial number 508, presents a confusing anomaly. This pistol has a concealed trigger bar located on the right side, under the frame. All other specimens seen have a disconnector bar on the left side, the protruding end of which is plainly visible. This bar lies on the outside of the frame, under the grip plate. This specimen has wood grip pieces (as would be expected from its low serial number), but it does not have any cartridge ejection port, such as is shown by No. 2477. Furthermore, to add still more to the confusion, this specimen bears the single patent number D.R.G.M. 625,263, which indicates that it was made previous to No. 6347, which specimen bears two patent numbers. The fact that it has any patent number at all and has no ejection port would indicate that it was made after No. 2477, but the presence of the unusual disconnector bar, together with the low serial number (508), seems to indicate a very early stage in production. The inconsistencies seem irreconcilable.

6.35 mm. "F.L."—The 6.35 mm. F.L. appeared commercially in two models, which are known as Modell II and Modell III. Presumably these were both made after World War I, but when they were introduced is not known. It has been rumored that the first 6.35 mm. pistol was of the same design as the 7.65, but this has not been confirmed. Certainly Models II and III are different from the 7.65 model. In these the slide and breechblock are not separate units held together by a stirrup, which is the most prominent and distinguishing feature of the larger model. Here disassembly is accomplished by means of a lever located on the right side of the slide, which actuates a locking mechanism. When this lever, which has an appearance similar to a mechanical safety lever, is turned the slide can be removed.

Mod. II is somewhat larger than Mod. III, as shown in Table 34.

Though the date of introduction of these smaller models is not known, it can be said that German catalogs of the early 1920's (Schilling and Lepper)

illustrate the design that later became known as the Modell II, though no such designation appeared in the illustration or text. It was stated, however, that the pistol could be had for either 6 or 8 rounds, and it would seem logical to assume that there were two grip (and magazine) lengths for the same model of pistol, to which no model designation had at that time been assigned. On the appearance of a new and definitely smaller model, however, it became necessary to assign model designations. The larger (and earlier) 6.35 mm. pistol thereupon became Modell II and the new model became Modell III.

Neither of these pistols is mentioned in the AKAH catalogs of 1922 and 1925, but Modell II is illustrated and described in the AKAH catalog of 1929, so this model at least was still available at that time. Specimens examined have been found to bear the name Langenhan (in script) instead of the F. L. SELBSTLADER inscription on the frame, and patent numbers are not present on any part of either model. Both have molded hard rubber grips with the letters F.L., together with a somewhat more elaborate floral design than that present on the 7.65 mm. model, in a semi-elliptical field on the grip pieces. No information is at hand regarding the system of serial numbering nor of the total number of these pistols produced. It is believed that the total production was not large, judging by the scarcity of specimens in circulation.

"Le Francais" pistols

The Le Francais series of automatic pistols, made by MANUFRANCE (Manufacture Francaise d'Armes et Cycles de St. Etienne, France), are of considerable interest because of their novelty of design and quality of workmanship. Four models were produced, in three calibers: the 6.35 mm. Modele de Poche (Pocket Model), the 6.35 mm. Policeman, the 7.65 mm. Le Francais (no other designation), and the 9 mm. Browning Long Le Francais (designed for military or police use). The 6.35 mm. models were designed during the years 1913–1914 by the Service Etudes (Research Department) of the firm and were based on ideas furnished by M. Mimard who was the founder Président Directeur Général at that time. Production of the 6.35 mm. models began in 1914, that of the 9 mm. Military model in 1928, and the 7.65 Le Francais was not produced until 1950, according to statements from the factory. The only pistols currently (1959) being manufactured are the 6.35 mm. models and the 7.65. The 9 mm. pistol was tested by the army but was not adopted. Manufacture of this Military model, which was naturally

TABLE 34
Data for two Langenhan 6.35 "F.L." pistols

Measurement	Mod. II	Mod. III
Length over-all, mm.	141	125
Barrel length, mm.	ca. 80	ca. 59
Weight, empty, gm.	503	410
Magazine cap., ctges.	7	5

designed for the 9 mm. French Long cartridge (much favored by the French but considered quite inadequate for military purposes by other nations), was discontinued in about 1938, according to information supplied by the manufacturer (Figs. 183 to 189).

All of the models operate in a similar manner, but differ in some details of construction. Minor differences also appear from time to time in the same model. As to total production of the three calibers, the following estimates were furnished by the factory (as of April 1959): 6.35 mm. models – ca. 215,000; 7.65 mm. models – ca. 10,000; and 9 mm. models – ca. 4,000.

The pistol is of the blowback type, with stationary barrel, and depends on a coil spring and inertia of moving parts to take up the force of recoil. In gen-

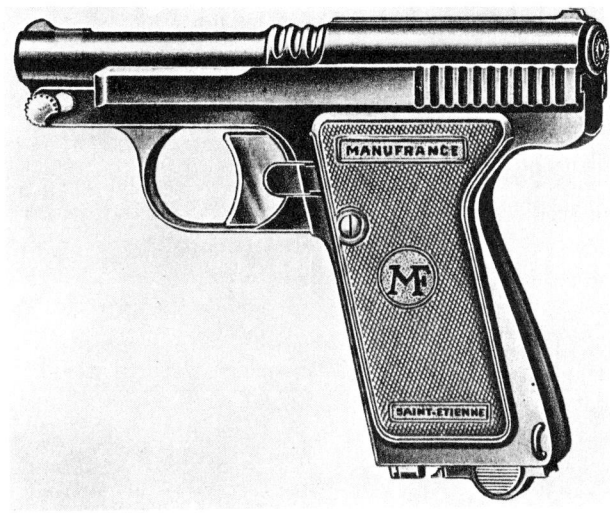

Fig. 185. 7.65 mm. "Le Francais" Pocket Mod.

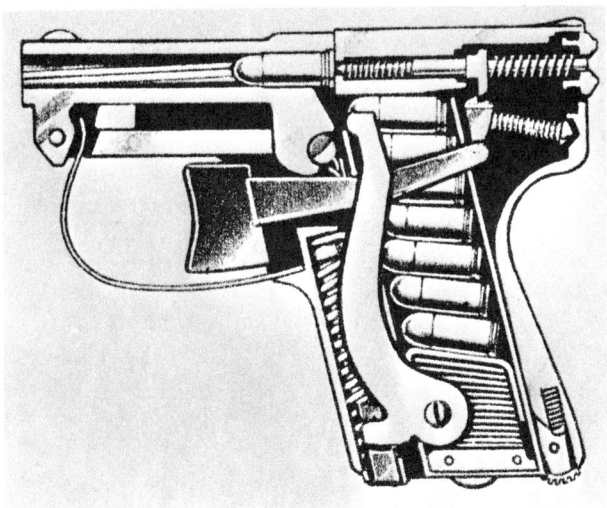

Fig. 183. 6.35 mm. "Le Francais" Pocket Mod. Sectional view.

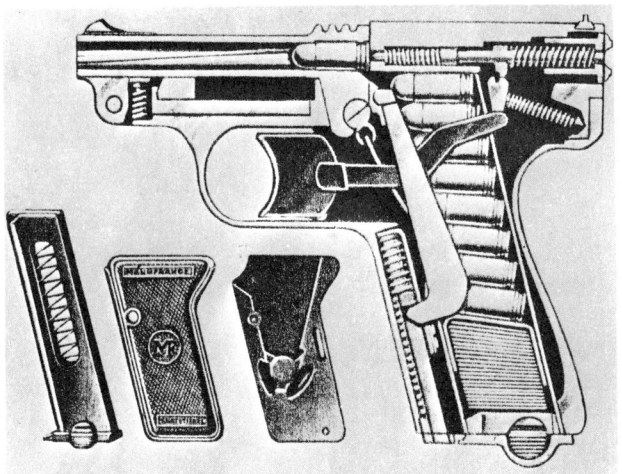

Fig. 186. 7.65 mm. "Le Francais" Pocket Mod. Sectional view.

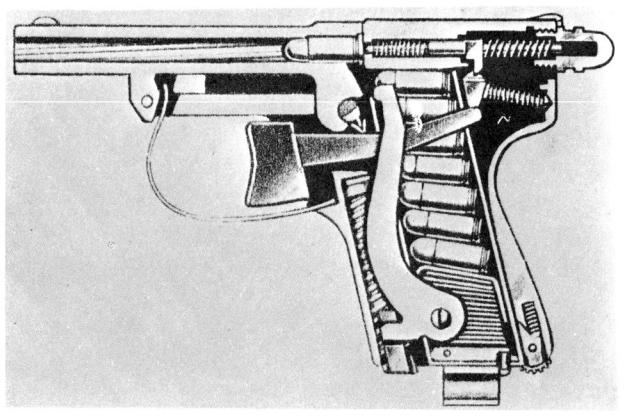

Fig. 184. 6.35 mm. "Le Francais" Policeman Mod. Sectional view.

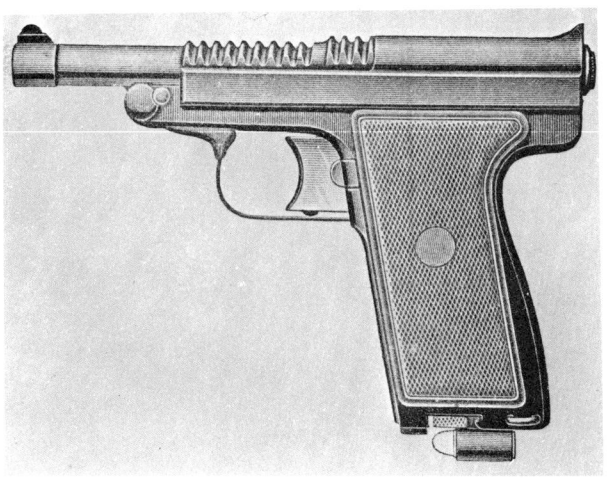

Fig. 187. 9 mm. "Le Francais" "Military Model." 219

eral it consists of three parts: barrel, slide unit, and receiver. The barrel is hinged to the frame at a point near the muzzle end. The large screw which serves as a pinion can be removed easily. There is a notched lug on the under side at the breech end, and when the barrel is in the closed position the lug engages a spring catch which is connected to and actuated by an outside lever on the right side of the frame. Pressing down on this lever causes the rear end of the barrel to flip up, due to the pressure of a spring just back of the pinion. In the 7.65 mm. model this spring is in the form of a vertically placed coil spring, while in the other models the slender

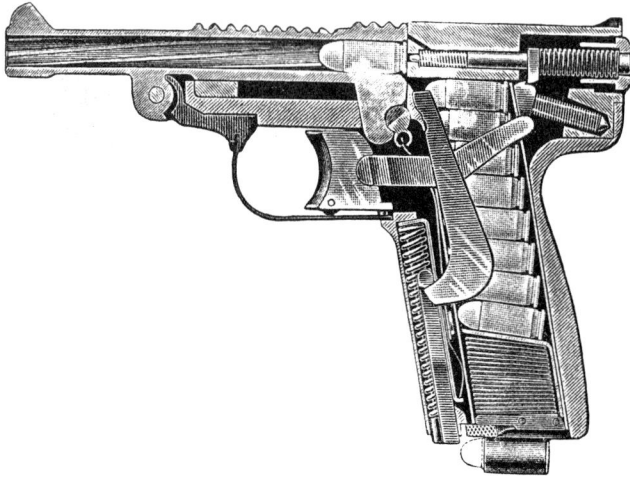

Fig. 188. 9 mm. "Le Francais" "Military Model." Sectional view.

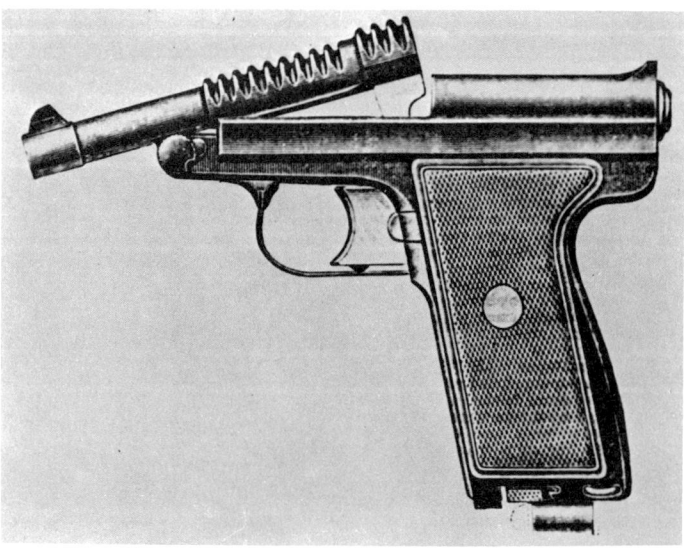

Fig. 189. 9 mm. "Le Francais" "Military Model." Barrel tilted for inspection or for loading an additional cartridge.

trigger guard acts as a spring. In the latter the trigger guard is a separate member, while in the 7.65 mm. model it is integral with the frame and much thicker.

When the magazine is removed the barrel automatically springs to the open position, so the arm cannot be fired when the magazine is out. The breechblock section is unique in several ways. The guides for the slide extend forward nearly to the point where the barrel is pinioned, and the lower part of the slide extends the same distance when the action is closed, thus affording a desirably long contact surface. The firing pin is of unusual design. It is longer than most pins, the rear half is greater in diameter, and at approximately the midpoint there is a square lug which acts as a bent for the sear. The front end of the pin carries a coil spring which holds the firing pin back of the hole in the breechblock until it is driven forward in the act of firing. Surrounding the rear and larger half of the firing pin back of the lug is a much heavier spring which, when compressed and released, drives the firing pin forward against the cartridge primer.

The pistol functions like a double action revolver, although it actually has no hammer. The trigger, trigger bar, and sear are all in one integral piece, which is free to slide back and forth as it has no pins or screws. When the trigger is pulled, the edge of the sear at the end of the trigger bar engages the lug on the firing pin, pushing the pin back and thus compressing the spring. When the spring is fully compressed the sear slips off the lug and the pin is driven forward to fire the cartridge. A small coil spring, mounted on a guide based against the back of the frame and pressing against the sear, causes the trigger assembly to move back into its original position as soon as the finger pressure on the trigger is released. Thus this mechanism functions as a double action, each shot requiring a pull of the trigger to cock and fire the arm, and it also acts as a disconnector as no second shot can be fired until the trigger returns to its original position. Also, and very importantly, should the cartridge fail to fire on the first pull of the trigger a second pull (or more) can be made on the same cartridge—a very desirable feature not present on the ordinary automatic pistol. In an emergency this might well save the shooter's life.

The recoil spring occupies an unusual position and operates in an unusual way. It is a rather heavy coil spring located in a tunnel directly in front of the magazine and is placed almost vertically. This spring connects with the slide through a flat lever located underneath the grip piece. As the slide recoils the lever causes the spring to be compressed, and then the compressed spring actuates the lever to return the slide to the closed position.

As the slide moves back upon firing, the fired shell is expelled by the force of the explosion without the aid of any extractor, none being necessary. As the shell leaves the chamber the base strikes the ejector lug which directs it to the right and upward. As the slide returns it picks off a fresh cartridge and chambers it in the usual manner.

It will be noted that this pistol is self loading, but not self cocking. Cocking is accomplished only by pulling the trigger. This constitutes an excellent safety feature, because there is no danger of accidental firing even when a cartridge is in the chamber. The forward spring around the firing pin holds the pin back so that the arm can not be discharged by jarring or a sudden shock, and a strong pull on the trigger is necessary to cock and fire the arm. In addition, as has already been stated, when the magazine

are merely thick low ridges, and few in number, it seems unlikely that they serve to dissipate much heat. Later issues of the 9 mm. pistol have more of these ridges than do the earlier and these may be a bit more effective.

The magazine catches are located at the bottom of the grip and vary in form in the different models and in different periods of manufacture of the same model. All models have rather low, fixed sights. The 6.35 and 7.65 mm. models use the Browning cartridge, while the 9 mm. uses the Browning Long which (as has been said), though favored in some European countries, is not elsewhere considered a satisfactory cartridge for military use.

In the earlier stages of production both of the smaller models had grips with straight, parallel sides, but later an integral rib was added to the rear of the grip frame, giving the pistols a better appearance and also improving the hold. The grip pieces are of molded rubber, with the exception that the

TABLE 35
Data for "Le Francais" pistols

Measurement	6.35 mm. Pocket Mod.	6.35 mm. Policeman	7.65 mm. Le Francais	9 mm. Brng. Long Military type
Total length	111 mm.	152 mm.	152 mm.	ca. 200 mm.
Barrel length	60 "	85 "	83 "	ca. 127 "
Height	84 "	84 "	122 "	ca. 130 "
Magazine cap.	7 ctges.	7 ctges.	8, 6 ctges.	8 ctges.
Weight	300 gm.	360 gm.	630 gm.	965 gm.
No. of grooves	6	6	6	6

is out the pistol cannot be fired, because removal of the magazine causes the rear end of the barrel to spring upward. Because of all of these safety factors no grip safety or mechanical thumb safety, as used on many other pistols, is necessary. This is probably one of the safest automatic pistols ever to be made.

The magazine is loaded and inserted in the usual manner. Then, customarily, an additional cartridge is slipped into the chamber before lowering the barrel, which locks automatically. The 7.65 and 9 mm. models have serrations on the slide to furnish finger grips, but the 6.35 mm. models do not. Of course when the finger grips are present the initial cartridge can be chambered by pulling back and releasing the slide in the usual manner. The magazines of the 7.65 and 9 mm. models may or may not have a little clip at the bottom to hold the extra cartridge needed for the chamber, in case such is desired.

The 7.65 and 9 mm. models have "cooling fins" turned on the barrel at the breech end. Since these

9 mm. model, designed for military use, was furnished with walnut grip pieces.

As mentioned earlier, there were two 6.35 mm. models, the Pocket Model and the Policeman. The latter had a longer barrel and a protruding knob at the rear end of the slide which was hollow, affording more room for the firing pin. Unscrewing this knob permits removal of the firing pin and spring. The smaller model had a similar closure plug, the end of which was nearly flush with the end of the slide.

Data for the "Le Francais" pistols are given in Table 35.

Factory rifling characteristics are known only for the 7.65 mm. model. They are: rifling, 6-Right; one turn of rifling in 240 mm.; width of grooves, 2.65 mm.; depth of grooves, 0.1 mm.

In addition to the 6.35 mm. models already described, a special target model was produced for a very short time. It is described in the 1929 and 1931 MANUFRANCE catalogues under the designation Le

221

Fig. 190. 6.35 mm. "Le Francais" Champion. Extension is for providing a better grip, not for increasing cartridge capacity.

Francais–Champion (Fig. 190).

In many respects this model resembles the Policeman but has two distinct differences other than the barrel length. The closure plug at the rear is much longer and the grip has an extension which slips on to the regular grip, thus increasing the length of the grip about 50 per cent and also increasing the front-to-back dimension somewhat, all of which serves the purpose of giving a much better hold for target shooting. The grip extension is not used for the purpose of increasing the magazine capacity, this being 7 rounds as for the Policeman model.

Evidently this model was not as well received as the others and was soon dropped, as descriptions do not appear in later factory literature. No specimens have been encountered and apparently this model is not well known.

Factory data for the Champion are as follows: total length, 235 mm.; barrel length, 150 mm.; length of rifled part, 133 mm.; distance between sights, 196 mm.; height (including grip extension), 111 mm.; weight, 462 grams.; 6-groove rifling, with right hand twist; width of grooves, 2.3 mm.; and depth of grooves, 0.08 mm.

In 1958 MANUFRANCE was offering a target pistol under the name Auto-Stand. This was a .22 cal. L.R. pistol obviously made by Mre. d'Armes des Pyrénées at Hendaye, France. It is very similar to the .22 cal. UNIQUE pistols formerly sold in the U.S. by Sears, Roebuck and Co. as the Higgins Mod. 85 and more recently by Montgomery Ward as the Western Field No. 5. Factory data given are: total length, 210 mm.; weight, 750 grams; magazine capacity, 10 cartridges. From the illustration the barrel length was calculated to be ca. 152 mm. and distance between sights ca. 161 mm.

Le Page pistols

The firm now known as Manufacture d'Armes Le Page, S.A., of Liége, Belgium, was established in 1790 and has long been known as a manufacturer of fine quality shotguns, rifles, and revolvers. At the time of the annexation of Belgium by France under the rule of Napoleon there was created the Manufacture Imperial d'Armes de Guerre, which kept as a Government monopoly the manufacture of all military weapons. This naturally created a great handicap to independent firms who had been supplying such arms. But in 1815 this monopoly ended with the end of French rule in Belgium and all firms were again in free competition. In 1810 the Banc d'Epreuve Officiel des Armes á Feu (Official Proof House for Firearms) had been established to control the quality of arms made in Belgium. This standardization, along with free competition, was of inestimable value to the members of the arms industry who were interested in making products of fine quality. In this situation the firm of Le Page flourished and for many years supplied military arms to many European countries, as well as arms for civilian use.

Immediately following World War I the firm of Le Page was reorganized as a Société Anonyme (stock company or corporation). A new workshop was built and equipped with modern American-made precision machines, and Le Page set out to capture a part of the American and British markets for firearms, but apparently with indifferent success.

After about seven years of research and development, according to company statements, Le Page added automatic pistols to their line (ca. 1925). While still offered for sale these pistols have never had a wide distribution in this country, probably because of the intense competition in this field. As foreign catalogs in general do not mention them it seems safe to presume that they were also not widely distributed in those countries either.

The Le Page pistols were made in four calibers —6.35 mm., 7.65 mm., 9 mm. Long, and the 9 mm. Browning Short (.380). The 7.65 and 9 mm. Long (Military) models are alike in construction and it is believed, but not verified, that the first 6.35 was also of the same construction and that it was superceded by a pistol of the Browning 1906 type.

The 7.65 and 9 mm. models were based on the design for which Le Page secured Belgian Patent No. 305,326. The pistol is of a simple blowback type, the force of recoil being taken up partly by a spiral spring located under the fixed barrel and partly by the inertia of the slide, which extends the full length of the arm. The upper part of the slide is cut away, exposing the entire length of the barrel (Fig. 191). The pistol has an external hammer which is located in a removable section constituting the rear edge of the frame. When the arm is completely assembled, this member, which is pinioned at the bottom of the frame, is held in place by the pin of the thumb safety.

To disassemble, the magazine is removed, the hammer is cocked, the safety is applied, and the slide is drawn back slowly to a point where the safety can be pulled out. The pinioned section containing the hammer can now be tilted back. The slide is now pulled back, the rear end is raised to disengage it from the guides and is then slid forward off the barrel. The operation is a very simple one and takes but a few seconds.

In addition to the thumb safety there is a magazine safety, which prevents firing when the magazine is out, and the hammer provides a third safety. The arm is therefore advertised as having "triple sûretés."

The 9 mm. model is constructed in the same manner, but has a greater magazine capacity (12 shots instead of 8), it has a detachable shoulder stock-case (in which the pistol can be carried), and it has an adjustable rear sight, calibrated for 100, 200, 300, and 500 meters. This model could be had either with or without the shoulder stock. The magazine release catch is at the bottom of the grip frame in both models, and the forward edge of the grip frame is "scalloped" to provide a more secure grip. Both models present a pleasing appearance and have good balance.

Catalog literature describing Le Page pistols infers, but does not specifically state, that there was available a 6.35 mm. pistol of the same construction. Circular literature, however, issued at a later time describes a 6.35 mm. pistol which is merely a conventional adaptation of the 1906 Browning. Specimens of this latter type, as well as the 7.65 mm., have been measured and photographed.

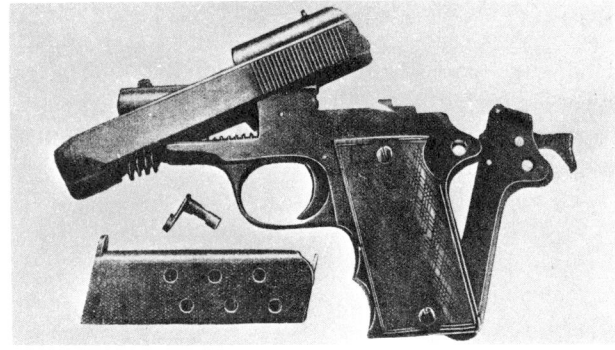

Fig. 191. 7.65 mm. Le Page. Partially disassembled.

Little Tom pistols

The Little Tom pistol was designed and apparently also produced by Alois Tomiška, a designer and manufacturer of firearms, in the town of Pilsen in Czechoslovakia. Reportedly this was in the period ca. 1908–1918. The pistol was made in 6.35 and 7.65 mm. calibers. The inscription on the left side of the slide of one 7.65 mm. pistol reads:

ALOIS TOMIŠKA - PLZEN - PATENT - LITTLE TOM
- 7.65 (.32)

Obviously these pistols were intended for sale in English-speaking countries, judging from the form of inscription. The design is a blowback, double action type possessing no particularly outstanding features. It is evidently a Browning adaptation. The mechanical safety lever is placed directly behind the trigger instead of at the rear of the frame, and there are two notches in the lower left edge of the slide. One is the safety notch, the other serves to keep the slide back in the open position when desired. The most characteristic feature of all Little Toms is the shape of the trigger guard. This is quite elongated, having an opening which can best be described as "egg shaped."

The manufacture of the Little Tom pistols was taken over by the Wiener Waffenfabrik of Vienna, Austria, at a date unknown. On the left side of the slide on one 7.65 mm. specimen seen by the author there is stamped the official commercial proof mark of the Vienna Proof House, below which appears the Austrian crown, all followed by the digits 2174.20. The number 2174 does not appear to be the serial number, as that (No. 33,406) is stamped in the customary position on the right side of the slide. The number 20 may indicate the year of production but may have some other significance—such as an inspector's number.

The 6.35 mm. Little Tom, as originally made at Pilsen, is very similar to those made by the Wiener Waffenfabrik, the principal difference being that the rear end of the slide is more nearly square in shape than the Vienna model, which is quite rounded. The Pilsen model has the AT monogram (letters superimposed) of A. Tomiška, whereas the Vienna model has the customary Wiener Waffenfabrik monogram. (See section on Trade Marks.) All 6.35 mm. pistols made in Vienna appear to have the Vienna Proof House marks, whereas the pistols made at Pilsen have no proof marks.

There appear to be at least two variations of the 7.65 mm. pistol made at Vienna. In one, the rear end of the slide has been cut away to expose more of the hammer, in order to provide a better grip

223

when it is cocked by hand. Cocking by hand would be difficult with the other model. On the first one referred to there is a small front sight and no rear sight, whereas the second has a rather high, semi-circular front sight and a notched rear sight. In the latter the slide projects beyond the forward end of the frame, whereas in the former the ends of the slide and frame are flush. The curves and other differences mentioned show clearly that the two models were not made on the same set of tools. The grip pieces on the two are different. Both have small, round, stubby spur hammers, similar to those on the 1907 Savage. Which of these variants was produced first is not known.

Vienna-made pistols have been observed to have serial numbers in the 20,000 and 30,000 range. It is not known whether the 6.35 and 7.65 mm. pistols were numbered in the same series, nor is it known where the numbering started. It could well have been at some rather high figure, such as 20,000, since the scarcity of specimens seems to indicate that the production of these pistols was not great.

The chief contribution made by Tomiška was that of the application of the double action principle to a small pocket arm, which allowed it to be carried safely in the pocket with a cartridge in the chamber ready for instant action, eliminating the necessity of either loading (which requires two hands) or consuming time in locating and operating a safety lever. As a defense measure this was an important contribution—one made use of later in such pistols as the Mauser Mod. HSc, Walther Mods. PP and PPK, and the Sauer Mod. 38(H).

It is stated that Alois Tomiška designed pistols other than the Little Tom, but little information concerning his activities is available. Lugs, a Czechoslovakian author, states that the Fox was designed by Tomiška and that this pistol, after some modifications, eventually became the CZ Model of 1922. Comparisons of the photographs of these seem to furnish corroboration.

M.A.B. pistols

The M.A.B. automatic pistols, made by Manufacture d'Armes Automatiques of Bayonne, France, are patterned after the Browning models. They are well made and are quite popular in the U.S. Production began in 1921, and up to and including World War II pistols were made in 6.25, 7.65, and 9 mm. Short (ACP) calibers. Following the war a .22 caliber model was brought out and some larger-caliber models were also added.

For a considerable period during World War II the plant was operated under the supervision of the occupying Germans. When operations were resumed by the owners at the close of the war the serial numbering, which had continued without interruption during German occupation, was set back (in some cases at least) to an approximation of where it was at the time of seizure of the plant. Not all of the vagaries in numbering can be explained so simply, however, because as late as 1949 the numbering of some models was set back to some arbitrary figure, even to No. 1 in some cases. Hence, it should be possible to find two M.A.B. pistols of the same model bearing the same serial number. In some cases the German acceptance mark will be found on one of them, but in other instances it will not.

Modele A—This pistol, originally without official nomenclature but later designated as Modele A, appears not to have had any systematic numbering system from the time of its introduction (1921) to 1925. In 1925 a French law required the registry of serial numbers, so at that time the use of consecutive numbers began. Since the serial numbers for the pistols made from 1921 to 1925 were not recorded, it is not known what the total production was for that period. From 1925 to some time in 1942 the numbers covered the range 10,001 to 109,240. When manufacturing was resumed by the owners in 1945, serial numbering was set back to start at No. 50,001. This does not mean that exactly 10,001 had been made up to 1925, nor does it mean that exactly 40,000 had been made by the French from 1925 to the time that the Germans took over. The figures are no doubt approximations, at best.

The Modele A resembles the Browning 1906 very closely. It has three safeties, including the grip safety. Very early specimens (one marked H28) and much later specimens (e.g., No. 79,354), as well as recent circular illustrations issued by the manufacturer, show the same appearance.

Modele B—This model, also in 6.35 mm. caliber, differs from Mod. A in some important respects, though still following the general Browning design. The upper part of the front half of the slide is cut away, exposing the full length of the barrel, and ejection of spent shells is upward rather than through a shell ejection port on the right side of the slide, as in Mod. A. Also the grip safety is absent, and Mod. B. has a fore sight, while Mod. A has no sights.

Production began in 1932 and this model is also in current production. Serial numbers started at No. 79,084 and are said to have progressed regularly until November of 1949, at which time the numbers reverted to No. 25,001.

Modele C–Modele C, originally a 7.65 mm. pistol, was later made in both 7.65 and 9 mm. Short (.380) calibers. It was introduced in September 1933 and serial numbering began at 10,504. By January 1946 the numbers had reached 114,690, at which time the numbering was set back to 68,821. Numbering was again interrupted at No. 71,015 in April 1949 and was set back to No. 1, from which it has proceeded.

The exact reasons for these (and similar) changes are not known but no doubt are connected with the German operation (or supervision) of the French plants during World War II.

While Mod. C looks much like an enlarged Mod. A, its method of disassembly is different and it is provided with sights, front and rear. The method of disassembly is much like that of the 1910 Browning and the Mod. 400 Astra. A short sleeve, with front end knurled, surrounds the muzzle of the barrel. The function of this sleeve is to retain the recoil spring, the forward end of which projects into it. The sleeve is held by a bayonet-type catch and is prevented from rotating accidentally by a bar catch (operated by a spring) placed below the muzzle. When the front end of this catch is raised, by depressing the rear end, the sleeve can be turned to a position where it is released, permitting withdrawal of sleeve and recoil spring. The slide is then removed to a point where the thumb safety can be engaged in the forward notch on the lower side of the slide, whereupon the barrel can be rotated to a position where it is disengaged and both slide and barrel can be removed.

Models C/D, D, E, and R, described below, disassemble in the same manner. Only one specimen of the Mod. C has been examined by the author and this was found (to his surprise) to have 5 grooves, right hand twist, one turn in ca. 12.0 inches and land width of 0.087 inch. Other models have six grooves.

Modele C/D–This is a more recent addition to the M.A.B. line, having been brought out in 1950. Serial numbering started at No. 1. The pistol is in current production.

Modele D–This is essentially a Mod. C pistol with a longer barrel. It presently is made in both 7.65 and 9 mm. Short (.380) calibers. External dimensions are the same for both calibers.

Production of this model began in September 1933. Serial numbering started at No. 10,730 and had reached No. 114,690 by October 1945, at which time the series numbering reverted to No. 50,001.

Modele E–This is a 6.35 mm. pistol of post-World War II design and has been manufactured since March 1949. Serial numbers started at No. 1. This pistol is considerably larger than either Mod. A or Mod. B (of the same caliber), in fact it is slightly longer than the 7.65 mm. Modele C. It has a longer and somewhat more streamlined grip than any M.A.B. pistol previously made. The magazine capacity is 10 rounds, whereas in the earlier 6.35 mm. models it was 6 rounds.

Modele R "Curt"–The R models come in several calibers. The Modele R "Curt" is somewhat larger than the Mod. D, but is of the same general construction and takes the 7.65 mm. ACP cartridge. The marked difference is the addition of an external hammer (present on all R models). As to the form of hammer, there are variants. Some have a solid hammer of the spur type while others have the ring type. Some of the R models have lanyard rings and others do not. Manufacture started in July 1951 and still continues. Serial numbers are said to have started at No. 621.

Modele R Long–This Modele R uses the French service cartridge designated as the 7.65 mm. Long. Production started in 1950, with serial No. 1, and still continues.

Modele R 9 mm. Parabellum–This is like the other members of the R model, but is chambered for the German 9 mm. Parabellum cartridge.

Modele F–In 1950 a .22 caliber model was added and given the designation Modele F. This model could be had with different barrel lengths. Factory literature states that lengths of 95, 152, and 185 mm. are available. Actually barrel lengths of 68, 113, and 172 mm. have been found on specimens examined in the author's laboratory. Another source, quoting factory records, gives the barrel lengths available with introduction dates and beginning serial numbering as follows: 105 mm., production began February 1951, serial No. 301; 153 mm., production began April 1951, serial No. 1; 173 mm., production began July 1950, serial No. 338.

Why the first to be produced should have the highest number and the last should have the lowest is a bit strange!

"Le Chasseur" Modele–This is a still more recent model in .22 caliber, appearing in 1953. It is an external hammer version of the Modele F and has a very elaborate and fancy grip, designed to fit the hand. One specimen has been measured and found to be 185 mm. in length with a barrel length of 113 mm. As this was No. 37 it is presumed that serial numbering started at No. 1.

Data given by the manufacturer relating to dimensions, weights, magazine capacities, etc., are summarized in Table 36.

Mann pistols

The 6.35 mm. Mann pistol was designed jointly by Fritz Mann and Otto Mann. The design dates from mid-1919 and production began in February or March of 1920 at the Fritz Mann Werkzeugfabrik at Suhl-Neundorf, Germany. Some of the Mann pistols produced later bear the inscription Mann Werke.

Manufacture of this model did not long continue.

Price List. This model is presumed to have been introduced some time during the year 1923. How long it was in production is not known nor how many were made. Serial numbers over 43,400 are known, however, for the 7.65 mm. pistol and over 42,000 for the 9 mm. Of course they may have been (and probably were) numbered in the same series. The numbering probably continued from the 6.35 mm. series. The 7.65 mm. pistol was still being offered for sale in 1928, but it has not been observed in catalogs of later date.

It is stated that Fritz Mann made some experiments toward the development of a more powerful bottle-neck cartridge of 6.35 mm. for use in a vest-

TABLE 36
Data from advertising circulars for M.A.B. pistols

Measurement	Mod. A	Mod. B	Mod. C	Mod. D	Mod. E	Mod. F	Mod. R (Long)
Total length, inches	4.5	4.13	6	7	6.1	10.65	7.48
Barrel length, inches	2.6	1.96	3.75		3.26	3.74	4.17
Weight, ounces	13	9.52	23	25	20	29.02	26.45
Caliber	.25	.25	.32	.32	.25	.22	.32
Magazine cap., ctges	6	6	7	9	10	10	9

Mod. C. Also in .380 cal. Magazine cap. 6 ctges. Mod. D. Also in .380 cal. Magazine cap. 8 ctges. Mod. F. Barrel lengths of 6″ or 7.28″ also available. Mod. R. Also in .380 cal. (8 ctges.); 9 mm. Long (7 ctges.); 7.65 mm. Short (9 ctges.); and 9 mm. Par. (9 ctges.).

Measurements on specimens examined have been found to vary from the data given by the manufacturer. This is particularly true as to barrel lengths.

It is listed in the June 1922 AKAH Catalog but not in the March 1925 edition. It appears in Genschow's Export List No. 33 (ca. 1921) but not in the 1924 price list. Manufacture evidently stopped prior to 1924 and quite possibly a year or two earlier.

This pistol is referred to in the AKAH Catalog as a "Westentaschen" (vestpocket) pistol, and it certainly fits that appelation as it is one of the smallest of automatic pistols. It is a blowback type and one of original design rather than being a copy of the 1906 Browning as most 6.35 pistols of that period were. Furthermore it had a most peculiar and unattractive appearance, which may account for its early demise.

Specimens ranging from No. 356 (dated 1920) to No. 15,427 (dated 1921) have been examined. Serial numbers over 17,000 are known but no figures as to total production are available.

The manufacturer intended to produce a 7.65 mm. pistol identical in design to the 6.35 mm. model, but this never materialized. However, a 7.65 mm. and 9 mm. Short model of more conventional design did appear and both are listed in the Genschow 1924

pocket type of pistol, but this never materialized.

Data for the Mann pistols are given in Table 37.

TABLE 37
Data for Mann pistols

Measurement	6.35 mm.	7.65 mm.	9 mm.
Over-all length, mm.	102	114-118	121
Barrel length, mm.	45	60	60
Height, mm.	68	78	78
Weight (empty) gm.	250	353*	378
Magazine cap., ctges.	5	5	5
Number of grooves	6	4	4
Dir. of twist	R	R	R

*This value taken from *Pistol Atlas*. Weights as given in catalogs vary from 360 to 410 grams.

Mannlicher pistols

Mannlicher rifles, designed by Ferdinand Ritter von Mannlicher (born in 1848), have long been known as among the most excellent of their time. They date back to about 1878 in design and 1880 in manufacture. Mannlicher soon became interested in the idea of producing a military weapon that

Fig. 192. 7.6 mm. Mannlicher Mod. 1894. Blow forward type. Packet loading.

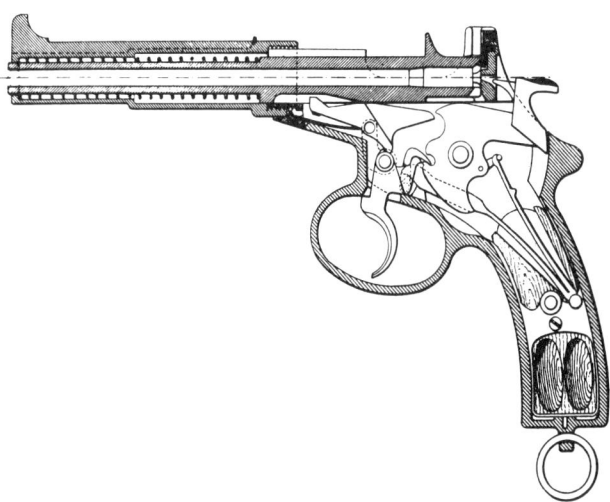

Fig. 193. 7.6 mm. Mannlicher Mod. 1894. Sectional view.

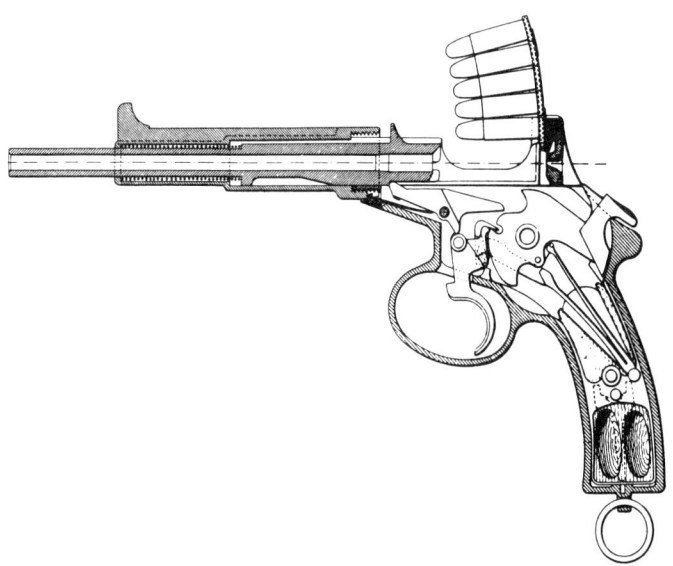

Fig. 194. 7.6 mm. Mannlicher Mod. 1894. Sectional view, showing loading operation.

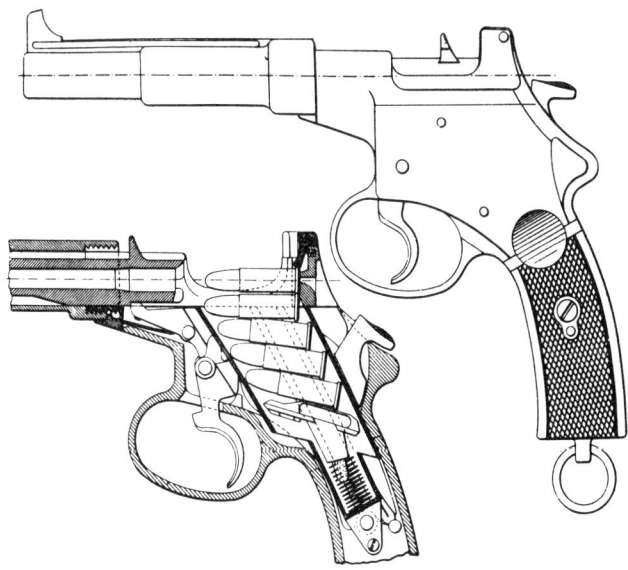

Fig. 195. 7.6 mm. Mannlicher Mod. 1894. Sectional view, showing cartridges in position in well.

would be "automatic" and in 1885 he brought out a light machine gun which embodied several of the features that later appeared in his first automatic pistol made in 1894. Many of his original conceptions appear in modern military arms, such as the Browning machine guns. His interest in the design of firearms seems to have continued up to the time of his death in 1903.

Modell 1894—The first Mannlicher automatic pistol reportedly was made at Fabrique d'Armes Neuhausen, in Switzerland, but very soon thereafter their production was moved to Steyr Werke, Steyr, Austria. It is stated that as originally designed it was intended to be of 8 mm. caliber, but, if so, it was soon changed to 7.60 mm. and cartridges of this cal-

iber were produced commercially. The pistol was also chambered for a 6.50 mm. cartridge, said to have been introduced in 1895. Both cartridges were produced by Keller and Co., according to White and Munhall* (Figs. 192 to 197).

Center Fire Metric Pistol and Revolver Cartridges, by H. P. White and Burton D. Munhall, Washington Infantry Journal Press. A companion volume deals with *Center Fire American and British Pistol and Revolver Cartridges*.

The specimens made in Switzerland are fully marked but do not have serial numbers, indicating that they were experimental models not intended for sale. The specimens made at Steyr bear the name Mannlicher and are fully numbered in several places, indicating that they were probably intended for the market. However, very few (possibly less than 100) were produced as they were soon superseded by an improved model, the Modell 1896. In any of its forms the 1894 model is a collector's item. Specimens marked "Modell 1895" have been encountered, but this is more of an indication of the year of production than a model designation, as it seems to have been the custom to assign a new model number each year for the arms produced in that year. Inasmuch as these 1895 models are at most only variants of the Modell 1894 it is more proper to consider them for what they are.

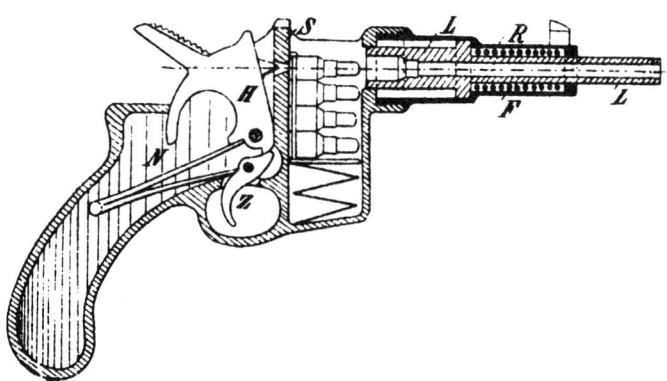

Fig. 196. 6.5 mm. Mannlicher (ca. 1895-96). Hammer down, no cartridge in chamber. 5 cartridges in magazine, which is "packet loaded."

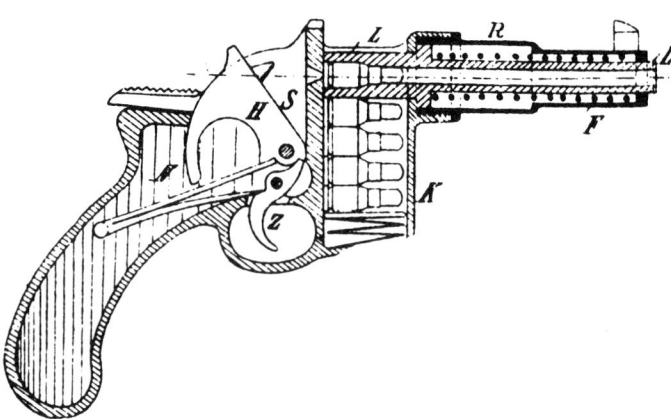

Fig. 197. 6.5 mm. Mannlicher. Cocking the hammer introduces a cartridge into the chamber.

228

The Modell 1894 (and variants) was quite different from the modern automatic pistol in that it was a "blow forward" type rather than the familiar blowback type. In this action the breechblock is in fixed position and the barrel, which is inclosed in a special concentric casing, moves forward at the moment of firing under the combined action of the gas pressure and the drag of the bullet due to friction against the bore. As the barrel moves forward it extracts and ejects the fired shell and locks in the open position if finger pressure is maintained on the trigger. As soon as the trigger is allowed to move forward, however, the barrel catch is released and the barrel slams back under the pressure of the spring which had been compressed during its forward motion. As it slides over the top of the magazine it picks up the top cartridge therefrom and chambers it. The pistol is thus reloaded, but it is not cocked. It may be thumb cocked, as it has an exposed hammer, or it may be cocked and fired by a steady pull on the trigger, as in the case of a double action revolver. The original pistol had no safety devices such as are present on the modern automatic pistol, because none were needed so long as the gun was not cocked.

Several modifications of the arm were made, one of which consisted of the elimination of the barrel catch which held the barrel in the forward position until released by removing the pressure on the trigger. While this feature made the pistol somewhat more "automatic" it was still only a "self-loading" pistol, as it had to be cocked in order to be fired. In still other variants the double action feature was omitted, thus necessitating cocking by hand. It is stated that still other experimental models showed grip safeties, presumably so that the pistol could be carried safely with the hammer in the cocked position.

Model of 1896—(Blowback design) The Modell 1896 (or perhaps more properly the Type 1896 Blowback) represents a transitional type. In it the blow forward principle which characterized the 1894 model was abandoned and the blowback substituted (Figs. 198, 199). The barrel was held in fixed position and the breechblock moved back into a housing upon firing of the pistol. This housing held a suitably stiff spiral spring which, together with the inertia of the moving parts, took up the force of the explosion to the desired degree.

Like the 1894 model, it was "half automatic" in that while it reloaded itself it had to be cocked before it could be fired. The hammer, instead of being exposed, was concealed within the frame and it was cocked from the outside by depressing the end of a lever which protruded from the rear of the frame.

The mechanism by which the pistol operated was novel but quite complicated compared to that of modern arms.

As in the 1894 model, the magazine was loaded from a charging clip. The system was referred to as "packet loading," a system very much favored by Mannlicher for his arms. The cartridges are first placed in position in the clip, where they are held by their rims, and then the end of the clip is inserted into guides above the magazine. The cartridges are then stripped from the clip by pushing them down into the magazine against a follower which is pushed upward by a coiled spring. The magazine is of the box type and is located in front of the trigger and below the line of the barrel. In this respect the pistol resembles the Military Type Mauser, but in most other respects it is quite different.

Modell 1900—Although designs for this model were patented in 1898 the first pistols were produced in 1900 and consequently were given the nomenclature "Modell 1900." As first produced, the pistol required a special experimental 8 mm. cartridge, details of which seem not to be known. Possibly because of the growing popularity of the German Mauser 7.63 mm. cartridge, it was soon decided to change the caliber of this new pistol to 7.63 mm. However, the Mauser cartridge was not used, but instead a new 7.63 mm. cartridge was developed, and in Austria this became known as the 7.63 mm. M.1900 Mannlicher. In Germany this cartridge was known as the D.W.M. 466 or 7.65 mm. Mannlicher to avoid confusion with the 7.63 mm. Mauser, which name applied only to the cartridge used in the 7.63 mm. Mauser Military Pistol. The two cartridges were not interchangeable, since the Mauser was of the bottleneck type whereas the Mannlicher had straight, tapered sides. The change in caliber resulted in a change of nomenclature for the pistol and it now became the Modell 1901 (Figs. 200 to 204).

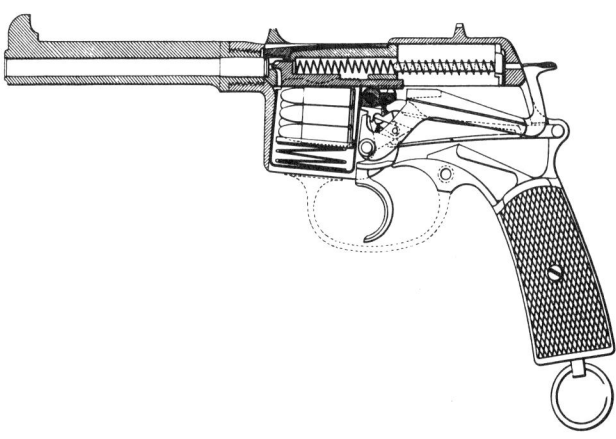

Fig. 198. Mannlicher Mod. 1896. Blowback, with fixed barrel. Packet loading, i.e., from a clip.

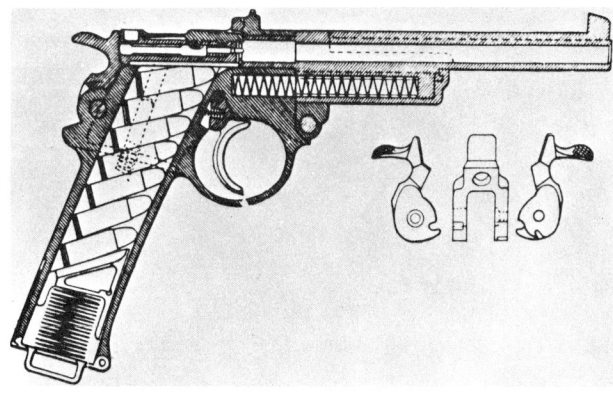

Fig. 200. 8 mm. Mannlicher Mod. 1900. Sectional view.

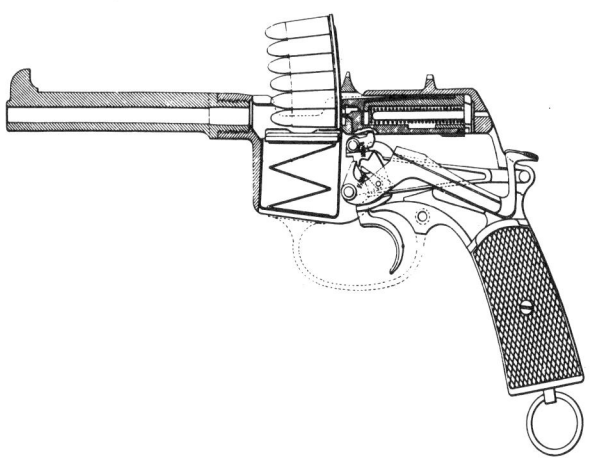

Fig. 199. Mannlicher Mod. 1896. Sectional view, showing manner of loading cartridges into magazine.

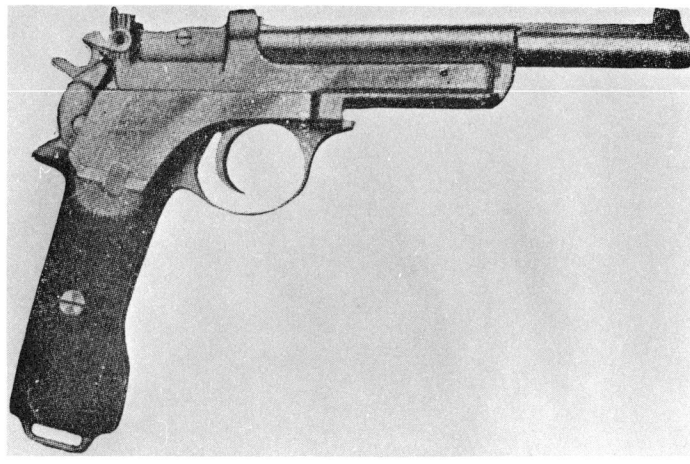

Fig. 201. 7.63 mm. Mannlicher Mod. 1901.

Fig. 202. 7.63 mm. Mannlicher Mod. 1901. This model had many variants.

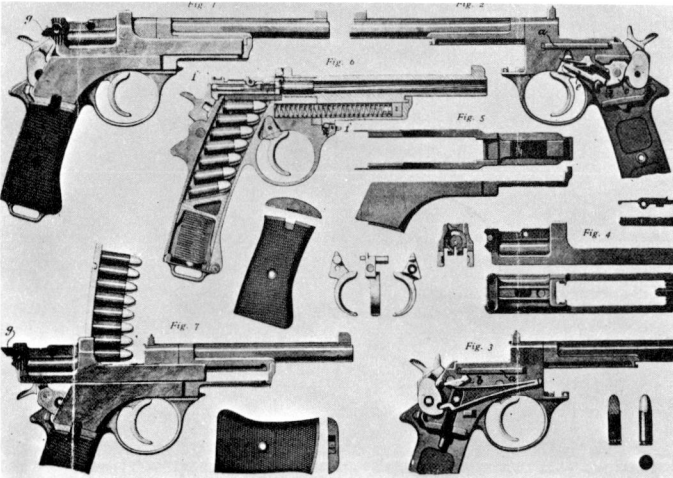

Fig. 203. 7.63 mm. Mannlicher Mod. 1901. Complete, sectional, and disassembled.

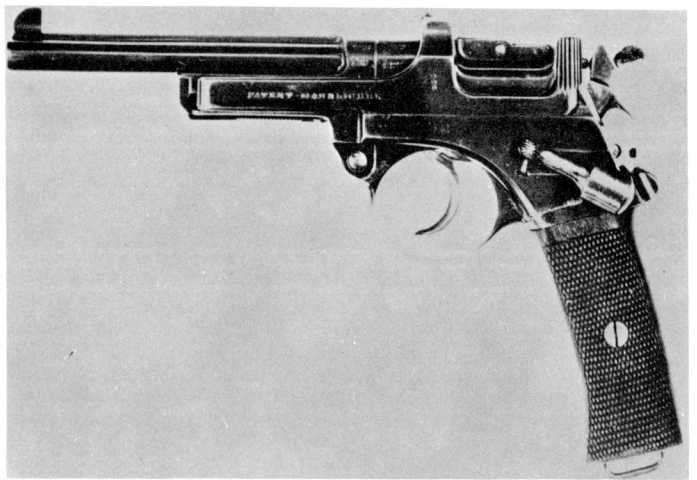

Fig. 204. 7.63 mm. Mannlicher Mod. 1901. One of many variants produced from 1901 to 1905.

The pistol was sold commercially, and apparently in very large quantities, up to the time manufacture was stopped in 1905. Considering the apparent popularity of the recognized excellent qualities the pistol possessed, it seems strange that production was not continued. Although it was very popular with Austrian Army officers who carried it as an unofficial side arm, the pistol was rejected for Austrian military use after official Army tests were made in 1904–05. This discouragement may have accounted for cessation of production. The pistol was very popular in South America and demands for ammunition in considerable quantity were made for many years after production of the pistol was stopped. Because of this continued demand, production of the 7.63 mm. Mannlicher cartridge was continued until the beginning of World War II. As the pistol had an excellent reputation and very considerable popularity in Europe and in South America it was naturally copied in Spain, but the pistols so produced were very inferior in workmanship compared to those made at Steyr.

The arm is a simple blowback in design, has an external hammer, and is simple and sturdy in construction. A considerable number of variant forms of this model were made. These may be found with markings such as Modell 1901, Modell 1902, Modell 1905, etc. and will show varying barrel lengths, different cartridge capacities, changes in safety styles, etc., but fundamentally they are all of the Modell 1901 type.

The original Modell 1900 had serial numbers starting at 1 (one) and this numbering continued through a transition 1900/01 form, but the whole series seems to have comprised less than 300 pieces. With the advent of Modell 1901 a new numbering series was adopted, again starting at 1 (one) and continuing in this series until cessation of production.

Factory records give the following data relative to rifling: number of grooves, 4; direction of twist, right; angle of twist, 5° 30′; one turn in 9.84 inches; groove depth, 0.0047 inch; groove width, .1154 inch; land width, .1212 inch; and groove diameter, .3012 inch.

Measurements of rifling made in the author's laboratory on specimens of this model show that these specifications were substantially followed.

Modell 1903 (Locked-breech, recoil-operated type)—Some authors prefer to call this the Modell 1896 because experimental models were actually produced in 1896, but the arm was actually put on the market in 1903 and because of this fact it is popularly known as the Modell 1903.

The novel system of locking, while similar to that

on the Military Type Mauser, was undoubtedly independently and concurrently arrived at, since, as stated, experimental models had already been produced in 1896, the year that the Mauser was introduced (Figs. 205 to 207).

The action is of the "short recoil" type and the breechblock and barrel travel together upon recoil until the barrel hits a stop. The breechblock then travels back alone into the breechblock housing, its motion being slowed down by camming and compression of the spring. At the moment that the barrel and breechblock separate, the shell is extracted and then ejected as the breechblock moves back. As in the 1896 blowback model, the hammer is completely concealed and is actuated by a lever, but in this model the lever is placed on the right side directly above the opening in the trigger guard. To cock the weapon the lever is pushed down with the right thumb into the horizontal postion. This lever contributes nothing to the appearance of the arm, which otherwise is very attractive.

The box magazine, made of sheet steel and detachable, is located in front of the trigger guard and is loaded by means of a charging clip. In the original model the clip held seven cartridges, but later when the 7.63 mm. cartridge was used it held only six. The special cartridge used in the original model of 1896 was replaced with a 7.63 mm. cartridge when the pistol was put on the market in 1903. The cartridge (D.W.M. 497) is known as the 7.63 M.1903 Mannlicher or M.1910 Mannlicher in Austria and as the 7.65 Mannlicher in Germany. The D.W.M. 466 and D.W.M. 497 are not identical. The 7.65 mm.

designation was adopted in Germany in order to distinguish it from the 7.63 Mauser, to which it is not identical. It is quite similar but has a lighter load, suitable for the Mannlicher. The Mauser cartridge, carrying a heavier load, should not be used in the Mannlicher as the locking device is not sufficiently strong and the pistol is likely to be ruined.

As in the case of other Mannlicher models, there were a number of variants of the 1903 model. One was a carbine type, having a rifle-type butt with pistol grip, a long barrel under which was a wooden forestock practically the length of the barrel, and a tangent rear sight adjustable to 400 meters. Another,

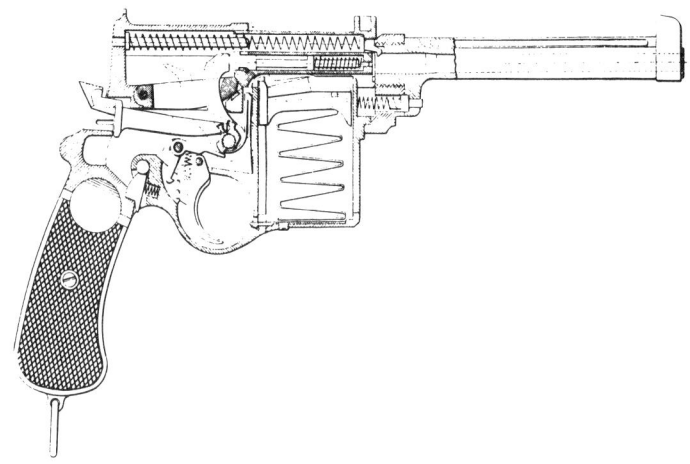

Fig. 206. 7.63 mm. Mannlicher Mod. 1903. Sectional view.

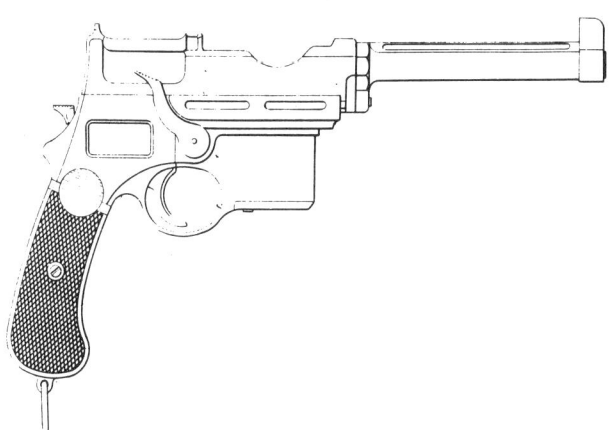

Fig. 205. 7.63 mm. Mannlicher Mod. 1903. Some authors call this a Mod. 1896, but it was first marketed in 1903. It was first designed for an 8 mm. (exptl.) cartridge, but used the Mannlicher 7.63 mm. cartridge when issued.

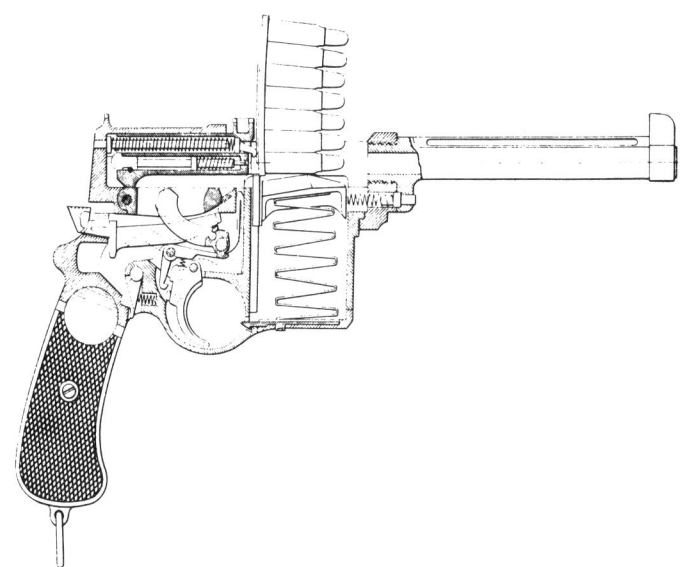

Fig. 207. 7.63 mm. Mannlicher Mod. 1903. Cartridges are stripped from a clip into the cartridge well.

more simple, variant consisted of a regular model provided with an adjustable rear sight (like the carbine) and a detachable butt-stock, thus converting it into a shoulder piece. Other variants had different barrel lengths and cartridge capacities, the incorporation of safety devices, etc.

The Modell 1903, though considered a more attractive and better balanced pistol with a better "feel," never attained the popularity which was achieved by the Mauser Military Pistol. This was probably due to the fact that the latter, though poorly balanced and awkward, was of much more rugged construction and better able to stand up under hard usage. How many Modell 1903 pistols were made is not known, but the sale was very limited indeed compared to that of the Mauser.*

Mauser military pistols (Recoil-operated, locked-bolt type)

In 1894 Paul Mauser, the inventor genius of the firm Waffenfabrik Mauser, of Oberndorf a/N, Germany, set himself the task of designing a military pistol which would possess certain characteristic features which he considered necessary.

The pistol should be of the recoil-operated, locked-bolt type, with magazine loading accomplished by stripping cartridges from a clip into a magazine well situated in front of the trigger, all of which principles had been so successfully used in the famous Mauser rifles. In addition, the pistol must have an external hammer (as a safety feature), must be constructed with interchangeable parts, must be capable of assembly and disassembly without tools; the barrel and extension thereof must be integral; the frame and action body should also be integral; and, finally, the action must remain open when the last cartridge is fired. His choice for a suitable cartridge was the 1893 7.65 mm. Borchardt, a cartridge which, with increased load, became known as the 7.63 mm. Mauser cartridge.

Early in 1895 a prototype model had been constructed, embodying the principles stated. It is believed that only one specimen was made in that year. This had a radial rear sight, checkered wood grip pieces, full Mauser markings, and no serial number. In 1896 further prototype specimens were made

*Full descriptions of the Mannlicher pistols, with drawings, will be found in a book entitled: *Mannlicher Rifles and Pistols*, by W. H. B. Smith, published by The Military Service Publishing Co., Harrisburg, Pa. Descriptions of some of them will also be found in *Handbook of Automatic Pistols*, by R. K. Wilson, Small Arms Technical Publishing Co., Plantersville, So. Carolina.

and as they seemed satisfactory it was decided to go into production. The first military adoption seems to have been by the Turkish Army, to which pistols were supplied during 1897 and 1898. These had full Mauser markings to which were added Turkish inscriptions. Later the Turks were supplied with pistols in the 7.65 Parabellum caliber. Soon after the Turks had adopted the pistol it was adopted for use by the Italian Navy, but the date is not known.

The 1896-type pistols were produced in four commercial and two experimental patterns. The commercial types included: a 6-round standard type, a 10-round standard type, a 20-round extended integral magazine type, and a 10-round carbine with long barrel and without a grip. The experimental patterns consisted of a 6 mm. type, built on a 10-round frame, chambered for a necked-down 7.63 mm. cartridge; and a 9 mm. type, also built on a 10-round frame, and chambered for a new 9 mm. cartridge designed by Mauser and later produced commercially.

The 1896-type pistols may be identified by the following points. The grip pieces are usually of wood, fully checkered, but occasionally in smooth finish, without serrations or checkering (Fig. 208). The head of the safety lever is solid, the hammer has a small-diameter hole through it and large bosses on either side with concentric rings which thicken progressively toward the center. The rear sight (on the 10- and 20-round and carbine models) is pivoted around a small-diameter pin. The thick ridges, running horizontally on both sides of the barrel extension just above the receiver, are smooth and without cutouts and grooves. All types are cut for a shoulder stock, and all have barrel extensions which are flat and smooth in the section below the rear sight and behind the ejector opening. The grip frame is large

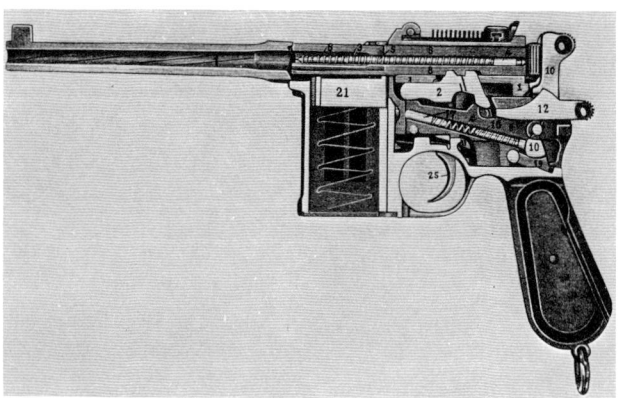

Fig. 208. 7.63 mm. Mauser Military Pistol. Sectional view.

and fully rounded. Serial numbers start at 1 (one). Rifling characteristics from original factory records are given in Table 38.

The number of these 1896 pistols which were made is not known, but it could not have been very large. The pistols are not common. Furthermore, the serial numbering on later types, which continued directly from the numbering of these 1896 types, is in the lower thousands.

1897, 1898, and 1899—Full production of the 6- and 10-round types continued through these years. Only minor external machining differences between these and the 1896 type can be noted. The grip pieces were changed to horizontally serrated wood plates. The safety lever head is pierced through, two long horizontal cutouts are machined into the thick ridges of the barrel extension above the receiver or frame. This is the pattern which is most frequently referred to as the Model 1898 or the Model 1899 Military Pistol. Neither of these designations is authentic, as the factory never gave any of these mod-

allowing engagement in the walls of the bolt. Somewhere around 1901–1904, a hammer with small head and flat sides was adopted for all models. A large-diameter pin was introduced for the rear sight assembly, and the so-called "Bolo" type oval-shaped grip pieces were introduced but not used on all models.

In this period the 9 mm. Mauser was introduced commercially, the earliest specimen seen having a number in the low 50,000's. This statement as to date is contrary to current literature, but is believed to be correct. The date of introduction usually given, 1908, is inconsistent with the serial numbering. During this period many combinations of variant characteristics were made. The pierced safety lever head was optional and continued to be for many years. Barrel extension side walls will be found flat (as in the 1896 type) or machined with a step (as in the 1898 and 1899 types). Machining with a step became standard procedure by 1905 and is found in all types thereafter.

TABLE 38
Rifling characteristics of Mauser 1896-type pistols

Number of grooves	4	Groove diam., max.	0.3118 inch
Direction of twist	Right	Depth of grooves	0.0047 "
Bore diam., standard	0.3004 inch	Width of grooves	0.047 "
Bore diam., maximum	0.3024 "	Width of lands	0.047 "
Groove diam., standard	0.3098 "	Twist (1 turn in)	9.84 inches

els a nomenclature. Serial numbers for this group are continuous from the early types and encompass the 10-round and 6-round versions, as each was manufactured. Generally speaking these range from 5000 to 15,000.

1899, 1900, 1902—In this period a number of important changes and modifications were made. The earlier, bossed hammer was replaced by a large-head, large-diameter hammer with flat sides, having a large pierced hole through it. This change is often erroneously given the date of 1905. The large-head hammer actually dates from 1899 and all types were provided with it up to about 1904.

A second important change consisted of a complete redesign of the firing sytem, which took place early in 1902 (starting with serial number around 30,000). In 1902, the safety lever was made longer and used a stud to control the hammer. The lever was swung up for the "safe" position, whereas in the pre-1902 types it was swung downwards. This and some other changes here mentioned are usually, but erroneously, stated to have been made in 1912. In 1902 the firing pin retaining plate was dropped in favor of placing wings on the rear of the pin and

From 1901 through 1902 an interesting variant was produced, on both an experimental and commercial basis. This is the type with a perfectly smooth receiver, having none of the cavities, flats, and cutouts of the type which preceded or followed it. Commercial pistols, in both the 6- and 10-round types, with serial numbers in the 20,000's will be found with the flat-sided receivers. Another interesting variant of this period was the so-called Officers Style, usually to be found with a shorter barrel, with a very small, rounded grip frame, not at all like the commercial models and having checkered-wood grip pieces. This pistol was produced in both the 6- and 10-round forms and would not accept the shoulder stock. It usually had the large hammer and the smooth receiver. Commercial serial numbers for this pattern are usually found to be in the 20,000's.

1905 to 1910—Manufacture of the Mauser pistol in this period settled down to four basic types (with minor variants in each): the 7.63 mm. in both 6- and 10-round capacities, and the 9 mm. in both 6- and 10-round capacities. The serial numbering in this period ranged from about 60,000 to 90,000. Only one hammer pattern was used, the small head with flat sides. The long up-swinging safety lever, with or without the pierced head, was used. The grip frame shape was confined mainly to the large, rounded-bottom style, originally used from 1896 to 1899. The so-called Bolo grip was also used. Around 1910 (in the 90,000 to 100,000 range) a very important change was introduced. Six-groove rifling was used for the first time on the Mauser Military Type pistol. For a time it appeared to be optional, but soon it became standard for both the 7.63 and 9 mm. pistols. The date for this change is usually given as 1912, but is believed to have actually been first used in 1910, to some extent at least. At just what serial number the permanent change from 4-groove to 6-groove rifling was made is not known, but the change is thought to have been complete at 120,000.

Fig. 209. Mauser experimental pistol Model of 1906/08. Recoil operated. Serial No. 16, based on German Pats. Nos. 198,894, 201,610 (both Sept. 21, 1907), and 207,083 (Dec. 5, 1907).

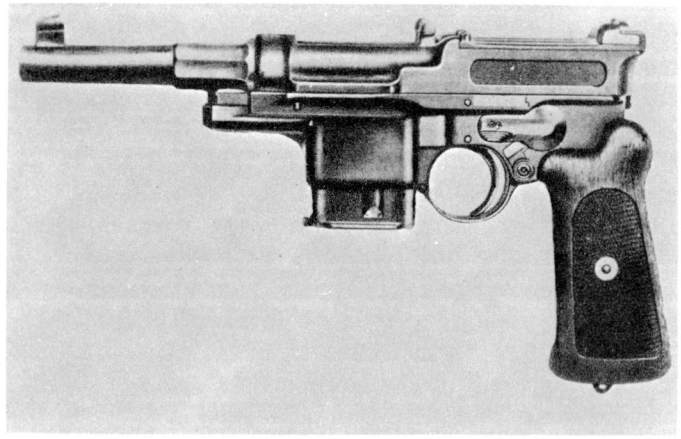

Fig. 210. Mauser experimental pistol Model of 1906/08. Another of several models. Serial No. 23. Has shorter magazine than No. 16 (Fig. 209) and barrel is octagonal at breech. Both are 9 mm.

Another model, which needs mention only since it was an experimental model which never reached the production state, is the so-called 1906/08 model (Figs. 209 and 210). It was of the recoil-operated type, with frontal magazine, and was designed for the 7.63 mm. Mauser cartridge. It followed the general outline of the commercial locked-bolt types. It was produced only as a working model of a rifle mechanism in which Mauser was interested. This, of course, is a collector's item. Still another experimental model, even more rare, is shown in Fig. 211.

1912 to 1920—By 1912 over 130,000 Mauser Military Pistols had been made, in 7.63 mm. Mauser and 9 mm. Mauser calibers and with several barrel lengths and magazine capacities (mostly 6- and 10-round). From 1912 to 1915 there were no major changes in design, but by 1915, as a result of the World War, the 6-round types and the 9 mm. types were discontinued. Annual production rose from 12,000 per year in 1909 to almost 40,000 per year by 1915.

In 1915–1916 an important improvement was made. This improvement is in the safety, and attention is drawn to it by the symbol ns (Neues Sicherung = New Safety) which is found superimposed on the rear edge of the hammer. At the same time a solid head, instead of a pierced head, was introduced on the safety lever. This change was made at a serial number somewhere around 280,000. The mechanical difference in the safety relates to the condition for application of the safety when the hammer is cocked. It is necessary to further depress the hammer, with the right hand, when the safety is applied.

In 1916 the GPK (Gewehrprufungs Komission) gave Mauser a contract to produce a 9 mm. Para-

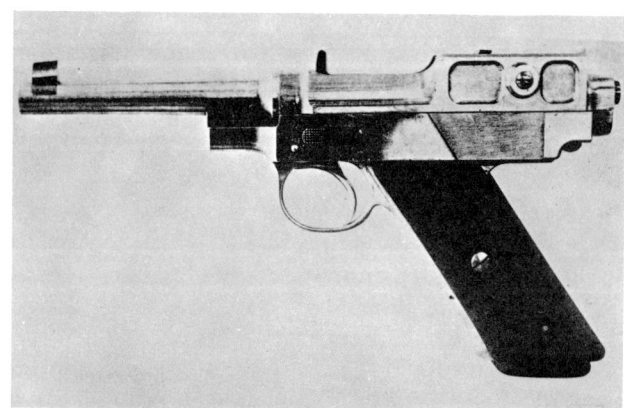

Fig. 211. 9 mm. Mauser experimental model. Has no factory model nomenclature. Recoil operated, magazine in frame, based on German Pat. No. 209,212 (Feb. 24, 1907).

bellum version, with full automatic firing. Although the design was completed the project was dropped before full production got under way. The use of the 9 mm. Parabellum caliber was retained, however, and about 150,000 pistols in that caliber were manufactured between 1916 and late 1918. These 9 mm. pistols were numbered in their own series, from 1 to about 150,000. The 7.63 mm. caliber continued the old series of numbers, and this rose into the 300,000's by late 1918 (Fig. 212).

1920 to 1937—When the war ended, the manufacture of pistols stopped for about two years. In 1920, when the new German Republic was allowed to equip its police and its 100,000-man army, the standard Mauser pistol and the Parabellum pistol,

particularly those in 9 mm. caliber, were counterstamped with the date 1920 to show officially authorized use. At the same time opportunity was taken to correct the safety devices on the 9 mm. Parabellum pistols. Mauser pistols found to have the date 1920 on the side of the barrel extension are usually of World War I manufacture and of postwar assembly from pre-1918 parts. The practice of dating all sorts of military-style pistols with the date 1920 became common, as this made them appear to be official. Consequently, one can find 7.63 Mauser pistols (unauthorized) with the 1920 date and also many types of pre-war and nonstandard barrel lengths in 7.63 Mauser and 9 mm. Parabellum with the 1920 date. Obviously, this 1920 date must not be confused with the serial number.

Commercial manufacture of the 7.63 mm. Mauser, in two barrel lengths and with 10-round capacity only, was resumed in 1922. From 1922 to 1929 the

Fig. 212. Comparison of mechanisms. *Upper:* Shows the fully automatic mechanism used in Mod. 712—the "Schnellfeuer Pistole." *Lower:* Conventional mechanism used in the Mod. 96 et seq. pistols.

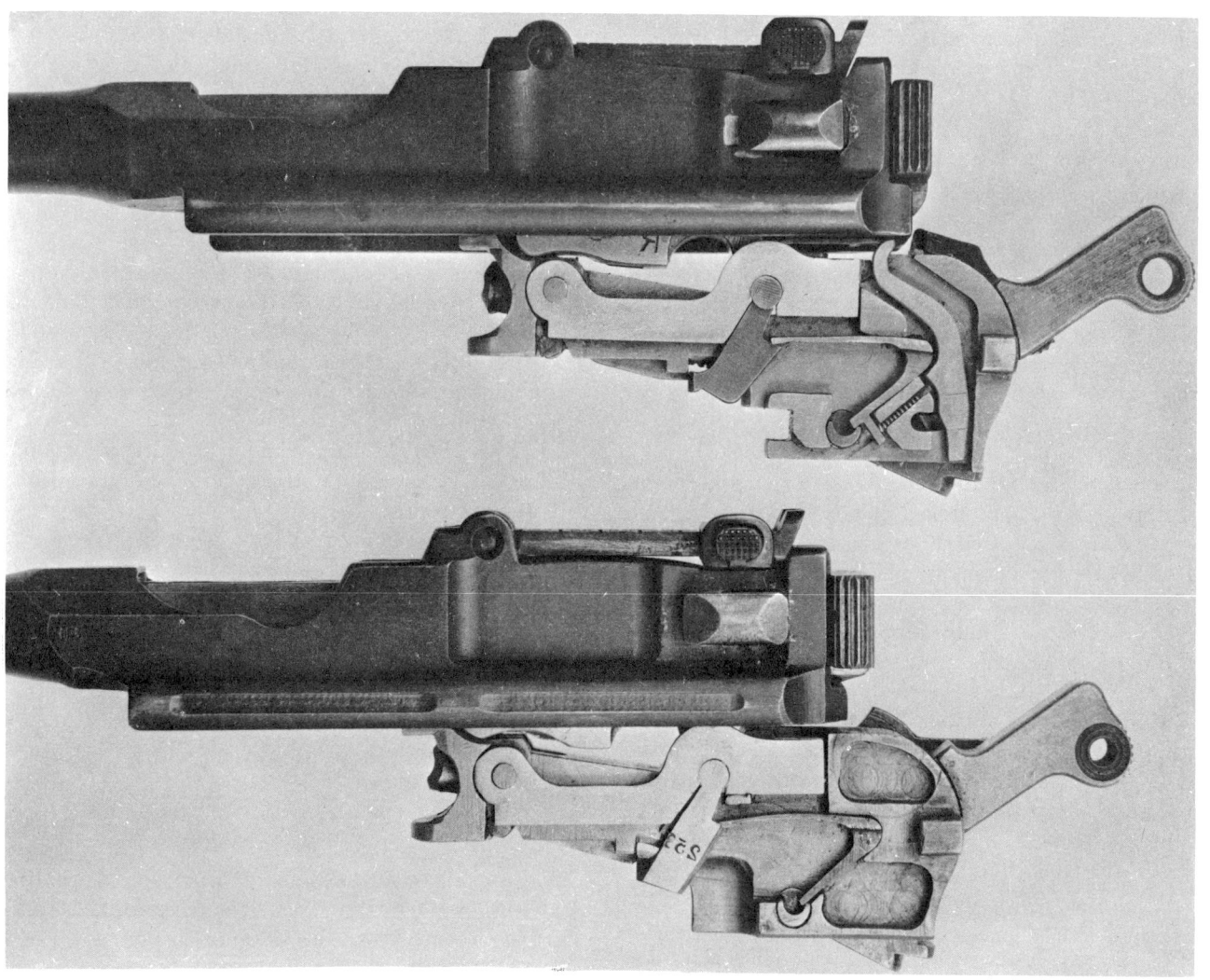

Asian market was very strong, particularly for the short-barrel (so-called Bolo) type, and the serial numbers, which continued from where they left off in 1918, rose to 700,000. Contrary to statements of many authors, the pistol was not sold in large quantities to the Soviets in this period. The market began to fall off in the Asian countries in 1919, due no doubt to the appearance of several unauthorized copies in Spain and to imitations which also appeared in India and China. Those produced in India and China show a great many variations, some being fairly exact copies and others merely imitations as to form. Some appear to be fairly good, particularly some made at the Government Arsenal in Shansei Province, where about 6000 were made. The first 3000 were made in 1929 (Pattern 18) and the second 3000 in 1930 (Pattern 19), the "Pattern" referring to the 18th or 19th year of the prevailing dynasty. Serial numbering started at 1 (one). Some, and perhaps all, of these were made in .45 caliber.

In 1929, with serial number ca. 800,000, the Mauser "universal safety" was introduced on the regular and Bolo models. This safety is identified by a return to the pierced safety lever head. In the summer of 1930 the selective-fire (reihenfeuer = successive) pistol was introduced. This pistol is variously known as the Schnellfeuer Pistole (in Germany), as the Model of 1932, or as Model 712. Fire was selective in that when a sliding plate on the left side of the receiver was pushed forward to the position marked "N" the pistol functions as a normal "semiautomatic" pistol, but when the plate is pushed back to the position "R" (for reihenfeuer) the pistol becomes a full automatic in action, i.e., a machine pistol. This pistol was numbered in a separate series, starting presumably at 1 (one) and running up to about 100,000. It was also copied in Spain.

Some Mauser factory records state that the manufacture of 7.63 mm. locked-bolt type pistols in both regular and selective fire models was stopped in 1935 to make way for production of the Parabellum. However, other factory records indicate that manufacture of the 7.63 mm. Mauser continued until late 1936 and that pistols were still being assembled and distributed in 1937.

While the total number of Mauser locked-bolt type pistols made between 1896 and 1937 is not known, it is believed that a reasonably good estimate can be made from the following considerations. Serial number 800,000 was reached in 1929. Production figures for 1935, 1936, and 1937 are given as 25,000, 30,000, and 30,000, respectively. About 10 per cent of these were in the Schnellfeuer model. On this basis it may be assumed that about 950,000 of the

original 7.63 and 9 mm. Mauser caliber pistols were made in the period 1896 to 1936, inclusive. Adding to this figure about 150,000 for the 9 mm. P'08 caliber and about 100,000 for the Schnellfeuer (both of which were numbered in separate series), and discounting the small number of 7.65 mm. caliber pistols that were made, it would seem that the total production up to 1938 must have been of the order of 1,200,000.

Mauser carbines—Although the Mauser Military Pistol could easily be converted into what was essentially a carbine by the attachment of the standard shoulder stock, it was very early decided to produce a "pistol carbine." One of these has already been mentioned—a 10-round type of 1896, without grip. In 1899 a second type was produced. This had the fixed stock with integral grip piece, a fore-arm, and a large-diameter barrel. Both the 1896 and the 1899 types were made in 7.63 mm. caliber. Around 1905 a limited quantity of carbines including the latest pistol characteristics were manufactured. These had the small flat hammer, the new long safety, large-diameter rear sight pin, etc. Between 1900 and 1905 several variant types appeared. The true carbines are scarce, as they were not made in quantity. It is reported that Mauser accepted an invitation to submit a Mauser Army Carbine in .45 caliber for testing in the U.S. Army Trials at Springfield but that the specimen was not completed in time for the trial.

Factory data for the 7.63 mm. Mauser Military Pistol, as issued ca. 1915–16, are given in Table 39.

Markings on 7.63 and 9 mm. Mauser pistols—The Mauser 7.63 pistol was adopted for use in the Turkish military service around 1899 but seems to have been dropped by 1902. Consequently, the so-called 1898 or 1899 Military Model (model designations were not used at that time) will be found with a Turkish crest on the left side panel of the frame. Some of the 7.63 mm. pistols were supplied to the

TABLE 39

Data for 7.63 mm. Mauser military pistol

Over-all length (without shoulder stock)	240 mm.
Length with shoulder stock*	640 "
Barrel length	140 "
Sighting radius	238 "
Height	150 "
Thickness	32 "
Magazine capacity, ctges.	10 (or 6)
Weight (with empty 10-ctge. mag.)	1150 gm.
Number of rifling grooves	6
Twist, right, 1 turn in	230 mm.

*This shoulder stock, being hollow, was also used as a case in which the pistol could be carried.

German military service from 1900 to 1905, and these are usually identifiable by the serial numbers and by the presence of German military proof marks. The Mauser 9 mm. caliber, commercial, was never distinguished by special markings from the 7.63 mm., and the 7.65 mm. Parabellum also was not distinguished by special markings. The 9 mm. Parabellum, however, was marked with a large, red-filled figure 9 cut into each grip piece.

After 1922, Mauser pistols were supplied to several Chinese and other Oriental police forces and were given appropriate markings. These pistols must not be confused with copies of native manufacture in those countries.* The pistol, in 10-round type, was supplied to the Persian military service in small quantities somewhere in the 1910–1915 period, and these were so marked. Specimens with Swiss and Russian markings are known, but it seems more likely that these markings were put on after delivery. All pistols, from 1896 on, were marked Waffenfabrik Mauser, etc. This is true even for the pistols which were manufactured after 1922, which was the date at which the name of the firm was changed to Mauser Werke. The Mauser Pocket Pistols were marked Waffenfabrik Mauser up to about 1930, at which time the Mauser Werke name was inscribed on them, but the name on the locked-bolt types was never changed.

Grip pieces—The original grip pieces were of checkered wood or of smooth wood (1896–97). In 1898 the horizontally serrated wood grip was introduced, and in 1899 the molded hard rubber grip piece with floral pattern was introduced. After 1900 the serrated grip pieces or the rubber grips with the floral pattern were used interchangeably, the floral pattern apparently being used less frequently. In 1900–1902 checkered wood grip pieces were used in limited numbers on special models. From 1902 on, the serrated wood grips are more common. Around 1906–07 a molded rubber grip with intertwined WM initials was introduced, and this form of grip was used intermittently up to 1914 on all models, including the blowback models (discussed elsewhere). From 1914 on, up into the late 1930's, the serrated grip (with varying patterns of serration)

was used on all of the Mauser locked-bolt types.

Serial numbers—The serial numbering of the Mauser locked-bolt type pistols began with No. 1 in 1896 and followed along continuously for the "standard" types, with the exception of small lots made for the German Government on special contract and other small lots for other countries. Separate numbering series were used for the 9 mm. Parabellum (P'08) and the Schnellfeuer types, of which there were approximately 150,000 and 100,000, respectively. Estimates of numbers produced are: 10,000 by 1899; 25,000 by 1901; 40,000 by 1903; 60,000 by 1907; 100,000 by 1910–11; 130,000 by 1912; 280,000 by 1915–16; over 300,000 by 1918; 800,000 by 1929; 1,200,000 by 1937 (all types).

Grip frame styles—The original pistols, about 1895–1896, have large, round-bottom grips which are the most common type. A smaller, oval-bottom type, known as the Bolo type, was introduced around 1903. These two types are considered standard. A small, rounded type was introduced, probably experimentally, in the short-lived Officers Model around 1900–01, but was not used elsewhere.

Caliber—The original pistol was of 7.65 mm. Borchardt M. 1893 caliber. From 1896 on, this was designated the 7.63 mm. Mauser, which carried a heavier load that was unsafe for the Borchardt pistol. The commercial models made from 1897 on are of 7.63 Mauser caliber. The 9 mm. Mauser caliber was especially designed to capture overseas trade, particularly in South America, Africa, and the Orient. This pistol is often referred to as the Export Model. Experiments on a 9 mm. caliber are said to have been made as far back as 1896, but it was not introduced commercially before about 1905 (some say 1908, but this is not consistent with known serial numbers). Its manufacture was discontinued in 1914 as was also the manufacture of the cartridge.

The 7.65 mm. Parabellum caliber pistols were reportedly made on a special contract for Turkey around 1899–1901 and again in the late 1920's in small quantity only. The 9 mm. Parabellum caliber was introduced during World War I, in 1916, in order to standardize ammunition.

9 mm. Experimental Pistol No. 40 (Gerät 40 Prägueausführung)—This experimental pistol, which was planned as a replacement for the P-38 but of which only five specimens were made, was designed by Altenburger, Seidel, and Starnanns of the Mauser Werke late in 1943. Although the prototype specimens were completed in 1944, the final design had not been finished at the end of the war.

The pistol was of the fully locked, recoil-operated type wherein the barrel engages cutouts in the roof

*Chinese copies of the Mauser Military Pistol of good quality are known. Some of these were made at the Hanyang Arsenal (near Hankow), one specimen of which is marked as having been made in the 14th year of the Chinese Republic (i.e., 1925). Other copies were made at the Shansei Province Arsenal, one known specimen of which is marked as having been made in the 19th year of the Republic (1930). Very likely, specimens made at other Chinese arsenals will be found.

of the slide. The outstanding feature, obviously intended to speed up and to reduce cost of production, was the use of stamped and formed sheet metal components throughout, except for the barrel, pins, and rivets.

The locking arrangement followed the Browning design in that a single cutout on the upper surface of the barrel held the slide and barrel together during recoil, followed by a downward and rearward unlocking motion of the barrel after firing. The arm was of the double action type. The safety system was patterned after that developed earlier for the HS series of blowback pistols. The pistol was naturally designed to use the standard 9 mm. Parabellum cartridge, so the P-38 magazine was adopted for this new pistol.

Mauser blowback pistols

The first Mauser patents on blowback type pistols date from 1907, and many patents were taken out from 1907 to 1915. Work on a fixed-barrel type of arms was first done on rifles in 1907, but in 1908 interest had shifted to experimental work on a hand gun of this type. Mauser's first attempt was to produce a military pistol in 9 mm. Parabellum caliber, and this resulted in a pistol designated as Modell 1909. Although an instruction book was issued, indicating that the pistol was expected to meet with approval, there was little demand for them and very few were made. This Modell 1909 is not to be confused with the later Modell 1912 and the Modell 1912/14, as it did not have the delaying or retarding devices which appeared on the Modell 1912. Successful functioning depended on the use of a special Parabellum cartridge with a lighter powder charge and lighter bullet, which was specially designed by Mauser for this weapon (Figs. 213, 214).

1910 and 1914 Types—In 1909–1910 Mauser developed and produced a 6.35 mm. pocket pistol which, except for size, minor machining, and assembly differences, was a copy of the 9 mm. Modell 1909, and this was put on the market later in 1910 or early in 1911. It is now referred to as the Mod. 1910, although at the time no model designation was assigned to it by the manufacturer. Model designations for the early smaller pistols were made only in the case of the 6.35 mm. vestpocket (W.T.P.) pistols and then only after the introduction of the second model.

Early issues of the 1910 Type are characterized by the presence of a lever on the left side of the receiver just above the trigger, the purpose of which is two-fold. The device combines a trigger pin and

on this pin is a latch which unlocks the front end of the side plate over the limb work. The rear end of this plate is rabbeted into the receiver. In the later issues of the 1910 Type pistol a simpler and less expensive scheme was used. In these later pistols the trigger pin is staked to the opposite (right) side of the receiver. To expose the limb work the slide is first removed and the side plate, which is rabbeted at each end, is simply lifted up at the rear end and removed.

Late in 1913 a new version of the 1910 type was announced, differing in a few details. Early in 1914 it was announced that a 7.65 mm. pistol was forthcoming, in which all of the latest features of the 6.35 mm. pistol would be incorporated. This ap-

Fig. 213. 9 mm. (Par) Mauser Mod. 1909. An experimental blowback model. Not successful and but few were made.

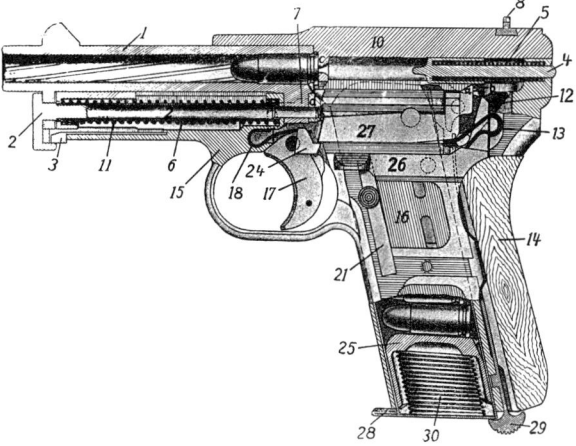

Fig. 214. 9 mm. (Par) Mauser Mod. 1912. An experimental pistol for which a special Parabellum cartridge with lighter bullet and powder charge was developed. Not accepted for military use.

peared late in that year or possibly early in 1915. Experimental models for a 7.65 mm. pistol had been made in 1912 and 1913, but the final form which was issued commercially was quite different in external characteristics from the experimental forms. The Model 1910 (but unofficial) designation seems to have remained as popular nomenclature for the early 6.35 mm. model (ca. 1910), the improved 6.35 mm. model (ca. 1913–14), and the first 7.65 mm. model (ca. 1914, commercially). Later the 7.65 mm. pistol became known as the Model 1914 in popular nomenclature. As time went on it appeared in several slightly differing forms, but essentially it remained the same.

The numbering of the 6.35 mm. pistols produced from 1910 to 1913 (inclusive) appears to have been from 1 to 61,000. The 7.65 mm. 1914 type seems to have been numbered first from 61,000 to 100,000, after which the numbers jumped to 200,000 and became intermingled with the numbers for the 6.35 mm. pistol. From the number 200,000 on, the 6.35 and 7.65 mm. pistols appear to have been numbered in the same series, which by 1939 had reached about 640,000. This statement does not include the W.T.P. models, however, which had their own series of numbering. Although the firm name had been changed from Waffenfabrik Mauser to Mauser-Werke in 1922, the new name was not used on the pocket pistols until 1929 or 1930, at about serial number 400,000.

1934–1939—From 1914 to 1934 there had been little change in the 7.65 mm. model, but in 1934 a change was made which altered its external appearance. This change consisted in the use of a more streamlined grip, which afforded a better hold. Instead of using two grip pieces the entire grip consisted of one piece, formed to fit the grip frame. A single screw on each side held it in place.

About this time Mauser began work on a design for a double action pistol and by 1937 they had developed one which they designated a Hahn Selbstspann (or self-cocking hammer). This system, generally referred to as the HS system, was much delayed in its development due to patent and legal difficulties engendered by Walther's natural desire to control the production of double action pistols. In 1937 Mauser produced a few of the new pistols, designated HSa, and circulated samples among firearms authorities, editors, etc. to get their reaction. As a result of recommendations and comments received, certain changes were made and a few of this revised form (known as HSb) were similarly circulated. Finally, a third form was arrived at and this was considered sufficiently perfected to warrant commercial production. This model was des-

ignated Modell HSc, and serial numbering started around 700,000. From the time that it was brought out, in 1938, until 1945 serial numbers had grown to about 955,000, indicating that more than 250,000 had been made in that period. This model was produced throughout World War II as a side arm for the Army and for the Luftwaffe, and very few were distributed commercially. Hence almost every specimen seen will have the German military acceptance mark (WaA). Not only did the military forces take over all of the HSc pistols produced, but also the last 100,000 or so of the 1934 type, consequently many specimens of the latter will also have the German military acceptance mark. Both of these 7.65 mm. pistols, being small, compact, and reliable, were desirable as light side arms. The Model HSc is an exceptionally fine pocket pistol.

Immediately after the war another 20,000 pieces were made for the French Government. These are regularly marked and should be numbered above 955,000. Naturally they will not have the German acceptance mark. There were several minor mechanical variations in this run. The Mod. HSc was also produced, experimentally, in .22 caliber and in 9 mm. Short (.380 ACP) but only in very small quantities. Consequently they are collectors' items.

Experimental models

As has been mentioned, Mauser's first attempt to devise a blowback pistol was aimed at producing a military model. After his Modell 1909 failed, work was continued and, by adding retarding bars under the slide, a fairly successful 9 mm. Parabellum design was attained by the end of 1912. This Modell 1912 was unique in that it was intended for a boat-tailed bullet. It could accept a holster-shoulder stock and was large in size. This model was adopted by Brazil in 1913 and Mauser was given a contract, but for what quantity is not known. Further improvements, particularly the incorporation of a radial rear sight, were made and the pistol was given the new designation of Modell 1912/14. Work was also started on a .45 caliber version of this new model, but the intervention of World War I put a stop to production of pistols on the Brazilian contract and to work on the .45. Several hundred of the 1912 and 1912/14 models were produced during the three-year period and these were put into German service in 1914 and 1915. In all, there are said to be at least a dozen minor variant forms of these 9 mm. pistols, but specimens of the .45 caliber pistols of this type are very rare indeed.

There was nothing particularly distinguishing about these 9 mm. types, as they were very much like the 7.65 mm. commercial type of 1914. Because of the small number made they are not likely to be encountered, except in collections (Figs. 215 to 218).

Another Mauser-designed pistol of interest is the Nickl-Mauser which was designed by Nickl, an engineer in the Mauser plant, in 1916. He designed a rotating barrel scheme which he placed on the 1914 type of Mauser pocket pistol frame. The design for

this pistol was licensed to the Czechs and became the basis for the Czech military pistol vz 22. Mauser, however, retained development rights and the pistol was made, experimentally, in various forms from 1916 to 1935. Specimens were made in the following calibers: 7.65 mm. Browning, 7.65 mm. French Long, 9 mm. Short Browning, 9 mm. Long Browning, and .45 ACP. Specimens dating from the early 1930's can be found in 9 mm. Parabellum, being service prototypes for the German army. All of these nonstandard-caliber pistols will be found with full commercial markings. None of these ever attained much approval in Germany, but the Czechs made good use of the design.

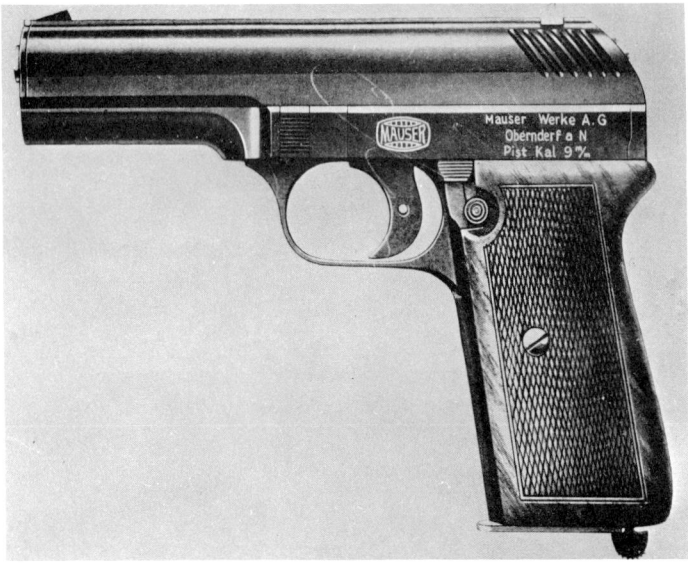

Fig. 215. 9 mm. Mauser Nickl Mod. Designed in 1916 by Mauser engineer (Nickl). Licensed to the Czech Government ca. 1921. With some modifications became the Czech Mod. 24 and was made until 1938.

Fig. 217. 9 mm. Mauser Nickl Mod. Showing method of disassembly.

240   *Fig. 216.* 9 mm. Mauser Nickl Mod.

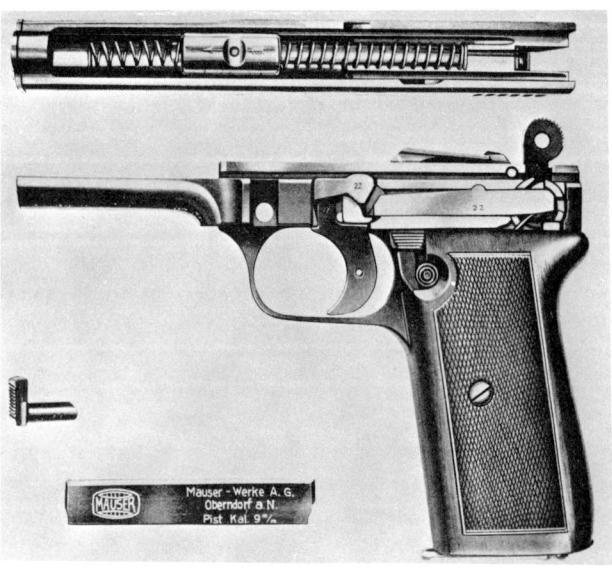

Fig. 218. 9 mm. Mauser Nickl Mod. Partially disassembled.

Mauser vestpocket models

The popularity of the 6.35 mm. F.N. Browning Baby (vestpocket) pistol, the Walther Model 9, and other very small pistols undoubtedly led Mauser to design a pistol of this size in order to get in on a good market. The result was a design which was patented in 1918 and to which was given the official nomenclature Mauser Westentaschen Pistole Kal. 6.35. This designation distinguished it from the Mauser Selbstlade Taschen Pistole Kal. 6.35 which they had introduced in 1910 and which continued in production. When a new model of this pistol was brought out later, a name had to be found to differentiate it from the original W.T.P. so it was referred to as the Modell II, and the earlier one then became Modell I.

Just when this pistol was first put on the market is not known, but the date was probably previous to 1923 as it is known to have been advertised early in that year. Serial numbering started at 1 (one) and had attained a figure of upwards of 50,000 when it was discontinued in favor of the new model, numbering of which appears to have started at around 50,000.

In 1936 or 1937 Mauser began the development of a new, more advanced design of vestpocket pistol, and this was introduced commercially in 1938 under the nomenclature of Mauser Westentaschen Pistole Kal. 6.35 Modell II, to distinguish it from the earlier model. This W.T.P. II was produced from 1938 to about 1939 or 1940 at which time all manufacturing facilities at Mauser had to be turned to wartime production of more important material. While this is not confirmed, it is believed that the serial numbering was continued from the earlier model, which would mean that the numbering started at about 50,000. Because of the short period of production it seems unlikely that the total production of this model exceeded 40,000 to 50,000 and probably it was less.

While there is much similarity between the two W.T.P. models there are some important differences. Neither has a grip safety but both have a magazine safety, which holds the action open after the discharge of the last cartridge. Each has a thumb safety, but in different locations. In Mod. I the thumb safety is located above the grip, below the rear end of the slide, whereas in Mod. II it is located in front of the grip and much of it is concealed by the grip, under which it operates. Considerably longer grip pieces are used on Mod. II, because more room is available on account of the relocation of the thumb safety. The grip is more streamlined, providing a better hold and a neater appearance. When cocked, the rear end of the firing pin protrudes a bit from the rear end of the slide, so that one can tell instantly, with the thumb, whether the arm is cocked. Of course it does not tell whether there is a cartridge in the chamber.

The original Mod. I bears the firm name Waffenfabrik Mauser whereas the Mod. II bears the name Mauser-Werke. The name change was made in 1922, consequently the fact that the Mod. I bore the original name might be thought to indicate that its introduction occurred prior to 1922. This, however, is not valid reasoning because, although the name change did occur officially in 1922, the original name of Waffenfabrik Mauser was used on pocket pistols until about 1930. The date of introduction of the first model may have been 1922, but the use of the original name form gives no valid information.

Factory data for the 6.35 and 7.65 mm. Mauser Pocket Pistols are given in Table 40.

TABLE 40

Data for Mauser pocket pistols

Measurement	Mod. 1910	Mod. 1914	W.T.P. 1st Mod.	W.T.P. Mod. II
Caliber, mm.	6.35	7.65	6.35	6.35
Length over-all, mm.	136	153	115	103
Barrel length, mm.	78.5	87	61	52
Sighting radius, mm.	117	127	100	90
Height, mm.	100	110	77	70
Thickness, mm.	22	27	21	21
Weight, empty, gm.	445	600	320	290
Magazine cap., ctges.	9	8	6	6

Mayor pistol

The 6.35 mm. (ACP) pistol bearing the marking MAYOR ARQUEBUSIER is a simple blowback in design. It appeared in two forms as to slide construction. In the earlier form the slide was of one-piece construction extending the entire length of the pistol and having a portion of the upper part of the front end cut away for the upward ejection of the fired shell, the extractor being located at the top of the slide at the rear of the cut away portion. In the later form of the pistol the slide extends the full length of the frame but consists of two separate sections. Upon firing the rear section moves back, extracting and ejecting the fired case to the right through the opening caused by the separation of the two sections, the extractor being located on the right side rather than at the top of the slide.

Both forms have a barrel which extends about ⅝ inch in front of the slide, both have a disassembly latch or lever extending from the front end of the

241

frame, and both have a mechanical safety located just back of the trigger guard on the frame. In the earlier form the safety was a thumb-operated lever (which was pushed forward or backward) while in the later form the safety was a thumb-operated sliding latch (which was pushed backward or forward). Disassembly is very easy, as all that is necessary is to push upward on the take down catch, thus releasing the slide.

Observed specimens are marked MAYOR ARQUE-BUSIER on the left side of the slide. On the left side of the slide there also appears a curious emblem (or trade mark) consisting of the outline of a fish above which is the letter R and below the letter N. This same design appears on the otherwise plain wood grip pieces. The serial number appears on the right side of the slide, and the later specimens carry the patent number.

Inasmuch as the name Mayor appears on all known specimens of this pistol it may be considered as correct nomenclature. The pistol is based on a design for which the inventor, Ernest Rochat of Nyon, received a Swiss patent dated February 11, 1919 (Pat. No. 86,863).

Sometime in 1917 or 1918 Rochat had asked the Mayor brothers, Francois in Lausanne and Ernest in Geneva, to make and distribute the pistol which he had designed. Ernest Mayor, who is still in business (1959) in Geneva, states that only a limited number of pistols were made by his brother, Francois, because he had only a small shop and consequently could not compete with the larger arms manufacturers.

A literal translation of the patent states that the design covers "A pistol comprising a mobile breech which opens and closes automatically by the firing of the cartridge, characterized by a helical spring placed co-axially in another helical spring which serves to bring the breech back to the front after each shot, the two opposed springs being mounted in a single chamber preceded by the mobile breech."

Menz pistols

August Menz (Waffenfabrik August Menz) of Suhl, Germany, made the 7.65 mm. Menta pistol during World War I. This pistol was one of the Beholla group, all made from the same drawings and already discussed. The Menta differed but little from the other three members of the group. During the later stages of production Stenda-Werke added a barrel assembly catch to the Stenda pistol. One 7.65 mm. pistol of this type, with Menz grip plate monograms but with no other markings, has been examined and found to have the barrel assembly latch (in slightly modified form). No pistol marked Menta or 7.65 mm. Menz on the slide has been found to have this catch. From the serial number, which is No. 72,322, it might be concluded that this was a continuation of the Stenda-Werke numbering rather than that of Menz. However, all other observed pistols made by Stenda-Werke are definitely so marked; furthermore, the rifling characteristics are not consistent for any pistol in the Beholla group. This pistol may have been one of a more or less experimental lot made by Menz after the war, but this is only a conjecture.

In addition to the 7.65 Menta made during the war, Menz made several other pistols. Some of these appear to have been produced in quantity, while others seem to have been of an experimental nature and not marketed. Menz also made pistols which were sold under other names, particularly the Bergmann Erben which were made for the successors (heirs) of Theodore Bergmann. The following notes, while admittedly incomplete, probably cover most of the pistols made by Menz.

Liliput—The Menz Liliput was made in two calibers, 4.25 mm. and 6.35 mm. The latter is designated Mod. I in the contemporary catalogs, while the former was given no designation other than the 4.25 Liliput. The two models are very much alike in design and operation, both being of the simple blowback type, striker-fired with a magazine capacity of 6 cartridges. The design bears a resemblance to the Menta in some respects.

The 4.25 mm. model is only 90 mm. (ca. 3.5 inches) in length, with a barrel length of 45 mm. and weight of 175 grams. Truly a "vestpocket" pistol. The cartridge used was a round originally designed for the Austrian Erika pistol, some time before 1914, and adopted by Menz when he brought out the Liliput in 1920. The Liliput soon displaced the Erika in the market, and though more popular than its predecessor it too was soon displaced. Cartridges of this caliber have not been made for many years.

Just when the 6.35 mm. model was introduced is not known, but it is thought to have been in 1925. Several specimens marked as Mod. 1925 and Mod. 1927 have been seen. The 4.25 and 6.35 models were apparently numbered in separate numbering series, as some specimens of the former have higher numbers than the lower numbers for the 6.35 model. The 6.35 mm. model is 105 mm. long, has a barrel length of 52 mm. and a weight of 270 grams. No production figures are available. The 6.35 mm. Liliput was reportedly also sold under the names Bijou, Okzet, and Kaba. The latter name was derived from the name of the dealer—Karl Bauer, of Berlin.

6.35 mm. Menta—The 6.35 Menta is a copy of the 7.65 mm. Menta and has the same markings. It is 118 mm. in length, barrel length is 63 mm., and weight is 384 grams. The magazine capacity is 6 rounds.

6.35 mm. Menz—While specimens of this pistol have not been available for examination, contemporary catalog illustrations show that it is not a copy of the Menta, though functioning in the same manner. The only feature that is exactly the same is the pattern of the grip plates. This pistol has a cocking indicator, a pin which protrudes from the rear end of the slide when the piece is cocked. The Menta does not have this feature. It also has a barrel assembly catch, probably taken from the Stenda but absent on the 6.35 mm. Menta. The top of the pistol is a straight line from end to end, not higher at the rear end as in the case of the Menta. Further details are lacking.

7.65 mm. Menz—The Menz Mod. II bears a very close resemblance to the 6.35 mm. Liliput or Menz Mod. I as it was also called. Even the monogram on the grip plates is the same. Apart from size, about the only discernible difference is a small change in the serrations of the finger grips.

The length of this model is 128 mm., barrel length is 67 mm., and the magazine capacity is 6 rounds.

Menz Mod. PB "Speziall"—This pistol represents an entirely different design from those previously used by Menz. The letters PB in the name represent the words "Polizei und Behörden" (indicating the pistol was for Police or other Official use).

In this model the barrel is fully enclosed, which was not so in previous models. It has double action with an exposed hammer. The thumb safety is located at the top of the slide at the rear end, instead of on the frame, and disassembly is accomplished by unlocking the trigger guard at the front (being pinioned at the rear end). The pistol is well designed, well made, and has an attractive appearance. According to Menz literature it came in 7.65 mm. caliber, with a kit containing a 9 mm. Short barrel and a 5.6 mm. practice barrel for center fire ammunition. Spent cartridges are ejected through a port on the right side instead of at the top, as with the previous models.

Menz P and B Mod. III and III-A—These 7.65 mm. pistols bear little resemblance to the PB Speziall or to any previous Menz pistol. The thumb safety is located at the top of the grip frame, close to the rear edge of the grip plate, instead of being on the slide. Disassembly is accomplished by pushing in

and turning a milled sleeve which surrounds the muzzle end of the barrel. Externally these two are alike except for a slight difference in the thumb safety and the grip plates.

Kersten (*Wapens en Munitie*) shows an illustration of a very similar Menz 7.65 mm. pistol which he calls the P.N.B. Mod. IV. The most obvious difference is in the location of the trigger. In the P and B Mod. III-A the trigger is at the rear end of the trigger guard opening, whereas in the P.N.B. Mod. IV the trigger is located in the center of the opening, as it also is in the Bergmann Erben 9 mm. Mod. II and the Menz PB Speziall. It is quite obvious that Menz did quite a bit of experimental work on pistol design, but it does not appear that his pistols had a wide sale.

Bergmann Erben "Speziall"—This pistol is the same as the Menz PB Speziall and was sold by Theodore Bergmann Erben (Bergmann's Heirs). The numbering seems to be in the same series; for example, the Bergmann Erben No. 3797 is identical to the PB Speziall No. 3267.

Bergmann Erben Mod. II—This pistol was made in both 7.65 mm. and 9 mm. calibers and was quite similar to the PB Speziall, but it differed in some details of construction. The magazine release is of the push-in button type, located at the front edge of the grip frame directly back of the trigger guard. Both are double action, with exposed hammer.

Bergmann Erben 6.35 mm. Mod. II—This 6.35 mm. pistol is strikingly like the 7.65 mm. Menz Mod. II. The forward end of the slide has been cut back somewhat farther on the underside, and the slide is a bit shorter, probably to decrease weight. The pattern of the serrations on the slide is somewhat different. The barrel lengths are the same, 67 mm., though the over-all lengths are not. The 7.65 Mod. II Menz is 128 mm. long, while the 6.35 mm. Bergmann Erben is 123 mm. in length. These latter pistols appear to be numbered in a special series, the first digit of which is 0.

Müller pistol

Though this pistol was never put on the market, and perhaps not more than a dozen prototype models were made, it is an arm that is of interest to collectors. No law enforcement officers are ever likely to encounter one. It was designed and patented by Bernhard Müller of Winterthur, Switzerland, and the models were constructed in ca. 1902 to 1907 (Fig. 219).

A specimen was submitted to the Swiss for Army Trials in 1904, but it was rejected. In U.S. Army

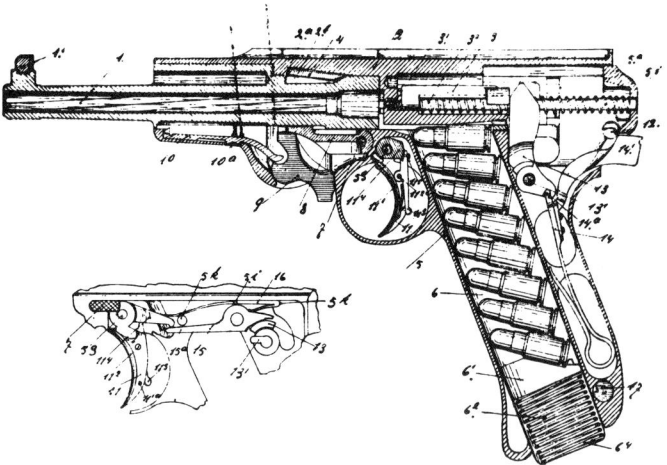

Fig. 219. Müller Experimental Mod. One of several models constructed between ca. 1902 and 1907. Sectional view.

Trials made in 1905 it suffered a similar fate. Admittedly it had some advantages over the Luger, with which the comparison was made, but in the opinion of the Board the disadvantages considerably outweighed the advantages. The advantages cited were that, compared to the Luger, it had fewer parts (27 as against 43), it was easier to assemble and disassemble, it had a simple cocking device and a device to show when the arm was cocked—the latter being a desirable feature because of the internal hammer. The disadvantages cited were these: it had greater weight, it had side ejection (though why this was a disadvantage was not stated), it had the possibility of premature firing (though none was cited as having been experienced in the tests), it had an inferior device for indicating whether the magazine was empty, too many misfires occurred, the ejection of fired shells was uncertain (resulting in frequent jamming), the trigger mechanism was uncertain, and the "safety" latch actually was unsafe because when it was in the "safe" position it could be jarred into the "ready" position merely by pulling the trigger several times. Even had the pistol passed the tests it is not likely that it would have been accepted, particularly as the desirability of the adoption of a .45 caliber arm (which was ultimately adopted) was being considered at the time.

The pistol did have some interesting and unusual features. For example, the recoil spring was located in the rear end of the slide, the hammer was enclosed and whether it was cocked or not could be told by observing the position of the external cocking lever. Cocking was performed by pressing the lever with the right thumb, and the arm could be uncocked by proper manipulation of the lever while

pulling the trigger. The pistol could be carried safely in the uncocked condition. In addition there was a thumb safety, but no grip safety was used.

The pistol was of the locked-bolt, short-recoil type, the barrel and breechblock being locked together at the moment of firing. After 6 mm. of recoil (the bullet having left the barrel at 3 mm. of recoil), the breech bolt was turned by an inclined plane which unlocked the breechblock from the barrel permitting it to move back its full length of travel, compressing the recoil spring and ejecting the fired shell while on the way. The arm had both an extractor and an ejector, and shell ejection was through a port on the right side. The designer put considerable stress on the claim that the shooter could adjust the trigger pull to suit himself and that with a "hair trigger" pull the arm was perfectly safe.

Data for this pistol are as follows: caliber, 7.65 mm. Parabellum; over-all length, 237 mm.; barrel length, 140 mm.; height, 145 mm.; thickness (max.), 32 mm.; weight (magazine empty), ca. 1000 gm.; and mag. cap., 8 ctges.

Oriental pistols (other than Japanese)

Information concerning pistols of Oriental manufacture, other than those made in Japan, is meager and often conflicting. Most of the pistols made in the Orient, other than Japan, are copies of pistols made by Mauser, Fabrique Nationale, and, occasionally, Colt. While there are many copies of the Mauser and F.N. there are but few of the Colt. The author has seen a quite good imitation of the .45 U.S. Army Model 1911A which was made at the Pusan Jin Iron Works in Pusan, Korea. The barrel, however, may have been made in the U.S. because the rifling is a little too good for Oriental manufacture, judging from experience. Automatic pistols of original design are very few in China. The Japanese pistols are discussed elsewhere.

Chinese pistols

Excellent copies of the Mauser Military Pistol have been made in China, and apparently in considerable numbers. These were produced in at least two arsenals—the Hanyang Arsenal and the Shansei Province Arsenal—and they may have been made at others. Those made at the Shansei Arsenal seem to be the ones most frequently encountered in the U.S., and they appear in both the 7.63 mm. Mauser and the .45 Colt calibers. They always are marked with Chinese characters. These indicate the Type (or Model) and the date of manufacture. This latter date is given in terms of the year after the founding of the Chinese Republic. For example, a .45 cal. copy of the Mauser Military Pistol has characters on the left side which (when interpreted) read "Style I" (or Type I), while on the other side the characters read "Made in the 19th year of the Chinese Republic," i.e., 1930 (Figs. 220, 221).

The Tokarev pistol has been used extensively in China, at first through importation from Russia of both completed pistols and parts which were assembled in China, and later through manufacture in toto in China with tools and machinery obtained from Russia. It is believed that since 1952 the Chinese have made most of the pistols going into service there.

Japanese Nambu Model 1914 (1925) guns have appeared in China, some of them bearing the inscription "North China - 19 Type" in Chinese char-

Fig. 220. Shiki First (i.e., Type I).

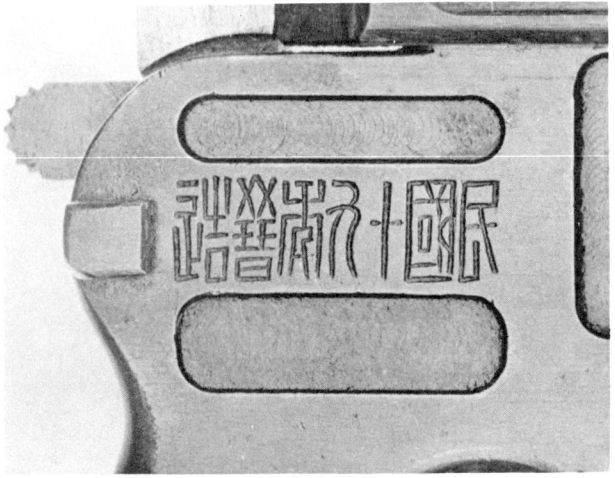

Fig. 221. 19th Year after founding of the Chinese Republic, i.e., 1930.

acters. Whether these were actually manufactured in China by the occupying Japanese (or by Chinese workmen under Japanese supervision) or whether they were made in Japan and given Chinese markings is not known. The latter would seem more probable. If this specimen was marked according to the Chinese custom, it would be the Model of 1930 (the 19th year of the Chinese Republic).

Many copies of the Model 1900 Browning made by the Fabrique Nationale have appeared in the U.S. and their manufacture is generally attributed to Chinese artisans, working independently. This very likely is true for many of them, but Donald Bady has pointed out (in a personal communication) some substantial grounds for the belief that some at least were made in India.

Some of these Oriental copies are imitations of the Model 1900 Browning, others are evidently copies of pre-1900 Brownings, i.e., of experimental or prototype models of 1898, particularly. In the discussion of the early Browning pistols it was mentioned that quite a number of these were marked with the Mauser insigne in the hope of interesting the Mauser firm in their manufacture. This hope was not realized. Apparently some of these pistols, by intent or otherwise, found their way to China and formed the basis for many imitations made there. While these imitations vary from specimen to specimen, as would be expected in hand-made pistols, they show a close resemblance among themselves and to the 1898 Browning. A comparison of a number of these pistols shows some points of considerable interest. For example, there is one group that bears the same serial number or senseless modifications of that same number. Several have the number 126,063, others have the number 26,063, and one has a number apparently intended for 26,063 but with the first 6 being clearly a 3 which faces the wrong way. Still another copy, which bears the earmarks of having been made by the same artisans, bears the serial number 1945. It bears the word HERSTAL on the slide, three times repeated and upside down in each instance. The word BROWNINGS is stamped on the frame. The grip pieces on the pistols in this group are checkered with no attempt at reproducing any type of FN monogram. Other imitations do show such an attempt.

The markings on these pistols make no sense. Two specimens, each bearing the number 126,063, (quite similar but not identical as to machining, etc.) bear quite different markings. One of them is marked GUERREHERSTAL on the slide and BROWNINGS-PATENT on the frame; the other is marked simply BELGIQUE on the slide but the name BROWNING does not appear anywhere on the gun. In this latter specimen both positions of the thumb safety ("Safe" and "Fire"), instead of being so marked, are marked EFR, a marking which might lead to slight confusion! But this is perhaps no more confusing than the inversion of the markings found on other specimens, where the "Safe" position is clearly marked "Feu" and the "Fire" position is marked "Sur." Still other variations are those in which both positions are marked "Feu," and in some cases no markings of either kind occur.

One other marking which invariably appears on this group is the Mauser name (Mauser insigne), which in some cases is a good imitation of that used on arms of legitimate Mauser manufacture. Evidently the artisans thought that this mark, copied from the F.N. specimen they had, made their product appear to be more legitimate. To add to this "legitimacy," one specimen of this group has the word NATIONALE on the slide, and for good measure the word is repeated three times and always upside down. This specimen bears the inscription BERSTAL-BERSTAL on the frame.

Specimen No. 9386 bears an "inscription" on the slide consisting of 43 closely spaced letters, some capital and some small letters, a number of which are faced in the wrong direction. This is followed by the capital letters EBPGR. On the frame there is another "inscription," consisting of two lines, the upper one of which is legible enough to be made out as GWMPNE-BPNBARE.

This specimen, which is better made than the group just discussed, has the straight-sided grip of the Browning Model 1900, rather than a streamlined (curved) grip, but otherwise it is similar to the Model 1898. It has grip pieces which carry the FN monogram but are dissimilar to those found on Mod. 1900. It does not, like the others, have the Mauser insigne. This may be a copy of an 1899 prototype of the Model 1900, and it may have been made in India. Like all the others, this specimen has a variety of proof marks. These are copies of Belgian marks, but the Belgian acceptance mark does not appear on this or any of the others mentioned.

Many photographs of other Asiatic pistols will be found in Part IV.

Ortgies pocket pistols

The Ortgies pistols are unique in design, although inevitably they have some features in common with other automatic pistols. The pistol was designed by Heinrich Ortgies, said to have been a German by birth but who was a resident of Liége, Belgium, until

about the close of World War I. The first prototypes are thought to have been made in Belgium in 1915–16. The pistol has an outward appearance similar to the F.N. Browning Mod. 1910, but internally it is quite different (Fig. 222).

To disassemble, the magazine is first removed and the slide is pulled back and then allowed to move forward slowly until it comes into a position where it can easily be lifted off. The barrel is pivoted at the rear end and can be removed by turning it at right angles, in which position it can be slid out. This pistol has but one safety and this is a grip safety which operates in an unconventional manner. When the grip safety is in the "in" position the gun can be fired by pulling the trigger, but when it is in the "out" position pulling the trigger alone, without depressing the safety, will not cause the gun to fire. To apply the safety, one must push in a little button which is located on the left side of the grip frame, below the rear end of the slide. This causes the safety to spring out, and when in this pisition it must be depressed before the trigger can be pulled. This safety device is certainly not one to be recommended because it is a very dangerous one. Firstly, when one pulls the slide back in the normal manner to transfer a cartridge from the magazine to the barrel chamber, the safety member is pushed in (as one grips the pistol) and it *remains there unless one releases it* by pushing in the release button. If one forgets this little detail he may be courting disaster. Secondly, in some specimens seen it is very easy to push the grip safety in accidentally, as the pressure required is very small. Cases are known where this has happened and accidental discharges have occurred in consequence. Any grip safety

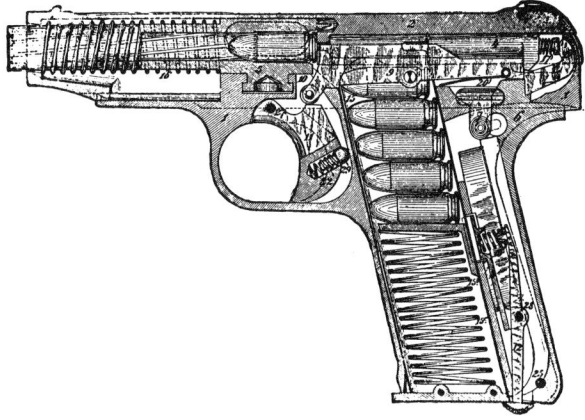

Fig. 222. 7.65 mm. Ortgies. Sectional view.

which does not require a substantial pressure to depress it is dangerous, and obviously more so when it automatically locks itself in this position when it is depressed—as is the case with the Ortgies.

Some time soon after World War I, Ortgies went to Erfurt where he organized the firm Ortgies and Co. to manufacture his pistol. Production of the 7.65 mm. pistol seems to have started in 1920, and because the weapons were attractive in appearance and were well made they soon attained popularity, which fact naturally attracted the notice of other manufacturers, including Deutsche Werke, A.G., of Erfurt. This firm purchased the rights, tools, designs, and unfinished parts from Ortgies and Co. but just when this purchase was made is not known. The 7.65 mm. caliber was the only one produced by Ortgies and Co., but apparently they had been tooling up for the 6.35 mm. model, because soon after Deutsche Werke took over the business a pistol of this caliber was produced. A short time later the 9 mm. Browning Short (.380) was brought out, but this did not enjoy the popularity attained by the smaller models. Production of the pistol in this caliber seems to have stopped somewhere around 1925–27. Deutsche Werke continued the manufacture of the pistol in the 6.35 and 7.65 mm. calibers until late in the 1920's.

An Ortgies manual, thought to have been issued in 1919, describes the 7.65 mm. model, listing it as available, and it also mentions but does not describe the 6.35 model. It also mentions a 9 mm. barrel, interchangeable with the 7.65, but does not infer that it was in production at that time. This was actually done later by Deutsche Werke.

Dealers lists of 1920 and 1921 include the 6.35 and 7.65 mm. models but do not mention a 9 mm. caliber. An Ortgies instruction booklet dated February 1922 describes the smaller-caliber pistols but does not mention the 9 mm. caliber. The first mention found of the 9 mm. caliber, as being in production, is in the AKAH Catalog of May 1922. From this it seems likely that the pistol was furnished in the 9 mm. caliber for the first time in about March or April of 1922.

The total number of Ortgies pistols made by either the original Ortgies and Co. or its successor, Deutsche Werke, A.G., is not known, but there were at least upwards of 250,000 and possibly more. The lowest serial number encountered in the author's laboratory for a pistol made by Ortgies and Co. (7.65 mm., of course) is No. 195, and the highest number seen on a pistol similarly marked is No. 10,614. The former has plain wood grips while the latter has wood grips with the HO (Heinrich Ortgies)

monogram. No Ortgies pistols with grips of material other than wood have been seen. It appears that Ortgies and Co. probably started their serial numbers at No. 1 and that they made upwards of 11,000 guns, at least.

The lowest serial number observed on an Ortgies marked as made by Deutsche Werke is No. 5834 and the highest is No. 227,576. Because of the overlapping of serial numbers it would seem that Deutsche Werke had its own serial numbering system. Whether the 6.35 mm. pistols were numbered along with the 7.65 in the same series or whether they were numbered in a series of their own is not known. The lowest number observed for a 6.35 mm. pistol is No. 283.

Pistols made by Ortgies and Co. had either plain wood grips or grips with the HO monogram. Pistols made by Deutsche Werke may be found to have plain grips with no monogram, or they may have grips with the HO monogram (probably from the supply of left-over parts at the time of purchase), or, more frequently, they will have a monogram which at first sight appears to be a rather fancy letter D (for Deutsche) but which when examined closely turns out to be a "lion couchant" with his tail raised to form the upper part of the letter D. This monogram usually appears also on the slide between the words Deutsche and Werke. A still different monogram is seen in the advertisements of the Ortgies pistol in the AKAH Catalog, consisting of the capital letters DW, the D being above the W. This monogram has not been observed on any of the large number of pistols examined, and whether it was actually used or not is not known.

O.W.A. pistol

This 6.35 mm. caliber pistol bears some resemblance to the Steyr but is not the same and was not made under any Pieper patent. The pistol is called the O.W.A. because of the presence of these letters in a monogram on the grips, the letters standing for Oesterreichische Werke-gws-Anstalt, a firm which apparently started up following World War I. It probably had some relation to O.W.G. and may have been manned by former employees of that firm. How long it was in operation is not known.

The pistol is different from the Steyr in that, while hinged at the front end, the whole slide tips up when the catch is released. In the Steyr, only the barrel tips up. Specimens Nos. 5626, 5906, and 18,315 (all dated 1922) are identical, with the exception of markings. The first two bear only the words PATENT ANGEMELDET (Patent Applied For) and the date on the left side of the slide and the words "MADE IN AUSTRIA" on the right. Pistol No. 18,315, however, bears the inscription

CAL 6.35 — ARSENAL VIENNA AUSTRIA
"Pat. I. A. KULTURSTAATEN"

on the left side of the slide and nothing on the right side. Pistol No. 37,161, dated 1924, (illustrated in the *Pistolen Atlas*) shows some differences in construction.

The unlocking lever is mounted on the right side of the slide instead of the left, and a lever has been substituted for a sliding catch to operate the mechanical safety. Like most of the non-Browning types of pistols, the O.W.A. is unnecessarily complicated.

Parabellum (Luger) pistols

The German Parabellum, or Luger as it is more commonly called in this country, is one of the best known and most widely used pistols in military history, having been the official weapon of several countries, and having been produced in tremendous numbers for use in two world wars.

Hugo Borchardt, a naturalized American living in Connecticut, designed an automatic pistol which had some unique features, the most outstanding of which was a toggle-joint locking system and a removable magazine which was inserted into the stock or grip. Unable to interest any American arms manufacturer he took his ideas to Germany where both he and his ideas met a quite different reception. He succeeded in interesting the Ludwig Loewe Co. of Berlin and they not only agreed to produce the pistol but also put him in charge of production, which began in 1893 (Figs. 223 to 225).

Despite its clumsy, awkward appearance and apparent lack of balance, the pistol was demonstrated to the U.S. Army authorities who rejected it though it gave a very convincing performance, particularly as to accuracy and lack of malfunctions. A number

of weaknesses in construction were noted. The Board did admit that the pistol had advantages over the service revolver then used. When attached to the stock, with which the pistol was provided, the balance and appearance were greatly improved, as was the accuracy of fire. In any case, however, it was not considered suitable as a military side arm.

Borchardt had designed a new cartridge for his pistol, in 7.65 mm. caliber. This is referred to as the Borchardt M. 1893 or M. 1894 cartridge and is sometimes spoken of as the forerunner of the 7.63 Mauser cartridge. Manufacture of this cartridge was continued for several years after the discontinuance of

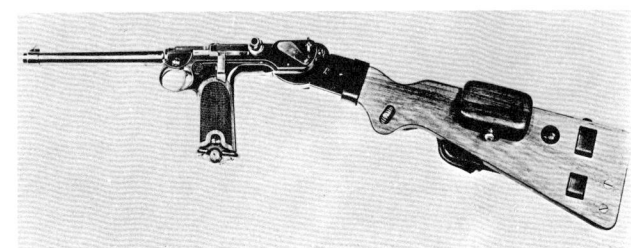

Fig. 224. 7.65 mm. Borchardt Mod. 1893. Provided with shoulder stock.

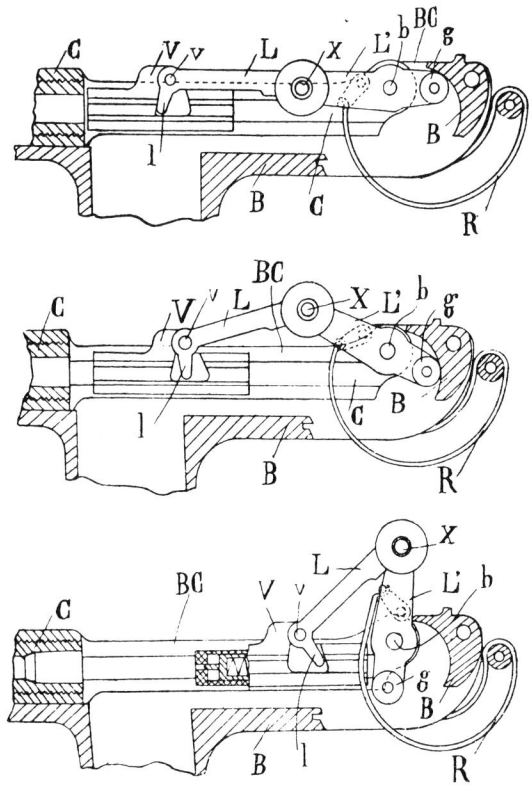

Fig. 225. Borchardt mechanism. Sketches showing three successive positions as action opens.

Fig. 223. 7.65 mm. Borchardt Mod. 1893.

the manufacture of the pistol itself, because of a continuing demand. This shows that there must have been a considerable sale of the pistol, even though its period of production was short.

In 1898 the Borchardt pistol was redesigned by Georg Luger, and prototypes were made at the Deutsche Waffen u. Munitionsfabrik, where he was an engineer. The earliest pistols were known by the combined name Borchardt-Luger. It is said that Borchardt was made the engineer in charge of production.

The Borchardt-Luger pistol as first produced used the Borchardt M. 1893 cartridge. In 1899 the Swiss Government authorities, who were testing the pistol for possible military use, requested a cartridge having less recoil. This resulted in the development of a new cartridge which was given the nomenclature of 7.65 mm. Parabellum. This name is said to have been derived from the fact that this was the code word for the D.W.M. firm. The pistol itself was soon known as the "Parabellum," the name "Luger" not being used in Germany. The widespread use of the name "Luger" for this pistol seems to have arisen, in considerable degree at least, to the fact that the firm of A. F. Stoeger, of New York City, registered this name and applied it to many of the pistols that they imported for sale in this country.

Modell 1900—Late in 1899 the pistol was considered ready for the market but it was not offered commercially until late in 1900. From the time of its appearance and up until about 1905 this model had no designation other than the "Selbstlade Pistole Parabellum," following the general European practice of not giving a model nomenclature to the first of a (possible) series of models. When and if a second or third model was produced the original model would then be given a special designation in order to avoid confusion. The Swiss adopted this first model of the Parabellum in April 1900, and they gave it the definite nomenclature of Pistole 1900. Deliveries of the Swiss order were made in 1901 and 1902.

This model of 1900 had a grip safety, a 4¾-inch slender barrel, a flat stable extractor, and a two-layer, laminated-leaf toggle main spring, the toggle heads being relieved at the rear. Three thousand of this model were delivered for Swiss service use. They may be identified by the "star-burst and cross" crest on the bridge of the receiver. The U.S. Army purchased 1000 in mid-1901, and these may be identified by the U.S. Eagle crest in the same location. In 1902 and 1903 field tests were conducted in several countries, including Austria, Bulgaria, Germany, Spain, and Sweden. In 1903-04 full-knurled

head toggles were introduced. Production of the 1900 model continued until mid-1906.

In 1902 a 9 mm. Parabellum pistol was produced in limited numbers. This had a heavier 4-inch barrel, and this heavier barrel may also be found on some specimens of the 7.65 mm. caliber. The receiver was shortened, for pistols of both calibers, but the practice was evidently not universal until 1905, since specimens dated 1903 and 1904 are found with the longer receiver.

The D.W.M. intertwined script initials (as a monogram) were used on all 1900, 1902, and later pistols. No official model nomenclature seems to have been given to the improved model or to the 9 mm. Parabellum model.

Modell 1904—In 1904 the Parabellum Marine Model 1904 was introduced. This was a 9 mm. weapon, using the long receiver and all features of the 1900 Model, but provided with a 6-inch barrel, a stock ridge on the rear edge of the grip frame (for attachment of a shoulder stock), and a two-step adjustable rear sight for 100 and 200 meters. This model was adopted into the German Naval Service in that year and was still in use by them during World War II. In the instance of military use of these pistols, the crowned M acceptance mark and date of manufacture will be found on the arm. None were made after 1920.

Parabellum Karabiner—This pistol, dating from 1903-04, had a forearm, provision for a solid wood butt-stock, and special sights. It was made commercially, fully marked but in limited quantity. A heavier toggle main spring made possible the use of heavier loads. Ammunition for this pistol is distinguished by having a black-oxidized brass cartridge case. It was not produced for many years as the model did not prove to be very popular.

In 1906 a number of changes in the then standard Parabellum pistol were made. The toggle main spring was replaced by a coil spring, the extractor was pivoted and marked to indicate whether the chamber was loaded. The Swiss adopted these new variations in their pistol, which they designated the Pistole 1900/06. These pistols were marked with the shield and cross crest on the receiver bridge. The 1900/06 for military use was marked with the "star-burst and cross."

The U.S. Eagle crest was used on pistols exported to this country, and 1900/06 pistols purchased by the Brazilian, Bulgarian, and Portuguese governments were supplied with their special markings. Pistols sold commercially either had the D.W.M. monogram or were without markings.

The 1902/06 variant represents the 9 mm., short

receiver, heavy barrel series to which were added the 1906 modifications. By 1906 the pistol was produced in a standard manner, with either the heavier, 4-inch or the slender barrel. The Marine Modell 1904/ 06 was produced in both 7.65 and 9 mm. calibers, the 9 mm. in Naval and commercial form, the 7.65 mm. in limited quantity for commercial sale.

In 1906–07 D.W.M. made two specimens of the 1906 form of the Parabellum in .45 caliber for trials at the U.S. Springfield Armory. An order for 200 additional pistols was received and accepted, but German acceptance of the pistol seems to have prevented the carrying out of this contract, and it was cancelled. No more .45 caliber pistols were made.

Pistole 08—Late in 1907 the grip safety was dropped for all models, and the so-called Modell 1908 appeared. This new 1908 type, without grip safety, was made with several barrel lengths, including 4, 6, 6½ inches, and a carbine type. It was made in both 7.65 and 9 mm. calibers. It was adopted by the German Army in 1908 and was given the official nomenclature of Pistole 08. The Naval model was also made in the 08 form. By 1911 a special long-barrel (8-inch) model, with adjustable rear sight was produced for military use. This has been erroneously referred to as the 1917 model. This long-barrel type was issued in lieu of carbines to machine gun troops and was widely used during World War I (Figs. 226 to 229).

With the adoption of this model into German service, the Government Arsenal at Erfurt was licensed

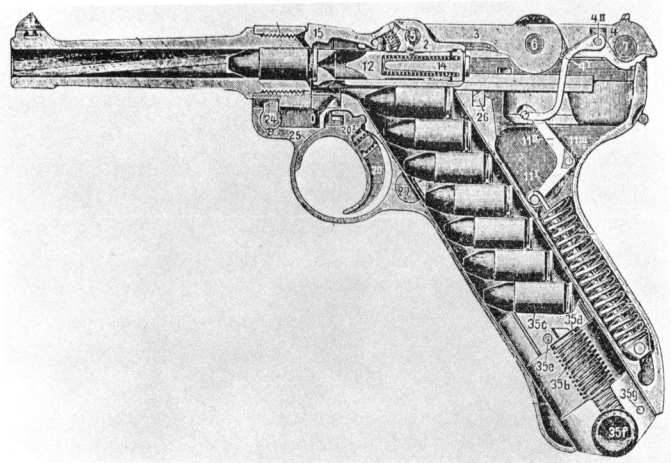

Fig. 226. Parabellum (Luger) Mod. 08. Sectional view.

Fig. 228. Parabellum (Luger) Mod. 08. With "Snail Drum" magazine.

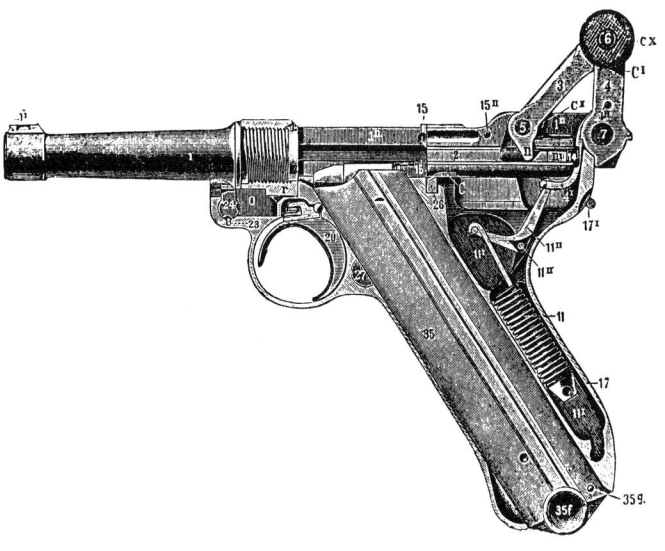

Fig. 227. Parabellum (Luger) Mod. 08. Sectional view, with action open.

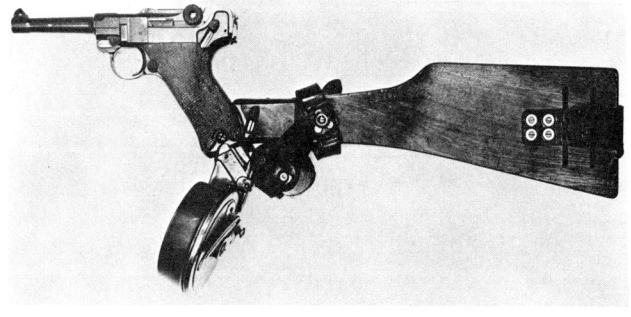

Fig. 229. Parabellum (Luger) Mod. 08. With shoulder stock-case and "Snail Drum" magazine. This magazine holds 32 cartridges.

by D.W.M. to make the pistol for service use. Specimens dated 1909 have been found, but actual production is said to have begun in 1910. Early service and commercial variants of the period will be found either with or without the hold-open device (later standardized) and with or without the stock ridge for shoulder stock (also later standardized). Pistols made at the Erfurt Arsenal are marked ERFURT. Production continued at Erfurt until 1918.

From 1908 to 1914 the Parabellum 1908 type was produced commercially by D.W.M. and with special markings for Chinese, Rumanian, and Turkish use. Several South American countries also used the pistol in 9 mm. caliber. Specially marked military issues of the 9 mm. 1908 pistol were made for Bulgaria and Serbia. Whether Serbia adopted it for service use is not known.

Because of World War I, supplies of the Parabellum to Switzerland and to Holland were naturally cut off. The Swiss decided to produce their own and ultimately did so with their Modell 1924 and, later, with their Modell 1906/29. The Dutch were assisted by the English firm of Vickers (agents for D.W.M.) who are said to have tooled up for the production of the pistol. There is some uncertainty as to the activities of the Vickers Co. in this connection. The Dutch Vickers pistols are clearly marked Vickers Ltd. and are otherwise identified by having large checkering on the grip pieces. All pistols used by the Dutch have brass plates brazed onto the left side of the receiver, and safety markings are in Dutch.

When World War I ended, several million parts, incomplete pistols, and completed wartime pistols were dumped onto the open commercial market. From 1919 to 1931 no standard, systematic manufacture of completely new Parabellum pistols took place but many were assembled from existing parts, plus special parts made to substitute for those of which there were shortages. Numerous variant barrel lengths and markings will be encountered.

Treaty limitations prohibited production of the 9 mm. pistol except for the 100,000-man army which had been authorized. The German staff was allowed to designate a single manufacturer to produce pistols for this specific use and they chose the firm of Simson and Co. of Suhl. Consequently, Parabellum pistols of the "08" style with Simson markings are found from 1920 on. In 1920 a wholesale modification of the safety device was made on many existing pistols. This modification consisted of shortening the blocking surface of the sear, so that the bolt could be partially withdrawn. Pistols so modified were usually counterstamped with the date at which the

modification was made, i.e., 1920. It is common, then, to find pistols marked with two dates, one being the 1920 date and the other the wartime date of original production of the specimen.

By the late 1920's, D.W.M. had been sufficiently reorganized to permit resumption of production. Commercial pistols and military shipments to Holland were undertaken. Simson, however, continued to produce the pistols used by the Germany Army. Early in the 1930's, Mauser Werke A.G. purchased the rights, tools, and fixtures for the 7.65 and 9 mm. Parabellum in all models. Up to 1934, toggle links and receivers with D.W.M. markings were used. Having used up all existing inventories of D.W.M. parts by 1934, Mauser began the commercial production of complete pistols. However, although the 7.65 mm. model was listed in factory literature as late as 1940, the pistol in that caliber was not produced after 1935. The 9 mm. Parabellum was made both for commercial sale and military use from 1935 on.

Pistols marked "42" were made by Simson and Co., whose production was stopped after 1937. Obviously the figure "42" has nothing to do with dates of production. It was simply the early manufacturer's code designation assigned to Simson since they happened to be the 42nd on the approved list of suppliers of the German Army after 1919. Pistols made by Mauser in the period 1937 to 1941 will carry either the mark "42" or "S/42." By 1940, all other types of the Parabellum were dropped in favor of the Pistole 08 with the 4-inch barrel.

Pistols are frequently encountered bearing the name (or initials) of Krieghoff. The firm of H. Krieghoff was one that had been very active in the refinishing and reassembly of surplus Parabellum pistols and parts after they were thrown on the market at the end of World War I. Up to 1938 they produced only reworked pistols to which they applied their own name, initials (HK), or trade mark. In 1939, however, the Luftwaffe gave them an order for 15,000 Pistole 08, of "full manufacture." Krieghoff produced these pistols, but this firm was not a large producer, compared to others. Yet they were of sufficient importance to be assigned the wartime code "fzs."

In 1934 two new safety devices, each of which could be added to existing pistols as well as incorporated in new ones, were devised at the Mauser factory. One of these is a dismounting safety which prevents the functioning of the pistol when the side plate is off and the other was a magazine safety. During 1934–35 these devices were added, either together or separately, to both the completely new

251

pistols and to those which were assembled, in part at least, from left-over D.W.M. inventories. Two specimens examined by the author, both with D.W.M. markings and the German WaA acceptance marks (which were introduced in 1933), are equipped with both of these safety devices. But the German military authorities did not approve of them, and they were dropped from the military pistols shortly after 1935. On the commercial models, however, Mauser continued the use of the dismounting safety. Many Mauser Parabellum pistols of post-1935 production show the holes for the dismounting safety but are without the bar itself. The magazine safety, on the other hand, had more (commercial) popularity and many pistols, even including some dating back to World War I in manufacture, will be found to be supplied with this device.

In 1941 the new three-letter manufacturer's code was introduced for all suppliers of military equipment, and Mauser was assigned the designation "byf" which appears on all pistols made by them for the German service until 1945. In addition to the pistols for military use, Mauser was permitted to continue limited production of the pistol for commercial consumption and police use up to 1942. The commercial pistol was marked with the Mauser trade mark and the date of production. All production of the Parabellum stopped in December 1942, at which time all of the Mauser facilities were concentrated on the manufacture of the Pistole 38 (Walther), or P-38 as it is marked. The last deliveries of the Parabellum, made in 1942, were to the Portugese government and these bore the Mauser trade mark.

As has already been stated, the Parabellum pistols in one form or another have been used as service pistols by many countries as far back as 1900. A list of these countries, which probably does not include them all, is as follows:

Brazil	Iran	Rumania
Bulgaria	Luxemburg	Russia
Chile	Mexico	Switzerland
China	Norway	Turkey
Holland	Portugal	

In addition to the successful service trials held in all of the above countries, unproductive trials were held in:

Austria	France	Serbia
Canada	Italy	Spain
Finland	Japan	Sweden
		United States

Original .22 caliber versions of the Parabellum pistol were produced experimentally by D.W.M. and also in Switzerland (Fig. 230). Conversion units, to

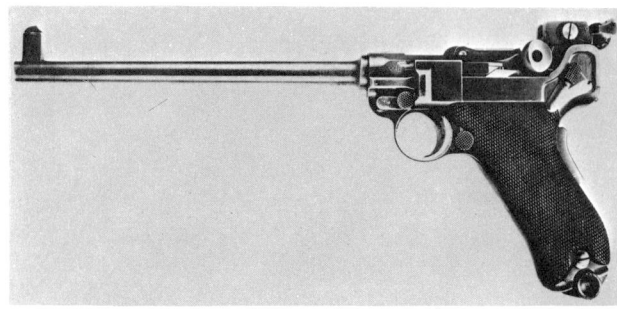

Fig. 230. .22 cal. Swiss Luger. Experimental model.

.22 caliber, were made by ERMA and sold commercially. They were used in the German military service from 1934 to 1940. The Swiss service also used a Swiss-made conversion unit.

For an excellent discussion of the Parabellum pistols the reader is referred to *The Luger Pistol* by Fred A. Datig, Fadco Publishing Co., printed by the Oxford Press, Hollywood, California, in 1955. A second edition appeared in 1959. This consists primarily of additional material secured by the author of the book during a visit to Germany.

N. Pieper pistols

Nicolas Pieper was an inventor and manufacturer in Herstal, Belgium, who made pistols bearing his name and who took out patents on automatic pistols which were licensed to others. Henry Pieper, his father, was for many years a manufacturer of shotguns and revolvers. Upon his death, the firm Henry Pieper S.A. became the S.A. Anciens Etablissements Pieper (generally known as A.E.P.) and used the name "Bayard" as its trade mark or trade name. N. Pieper reportedly sold some of his patents to this firm but apparently they were not used in making automatic pistols, at least, for the Bayard pocket pistols are based on patents taken out by B. Clarus. None of the patents used by N. Pieper in making his own pistols or those later licensed to the Austrian firm Oesterreichische Waffenfabrik Gesellschaft (O.W.G.) were sold or licensed to A.E.P.

Some of the features of the N. Pieper pistols have been attributed to J. Warnant who obtained patents in 1904 and 1905, upon which the Warnant automatic pistol was based. The N. Pieper pistols are not, however, copies of the Warnant. They were based on patents taken out by N. Pieper in 1906 and 1907; the first model or models seem to have appeared in 1907. Later patents secured by Pieper were assigned to (or licensed to) O.W.G. and became the basis for the Steyr pocket pistols. It is therefore not

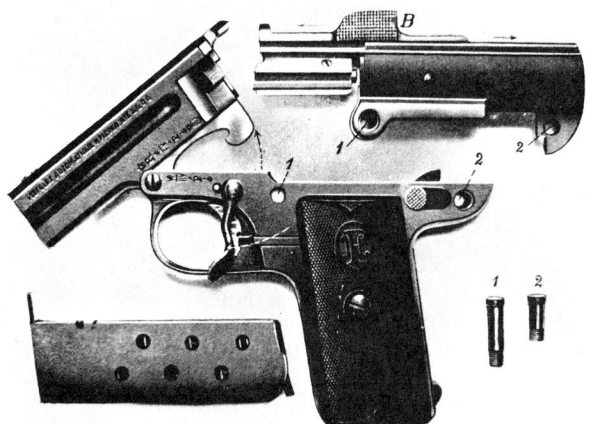

Fig. 231. 6.35 mm. N. Pieper 1908 Mod. "Basculant" type, partially disassembled.

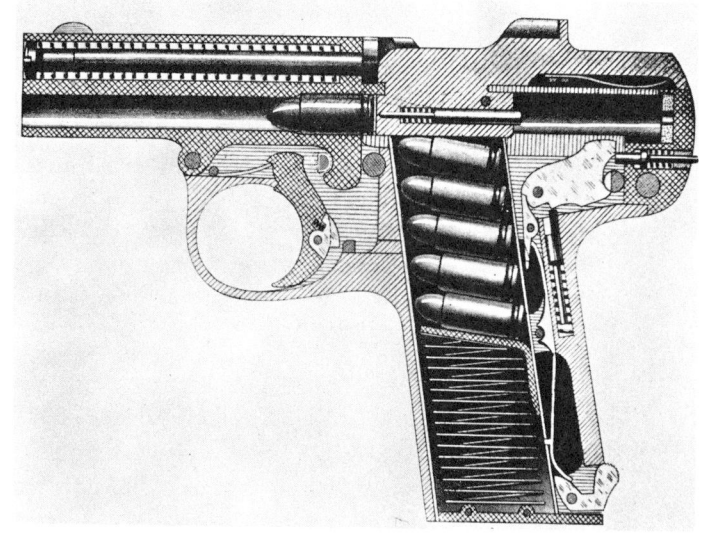

Fig. 232. 7.65 mm. N. Pieper 1908 Mod. Sectional view of "Basculant" type.

strange that the N. Pieper and the Steyr pistols bear a marked resemblance. For a description of the latter, see the section on Steyr pistols (Figs. 231, 232).

Three types of N. Pieper pocket pistols have appeared: (A) the Basculant type, in which the forward end of the barrel is hinged underneath so that it tips up from the rear (a feature which Pieper claimed to have originated); (B) the Demontant type in which the barrel and slide can be lifted up and removed as a unit by turning a lever on the left side of the frame, after which the barrel and slide can be separated (disassembly is easy, as the name indicates); and (C) a third type which more closely resembles the Browning but which has some original features.

An early catalog of the firearms sold by J. B.

(ca. 11 oz.), barrel length 51 mm. (ca. 2¹⁄₁₆″). A 9-cartridge magazine was also available. Reportedly in production in 1923.

Mod. N—7.65 mm. Brng. "Basculant" (i.e., tip-up barrel). Large model. 7 shots. 595 grams (ca. 21 oz.), barrel length 77 mm. (ca. 3⅛″), over-all length 148 mm. (ca. 5⅞″).

Mod. O—Same as Mod. N, except 6 shots. 567 grams (ca. 20 oz.), barrel length 71 mm. (ca. 2⅞″).

Mod. P—6.35 mm. Brng. "Basculant". Small model. 6 shots. 312 grams (ca. 11 oz.), barrel length 56 mm. (ca. 2¼″), over-all length 115 mm. (ca. 4½″).

TABLE 41
Catalog data for N. Pieper pistols

Measurement	Mod. N	Mod. O	Mod. P
Caliber	7.65 mm. Brng.	7.65 mm. Brng.	6.35 mm. Brng.
Over-all length	154 mm.	145 mm.	126 mm.
Barrel length	81 "	73 "	58.5 "
Height	110 "	97.5 "	86 "
Weight, empty	600 gm.	570 gm.	310 gm.
Magazine cap.	7 ctges.	6 ctges.	6 ctges.

Ronge Fils, of Liége, lists the following N. Pieper models:

Mod. A—7.65 mm. Brng. "Large Army Mod." 7 shots. 595 grams (ca. 21 oz.), barrel length 77 mm. (ca. 3⅛″).

Mod. B—7.65 mm. Brng. "Large Mod." 6 shots. Otherwise same as Mod. A.

Mod. C—6.35 mm. Brng. "Demontant" (i.e., no tools required for disassembly). 6 shots. 312 grams

Data taken from an N. Pieper catalog describing his 1920 Modeles differ somewhat from the figures given above for these models. They are as given in Table 41.

In addition to the models listed above, a circular issued by N. Pieper in 1920 shows a Mod. D (or Modele 1920) of the Basculant variety, resembling Mod. C, but differing somewhat. Data given are: 6.35 mm. Brng., magazine capacity 6 ctges, weight

330 grams (magazine empty), barrel length 54 mm. (ca. 2⅛ inches), over-all length 115 mm. (ca. 4½ inches), 6 grooves with right hand twist.

"Legia" pistol—Pieper literature states that this pistol is the only Pieper pistol made wholly at the Pieper factory in Paris. Data given are as follows: 6.35 mm. Brng., 6 shots, 350 grams (ca. 12.4 oz.), barrel length 55.5 mm. (2¼ inches), over-all length 114 mm. (ca. 4½ inches).

This is a modified Browning type, with some distinctive features. Instead of using the barrel-locking device which requires only about a quarter turn to release the barrel, the barrel in this pistol is actually screwed in as in the case of many revolvers, there being nine threads at the rear end of the barrel where it is reduced in size.

To disassemble the pistol the slide is drawn to the rear and locked in that position by turning a lever on the right side of the frame. Then the barrel (which is fluted at the front end to provide a better grip) is grasped and unscrewed by the fingers or by means of a wrench which is provided.

New Pieper Brevete—This pistol though marked PIEPER BREVETE appears to be practically identical to the Legia, with the important exception that it is provided with two magazines. One takes 6 cartridges (as does the Legia) while the other takes 10. The lower end of the lengthened magazine is provided with side plates which match the regular grip plates and consequently give the arm an attractive appearance.

Factory literature at hand does not give data for this model, but presumably they are about the same as (if not identical to) those for the Legia. No statement is made as to whether this model is made at the Paris factory or that in Liége.

It is reported that barrels for the Pieper pistols were rifled by Orban and Gilman in Liége. Whether this applies to the pistols made in the Paris factory is not known. All barrels had six grooves with right hand twist.

Radom (VIS 35) pistol

Previous to 1935 the Polish Army had been supplied with a variety of side arms, including the F.N. Browning, Colt, Luger, Mauser, and Steyr automatic pistols and the Nagant revolver. For obvious reasons this was not desirable, and the army officials decided to standardize on a single weapon. Manufacturers were invited to submit specimens for official testing in 1935. The firms Breda, Mauser, Skoda, and two Polish engineers by the names of Wilniewczyc and Skrzypinski entered the competi-

tion. As a result of the tests, the model submitted by Skoda and the two engineers was selected. License was procured by the Government and production of the pistol was turned over to the Government Small Arms Factory at Radom (Fabryka Broni w Radomiu).

The pistol was given the name VIS, and the pistols were marked

F.B. RADOM VIS MOD. 35. Pat. Nr. 15567.

The pistol has become generally known as the Radom, though the correct name is VIS mod. 35 (frequently shortened to VIS 35). The name VIS is said to have been derived from the names of the two engineer designers—V for *Wilniewczyc* (as W is pronounced V), I for the word *and*, and S for *Skrzypinski.*[*]

Manufacture of the pistol actually began in 1936 and was continued by the Poles until war broke out and Poland was occupied. The Germans took over the plant, as they did in other occupied countries, and manufacture continued under their supervision. Pistols so made, and apparently pistols confiscated by them, were marked with the Waffenamt acceptance marks. Some of the pistols made during the German occupation will be found to be marked "P-35 (p)," rather than with the inscription given above. Incidentally it may be remarked that not only were some undesirable changes made in the construction of the pistol, but also the workmanship deteriorated considerably. Part of this was doubtless due to the intense pressure put on production, but one may surmise that in part it was due to the distaste for the job on the part of "slave labor."

How many pieces of this arm were produced is not known, and the prefix letter system of numbering does not help in making an estimate. From the number that have appeared in this country it is safe to say that many thousands must have been made. The official side arm of the Polish Army is now the Tokarev, naturally.

To a considerable extent the VIS 35 resembles the U.S. Mod. 1911A1, but in many respects its construction is different. Some of these differences are in the method of locking and unlocking the barrel, the recoil assembly, the method of disassembly (field stripping), and the manual safety (decocking device). Instead of using the Colt type of barrel link, a stud is forged (or machined) onto the under side of the breech end of the barrel. The barrel and

[*]The fact that the name chosen was VIS rather than WIS may well have been because of the Latin word "vis" which means power. Either V or W could have been used because in Polish they have the same sound, but for foreigners generally the sound is better expressed by the letter V.

slide remain locked together until the bullet emerges from the barrel. The pistol is classed as a short-recoil arm, as the barrel and slide recoil together for only ¼ inch, at which point a beveled surface on the barrel stud strikes the unlocking cam in the receiver, forcing the end of the barrel down and unlocking the slide from the barrel. The released slide moves to the rear, ejecting the fired shell in route, and picks up and chambers a fresh cartridge on its return. This locking and unlocking device is quite similar to the system used on some of the early Japanese pistols.

The recoil spring assembly is somewhat different from that in the Colt and is certainly no improvement. As to safety features, all specimens observed have had a grip safety which effectively prevents firing unless the grip is grasped by the hand. In addition, the early pistols had a thumb-operated decocking lever which permitted carrying the pistol with a cartridge in the chamber but with the hammer down. Pushing down on the lever brings a steel block between the hammer and the firing pin and then trips the sear, allowing the hammer to fall safely. As soon as pressure on the lever is removed a spring automatically returns the block to its former postion. As the pistol is not of the double action type, the hammer has to be cocked by hand if it is down while a live cartridge is in the chamber. In the later stages of production this decocking lever was omitted, in order to speed up manufacture. No conventional thumb safety is present on this pistol.

Field stripping is simple as it consists of the removal of the slide, barrel, and recoil assembly, only. As first made, there was a special slide-locking lever located on the frame below the rear end of the slide, on the left side. To lock the slide in proper position for stripping, the slide is pulled back until the catch on this lever can be pushed into a rectangular notch on the under side of the slide, 1¾ inches from the rear end. This brings the pin at the forward end of the slide stop directly below a semicircular notch in the slide and permits removal of the stop by pushing out the pin from the right side, in the same manner as for the Colt .45. The slide may now be pushed forward off the guides.

Some time during the German occupation period this extra slide locking device was omitted to simplify production. When this is absent the slide is drawn back into the proper position and held there by hand while the pin is withdrawn. After removal of the slide the spring assembly can be removed by rotating it and lifting it, and the barrel can be removed by lifting the breech end and pulling it back.

Some specimens will be found to have a slot for a shoulder stock in the back strap at the bottom of the grip, and they may or may not have a lanyard "ring," while still others will have the ring but no slot for a shoulder stock.

Dimensional data are as follows: caliber, 9 mm. Parabellum; over-all length, 8¼ inches; barrel length, 4⁹⁄₁₆ inches; height, 5⅛ inches; weight (empty), 36½ oz.; magazine cap., 8 ctges.; and number and dir. of grooves, 6-Right. These data were taken from a particular specimen. Dimensions and weights will be found to vary with specimens.

Reising pistol

This is a .22 caliber target pistol which was designed by Eugene G. Reising, a resident of East Hartford, Conn., to whom basic patents were issued on May 16, 1916, and October 25, 1921, according to inscriptions on the pistols. His first application relating to "a new and improved trigger mechanism for automatic fire arms" was filed on June 19, 1915. U.S. Pat. No. 1,183,115 was granted on this application on May 16, 1916. An application for a patent on "a new and improved fire arm," actually relating only to a new safety device to prevent accidental discharge, was filed on October 17, 1917, and U.S. Pat. No. 1,359,746 was granted on this application on November 23, 1920. On January 2, 1917, two aplications were filed, one for an improved extractor and the other for an improved ejector, upon which U.S. Pats. Nos. 1,309,337 and 1,309,338 were granted on July 8, 1919.

The date at which full production began is not known, but the arm was first made by the Reising Arms Co. of Hartford, Conn., and these will be found to be so marked on the left side. The serial numbers, also on the left side, apparently started at No. 1. On the right side of the pistols of this first series appears the two-line inscription "PATENTED MAY 16, 1916–OTHER PATENTS PENDING." The series is characterized not only by the presence of the Hartford markings and this inscription but also by the use of 12 V-shaped oblique serrations forming the finger grips on the slide. There are a number of small structural variations in this series and differences in the sights used. Reportedly, serial No. 1 had checkering on the trigger. Whether other specimens of the first production had such checkering is not known, but if so it was soon given up.

Presumably the October 25, 1921, patent date was put on pieces made soon after that date. Inasmuch as specimens bearing only the 1916 patent date are known to have serial numbers above 2800, it appears safe to conclude that at least that number of pistols had been produced by the latter part of 1921. Somewhere around 1922 the firm moved to New York City and took the name The Reising Corporation, which implies that there was a reorganization.

Serial numbering on pistols produced in New York starts at 10,000, which no doubt is an arbitrary figure and gives no clue to how many were actually made at Hartford. The highest serial number reported for the Hartford series is slightly above 3500 and the total number produced very likely did not exceed 5000. The first of the New York series seem to contain various components left over from the Hartford production. For example, the 12 V-shaped serrations in the finger grips still appear and certain machining characteristics of the Hartford series are also evident, but they are not present in the later specimens of the New York series. The Hartford characteristics mentioned continue to appear in the numbering range 10,000 to about 10,400, at which point a new type of serrations for the finger grips on the slide was adopted. These are nine in number and are square cut, resembling those used on the Savage pistol. Observed specimens also have a long cross-serrated ramp back of the foresight and an adjustable rear sight. Otherwise, the pistols of the two series are very much alike. The foresight is naturally mounted on the barrel, while the rear sight is mounted on the slide, a feature considered as undesirable by many expert shooters. Alignment of the sights is more permanent when they are both mounted on the same piece of rigid metal.

The number of pistols made in New York is not known, but it has been conjectured that it probably did not exceed 1000. The pistol was tested for gallery practice by the Army on August 21, 1921, but was found to be unsatisfactory. In 1924 there were additional tests, indicating that the pistol was still in production in that year. Again the pistol was rejected and it appears that production ceased not long thereafter.

The Reising pistol was comparatively simple in construction and appeared to possess many good features, but unfortunately it faced very serious competition at a time when such pistols had not become highly popular. It consists of three principal sections: the barrel (hinged type), the receiver, and the slide (Fig. 233). No barrel locking device was necessary because of the relatively low pressure produced by the .22 cal. L.R. ammunition used. The force of the explosion is absorbed by the recoil spring and the inertia of the slide and other moving parts. The frame of the receiver extends forward well beyond and above the trigger guard and the front

end is hinged to the barrel by means of a snugly fitting transverse bolt which can be easily removed if desired. At the rear end of the barrel is a locking lug on the lower side which, when the barrel is lowered into position, engages a turning bolt and locks the barrel securely. Upon rotating this bolt, by sliding a button on the left side of the receiver, the barrel is unlocked and the rear end can be raised for inspection or cleaning.

The breechblock is an integral part of the slide and contains the spring loaded firing pin and extractor. The recoil spring is located in a tunnel below the rear part of the barrel. This spring contains a plunger at the forward end, and an arm pushes against the head of this plunger, when the pistol is fired, thus forcing back and compressing the spring as the slide moves back. The rear end of the slide pushes back the external hammer to the full cock position, at the same time compressing the spring which operates the hammer. This coil spring is located in the grip frame, back of the magazine. As the slide passes over the disconnector the latter is forced down to disengage the trigger from the sear. As the hammer comes into the fully cocked position, the sear is forced by a spring to engage in a notch, thus holding the hammer at full cock. The sear bar and sear remain disconnected until pressure on the trigger is released, allowing the sear spring to force the trigger back to the firing position. As the breechblock flies forward under the pressure of the compressed recoil spring it strips a cartridge from the top of the magazine and chambers it, and the extractor hook rides over the rim of the cartridge in position to extract it after firing. Because of the construction of this pistol no shell ejection port is necessary, thus making the arm more water- and dirt-proof.

As a safety feature the pistol has an automatic disconnector, operating on the principle of that used

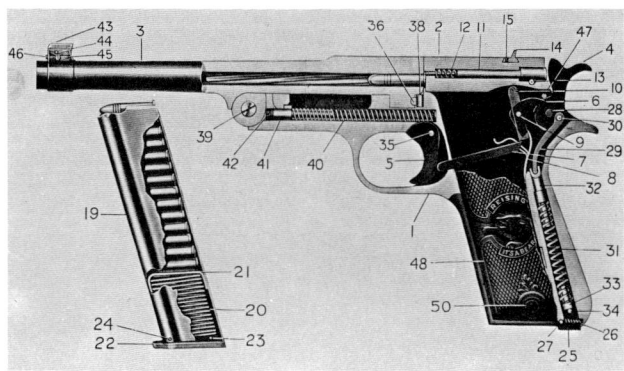

Fig. 233. .22 cal. Reising Target Pistol. Sectional View.

in the Colt, preventing more than one shot being fired for each pull on the trigger. Also the arm cannot be fired unless the breech face and the rear end of the barrel are firmly in contact, thus preventing premature firing. There is also a magazine disconnector which prevents firing when the magazine is out. And, lastly, the exposed hammer is a safety feature, not only because it shows whether the arm is cocked but also because it has a long spur which makes it possible to lower it to a safe position, i.e., at "half cock."

The magazine has an unusual capacity of 14 cartridges. As is the case for many other pistols, the magazine has perforations which makes it easy to see how many cartridges are in it.

Remington pistols

Model 51—The Remington automatic pistols, manufactured by the well known Remington firm of Ilion, N. Y., which has operated under various names since its founding in 1816 by Eliphalet Remington, were based on designs originating with John D. Pedersen. His first patent application relating to automatic pistols was filed on July 30, 1915, and was renewed on July 17, 1919. The basic patent was issued on August 3, 1920, and bears Pat. No. 1,348,733. Several additional patents were issued in 1920, one of them to Crawford C. Loomis, and another was issued in 1921.

This arm operates on the blowback principle, but is unique in some respects. The breechblock mechanism is constructed in a manner which lessens recoil, while still affording sufficient force to operate the necessary functions of ejecting the fired shell, reloading, and cocking the hammer (Fig. 234). The breechblock unit is not an integral part of the slide but is a separate unit which is set into the rear

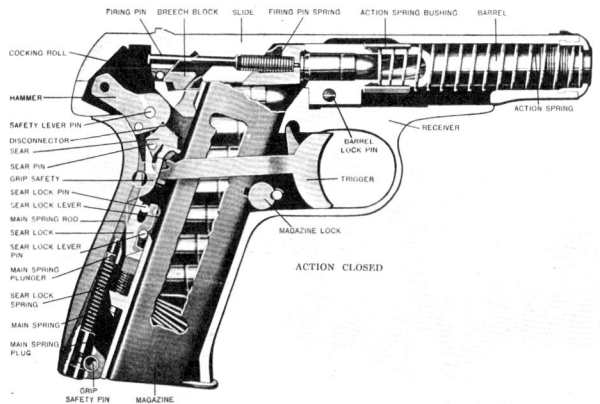

Fig. 234. Remington Mod. 51. Sectional view.

portion of the slide. This unit consists of two parts, a lighter one carrying the breech face and a heavier inertia supporting "block" which is in contact with the lighter portion at the moment of firing. The impact of the base of the cartridge against the breech face drives both back, but a resisting shoulder catches and holds the lighter breech face section after it has traveled about 3/16 inch. The inertia section, to which force has been transmitted through the lighter forward section, continues its backward travel to a point where it releases the forward section, allowing it also to move back and rejoin the inertia unit for the completion of the recoil cycle. The Pedersen device has been variously described as one which supplies a "hesitation," "delayed," or "semilocked" action. The important thing, as far as the shooter is concerned, is that the lessening of the force of recoil makes the arm a pleasanter one to shoot.

The arm is a particularly safe one since it has three excellent safety features. These consist of (1) a grip safety of good design which prevents firing without squeezing the grip, (2) a thumb safety, located on the frame under the rear end of the slide, which prevents firing when turned to the "up" position, and (3) a magazine safety which prevents firing when the magazine is out of the gun. Partial insertion of the magazine will, however, remove this safety feature making it possible to fire the pistol if one is sufficiently careless. For some reason the "Safe" and "Fire" positions of the thumb safety lever are not marked.

When the hammer is not cocked the grip safety is not in the operating position, but as soon as it is cocked the grip safety member springs out. By looking at the grip safety, or by pressing it, one knows at once whether the pistol is cocked. The thumb safety also acts as an indicator of the hammer position, because it cannot be turned up into the "Safe" position unless the hammer is cocked. All in all, the safety features are good and far superior to those found on many automatic pistols.

The magazine release is of the "push in" type and is located on the frame back of the trigger guard. When it is pressed in, the magazine is not only released but is forced out by a spring so that it can be easily grasped for removal.

The shape, size, and angle of the grip are particularly to be commended. The pistol almost "points itself" because of the excellence of the grip design. The top of the slide is flattened and is matted, to prevent reflections. The sights are of the "square" type, i.e., the opening in the rear sight is square and the front sight, when viewed through the rear sight, presents a square appearance. The front edge of the front sight is beveled.

The Model 51 was made in two calibers, .32 and .380 (ACP). The .380 was the first to be put on the market. Commercial shipments, starting with serial No. 24, began in September 1919. Manufacture of this model stopped early in 1927, at Serial No. 60,800, and sales ceased in 1934. Though the numbering of the .380 pistol began at No. 1 and stopped at No. 60,800, there appears to have been a gap in numbering somewhere between ca. 49,000 and ca. 56,000. One suspects that it may have had something to do with plans for the forthcoming .32 caliber model.

Commercial shipments of the .32 caliber M-51 began in September 1921, with Serial No. 60,829. The numbering of this model is said to have been started at 60,801 and continued to 70,280 at which point there was a break in numbering (perhaps to allow for a contemplated resumption of production of the .380 model), and the numbering was again resumed at 90,501 and continued to 92,627, at which point (in the year 1927) manufacture ceased. Commercial shipments ceased in 1934, when stores were exhausted.

The first specimens of the .380 model had plunge-milled serrations which, though perhaps more attractive in appearance, do not give as good a grip as do slanted serrations, with sharp edges. Slanted serrations were adopted later—probably some time in 1920, as it seems to have occurred somewhere between Serial Nos. 24,346 and 47,509, these guns having plunge-milled and slanted serrations, respectively. The change over to the new type of serrations was not an abrupt one, however, as there appears to be some overlapping. For example, specimen No. 24,346 has the slanted serrations while Nos. 26,905 and 32,400 have the plunge-milled type of serrations. The .32 caliber M-51 pistols naturally have the slanted type, because their production began after the change had been fully consummated. Both the .32 and .380 caliber pistols had the same dimensions, being 6⅝ inches (168 mm.) in length, 4¼ inches (107 mm.) in height, and with barrel length of 3½ inches (88 mm.). The .380 cal. pistol weighs 21.1 oz. (498 grams). Both have 7-groove rifling, right hand twist, nominally one turn in 16 inches. The magazine capacities for the .32 and .380 are 8 and 7 rounds, respectively.

The inscriptions to be found depend on the time of manufacture, as the name of the Remington firm was changed during the period of manufacture. The inscription (found on the milled rib) for the earlier production will read

THE REMINGTON ARMS-UNION METALLIC
CARTRIDGE CO. INC.
REMINGTON ILION WKS. ILION, N.Y.
PEDERSON'S PATENTS PENDING

The grips carry a circular medallion type of monogram with the word REMINGTON and the letters UMC, below which are the words Trade Mark (in smaller type). The word REMINGTON with the words TRADE MARK (below) also appears on the right side of the frame.

On some of the later production of the .32 cal. model the inscription reads

REMINGTON ARMS CO. INC.
ILION, N.Y. U.S.A.
PEDERSON PATENTS. PAT'D. MAR. 9, 20;
AUG. 3, 20; OCT. 12, 20; JUNE 14, 21.
OTHERS PENDING

The reason for the change in the inscription lies in the fact that in 1910 the company had joined with the Union Metallic Cartridge Co. and operated under the joint name Remington Arms-Union Metallic Cartridge Co., Inc. until 1920, at which time the name was changed back to the former name of The Remington Arms Co., under which it had operated from 1888 to 1910.

The caliber of the M-51 pistol is stated on the barrel and can be seen through the shell ejection port. It does not appear on the slide or frame. The serial numbers are always prefaced by the letters PA and appear on the left side of the frame.

.45 Caliber model—Previous to the introduction of the .380 cal. M-51, an experimental model in .45 caliber had been made and submitted to the navy for testing in 1919. The pistol was highly regarded and was tentatively adopted in 1920, but later it was rejected because it was considered undesirable to have two different models of automatic pistols in the armed services. The pistol was also submitted to an Infantry Board in 1920 and was again rejected. None of the pistols in this caliber were ever offered for commercial sale. This experimental model was 8½ inches in length, with a 5-inch barrel, and weighed 2 pounds, 3 ounces (with empty magazine).

It seems regrettable that the demand for the M-51 pistols was not sufficient to warrant continuation of their production. While more intricate than some of the competing pistols, and presumably more costly to manufacture, the pistol had many features that made it very attractive.

Robar pistols (Jieffeco and Melior)

The Jieffeco pistol was designed by H. Rosier

and, in its first form, appeared in about 1910. It is advertised in the ALFA Catalog of 1911. An earlier form was designed by Rosier around 1906–07, but this did not come on the market.

The Jieffeco pistols were made by Robar and DeKerkhove, in Liége, Belgium, under S.G.D.G. patent No. 24875. (S.G.D.G. = Patent Without Government Guarantee) The brand name (or "mark") Jieffeco was no doubt derived from the name Jannsen Fils et Cie., who owned it and for whom the pistols were made. This firm, long prominent as a dealer in various types of firearms, is no longer in business, having been liquidated in 1958.

The date of organization of Robar and DeKerkhove is not known, but in 1927 the name was changed to L. Robar and Co. In 1933 the name Robar and Co. was being used, but in July 1935 they had gone back to L. Robar and Co. In 1948 they were using the name Sociéte Robar et Cie. The firm is sometimes referred to as the "Etablissements Robar." It was in the hands of a receiver in 1959.

Although the Jannsen firm owned the name Jieffeco, they apparently did not have exclusive control over sales made in that period because the same pistol was marketed under the name Melior. The pistols are identical in all respects (including patent numbers) except for the change of name on the slide and on the grips. They are known to have been numbered in the same series.

New models of the 6.35 and 7.65 mm. Melior pistol were introduced in January 1921 and, presumably, the name Jieffeco was dropped at that time. The Jannsen firm took over the sales of the Melior, to a considerable extent at least, and continued selling them until they went out of business. In 1953 correspondence they stated that they had a monopoly on sales "in a few countries—not including the U.S." The Melior has been sold quite continuously in this country, however, by various sales agencies.

Serial numbers for the 6.35 mm. "Old Mod. Melior" (including those used on the Jieffeco) ran from No. 1 to No. 38,978, and serial numbering of the 6.35 mm. "New" model began at No. 38,979. For the 7.65 mm. "Old Mod. Melior" (and Jieffeco) the numbering ran from No. 1 to No. 27,350, and for the "New" Mod. Melior the numbering began at No. 27,351.

The Jieffeco (or Old Mod. Melior) was produced in only the two calibers, 6.35 and 7.65 mm., although it appears that a 9 mm. version was planned at one time. The design for the two calibers is the same and is a simple blowback, striker-fired type. The recoil spring is above a fixed barrel and both

are in a housing that can be removed to the front by taking out the recoil spring nut. Only the breechblock recoils. It carries the extractor and a rod to compress the recoil spring. There is no ejector, as the fired shell pivots off the end of the striker. The trigger bar is exposed on the right side until covered by the grip. The magazine is of the conventional sheet metal type and has a push button release located near the bottom of the grip frame. There is a thumb-operated safety located very near the rear edge of the frame. All 6.35 mm. specimens seen have serrations on both the front end of the barrel and on the spring housing beneath, as well as on the rear end of the slide. The illustrations issued in 1911, however, do not show the serrations on the forward part of the pistol. Observed specimens of the 7.65 mm. model show serrations only on the rear end of the slide.

Catalog data for the 6.35 mm. pistol are: total length, 110 mm.; weight, 400 gm.; and magazine capacity, 6 ctges. Data for the 7.65 mm. pistol are: total length, 160 mm.; weight, 650 gm.; and magazine capacity, 8 ctges.

A 6.35 mm. specimen marked simply PHOENIX LOWELL, MASS. U.S.A. PATENT, bearing serial No. 108 has been examined. Other than the inscription above and the word PHOENIX on the grip plates, the gun has no markings. This specimen differs from the Jieffeco only in that it has a magazine release of the conventional snap type at the bottom of the grip frame.

Melior "New Model"—This designation of New Model is not an official designation, but is used here and elsewhere to distinguish it from the former model of the Jieffeco type. Factory literature designates it as Model 1920.

This model was first made in 6.35 and 7.65 mm. calibers only, but in later years .22 cal. and 9 mm. (.380) versions have been added. The .22, 7.65 mm., and 9 mm. pistols are all built on the same frame. The 6.35 mm. arm is built on a smaller but similar frame.

This is the fixed-barrel type, the barrel being fixed securely in position. Near the rear end of the slide there is a slot extending not only through the slide but also through the breechblock unit which carries the breechblock, extractor, firing pin, and its spring. A sliding block fills the slot and locks the slide and breechblock units together. This little block may be removed by raising a spring-loaded latch which extends toward the rear. In the case of the 6.35 model, the rear sight is mounted on this sliding block, but on the 7.65, 9 mm., and .22 cal. models the rear sight is mounted in front of the block. Removal of

259

this block releases the slide, which can be slid forward over the barrel, and also releases the breechblock unit, which can be slid off the rear of the frame. The recoil spring, together with a sleeve which covers its rear portion, remains in the slide and can only be removed by unscrewing a small, threaded, circular plate against which the front end of the spring rests. The sleeve surrounding the rear end of the spring serves not only as a stop for the spring but it covers about half of the shell ejection port (to keep dirt out), as in the Walther Mod. 7, when the action is closed.

The earlier issues of the 6.35 mm. pistol have a grip safety in addition to the conventional thumb-operated safety and magazine safety, but later this grip safety was omitted. Specimen No. 102,971 and those having lower numbers have the grip safety, while specimen No. 112,470 and those having higher numbers do not. Evidently the change took place somewhere between these numbers, but at what date is not known.

The Meliors of this newer type, in all calibers, are made under the design covered by patents Nos. 259,178 and 265,491. Catalog data for the 6.35 mm. pistol are: total length, 120 mm.; weight, 360 gm.; and magazine capacity, 6 ctges. Data for the 7.65 mm. gun are: total length, 150 mm.; weight, 635 gm.; and magazine capacity, 7 ctges.

Specimen No. 41,765 is interesting because it shows that Melior pistols of the newer type, as well as those of the Jieffeco type, were supplied to dealers to be sold under a different name. This pistol bears the following inscription: MRE. LIÉGEOISIE D'ARMES À FEU BREVETS 259178—265491—LIÉGE—BELGIUM.

The pistol has a grip safety, as would be expected from its low serial number.

A 6.35 mm. Melior pistol, bearing the serial number 12,281, has recently come to the attention of the author, and this pistol presents a problem. It very definitely is not an original Melior, in spite of its low serial number. On the other hand, it is unlike the New Model of 1920, though some of its features are similar. It has the same sliding block mounted in the slide, the removal of which permits disassembly, but this block is mounted considerably farther forward, and the sight is on the front edge. This model has the grip safety; it has a disconnector bar on the right side; and the ejection of fired shells is upward rather than through a port on the right side. The patent numbers are the same as for the 1920 model, but many features are quite different. The low serial number suggests that this is a newer model and that with its appearance a new series of numbering started. This, however, is only a conjecture.

This pistol is shown in Part V.

Römer pistol

The Römer was made by the Römerwerk Aktien Gesellschaft of Suhl, Germany, in the mid-1920's. It was provided with two interchangeable barrels with lengths of ca. 2½ to 3 inches and ca. 6½ inches. Different specimens show variations in lengths. Interchangeability of barrels enabled one to convert the pistol quickly from a pocket pistol to one for target use. Some specimens will be found to have an adjustable front sight for the longer barrel. A 26-inch barrel has been reported but not confirmed. If such a barrel was ever supplied there presumably was also a shoulder stock.

The pistol was made for the .22 L.R. cartridge and is of the usual blowback type. An unusual feature was the telescoping of the forward end of the breechblock into the rear end of the barrel to the extent of about one-half inch. This was done to provide an effective gas seal as a safety feature and is believed to be unique. Because of this construction a semielliptical cutout was made on the right side of the breech end of the barrel to provide the necessary clearance for the ejection of the fired shells. When the action is closed this port is closed by the machined-down front end of the breechblock which projects into the machined-out portion of the barrel breech, thus providing a seal against the entrance of dirt or water.

The magazine is unusual in that the sides are split and provided with follower buttons, one on each side. By grasping these with the thumb and finger of one hand and pushing down, the follower spring is compressed, making the introduction of cartridges very easy. This is a feature which might well be used in several larger-caliber pistols whose magazines are hard to load.

A thumb safety is located at the top of the grip frame, back of the grip plate. This is rotated 180° from the forward ("fire") to the rear ("safe") position.

The interchange of barrels can be accomplished in a few seconds. The barrel is inserted into the guides, pushed back into position, and securely locked by a wedge which rises from the receiver above the trigger guard. To remove the barrel a thumb screw, located at the front of the trigger guard, is pressed forward to unlock the wedge and permit the barrel to be slid forward off the guides.

No figures as to total production are at hand, but

as the pistol was offered for sale for only a short time the output must have been small. Specimens ranging from Serial No. 614 to No. 1599 have been examined.

Factory data are as follows: total length, 133 or 240 mm.; barrel length, 77 or 180 mm.; height, 83 mm.; thickness, 21 mm.; weight (magazine empty), 375 or 450 gm.; and magazine capacity, 7 ctges.

Roth-Sauer pistol

This 7.65 mm. pistol was manufactured by J. P. Sauer u. Sohn in Suhl, Germany. It was invented by Georg Roth of Vienna, Austria, and appeared on the market in about 1905. The arm is based on patents issued in 1898, but it also has features which appeared in an earlier pistol designed by Karel Krnka in 1895.

The cartridge, known generally as the Roth-Sauer cartridge, but also as the Roth-Frommer in Hungary, is identical except for powder loading to a cartridge developed by Frommer for his Mod. 1906 pistol. The latter appears to have been derived from a still earlier Frommer cartridge. The powder charge in the Roth-Sauer version, being lighter, will not cause the Frommer pistol to function.

How many Roth-Sauer pistols were made is not known. It is sometimes referred to as "a little known" pistol. Facts concerning the production of this unusual cartridge do not bear this out, however. The cartridge was not only manufactured in Europe but the demand in this country was considered sufficient to warrant its production in the U.S., and it was produced in this country for several years. Production is said to have ceased here in the 1920's, but production in Europe continued until the late 1930's. From this it would seem that a considerable number of these pistols must have been produced, though it must be admitted that specimens in this country are rare enough to be collectors' items.

Factory literature describes this pistol as "an automatic recoil pistol, with back sliding barrel and solid cylindrical breech block, fitted with a positive locking device, the locking of which is achieved by the adjustment of massive knobs." This is considered to be the most distinguishing feature, as compared to other automatics then on the market. Quoting further, "The working of the Roth-Sauer pistol is based on the principle of using the recoil force, so that the opening of the lock, ejecting of the exploded shell, inserting of a new cartridge from the magazine into barrel and rebolting of the lock preparatory to the next shot are made without any manipulation by hand."

Great stress is put on the safety of the locking mechanism. "A turn of 25° of the breechblock with respect to the two solid locking knobs in the breechblock chamber (which is screwed fast to the barrel) prevents not only separation of lock from barrel before the charge has left the muzzle, but also prevents gases from entering the loading chamber." To this is added another important feature, namely, "the working of the breechblock connection with the firing pin, which join just before the cartridge is fired, thus positively closing the barrel at the breech."

The pistol is loaded from a clip which holds the seven cartridges. The loaded clip is inserted into the cartridge well until the clip rests on a track in the breechblock chamber, then the cartridges are released from the clip by pushing down on the movable slide at the top, and the empty clip is removed.

Dimensions and weight of the pistol, as given by Sauer u. Sohn, are: caliber, .301 (7.65 mm.); overall length, 6⅝ inches; height, 4⁹⁄₁₆ inches; weight, 23 ounces; and magazine capacity, 7 ctges.

Roth-Steyr pistol

The 8 mm. Roth-Steyr military pistol was based on patents taken out during the years 1898 to 1900 by Georg Roth, G. Krnka, and K. Krnka, well known Austrian firearms designers. The ancestry of this pistol may be said to go back to a pistol developed by Karel Krnka in 1895, as certain features present in that pistol also appear in the Roth-Steyr (Fig. 235). Though brought out in 1904 it was not adopted officially by the Austrian military forces, particularly for use by the cavalry, until 1907. The official

Fig. 235. Krnka automatic pistol. Developed by Karel Krnka in 1895.

nomenclature for this pistol was the Repetier Pistole M-7. Later, during World War I, it was used by other units of the K u. K (Kaiserliche Königliche Armee), one of the three armies of the Austro-Hungarian Empire. Other military armies or groups used the Steyr Mod. 1912 and the Hungarian Militia (Honved) was equipped with the 7.65 mm. Frommer pistol as a side arm (Figs. 236 to 240).

Two large firearms manufacturers, the Oesterreichische Waffenfabrik Ges., in Steyr, Austria, and Fegyvergyar in Budapest, Hungary, produced the pistol in large numbers. Each pistol was marked with the official government mark and the right hand grip piece of many had a round metal insert with markings stamped on it indicating the unit to which it was issued.

The pistol is of the locked-breech type, with a recoiling and rotating (90°) barrel, a feature much favored by the Krnkas. It has no removable magazine, as used in later automatic arms, the cartridges lying in a well in the butt between the grip plates. To load, the action is opened and a clip containing 10 cartridges is inserted into a guide and pushed down, after which the clip is withdrawn.

No grip or mechanical safety was provided, nor is one necessary, because, though the pistol ejects the fired shell and moves a fresh one into the chamber, the piece has to be "cocked" for each shot. This is done by pulling back the firing pin by a strong, long pull of the trigger. This feature provided

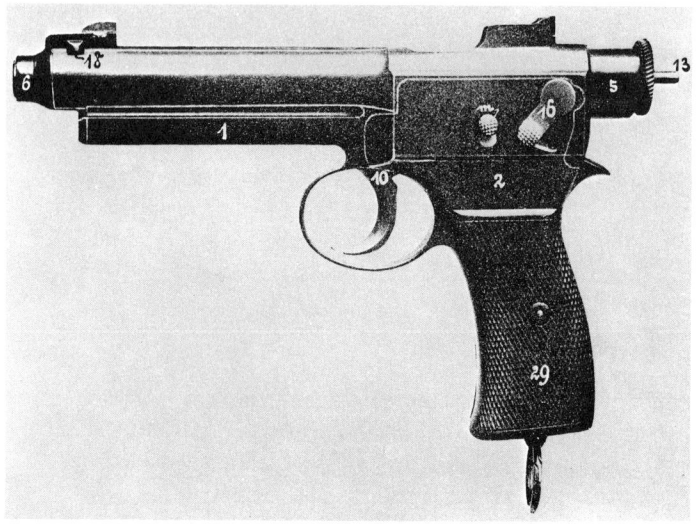

Fig. 236. Roth Mod. II (1904) 7.65, 8, and 10.2 mm. calibers. Predecessor of the 1907 Roth-Steyr.

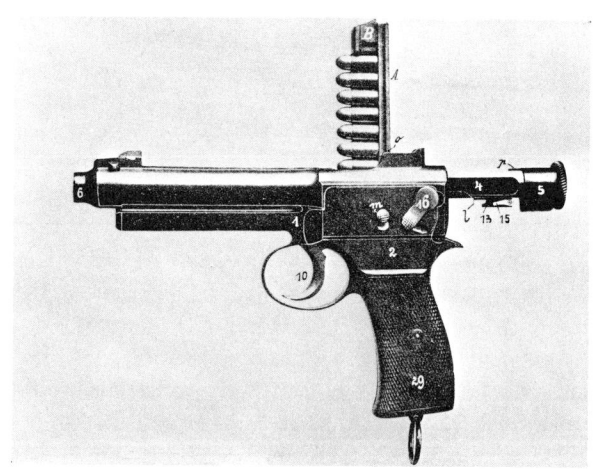

Fig. 238. Roth Mod. II (1904). Showing method of loading.

Fig. 237. Roth Mod. II (1904). Based on Patents by K. Krnka and Georg Roth.

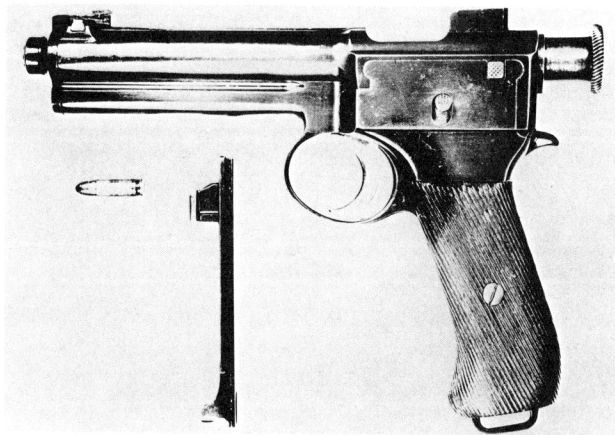

Fig. 239. 8 mm. Roth-Steyr Mod. 1907. A 10.2 mm. version was submitted for U.S. Government tests in 1911.

adequate safety, certainly, but is a very undesirable way of solving the safety problem because the muscular effort required to pull back the trigger (through a considerable distance) makes accuracy of aim almost impossible. Furthermore, rapidity of fire (considered one of the chief assets of an automatic weapon) is lost. By modern standards these pistols are of historic interest only, though, of necessity and because stores of them were still available, they were used to some extent in World War II. The most recently made specimen examined was dated 1927.

Ruger pistols

The Ruger pistols, made by Sturm, Ruger and Co., of Southport, Conn., are comparative newcomers in the field, having been first brought on the market in 1949. They are deservedly popular because of their simple design, excellent performance, and price. The pistol is characterized chiefly by having an exposed barrel, a true bolt action rather than the common slide construction, and a streamlined grip frame fabricated from sheet metal stampings. The bolt is cylindrical in shape and is housed in a tubular receiver, into which the barrel is firmly screwed. The barrel and receiver thus form practically a one-piece base for the sights, thus assuring permanent alignment. This is an important feature for a target pistol.

The receiver is fastened to the frame by heavy steel lugs which are firmly locked when the arm is assembled. A hardened chromemolybdenum steel pin $5/16$ inch in diameter furnishes a positive arrest for the bolt in its rearward travel. The rear end of the protruding bolt has milled projections ("bolt ears") which furnish a good grip for pulling back the bolt.

William B. Ruger filed his first patent application,

containing the basic data for the design of this pistol, on November 5, 1946, and the patent (No. 2,655,839) was issued on October 20, 1953. In the meantime other applications on improvements had been filed and patents No. 2,585,275 and 2,624,969 were issued on February 12, 1952, and January 13, 1953, respectively.

The first prototype model was made in 1947 and a second in 1948. In January 1949 the firm of Sturm, Ruger and Co. was formed and all the Ruger patents were assigned thereto. By August of 1949 a small number of pieces had been completed, and full production got under way in September. Early in 1951 a Mark I Target Pistol was introduced, with a 6⅞-inch barrel, and in 1953 a 5¼-inch barrel was also made available for this new model. To distinguish this model from the earlier one the nomenclature Standard Model was introduced for the first model produced. The 6⅞-inch barrel for the Mark I has an undercut front sight while the 5¼-inch barrel has a square-cut sight. In 1954 a muzzle brake was made available for the Target model.

The serial numbering of the Standard model started at No. 1 and increased consecutively to No. 661, at which it was discontinued and begun again at 2000. The initial numbering of the Mark I Target model began at X1 and continued to X32, at which point the numbering was incorporated into the same series as that used for the Standard model, and the first run of the Mark I received serial numbers in the 15,000 range. Blocks of numbers, in alternation, were set aside for each model. By 1957 the total production was reported to be in the 160,000 range, which is an indication of its popularity.

Between January and November of 1956 a total of 4600 Mark I Target pistols was supplied to the U.S. Ordnance Department for distribution to the army for training purposes. Specimens of these will be marked "U.S." on the top of the receiver.

Factory data are given in Table 42.

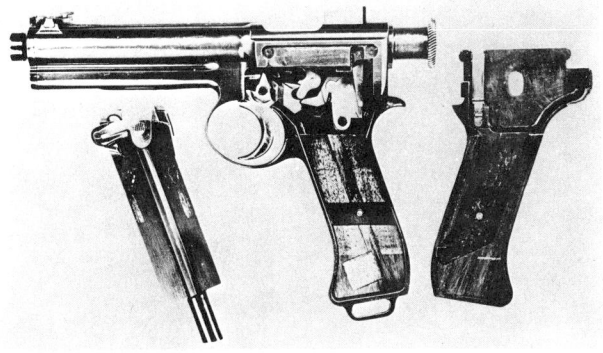

Fig. 240. 8 mm. Roth-Steyr Mod. 1907. Partially disassembled.

TABLE 42

Factory data for Ruger pistols

Measurement	Standard model	Mark I target model
Total length	8¾ inches	10⅞ or 9¼ inches
Barrel length	4¾ "	6⅞ or 5¼ "
Weight	36 oz.	42 or 39 oz.
Magazine cap.	9 ctges.	9 ctges.
Front sight	Partridge style Width .093 inch	Partridge style Width .125 inch
Rear sight	Square notch type	Micro, with click adj. for windage and elevation
Rifling 6-Right, 1 turn in 14 inches for both*		

*See Appendix II for specifications.

Sauer pistols

J. P. Sauer u. Sohn, of Suhl, Germany, in 1900 brought out a unique 4-shot repeating pistol of 7 mm. caliber, which was patented not only in Germany but also in Belgium, England, the U.S., and Russia. This pistol evidently became very popular in Europe.

Their first venture into the field of automatic, or self-loading, pistols appears to have been in connection with the production of the Roth-Sauer, one of two pistols designed by G. Roth of Vienna. The larger model, known as the Roth II was made in Austria and was used as a cavalry pistol by the Austrian Army. This pistol is described elsewhere.

7.65 mm. models

1913 Model—The 7.65 mm. Sauer pistol was the first to be brought out and is properly called the 1913 Modell as it was introduced in that year. It frequently is referred to as the Old Model. As a matter of fact, no model designation was assigned to it until early in the 1920's, when a smaller version of the same model appeared in 6.35 caliber (Fig. 241).

The 1913 Mod. is characterised by its rather unique appearance. The barrel is housed in a rather large tube or cylinder, with a spiral recoil spring surrounding it. It has a separate breechblock unit which is inserted from the rear, somewhat after the fashion of the American Savage which appeared in 1907 and which may have furnished the idea. The breechblock unit is disengaged by pressing down the rear sight and turning a large milled cap at the rear end of the slide. When this is unscrewed suffi-

ciently the breechblock unit can be removed and the slide can be pushed forward off the barrel.

The pistol is of the blowback type, having a concealed firing pin (striker). The magazine holds 7 Browning 7.65 mm. cartridges. There is a manual safety on the left side, just back of the trigger guard, which is manipulated with the thumb. When the safety lever is turned with the slide open the slide is locked in that position. The grip is straight, not streamlined as in later models, and does not afford as good a hold. Like all Sauer products the gun was well made. From 1913 to about 1920 there seem to have been no changes, after which some changes in the firing mechanism and different forms of grip pieces were tried out, with no change in model designation, however. When production of this model ceased is not known, but it was still offered on the market in 1929.

Factory literature gives the following data for the 1913 Model, as originally issued: total length, 144 mm.; barrel length, 78 mm.; height, 98 mm.; rifling, 1 turn in 420 mm.; number of grooves, 6; weight, empty, 565 gm.; and magazine cap., 7 ctges.

"Berhorden" Modell—In most details the Behorden (i.e., Authority) model, or 1930 Modell as it is also called, is very much like the 1913 Mod., but it has a more attractive appearance in that it has a streamlined grip affording a much better hold. Work on this model is said to have been started in 1927, but it did not appear commercially until 1930. Serial numbering started where the numbering of the 1913 Mod. left off, apparently somewhere around the number 175,000. As was hoped, this model was adopted to some extent for police use. The Dutch Naval Service and Police Service adopted it for such use, in the regular commercial form; and it is reported that a special form was furnished for Dutch police use (Fig. 242).

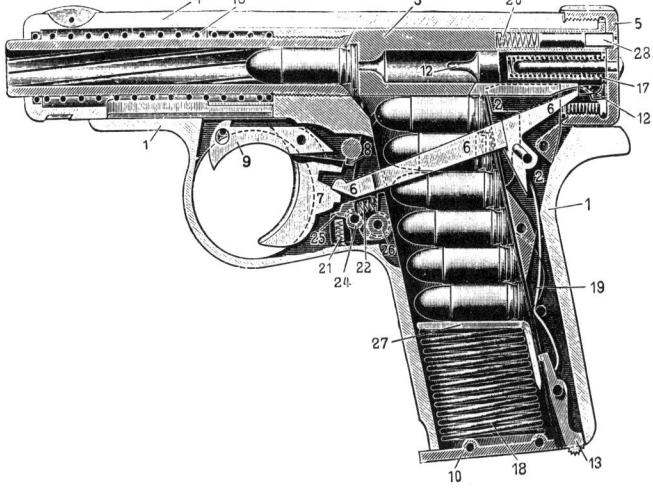

Fig. 241. 7.65 mm. Sauer Mod. 1913. Sectional view.

Fig. 242. 7.65 mm. Sauer Behorden Mod. With auxiliary barrel to shoot center fire 4 mm. "Zielmunition 20."

Several styles of grip piece and slide markings will be found, and a light (duralumin) frame variation may also be encountered.

Modell H(38)—As early as 1932 Sauer began experimenting with double action firing systems. O. Zehner has been named as the leading engineer on this project. From 1932 to 1937 several experimental models were made, apparently with the idea of incorporating this feature into the Behorden model. However, in 1938 a completely new pistol had been produced as a replacement for the "Behorden" model. This pistol was first called the Sauer Selbstladepistole - Modell H - Kal. 7.65. The letter H stood for Hahn (hammer), as this was a "Hahn Selbstspannung" (hammer, selfcocking) pistol. The nomenclature was soon changed and the pistol is now known as the Modell 38(H) (Fig. 243).

This pistol is unusually attractive in appearance and functions well. The top of the slide is ribbed and checked, which aids in sighting and improves the pistol's appearance. There are some good features in design. When the magazine is out the pistol cannot be fired, but when it is pushed in all the way the mechanism is unlocked and the arm can now be discharged (if there is a cartridge in the barrel) by pulling the trigger, which both cocks and fires, because of the "double action." With a cartridge in the barrel, the hammer may be lowered by pressing down the cocking lever, thus putting the pistol into a safe though fully loaded condition. If it is desired to cock the arm before firing, in order to take better aim, this can be done by pressing down the cocking lever and giving the trigger a strong pull. This double action firing system is one of the best that has been produced. In addition there is also a me-

chanical safety, operated by a lever or thumb piece on the left side of the slide, back of the trigger guard. When the last shot is fired, the slide remains in the open position, indicating that the arm is empty.

No production figures are available, but hundreds of thousands were made for the German Luftwaffe, who took over the entire production in the war period, up to the close of the war in 1945. The serial numbering was a continuation of that used for the "Behorden" model, and specimens having numbers above 500,000 have been examined.

As the war progressed, some minor changes and some simplifications in design were made, the most important of which was the elimination of the cocking lever (or hammer safety) on the rear of the slide. This change, judging from serial numbering, seems to have occurred in 1944. Just why this seemingly very desirable feature (possessed by no other arm) was eliminated is not known. Presumably it was done to speed up production and may not have been considered of vital importance in a military weapon. While the pistols produced during the wartime did not have the excellent finish found in pre-war specimens, and often had wood grip pieces, the quality of workmanship on the essentials seems not to have suffered.

Experimental models with light (duralumin) frames were made, and experimental work on adaptations of this model to pistols of 6.35 mm. and 9 mm. Short calibers are reported to have been made. Unconfirmed reports have also appeared that some work was done on a .22 caliber pistol as well. Apparently these experimental types were not successful or were not put into production because of the war.

It is reported that some experimental work was done on design for a fully locked, recoil-operated type of military pistol to handle the 9 mm. Parabellum cartridge. This has not been fully verified, and no specimens have been seen. However, considering Sauer's reputation for skill in design and excellent workmanship, it would seem logical that they may have been asked to undertake such work.

6.35 mm. models

The first 6.35 mm. Sauer pistol appeared on the market some time between 1920 and 1922. The original pistol in this caliber was an exact copy of the 1913 7.65 mm. model. As time went on some small changes were made, particularly in the mechanical safety and in the use of different forms of grip pieces. Manufacture continued through the 1920's, and it was still offered for sale in 1929 (and possi-

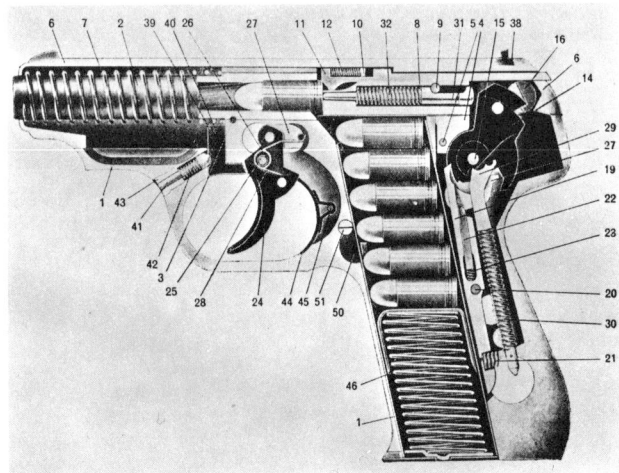

Fig. 243. 7.65 mm. Sauer Mod. H(38). Sectional view.

bly later) at which time it was referred to as the Grosses Modell of 6.35 caliber, other smaller models having been introduced. When production ceased is not known. Specimens in the 48,000 range have been examined, but many more may have been produced.

Factory literature of the early 1920's, describing the 7.65 mm. model as then issued and the newly introduced 6.35 mm. version, show that some changes had been made in the 7.65 mm. model. The specifications given are shown in Table 43.

Some time later (but prior to 1925) a new and quite different 6.35 mm. Sauer pistol was brought out as the W.T.M. (Westentaschen Modell). This bore no resemblance to the earlier model, being more like (though not identical to) the Walther Mod. 9. Ejection of fired shells was from the top, as with the Walther. This first W.T.M. is easily identified by the flutings (or serrations) which are present on the forward end of the slide as well as on the rear, where they form the finger grips. Possibly it was thought that they improved the appearance of the arm. It is clear that a new numbering series was started for this new model, as low-numbered specimens have been examined. This vestpocket model is based on the D.R.P. No. 453,654, though this patent was not cited until a later model came out.

The first W.T.M. described above was succeeded (in late 1927 or early 1928) by a new and smaller vestpocket model, to which was assigned the nomenclature Modell 28. As first issued, this model had much the same appearance as the preceding model, the most obvious difference being in the pattern of serrations (slanted instead of vertical) on the rear end of the slide and the absence of serrations on the forward end of the slide. It retained the exposed barrel section in the slide, through which expended cartridges were expelled. The pistol had grip pieces which bore the inscription Cal. 6.35. 28, as well as the name Sauer. Specimen No. 11,158 was found to be of this type and is evidently in the same numbering series as the first W.T.M.

Some time later a change was made in this model.

TABLE 43

Data for Sauer pistols (Early 1920's)

Measurement	6.35 mm. Mod.	7.65 mm. Mod.
Total length	125 mm.	144 mm.
Barrel length	65 "	78 "
Height	90 "	98 "
One turn of rifling in	220 "	360 "
Number of grooves	6	6
Weight (empty)	ca. 400 gm.	ca. 530 gm.
Magazine capacity	7 ctges.	7 ctges.

A cartridge ejection port was provided on the right side of the slide, and the barrel was completely inclosed in the slide, with the exception of this port. When this change was made is not known. No figures on total production are available, but specimens in the 250,000 range have been examined, and production is said to have continued until late in the 1930's.

Some idea of the relative sizes of the different 6.35 mm. models may be obtained from the data in Table 44.

TABLE 44

Data for three 6.35 mm. Sauer pistols

Measurement	1913 Model	W.T.M.	Model 28
Total length	125 mm.	105 mm.	100 mm.
Height	90 "	69 "	69 "
Weight	420 gm.	330 gm.	275 gm.
Magazine cap.	7 ctges.	6 ctges.	6 ctges.

Savage pistols

The original design for the automatic pistol which later became known as the Savage, since its production was taken up by the Savage Arms Co. of Utica, N. Y., seems to have been the work of William Condit. The first development and prototype manufacture appear to have taken place in the first months of 1904. Later in that year Condit joined with Elbert H. Searle with whom further improvements were jointly made. By 1905 two distinctly different models had been produced in prototype form: (1) a fixed-barrel, retarded-blowback design and (2) a moving-barrel, recoil-operated design. Patents were issued by the U.S. Patent Office on November 21, 1905, and at the end of that year both designs had been licensed for manufacture by the Savage Arms Co. At this time Condit dropped out of the picture and Searle represented their interests at the Savage plant.

It was the original intention of the Savage Co. to bring out a .32 caliber version of the blowback pistol only, but when the U.S. Ordnance Department invited manufacturers to submit automatic pistols for trial at the Springfield Armory in 1907 they began constructing .45 cal. versions of both the blowback and the recoil-operated types. One .45 cal. blowback pistol had been completed by December 1906, and this weapon (which was quite different from subsequent pistols of this caliber) was submitted to the Springfield Armory. It was found not to be acceptable for military use.

By mid-1906 the firm had decided to resume planning for a .32 cal. blowback type pistol, and they started tooling up for production in the winter of 1906. Judging from the time that elapsed before production began it is surmised that several prototype specimens were probably made before a final one was accepted. The .32 cal. Savage was introduced in August 1907, with the official nomenclature Savage Automatic Pistol, Pocket Model, Caliber .32. This very specific designation was used to distinguish it from the .45 caliber specimen which (as well as later .45 cal. types) was referred to as the Government Model. The September 1907 issue of *Outdoor Life* contained what is said to be the first public mention of this new pistol, in an unauthorized article written by a man who seems to have had only a superficial knowledge of his subject, much to the annoyance of some persons in the Savage Co. (Fig. 244).

The earliest form of the pistol is distinguished by the absence of lettering at the safety lever and by the small-sized letters in the insigne on the grip pieces. A further characteristic is the fact that the checkered head of the safety is a complete circle, the edge of which overlaps the grip piece when it is in the "Fire" position. Serial numbering began at No. 1. By 1909 the left grip piece was recessed to partially accept the safety lever when in the "fire" position, and the words "Fire" and "Safe" were added at the appropriate places on the frame. The checkered head was also partly cut away on the left side (in "Fire" position).

The .380 caliber model was introduced in 1913, with serial numbering starting at No. 1, and with the letter B added. Curiously, in some specimens this letter is used as a prefix to the serial number while in other specimens it will be found used as a suffix

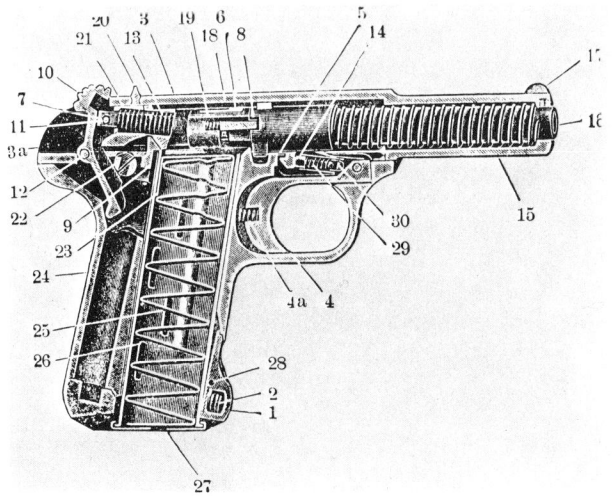

Fig. 244. .32 cal. Savage Mod. 1907. Sectional view.

thereto. This pistol followed the design of the .32 cal. 1907 Model. In 1915, however, a modified version of both the .32 and .380 appeared; this modification consisted of the addition of a grip safety (which was commendable) and the elimination of the hammer-shaped cocking lever that was exposed at the rear end of the slide in the original model. This 1915 version is usually referred to as the Hammerless Model, though that is a misnomer since no Savage pistol has a hammer. The new model was numbered in continuation of the same series as the original .32 and .380. The Hammerless model was short lived, as its manufacture was discontinued in 1917 in favor of a new-style external cocking lever, which had a spur shape rather than the smaller, rounded (or dome shaped) piece formerly used. This was a desirable change for three reasons. The spur-shaped cocking piece made it easier to cock the weapon by hand, and its observable position told the user whether the arm was cocked or not. It also made it possible to carry a cartridge in the barrel with the arm uncocked, by letting down the cocking piece (carefully) after a cartridge had been chambered by pulling back the slide. With the original cocking piece this was a very dangerous procedure and with the Hammerless model obviously impossible. With the Hammerless model one could not tell, from external examination, whether there was a cartridge in the chamber. The new model still retained one undesirable feature (present in all models) in that the recoil spring is so stiff that drawing back the slide to chamber a cartridge is a difficult operation—almost as difficult as in the case of the Dreyse. Another noticeable change which has been observed on Mod. 1907 pistols of late issue (serial numbers above 200,000, presumably ca. 1917) is the style of the serrations in the finger grips on the rear of the slide. Originally these were wide, deep, and 9 in number, while in the later issue they were much narrower and 28 in number.

Late in 1917 a new, enlarged, and much-better-shaped grip was introduced. The grip pieces were provided with a new Savage monogram, still carrying an Indian head (and an extended arm holding a gun), quite different from the original. For some unaccountable reason the grip safety was eliminated—a change not to be praised. The spur-shaped cocking piece was retained, however. Both the earlier 1907 and the Hammerless models were dropped at the end of 1917 and only the .32 and .380 cal. Model 1917 was manufactured from that time on. Serial numbering appears to have been in continuation of the earlier numbering series. Production of Model 1917 was discontinued in 1928 and has never been resumed. Competition with better-designed and better-known automatic pistols made continuation unprofitable.

Despite the unsatisfactory showing of the .45 cal. Savage pistol submitted to the Ordnance Department early in 1906, the Savage Co. was given an order for 200 pistols in .45 caliber in an improved design. Many of the features of the pistol as originally submitted were highly praised by the examining Board, even though it was not accepted. The order was not completed until the fall of 1908, at which time some 230 numbered specimens and at least a dozen unnumbered and otherwise variant specimens had been made. These 230 pistols were delivered for field trials in 1909 and 1910. Having proved to be unsatisfactory for military purposes they were sold at public auction in 1912. At least four other forms of .45 cal. automatic pistols were produced in small quantity from 1909 to 1911 and are now collectors' items. No Savage automatic pistol was ever adopted by the U.S., but the Portugese Government adopted the .380 cal. Model 1917 and used it as their official side arm until manufacture was discontinued in 1928. Whether these pistols supplied to the Portugese were especially marked or especially numbered is not known.

Shortly before World War I Savage decided to bring out a .25 caliber pistol. A set of tools was started and several dozen prototype specimens were made, but the arm was never offered for sale. Known prototype specimens are numbered in a series starting at 100,001. They had grip safeties and were finished in a commercial manner, as if they were intended for sale.

Another .25 cal. Savage, having a shorter barrel and frame, but otherwise like the former, has been reported—the design of which dates from 1916 or 1917. The entry of the U.S. into the World War seems to have prevented this pistol from being offered commercially. After the war, sometime in 1919, plans for its manufacture were resumed and a few were made, fully marked and bearing serial numbering which started at 1000-M. Only a very few have been seen and, no doubt, most of those that were made are now in the hands of collectors.

Between 1910 and 1915 several minor variant forms of the .32 cal. Mod. 1907 pistol appeared. These included types with lanyard loops, cartridge-indicating collars around the barrel at the chamber, and variant styles of sights. The types that were fitted with lanyard loops may have been furnished on contract for police use, since they usually have registry serial numbers on the right side of the frame.

Schmeisser pocket pistols

These pistols were made by the C. G. Haenel Waffen und Fahrradfabrik in Suhl, Germany, which was founded in 1840. In 1945, at the close of the war, it became the Ernst Thälman-Werk VEB, who presently make double barreled guns, based on Schmeisser's patents, and sewing machines.

The Schmeisser pistols (or Haenel-Schmeisser as they are sometimes called) were designed by Hugo Schmeisser, son of Louis Schmeisser who is said to have been the designer of the very first Bergmann self-loading pistols early in the 1890's. Hugo Schmeisser was not only a designer but also the Chief Engineer of the Haenel Company and was responsible for the design of several machine pistols.

Hugo Schmeisser was with Haenel during World War II and through 1945, but when the Soviet forces took over he "went east." Whether this was done voluntarily or not is not known. The current Soviet rifle is said to be "a bare-faced imitation" of Schmeisser's last German design, the MP45 Haenel.

The design of the pocket types dates from 1918 to 1919, and production of the first type, which at the time had no model designation, began in 1920. The design is of the blowback type. During the first two years there were a few minor, but no major, changes.

The Schmeisser pistol has one unique feature that relates to safety. A number of automatic pistols have been so constructed that when the magazine is withdrawn the action is locked and the pistol cannot be fired by pulling the trigger. In these pistols the action is unlocked when the magazine is fully reinserted, and the pistol can then be fired. Schmeisser, in his design, went one step further as regards safety. In this pistol the magazine cannot be withdrawn unless the safety is on and, since it remains on, the pistol cannot be discharged when the magazine is out. Upon reinsertion of the magazine the pistol still cannot be fired until the safety lever is put in the "off" position. Unlike the other pistols the mere reinsertion of the magazine does not suffice to put the pistol in firing condition. Making it impossible to fire an automatic pistol when the magazine is out is a feature that undoubtedly would have saved many accidents had it been universally used.

Another desirable feature, but not unique to the Schmeisser, is the pin indicator which protrudes from the rear of the slide so that one can tell by a touch of the thumb whether the gun is cocked or not. Another feature which seems a desirable one is the absence of a cartridge ejection port, the presence of which always makes it easier for dirt, dust, and water to get into the mechanism. The Schmeisser pistols are well designed and well made, as would be expected, and they are attractive in appearance.

The only pocket pistols made were of 6.35 mm. caliber and used the Browning cartridge. There were two models, now designated as Mod. I and Mod. II. As is customarily the case, no model designation was used for the first pistol produced. Later, when the smaller "vestpocket" (Westentaschen) model appeared it became necessary to distinguish between the two, so the new pistol was given the official nomenclature Modell II, whereupon advertisers and others called the first type Modell I (Figs. 245 to 247).

The first type pistol (now called Mod. I) is de-

Fig. 245. 6.35 mm. Schmeisser Mod. I.

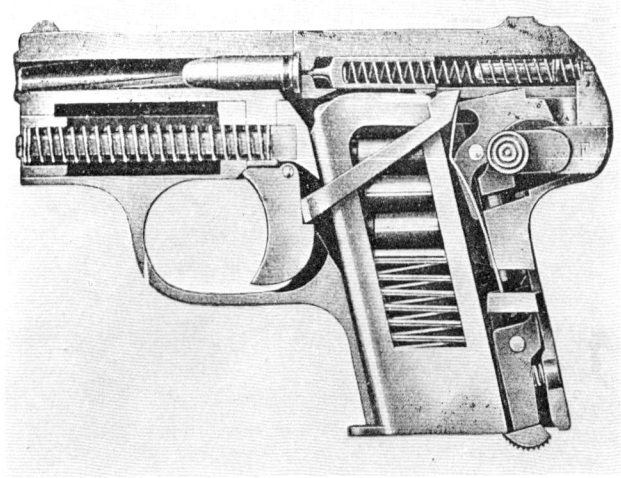

Fig. 246. 6.35 mm. Schmeisser Mod I. Sectional view.

Fig. 247. 6.35 mm. Schmeisser Mod. II.

scribed in the 1923 edition of Bock, but the Mod. II is not mentioned. Similarly the first model was also advertised in the 1922 and 1925 editions of the AKAH Catalog and by Christian Hansen (Hamburg) in 1923, but Mod. II was not mentioned. However, both Mod. I and Mod. II are advertised in the 1929 edition of the AKAH Catalog, so it appears that Mod. II appeared some time between 1925 and 1929.

Both pistols have the safety feature already described, but in the Mod. II the safety lever, which in each case is operated by the right thumb, is located in front of the left grip piece, directly back of the trigger, whereas in the Mod. I the lever is located near the rear end of the frame, back of the grip piece. This is a more natural position for an operation to be performed by one hand, as the lever is directly under the thumb and is easily pushed downwards.

There is considerable difference in the sizes of the two models as is shown by the data in Table 45.

No production figures are available, nor is it known when production ceased. It is doubted that

TABLE 45

Data for Schmeisser pocket pistols

Measurement	Mod. I	Mod. II
Length over-all	115 mm.	110 mm.
Length of barrel	55 "	52 "
Height	77 "	67 "
Weight	350 gm.	250 gm.
Magazine cap.	6 ctges.	6 ctges.

269

they were made after about 1930. This would account for the rarity of specimens, particularly of Mod. II.

Schmeisser "Machine pistols"*

The basic designs for these pistols were patented in the period 1930–1936, by Hugo Schmeisser, Chief Engineer of the C. G. Haenel Waffen und Fahrradfabrik of Suhl, Germany. The prototype version, known as the Maschinenkararabiner 36 (marked MKb 36) may have been hand-made at the Haenel plant. The MKb 36 was chambered for the 9 mm. Parabellum cartridge. It had a full-length barrel and a full wood stock. After certain modifications and improvements were made it was adopted into the German service some time in 1938. The weapon was then given the designation Maschinenpistole 38.

This pistol was manufactured by ERMA (Erfurter Maschinen u. Werkzeugfabrik bei Geipel, G.m.b.H.) of Erfurt. The pre-1941 code designation for this firm was "27," the post-1941 code was "ayf," and the permanent Waffenamt Abnahme inspector's number was 280. As far as is known Haenel supplied only the magazines for this weapon, the manufacture of the weapon itself being confined to ERMA.

In the summer of 1940 a simplified version of the MP38 was brought out, and this was designated the Maschinenpistole 40 (or MP40). Prior to 1941 the MP40 was produced by ERMA and from late 1940 on by Steyr-Daimler-Puch A.G., at Steyr, Austria. The pre-1941 code designation for this firm was "660," which was changed to "bnz," and the WaA number was 623. In 1942 Haenel received its first contract to manufacture the MP40. The code designation for this firm was "fxo," and the WaA number was 37.

Two other firms manufactured components for the MP40, and their code designations will appear on various parts of the weapons as well as the codes of the principal manufacturer. These firms were: Merz-Werke Gebrüder Merz, Frankfort (code "cos"), and the National Krupp Registrier Kassen G.m.b.H. (code "cnd"). A third firm, not identified, produced triggers and the WaA number 815 appear on them.

A commercial version of the MP40, known as the Maschinenpistole 41 (MP41), was produced by Haenel for sale to friendly nations (Portugal, Rumania, etc.). These weapons are characterized by the use of a full wood stock, and full commercial markings of the manufacturer: C. G. Haenel Waffen u. Fahrradfabrik, Suhl. Such markings of course do not appear on weapons designed for German military use.

Schouboe pistols

This group of pistols originated in a design produced by Jens Theodor Suhr Schouboe, Technical Manager of the Dansk Rekyriffel Syndikat in Copenhagen, and for which he secured Danish Patent No. 6135 dated December 2, 1902. Although many changes and modifications were made in later years, it appears that he secured no further patents (Figs. 248, 249).

Manufacture of the Schouboe pistols began with a 7.65 mm. pocket model intended for commercial sale. As there was little demand for it, less than 1000 pieces were made and production ceased in 1910.

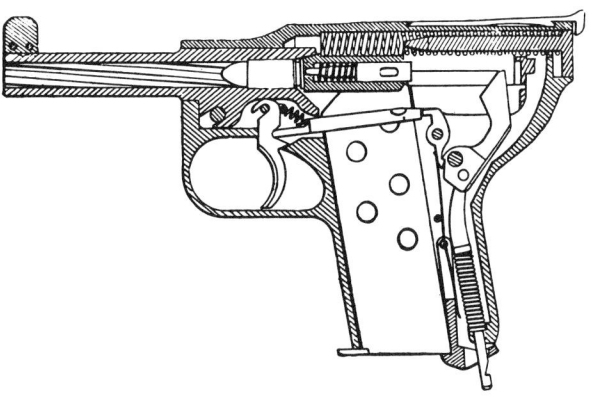

Fig. 248. 7.65 mm. Schouboe. One of several models of this caliber.

Fig. 249. 11.35 mm. Schouboe Mod. 1912. Submitted for U.S. tests in 1912.

*These are, of course, submachine guns rather than automatic pistols.

In 1904 a larger model in 11.35 mm. caliber was made experimentally. Three years later this had been perfected and was offered for military and commercial use as Model 1907. Later on still other improvements were incorporated in models which appeared as Model 1910 and Model 1912. The last 11.35 mm. Schouboe to appear was the Model 1916, which again embodied still further changes and improvements. None of these 11.35 mm. models were successful, however, and less than 1000 pieces in all the different styles combined were made. Inasmuch as these pistols were practically hand made it is not surprising that they vary from specimen to specimen as far as details are concerned. Apart from the 7.65 mm. model, the 11.35 mm. models and some three pieces in 9 mm. caliber, which were made as exercises in tool work and machining (presumably by apprentices), represent the entire activities of the D.R.S. in the field of automatic pistols, as they ceased entirely when Schouboe left the firm in 1917.

The cartridge for the 7.65 mm. model was the regular Browning (.32 ACP), but for the 11.35 mm. pistol a curious cartridge was developed by the Deutsche Waffen und Munitionsfabriken. This consisted of a straight, rimless case and a light-weight bullet having a wood core and aluminum base plug. While this cartridge gave the bullet a high velocity, it was very inadequate as to stopping power and was not accurate. Consequently, it was not considered at all suitable for military purposes. The pistol was barred from the U.S. Army Trials because it was not designed to use the specified .45 caliber bullet weighing 230 grains.

Schouboe pistols made in the earlier years were fitted with checkered or smooth sheet steel grip pieces, but by 1912 checkered wood grip pieces were in use.

Factory data are given in Table 46.

TABLE 46

Data for Schouboe pistols

Measurement	7.65 mm. Mod.	11.35 mm. Mod. 1907
Total length	170 mm.	203 mm.
Barrel length	90 "	130 "
Height	95 "	119 "
Thickness	20 "	. . . . . .
Weight (without mag.)	550 gm.	890 gm.
Magazine capacity	6 ctges.	6 ctges.
Initial velocity	330 m./sec.	500 m./sec.

Schwarzlose pistols

Although production of his pistols has long since ceased, Andreas Wilhelm Schwarzlose of Berlin, Germany, made some fundamental contributions to the development of self-loading pistols. His first design was brought out in 1893, a year after the Schonberger, which has the distinction of being the first automatic pistol that functioned well enough to be marketed. The 1893 Schwarzlose was not so fortunate, however, and only a few were made.

Though recoil operated, this pistol bears little resemblance to those developed later. It had an external hammer which had a long, curved firing point which passed through a curved hole in the breechblock. The hammer and breechblock were both pivoted at the same point and moved back in the same plane under pressure of the recoiling barrel. The magazine well was located horizontally beneath the barrel and the 7 cartridges therein were pointed downward. The cartridges were naturally of the rimmed type, not bottle-necked.

When a cartridge was fired, the barrel recoiled and drove back both the hammer and breechblock, through an arc, thus cocking the hammer for the next shot, and also operating the ejector. A new cartridge was brought up into horizontal position, in line with the bore of the barrel, by a 90° rotation of a cartridge carrier located at the rear end of the magazine. At the end of its arc the breechblock then moved forward smartly, picked the cartridge off the cartridge carrier and forced it into the chamber, the carrier meanwhile rotating back through a 90° arc to pick up a fresh cartridge thus completing the cycle. While this was an ingenious invention the gun was not practical and but few were made.

Schwarzlose, being a true inventor, was not unduly discouraged by this failure and proceeded with his designing and experimenting. By 1898 he had produced a design which he considered worth putting into production and did so. It was a recoil-operated, turning-bolt design and was the first application of the turning bolt idea to an automatic pistol.

The pistol had a long, tapering barrel which had an enlarged section at the rear of the chamber proper to provide space for recesses for the locking lugs on the "bolt," the diameter at this point being the same as that of the "bolt." The "bolt" consisted of a sliding unit which contained the breech face, firing pin, large, coiled spring, and ejector. The forward end of the bolt (somewhat smaller in diameter than the remainder) carried four integral locking lugs, the upper two being set at right angles and the lower two at an angle of 60°. When the action was closed these lugs engaged in the recesses provided for them in the rear of the barrel section, thus locking the two sections securely together.

The rear end of the bolt had a guide ring (pinned

271

to the action body) on the underside of which was a slot which acted as a guide; the first half of this slot was parallel to the axis of the bolt, but the rear half made a helical counterclockwise turn. An integral lug on the lower side of the guide ring engaged in this slot. Upon firing, the barrel and bolt (being locked together) moved back together until a turning motion was imparted to the bolt, thus unlocking it from the barrel section. At the same time the backward motion of the barrel was stopped while the bolt continued back, making a turn of about 45°.

The barrel, upon its release from the bolt, sprang forward a short distance, due to the force exerted on it by the pressure of a compressed spiral spring which was located in a channel below the rear end of the barrel. The barrel was stopped at this point by a detaining device. During its backward travel the bolt drew back a lever which functioned both as an extractor and a sear; and, near the end of its travel, a lug on the lower surface operated the ejector which threw the fired shell upward. The bolt, after recoiling to the end of its path, was forced forward by a stiff coiled spring and in passing over the magazine picked off the top cartridge and forced it into the chamber. While moving forward the bolt was rotated by the guide ring so that when the barrel and bolt sections came together they were securely locked, the barrel was simultaneously released and moved forward to its original position.

The striker was quite different from the modern type. It consisted of a long pin, the rear end of which always protruded from the rear end of the bolt, terminating in a knob. Surrounding the striker is a stiff, coiled spring which acts as the main spring and also as a spring for the striker. To cock the piece, initially, the knob on the bolt was seized by the fingers and pulled back as far as it would go.

When the last cartridge was fired the action remained open—a feature which was used for the first time in any commercial pistol. Schwarzlose, therefore, introduced two features which were used extensively by others. These were the turning bolt and the lock-open feature just mentioned.

The fore sight was necessarily very high because of the very considerable taper of the barrel, and it was integral with the barrel instead of being attached. The rear sight was mounted on the rear end of the barrel rather than on the rear end of the pistol, thus decreasing materially the sighting radius. This sight could be adjusted as to height by turning a milled, eccentric wheel, provided with clicks to indicate its position. The sight was graduated from 100 to 500 meters.

While the pistol had some considerable sale in

Germany and a lesser amount in England and the U.S., it was faced with tough competition in the form of the Mauser which was currently becoming very popular and was being pushed by a well-established and powerful company. While well-made as far as workmanship was concerned, the Schwarzlose was by no means as rugged a pistol and was quite unsuitable as a military weapon. It was also too complicated. Many liked its balance better than that of the Mauser, quite understandably, but it was less reliable under heavy usage.

The model described above is referred to as the "Standart" model, and was chambered for the original 7.63 mm. Mauser cartridge which was much weaker than the one developed later and currently used. Even so, the cartridge used put a heavy strain on the rather light mechanism. The pistol had an over-all length of 10¾ inches, barrel length of 6½ inches, and weighed 23½ ounces. The rifling had four grooves, with right hand twist.

It is said that in 1905 Russian revolutionists bought up the entire stock of pistols, which was considerable, in preparation for the uprising that occurred during the Russian-Japanese War of that year, but that only a portion actually reached their destination as a great many were confiscated at the border.

A second model of the Schwarzlose, similar but larger and heavier and chambered for a special 7.65 mm. cartridge, is reported. The cartridge was said to be similar to the Mauser cartridge but not interchangeable with it. This model, designated the Perfect, also had four-groove rifling with right hand twist. Little is known about this model. It is doubted that it was ever produced in quantity. Specimens seem to exist only as collectors' items.

Pocket Model 1908—In 1906 or 1907 Schwarzlose began work on a pocket model and by 1908 had perfected one having some unique features of design. This was put into production in 1908 by the firm A. W. Schwarzlose, G.m.b.H. of Berlin, and most specimens will be found so marked on the left side. On the right side the Schwarzlose machine gun trade mark will usually be present. Actual sales did not begin until sometime in the latter half of 1909. In Germany the firm of G. C. Dornheim were sales agents, while in the U.S. the Warner Arms Co. of Brooklyn imported and sold the pistol until its manufacture was discontinued in 1911. They then assembled the pistol in Brooklyn until sometime in 1913 from parts which had been purchased from Schwarzlose. There is some evidence, not as fully confirmed as one would like, that Warner Arms also bought the Schwarzlose machinery and tools when manufacture was stopped in Germany. Pistols sold in the U.S. will be found to have the Warner Arms Co. monogram (W.A.C.) on the grip pieces, in addition to the original Schwarzlose markings. The pistol was also sold to some extent in other countries, but in no considerable numbers (Figs. 250, 251).

This pistol is unique in one respect; it is the only "blow forward" type ever to be marketed. The breechblock is integral with the frame and consequently is immovable. Only the barrel can slide, and there is no locking device or cam action to assist in absorbing shock. Below the barrel is a stiff spiral spring (surrounding a guide rod) which is compressed as the barrel jumps forward under the force

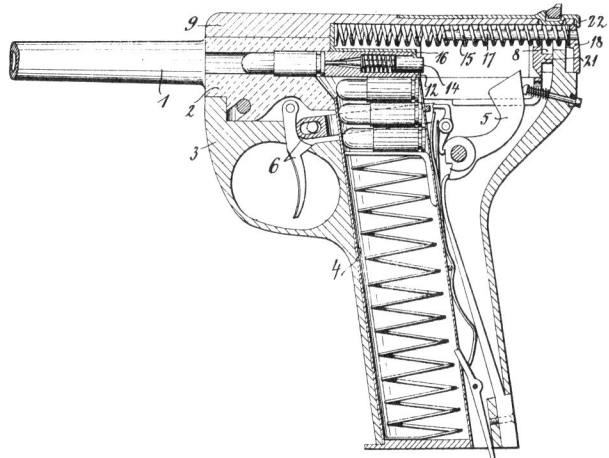

Fig. 250. 7.65 mm. Schwarzlose. From U.S. Patent drawings of 1903. No model designation known.

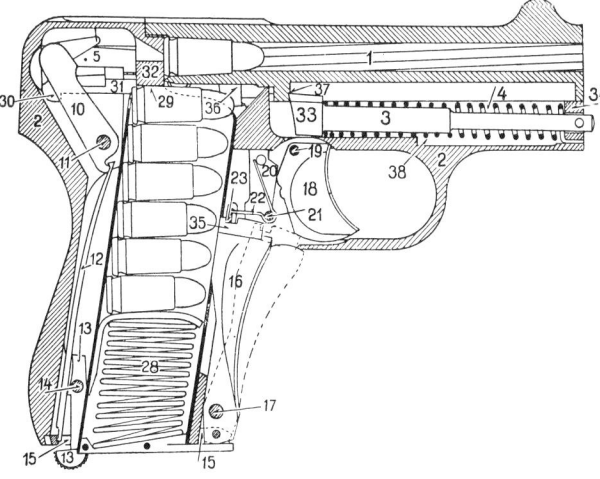

Fig. 251. 7.65 mm. Schwarzlose Mod. 1909. Sectional view. First put on market in 1909.

of the explosion. The extractor is located in the breechblock, as usual, and as the barrel moves forward the ejector (located in the rear end of the barrel section) throws the fired shell out to the right. As the barrel returns, under pressure of the compressed spring, a fresh cartridge is picked up from the top of the magazine and chambered.

The pistol has an internal hammer of the revolver type, actuated by a flat spring located back of the magazine. Some specimens have a safety grip while others do not. The grip safety is unusual in that it is located on the front of the grip rather than on the back strap, and consequently is squeezed by the fingers rather than by the palm. A mechanical safety is located on the left side of the frame directly back of the trigger guard. In some specimens this is actuated by turning a lever while in others it is operated by a sliding button.

The magazine is inserted into the grip in the usual way, a catch at the bottom of the frame holding it in position. To load an initial cartridge into the chamber, the checkered (or, in some cases, serrated) finger grips on the rear end of the barrel are grasped by the fingers and the barrel is pushed forward as far as it will go and released. Since the spring is necessarily a very stiff one in this blow-forward type of pistol, where the unassisted spring must absorb much of the shock of explosion, the force required to push the barrel forward is very considerable.

The pistol was not a pleasant one to shoot. The use of an immovable breechblock may have added protection to the shooter (as was the intention) but the absence of a recoiling breechblock unit to take up part of the force of the explosion necessarily increased the "kick." There was naturally a practical limit to the stiffness that could be put into the spring. Too stiff a spring would interfere with the proper functioning of the arm and would make pushing forward the barrel in loading too difficult.

This Schwarzlose pistol was 138 mm. (5⁷⁄₁₆ inches) in length, the barrel length was 105 mm. (ca. 4⅛ inches), and the weight (which varied from specimen to specimen) was ca. 533 grams (ca. 18¾ ounces). The magazine capacity was 7 cartridges, 7.65 mm. (ACP). The gun has a front sight only. Rifling consisted of four grooves, right hand twist with one turn in ca. 8 inches.

Compared to many other automatic pistols, the construction of this one was fairly simple, with relatively few parts. Externally the design was pleasing in shape, the streamlined grip gave a comfortable hold, and the balance of the piece was good. But the disadvantages of frequent jamming, extraction and ejection failures, coupled with the disagreeable jarring upon discharge, outweighed these advantages. No figures as to total production are available, but the arm was never very popular and was made for a very short time, so the total number produced must have been small.

Sharp Shooter (and JO-LO-AR) pistols

The Sharp Shooter automatic pistols were of a simple blowback type which followed the design shown in Spanish Patent No. 68,027. The JO-LO-AR pistols are of the same design and bear the same patent number, with the addition of Spanish Patent No. 70,235. The former patent covers the design of the pistol, while the latter covers the addition of a cartridge case extractor, which was granted to José de L. Arnaiz on September 12, 1919. It is conjectured that the name JO-LO-AR was derived from the name of this patentee. Since these pistols are essentially alike, except for the extractor, they are being considered together. Both were made by Hijos de Calixto Arrizabalaga of Eibar, Spain, according to the Spanish Ministry of Munitions and the Eibar Proof House. The Sharp Shooter was marketed by Ojanguren and Vidosa, whose monogram appears on the grip pieces, and also by Hijos de José J. Aldazabal.

The Sharp Shooter is known to have been made in 6.35 and 7.65 mm. calibers and may have been made in 9 mm. also, though none have been seen. The JO-LO-AR was made in 6.35 mm. according to the Spanish Ministry, but none have been encountered. It is stated by the Eibar Proof House that it was made in 7.65 mm. as well as in the 9 mm. model, which latter has been seen. This specimen bore the number 5928, the date 1924, and both of the above-mentioned patent numbers. The extractor, which particularly differentiates the two pistols, is shown in the photograph of the pistol in Part IV.

As mentioned, the Sharp Shooter is of the blowback type, having an external hammer and a fixed and exposed barrel which is hinged at the forward end. By pressing a catch, which releases the barrel, the rear end may be tilted upward for examination, loading, or cleaning. The top part of the slide is, obviously, cut away for the entire length of the barrel. The force of the recoil is largely absorbed by the usual spiral compression spring, housed under the barrel, and by the inertia of the rather heavy slide. The arm is very sturdily built and rather heavy for the ammunition used. For example, the 7.65 mm. model weighs ca. 763 grams, or nearly 27 ounces.

The dimensions of the three models are given in Table 47.

TABLE 47
Data for Sharp Shooter and JO-LO-AR pistols

Measurement	6.35 mm. S. S.	7.65 mm. S. S.	9 mm. JO-LO-AR
Total length	133 mm. (5¼″)	162 mm. (6⅜″)	217 mm. (8⁹⁄₁₆″)
Barrel length	76 " (3¹⁄₁₆″)	98 " (3⅞″)	155 " (6⅛″)
Height	87 " (3⁷⁄₁₆″)	116 " (4⁹⁄₁₆″)	136 " (5⅜″)

S.I.G.-Neuhausen pistols

The first military automatic pistol used in Switzerland was the German Parabellum (Luger), which they selected for use in 1901. From that time to sometime in 1914, when World War I broke out, the Swiss were provided with these pistols from the D.W.M. factory in Berlin. As further supplies were cut off, it became necessary to develop another source, so the Government arsenal at Berne undertook their manufacture. Actual production seems to have started around 1920, but this first Swiss-made Luger became known as the Mod. 1924. Serial numbering up to nearly 20,000 has been observed for this model. This first model was a duplicate of the German pistol, except for Swiss markings and proofs. Sometime later a newer model of the Parabellum was developed, and this was designated the Modell 06/29. It is reported that about 30,000 of this model were made and that production ceased in about 1940. The firm S.I.G. produced the major parts for this new model and the pistols appear to have been assembled at Berne. After the adoption of the Mod. SP 47/8 as the official side arm, the remaining stock of the Mod. 06/29 were put on commercial sale, with the addition of the letter P (for Privat) as a prefix to the serial number.

The firm S.I.G. (Schweizerische Industrie Gesellschaft),* located at Neuhausen, became interested in a pistol whose design had been patented in France on March 4th, 1934, by an engineer named Petter who was in the employ of the Sociéte Alsacienne de Construction Mécaniques (S.A.C.M.) in Cholet. The design for this recoil-operated pistol was so highly regarded at the French trials of 1935 that the pistol was adopted for the French military services as the Pistole Automatique Modele 1935A, generally now referred to simply as Mod. 1935A, and government orders were given to S.A.C.M. for its production. The pistol superseded the outmoded

*This firm is also known by the French name Sociéte Industrielle Suisse. It was founded in 1853 and has manufactured military and other arms and parts since 1860.

Modele 1892 revolver which had been the French official side arm. The pistol was chambered for the French 7.65 mm. Long cartridge which at the time was the ammunition used in the service machine gun.

In 1937 S.I.G. secured a license to manufacture pistols based on the Petter patent and to conduct research toward the improvement of the design. The first specimens produced were known as the Selbstladepistole Petter and were in 7.65 mm. Parabellum caliber, as that was the caliber of the automatic pistols then in use. Some few specimens seem to have been made in the original French 7.65 mm. Long caliber, also. Feeling that a larger caliber was desirable, the pistol was soon redesigned for the use of the 9 mm. Parabellum cartridge, and this was designated the Neuhausen Pistole Kal 9 mm. The 7.65 mm. pistol had 4 grooves in its rifling and a magazine capacity of 8 rounds, while the 9 mm. Parabellum type had 6 grooves and a magazine capacity of 8. In general, these first pistols followed the original Petter design, with some minor variations. None of these pistols, in either caliber, were made in any quantity and they were not marketed.

Apparently S.I.G. was not satisfied either with the original Petter design or with the modifications they had made, and in the period 1942–1944 no less than eleven different proto type specimens of a new group of pistols appeared, in which many new ideas were incorporated, while retaining some of the original Petter features, such as the self-contained firing system and self-contained recoil assembly.

In 1944 actual manufacture of a 9 mm. Selbstladepistole Neuhausen 44/16 and also one with smaller magazine capacity (8 rounds instead of 16) was projected and instruction booklets were printed and distributed. These pistols, however, were never produced in quantity. It had been hoped that the 9 mm. 44/16 might be accepted for Swiss military service, and trials were held in the period 1942–1945, but at the end of the war the trials were postponed, indefinitely.

In 1947, after a year or so of experimentation with a new design, a model had been sufficiently developed and tested to warrant commercial production, in both the 7.65 and 9 mm. Parabellum calibers, with interchangeable barrels—a new and important feature (Fig. 252). The Selbstladepistole 47/8 is a very different and much improved pistol over the original pistols of Petter design. The basic arm is the 9 mm. caliber, but by replacing the barrel and recoil spring the pistol can be quickly converted to fire the 7.65 mm. Parabellum cartridge. Furthermore, by replacing the magazine, slide, bar-

rel, recoil spring and recoil guide (with a separate unit in which they are contained), the pistol can be converted to handle .22 L.R. ammunition. Later a 4 mm. practice unit was devised and made available. In addition, a target version of the pistol, in either 7.65 or 9 mm., can be had.

The 9 mm. Parabellum pistol was adopted by the Swiss military service in October 1948 and was given the official designation Pistole Modell 1949. It was carried by officers, including N.C.O., as a replacement for the 7.65 mm. Luger and the 7.5 mm. revolver previously used. Pistols for Swiss military use are marked with the Swiss Cross insigne, and serial numbers have a prefix letter A. Pistols supplied to the German border police have the letter D as a prefix to the serial number. Those sold commercially have the letter P for the prefix, and serial numbering for these started at 50,001.

The 9 mm. pistol was adopted for Danish military service in August 1948 and was given the official nomenclature Pistol M/1949. Serial numbers of the pistols for Danish use are in a separate series, starting at No. 1. Several Swiss police departments have adopted the SP 47/8, e.g., those at Basel, Lausanne, and Zurich.

This pistol is, without question, one of the finest automatic pistols ever designed. It represents the finest in Swiss workmanship, which is high praise for any pistol.

Fig. 252. 9 mm. S.I.G. Mod. 47/8. Shown with interchangeable slide and .22 cal. barrel. A 7.65 mm. barrel also available. This barrel is interchangeable with the 9 mm. barrel, requiring no extra slide.

TABLE 48
Data for S.I.G. pistols

Measurement	Mod. 44/8 9 mm. Par.	Mod. 44/16 9 mm. Par.	Mod. SP 47/8		
			9 mm. Par.	7.65 mm. Par.	.22 cal.
Over-all length, mm.	215	215	215 (8½″)	215 (8½″)	215 (8½″)
Barrel length, mm.	120	120	120 (4¾″)	120 (4¾″)	120 (4¾″)
Length of line of sight, mm.	...	....	164 (6½″)	164 (6½″)	164 (6½″)
Height, mm.	130	143	...	...	...
Thickness, mm.	32	40	...	...	...
Weight (mag. empty), gm.	900	1095	985 (34¾oz.)	995 (35 oz.)	945 (ca. 33 oz.)
Magazine capacity, ctges.	8	16	8	8	8
Twist, right, 1 turn in, mm.	250	250	250 (9⅞″)	250 (9⅞″)	450 (17¾″)
Number of grooves	6	6	6	4	6

Smith and Wesson automatics

S & W Model 1913—The great popularity of the automatic pistol in the early part of the century resulted in a plethora of designs and models. Arms manufacturers were naturally anxious to cash in on this increasing demand for something new. Among the resulting productions was the ".35 caliber" S & W automatic which was based on patents acquired from Charles Ph. Clement of Liége, Belgium. Just why this poorly designed pistol was chosen as a starting point is not known, but it may have been because the design was something out of the ordinary, or it may have been a matter of possible protection, inasmuch as three patents on the Clement design had been taken out in the U.S. prior to 1913. As produced, the pistol was by no means a copy of the Clement.

The nomenclature ".35 caliber" (though incorrect and misleading) was chosen deliberately in order to differentiate the new cartridge, especially designed and made for this pistol alone, from the regular .32 caliber ACP cartridge which it closely resembles. In this special cartridge the case is somewhat enlarged to accommodate a bullet of special design. The exposed end of the bullet (only slightly larger in diameter than the regular .32) was jacketed, while the rear portion, which was still larger in diameter and completely enclosed in the case, was not jacketed. The theory was that the jacketed, exposed end would, as usual, prevent the cartridge from jamming and prevent scarring or damage to the bullet from the magazine or the loading operation, while the exposed lead on the more cylindrical part of the bullet would cause it to engage better in the rifling and also reduce wear on the rifling, thus prolonging the life of the barrel.

Even had the pistol been well designed otherwise, the handicap of requiring a special cartridge (not everywhere obtainable) would have been a severe detriment to its sales appeal. The combination was

too much and, although well made, as all Smith and Wesson products are, the production life was short (1913 to 1921) and the total number produced was relatively small.

Compared to other automatics this was a curious weapon in several respects. Instead of having a slide, as most blowbacks do, it had a rectangular bolt of light construction, on the exposed sides of which were ribs (rather than sharp serrations) which served as finger grips for drawing the bolt back in the act of loading and cocking. The bolt, which appeared solid from the external view, had a vertical slot starting back of the breech face and extending back to and around the vertical post to which the barrel extension was hinged. The bolt carried the extractor and the spring-loaded firing pin as well as the breech face, and it moved shuttlewise between the receiver and the barrel extension. A hammer, actuated by a nearly vertically placed coil spring, was located back of the magazine well. In firing, the hammer extended up into the slot in the bolt to strike the end of the firing pin.

The barrel section contained a powerful recoil spring in a tunnel above the barrel, and to the rear of this was an integral extension which was hinged to a vertical post at the rear end of the frame. This section was locked down in place on the receiver by a catch which was operated by the trigger guard. Pulling the end of the guard out and pushing it down released the barrel section so that the muzzle end could be swung upward. The barrel could thus be cleaned from either end.

The recoil spring was necessarily very heavy and stiff because the force of the recoil had to be absorbed almost wholly by the spring, due to the absence of the customary heavy slide and to the light construction of the bolt, both of which usually assist the spring. The presence of this unusually stiff spring would make loading and cocking quite difficult if it were not for a unique feature which permitted "by passing" of the spring. There was a spring-loaded release catch on the left side of the bolt which, when pressed, disconnected the bolt from the recoil spring, making it possible to draw back the bolt without having to compress the spring. This made loading and cocking very easy.

The manual safety, instead of being operated by a lever placed on the side of the arm, consisted of a small wheel with milled edges located (of all places) on the left edge of the back strap of the frame, just below the shoulder of the grip. This wheel had to be rotated to lock and unlock the sear. This was a poor feature. The grip safety was located on the front edge of the grip below the trigger guard, but instead of being a long member which is automatically depressed by the grasp of the hand it was a short curved piece which requires a special technique involving movement in two directions. Obviously this was not conducive to speed in operation and was a bad feature.

Compared to modern automatics, complete disassembly and assembly (particularly) were not simple operations. Very detailed operations were involved.

While the proper ammunition to use in this pistol is the now obsolete (since 1940) special .35 caliber S & W cartridge it is possible to use the regular .32 caliber ACP cartridge. The bullets will not properly fill the grooves, as the groove diameter is about 0.009 inch greater than it should be for this bullet. The .32 caliber cartridges will load and eject with no difficulty. On account of the greater chamber size the fired cases will be bulged but not ruptured. Experiments reported by H. P. White and B. D. Munhall* show that the velocity attained by the .32 caliber bullet is about the same as that for the special .35 caliber bullet, but that neither furnish the velocity that is attained when the .32 caliber cartridge is fired in a good automatic (Mauser) having the same barrel length.

The special cartridge designed for this pistol certainly had nothing to commend it. As for the pistol itself it had a number of undesirable features.

S & W Model 1925—This model, introduced in February 1924, was a modified version of the .35 caliber pistol and differed in some important respects. Whereas the former model had three principal parts this one had four: (1) a fixed barrel and spring assembly, (2) a slide, (3) a bolt, and (4) the receiver. Unlike the previous model the barrel was not hinged but was fixed to the receiver, and it had guides to receive a slide which extended the entire length of the pistol. The recoil spring was mounted

Centerfire American and British Pistol and Revolver Cartridges by White and Munhall, The Combat Forces Press, Washington, D.C.

in a groove above the barrel and here again the recoil spring was quite a stiff one. This spring was "by passed" in the same manner as for the previous model, by pushing in a stud which projected from the left side of the bolt. The bolt was a separate moving section, of light construction as in the former model, and was not a part of the slide. Its construction was essentially the same.

Upon firing, the bolt and slide recoiled together, thus compressing the recoil spring. It extracted and ejected the shell, cocked the hammer, and moved forward to chamber a fresh cartridge which it stripped off the top of the magazine.

Unlike the former model, this pistol did have a magazine safety, which made it impossible to fire the arm when the magazine was out. It did not have the wheel-like (or any other) thumb safety, but it did have the objectionable grip safety present on the earlier model.

Although this model used a more satisfactory type of ammunition and had some desirable changes in design, it too was apparently not sufficiently popular to warrant continued production. Manufacture was discontinued in 1937.

9 mm. Parabellum—The S & W 9 mm. Parabellum pistol is comparatively new, having been introduced in 1955. Two models were developed, one being of the single action type and the other double action. As this is written only the double action model has been put into production. If and when the single action is produced it will be like the double action except that the double action draw bar will be eliminated. In principle, this pistol is a modified Browning, with recoil spring assembly below the barrel.

Disassembly is quite simple, up to a certain point, but complete disassembly is not recommended. Unlike the .45 Colt, the bushing around the muzzle of the barrel is not removed to take out the spring assembly. Takedown is accomplished by first removing the slide stop, by drawing the slide to the rear until the little recess in the lower left edge of the slide is lined up with the forward end of the slide stop and pushing out the stop from the right side. The slide can then be pushed forward off the frame. The recoil spring is next compressed a bit and the spring assembly is lifted out. Finally the barrel bushing is rotated to the left and drawn out, whereupon the barrel can be removed by lifting the rear end back and out of the slide.

The pistol has no grip safety, as one is not considered necessary, but it does have the customary thumb safety located at the rear end of the slide, on the left side. When the thumb safety is in the

Fig. 253. .22 cal. Smith & Wesson Mod. 41. Disassembled.

"safe" position, a steel block is interposed between the hammer and the springloaded firing pin. A blow on the hammer will therefore not cause discharge because of this blocking and also because the firing pin is of the inertia type. Furthermore, a cartridge inadvertently left in the chamber cannot be discharged when the magazine catch is disengaged for removal of the magazine. After the last shot the slide remains in the open position, ready for a newly charged magazine to be inserted.

The over-all length is 7½ inches, barrel length 4 inches, and sight radius 5½ inches. The rifling has 6 grooves, right hand twist, with one turn in 10 inches. The width of lands is specified as being 0.071 inch and groove widths 0.115 inch. The weight of the gun, with empty magazine, is 28 ounces.

Magazine capacity is 8 cartridges.

Some minor, but no major, changes seem to have been made since first issued. The weapon is well constructed and of pleasing appearance.

Model 41 target pistol—A design for a .22 caliber automatic target pistol was evolved and a prototype built in 1941. For this reason the pistol has the nomenclature Model 41 although it was not produced until many years later. The intervention of World War II put all plans for the new pistol on the shelf for the time being. At the close of the war, plans were revived and the pistol was to be produced in 1950, but again they had to be put aside because of the Korean war. In 1957, however, production finally got under way.

In every respect this pistol seems to be a first class job. It is a simple blowback in principle, consisting of three principal parts: the barrel assembly, slide, and receiver (Fig. 253). The barrel has an integral extension running back the full length of the pistol. The sights are mounted on this single piece of metal, which assures permanent alignment, and they provide a sighting radius of 9⁵⁄₁₆ inches. The barrel is locked to the receiver by a simple locking device which permits its easy removal. All that is necessary is to pull the forward end of the trigger guard out of its socket and push it down as far as it will go. This releases the barrel which then can be picked off. If it is desired to remove the slide, this is done by pulling it back, raising the rear end slightly, then pushing it forward.

The top of the barrel has a ¼-inch strip of dull finished, serrated grooving between the sights. The sights are of the Partridge type, the front sight being ⅛ inch wide and undercut at the rear to prevent troublesome reflections. The blade of the rear sight has a wide rectangular notch and is slanted back at the same angle as the back of the front sight. The back end of the rear sight is serrated and both the top of the barrel and rear surfaces of the frame have a dull matte, sandblasted finish. The rear sight has click adjustments for both elevation and windage. At a distance of 50 yards the point of impact of a bullet is changed ⅜ inch and ¼ inch, respectively, for each click.

The pistol has the customary thumb safety, on the left side near the end of the frame, and a magazine safety which prevents accidental discharge when the magazine is out. The magazine release is of the push-in type and is located behind the trigger guard. An automatic stop holds the breech open after the last shot is fired. In front of the thumb safety there is a release for the slide stop. The capacity of the magazine is 10 rounds.

As issued from the factory the pistol has an aluminum alloy muzzle brake weighing ⅜ ounce as standard equipment. It fits over a short section of the barrel of reduced diameter and is held in place by a screw which also holds in place a counterweight of aluminum weighing ⅜ ounce or an optional steel weight weighing 1½ ounces. If desired, the shooter may obtain a very versatile set of balancing weights which may be attached on the underside of the barrel in a variety of combinations to suit his particular need or whim. These adjustments are easily made.

An excellent feature, present on some other automatics but not often found on target pistols, is an indicator which shows whether the gun is cocked or not. This consists of a pin which protrudes from the rear of the frame about ¹⁄₁₆ inch when the hammer is in the cocked position, but which is withdrawn into the frame out of sight (and feel) when the hammer is down. This is a very desirable safety feature.

The over-all length of the pistol is 11⅞ inches (including muzzle brake) and the barrel length is 7⅜ inches, of which 6⅝ inches is rifled, and the weight (with brake and empty magazine) is 2 pounds. The rifling consists of 6 lands and grooves, right hand twist with one turn in 15 inches.

Reports on the accuracy of fire of this pistol indicate a rather phenomenal performance which promises a great future for it in target shooting if it has the needed durability. Time will tell, but the past performance of the products of this company are such that the pistol will probably prove itself satisfactory in this respect.*

Star, Bonifacio Echeverria

The firm of Bonifacio Echeverria (or STAR, Bonifacio Echeverria, S. A., as it is now known) is one of three manufacturers who are now allowed to make automatic pistols in Spain. Their products have been widely and favorably known in many countries, including the United States, where they seem to be enjoying a wide sale.

The early history of the company is not clear, and accurate information as to its early activities is difficult to get because all records were destroyed by fire in the Spanish Civil War in the 1930's. Unfortunately, such information as is available is, at times, inconsistent and confusing. From what can be patched together it appears that a Julian Echeverria started producing pistols early in this century, at least he was granted patents on pistol design as early as 1907. One specimen examined by the author, Serial No. 57, has been identified by the present firm as having been made in "about 1906." Presumably this is one of the first Echeverria pistols made. It is of interest to note that this pistol bears the inscription AUTOMATIC PISTOL—STAR—PATENT, but it does not bear the impression of a star, such as appears on Star pistols of later vintage. Nor does it bear the Echeverria name. Just when the impression of a star (with radiating rays) was first used is not known, but an illustration of the 6.35 mm. Star pistol in the ALFA Catalog of 1911 shows a pistol very much like No. 57 but differing in a few respects, and this has the impression of a star stamped on the left side of the slide, near the rear end, where it appeared on some later models. This seems to fix the introduction of the six-pointed star

---

*For a fuller account of this pistol see General Hatcher's article in the January 1958 issue of *The American Rifleman.*   279

as an identifying mark at some date between 1906 and 1911.

Specimen No. 20,873 in 7.65 mm. caliber bears the inscription

AUTOMATIC PISTOL—STAR

PATENT FOR THE 7.65 CARTRIDGE

MADE IN SPAIN

This pistol was evidently made after 1911 and before 1919, as it does not have the method of disassembly present on the 1919 Type. A Star pistol quite similar in design, but differing in some respects, bearing the Serial No. 58,276 has exactly the same inscription as that shown in the ALFA illustration of 1911. This, as will be shown, is a 1919 Type, credited to Bonifacio Echeverria.

It appears that there may have been a firm operating under the name Julian Echeverria y Orbea and that this firm merged with a firm by the name of Orbea y Cia. to form the firm bearing the name Bonifacio Echeverria. Another firm, Orbea Hermanos, operated separately. None of this has been confirmed, however.

Just when the firm bearing the name Bonifacio Echeverria came into being is not known, but patents on firearms design and a trade mark patent were issued to him in 1919. The trade mark patent (Mar. 36.635) was issued on November 16, 1919. It covered the name Star and also the legend "Bonifacio Echeverria, Eibar." At the time of issuance of all of these patents his address appeared as Ronda Universidad 17, Barcelona. Whether Star pistol manufacture started in Barcelona and later was transferred to Eibar is not known.

Bonifacio Echeverria was granted patents on two model designs in March 1919; these were patents Mo. 2.533 and Mo. 2.534. The design shown in Mo. 2.534 is identical to specimen No. 58,276 and therefore should properly be called the 1919 Type, no model designations being yet used. Another specimen examined, of 7.65 mm. caliber and bearing the Serial No. 37,364, is identical to the design shown in patent Mo. 2.533, and this also should properly be referred to as the 1919 Type, for the same reason. This pistol (No. 37,364) is the first one encountered which bears the name of Bonifacio Echeverria, the inscription on the slide reading:

BONIFACIO ECHEVERRIA (ESPAÑA)—EIBAR

PISTOLA AUTOMATICA

Specimen No. 58,276, in 6.35 mm. caliber, does not carry the name of Echeverria. This may indicate that the two calibers were numbered in separate numbering series, but this is doubted. The two specimens, Nos. 37,364 in 7.65 mm. and 58,276 in 6.35 mm. caliber, are practically alike except for caliber and size. The only other observable differences are in the shape of the exposed hammer, the absence of the Echeverria name on the smaller one, and the absence of the word Star on the grips of the 7.65 mm. specimen.

Some of the 1919 Type pistols continued in production for some years, during which time a considerable number of modifications were made. The early Echeverria pistols seem to have an unusual number of variants. The first to be discontinued was the 9 mm. model, production of which stopped in 1921. Both the 6.35 mm. and the 7.65 mm. models were discontinued in 1929 (Figs. 254, 255). These models were replaced with new ones, but just when and in just what order they appeared is not known. The Star Catalog of 1934 lists the pistols which were in producton at that time. In order of their appearance in the catalog, they are as follows:

Mod. E—6.35 mm. Vestpocket Model. 6 shots, weight 280 grams. This was one of the smallest pistols ever produced, being only 100 mm. in length

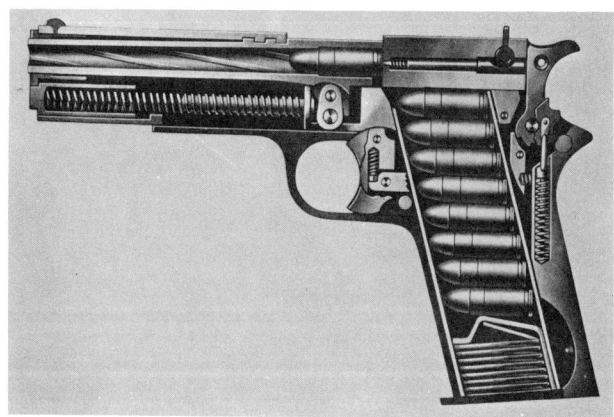

Fig. 254. 9 mm. (.380) Star Mod. 1922. Sectional view.

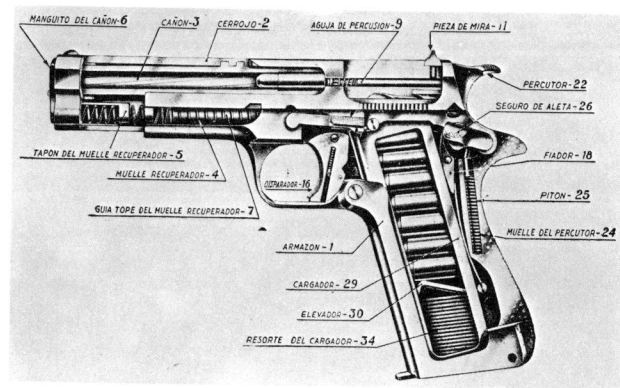

Fig. 255. Star pistols. Sectional view. Models: S, SI, A, B, M, and P.

—about the size of the more familiar Walther Mod. 9 and the Mauser Mod. W.T.P. II. Mod. E was discontinued in 1941.

Mod. C.O.—6.35 mm. Pocket Model. 8 shots. This was distinctly larger than Mod. E, its length being 120 mm. and weight 400 grams. Mod. C.O. was discontinued in 1957 when it was replaced by Mod. C.U.

Mod. H—7.65 mm. Pocket Model. 7 shots. A special magazine for 15 shots was obtainable. This model is a duplicate of Mod. C.O. in design. The model was discontinued in 1941.

Mod. I—7.65 mm. Police Model. 9 shots. A special magazine for 15 shots was obtainable. This pistol is similar in design to Mod. H, but is larger and heavier. It has a streamlined grip (a "comb") and a lanyard ring. The barrel is 123 mm. long instead of 70 mm., and the weight is 690 grams as against 580 for Mod. H. Mod. I is apparently still in production with some modifications.

Mod. D—9 mm. (.380) Spanish Police and Pocket Model. 6 shots. A special magazine for 15 shots was available. Regulation pistol for the Spanish Police. This is a transition model, having most of the features of the Colt Mod. 1911 (without the grip safety), but retaining some of the features of the previous Star models, such as the safety. Mod. D was discontinued in 1941.

Mod. "F.T.B."—.22 caliber Target Pistol. 11 shots. This pistol had a 190-mm. barrel, over-all length of 250 mm., and weighed 750 grams. It appears to be identical in design to model I, except for caliber and length of barrel. This later became the Mod. F. It is still in production.

Mod. A—7.63 caliber. For the Mauser cartridge. War and Police Model. 8 shots. 180 or 200 mm. barrel. Had an adjustable sight, to 1000 meters. This model had the straight grip, as on the 9 mm. Mod. A. The catalog stated that this model could also be obtained in 9 mm. Bergmann or Colt .45 calibers.

Mod. B—9 mm. Parabellum. War and Police Model. 8 shots. 105, 130, and 160 mm. barrels available. This model had the improved grip, with comb, as on the 9 mm. Mod. A.

Mod. C—9 mm. Long. War and Police Model. 8 shots. This model is the same as Mod. B except for caliber. Barrel length either 105 or 139 mm.

The Mod. A could be provided with a shoulder stock in the following calibers: 9 mm. (.38), 9 mm. Bergmann, and 7.63 mm. Mauser. For the .38 and the 9 mm. Bergmann calibers, special magazines were available for either 16 or 32 cartridges. The shoulder stock was of the case type, like that for the Mauser Military Pistol, permitting carrying the pistol in it while attached to the belt.

A list of models "currently manufactured," as supplied by the manufacturers in 1953, includes the models named below. Some of these are new, while in several others considerable modification had been made.

Mod. C.O.—6.35 mm. Pocket Model. Discontinued in 1957 and replaced by Mod. C.U., having a light aluminum alloy frame.

Mod. I—Continued, with modification.

Mod. F—.22 cal. Continued. 110 mm. barrel.

Mod. F. Target—.22 cal. Target Model, 180 mm. barrel.

Mod. F. Sport—.22 cal. 150 mm. barrel.

Essentially these are the same except for barrel lengths.

Mod. F Olimpic—.22 cal. Short. Essentially the same as the other F model, with the addition of adjustable sights (for windage and elevation), balance weights, and gas check. Barrel length 180 mm., over-all length 255 mm., and weight 1510 grams.

Mod. SI—7.65 mm. This model has been discontinued.

Mod. S—9 mm. (.380). The S and SI models are alike except as to caliber. They are closely modeled after the .45 1911 Colt, but without the grip safety.

Mod. Super SI—7.65 mm. This model has been discontinued.

Mod. Super S—9 mm. (.380) The Super S and Super SI models are identical except as to caliber. They also are close copies of the .45 1911 Colt in general design, but with modifications. They have fancy grips, with no grip safety, but the most important change is in the method of disassembly. The disassembly device is mounted on the right side. By simply rotating a lever the slide can be removed. This appears to be an excellent improvement.

Mod. A—9 mm. (.38). 8 shots.

Mod. B—9 mm. Parabellum. 9 shots.

Mod. M—.38 auto. 9 shots.

Mod. P—.45 auto. 7 shots.

These four models are identical in form and are almost exact copies of the .45 1911 Colt, without the grip safety. All have 125-mm. barrels.

Mod. Super A—9 mm. (.38) 9 shots.

Mod. Super B—9 mm. Parabellum. 9 shots.

Mod. Super M—.38 auto. 9 shots.

Mod. Super P—.45 auto. 7 shots. This model has been discontinued.

These four Super models, like those of the S series, have the improved method of disassembly. Just when they appeared is not known, but they were adopted as regulation service pistols by the Spanish

Army in July 1946 and by the Spanish Navy in October 1946.

Mod. MD—This model is unique among the Star pistols in that it can be instantly converted from a semi-automatic to full automatic pistol by manipulating a vertical member set into the right hand side of the slide. It was made regularly in 9 mm. (.38), 7.63 mm. (Mauser) and .45 ACP calibers, and could be obtained in "less usual" calibers, on demand. The pistol was provided with a wood case which also served as a shoulder stock. One specimen

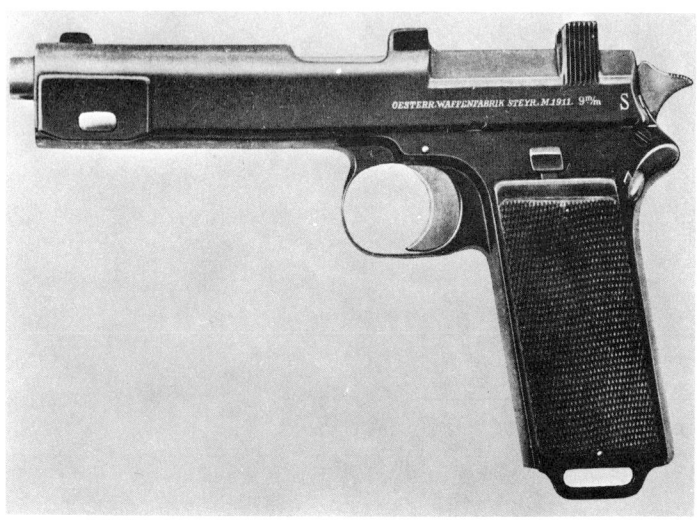

Fig. 256. 9 mm. Steyr Mod. 1911. Also known as the Steyr-Hahn.

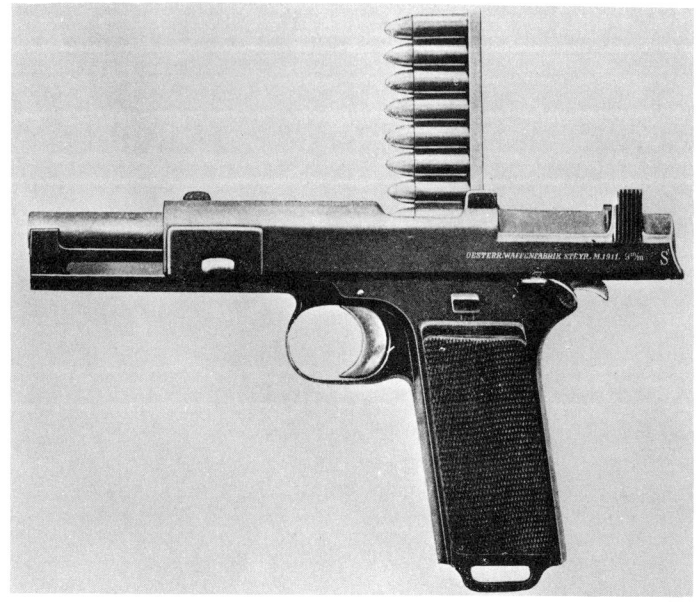

Fig. 257. 9 mm. Steyr Mod. 1911. Showing method of loading.

examined was of .45 cal. and was marked GUARDIA NACIONALE NICARAGUA on the right side. This specimen bore the Serial No. 3956.

Mod. HF—.22 caliber. Vestpocket Model. This pistol seems to be unlike any other model of the Star line. The serial number (No. 519,344) on the one examined would indicate that it is of fairly recent production. No description of it has been seen in factory literature. In appearance it somewhat resembles the earlier Mod. H (or HN), but it has a mechanical release like that on the .45 Colt Mod. 1911, and the magazine release is similar to that of the Colt. It is 137 mm. in length and 102 mm. high. Unfortunately the rifling could not be measured.

In 1958 a new Modelo DK in 9 mm. (.380) was introduced. This has a light aluminum alloy frame. It is a very neat, compact pistol, being only 145 mm. in length and 100 mm. in height. It has a very streamlined grip, affording an excellent hold for a medium-sized hand. It appears that it would be an excellent arm for self-defense, for which it presumably was intended. Why the model designation Modelo DK, formerly used for a .22 caliber pistol, was revived and assigned to this 9 mm. pistol is not known.

Steyr (Steyr-Hahn) military pistol

This 9 mm. recoil-operated, rotating barrel (60°), was designed, patented and manufactured by the Oesterreichische Waffenfabriks Gesellschaft at Steyr, Austria (Figs. 256 to 259). The name Steyr-Hahn

Fig. 258. 9 mm. Steyr Mod. 1911. Partially disassembled.

(i.e. Steyr-Hammer) was used to distinguish it from the Steyr-Roth pistol which did not have a hammer. The name is not official nomenclature. Actual designing seems to have begun in 1910, production in 1911, and distribution in 1912. The first version of this arm established the official nomenclature, the inscription on the left side reading OESTERR. WAFFENFABRIK. STEYR. M. 1911. 9 mm.

The serial numbering started at No. 1 and the pistols were marked with the official government proof mark used for pistols made for commercial use. This mark appears on the left side of the slide. In this original commercial form of the pistol the rear sight is a separate block dovetailed into the sight box at the rear of the slide. It appears that only a comparatively small number of these commercial specimens were made. This is borne out by the fact that one observed specimen, dated 1911, bears the serial No. 867 on the slide and the No. 4070-j (a military number) on the frame which is dated 1912. The slide and barrel are a part of the original commercial production, while the frame was part of a military production.

In mid-1912 the pistol was adopted into the Austrian military service as the 1912 Selbstlade Pistole-Steyr. It appears that the Hungarian forces of the Austro-Hungarian Army were equipped with the 7.65 mm. Frommer pistol during World War I. For military purposes the numbering system was changed so as to avoid the use of very large numbers. This system, like the German, uses a maximum of four digits, and a suffix letter. The first (or possibly second) 9999 would be numbered from 1-a to 9999-a, then from 1-b to 9999-b and so on. The M-12 or military type differs from the earlier commercial type in that the rear sight was made in one piece,

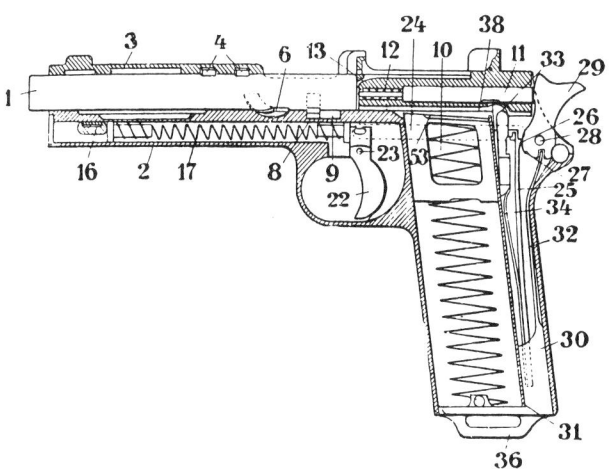

Fig. 259. 9 mm. Steyr Mod. 1911. Sectional view.

the commercial Vienna proof mark was dropped and the Austrian military mark substituted, appearing on the upper part of the trigger guard (right side), together with the official government mark (Wn for Wien), followed by the Austrian Eagle and two digits (probably an inspector's number). The M-12 has a simple inscription, consisting of the word STEYR followed by the year in which the arm was made. Specimens examined were dated from 1912 to 1918. No figures are available as to the total production of the M-12 for the Austro-Hungarian forces, but the number probably ran into the hundreds of thousands. Specimens in the z series (dated 1919) have been examined. If all the letters from a to z were used as suffix letters, and if each group were filled (which probably was not the case), the total number produced would be well over 250,000. That a great many were produced is evident from the fact that in 1938 there were still so many of them in military stores in Austria that the Germans confiscated them for use of the Nazi police forces stationed in Austria. In order to simplify the ammunition problem these confiscated pistols were rechambered to take the 9 mm. Luger (Parabellum) cartridge, which in German military parlance is called the Patrone 08. Pistols so modified will show the digits 08 stamped on the slide and should show the German Nitro proof mark on the left side and the military proof on the right side of the frame. No new nomenclature seems to have been given to these modified pistols by the Germans, and since there was no renumbering the serial numbers represent the original numbering put on at the factory.

The O.W.G. manufactured the M-12 pistol on contract for the Rumanian government in 1913 and 1914, but only before World War I started. The Rumanian nomenclature for the pistol is the same as the Austrian, viz. M-12. On the left side of the slide will be found the Rumanian Crown beneath which is inscribed "Md. 1912." The serial numbers are believed to have started at 1 and probably did not exceed 10,000. One variant for the Rumanians, and apparently not made in quantity, was a style provided for a shoulder stock attachment.

Prior to World War I, the O.W.G. also executed a contract for Chile. These pistols were identical to the Austrian M-12, with the exception of the markings. On the left side there appears the Chilean coat of arms and on the right the words EJERCITO DE CHILE. How many pistols were furnished on this contract is not known, nor what system of numbering was used. After the war, however, Chile acquired a large number of service weapons and added their own markings. In consequence it is possible to find

Austrian numbered and proofed M-12 pistols which also show Chilean markings. The pistols furnished on contract were not proofed.

The M-12 pistol is a simple, quite strong, well-made pistol which was found to be very reliable in action. Some cracked barrels have been reported, however, indicating that the barrels were too thin. The pistol requires a special cartridge designed for use with this pistol, but thought to be still available. Like the Roth-Steyr, the magazine well is loaded with cartridges by inserting the end of a clip into a guide and pushing the cartridges downward, after which the clip is removed. The clip carries 8 cartridges. Following World War I, production of this pistol was stopped and none have been made since.

Factory data for the 9 mm. Mod. 1911 Steyr are as follows: total length, 205 mm.; length of barrel, 126 mm.; weight, 960 grams; magazine capacity, 8 ctges.; rifling grooves, 4-Right; initial velocity, 340 m./sec.

Steyr pocket pistols

As has been stated elsewhere, Nicolas Pieper of Herstal, Belgium, took out patents on various designs of pocket pistols, some of which he manufactured and some of which were licensed to others. Among the latter, the pistols made by the Oesterreichische Waffenfabrik Gesellschaft at Steyr, Austria, are important. These were based on early Pieper patents, as is stated on every specimen. Patents on these pistols were taken out in England and in Switzerland, also. Pistols based on Pieper patents show a strong influence of the Warnant designs, patents for which preceded those of Pieper. Steyr and Pieper pistols show considerable resemblance.

Mod. 1909—The October 1909 issue of *Schuss u. Waffe* contains the first mention of the Steyr pocket pistol, in both the 6.35 and 7.65 mm. caliber (Fig. 260). The November issue of this periodical contains the first advertisement of these weapons and gives the nomenclature Steyr Modell 1909. The numbering of the 7.65 mm. model is said to have started at 1001. Just where the numbering of the 6.35 mm. pistols began is not known, but it would seem that they must have been numbered in a separate series, for two reasons. First, all 6.35 mm. pistol serial numbers include the suffix letter A; second, the serial numbers on some 6.35 mm. pistols marked as made in 1910 are higher than those on 7.65 mm. specimens marked as having been made in 1911, and 6.35 mm. pistols marked 1921 have higher numbers than the 7.65 pistols made in 1928.

As production went on, there were some slight changes in the 7.65 mm. model. At what point in numbering, or on what date, these changes were made is not known but the following observations have been made. Specimens Nos. 1009 (dated 1909), 9348 and 11,607 (both dated 1910), and No. 25,084 (dated 1911) are identical. Those in the 50,000 range are found to be slightly different, and these have the letter P added to the serial number. The differences relate to bolt and slide construction. Obvious external differences are as follows. The earlier specimens have slanted grip serrations, always located at the rear end of the slide on an integral "block." On specimen No. 55,528P the grip serrations appear in vertical form and are below the "block," which in this instance has a smooth surface. But on specimen No. 57,478 the serrations constituting the finger grips have been moved back to their original position (on the "block") and are vertical instead of slanted as in the early production. Another difference is in the size of the serrated integral "block" at the rear end of the barrel, by means of which the barrel is forced down into the locking position. The barrel is pinioned at the forward end and is released by an unlocking lever, positioned below the "block" referred to. This "block" is considerably longer in the 1928 specimens. The earlier specimens do not have a lanyard loop, while the later specimens are so provided. The 1928 specimens have the STEYR monogram on the grips while the earlier ones have the O.W.G monogram.

The 6.35 mm. Steyr Mod. 1909 is a smaller version of the 7.65 mm. type, mechanical details being the same as those in the earliest form of the latter. Spe-

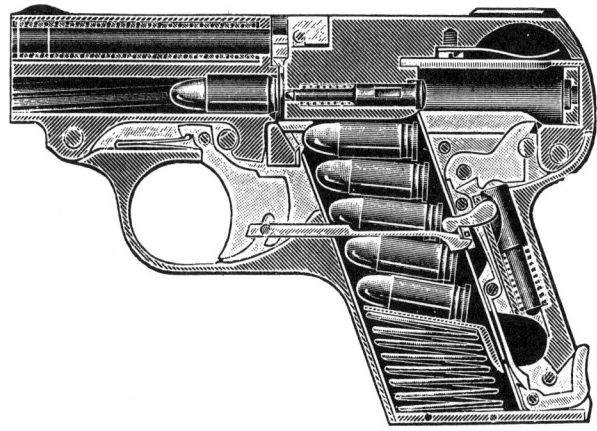

Fig. 260. 6.35 mm. Steyr Pocket Mod. Sectional view.

cimens manufactured as late as 1924 (No. 118,759 A) still show the same mechanical features.

Though the original name of the firm manufacturing the Steyr pistols (O.W.G.) was apparently retained during the 1920's, the owg monogram was superseded by a monogram consisting of the encircled word STEYR as early as 1921, as shown on pistol No. 99,955 A, which is so dated. By the mid 1930's the name of the firm had been changed to Steyr-Daimler-Puch A.G.

The manufacture of Steyr pocket pistols naturally ceased during World War I and seems to have been resumed ca. 1921. Production again was stopped in 1939 because of World War II and appears not to have been resumed.

TABLE 49

Factory data for Steyr pocket pistols

Measurement	6.35 mm. Mod.	7.65 mm. Mod.
Total length	115 mm.	162 mm.
Length of barrel	54 "	95 "
Height	79 "	102 "
Thickness	19.5 "	25 "
Weight, empty	330 gm.	605 gm.
Magazine capacity	6 ctges.	7 ctges.
Rifling grooves and twist	6-Right	6-Right
Initial velocity	210 m./sec.	275 m./sec.

Stock pistols

The Stock pistols, made by Franz Stock of Berlin, Germany, are of a simple blowback type. They came out in the early 1920's in all three calibers: .22, 6.35 mm., and 7.65 mm. The first two to be produced were evidently the 6.35 mm. and the 7.65 mm. as they are the only ones mentioned in the 1923 edition of Bock. The AKAH Catalog issued in March 1925, however, shows all three as being available (Fig. 261).

The pistol has a fixed barrel. The slide, which extends the entire length of the barrel, has a portion cut away, exposing about two thirds of the top of the barrel. The breechblock unit, which also contains the firing pin (striker) and spiral spring, is set into the rear end of the slide and the extractor bar holds the unit in position. The extractor is located at the top of the breechblock unit, and expended shells are thrown upward by its operation. Removal of the magazine, which holds 7 cartridges in the 6.35 and 8 in the 7.65 mm. model, locks the action so that the pistol cannot be fired when the magazine is out, even though a cartridge is in the chamber.

To disassemble, the magazine is removed and the slide is pulled back as far as it will go and locked in that position by turning the thumb safety upwards. A large-headed screw, located in the rear end of the slide, is removed, whereupon the firing pin with its encircling spring can be shaken out. The forward end of the extractor bar is now lifted, thus unlocking the breechblock unit, which can now be slid forward and lifted out. Then the slide is drawn forward over the muzzle end and the spiral compression spring is removed. The whole operation need not take more than 30 seconds, and reassembly is as easy.

For the 6.35 mm. model the lowest serial number seen is No. 460 and the highest No. 9319; for the 7.65 mm. model the lowest is No. 6162 and the highest No. 17,322. No information is at hand concerning the total production of any of the models, nor is it known when production was stopped.

Only one .22 caliber Stock has been measured. While this model is of the same general type of construction there are some minor differences. The extractor is not at the extreme top of the breechblock, but is set at an angle, a little lower on the right side, so that expended shells are thrown to the right and upward rather than directly upward as in the other models.

The over-all length of the specimen examined (Serial No. 289) was 205 mm., length of barrel 138 mm., and height 100 mm. The sighting radius is long, as it should be for a target pistol, being 180 mm. The magazine capacity for this model is 10 rounds. The pistol could be obtained with different barrel lengths. For example, it could be obtained with a 190 mm. barrel and over-all length of 260 mm. With this barrel the weight would be 700 grams.

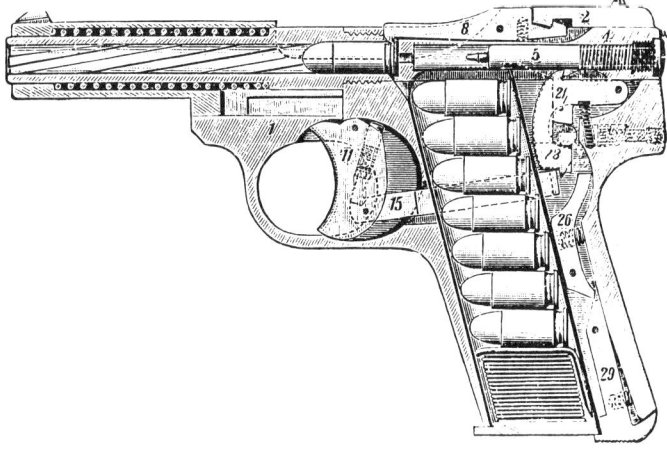

Fig. 261. 7.65 mm. Stock. Sectional view.

The 6.35 and 7.65 mm. pistols have good balance, but the .22 cal. model is not so well balanced, having a longer barrel and a short grip. All of the pistols are well designed and very well made.

TABLE 50
Factory specifications for Stock pistols

Measurement	6.35 mm.	7.65 mm.
Over-all length	118 mm.	170 mm
Barrel length	63 "	100 "
Height	84 "	108 "
Thickness	22 "	30 "
Sighting radius	105 "	148 "
Weight, empty	360 gm.	690 gm..
Magazine capacity	7 ctges.	8 ctges.

Tokarev pistols

Until the development of the Tokarev automatic pistol, the side arm used in Russia was the revolver, either the 7.62 mm. Nagant or the Belgian Pieper of the same caliber. These pistols are practically alike. The last Belgian contract expired some time in 1898 or 1899 and manufacture of the Nagant began at Tula in 1900. The Belgian numbering series was continued through 1917, when manufacture was interrupted. When it was resumed in 1921 a new numbering series, starting with No. 1, was instituted; and this continued until about 1935 when a two-letter prefix numbering system was adopted and used until the Tokarev pistol superseded the revolver.

The Tokarev pistol was developed in the 1920's by F. V. Tokarev, who had been an officer in the Russian army in World War I and later was employed in the Tula arsenal. The pistol was given the official nomenclature Tokarev 30, from the year of its production. The U.S. Army Model 1911 pistol was of course known in Russia, and it is likely that the developments taking place in France (by Petter at Cholet) and at Neuhausen in Switzerland were also known. It is of course not to their discredit that they took the best features of existing automatics and added to them features and simplifications of their own.

The Tokarev pistol was built for practical service rather than for looks, which is not to say that it is clumsy or unwieldy in appearance. It does not have the beautiful, precise machining and the excellent finishes of the Swiss Neuhausen or the German Walther pistols. Its most outstanding features are its ruggedness, its certainty of action, and its simplicity of construction, which not only make it easy to assemble and disassemble but, most importantly, makes it cheap to produce in quantity. Obviously these are qualities most desirable in a military weapon.

Basically the pistol is a Colt (or Browning), but with many changes and simplifications. Some were made to add strength where it was needed, and others were made for purposes of simplification and economy. The grip safety and mechanical safety on the side were eliminated, the only safety being a half cock safety. The magazine holds 8 cartridges and is unique in construction in that it can be taken apart for repairs. Cartridges are guided into the chamber in a very positive manner not dependent on the lips of the magazine, which in this instance are quite flat. Cartridge jamming consequently is rare. In 1933 the original Mod. 30 was improved, the barrel-locking lugs being replaced with an integral circumferential band, which provided more strength. This also reduced cost as it permits lathe production. The original Mod. 30 had a separate "back strap" or rear frame edge which was replaced by an integral grip frame edge. Neither the original nor the 1933 modification had a grip safety, though photographs of the original model might give that impression. The new model had a slightly different disconnector arrangement. This changed model is often referred to as the Model 33 Tokarev, but it is not believed to be official nomenclature.

The year of manufacture is stamped on the left side of the frame, as is also the serial number, which seems to have started at No. 1 with the original model and continued with the newer version. The earlier pistols, in both versions, have serial numbers without prefix letters. Observed specimens dated as late as 1935 (No. 45,311, for example) do not have them, but it is believed that the two-letter prefix system was started at about that time. Sometime between 1943 and 1947 the pattern of serrations in the finger grips on the slide was changed. Earlier specimens have a pattern consisting of 7 wide and 7 narrow alternating serrations. This was changed to 24 narrow serrations of equal width.

The caliber of 7.62 mm. was no doubt selected because it was a traditional one for Russian arms. The Nagant and Pieper revolvers, machine guns, the infantry rifle and submachine guns used that caliber. Curiously, one of the principal artillery pieces has a caliber of 76.2 mm. The particular cartridge used is almost identical to and interchangeable with the German Mauser 7.63 mm. cartridge, thus simplifying the ammunition problem for whoever captured the other's ammunition dumps! Occasional failures to extract may occur. These can be eliminated by grinding off the inner surface of the extractor hook.

The Tokarev pistol is known to have been in production as late as 1954 and possibly later. While the original Mod. 30 was made only at the "Principal

Arsenal" at Tula, the 1933 version was made at other arsenals or shops in Tula and in several other places. Some of these arsenals (or factories) used variant markings during World War II. Rather crude checkered wood grip pieces were used by some, though most of them used serrated black plastic grip pieces, bearing a circled star and the initials CCCP (equivalent to our USSR). One arsenal at Tula used checkered hard rubber grip pieces with a circled triangle containing an arrow with the letters CCCP outside the triangle.

Following World War II the Tokarev pistol has been made in other countries, the earliest of which may well have been China. There it was given the official nomenclature of Shiki 51 (i.e. Type 51). The first specimens contain parts made in Russia. It is not known definitely whether these pistols were assembled in Russia or in China. It is known, however, that equipment was supplied to China so that they were able to make their own pistols, and that they have done so since some time in 1952. One specimen, No. 19,696 (with no letter prefix), dated 1952 and having Chinese characters on the right side has been encountered. This pistol was definitely made in Russia, as it corresponds in all respects with the known Soviet-made pistols, with the exception of the number and Chinese marking. Serial numbering of the Type 51 evidently began with No. 1, with the pistols supplied from Russia, and at last report was well over 100,000 and probably actually much larger. The Chinese-made Tokarev is identical to those made in Russia, with the exception of the grip plates, the lack of prefix letters in the numbering, the arsenal marks (there appear to be two arsenals), and the Chinese characters on the right side.

The Tokarev was also manufactured, and still may be, at the Fabryka Bronn Radom in Radom, Poland. As manufactured there, it has the serrations (7 wide alternating with 7 narrow) used in the earlier Soviet-produced pistol, but otherwise it is the same as the early 1933 version made in Russia. The presence of the earlier serration pattern suggests that the Polish pistols were made on old tools and fixtures supplied from Russia.

The grip pieces are, naturally, different and they reflect the Radom VIS 35 influence. The left grip piece has a large triangular panel containing the letters FB (for Fabryka Bronn), the design being the same as the present on the VIS 35; the right grip piece also has a large triangle, but this contains the overlapping letters WP. The serial numbers appear to start at A-1, and letter prefixes as high as K have been observed. The number of digits in the serial number may run as high as five. If all of the letters from A to K were used (which, of course, is not a known fact) it would appear that a good many Tokarev pistols had been made in Poland. Unlike the pistols made in Russia and in China, the year of manufacture is not stamped on the pistol.

A slight variant of the Polish-made Tokarev appeared in East Germany, probably made at Radom as it appears identical to the one known to be made there, the only apparent difference being in the use of plain, unmarked, serrated grip pieces.

The Tokarev has also appeared in Hungary, where it is known as the 48 Minta Piztoly (i.e., 48 Model Pistol). It may possibly have been made in Hungary, but it seems more likely that it was furnished from Russia. It is like the Russian-made pistol, except that the grip pieces bear the Hungarian Communist crest, consisting of a symbolized sheaf of wheat.

Since 1950 the Soviet small arms formerly used are being replaced. Two new pistols are now in use. These are the 9 mm. Stechkin (APS) which is of the selective fire type and is provided with a shoulder stock-holster similar to the one furnished by Mauser for their military pistol. The other new pistol is the Makarov (PM), a more compact arm than the Stechkin and having a Walther-type double action and safety. There has been no opportunity to examine these pistols. It is interesting to note that the Soviets are moving toward larger-caliber pistols while the NATO countries are moving in the opposite direction.

"UNIQUE" (and related) pistols

The "UNIQUE" pistols are a product of the firm Manufacture D'Armes des Pyrénées located at Hendaye in the southwestern part of France near the Spanish border. In addition to the pistols bearing the brand name "UNIQUE", the firm made many others which bore the brand name of the dealer to whom they were supplied. Some of these were identical (or practically so) with the "UNIQUE" line, while others were of different design. Both will be dealt with later.

Factory literature indicates that the production of "UNIQUE" pistols started in 1923. Between that date and 1940 eleven models were produced; many of these represented only slight differences, however. During World War II the Germans took over control of the plant and continued to produce the same type of pistols under the same name. The first to be so produced was practically identical to an existing model (No. 17, to be described later) but with changed grip plates. Each pistol made in this period will be found to bear the German military acceptance mark, indicating that they were being made for military use.

Later in the war certain other changes were made, giving rise to a new nomenclature—the Kriegsmodell. This will be discussed more fully later.

Early "UNIQUE" models (1923-1940)

Undated booklets issued by the factory at some time prior to World War II give short descriptions of the eleven models which had been developed. These models are given catalog numbers which are not consistent with the dates of introduction of the various models. Obviously model designations were not assigned to each model at the time of its introduction, but were chosen at some later date for the probable purpose of identification of the different types available to the customer and to assist him in ordering. The model numbers start at No. 10, for some unexplained reason, and continue to Mod. No. 21. They appear in 6.35, 7.65, and 9 mm. calibers. No .22 caliber pistols were produced until after the end of World War II. Each of the eleven pre-war models will now be discussed briefly.

Mod. No. 10—This 6.35 mm. model with its counterpart in 7.65 mm. caliber is referred to as the Modele Classique and, no doubt, is the first model to bear this brand name. It is a typical copy of the 1906 Browning and, like most, does not have the grip safety. It has two safety features, the customary thumb safety and the magazine safety. Removal of the magazine renders the action inoperable. Like most Browning imitations, the thumb safety is located just back of the trigger guard in front of the left grip plate. This is also true for the other ten of these early models.

Mod. No. 11—This model is essentially the No. 10 with the addition of a grip safety and a cartridge indicator. The cartridge indicator is located in the top of the slide and tells whether there is a cartridge in the chamber. Models Nos. 10 and 11 were made from 1930 to 1940.

Mod. No. 12—The omission of the cartridge indicator gives rise to this new nomenclature. Otherwise this pistol is identical to the No. 11, and it too is stated to have been produced from 1923 to 1940.

Mod. No. 13—By increasing the magazine capacity from 6 to 7 cartridges a "new" model is created. No. 13 and No. 12 are identical except for this one feature.

Mod. No. 14—To increase fire power still further, the length of the magazine was increased to take 9 cartridges. Otherwise, only minor differences are to be noted, such as a slight change in the location of the thumb safety, a change in shape of the maga-

zine release, a change in shape and design of the grip plates and in the pattern of the finger grip serrations on the slide. Fundamentally, it is of the No. 10 design and was made over the same period of time, i.e., 1923 to 1940.

Mod. No. 15—Here we have the first 7.65 mm. "UNIQUE" to be described. Except for size and caliber this is the same Modele Classique as No. 10 and was also produced over the same period of time, i.e., 1923 to 1940. There are a few minor differences, such as the slightly raised position of the thumb safety and a notch on the lower edge of the slide for the engagement of the hook of the thumb safety, a change in the lion monogram on the grips, and the use of narrower serrations on the finger grips on the slide. It was advertised as a pistol suitable for police work, guard duty, etc.

Mod. No. 16—This 7.65 mm. pistol is the same as No. 15 except that the magazine capacity has been increased from 6 to 7 cartridges. Like No. 15 it was made from 1923 to 1940.

Mod No. 71—This is a somewhat larger pistol than Nos. 15 and 16 and has a magazine capacity of 9 rounds, but it is similar in design to the smaller models. This was advertised as an *"Arme de Guerre, made in accord with the conditions and tolerances enumerated in the Specifications of Artillery . . ."* This model and those following were provided with a lanyard ring. The pattern on the grips is slightly different in form from any seen on the preceding models, the name "UNIQUE" being curved, concave downward.

Mod. No. 18—Here we have a decided departure in design from all of the preceding models, all of which had a spiral recoil spring located below the barrel, as in the 1906 Browning. Mod. No. 18 has a recoil spring surrounding the barrel, as in the 1910 Browning, and disassembly is accomplished in the same manner. The recoil spring is held in place by a sleeve (or ring) having a knurled edge. When this sleeve is rotated into the proper position it is unlocked (bayonet catch) and can be removed, together with the spring. The slide is then moved back until the hook of the thumb safety is engaged in a notch. The barrel can then be rotated until it is free and the slide and barrel can be removed. Only the thumb safety and magazine safety are provided. The magazine holds 6 cartridges. Markings are similar to those on No. 17.

Mod. No. 19—By simply increasing the magazine capacity from 6 to 7 cartridges a "new" model is created. This model is simply No. 18 with increased magazine capacity.

Mod. No. 20—Here again a "new" model is created

by simply increasing the magazine capacity of No. 18 from 6 to 9 cartridges. The length of the two is the same but No. 20 is naturally higher and heavier.

Mod. No. 21—This is the only 9 mm. caliber pistol made in this period. It is of the same design as Nos. 18 and 19, and the dimensions are the same as those for No. 19. As it has a magazine capacity of six rounds and because of the increased bore (leaving less metal) the weight is less, being 605 grams as against 615 for No. 19. Like the others it has only two safeties, the thumb safety and magazine safety. None of the 7.65 or 9 mm. models have the grip safety.

of slanted for vertical serrations on the slide. The frame has a pointed extension at the shoulder, below the rear end of the slide, also to improve the grip. The grip pieces are of the same design as those used on the earlier war-produced models.

It would appear, from the fact that a four-page circular describing the Kriegsmodell was issued in the German language, that these pistols must have been offered for commercial sale in Germany during the war, perhaps for civilian defense. The illustration shows the pistol to be the same as the one used for military purposes (with German acceptance marks), except that different grip plates were used.

TABLE 51

Catalog specifications for " UNIQUE" pistols (Pre-1940 models)

Measurement	Model Number											
	10	11	12	13	14	15	16	17	18	19	20	21
Caliber, mm.	6.35	6.35	6.35	6.35	6.35	7.65	7.65	7.65	7.65	7.65	7.65	9
Total length, mm.	104	104	104	104	112	126	126	155	145	145	145	145
Barrel length, mm.	. . .	. . .	. . .	. . .	. . .	66	. . .	. . .	. . .	. . .	. . .	88
Height, mm.	70	70	70	70	100	91	96	120	96	96	110	96
Weight, grams	370	360	360	385	400	570	610	785	. . .	615	650	605
Magazine cap., ctges.	6	6	6	7	9	6	7	9	6	7	9	6

Note: Some advertising circulars give dimensions which vary somewhat from those stated above. From this it would appear that the dimensions were changed a bit from time to time.

World War II production

As has already been said, the Germans took possession of the plant when they overran France, and production of "UNIQUE" pistols continued under their supervision. While accurate figures are not at hand, it is reported that about 15,000 were produced in 1942 and 20,000 in 1943. Other figures are lacking.

The first 7.65 mm. "UNIQUE" pistols to be seen having German military acceptance marks are practically identical to the Mod. No. 17, described above, but they have black, fluted grip pieces which are marked 7.65 m/m 9 SCHUSS. The shape of the grip frame, which is more streamlined, and the sharper angle of the rear end of the frame at the shoulder appear to be the only features which differ from those on the No. 17. Specimens Nos. 40,313, 48,227, and 55,898 are examples of this type of design. Later production, still under German supervision, resulted in a model showing more changes, while retaining the same general system. This model was given the nomenclature Kriegsmodell by the Germans. While retaining the early Browning arrangement of barrel and recoil spring (below the barrel), an external hammer was incorporated (for the first time on a "UNIQUE") and a rib (or ridge) was added to the lower part of the back strap, to give a better grip. Another, but minor change, was in the substitution

These are checkered instead of being fluted, and have the name "UNIQUE" in a circle instead of 7.65 m/m 9 SCHUSS. The inscription on the slide for the pistols marked for military use reads:

7.65 COURT 9 COUPS "UNIQUE"
MANUFACTURE D'ARMES DES PYRÉNÉES HENDAYE,

while the pistol described in the German pamphlet bears the inscription: MANUFACTURE D'ARMES DES PYRENEES F^{SS} HENDAYE.

Specimen No. 61,416 bears German military acceptance marks and is of the later type produced during the war. Specimens Nos. 72,100 and 72,154, however, are identical to Mod. No. 17 made prior to the war, and they bear pre-war markings. Furthermore, no German acceptance marks are present. The serial numbers would indicate that they were made after the war, but information from the factory implies that the manufacture of No. 17 was not resumed following the war. If such is the case, it must be that the serial numbering used by the Germans during their control of the factory was not a continuation of the pre-war numbering.

Post-World War II developments

Modele C—This 7.65 mm. pistol follows a new design. While resembling the early Browning, in that the recoil spring (and its guide) are located below the barrel, the arm has an external hammer and also an indicator which tells whether the pistol is cocked.

Several safety features are stressed: (1) the customary thumb safety is present and in an easily accessible postion; (2) the presence of an external hammer in itself is a safety feature since its posi-tion is easily determined and, in addition, the gun can be carried in safety when the hammer is in the "half cock" position; (3) the position of the exposed end of the extractor is determined by the presence or absence of a cartridge in the chamber

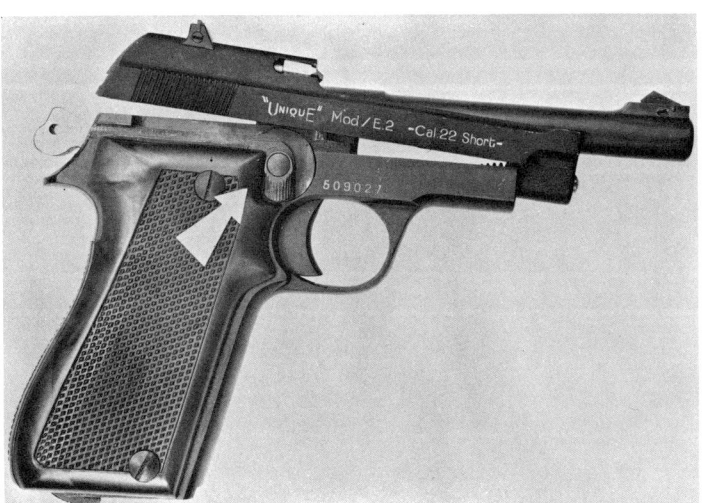

Fig. 262. .22 cal. "UNIQUE" Mod. E-2

Fig. 263. .22 cal. "UNIQUE" Mod. E-2. Arrow points to lever which, when turned, releases the slide.

(it projects when the chamber is empty); (4) the arm cannot be fired when the magazine is removed; and (5) it cannot be fired unless the action is completely and firmly closed.

Modele F—Mod. F is the same as Mod. C except that it is of 9 mm. Short (.380) caliber. The dimensions and weight are the same. Length - 145 mm., height - 120 mm., weight - 650 grams. The magazine capacity of Mod. C is 9 rounds while that of Mod. F is 8.

Pistols of .22 caliber

Up to and during World War II no .22 caliber pistols were made by this firm, but in about 1950 attention was turned to the production of such pistols.

Modele Rd—While this is the factory designation, the pistol was sold under the name Ranger and was so marked on the grip plates. It is a rather conven-

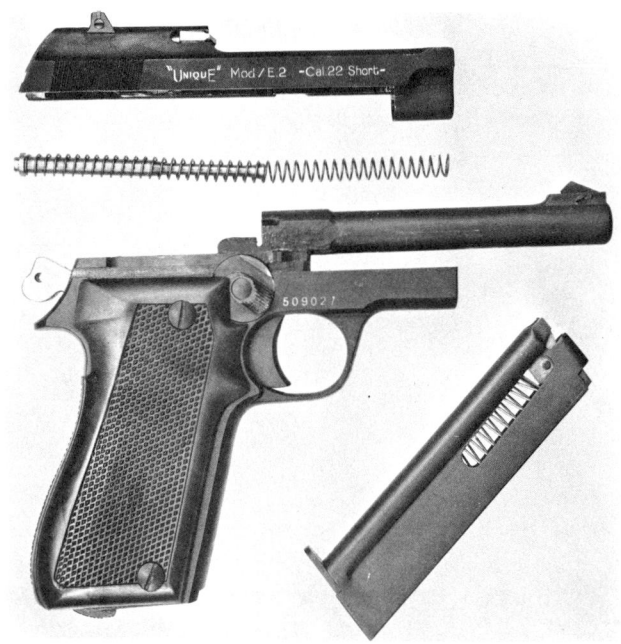

Fig. 264. .22 cal. "UNIQUE" Mod. E-2. Partially disassembled.

tional type, modeled to a very considerable extent after the 7.65 mm. pistol made in the later portion of World War II. It has much of the external appearance of the Kriegsmodell, with the exception of the size, caliber, and length of barrels. Barrels were available in three lengths, varying from about 90 mm. to nearly 190 mm. Some long-barreled specimens have a muzzle brake while others do not. Measurements for specimens examined are: length 254 mm. (10″), barrel length 184 mm. (7¼″), and height 125 mm. (ca. 5″). While most .22 caliber "UNIQUE" pistols have one turn of the rifling in ca. 12.0 inches, one Ranger was found to have one turn in 18.0 inches.

Modele 52—This pistol (presumably introduced in 1952), chambered for the .22 L.R. cartridge, is unlike the Ranger model in that nearly two-thirds of the upper part of the front end of the slide is cut away, exposing the barrel. It has an external hammer and the shape of the grip is very similar (though not identical) to that of the 7.65 pistol produced in the later war period and to the grip used on the Ranger model.

As this is a fixed-barrel type of pistol, a new type of disassembly was necessarily devised. On the right side of the frame, in front of the grip plate, is a short lever which can be forced down with the thumb. This releases the slide which can be removed by raising the rear end to a point where it is possible to push the slide forward over the muzzle. The

recoil spring, which is below the barrel, is released as the slide moves forward.

In the specimen examined the sights were not adjustable, the barrel being too short to require such. Measurements of the specimen examined are: length 145 mm. (5⅝″), barrel length 80 mm. (3⅛″), and height 120 mm. (4¾″).

Modele L—This pistol, in .22, 7.65 mm., and 9 mm. calibers, is a comparatively new model. It has an exposed hammer, a full length slide with the top part of the slide cut away the full length of the barrel, and conventional spiral recoil spring located beneath the barrel. Two safeties are provided, the usual thumb safety which is located in front of the left grip plate and a magazine safety. The magazine release button, of the push-in type, is located near the bottom of the grip frame at the rear edge. The grips are streamlined, have a curved thumb rest, and contribute materially to the pleasing appearance of this model. This pistol, in all calibers, may be obtained with either steel or light alloy frames. Data for this model are given in Table 52.

TABLE 52
Data for "UNIQUE" Model L pistol

Measurement	.22 L.R.	7.65 mm. (.32)	9 mm. Short (.380)
Model designation	Ld	Lc	Lf
Total length	148 mm.	148 mm.	148 mm.
Barrel length	ca. 80 "	ca. 80 "	ca. 80 "
Height	100 "	100 "	100 "
Weight (steel frame)	610 gm.	645 gm.	645 gm.
" (alloy frame)	430 "	475 "	465 "
Magazine capacity	10 ctges.	7 ctges.	6 ctges

Models 1, 2, 3, and 4, Types D and E—This series of pistols was introduced in 1954. They are of the fixed barrel type, all have external hammers, operate in the same manner as the Mod. 52, and disassemble in the same manner. The chief differences are in the barrel lengths, sights, grip designs, and accessories (Figs. 262 to 266).

Those guns chambered specially for the .22 L.R. cartridge are designated by the capital letter D, while those specially chambered for the .22 Short are designated by the capital letter E. Models, of which there are four, are designated by numbers, hence we have (for the full series) the nomenclatures: D-1, D-2, D-3, and D-4 (for the .22 L.R.) and E-1, E-2, E-3, and E-4 (for the .22 Short). These pistols were obviously developed from the earlier Ranger (1948–1951) and RF (1951–1954) models.

The safety features are similar to those provided in the earlier models: an external hammer, which can be carried at "half cock," the customary thumb

Fig. 265. .22 cal. "UNIQUE" Mod. E-2. With grips removed.

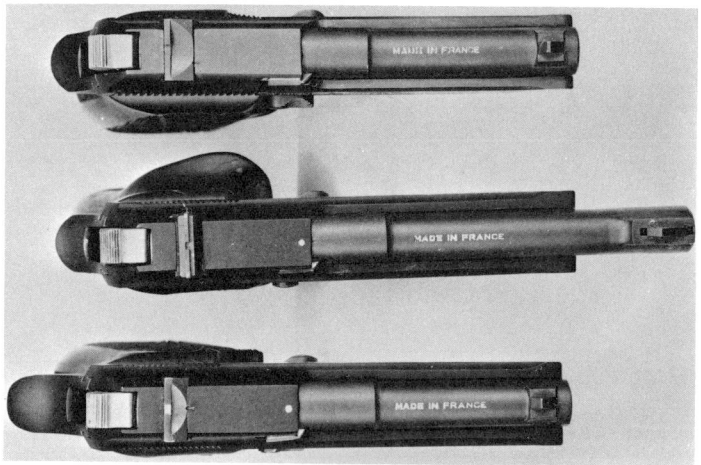

Fig. 266. .22 cal. "UNIQUE" automatic pistols. *Top:* Model D-1. *Middle:* Model E-2. *Bottom:* Model E-1.

safety and the magazine safety (which prevents firing when the magazine is out). For the L.R. (or D) models the action stays open after the last shot is fired, but for the Short (or E) model this is not so.

Models 2, 3, and 4 have adjustable sights. Mod. 1 has fixed sights. Mods. 3 and 4 (in either D or E type) can be had with adjustable balancing weights (three weights in the set), and Mods. D-4 and E-4 (also called the Olympic model) can be had with a muzzle brake.

Catalog specifications for these four models, in the two types, issued in 1954, are given in Table 53.

Pistols other than the "UNIQUE" made by the same firm

As has already been mentioned, pistols with names other than "UNIQUE" were manufactured,

some for sale by the manufacturer and others to be sold by certain dealers.

Mikros—The Mikros is an example of the former (i.e., marketed by the manufacturer). It was made in both 6.35 and 7.65 mm. calibers, and was sold from 1934 until 1939.

This pistol is quite different in design from the "UNIQUE". The barrel and frame are integral, and the recoil spring is housed in a channel below the barrel. Some of the other pistols were described as having fixed barrels, but they were different in that barrel and frame were not made from one piece of metal. At the rear end of the slide is a button which, when pushed in, releases the support block for the firing pin and spring. The slide is also released and can be slid forward over the muzzle.

The pistol has the two customary safety features: a thumb safety and a magazine safety, the latter preventing firing when the magazine is out. The thumb safety is operated by a flat lever which projects forward from under the left grip piece. It may be moved up or down, into the "Fire" or "Safe" positions, respectively.

Catalog specifications for the 6.35 mm. Model are as follows: total length, 100 mm.; barrel length, 52 mm.; height, 67 mm.; weight, 240 grams. Those for the 7.65 mm. Model are as follows: total length, 110 mm.; barrel length, 59 mm.; height, 80 mm.; weight, 400 grams.

The 6.35 mm. model is one of the very smallest of automatic pistols of its caliber, being practically the size of the Mod. No. 9 Walther and smaller than the 6.35 mm. Mann. Since the Mikros and the Walther No. 9 are alike, it probably is not entirely a coincidence that the booklets for the two are also just alike in format. The 7.65 mm. model is also extraordinarily small for its caliber.

Mikros-1958 Model—After a lapse of nearly 20 years the name Mikros was revived and applied to a new model of different design which came out in 1958. This pistol bears some resemblance to the 1934 Mod. of the Beretta, in that it has an external hammer, a similar (but not identical) barrel fastening, and much the same method of disassembly. It is not, however, a copy of the Beretta.

It is a blowback type, without any distinguishing or unique features, in which the force of the recoil is taken up by a spiral spring (located below the barrel) and the inertia of the moving parts. It is obtainable in .22 Short and 6.35 mm. calibers. The same frame, slide, etc. are used for both. The normal barrel length is 57 mm., but a special barrel 102 mm. in length can be obtained in .22 caliber, only. Alloy frames may be had if desired.

TABLE 53

Data for "UNIQUE" Model 1, 2, 3, and 4, Types D and E

Measurement	Model designation							
	D-1	D-2	D-3	D-4	E-1	E-2	E-3	E-4
Total length (approx.), mm.	154	184	290	310*	154	184	290	310*
Barrel length, mm.	78	108	210	230*	78	108	210	230*
Length of line of sight, mm.	104	128	231	250	104	128	231	250
Height (approx.), mm.	125	127	127	127	125	127	127	127
Magazine capacity, ctges.	10	10	10	10	6	6	6	6
Weight, magazine empty, gm.	645	695	785	815	610	655	740	770
Set of 3 balancing weights (approx.), gm.			700	700			700	700
Revised specifications — 1959 factory literature (Models D-1 and E-1 not mentioned; presumably no longer made)								
Total length, mm.		184	290	299*		184	290	299*
Barrel length, mm.		107	210	217*		107	210	217*
Height, mm.		127	127	127		127	127	127
Magazine cap., ctges.		10	10	10		6	6	6
Weight, magazine empty, gm.		680	770	790		650	740	755

*Length includes integral muzzle brake. Models D-2 and E-2 for defense and sport. Models D-3 and E-3 for target shooting. Models D-4 and E-4 for Olympic target shooting. D types, .22 L.R.; E types, .22 Short. Sights adjustable vertically and horizontally on Models 2, 3, and 4. Adjustable counterweights obtainable for Models 3 and 4.

Having an external hammer adds a measure of safety, as the position of the hammer indicates whether the gun is or is not cocked. Furthermore the pistol can be carried uncocked with a cartridge in the chamber, and can be cocked and fired with one hand. In case of a misfire the gun can be cocked again almost instantly for a second try. These are important features in case of an emergency, where time may be very important.

In addition there are the usual modern safety features, consisting of a thumb-operated mechanical safety and a magazine safety which prevents the arm from being fired when the magazine is out. The thumb safety has red and white dots, which are alternately exposed, to indicate the "Fire" and "Safe" positions.

Disassembly is simple. The slide is drawn back and locked in the open position with the thumb safety lever, the magazine is removed while pressing the release button on the left grip piece, the barrel is pushed back a bit to unlock it and is then lifted out, the thumb safety is now turned to release the slide which can be removed by sliding it forward, and the spring and guide can be removed after the slide is off.

Audax—The Audax pistol was made in both 6.35 and 7.65 mm. calibers and was marketed exclusively by La Cartoucherie Francaise in Paris, according to information supplied by the factory. It was produced from 1931 to 1939.

The 6.35 mm. model is practically identical to the "UNIQUE" No. 11 which had been introduced in 1930. The dimensions, however, as stated in advertising literature, are slightly different. The Audax is slightly longer and higher, but of the same weight. The position and shape of the thumb safety are different, in that the lever projects forward from under the left side of the left grip plate. The arm is disassembled in the same manner as the "UNIQUE" and other Browning 1906 types. Like the "UNIQUE" No. 11,

TABLE 54

Catalog data for Mikros-1958 Model pistol

Measurement	.22 cal. and 6.35 mm.*	.22 cal. with long barrel
Total length	112 mm. (4⁷⁄₁₆″)	157 mm. (6³⁄₁₆″)
Barrel length	57 " (2¼″)	102 " (4″)
Height	74 " (2¹⁵⁄₁₆″)	74 " (2¹⁵⁄₁₆″)
Weight (steel frame)	350 gm. (ca. 12.3 oz.)	375 gm. (ca. 13.2 oz.)
Weight (alloy frame)	265 " (ca. 9.35 oz.)	290 " (ca. 10.23 oz.)
Magazine capacity	6 ctges.	6 ctges.

*Note that dimensions and weights are stated to be the same in spite of the difference in bore. The 1958 is designated the K Model, the .22 being the Ke and the 6.35 the Kn.

it has a grip safety in addition to the thumb safety and magazine safety.

The 7.65 mm. Audax closely resembles, but is not identical to, the "UNIQUE" Mod. No. 19. The magazine capacity (7) is the same for each. The length is stated to be 150 mm., length of barrel 97 mm., height 99 mm., and weight 570 grams (empty)— as compared to a length of 145 mm., height 96 mm., and weight of 615 grams for the No. 19 "UNIQUE".

The thumb safety lever (slightly different in form) is located in the same relative position and functions in the same manner as for the 6.35 mm. model. Instead of having the magazine release catch at the bottom of the grip frame, as in the 6.35 pistol, the release is of the push-in type and is located on the frame directly back of the lower part of the trigger guard. There is also a short rib on the lower end of the back strap which is not present on the smaller model. The name of the manufacturer does not appear on either model, the inscription on the 7.65 mm. pistol (and that on the smaller one is similar) reads:

PISTOLET AUTOMIQUE CAL. 7.65 m/m
"AUDAX" MARQUE DEPOSEE
FABRICATION FRANCAISE

"UNIQUE" *pistols sold under other brand names*

Correspondence from the factory states that in the years 1923 to 1939 "UNIQUE" pistols were supplied to many dealers who sold them under their own brand names. They list the following:

6.35 mm. caliber
Le Sans Pareil (marketed by Piot Lepage in Paris)
EBAC (same as Le Sans Pareil)
7.65 mm. caliber

Burgham	Mars (name used in several countries)
Cesar (a "Cesar" was also made in Spain)	Perfect
Capitan	Prima
Chantecler	Rapid-Maxima
Chimere Reinor	Reina
Colonial (name also used in Spain)	St. Hubert
Demon "Marine"	Selecta
Elite	Sympathique
Furor	Touriste
Gallia	Triomphe Francais
Ixor	Unis
Le Tout Acier "DUC"	Vindex

The great preponderance of 7.65 mm. pistols listed, coupled with the known popularity of the 6.35 size, leads one to suspect that the list is not complete as far as the 6.35 mm. pistols are concerned.

Walther pistols

The Waffenfabrik Walther was founded by Carl Walther in Zella-Mehlis (then known as Zella St. Blasii) in the year 1886. Walther came from a long line of ancestors who had engaged in the manufacture of weapons. One ancestor, Matthias Konrad Pistor, established a weapons factory in 1745. For many years the principal products of the Walther factory were hunting arms and target rifles. In 1908, together with his cousin, Friederich Pickert (a well-known revolver manufacturer), and also assisted by his son, Fritz, Walther designed and produced the first successful German-made 6.35 mm. self-loading pistol. This was followed by other models and up to the outbreak of the first World War, in 1914, four other models had been developed and produced. The advent of war necessitated greatly increased facilities, because of ever-increasing orders, and an entirely new factory was built.

After the death of Carl Walther in 1915, the firm was taken over and operated by his three eldest sons: Fritz, Georg, and Erich. In both World Wars this firm was one of the principal producers of military type pistols. At the close of World War I, it was confronted with the problem of turning their enormously increased facilities to the production of peace-time products, the further production of military type weapons being forbidden by the terms of the Versailles Treaty. As we shall see later, however, this treaty was violated in preparation for World War II. Production of small-calibered rifles, target rifles, sporting rifles, double barreled shotguns, signal pistols, and self loading pistols in calibers under 9 mm. was resumed. Calculating machines were also made. At the time of their 50th Anniversary, in 1936, they had produced over 1,000,000 pistols, of which some 200,000 were the 6.35 cal. Mod. VIII. Parenthetically, it may be stated here that this pistol was also produced throughout World War II, because of its popularity with German officers.

Following World War I, several new models were introduced. Some of these, such as the Mods. PP and PPK, were well suited to military use and by 1941 nearly 400,000 are said to have been made. Soon after the middle of the 1930's, if not before, attention was turned toward development of military types, in probable anticipation of approaching war. All through World War II, Walther was one of the principal manufacturers of pistols. Several new models, of 9 mm. military types, were developed prior to and during World War II. At the close of the war the plant was intact, having never been seriously bombed (if at all), but when the U.S. forces took possession, the workmen who were largely prisoners of war made attempts to wreck the machinery in the plant. Later the plant was turned over to the Russians who occupied the Zella-Mehlis area. Operations have been moved to Ulm a.D.

Notes on models

First model—The first automatic pistol made by Walther was a pocket pistol of 6.35 mm. caliber, using the Browning cartridge. All succeeding pistols used the Browning cartridge, except those designed for the 9 mm. Parabellum cartridge. The first model, or type, was without factory model designation, and was only called Modell I after the introduction of a second model. At this time the F.N. and Colt small pocket types had attained great popularity, and it was natural that Walther would want to share in this large market. While national pride may have played some part in their decision, it is more likely that the profit motive had more weight.

This pistol is of simple blowback design, with barrel integral with the frame and with a firing pin housed in the breechblock section. The slide is cut away on top leaving the forward end of the barrel exposed. Fired shells are ejected upwards as the slide moves back to its extreme position. The recoil spring and guide are housed below the barrel and this spring is compressed as the slide moves back. The magazine release is of the push through type and is located at the top of the frame, behind the grip.

To disassemble, a spring latch located in front of the trigger guard is pushed down. This pivots the upper end of the catch out of the path of the slide. The slide is then drawn back, the rear end is lifted up, as its grooves clear the guides, and the slide is then pushed forward over the end of the barrel.

Modell II—This model, marked as having been made in Zella St. Blasii (Thur.), was brought out in 1909. In this improved model the slide completely surrounds the barrel, except for a shell ejection port, located on the right side. In this model the recoil spring surrounds the barrel, instead of being below it, and the barrel itself serves as the guide. The front end of the spring presses against a removable bushing, and the spring is compressed as the slide moves back. Also, in this model a concealed hammer is present, instead of a simple rod-like firing pin surrounded by a spiral spring. The magazine is released by a catch placed at the bottom of the grip frame.

When the chamber is empty, that fact is indicated by the position of the rear sight, it being in a depressed position. When a cartridge is chambered the sight rises into proper position for use in aiming. Disassembly is very easy. The knurled bushing surrounding the front end of the barrel is turned until it is disengaged, whereupon the slide can be removed from the front. This model was very well received and became very popular.

Modell III—This is the first 7.65 mm. caliber pistol produced by Walther and came onto the market in 1910. In many respects it is similar to Mod. II. One important and curious change, however, was made in the location of the shell ejection port, which appears on the left side. This might be an advantage to a left handed shooter, but scarcely to one who is right handed.

The method of disassembly is practically the same as for Mod. II, except that the knurled bushing, which extends out in front of the end of the slide in Mod. II, is replaced by a sleeve section of the slide which extends out to the end of the lengthened barrel. This sleeve must be pushed in and turned, an operation somewhat more difficult than for Mod. II, particularly because of the absence of knurling. As in Mod. II, the barrel is surrounded by a spiral recoil spring and the hammer is retained. The hammer may be locked in the cocked position by a thumb safety located on the left side of the slide. This model presents a considerable improvement in workmanship and appearance over previous models.

Modell IV—The 7.65 mm. Mod. IV, both larger and heavier than Mod. III, was also introduced in 1910. A longer magazine permits carrying 8 cartridges, instead of 6, as in Mod III. Being considerably longer, and having raised sights at the ends of the slide, it provides a better sighting radius. These features combine to make the pistol a much more desirable one for military purposes than its predecessor, and it was widely used by German officers as a side arm in World War I.

As in Mod. III, the shell ejection port is placed on the left side of the slide, and firing is accomplished by a concealed hammer that can be locked in the cocked position (or unlocked) by turning a thumb lever. To prevent the firing of more than one shot with each trigger pull, there is a feature that acts as a disconnector. The trigger bar is curved and seats in a niche on the under side of the slide when the pistol is fully closed and the trigger is released. Pulling the slide back cocks the arm, the hammer being pushed back into the cocked position, where it is held by a sear operated by a spring, the sear being forced into position ahead of the hammer strut. As the slide moves forward to chamber a cartridge, the hammer remains at full cock. A hook at the end of the trigger bar reaches the sear to disengage the hammer only when the trigger is pulled.

As first issued, the hammer-trigger connector bar is exposed in part, as it lies on the outside of the frame but under the left side grip plate, while in later issues this connector bar is fully concealed. Specimen No. 103,361 (marked as made in Zella St. Blasii) has the bar partly exposed, whereas specimen No. 253,782 has it fully concealed. At what time, or serial number, the change was made is not known. Other changes noted are, the absence of a rear sight in the earlier specimens, but present in later ones; and the type of serrations forming the finger grip on the rear end of the slide. In the early specimens the finger grip pattern consists of 7 square-cut, rather wide grooves, whereas in the later specimens the serrations are narrow V-shaped grooves and 16 in number.

Modell V—This 6.35 mm. model is essentially an improved version of Mod. II. It shows better workmanship and has a better appearance. Several specimens have been seen in the 77,000 to 93,000 serial number range, and all possess the same features. The pistol was introduced in 1913.

Modell VI—Mod. VI is a 9 mm. Parabellum version of Mod. IV and was produced for military use in 1917 because of a shortage of side arms. Because of the much more powerful cartridge, the pistol necessarily had to have a much more powerful spring which, together with the use of heavier parts, was expected to take the greatly increased shock. The strong locking device, carried over from the Mod. IV, seemed to suffice for the Parabellum cartridge of that period. Later the pressures in the Parabellum cartridge were stepped up to such an extent that, while the shooter may not necessarily be in danger, the mechanism of the gun is likely to be damaged by the increased shock.

In this model, ejection of fired shells is through a port placed on the right side of the slide. The slide locking device is similar to that on Mod. IV, and disassembly is accomplished by pushing in the sleeve at the front end of the slide, and turning it until it disengages—the same type of "bayonet lock" being used. As in the Mod. IV, the front sight is mounted on the end of the slide extension, to give as long a sighting radius as possible. Only a few thousand of this model seem to have been made, probably because it was realized that the type of mechanism was scarcely suitable for so powerful a cartridge. While advertisements have been seen by the author for Mods. IV, V, VII, VIII, and IX, none has been seen for Mod. VI and it is doubted that any of this model were ever offered for commercial sale. These pistols probably had their own series of numbering, and some at least were marked as being

made in Zella St. Blasii (No. 710, for example). Zella St. Blasii and the adjoining town of Mehlis combined in 1919 and took the name Zella-Mehlis. Walther pistols made after this date are naturally marked WAFFENFABRIK WALTHER ZELLA-MEHLIS.

Modell VII—This is a 6.35 mm. caliber version of Mod. VI, and it also was brought out in 1917, to meet the demands of German officers for a small, easily concealed pocket pistol—possibly for use in case of capture. At any rate it seems to have been quite widely carried. As it was a copy of Mod. VI, no further description is necessary.

Modell VIII—This model, of 6.35 mm. caliber, was first produced in 1920, by permission of the League of Nations, as it did not violate the provisions of the Versailles Treaty (Figs. 267, 268). Like its imme-

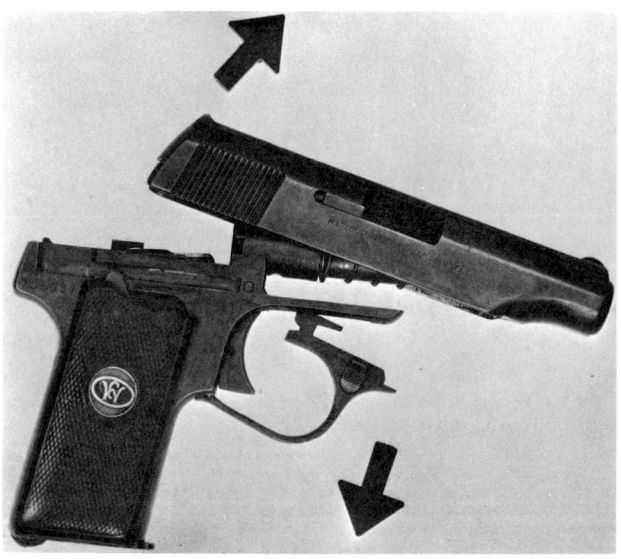

Fig. 267. 6.35 mm. Walther Mod. 8. Showing method of disassembly.

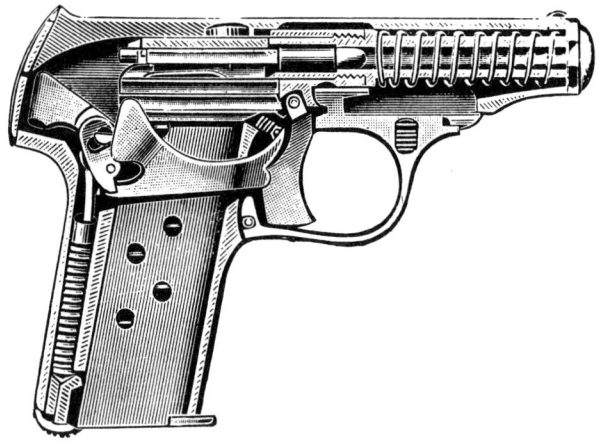

Fig. 268. 6.35 mm. Walther Mod. 8. Sectional view.

diate predecessors, it is of the concealed-hammer type, but has a single unit slide and a different method of disassembly. The barrel is completely concealed, except for the shell ejection port located on the right side. The front end of the trigger guard (which is pivoted at the back end and which is made lightly so that it will spring) when in the closed position passes through a slot in the receiver and thus locks the slide.

Some specimens, of early issue, had a latch (or catch) on the forward end of the trigger guard which, when pulled down, released that end of the trigger guard allowing it to be pulled down. In later specimens this catch is missing, but the trigger guard, being of fairly light construction, can be sprung by pushing it back, whereby it is released and can be lowered. Specimen No. 466,935 has the catch, whereas specimen No. 720,440 does not. In either case, when the trigger guard is pulled down and back the slide is released and can be drawn back, lifted at the rear end, and pushed forward over the end of the barrel.

This model has a longer magazine, holding 8 cartridges, and consequently a longer grip which gives a better hold than is found in the other 6.35 mm. models. The shape of this hold could have been improved by streamlining the grip, and the appearance of the arm would have been much improved also. Light weight (aluminum alloy) frames are to be found on some specimens, and these reduce the weight about 3 ounces, but most specimens do not possess this feature.

Modell IX—This is the "baby" of the Walther pistols and is truly a vestpocket type, as it is barely 100 mm., ca. 3¹⁵⁄₁₆ inches, in length. It is one of the smallest 6.35 mm. caliber pistols and is a very attractive piece. It was put on the market in 1921 to compete with several other "Westentaschen" and "Baby" models of other makes (Fig. 269).

In many respects this model resembles the first one that Walther made, more than it does the later ones. Like the first model it has a barrel integral with the frame and a rod-like firing pin surrounded by a spiral spring, rather than possessing a hammer. The rear end of the firing pin protrudes from the rear end of the slide when the arm is cocked, and disappears when it is not. This feature is, of course, not unique. The upper part of the slide is cut away to expose the full length of the barrel, and fired shells are ejected upward as the extractor is at the top of the breech face. As there is no ejector the shell pivots on the end of the firing pin, which serves as an ejector. The thumb safety is on the left side, in front of the grip plate where such a device should

be for convenience, and has to be pushed upwards to fire. The spiral recoil spring, as in the first model, is located below the barrel and in this model has no guide.

Disassembly is very easy. A little catch at the rear end of the slide will be observed in a small dumbbell-shaped unit. When this unit is pressed in and the catch is raised (which can be done with the thumb nail) this little unit slides back, permitting the rear end of the barrel to be raised and slid forward over the muzzle end of the barrel. The firing pin and its spiral spring can then be drawn out of the slide. Assembly or disassembly can be accomplished in 10 seconds, after a little experience. The lock work can be exposed by removing the two single screws that hold the grip plates onto the frame. All features considered, this is one of the simplest and most attractive vestpocket pistols ever produced, though many would prefer that it have a grip safety as an additional safety precaution.

Modell PP—The name of this pistol comes from the German words "Polizei Pistole," and it was intended for police (and similar) use, as the name implies. However, it was not limited to such use, by any means, as it was used extensively in World War II, the advent of which may or may not have been foreseen when it was introduced in 1929. It first appeared in 7.65 mm. caliber, but later it was also made in .22 L.R. and 9 mm. Short (.380 Browning) calibers (Fig. 270).

While this is a blowback in design and possesses many of the features present in the earlier Walther pistols, it has some important new ones. Perhaps the most important new features are the presence of an external hammer which drives forward a firing pin,

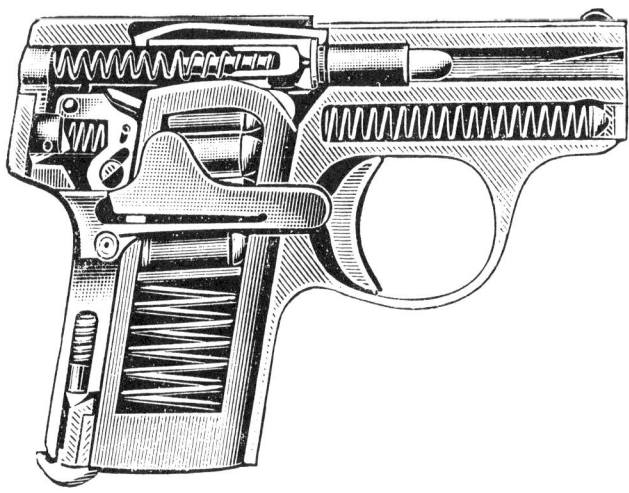

Fig. 269. 6.35 mm. Walther Mod. 9. Sectional view.

Fig. 270. 7.65 mm. Walther Mod. PP. Sectional view.

and its double action. Another new feature, and one believed to be unique, is a "signal pin" which, together with its surrounding coil spring, is mounted in the slide directly above the firing pin. If the chamber is empty the spring forces the end of this pin through a small hole in the breech face so that the rear end of the pin does not protrude, but when a cartridge is in the chamber the forward end of the pin rests against the base of the cartridge and consequently is pushed back a bit so that the rear end does protrude, where it can either be seen or felt with the thumb. Unlike the pin present in the Mod. IX, which only indicates whether the arm is cocked (irrespective of whether there is a cartridge in the chamber or not), this signal pin tells whether there is a cartridge in the chamber and has nothing to do with the cocking of the arm. While this device appears to be an excellent one, it was eliminated later on under the stress of war production near the end of the war. The device is not suitable for rim fire cartridges, for obvious reasons.

As has been mentioned, this pistol is of the double action variety, considered by many to be a very desirable feature in a military arm. It is provided with unique and adequate safety devices. Drawing back the slide cocks the arm and when the slide is released a cartridge is chambered, as usual. The hammer may be lowered safely by pushing down the safety catch on the left side. The hammer is blocked by the rotation of a member into a position which prevents the hammer from hitting the firing pin. In addition, the pistol has another safety device, which is automatic. This one prevents the accidental discharge of the arm by something accidentally striking the hammer when the hammer is down, so that even though the thumb safety may

not have been applied a blow on the hammer cannot cause the hammer to hit the firing pin. A safety block, which prevents accidental firing, rises to a point where the hammer may pass it only when the hammer is in the fully cocked position. This device is somewhat similar, in principle, to the "Hammer the Hammer" safety device used in the Iver Johnson revolvers. The PP pistol may be carried in perfect safety with the hammer down, and the arm may be fired by a strong pull on the trigger which cocks and discharges it, because of the safety double action principles incorporated therein.

When the thumb safety is applied the firing pin is blocked, and when the slide is drawn back to open the mechanism the decocking lever is tripped automatically in such a manner that as the slide moves forward again the hammer follows to the uncocked position, without the possibility of accidental discharge in the process of loading or unloading.

Another feature, not used on previously made Walther pistols but common to many others, is the button magazine release situated below the slide and between the trigger guard and the left grip plate. In previous models, with the exception of Mod. I, the release was at the bottom of the grip frame.

Modell PPK—This model is a somewhat smaller and lighter version of the Mod. PP and was especially designed for the use of detectives and others who desired a more compact pistol that could be concealed more easily. Its name comes from the words "Polizei Pistole Kriminal," indicating its special police work application. This model was introduced in 1931 and it immediately became popular (Figs. 271, 272).

Several styles of grip plates will be found, but the most interesting and attractive grip was a one-piece plastic grip which was molded to fit the hand and which slips on over the grip frame, to which it is held by a single screw on each side. This affords a very fine hold as well as presenting a good streamlined effect. A cheaper and less attractive one-piece type of grip was made of wood. Wartime production pistols often have these. Some pistols of each type (PP and PPK) had plastic extensions of the magazine to provide a better hold, especially for a large hand.

Both the PP and PPK models were later made in .22 Long and in 9 mm. Short (.380) calibers. The external dimensions were the same as for the 7.65 mm. models. The magazine capacities were: for each of the .22 models - 8 rounds; for the 9 mm. PP - 7 rounds; for the 9 mm. PPK - 6 rounds. The weights were: ca. 675 grams for the .22 Mod. PP; ca. 560

Fig. 271. 7.65 mm. Walther Mod. PPK. Partially disassembled.

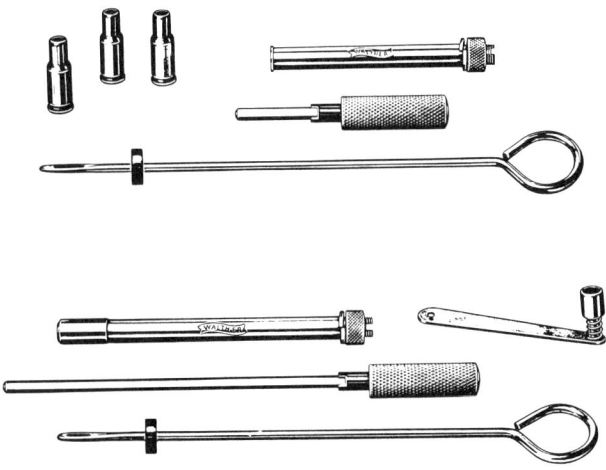

Fig. 272. Adapter sets for Mods. PP & PPK.

Modell MP—This model was developed secretly as it was a distinct violation of the Versailles Treaty which forbade the making of pistols of larger caliber than 7.65 mm. Both of the principal manufacturers of automatic pistols in Germany, Mauser as well as Walther, were violating the provisions of the treaty several years before the beginning of World War II.

This new Mod. MP was essentially a copy of the authorized Mod. PP, except that it was much larger and was chambered for the 9 mm. cartridge. Use of this powerful cartridge necessitated a much more powerful recoil spring. Since the pistol was designed for military use it was provided with a lanyard ring.

The use of such a powerful cartridge as the Parabellum (or 08) cartridge in a pistol of the blowback type, and particularly those developed for use in machine guns, puts a strain on the mechanism that, sooner or later, is likely to cause trouble. Possibly for this reason the production of this pistol was soon dropped. Certainly it was not used extensively in World War II. For obvious reasons it was never offered for sale commercially and specimens of it are rarely found.

Heeres Pistole—The Heeres (Army) model, chambered for the 9 mm. Parabellum cartridge, was fully developed by 1937. It is very much like the P-38, its successor, although parts are not interchangeable. Experimental models are said to have been made for the use of the U.S. .45 and the .38 ACP cartridges, but these never went into production. Reportedly some 25,000 were made for some foreign power in 1942. Several specimens (Nos. 12,791, 14,007, 22,502, and 23,013), presumably from this

TABLE 55
Data for Walther pocket pistols

Measurement	Model Number
	I	II	III	IV	V	VI	VII	VIII	IX	PP	PPK
Total length, mm.	110	106	127	150	106	209	132	130	100	176	149-154
Barrel length, mm.	53	54	66	88	54	120	76	73	51	98	83-87
Height, mm.	79	77	...	105	75	130	90	90	69	108	108
Weight, gm.	320	277	471	535	272	964	334	350	259*	650	ca. 539
Magazine cap., ctges.	6	6	6	8	6	8	8	8	6	8	7
Cartridge	6.35	6.35	7.65	7.65	6.35	9 Par.	6.35	6.35	6.35	7.65	7.65

*Catalogs give 235 gm.
Note: All calibers are Browning (ACP).

grams for the .22 PPK; ca. 710 grams for the 9 mm. PP; ca. 580 grams for the 9 mm. PPK.

An auxiliary, insertable barrel was available for the 7.65 mm. models, which permitted the use of the 4 mm. "Zielmunition 20" cartridges for target practice up to about 10 yards.

lot, have been seen, all of which showed the same full commercial markings and the absence of German military acceptance marks. It seems a bit strange that the Germans should be making military pistols for any foreign power (except an ally) at a time when pistols were so desperately needed by their own forces that they had to resort to the use of nonmilitary types, many of which were of inferior quality. The Heeres pistol was of splendid workmanship typical of Walther's normal production.

Modell P-38—Of all of the pistols developed during World War II, the Mod. P-38 is the most notable. It is a very fine pistol and, until late in the war, every specimen showed fine workmanship. It is, however, very complicated and many of its parts are too expensive to produce for a weapon designed for military use. Compared to the simplicity of the U.S. Army .45 or the Russian Tokarev, it is not well designed for a "production job."

The P-38 follows directly from the Heeres model, having many of the same features. Specimens of the late production of the Heeres, which are marked with the letters H.P. on the left side of the slide, are externally undistinguishable from the early P-38 production, which bear military markings and do not carry the Walther name. In both of these models the button type of magazine release was dropped in favor of the earlier type of release, situated at the bottom of the grip frame.

The firing pin safety system in the Heeres pistol, one of the safest ever devised, was used in the early production of the P-38, but as war pressure increased this was simplified. Even so it is a pretty good one. Whether the original or the simplified system is present in a P-38 can be told by examining the exposed end of the firing pin when the hammer is raised. In the Heeres pistol, and in the early specimens of the P-38, the end of the firing pin has a rectangular appearance, while in the war model P-38 the end is circular.

As has already been suggested, as the war went on and pressure on production increased the quality of workmanship deteriorated and the P-38 pistols made near the close of the war are by no means the fine specimens that were produced at the outset. This no doubt was due in part to the fact that many of the workmen in the plant in the later war years were drawn from the many prisoners of war then available. Such men could not be expected to take pride in Walther standards of workmanship! There certainly was no incentive to excel.

The P-38 was made not only by Walther (specimens of which are marked with the code ac and the last two digits of the year of manufacture) but by Mauser (code byf) and in smaller quantities by the Spreewerk in Berlin-Spandau (code cyg). Specimens have also been found marked $\frac{SVW}{45}$ and dated as having been made in 1945. Pistols so marked were made by Mauser, who used this code

for the year 1945, only.

Experimental models of the P-38 in .22 caliber were made by Walther but were never put into production. One of these is said to have been made in 1942 and was designed for military service target practice. Another experimental model, on the P-38 style, differed in that it had a floating chamber. Experimental models of a "Volkspistole" (for citizen use) date back to 1937. These were made along the lines of the P-38 and were made largely of sheetmetal. Some were produced in 1944–45, in two different types, and one type by Gustloff Werke in Suhl.

In spite of the wanton destruction of machinery,

Fig. 273. 9 mm. Walther Mod. P-38. Post-World War II production.

Fig. 274. 9 mm. Walther Mod. P-38. Post-World War II. Partially disassembled.

drawings, specifications and records at the Zella-Mehlis plant at the end of the war, production of the Mod. P-38 has been resumed at Ulm-Donau (Figs. 273, 274).

"Armeepistole" or *"Hammerless"* Model—Unlike the PP Mod. and the P-38, this pistol has a fully concealed hammer, but otherwise it has features of both. The stock or grip resembles that of the PP Mod. while the slide, in some respects, resembles that of the P-38. It has a different style of safety, however, and also has a different type of locking pin. The double safety device appears to be quite efficient. The pistol is chambered for the 9 mm. Parabellum cartridge (Figs. 275 to 277).

It has been stated that these fine pistols, which are excellent examples of the best of Walther workmanship, were never intended for the market but were made exclusively as private presentation pieces. They were made in a variety of slightly differing forms, very few of which were alike, and the whole production is thought not to have ex-

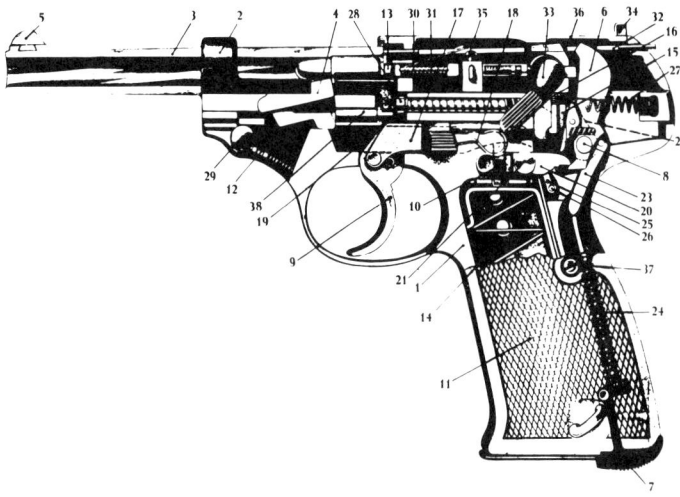

Fig. 277. 9 mm. Walther Armee Pistole. Sectionalized.

ceeded 50 or so specimens. They are numbered in a special series, each number starting with 0 (01 to 050).

Barrel lengths vary (2, 4.9, and 7 inches), some have steel slides while others have slides made of aluminum alloy, and some are grooved to accept shoulder stocks. These last have two-leaf target sights, while the others do not. One specimen is reported to be in .45 caliber, but this is questioned.

Target pistol—In 1932 Walther brought out a .22 Target Pistol, designed for use at the Olympic competitions (Figs. 278 to 280). The pistol bore considerable resemblance to the first pistol (or Mod. I), particularly in slide design and in the use of a rod-like firing pin surrounded by a coiled spring, rather than being a hammer model. As the slide moves back it draws the firing pin back and compresses the surrounding coil spring; the pin engages and is held by the sear. Pressure on the trigger is transmitted to the sear and the firing pin is released. Since the sear bar connects with the sear only when the slide is in the closed position, permitting it to rise into a slot on the under side, it acts as a disconnector. Consequently a separate pull on the trigger, is required for each shot. This model appeared in two barrel lengths, 9 inches for competition shooting and 6 inches for other use. This model did not have balancing weights, as did the Olympic model.

Olympic Modell—This model appeared in several different forms, depending on the use for which each was intended, and it differed markedly in construction from the earlier (1932) target pistol. Although it has an enclosed hammer like the Target

Fig. 275. 9 mm. Walther Armee Pistole.

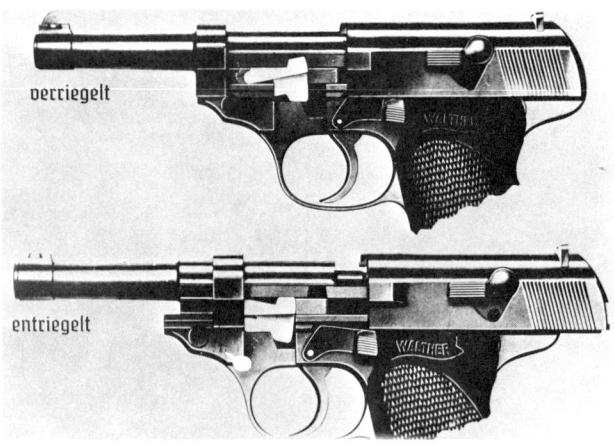

verriegelt

entriegelt

Fig. 276. 9 mm. Walther Armee Pistole.

301

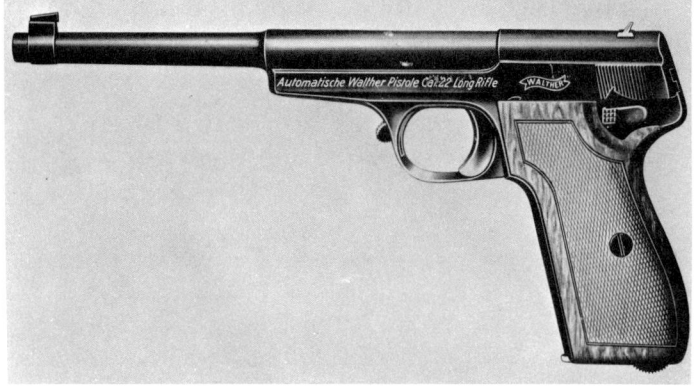

Fig. 278. .22 cal. Walther Target Pistol.

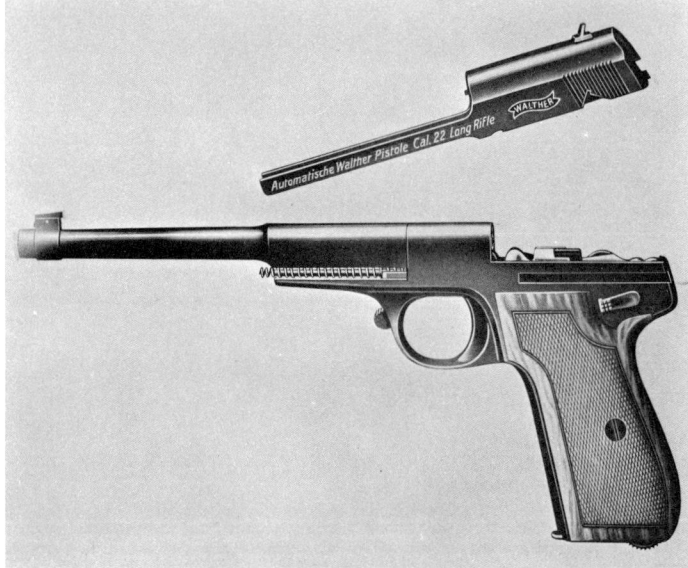

Fig. 279. .22 cal. Walther Target Pistol. Showing method of disassembly.

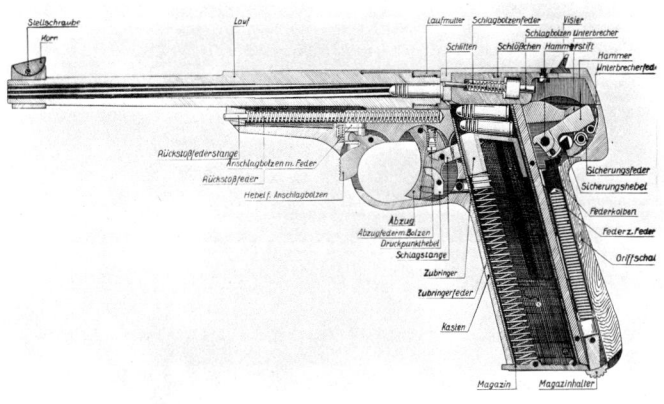

Fig. 280. .22 cal. Walther Target Pistol. Introduced in 1932. Sectional view.

Pistol, it has more resemblance to the PP model in other respects (Fig. 281).

Like the Olympic models made by other manufacturers, the pistol had adjustable balancing weights which permitted an adjustment of balance to suit the need or whim of the individual shooter. Some were made for .22 L.R. and some for .22 Short cartridges, and interchangeable barrels were obtainable for some models. Also some specimens were made with aluminum alloy slides. Four particular models were made, beside which there were numerous variants.

1. Sport Model—This designation may or may not be an official one, but it is the one generally used. Eleven shots could be fired (10 cartridges in the magazine). Total length was 272 mm., barrel length 190 mm., sighting radius 235 mm., weight 860 grams. It was available with or without weights.

2. Jägerpistole—For use in the Deutschen Jägerschaft competitions. Barrel length was 100 mm., weight 725 grams, magazine capacity 10. It was designed for .22 L.R. cartridges.

3. Fünfkampf Modell—Total length was ca. 330 mm., barrel length 240 mm., weight 1000 grams, and magazine capacity 10. It was designed for L.R. cartridge. A set of four balancing weights was available. Widely differing weights for this model have been reported.

4. Olympic Schnellfeuer Modell—This was the same as No. 1 above with the following exceptions: weight 785 grams, one adjustable weight of ca. 351 grams, magazine capacity 6, chambered for .22 Short cartridge.

Statements as to weights, total length, barrel length, etc. will be found to vary, indicating that there were a number of variants. All are agreed, however, that this is an excellent target pistol and that it shows workmanship conforming to Walther's high standard.

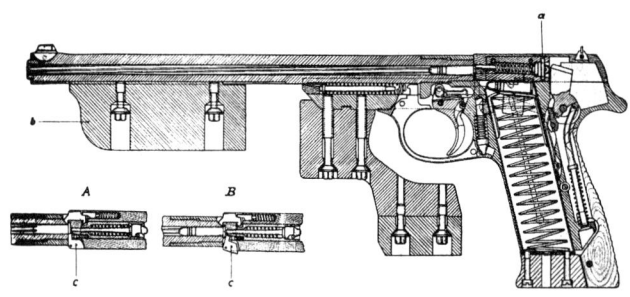

Fig. 281. .22 cal. Walther Olympia Pistole. Sectional view.

Walthers of foreign manufacture

Some time after the close of World War II, manufacture of the 7.65 mm. Mod. PP Walther was started by the firm Mre. de Machines du Haut Rhin at Mulhouse/Bourtzwiller, France, under license from Walther (Figs. 282, 283). Later a .22 cal. model also appeared. These pistols seem to be of excellent quality, as would be expected if, as reported, they are produced under the supervision of Walther.

In 1948 the manufacture of a copy of the 9 mm. Mod. PP Walther, known as the Kirikkale, was begun at the government factory Kirikkale Tüfek Fabricular (Kirikkale Rifle Factory) in Turkey. Serial numbering started at 10,001 and apparently about 10,000 were made. Two years later, copies of the 7.65 Mod. PP appeared, but apparently were made in small quantity as there was little commercial demand. In 1951 a dozen or so copies of the Walther P-38 Mod. were made, probably with the expectation of Army adoption. Serial numbering for these started at 5001. Manufacture of copies of the Walther pistols at Kirikkale seems to have ceased in 1952. Whether it has been resumed or not is not known.

Another copy, no doubt unauthorized, is the Hungarian Pistol Mod. 48 (Madarska Pistole vz 48),

Fig. 282. .22 cal. Walther Mod. PP Sport. Made under license by Manhurin.

Fig. 283. .22 cal. Walther Mod. PP Sport. Disassembled.

made at the Fémáru es Szerszamgepgyar, N.V., at Budapest. This appears to be an exact copy of the Mod. PP Walther.

Warner pistols

The history of the Warner Arms Corporation is not entirely clear and its activities are relatively unimportant but do merit some consideration. F. B. Warner, then of Brooklyn, N. Y., imported and sold the German-made Schwarzlose 7.65 mm. pistol which had been patented by A. W. Schwarzlose on April 13 and August 24, 1909. Just when Warner began selling this pistol is not known, but it is stated on good authority that its manufacture was discontinued in 1912 and that the machinery, tools, unfinished parts, etc. were purchased by Warner who set up a factory in Brooklyn for the assembly (and possible future manufacture) of the pistol. This venture had a very short life, as production of this pistol, called the Warner Automatic, ceased in 1913.

The original Schwarzlose pistol bears the inscription A. W. SCHWARZLOSE G.M.B.H. BERLIN on the left side and the Schwarzlose trade mark on the right side. The patent dates may or may not be present. The pistols imported and sold by Warner have the inscription

WARNER ARMS CORPORATION
BROOKLYN N.Y. U.S.A.

on the right side, in addition to the regular Schwarzlose markings.

Specimen No. 245 represents somewhat of an enigma. On the left side of the frame it bears the customary authentic Schwarzlose inscription, reading

A. W. SCHWARZLOSE g.m.b.h. BERLIN
PAT'D APR. 13 and AUG. 24, 1909

and on the right side, below the Schwarzlose trade mark, is the inscription

WARNER ARMS CORPORATION
BROOKLYN, N.Y. U.S.A.

The grip pieces are of molded hard rubber and carry the WAC (Warner Arms Corporation) trade mark.

This specimen is not the conventional Schwarzlose pistol in several respects. The most striking difference is in the omission of the grip safety. The sliding thumb safety has been replaced by the conventional type of turning thumb safety, which is much easier to manipulate, and the magazine catch has been changed. The finger grips on the slide consist of rolled die hatching instead of milled grooves. Finally, the serial number does not appear in the usual place, on the right side directly under the finger grip. The number does appear on the back of the standing breech and on the inside on the left hand barrel extension which carries the ejector. The smallness of this number (245) and the features of its construction seem to indicate that it was a late rather than early model, numbered in a different series.

Whether this specimen was one of a new model (contemplated or actual) being put out by Schwarzlose, or whether it was made up on a special order for Warner is not known. The absence of German proof marks may indicate the latter.

"The Infallible"—The Schwarzlose having proved to be weak in sales appeal, Warner became interested in a design being developed by Andrew Fyrberg of Worcester, Mass., who had taken out numerous revolver patents which had been assigned to Iver Johnson. Warner made arrangements to manufacture a pistol of a design covered by a patent issued to Fyrberg on July 28, 1914. Application for this patent had been made on March 13, 1913, and assignment of the prospective patent was made to Warner. Whether the development of this design was made in Worcester or Brooklyn is not clear, but the drawings seem to have been made from a completed prototype and may well have been made at the Warner plant. It seems very likely that experimental models of this .32 cal. pistol were made in conjunction with Warner and that specimens were offered for sale for the reason that specimen No. 529 bears the patent date of July 28, 1914, indicating that at least that number of pistols had been made before the patent was granted.

It is stated in records made in the early 1920's that the Warner Arms Corporation moved to Norwich, Conn., in 1913, and this seems probable because specimen No. 529, marked as having been made in Norwich, bears but the one patent date—July 28, 1914. On March 9, 1915, a second patent was issued to Fyrberg and assigned to Warner. Specimens in the 900 range and above bear both patent dates and were made in Norwich.

Presumably, financial difficulties were encountered—not an uncommon experience in the precarious business of firearms manufacture, especially with small firms trying to introduce a new and inferior model—and in 1917 the Warner Arms Corporation merged with the much older firm of N. R. Davis and Sons of Assonet, Mass. The manufacture of the pistol was continued by this new firm, the Davis-Warner Arms Co., for only two years. In 1919 the firm moved to Norwich and apparently became inactive not long thereafter. In 1930 it appears to have been resurrected for the purpose of merging with the Crescent Arms Co. to form the new firm

of Crescent-Davis Arms Corporation. The name Warner having disappeared, the changing fortunes need be pursued no further.

When the Davis-Warner Arms Co. took over production of the pistol, the name The Infallible was changed to Infallible. The first pistols produced by this new firm were very similar to those previously made at Norwich. Later, some slight changes were made, including the use of a new monogram for the grip pieces, but the general design remained essentially the same. No figures as to total production are available, but it is certain that the number was not large as the arm was never popular.

Webley pistols

The only English-made automatic pistols which have been produced in considerable numbers are those made by Webley and Scott, Ltd. of Birmingham and London. An experimental model was built in 1903, based on a design patented in the same year by W. J. Whiting (Brit. Pat. No. 19,032 - 1903). This pistol was of the locked-breech type with recoiling barrel, under which was a spiral recoil spring. Only a few specimens were made as it was not considered a success.

Webley 1904 model—In 1904 Whiting produced a new design, covered by Brit. Pats. Nos. 3820, 17,856, and 25,028 (all of 1904). This pistol also employed a locked breech with recoiling barrel, with a locking system of the prop-up type. Unlike the 1903 prototype, however, a stiff V-shaped spring and recoil lever, located under the right hand grip piece, replaced the spiral spring. This idea came from the Webley revolvers, where such a spring had long been used.

This pistol was very heavy, was awkward in appearance, and consisted of too many parts, a number of which required exacting milling operations, making it expensive to produce. This model was never adopted for armed forces use and but few were made, there being no commercial market for such a weapon.

Webley Mark I—By 1913 an improved .455 caliber pistol had been developed and it was adopted in that year for use by all British Naval units and by the Royal Marines. This pistol also had the locked-breech system, necessary for a pistol of this power. The mechanism, though excellently made to exacting specifications, was very complicated and consequently expensive to manufacture. Like the Model 1904, the recoil spring was of the V type, located under the right grip plate. These plates, usually made of ebonite, were brittle and easily broken. As the spring was covered by this plate a broken plate led to trouble. On some specimens wood grip plates are to be found.

Other variants also appeared. Some pistols had grip safeties while other specimens show the safety to have been omitted. In the case of those that had the grip safety the hammer (always placed externally) is located on the grip, and pressure on the grip causes the whole lock assembly (hammer, sear, and sear lever) to move inwards. Other variants appear as to the type of sights used. All specimens show a lanyard ring.

The over-all length of the Mark I is 8½″ (216 mm.), barrel length 5″ (127 mm.), height 5½″ (140 mm.), and weight 39½ oz. (1120 grams), with empty magazine. The magazine capacity is 7 rounds. Whereas the .455 Webley revolver had 7 grooves with right hand twist of one turn in 20″, the Mark I automatic has 6 grooves with right hand twist of one turn in 10″.

When the magazine is pushed in partially, to a point where a "catch" holds it, the arm may be used as a single-shot pistol by inserting cartridges directly into the chamber, the action remaining open after each shot. Pushing the magazine all the way in converts the pistol into the conventional self loader.

Despite the excellent workmanship used in its manufacture, this pistol is not considered to be a satisfactory military arm. It is too complicated and has too many parts, many of which require very exacting milling and machining operations to insure the proper functioning of the weapon, all of which makes it an expensive arm to produce. In these respects it is the antithesis of the Russian Tokarev. While the Webley can be disassembled fairly easily for such a complicated weapon, this operation has to be performed all too frequently because a very small amount of foreign matter in the mechanism is likely to cause it to malfunction.

Webley .38 cal. model—The Webley .38 caliber model, introduced in 1910, was brought out to satisfy a natural demand for a lighter automatic pistol than the Mark I. In general this new pistol was a copy of the Mark I, but it was furnished with an internal striker of the non-inertia type instead of the external hammer. Like its progenitor, it is prone to malfunction if dirt, dust, or too-heavy oil gets into the mechanism.

The pistol was 8″ (203 mm.) in length, and weighed about 33 oz. (935 grams). This model was not long in production.

Webley 9 mm. "High Velocity" model—This model was designed to take the Belgian 9 mm. Browning

Long cartridge and was introduced in 1913. While it resembles the .455 Mark I in having an external hammer and the same type of grip safety, the action is quite different, being of the blowback type with a stiff recoil spring. The use of the blowback principle, rather than the locked bolt, was possible because of the relatively weak cartridge used. Some specimens of this model are reported to be without the grip safety.

Like the other blowback pistols made by Webley and Scott, the barrel is held in position by the trigger guard. Disassembly is accomplished by inserting the finger in the trigger guard and pulling down and forward. The recoil spring is of the characteristic V type. The magazine holds 7 cartridges. In some specimens the magazine release catch will be found to be on the frame back of the trigger guard while in others it will be found at the bottom of the grip frame.

The over-all length is 8″ (200 mm.), weight 32 oz. (ca. 907 grams), and the magazine capacity 7 cartridges. An interesting feature of this arm relates to the loading. As in many other automatics, when the last shot is fired the action remains open. In this pistol the magazine follower pushes the slide catch up and holds the slide in the open position. To load, the magazine is pushed all the way in and then a stud located on the top of the slide is pressed in, thus releasing the catch which holds the slide back, whereupon the slide (impelled by the compressed recoil spring) rushes forward stripping off the top cartridge and chambering it.

This pistol was adopted for use by the South African Police and reportedly was also used at one time by the Egyptian Police. It is often called the New Military and Police Model, but it is doubtful that this is official nomenclature.

Both the .38 cal. model and the 9 mm. High Velocity model have rectangular, fixed lanyard "loops," rather than the loose rings found on the .455 models.

Webley .32 cal. model—The .32 cal. model was first manufactured in 1906, following the design covered in British Patent No. 15,982 (1905). It became known as the Metropolitan Police Model, as it was so used for a number of years. It was supplanted by revolvers for police work and was discontinued many years ago.

The pistol is of the blowback type, having much the same lines as the larger-calibered models. It has the V-type spring and recoil lever, located under the right grip plate. It has an external hammer and spring-loaded inertia firing pin. A thumb safety is mounted on the frame below the slide back of the trigger guard.

To disassemble, the hammer is raised to full cock, the safety lever is turned to the "Safe" position, the magazine is withdrawn and, by placing a finger through the trigger guard and pulling it toward the muzzle, the barrel is freed. The barrel and breech-block can then be withdrawn.

The over-all length of the pistol is 6¼″ (158 mm.), barrel length 3½″ (89 mm.), height 4½″ (114 mm.), weight (magazine empty) 20 oz. (567 grams), capacity of magazine 8 rounds. The front sight is semicircular in shape, and the rear sight (when present) is a simple notched type. Some were not supplied with any rear sight. The magazine catch is at the bottom of the grip, at the rear of the magazine, and is pushed in to release the magazine. Some specimens reportedly were made with a grip safety, but most were not. There is no provision for a lanyard on the .32 or .25 caliber models.

The .32 Harrington and Richardson automatic is a hammerless type based on this model, but possessing a modified firing system and a grip safety. It was made for only a short time as the demand for it was too limited.

Webley .380 model—This pistol is like the .32 cal. pistol just discussed but chambered for the .380 (9 mm. Short Browning) cartridge. The characteristics are the same except for the caliber and the magazine capacity, which is 7 instead of 8 rounds.

Webley .25 cal. model—The Webley .25 caliber pistol is practically a copy of the .32 cal. model. It appears in two forms, with and without external hammer. An undated Webley and Scott circular shows only the hammer model, and the ALFA Catalog of 1911 shows but this one model. An English (*Personne*) catalog, of about 1920, shows both the hammer and hammerless types. Presumably the hammer type was the first to be introduced. Specimens Nos. 83,423 and 133,249 have the external hammer. They also have a slide whose top is continuous for its entire length, except for a shell ejection port on the right side; and they have a finger grip pattern which consists of either 11 or 12 serrations. Specimens Nos. 107,781 and 139,534, however, do not have the external hammer. The top of the slide is not continuous from end to end, but is cut away for about one third of its length, exposing the top of the barrel (in much the same manner as with the Vest Pocket Sauer and the Stock pistols). This type has both front and rear sights, the hammer type has none. The serrations comprising the finger grip pattern are coarser and eight in number. This overlapping of serial numbers for the two types indicates that either (1) there was no abrupt change over from one type to the other and that both types were

being made simultaneously in the same numbering system, or (2) that a separate numbering system was used for each type. The former conjecture appears more likely.

The .25 caliber types do not have grip safeties. Circular literature states that either the .32 or .25 cal. pistol, because of its efficient thumb safety, may be "carried at full cock without danger of accident." The hammer model permits the lowering of the hammer on a loaded chamber for additional safety, however. As with other hammer models of the Webley line this is a procedure which requires care because of the shape of the hammer, which is not well designed for this operation.

The over-all length of the .25 cal. pistol (hammer type) is 4¼″ (108 mm.); barrel length, 2⅛″ (54 mm.); height, 3⅛″ (79 mm.); weight (without magazine) 11 oz. (ca. 312 grams); magazine capacity, 6 rounds. The dimensions of the hammerless type are approximately the same, but the weight is about 5 grams less.

Variants are to be found, particularly as to the design of the grip plates.

Webley and Scott, Ltd. do not now manufacture automatics but continue to manufacture revolvers.

Yugoslav pistols

The only manufacturer of pistols of any importance in Yugoslavia is the Voino Tekhnichki Zavod (Army Technical Factory) located at Kragujevac. It is not known when this firm originated, but it had been in operation many years before World War II. About 5000 workers were employed. During the war the Germans bombed the plant, but soon thereafter they rebuilt it and installed considerable modern German machinery, which was left behind when they retreated.

Many foreign-made pistols had been imported from Belgium and Spain in the years before the war. Some pistols which are identical to the 7.65 mm. Eibar Type (a Browning modification) developed by Gabilondo, but made by many other Spanish manufacturers as well, for sale to the French during World War I, are found with Yugoslav markings but with the "Fire" and "Safe" positions of the thumb safety marked in French (following the Spanish custom). One such specimen which is identical to the Eibar Type pistol made by Echave and Arizmendi in Eibar is marked (in Serbian) PISTOL 7.65 mm. F V T Z 1923, which indicates that it is a Model 1933 Pistol made by Voino Tekhnichki Zavod, or at least marked to give that impression. Whether it was made in Spain or not is not known, but other pistols known to have been made in Yugoslavia do not have French markings to indicate the position of the thumb safety.

Still another, a 9 mm. F.N. Browning Model 1922, with authentic markings on the left side of the slide (including the name of the manufacturer) has on the right side a Serbian inscription which reads ARMY-STATE No. 11954, meaning that this gun is the property of the state. The number coincides with the serial number put on by F.N., and the specimen is no doubt one of a large shipment made to Yugoslavia just before the war. On the top of the barrel there is stamped an interesting coat of arms, which, incidentally, is also found on an F.N. Browning 7.65 Model 1910 having similar markings. Yogoslav importations for military purposes were not limited to weapons of 9 mm. caliber.

The coat of arms is that of the Kingdom of the Croats, Serbs, and Slovenes (Yugoslavia). This coat of arms was used not only on weapons but on holsters and as shoulder patches and indicated that the bearer had fought in Mikhailovich's army against the Communists. A Communist, whose equipment bore the hammer and sickle, would hesitate to be found with any equipment bearing the Yugoslav coat of arms.

One Yugoslav pistol which is of native origin is the 9 mm. Yovanovitch. L. Yovanovich was an officer-engineer-inventor who designed and developed this pistol, then sold it to the Yugoslav Government. It was manufactured by the Voino Tekhnichki Zavod.

Only one of these has been seen and measured. This had a total length of 7¼″, barrel length of 4¼″, and height of 4⅝″. The barrel and bolt are contained in a tapered tubular housing which runs the entire length of the arm. The pistol is disassembled by turning a milled head at the rear of the housing. It has a mechanical thumb safety located in front of the left grip piece—a lever set in a vertical position with the "Safe" and "Fire" positions indicated in Serbian. The grips are of plain wood, without serrations or checkering. The inscription on the barrel reads

PATENT L. YOVANOVITCH

MODEL 1931

There are no proof marks or other markings.

As to rifling, the pistol has 6 grooves, right hand twist, with one turn in 8.4 inches. The bore diameter is 0.3508, groove diameter 0.3590, and land width 0.045 inches. All the above data were taken from one specimen (No. 3344), the rifling of which was in good condition.

It is said that a substantial order for pistols was obtained from Haile Selassie of Ethiopia in 1954 and that these were made and delivered. This statement has not been confirmed, but, if true, it is likely that they were the 9 mm. Yovanovitch.

A former officer in the Mikhailovitch Army states that pistols of both 7.65 mm. and 6.35 mm. calibers, of the same deisgn, were made. The former were for police and similar use, rather than for military use.

Zehna pistol

The Zehna pistol, of 6.35 mm. caliber, was designed by Emil Zehner in about 1919–1920 and prototype forms were made in 1920 and perhaps in early 1921. When commercially produced, in mid-1921, the pistol differed somewhat from the prototypes. It was manufactured by the Zehner Metallwarenfabrik at Suhl, Germany. While it appears to have been moderately successful its production seems to have ceased somewhere around 1928. It appears in the 1927 Genschow Catalog but is not in the 1928 edition.

The Zehna is remarkably like the Mod. I Schmeisser, sometimes referred to as the 1920 Mod., which in fact pre-dates the Zehna by only a year or so. The Schmeisser pistol was manufactured by C. G. Haenel, also of Suhl. The similarity of the two pistols may have had something to do with the termination of production of the Zehna. Though the similarity is great the two are not identical as to dimensions, as will be seen from the data in Table 56.

TABLE 56

Data for Schmeisser and Zehna pistols

Measurement	Schemisser Mod. I	Zehna
Over-all length	115 mm.	125 mm.
Height	76 mm.	80 mm.
Thickness	23.5 mm.	23 mm.
Weight	350 gm.	410 gm.
Magazine capacity	6	6
Number of rifling grooves	4	4
Direction of rifling twist	Right	Right

APPENDICES

INDEX

Class characteristics of shell markings

by Mezger, Hees, and Hasslacher

The following translation from *Archiv für Kriminologie*, Vol. 89, pp. 1–32 and 93–116, is quoted by permission from the *American Journal of Police Science*, Vol. II, pp. 473–99, and Vol. III, pp. 124–45.

Breech Face Markings

It is a well-known fact that at the moment when the cartridge is fired, the empty shell is hurled violently against the breech face, as a result of the recoil. The primer and shell head receive certain imprints from the breech face, differing somewhat according to the pressure developed within the individual cartridge (Fig. 284). These impressions vary

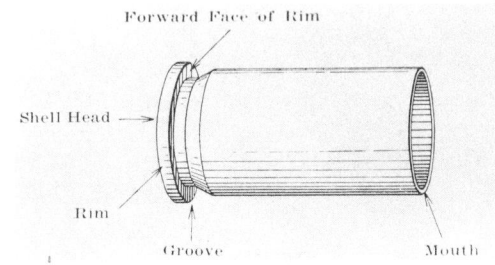

Fig. 284. Sketch showing various parts of an unfired shell.

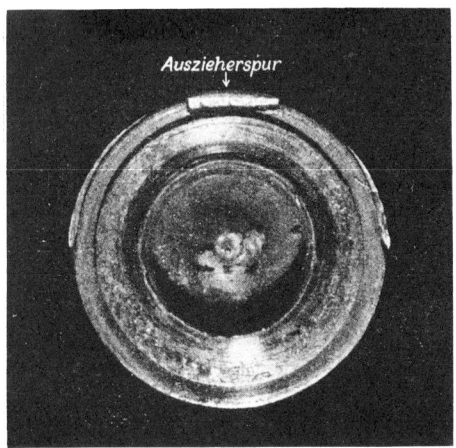

Fig. 285. Head of shell fired from Model 2 Schmeisser pistol. Auszieherspur—Extractor mark.

considerably in their nature, and may be of great value in determining the type or even the particular make of weapon used. As a further result of the recoil, the breechblock glides back. At the same time, the recoil spring and the firing pin spring are compressed. According to the particular construction of pistol, the fired shell is ejected either by an ejector stud on the firing pin or by the usual ejector.

The ejector is attached to the frame of the pistol, and ejects the fired shell as the breech block slides rearward. Occasionally, as in the case of the Webley and Scott pistols of caliber 7.65 and 6.35 (with hammer) and the MAB pistol, one of the magazine lips acts as an ejector. The extractor, which catches hold of one side of the shell as the slide glides back, acts as the pivot for the shell as it is being ejected. As a result the extractor hook usually scratches clearly visible marks on the shell head (Fig. 285).

Anyone who wishes to work with shells for the purpose of determining the numerous types of arms used, must necessarily become acquainted with the exact processes and mechanisms of various pistol models, in order to be able to distinguish for himself the several kinds of markings. It will make matters easier if the cartridges to be employed in experimental tests are painted with a mixture of spirit varnish and castor oil. If this is done, the various marks will become more easily visible. During our early studies of breech face impressions on the shell head and primer, we pasted small discs of copper, 0.05 mm. thick (which had been softened by heating in a stream of hydrogen) on the shell head before firing the cartridge. This method is especially valuable in determining whether any of the boundaries of the breech face fall within the area of the shell

311

head, and can be counted on to produce characteristic imprints thereon. After some practice in recognizing breech face impressions, it is well to use cartridges without the head stamps (the letters and numbers commonly imprinted in the course of manufacture), as these make it more difficult to see the markings, and their presence sometimes masks entirely any imprint which may be acquired. Furthermore, cartridges with copper primers are better for our purposes than those with brass ones, because the impressions in the copper are clearer.

Extractor Marks

Among the most important marks on a shell are those made by the extractor, not because it is possible to determine from them definitely what type of pistol was used, but because these serve as an excellent starting point for deciding from an examination of a shell found at a scene of a crime what type of weapon was used, and also because they are valuable in checking our other observations. These impressions give the examining officer the first clue as to the position of the shell in the chamber at the time of firing. As previously stated, they are found on the forward face of the shell rim. They usually consist of a few slight striations readily distinguishable in the surrounding powder smudging. These striations can be seen best under a lateral light.

The smudge surrounding the extractor marks results from the powder gases emitted when the cartridge is fired, and enables us to distinguish these striations from any other marks that may have gotten on the shell previously. The lack of any trace of powder smoke at the point on the chamber rim occupied by the extractor is due in our opinion to the fact that the powder gases cannot condense there. If the extractor hook has only a slight hold of the shell head, this hook may, as the fired shell is ejected, glide over the rim of the shell head and thus produce distinct scratches thereon. *Only the markings on the forward face of the shell rim are significant* in locating the extractor markings and in determining the position of the cartridge in the chamber at the time of firing. If this is not kept in mind, it will often be impossible to avoid confusing these imprints with different marks, such as those produced by the magazine, or arising from other causes.

The extractor markings may be significant in determining the type of pistol used due to the fact that there are at least two types of pistols that have no extractors, the Steyr Pistol, caliber 6.35, and the Steyr Pistol, caliber 7.65, up to No. 50,000. Steyr Pistols above No. 50,000 have extractors. This fact is interesting because it shows unmistakably that in the act of shooting the extractor does not actually extract, but that the pressure of the powder gases is in itself sufficient to hurl the shell and the breech block backwards. The extractor functions as such only if a cartridge fails to go off, or in case one wishes to unload a pistol for the sake of practice. If, therefore, it can definitely be shown that there are extractor marks on a shell, this will establish the fact that one of the extractorless Steyr Pistols was not used in a particular case. On the other hand, it is not safe to conclude, in the absence of extractor marks, that this type of Steyr Pistol was necessarily used, because the extractor may not have left any imprint because of a defect, or for some other reason.

Often the extractor marks on the forward face of the shell rim will give some clue concerning the form and position of the extractor hook itself; for sometimes the outlines of this hook are plainly visible on this area, which lies against the rear face of the barrel. Inasmuch as the various makes of pistols have entirely different extractors, and since those of any particular make are quite uniform, the imprint of the extractor hook may give a likely clue as to the make of firearm used.

Extractor Basic Forms

We have classified the fundamental forms of the extractor marks, on the basis of our researches, into four groups, for the purpose of determining the particular type of pistol involved. Figure 286 illustrates these four basic forms of extractor imprints, as

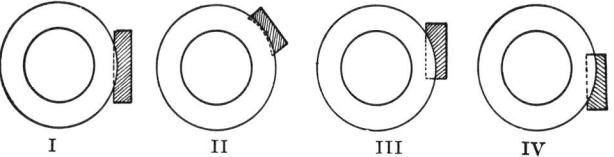

Fig. 286. Extractor basic forms.

they appear on the shell head, assuming that these latter are transparent. The broken lines in each case show the part of the extractor hook that will leave a mark. In the case of form No. I, the extractor hook lies straight up and down, more or less on a tangent to the shell. The imprint of the extractor, therefore, appears as a segment, or if the hook is narrow enough, it forms a rectangular mark on the shell head. In the case of form No. II, the shape of the extractor hook corresponds to the arc of the shell rim, and consequently an arc-shaped mark is made, parallel to the rim and often easily visible, even when only one side of the hook has taken hold of the shell. In those cases where a rectangular hook is located above or below the firing pin aperture in the breech face, we get the forms shown as Nos. II and IV. These latter two can be distinguished from No. I only in case the horizontal edge of the triangle makes a sharp impression. Of course there are intermediate forms, and in such instances it is necessary also to examine the illustrations of the various breech faces as shown in the charts to determine the form of the extractor. An exception in the usual classification of extractors is found in the Mann Pistols of 6.35, 7.65, and 9 mm. caliber. In the case of these Mann Pistols, the extractor is a part of the breech face and covers about one-fourth of the shell. It is relatively easy to determine that one of these pistols has been used because of the very large extractor marks, which take up about 90 degrees of the shell's circumference. Another peculiarity of these pistols is the fact that it is impossible to load them by placing an individual cartridge in the chamber because the extractor cannot be snapped over the rim of the cartridge head on account of its springless attachment to the breech face.

Imprint of the Breech End of the Barrel

If we examine the shell head from both sides, beginning at the extractor mark, we come upon the deformations on the forward face (edge) of the shell rim mentioned in the first part of this article, provided the cylindrical part of the shell fits far enough into the chamber so that the shell head is flush with the breech end of the barrel. Strangely this latter condition does not exist in the case of most Spanish pistols, and in the case of the Mann Pistols (calibers 6.35 and 7.65) the cartridge fits into the chamber only to the end of the cylindrical part of the shell. Consequently, the absence of the chamber rim marks is quite characteristic for this type of pistol. With regard to all other firearms, these marks practically always appear, whether the cartridge is automatically inserted in the chamber from the magazine, or is placed there by hand; for the surface of the shell at the breech end of the barrel is so small that as the breech block snaps forward it represents a relatively large force. For this reason there are often swollen formations on the shell rim. Of course, a mark of this type is made on the shell every time the breech block comes in contact with it, assuming a cartridge is inserted more than once for the sake of practice. However, the last imprint made on the shell is easily recognizable because of its relation to the extractor mark and powder smudging, etc. We have especially noticed chamber marks on the shell heads in the case of pistols having a little rim for the protruding part of the shell head, so that the head of a cartridge placed in the chamber is to a certain

extent depressed, that is, it is flush with the breech end of the barrel. Always in the case of the lower half of the rim of the chamber in automatic pistols there is a ramp to facilitate the transfer of the cartridge from the magazine into the chamber. Besides, a small opening is left on the chamber rim for the extractor. Inasmuch as the shell does not touch the chamber rim at the two places mentioned above, no deformation results here; and because the position of the opening of the extractor cut in the chamber rim must tally with the location of the extractor itself in the breech face, it is possible to determine from the nature and position of the deformations on the forward face side of the cartridge rim, whether the extractor of a particular gun is located vertically (at the top of the breech block), or at some intermediate position to right or left. *The ascertainment of this fact is of the utmost importance in locating other characteristic markings and in determining the types of arms involved.*

We have classified these basic forms into eight groups, with three chief forms of chambers. These are illustrated in Figure 287 in such a way as to show the shell heads in their position in the chambers. The points of contact on the chamber at which deformations to the shell might result are shown by dotted lines on the illustrations. The several basic forms have been numbered according to the frequency with which they occur in automatic pistols. Basic Form No. 1 shows a picture of the chamber of a pistol

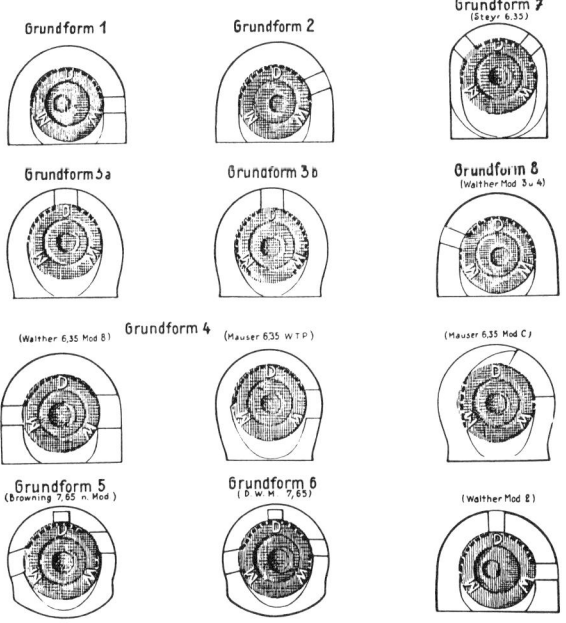

Fig. 287. Basic forms of chamber rim markings. Used to determine orientation of cartridge in gun.

313

ejecting to the right, in which the extractor is on the right side of the firing pin aperture, either level with this hole or below it. The deformation of the forward face of the cartridge rim in the case of these pistols begins to the right of, and very close to, the extractor mark, runs counter-clockwise parallel to the edge of the shell, and at about the middle of the shell deviates to the left at a sharp angle, because at this point the trough-like space of the ramp begins. In the case of Basic Form No. 2 we have another pistol ejecting to the right, with the extractor in a somewhat higher position. As a result, the little corner to the right which forms the lower limit of the opening for the extractor in the chamber rim, also makes an imprint upon the shell. There are of course pistols the basic forms of which lie between Forms 1 and 2, and in such cases the little corner to the right of and below the extractor opening may be so small as to leave no such imprint upon the shell. Such pistols are therefore classified under both Basic Forms 1 and 2. Basic Form 3 is especially conspicuous, because the extractor in this instance, is set at the top of the breech face, resulting in a division of the latter and the corresponding opening in the breech of the barrel into two equal halves. Up to the present time in the case of all shells fired from such pistols, we have been able to recognize this particular location of the extractor by the symmetrical markings of the chamber rim on both sides of the extractor mark. Another peculiarity of this type of pistol is the fact that the deformations on both sides of the extractor mark are characteristically long. Only if a special supporting edge is made for the shell rim by boring out the chamber, do the two symmetrical (deformation) marks extend below the center of the shell (Basic Form 3b), whereas in the case of other pistols, without a special supporting edge, the marks are relatively short (Basic Form 3a).

There are a number of other makes of pistols, the chamber rims of which have such distinctive shapes that it is possible definitely to determine the type of pistol involved from the impression left by the chamber rim. Our first example of such a chamber form is shown in the central sketch in the row next to the bottom in Figure 287. This illustrates a Mauser vest pocket pistol, caliber 6.35 (Mauser 6.35 W.T.P.). From the drawing it will be seen that the opening of the lower half of the chamber rim does not begin gradually at the left side but starts off at a considerable angle, and as a result when one examines the ribbon-shaped marking of the chamber rim on the shell, it appears to be sharply cut off. The same kind of imprint on the shell results if the chamber

rim has an actual opening at this point, as happens in the case of the Walther Pistol of the same caliber, Model 8, old style. (See sketch just to the left of the one described.) The purpose of the opening in the chamber rim, in this instance, was to provide room for a cartridge guide in the breech face opposite the extractor. In the newer style of Walter Pistol, Model 8, the entire upper half of the breech face is countersunk, which makes the guide-pin and the opening above the chamber for it entirely superfluous. Since both chambers (that of the Mauser Vest Pocket Pistol and that of the Walther Model 8, old style) are identical as to the markings on the shell, we have designated them as Basic Form 4. The chamber rim of the original Browning Pistol (F.N.) caliber 7.65, Model 1910, is similar to that in this Walther Pistol, the Browning likewise having a guide-pin in its breech face, corresponding to the opening in the chamber. One purpose of this pin is to guide the cartridge as it comes from the magazine, but more especially it acts as a counter-support for the shell after firing, preventing it from being ejected sideways. However, the Browning Pistol has an added characteristic in that the little corner of the chamber located to the right of and below the extractor opening is stamped into the shell rim, as shown in Basic Form 5 in Figure 287. Another interesting variation is found in the chamber rim of the D.W.M. Pistol, caliber 7.65 (the former Deutsche Waffen und Munitionswerke, Berlin). Although this latter pistol is identical in construction and external appearance with the Browning Pistol 7.65, Model 1910, and although both of these models are the same in that there is a little supporting rim for the shell head due to the countersinking of the chamber, we nevertheless have noticed that usually, in addition to the little corner to the right of and below the extractor opening in the chamber rim which is found reproduced on the shell rim in the case of the Browning Pistol, the D.W.M. Pistol has another little corner producing a second imprint. This additional little corner is located to the left of and below the opening in the chamber for the guide pin. (See Basic Form 6, Figure 287.) According to information received from Chief Engineer Hoffman of Berlin, this added little corner was not accidental, but the manufacturers intentionally slightly countersunk the chamber unlike the original Browning Pistol so that it would be of stronger construction. To be sure, it must be borne in mind that this little corner sometimes will not leave an imprint, especially if the boring of the chamber has been somewhat irregular. We actually came across such a case. But usually it is possible, by means of this slight characteristic mark, positively to determine whether shells have been fired from a D.W.M. Pistol, caliber 7.65 or from a 7.65 caliber Browning Pistol. At least, we have never found this second characteristic imprint on shells fired from a Browning Pistol.

Basic Form 7 represents the chamber rim of the Steyr Pistol, calibers 6.35 and 7.65 up to serial number 50,000. As mentioned in the early part of this treatise, these models have no extractor and consequently are without any corresponding extractor opening in the chamber rim. However, there are two symmetrical grooves running toward the center of the barrel, the limits of which are usually at least partially visible. As the Steyr Company informed us, these grooves serve as means of escape for superfluous powder gases, that is, as a kind of safety valve in case defective cartridges are used, resulting in a burst shell. (Cf. Dr. Kraft's article "The Schmoller Murder Case, *Archiv für Kriminologie,* vol. 88, pp. 133.) Attention is called also to the fact that in the case of pistols ejecting to the left, in which the extractor is located in the left side of the breech face, the markings of the chamber rim on fired shells are located on the opposite side from that of pistols ejecting to the right. We know of only two such pistols ejecting to the left, namely, Walther Pistols, caliber 7.65, Models 3 and 4. In the case of Mauser Pistol, caliber 6.35, large Model C, up to No. 286,000 (Year 1921), and occasionally also in the case of Mauser Pistol, caliber 7.65, older type, the upper side of the chamber is cut off to one side, so that the shells do not touch the breech end of the barrel. As a result the chamber rim of this type of pistol makes only a lateral imprint on the forward side of the cartridge head (Cf. Figure 287). This marking, however, is not entirely characteristic, because usually the imprints of the chamber rim, in the case of all of the basic forms, are much weaker below the upper rim of the shell than laterally. Sometimes, in fact, the former imprints are entirely invisible, because of the depression of the cartridge in its relatively roomy chamber. If the impression from the chamber is lacking in the center above, it is not safe to conclude that this represents the space for the extractor; the extractor mark on the shell is the determining factor here. To our knowledge, the Walther Pistol, Model 2, is the only one having an opening on the top and in the middle of the chamber rim, which is intended not for the extractor, but for an indicator pin (see Figure 287). As we shall explain in Section 7, of this treatise, this indicator pin likewise leaves a mark upon the shell rim, and might, therefore, be easily mistaken for an extractor

mark. However, in the case of shells fired from a Walther Pistol, Model 2, the extractor mark is located laterally and on the right side of the shell rim.

Ejector Marks

The description of the ejector marks introduces us to the characteristic imprints to be found on the shell head. We shall first discuss the pistols equipped with special ejectors. Whenever an examination of the imprints on the shell head is undertaken, it is essential to determine first the exact position of the shell at the time of firing. Usually it will be possible to do this, as explained above, on the basis of the extractor and chamber rim marks. In the discussion which follows, we shall describe the position of the various markings as "right," "left," "above," or "below." At the same time we shall keep our eye on the shell in the chamber, using the same method of observation as was employed for the extractor marks and the imprints of the chamber rim. A correct determination of the position of the shell head in the chamber is especially essential in examining the ejector marks.

We have previously indicated that the ejector marks are of secondary origin, as compared with the imprints on the shell head made as a result of its recoil against the breech face; for whereas the shell receives imprints from the breech face while still lodged in the chamber, before it rebounds upon the ejector it must travel backwards for a considerable distance together with the breech block, and thus has a chance (although held gently by the extractor on one side) to change its position slightly. The result is that, unlike the imprints of the breech face, the ejector marks are not always made in the same way or the same relative position, even on shells fired from a particular pistol. Slight chamber variations may make a difference in this connection. Occasionally an ejector that has made a clear imprint on one shell, may at another time merely touch the edge of the shell head, or not even reach the shell at all. Furthermore, the ejector marks on a shell are sometimes clearly outlined and at other times appear as a mere scratch, depending on the force of the contact of the shell and the ejector. Consequently, it is not always an easy task to discover these markings, and there is danger to the uninitiated of confusing such marks with others that may be formed on the shell. It is possible to determine beforehand in what part of the shell head the ejector mark is to be found, by ascertaining the position of the shell in the chamber when fired. It is easy, therefore, to decide whether a certain mark is an ejector mark, or merely an accidental marking. Usually, the ejector is attached in a position opposite to the extractor, because the ejector is most efficient when so placed. Thus, if the extractor is on the right side, the ejector will be found on the left; and if the extractor is on the left side, as in the case of the Walther Pistols, Models 3 and 4, mentioned above, the ejector is on the right. If the extractor is in the upper part of the line of vision of the pistol (i.e., at the top of the breech block) one would expect to find the ejector below in the center (at the bottom of the breech block) as is the case, for example, of the Pickert Pistol, caliber 6.35. However, since the ejector if so located can be attached to the pistol frame only behind the magazine (a relatively unsatisfactory position), we usually find it as in the case of pistols with extractors on the left or right side toward the front of the frame and directly to the right or left of the magazine. The Mauser Pistol, caliber 7.65 and the very similar Czechoslovakian "N" Pistol, caliber 9 mm. short (Brünn) are peculiar in that in spite of the lateral position of the extractor with respect to the magazine there is a slot (groove) left for a hook, which serves to hold the slide in its rearward position after the magazine is removed, and acts also as an ejector after a cartridge is fired. To be sure, there are seldom marks from it on the shells; and in the case of the very similar Mauser Pistol, caliber 6.35 (large model C) there is never a mark of this kind on the shell because the arresting stud is set too deep, due to the smaller diameter of the shell. Instead, the firing pin acts as the ejector in this model.

In Figure 288 we illustrate the various possible Basic Forms of ejector imprints on shells and their relation to the extractor marks. Of course, it is relatively unusual for them to appear in such perfection, but is ordinarily possible to classify a given shell according to one of these forms if we keep in mind the position of ejector marks with relation to those of the extractor, even though only parts of these imprints are visible. In the case of pistols ejecting to the right, Basic Form No. 1 is by far the most common. It consists of a right angled triangle, the hypotenuse of which is made by the shell rim. The extractor, marked "A," may occupy any of the positions indicated in Forms 1a, 1b, and 1c. Forms 2a and 2b show the same kind of triangular marking in the reverse position, as with respect to pistols ejecting to the left (e.g., Walther models 3 and 4, caliber 7.65); and Form 2c illustrates the ejector imprint of the Spanish model "Star" with the extractor mark directly on top. There is no danger of confusing Forms 1 and 2 by turning the shell about, if the chamber rim marks are also kept in mind. Furthermore, it is possible to identify form No. 2 by the fact

that the long side of the triangle always points downward. Additional important ejector marks are shown in Forms 3a, 3b, and 3c. These are in the form of a square or rectangle on one side of the shell rim. Form 3a is the most usual of this group, and is found in the case of a large number of pistols ejecting to the right. In pistols of this class, the extractor and ejector marks are directly opposite each other. If the two corners of this rectangle are not visible on the shell head, as often occurs, it is possible to see only a segment-like mark. In the case of the Mauser Pistol, caliber 7.65, the extractor and ejector marks are in the relative position shown in Form 3b. This form as well as 3c, representing the Pickert Pistol, caliber 6.35, previously mentioned, shows a mark that is smaller and more nearly square. Form 4 illustrates the semi-circular ejector mark of the Oewa Pistol, caliber 6.35. Here too the extractor mark "A" is directly opposite the ejector mark, even as in Form 3a. The Praga 7.65, Delu 6.35, and Webley and Scott 6.35 hammerless are easy to recognize because they have two symmetrical ejector marks with the extractor imprint located directly opposite. Form 5 represents the Praga and Delu pistols, and Form 6 illustrates the aforementioned Webley and Scott pistol. Inasmuch as most makes of pistols leave ejector marks of the 1a, 1b, or 1c group, we have raised the

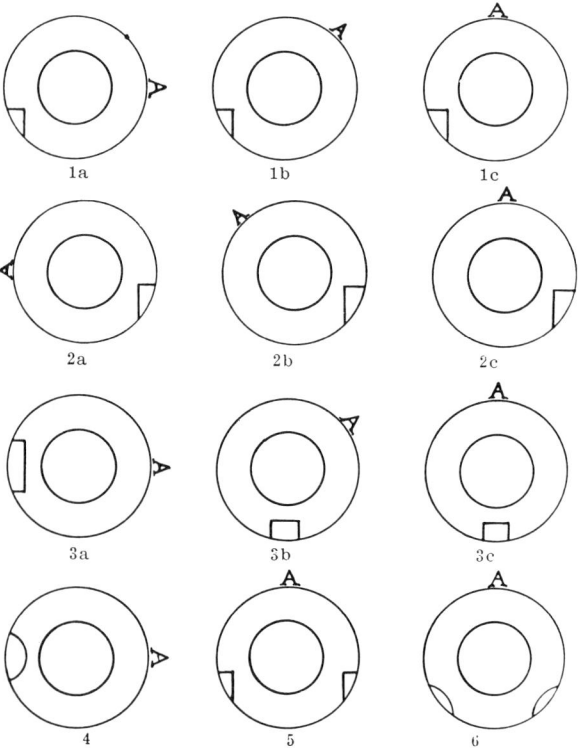

Fig. 288. Ejector basic forms.

question as to whether it would not be possible to make a further subdivision of these forms by measuring the angle made by the extractor mark, the ejector imprint, and the center of the shell. In this connection we used the instrument described by Pietrusky in vol. 77, p. 95, of the *Archiv für Kriminologie*. Instead of dividing the graduated drum into 100 parts, we used one with 360 possible readings to which we attached a pin that causes the drum to stop at the zero point. We employed this instrument to measure hundreds of shells with ejector marks. However, our results varied to such an extent (sometimes there were differences of 30°) whether the shells were fired from the same pistol or from pistols of the same make, that it was impossible to use this method of classification. Basic Form 1c, in which the extractor is in the vertical line of the pistol, was the only one in which such classification proved possible; for in this case we found that the angle between the ejector and extractor marks, measuring from the center of the ejector mark counter-clockwise, was always more than 210°, whereas in the case of all other pistols it is less than 210°. In actual practice, however, it is best to use the chamber rim marks on the forward side of the shell rim as a starting point, or, if these are not present, to classify the shells on the basis of the ejector forms shown in Figure 288. For these reasons it is just as well not to attempt the above-mentioned angle measurements. The variations in these measurements are due mainly to the irregular position of the ejector marks on the shell, and also to the fact that the same part of the extractor claw does not always take hold of successive shells. As to the inability of the instrument to take measurements with absolute exactness, this is a far less serious criticism.

We estimate that about two-thirds of the various kinds of pistols now on the market are equipped with special ejectors, and that the remaining third, as stated in our introductory comments, employ the firing pin as an ejector. The ejector mark is, therefore, a convenient means of distinguishing these two large classes of pistols from one another, assuming that there are such marks on the shells. If the ejector does not make any visible mark, it is of course

difficult to make this classification. We have found that besides the Mauser Pistol, caliber 7.65, already mentioned, there are a number of Spanish 7.65 automatic pistols, equipped with special ejectors, as well as Savage Pistol 7.65, the Heim 6.35, and Webley and Scott's 7.65 and 6.35 (with hammer), which sometimes leave no ejector imprint on a shell, although in every case the shell is successfully ejected. In the case of the two last-named models, this is due to the fact that one of the lips of the magazine acts as an ejector, and for this reason it is easily bent or broken off.

If a shell shows no trace of an ejector mark, it may have been fired either from a pistol with or without a special ejector. It is only in rare cases that it can be definitely established that a shell was fired from a pistol with a firing pin ejector, that is, in case there is a second weaker imprint on the primer besides the firing pin impression. We have never found such a second firing pin impression on a shell fired from a pistol with a special ejector. Such a second imprint is not always visible upon shells fired from a pistol with the firing pin serving as ejector because the firing pin, when so acting, usually reenters its original imprint. If there is a second impression, it is either circular in form like the original one, and similar in its characteristics to the latter; or, it may be eggshaped (elliptical), due to the movement of the shell during firing. It was Raestrup who first called attention to the possibility of using such secondary firing pin impressions as a means of identification. (*Archiv für Kriminologie*, 1926, p. 242) He considered their presence as characteristic only in the case of D. W. Pistols (formerly Deutsche Werke, Erfurt), whereas, of course, they may be found on all pistols similarly constructed. (*End of quoted material.*)

Illustrations of the Eight Basic Forms:

The eight Basic Forms of extractor and breechblock types recognized by Mezger, Hees, and Hasslacher are illustrated, with numerous examples, on the following seven plates. In each photograph the breech face and extractor are shown as they appear from the front.

Plate 1. Examples of Extractor Basic Form 1 as used on various guns

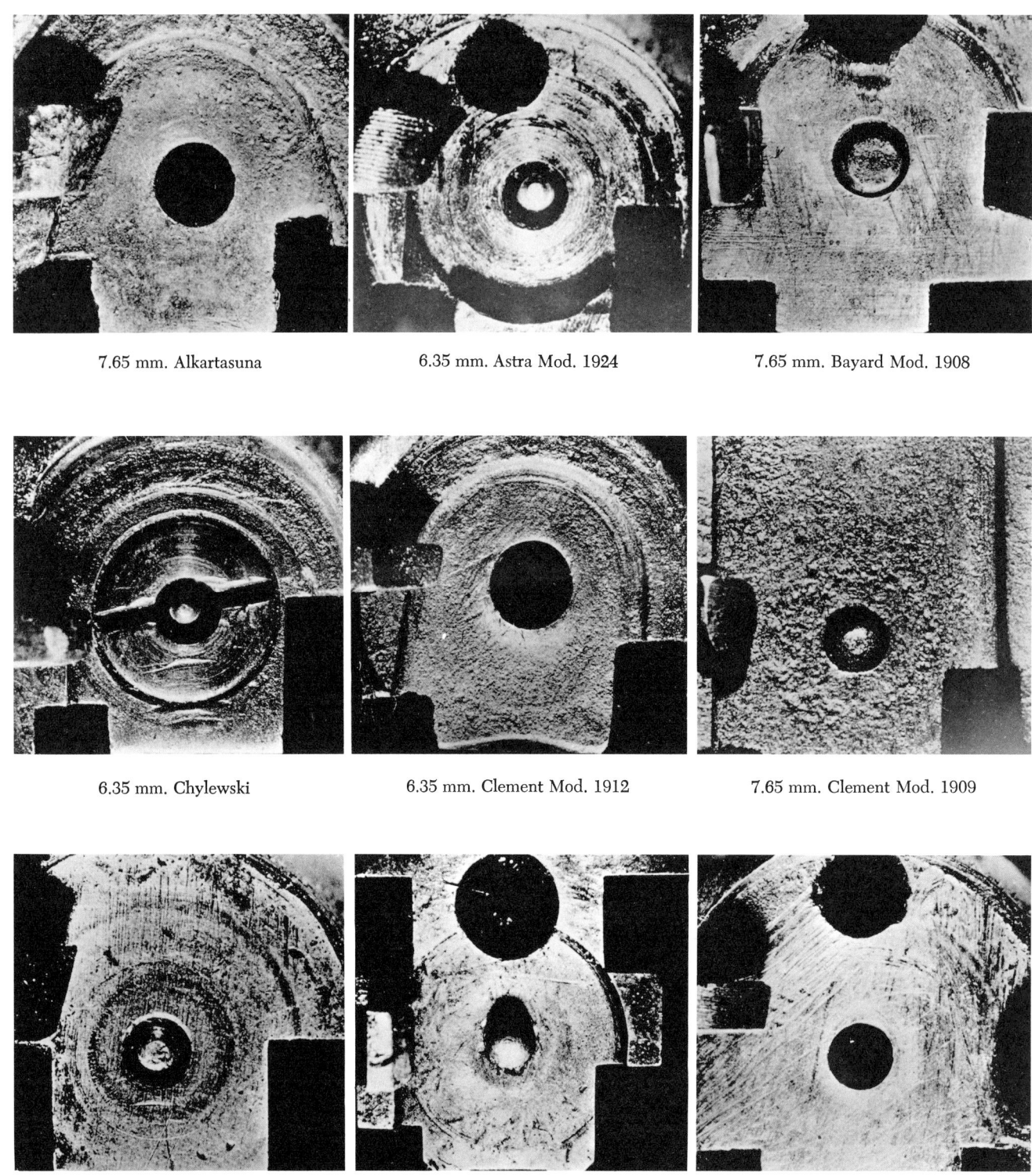

7.65 mm. Alkartasuna	6.35 mm. Astra Mod. 1924	7.65 mm. Bayard Mod. 1908
6.35 mm. Chylewski	6.35 mm. Clement Mod. 1912	7.65 mm. Clement Mod. 1909
.380 cal. Colt	7.65 mm. F.N. Browning Mod. 1900	9 mm. F.N. Browning Mod. 1922

Plate 2. Examples of Extractor Basic Form 1 as used on various guns

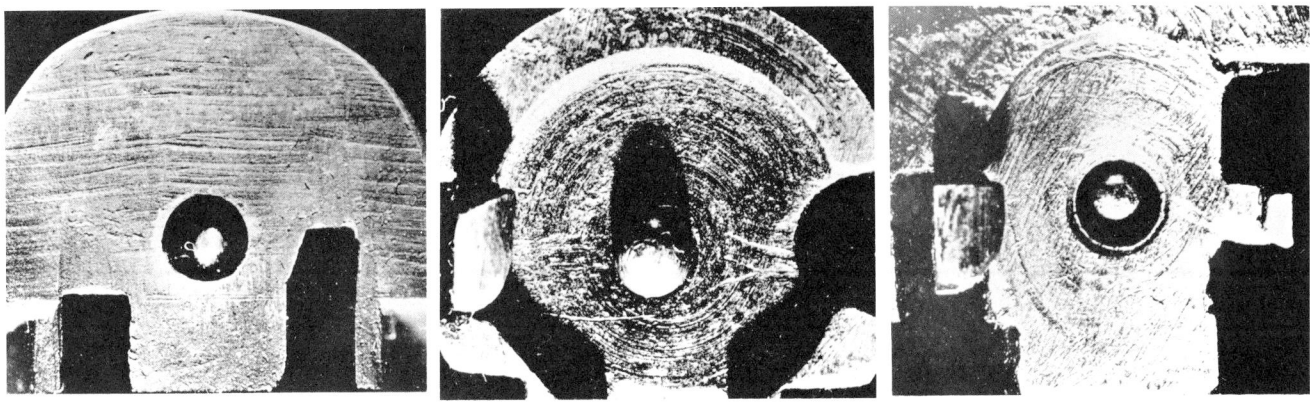

6.35 mm. Le Francais   .32 cal. The Infallible   6.35 mm. Langenhan Mod. II

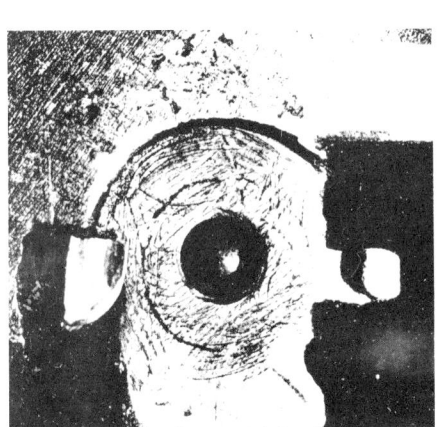
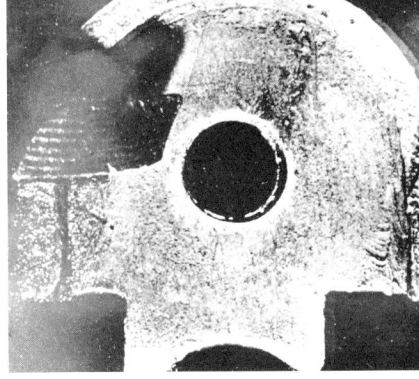
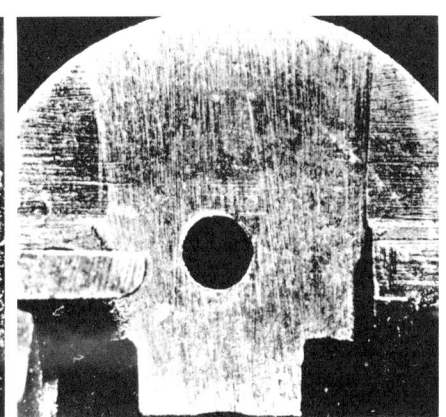

6.35 mm. Langenhan Mod. III   7.65 mm. Leonhardt   6.35 mm. Menz

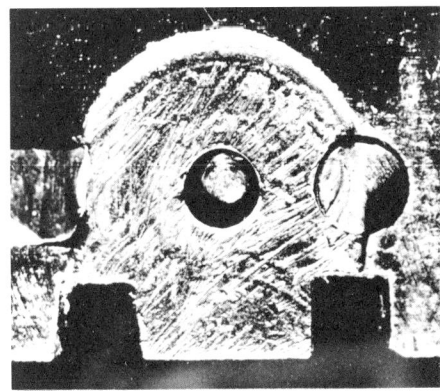
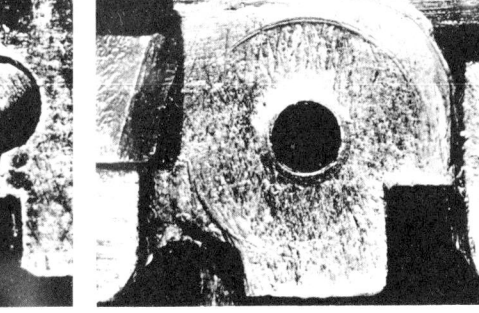
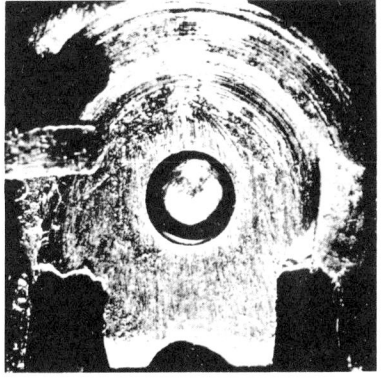

6.35 mm. O.W.A.   .32 cal. Remington   6.35 mm. Ruby (G.C.)

Plate 3.   Examples of Extractor Basic Form 1 as used on various guns

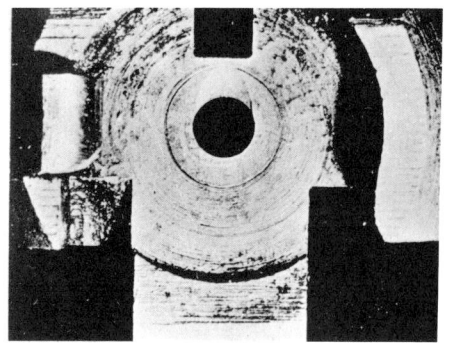

7.65 mm. Sauer—Behorden Mod.

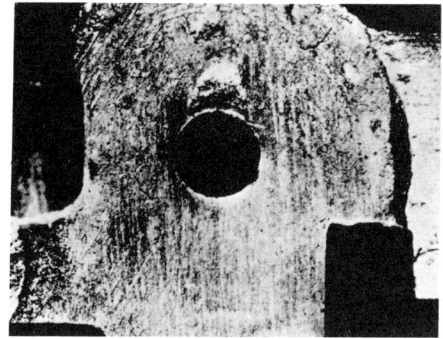

6.35 mm. Sauer—1913 Mod.

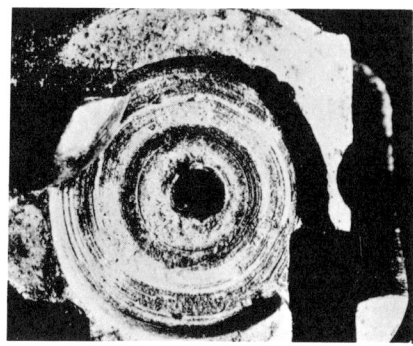

.32 cal. Savage—1917 Mod.

.32 cal. Smith & Wesson

7.65 mm. Stenda

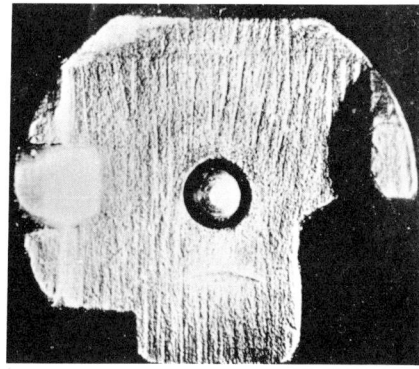

7.65 mm. Steyer

6.35 mm. Titanic

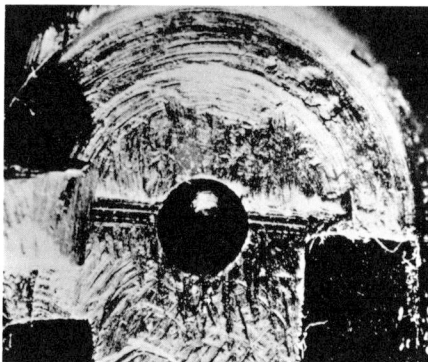

6.35 mm. Tiwa

6.35 mm. Unceta Fortuna

Plate 4. Examples of Extractor Basic Form 1 as used on various guns

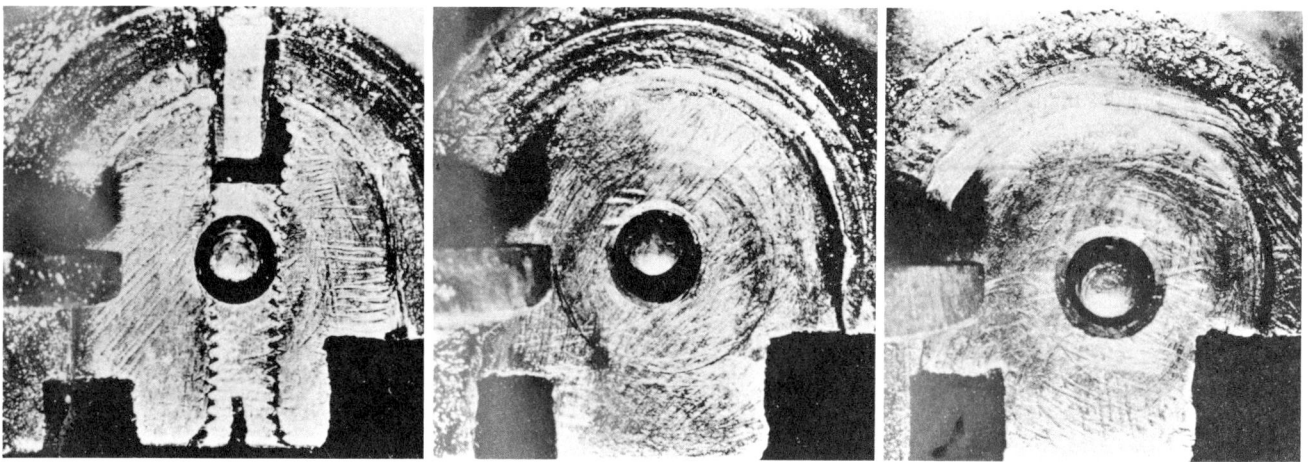

6.35 mm. Walther Mod. 2   6.35 mm. Walther Mod. 5   6.35 mm. Walther Mod. 7

6.35 mm. Walther Mod. 8   7.65 mm. Walther Mod. P.P.   6.35 mm. Walther Mod. P.P.

Plate 5. Examples of Extractor Basic Form 2 as used on various guns

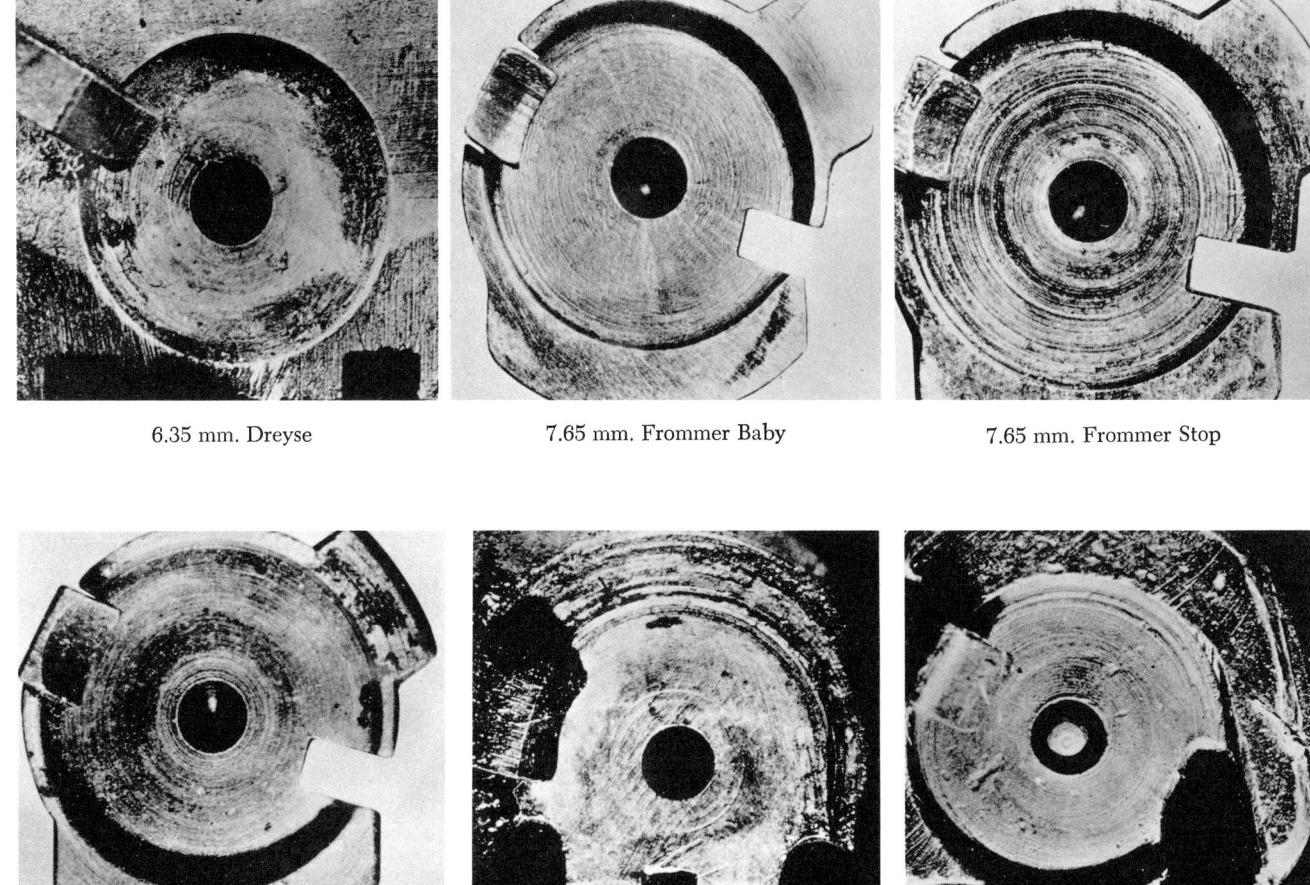

6.35 mm. Dreyse   7.65 mm. Frommer Baby   7.65 mm. Frommer Stop

9 mm. Frommer Stop   7.65 mm. Mauser Mod 1914   7.65 mm. Rheinmetall

Plate 6. Examples of Extractor Basic Form 3 as used on various guns

7.65 mm. Beretta Mod. 1915

.32 cal. Harrington & Richardson

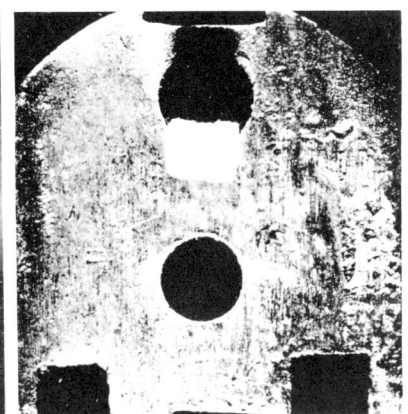

6.35 mm. Mikros

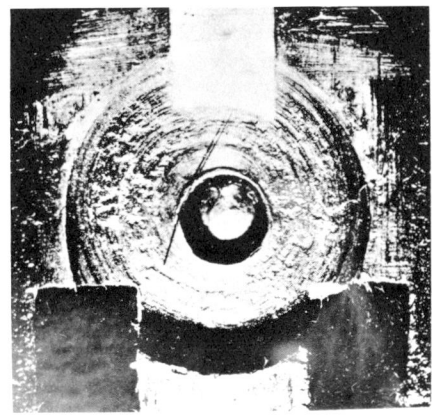

6.35 mm. Star

6.35 mm. Walther Mod. 9

.25 cal. Webley & Scott

Plate 7. Examples of various Basic Forms of Extractors on various guns

Basic Form 4
6.35 mm. Mauser Mod. W.T.P.

Basic Form 5
6.35 mm. Delu

Basic Form 6
.25 cal. Harrington & Richardson

Basic Form 7
6.35 mm. Steyr

Basic Form 8
7.65 mm. Walther Mod. 3

Basic Form 8
7.65 mm. Walther Mod. 4

Rifling specifications

The following tables of rifling specifications are by no means complete, but they do cover a very large number of rifled arms that the firearms examiner is likely to encounter. While this book is devoted mainly to hand guns it was thought desirable to include rifling specifications for many rifles as well, since they are frequently used in the commission of crimes.

As pointed out in the text, it must be remembered that specifications represent an ideal rather than an actual accomplishment. In a few cases it appears that they represent "window dressing" rather than performance. A good many manufacturers, however, do make a serious attempt to follow their specifications, but (and this was particularly true in the past)

tools do wear and the resulting rifling naturally shows the effects. With the advent of the newer methods now being used by an ever increasing number of manufacturers, it may reasonably be hoped that specifications will be followed more closely because of the much greater hardness of the rifling tools. Whether specifications are actually met or not, at least there should be more uniformity in the product because of the decrease in wear on the rifling tools. If specifications are not met, it will be largely because the broaches or the button swages as originally formed did not meet the prescribed specifications rather than being due to changes while they are in use, but eventually they too will wear away.

TABLE A–1

Astra-Unceta y Cia., S.A., Guernica, Spain

Automatic pistols (received March 1958)

Caliber	Dir. of twist	No. of grooves	Inches per turn	Bore diam., in.	Groove diam., in.	Land width, in.	Groove width, in.	Rifling Method
.22	Left	6	9.48	.212	.219	.059	.055	Button
.25 (6.35 mm.)	Left	6	9.48	.244	.251	.049	.083	Button
.32 (7.65 mm.)	Right	6	9.48	.302	.310	.083	.079	Button
.380 (9 mm.)	Right	6	9.48	.350	.359	.112	.075	Button
9 mm. Parabellum	Right	6	9.48	.348	.357	.069	.118	Button

TABLE A–2
Pietro Beretta, Gardone V.T. (Brescia), Italy
Automatic Pistols

Caliber (or Ctge.)	Model	No. of grooves	Dir. of twist	Inches per turn	Groove width, in.	Groove diam., in.
.22 Short R.F.	Mod. 950 (Minx M-4 and Minx M-2)	6	Right	13.78	.084-.088	.219-.220
.22 L.R., R.F.	Mod. 949 (Olimpionica)	6	Right	13.78	.084-.090	.219-.221
.22 L.R., R.F.	Mod. 948 (Plinker)	6	Right	13.78	.084-.092	.219-.221
.25 ACP (6.35 mm.)	Mod. 418 (Panther) and Mod. 950 (Jetfire)	6	Right	10.0	.088-.093	.251-.253
.32 ACP (7.65 mm.)	Mod. 935 (Puma)	6	Right	9.85	.108-.116	.309-.311
9 mm. Par.	Mod. 51 (Canne F.A.E.)	6	Right	9.84	.130-.140	.355-.357
9 mm. Par.	Mod. 51 (Also called 951 and 1951 Brigadier)	6	Right	9.84	.131-.139	.355-.357
.380 ACP (9 mm.)	Mod. 934 (Cougar)	6	Right	9.84	.131-.136	.357-.359

TABLE A–3
Colt's Pt. F.A. Manufacturing Co., Hartford, Conn.
(Dated as of 11/20/45)

Model name	Caliber	Bore diam. Min., in.	Bore diam. Max., in.	Groove diam. Min., in.	Groove diam. Max., in.	Groove depth, in.	Groove width, in.*	Land width, in.*	Inches per turn Before 4/23/53	Inches per turn After 4/23/53
Automatics										
Sport Woodsman	.22 L.R.	.214	.215	.221	.222	.0035	.073	.038	14	14
Target Woodsman	"	"	"	"	"	"	"	"	"	"
Match Target Woodsman	"	"	"	"	"	"	"	"	"	"
Challenger	"	"	"	"	"	"	"	"	"	"
Gov. Model Automatic Pistol	.45 ACP	.442	.444	.449	.451	.0035	.158	.071	16	16
National Match Automatic Pistol	"	"	"	"	"	"	"	"	"	"
Eley Colt Automatic	.455	.450	.451	.457	.458	"	"	.074	"	"
Ace Automatic Pistol	.22 L.R.	.214	.215	.221	.222	"	.073	.038	"	"
Super .38 Automatic	.38 Super	.346	.347	.353	.354	"	.122	.057	"	"
Super Match .38 Automatic	"	"	"	"	"	"	"	"	"	"
Conversion Unit	.22 L.R.	.214	.215	.221	.222	"	.073	.038	12	12
Lightweight Automatic Pistol	.45 ACP	.442	.444	.449	.451	"	.158	.071	16	16
"	.38 Super	.346	.347	.353	.354	"	.122	.057	"	"
"	9 mm. Par.	.348	.349	.355	.356	"	.125	.057	"	"
Colt Automatic	.32	.304	.305	.311	.312	"	.108	.049	"	"
"	.380	.348	.349	.355	.356	"	.123	.058	"	"
"	.38	"	"	"	"	"	"	"	"	"
"	.25	.243	.244	.250	.251	"	.008	.038	"	"
Revolvers										
Official Police	.38 Spec.	.346	.347	.353	.354	.0035	.122	.057	16	14
" "	.22 L.R.	.214	.215	.221	.222	"	.073	.038	"	"
Colt Border Patrol	.38 Spec.	.346	.347	.353	.354	"	.122	.057	"	"
Colt Army Special	.32-20	.304	.305	.311	.312	"	.108	.049	"	"
" " "	.38-40	.394	.395	.401	.402	"	.144	.059	"	"
" " "	.41	"	"	"	"	"	"	"	"	"

(Continued)

TABLE A–3 (Continued)

Model name	Caliber	Bore diam. Min., in.	Bore diam. Max., in.	Groove diam. Min., in.	Groove diam. Max., in.	Groove depth, in.	Groove width, in.*	Land width, in.*	Inches per turn Before 4/23/53	Inches per turn After 4/23/53
Officers Model Match	.38 Spec.	.346	.347	.353	.354	.0035	.122	.057	16	14
" " "	.22 L.R.	.214	.215	.221	.222	"	.073	.038	"	"
Officers Model Target }	.22 and	"	"	"	"	"	"	"	"	"
Officers Model Special }	.38	.346	.347	.353	.354	"	.122	.057	"	"
Colt .357	.357 Mag.	"	"	"	"	"	"	"	"	"
Colt Trooper	.38 Spec.	"	"	"	"	"	"	"	"	"
"	.22 L.R.	.214	.215	.221	.222	"	.073	.038	"	"
Police Positive Special	.32 N.P.	.304	.305	.311	.312	"	.108	.049	"	"
" " "	.38 N.P.	.346	.347	.353	.354	"	.122	.057	"	"
" " "	.38 Spec.	"	"	"	"	"	"	"	"	"
" " "	.32-20	.304	.305	.311	.312	"	.108	.049	"	"
Cobra	.32 N.P.	.304	.305	.311	.312	.0035	.108	.049	16	14
"	.38 N.P.	.346	.347	.353	.354	"	.122	.057	"	"
"	.38 Spec.	"	"	"	"	"	"	"	"	"
Detective Special	.32 N.P.	.304	.305	.311	.312	"	.108	.049	"	"
" "	.38 N.P.	.346	.347	.353	.354	"	.122	.057	"	"
" "	.38 Spec.	"	"	"	"	"	"	"	"	"
Aircrewman	.38 Spec.	"	"	"	"	"	"	"	"	"
Colt Courier	.22 L.R.	.214	.215	.221	.222	"	.073	.038	10	10
" "	"	"	"	"	"	"	"	"	12	12
" "	.32 N.P.	.304	.305	.311	.312	"	.108	.049	14	14
Camp Perry Model	.22 L.R.	.214	.215	.221	.222	"	.073	.038	16	16
Police Positive Target	.22 L.R.	"	"	"	"	"	"	"	"	"
Police Positive Target	.32	.304	.305	.311	.312	"	.108	.049	"	"
Pocket Positive	.32	"	"	"	"	"	"	"	"	"
Police Positive	.32	"	"	"	"	"	"	"	"	"
Police Positive	.38	.346	.347	.353	.354	"	.122	.057	"	"
Single Action Army	.32-20	.304	.305	.311	.312	"	.108	.049	"	"
" " "	.38-.40	.394	.395	.401	.402	"	.144	.059	"	"
" " "	.40	"	"	"	"	"	"	"	"	"
" " "	.45	.444	.445	.451	.452	"	.158	.071	"	"
New Service Target	.38 Spec.	.346	.347	.353	.354	"	.122	.057	"	"
" " "	.44 and .44-.40	.419	.420	.426	.427	"	.152	.066	"	"
" " "	.45	.444	.445	.451	.452	"	.158	.071	"	"
" " "	.455	"	"	"	"	"	"	"	"	"
New Service	.38-.40	.394	.395	.401	.402	"	.144	.059	"	"
" "	.44 and .44-.40	.419	.420	.426	.427	"	.152	.066	"	"
" " †	.45	.444	.445	.451	.452	"	.158	.071	"	"

*Measurements for groove and land widths are with accuracy of ±.002 inch.

†Replacement order barrels are broached (a) .442-.444, (b) .449-.451 as of March 1949.

TABLE A–4

Hammerli A/G, Lenzburg, Switzerland

Model	Caliber and cartridge	No. of grooves	Dir. of twist	Inches per turn	Bore diam., in.	Groove diam., in.	Groove width, in.	Remarks
MP 33 Match	.22 cal. Ex. Long	6	R	17.72	.212-.2132	.222-.2232	.087	S.S. pistol, Obsolete
45, KK-SD, KB-44	.22 cal. Ex. Long	6	R	17.72	.212-.2132	.222-.2232	.087	S.S. rifles, Obsolete
101 and 102 Match	.22 L.R.	6	R	17.72	.216-.2168	.222-.2232	.079	S.S. pistol
200 and 203 Olympia	.22 Short	6	R	17.72	.213-.215	.222-.224	.065	Hammerli-Walther Semi-auto-pistol
200 and 203 Olympia, 204 and 205 American	.22 L.R.	6	R	17.72	.216-.2168	.222-.2232	.079	Same as above
503 and 504 Match, 507 Flobert	.22 L.R.	6	R	17.72	.216-.2168	.222-.2232	.079	Bolt action S.S. rifles

All models use rim fire cartridges.

TABLE A-5
High Standard Manufacturing Corporation, Hamden, Conn.

Model	Caliber and cartridge	No. of grooves	Dir. of twist	Inches per turn	Bore diam., in.	Groove diam., in.	Groove width, in.
H-D Military	.22 L.R.	6	R	14	0.212	0.217	0.031
Duramatic and Higgins M80	.22 L.R.	6	R	16	.2165-.2175	.2225-.2230	.055-.062
Field King, Sport King, and Supermatic	.22 L.R.	6	R	16	.2165-.2175	.222-.2225	.055-.062
Flite King LW and Olympic O	.22 Short	6	L*	24	.2165-.2175	.222-.2225	.055-.062
Olympic Citation 102 and Flite King 102	.22 Short	6	L*	24	.2165-.2175	.222-.223	.055-.062
Supermatic, Citation, and Trophy	.22 L.R.	6	R	16	.2165-.2175	.222-.223	.055-.062
Sentinel Revolver and "J. C. Higgins" M80 Rev.	.22 L.R.	6	R	16	.218-.219	.2245-.2250	.055-.062
W-101 Double-Nine Revolver	.22 L.R.	6	R	16	.219-.220	.2245-.225	.055-.062
"J. C. Higgins" Bolt Action Rifle-M52	.222 Rem.	6	R	16	.218-.219	.2245-.2250	.055-.062
"J. C. Higgins" Rifles M30, M30-A, M31, M33, M29	.22 L.R.	6	R	16	.2165-.2175	.222-.2225	.055-.062

*Since ca. August 1958 all rifling is currently done by the button swage process.

TABLE A-6
Iver Johnson's Arms & Cycle Works, Fitchburg, Mass.
Revolver and rifles

Caliber	Rifling Pitch 1 right turn in	Land width, in.	Groove width, in.	Groove diam., in.	Bore diam., in.	No. of grooves
Rev. .22	15.75 Inches	.0675	.069	.225	.217	5
" .32	23.33 "	.0955	.095	.312	.303	5
" .38	23.33 "	.1148	.105	.360	.350	5
Rifle .22	20 "	.0427	.072	.224	.219	6

Models manufactured
.22 Regular 7-Shot; Sealed 8 Model 8-Shot; .32 & .38 5-Shot; .32 Special 6-Shot

Models	Calibers—Rim & Center Fire
I. J. Safety Hammer Auto. Revolver	.22 Cal. R.F. & .32 & .38 Cal. C.F.
I. J. Supershot 9- or 7-Shot	.22 Cal. only R.F.
I. J. Supershot Sealed Eight—8-shot	.22 Cal. only R.F.
I. J. Protector Sealed Eight—8-shot	.22 Cal. only R.F. 2½″
I. J. Champion Single Action—8-shot	.22 Cal. only R.F.
I. J. Trigger Cocking—8-shot	.22 Cal. only R.F.
I. J. Safety Hammerless Auto. Revolver	.22 Cal. R.F. & .32 & .38 Cal. C.F.
I. J. Special Hammer Auto. Revolver	.32 Cal. C.F. only 6-shot
I. J. Special Hammerless Auto. Revolver	.32 Cal. C.F. only 6-shot
I. J. Model 1900 Double Action	.22 & .32 R.F. & .32 & .38 Cal. C.F.
I. J. Target—9-shot	.22 Cal. only R.F.
I. J. Target Sealed 8—8-shot	.22 Cal. only R.F.
U. S. Hammer Auto	.22 Cal. R.F. & .32 & .38 Cal. C.F.
U. S. Hammerless Auto.	.32 & .38 Cal. C.F.
U. S. Double Action	.22 & .32 Cal. R.F. & .32 & .38 Cal. C.F.
I. J. Bolt Action Safety Rifle Mdl. X	.22 Cal. R.F. only
I. J. Bolt Action Safety Rifle Mdl. 2-X	.22 Cal. R.F. only
I. J. Bolt Action Safety Rifle Mdl. 2-XA	.22 Cal. R.F. only

*This model discontinued.

Note: The specifications given above were adopted in 1903 and were used up to 1955, at which time all production of rifles ceased. New models of .22 cal. revolvers No. 55 and 55S were introduced in 1955, No. 57 in 1956 and No. 66 ("Trailsman" — with chrome-lined barrel) in 1958. All production of other revolvers ceased with the introduction of these new models, and no revolvers of larger caliber are now (1958) being made, although they are planned for some time in the future.

Present rifling specifications are: 6 lands and grooves, right hand twist; groove diameter 0.225″; land width—0.058″; one turn of rifling in 15.0″. Rifling is done by the swaging method.

TABLE A-7
Manufacture D'Armes Automatiques, Bayonne, France
Automatic pistols

Caliber	Dir. of twist	No. of grooves	Inches per turn	Bore diam., in.	Groove diam., in.
.22	Right	6	12.2	.212	.2201
6.35 mm.	Right	6	12.2	.2492	.2516
7.65 mm.	Right	6	12.2	.3012	.3114
9 mm.	Right	6	12.2	.348	.3551

Data given above are from official factory records of 1954. Widths of lands and grooves were not given.

TABLE A-8
Manufacture D'Armes des Pyrénées Francaises, Hendaye, France
Automatic pistols and rifle

Caliber	Dir. of twist	No. of grooves	Inches per turn	Bore diam., inches	Groove diam., inches	Land width, inches
.22 L.R. and Short	Right	6	12	.212	.220	.059
6.35 mm.	Right	6	12	.245	.248	.059
7.65 mm.	Left	6	12	.302	.310	.039
9 mm.	Left	6	12	.348	.355	.039
.22 cal. Rifle	Right	6	17.68	.216	.222	.059

Date of adoption of above specifications: May 5, 1958.

TABLE A-9
Marlin specifications from 1932

Model No.	Name of model	Caliber— (cartridge)	Bore diam., in.	Groove diam., in.	Groove width, in.	No. of grooves	Dir. of twist	Inches per turn	Date of specifications
39-A	Lever Action Rifle	.22 L.R.	.2185	.2225	.069	6	R	16	1932-1945
39-A	Lever Action Rifle	.22 L.R.	.215	.2215	.075	5	R	16	1945-1948
39-A	Lever Action Rifle	.22 L.R.	.2175	.2225	.069	6	R	16	1948-1953
80, 81, 88, 100	Marlin Rifles	.22 L.R.	.215	.2215	.075	5	R	16	Up to 1950
80, 81, 88, 100	Marlin Rifles	.22 L.R.	.218	.2225	.069	6	R	16	1950-1953
89	Semi Auto. Rifle	.22 L.R.	.218	.2225	.069	6	R	16	Up to 1953
56	"Levermatic" Rifle	.22 L.R.	.2195	.2225	.013-.015	16	R	16	Since May 26, 1955
39-A, 80, 81, 88, 89, 100	Marlin Rifles	.22 L.R.	.2195	.2225	.013-.015	16	R	16	From 1953 on
322	Bolt Action Rifle	.222 Remington	.2215	.2235	.014-.016	16	R	14	From 1954 on
336	Lever Action Rifle	.219 Zipper	.2215	.2235	.014-.016	16	R	14	Since May 26, 1955
36	Lever Action Rifle and Carbine	.30-30 W.C.F.	.300	.308	.0933	6	R	10	Up to 1946
36	Lever Action Rifle and Carbine	.30-30 W.C.F.	.300	.308	.177	4	R	10	1946 and 1947
336	Lever Action Rifle and Carbine	.30-30 W.C.F.	.300	.308	.177	4	R	10	From 1948 on
36	Lever Action Rifle and Carbine	.32 Winchester Spl.	.313	.318	.0983	6	R	16	Up to 1946
36	Lever Action Rifle and Carbine	.32 Winchester Spl.	.313	.318	.177	4	R	16	1946-1947

(Continued)

TABLE A-9 (Continued)

Model No.	Name of model	Caliber—(cartridge)	Bore diam., in.	Groove diam., in.	Groove width, in.	No. of grooves	Dir. of twist	Inches per turn	Date of speci-fications
336	Lever Action Rifle and Carbine	.32 Winchester Spl.	.313	.318	.177	4	R	16	From 1948 on
336	Lever Action Rifle and Carbine	.35 Remington	.349	.359	.110	7	R	16	From 1950 on
57M	Lever Action Rifle	.22 Winchester Magnum	.2215	.224	.022	20	R	16	
455	Bolt Action Rifle	.30 Govt. M 1906	.3045-.305	.308	.024	22	R	10	

TABLE A-10
Marlin Firearms Company, New Haven, Conn.

Model No.	Caliber	Bore diam., in. ±.0005	Groove depth, in.	Groove width, in.	Land width, in.	No. of grooves	Inches per turn	Dir. of twist
18	.22	.217	.0015	.0691	.0445	6	16	Right
20	.22	.217	.0015	.0691	.0445	6	16	"
25	.22- short & caps only	.217	.0015	.0691	.0672	5	20	"
37	.22	.217	.0015	.0691	.0445	6	16	"
38	.22	.217	.0015	.0691	.0445	6	16	"
39	.22	.217	.0015	.0691	.0445	6	16	"
92	.22	.217	.0015	.0691	.0445	6	16	"
97	.22	.217	.0015	.0691	.0445	6	16	"
27	.25/20	.250	.0020	.0785	.0520	6	12	"
94	.25/20	.250	.0020	.0785	.0520	6	12	"
93	.25/36	.250	.0020	.0785	.0520	6	9	"
93	.30/30	.301	.0020	.0933	.0643	6	10	"
93 CS	.30/30	.301	.0020	.0933	.0643	6	10	"
92	.32 R & C	.302	.0025	.0949	.0632	6	22	"
93	.32 Special	.313	.0025	.0983	.0656	6	16	"
93 CS	.32 Special	.313	.0025	.0983	.0656	6	16	"
27	.32/20	.305	.0025	.0958	.0639	6	22	"
94	.32/20	.305	.0025	.0958	.0639	6	22	"
93	.32/40	.313	.0025	.0983	.0656	6	16	"
94	.38/40	.395	.0025	.1240	.0827	6	36	"
93	.38/55	.370	.0025	.1162	.0775	6	20	"
95	.38/56	.370	.0025	.1162	.0775	6	20	"
95	.40/65-70, 82	.397	.0025	.1247	.0831	6	20	"
94	.44/40	.418	.0025	.1313	.0875	6	36	"
95	.45/70-85, 90	.449	.0025	.1410	.0940	6	20	"
50	.22 Automatic	.216	.0023	.0691	.0439	6	16	"
80	.22	.216	.0023	.0691	.0439	6	16	"
*80	.22	.216	.0023	.0691	.0666	5	16	"
A1	.22	.216	.0023	.0691	.0439	6	16	"
*A1	.22	.216	.0023	.0691	.0666	5	16	"
100	.22	.216	.0023	.0691	.0439	6	16	"
*100	.22	.216	.0023	.0691	.0666	5	16	"

*Rifling changed to 5 grooves August 6, 1937.

TABLE A-11
Remington Arms Co., Inc., Ilion, N. Y.

Model	Caliber	Bore diam., in.	Groove diam., in.	No. of grooves	Groove width, in.	Inches per turn	Dir. of twist	Magazine capacity
4, 6	.22 S., L., and L.R.	.217	.222	5	.085	16	R	Single shot
4	.25 Stevens	.250	.256	5	.095	16	"	" "
4, 6	.32 S. and L.	.304	.311	5	.115	20	"	" "
8	.25 Rem., Auto.	.250	.256	6	.095	10	"	5
8	.30 Rem., Auto.	.300	.306	7	.105	12	"	5
8	.32 Rem., Auto.	.312	.319	7	.110	14	"	5
8	.35 Rem., Auto.	.349	.357	7	.115	16	"	5
12A	.22 S., L., and L.R.	.217	.222	5	.085	16	"	15, 12, and 10
12A	.22 Short	.217	.222	5	.085	24	"	15
12B	.22 Short	.217	.222	6	.085	24	"	16
12C	.22 S., L., and L.R.	.217	.222	6	.085	16	"	16, 12, and 11
12CS	.22 Rem. Spl. or W.R.F.	.220	.226	6	.085	16	"	9
14A, 14R	.25 Rem.	.250	.256	6	.095	10	"	5
14A, 14R	.30 Rem.	.300	.306	7	.105	12	"	5
14A, 14R	.32 Rem.	.312	.319	7	.110	14	"	5
14A, 14R	.35 Rem.	.349	.357	7	.115	16	"	5
14 1/2A, 14 1/2R	.38 Rem.	.392	.398	6	.170	36	"	Full-11, Half-9
14 1/2A, 14 1/2R	.44 Rem.	.418	.424	6	.170	20	"	Full-11, Half-9
16	.22 Rem., Auto.	.220	.226	6	.085	16	"	15
24	.22 Short	.213	.218	5	.070	24	"	15
24	.22 L.R.-O.S., Auto.	.213	.218	5	.085	16	"	10
24	.22 L.R.-N.S., Auto.	.217	.222	5	.085	16	"	10
25A, 25R	.25-20	.250	.256	6	.095	14	"	25A-10; 25R-6
25A, 25R	.32 W.C.F.	.3035	.310	6	.105	20	"	25A-10; 25R-6
30A, 30S	.25 Rem.	.250	.256	6	.095	10	"	5
30S	.257 Rem. Roberts	.250	.256	6	.095	10	"	5
30A	.30 Rem.	.300	.306	7	.105	12	"	5
30A	.32 Rem.	.312	.319	7	.110	14	"	5
30A	.35 Rem.	.349	.357	7	.115	16	"	5
30A, 30S	.30-06	.300	.3075	4	.175	10	"	5
30A, 30S	7 m/m	.276	.283	6	.105	9	"	5
33	.22 S., L., and L.R.	.217	.221	5	.085	16	"	Single shot
34	.22 S., L., and L.R.	.217	.222	5	.085	16	"	22, 17, 15
37	.22 L.R.	.217	.219	6	.088	16	"	5
40	.30-06	.300	.3075	4	.175	10	"	5
40	7 m/m	.276	.283	6	.105	9	"	5
41	.22 Short	.217	.221	4	.085	24	"	Single shot
41	.22 S., L., and L.R.	.217	.221	4	.085	16	"	Single shot
41	.22 Rem. Spl.	.220	.226	6	.085	16	"	Single shot
51	.32	.3035	.310	7	.105	16	"	8
51	.380	.348	.354	7	.115	16	"	7
81	.25 Rem. Auto	.250	.256	6	.095	10	"	5
81	.30 Rem., Auto.	.300	.306	6	.115	10	"	5
81	.32 Rem., Auto.	.312	.319	6	.120	14	"	5
81	.35 Rem., Auto.	.349	.357	6	.125	16	"	5
95	.41 Short R.F.	.393	.400	5	.170	10	L.	Two shot
121	.22 Short	.217	.222	5	.085	24	R.	20
121	.22 S., L., and L.R.	.217	.222	5	.085	16	"	20, 15, and 14
121	.22 Rem. Spl. or W.R.F.	.220	.226	6	.085	16	"	12
141	.30 Rem.	.300	.306	6	.115	10	"	5
141	.32 Rem.	.312	.319	6	.120	14	"	5
141	.35 Rem.	.349	.357	6	.125	16	"	5
241-SA	.22 Short, Auto.	.213	.218	5	.070	24	"	15
241-LA	.22 L.R., Auto.	.217	.222	5	.085	16	"	10
341	.22 S., L., and L.R.	.217	.222	5	.085	16	"	22, 17, and 15
81	.300 Savage	.300	.3075	4	.175	10	"	5

(Continued)

TABLE A–11 (Continued)

Model	Caliber	Bore diam., in.	Groove diam., in.	No. of grooves	Groove width, in.	Inches per turn	Dir. of twist	Magazine capacity
411	.22 C. B. Cap	.217	.221	4	.085	16	R	Single shot
510, 510P	.22 S., L., and L.R.	.217	.222	4	.085	16	"	Single shot
511, 511P	.22 S., L., and L.R.	.217	.222	4	.085	16	"	6
512, 512P	.22 S., L., and L.R.	.217	.222	4	.085	16	"	22, 17, and 15
513S, 513SP	.22 S., L., and L.R.	.217	.221	6	.088	16	"	6
513-T	.22 L.R.	.217	.221	6	.088	16	"	6
550, 550P	.22 S., L., and L.R. Auto.	.217	.222	5	.085	16	"	22, 17, and 15
550-1	.22 S., L., and L.R.	.217	.2195	6	.084	16	"	
550-2G	.22 Short	.217	.2195	6	.084	16	"	
521-T	.22 L.R.	.217	.222	4	.085	16	"	6 shots (1949 tables)
521-T	.22 S., L., and L.R.	.217	.2195	6	.084	16	"	(1958 tables)
514	.22 S., L., and L.R.	.216	.2195	6	.080	16	"	Single shot
552	.22 S., L., and L.R.	.2175	.220	6	.084	16	"	
552-GS	.22 Short	.2175	.220	6	.084	16	"	
572	.22 S., L., and L.R.	.2175	.220	6	.084	16	"	
40X-S1	.22 L.R.	.218	.222	6	.087	16	"	
40X-H1	.22 L.R.	.218	.222	6	.087	16	"	
721	.30-06 Springfield	.300	.308	6	.115	10	"	4
721	.300 H. & H.	.300	.308	6	.115	10	"	3
721	.270 Winchester	.270	.277	6	.105	10	"	4
721	.300 Magnum	.300	.308	6	.115	10	"	3
720R	.257 Rem. Roberts	.250	.256	4	.140	10	"	5
720R	.270 Winchester	.270	.277	4	.160	10	"	5
720R	.30-06 Springfield	.300	.3075	4	.1797	10	"	5
720A	.257 Rem. Roberts	.250	.256	4	.140	10	"	5
720A	.270 Winchester	.270	.277	4	.160	10	"	5
720A	.30-06 Springfield	.300	.3075	4	.1797	10	"	5
720S	.257 Rem. Roberts	.250	.256	4	.140	10	"	5
720S	.270 Winchester	.270	.277	4	.160	10	"	5
720S	.30-06 Springfield	.300	.3075	4	.1797	10	"	5
722	.257 Roberts	.250	.256	6	.095	10	"	4
722	.22 Rem.	.219	.224	6	.080	14	"	5
722	.308 Winchester	.300	.308	6	.115	10	"	4
722	.244 Rem.	.237	.2435	6	.090	12	"	4
722	.222 Rem. Magnum	.219	.224	6	.080	14	"	5
725	.30-06	.300	.308	6	.115	10	"	4
725	.270 Winchester	.270	.277	6	.105	10	"	4
725	.280 Rem.	.277	.283	4	.160	10.5	"	4
725	.244 Rem.	.237	.2435	6	.090	12	"	4
725	.222 Rem.	.219	.224	6	.080	14	"	5
740	.30-06	.300	.308	6	.115	10	"	4
740	.308 Winchester	.300	.308	6	.115	10	"	4
740	.280 Rem.	.277	.283	4	.160	10.5	"	4
740	.244 Rem.	.237	.2435	6	.090	12	"	4
760	.30-06	.300	.308	6	.115	10	"	4
760	.308 Winchester	.300	.308	6	.115	10	"	4
760	.35 Rem.	.349	.357	6	.130	16	"	4
760	.270 Winchester	.270	.277	6	.105	10	"	4
760	.222 Rem.	.219	.224	6	.080	14	"	5
760	.244 Rem.	.237	.2435	6	.090	12	"	4
760	.280 Rem.	.277	.283	4	.160	10.5	"	4
51	.32 Rem. Auto. Pistol	.3045	.311	7	.105	16	"	8
51	.380 Rem. Auto. Pistol	.349	.355	7	.115	16	"	7

TABLE A–12
Savage Arms Corporation, Chicopee Falls, Mass.
Rifles

Model	Cartridge	Land diam., in.	Groove diam., in.	Groove width, in.	Inches per turn
3, 4, and 5 Savage Bolt Action	.22 Long Rifle	.2175-.2185	.223-.225	.090	16
6 Savage Automatic Rifle	Same	Same	Same	Same	Same
23-AA	.22 S., L., and L.R.	.217-.218	.223-.224	.090	16
29 Savage Slide Action	.22 S., L., and L.R.	.217-.218	.221-.225	.090	16
99 Savage Lever Action	.22 Savage H.P.	.221-.223	.227-.228	.068	12
322 Stevens Bolt Action	.22 Hornet	.217-.218	.223-.225	.087	16
23-D Savage Bolt Action	.22 Hornet	.217-.218	.223-.224	.090	16
342 Savage Bolt Action	Same	Same	Same	Same	Same
101 Savage S.S. Pistol	.22 Long Rifle	.217	.227	.085-.093	
24 Savage Combination Gun- .22 and .410 gauge	.22 Long Rifle	.217-.218	.223-.225	.087	16
24 Savage Combination Gun- .22 and .410 gauge	.22 Winchester R.F. Magnum	.219-.220	.224-.225	.087	16
340 Savage Bolt Action	.222 Remington	.2185-.220	.223-.225	.087	14
15 and 15-Y Stevens Bolt Action S.S. Rifle	.22 Long Rifle	.217-.218	.223-.2245	.059	16
84 and 86 Stevens Bolt Action Repeating Rifle	.22 Long Rifle	.217-.218	.223-.225	.087	16
85K, 87 and 87K Stevens Auto. Rifles and Carbines	.22 Long Rifle	.217-.218	.223-.225	.087	16
99 Savage Lever Action	.243 Winchester	.237-.238	.243-.2445	.090	10
99 Savage Lever Action	.250-3000 Savage	.250-.252	.257-.2585	.088	14
40 and 45 Savage Bolt Action	Same	Same	Same	Same	Same
23-B Savage Bolt Action	.25-20 W.C.F.	.250	.256	.088	14
110 Savage Bolt Action	.270 Winchester	.270-.2715	.277-.2785	.086	10
40 and 45 Savage Bolt Action	.30 Govt. M-06	.300-.302	.308-.3095	.100	12
110 Savage Bolt Action	.30 Govt. M-06	.300-.3015	.308-.3095	.100	10
325 Stevens Bolt Action	.30-30 W.C.F.	.299-.301	.308-.3095	.100*	12
340 Savage Bolt Action	Same	Same	Same	Same	Same
219 Savage S.S. Rifle	.30-30 W.C.F.	.300-.302	.308-.3095	.100	12
40 and 45 Savage Bolt Action	.300 Savage	.300-.302	.308-.3095	.100	12
99 Savage Lever Action	.303 Savage	.300-.302	.308-.3095	.100	12
99 Savage Lever Action	.308 Winchester	.300-.302	.308-.3095	.100	12
23-C Savage Bolt Action	.32-20 Winchester	.3045	.3105	.115	20
99 Savage Lever Action	.358 Winchester	.350-.3518	.358-.3595	.110	12
Automatic pistols					
1907, 1915 and 1917	.32 ACP	.3045	.3105	.115	12**
1915, 1917	.380 ACP	.349	.355	.125	12†

Note: All rifles and pistols have right hand twist. Mods. 19, 23-AA, 23-D and 29 have 4 grooves, all other have 6.
*Mods. 325, 325A, 325B were 0.116″, and Mod. 325C was 0.116″ but changed to 0.110″.
**Very early specimens have 1 turn in 16″, later changed to 12″.
†Late specimens had 1 turn in 16″, whereas early specimens had 1 turn in 12″.

TABLE A–13
Schweizerische Industrie Gesellschaft, Neuhausen, Switzerland
Mod. P 210 automatic pistols

Caliber	Dir. of twist	No. of grooves	Inches per turn	Bore diam., inches	Groove diam., inches	Groove width, inches
.22 L.R.	Right	6	17.72	.2138-.2158	.220-.222	.067-.078
7.65 mm. Parabellum	Right	4	9.84	.301-.3026	.309-.311	.118-.130
9 mm. Parabellum	Right	6	9.84	.3468-.3488	.356-.358	.102-.114

Barrels rifled by the scrape cutter process.

TABLE A-14
J. Stevens Arms Company, Chicopee Falls, Mass.
(Now owned and operated by Savage Arms Corporation)
Stevens rifles as of 1932*

Caliber	Dir. of twist	No. of grooves	Inches per turn	Bore diam., inches	Groove diam., inches	Land width, inches	Groove width, inches
.22	Right	6	25 (Short) 16 (L. & L.R.)	.2175 +.0005 −.0000	.224 +.0000 −.0005	.0102	.100
.25	Right	6	17	.2495 +.0005 −.0000	.256 +.0000 −.0005	.0116	.115
.32 S. and L. R.F. and C.F.	Right	6	25	.2985 +.0005 −.0000	.309 +.0000 −.0005	.0219	.130

*Specifications furnished in 1932 "show practice we have followed for many years and we have no earlier specifications." In 1936 Stevens Arms Co. (previously a subsidiary) became a Division of Savage Arms Corporation and soon thereafter the following change in specifications for the .22 was noted: Land width .032″ (instead of .0102″); Groove width .086″ (instead of .100″). All other dimensions unchanged.

TABLE A-15
Sturm, Ruger and Company, Inc., Southport, Conn.
Revolvers and automatics

Model and caliber	Dir. twist	No. of grooves	Inches per turn	Bore diam., inches	Groove diam., inches	Groove width, inches
.22 Single Six Revolver, Prior to Dec. 1959	Right	6	14	.215 +.002 −.000	.221 +.002 −.001	.065
After Dec. 1959	Right	6	14	.219	.224−.225	.065−.075
.357 Magnum Revolver, Prior to Jan. 1960	Right	6	16	.3475±.001	.357±.001	.116
After Jan. 1960	Right	8	16	.350−.3515	.357−.3585	.075−.080
.44 Magnum Revolver	Right	6	20	.417±.001	.430±.001	.125
.22 Standard automatic	Right	6	14	.215 +.002 −.000	.221 +.002 −.001	.065

TABLE A-16
Webley and Scott, Ltd., Birmingham, England
Revolvers and automatic pistols

Model	Cal.	Cartridge	No. and dir. of twist	Inches per turn	Bore diam., in.	Groove diam., in.	Land width, in.	Groove width, in.
All .22 pistols and revolvers	.22	.22 R.F.	7-R	15	.216-.218	.222-.228	.0299	.070
W.P. Hammer and W.P. Hammerless, D.A. Rev.	.32	.320 C.F.	7-R	15	.301-.303	.309-.315	.0351	.100
Mark IV and Mark IV Pocket Rev., D.A.	.32	.32 S & W Long	7-R	15	.301-.303	.309-.313	.036	.100
No. 5 D.A. Rev.	.38	.360 No. 5	7-R	15	.355-.357	.363-.369	.0343	.125
Mark IV and Mark IV Pocket Rev., D.A.	.38	.38 S & W	7-R	15	.350-.352	.358-.362	.032	.125
Mark I and Mark III D.A. Rev.	.38	.38 S & W	7-R	15	.350-.352	.358-.364	.032	.125
Mark III (Original Mark IV) D.A. Rev.	.38	.38 S & W	7-R	18	.350-.352	.358-.362	.032	.125
Gov't. Mark IV D.A. Rev.	.38	.38 S & W	7-R	18	.350-.352	.358-.364	.032	.125

(Continued)

TABLE A-16 (Continued)

Model	Cal.	Cartridge	No. and dir. of twist	Inches per turn	Bore diam., in.	Groove diam., in.	Land width, in.	Groove width, in
Webley-Fosbery Semiautomatic Rev.	.38	.38 ACP	7-R	15	.350-.352	.358-.364	.032	.125
.44 Russian, D.A. Rev.	.44	.44 S & W Russian	7-R	15	.417-.419	.425-.431	.0471	.140
W.G. and W.G. Target D.A. Rev.	.455	.455 Rev.	7-R	15	.445-.447	.453-.459	.0506	.150
Webley-Fosbery Semiautomatic Rev.	.455	.455 Rev.	7-R	20	.441-.443	.449-.455	.0479	.150
Mark I, II, III, IV, V, and VI D.A. Revs.	.455	.455 Rev.	7-R	20	.441-.443	.449-.455	.0429	.155
Bull Dog, 83/.455, R.I.C., Wilkinson Webley D.A. Rev.	.455	.455 Rev.	7-R	15	.447-.449	.455-.461	.0506	.150
Automatic Pistol, Hammer & Hammerless	.25	.25 ACP	6-R	10	.245-.247	.253-.259	.0283	.100
Automatic Pistol	.32	.32 ACP	6-R	10	.303-.305	.313-.319	.0286	.130
Automatic Pistol	9 mm.	9 mm. Brng. Long	6-R	15	.353-.355	.361-.367	.0498	.135
Automatic Pistol	.380	.380 ACP	6-R	20	.350-.352	.360-.366	.0384	.145
Automatic Pistol	.38	.38 ACP	6-R	10	.350-.352	.358-.364	.0382	.145
Automatic Pistol	.455	.455 SLP	6-R	10	.447-.449	.455-.461	.044	.190

Note: All revolvers and pistols rifled by hook cutter method. Data from Webley and Scott, August 1958, courtesy of H.P. White Laboratory.

TABLE A-17
Carl Walther, Ulm-Donau, Germany

Model	Cartridge	Bore diam., in.	Groove diam., in.	No. of grooves	Groove width, in.	Inches per turn
KKJ, KKM, KKS Bolt action rifles	.22 L.R.	.216-.2168	.222-.2236	8	.047-.051	15.75
KKJ-H Bolt action rifle	.22 Hornet	.217-.2186	.222-.2236	8	.041-.045	15.75
A and B Rifle, and A and B Carbine	7 x 64 mm.	.275-.277	.285	4	.108	8.66
A and B Rifle, and A and B Carbine	8 x 57- J and JR	.309-.311	.319-.3198	4	.157-.169	10.63
A and B Rifle, and A and B Carbine	8 x 57- JS	.311-.313	.322-.324	4	.157-.169	10.63
Automatic Pistol Mod. P-38	9 mm. Par.	.347-.3494	.357-.359	6	.091-.095	9.84

The following Walther Pistols are made by Mre. de Machines du Haut-Rhin (Manhurin), Mulhouse-Bourtzwiller, France, on license from Walther

Automatic Pistol Mods. PP and PPK	7.65 mm.	.301-.303	.309-.311	6	.100-.106	9.84
Automatic Pistols Mods. PP and PPK	9 mm. (.380)	.350-.357	.358-.360	6	.126-.132	9.84

Note: Barrels for A and B rifles and carbines are furnished by Hammerli, Lenzburg, Switzerland. All Walther rifles and pistols have right hand twist.

TABLE A-18
Whitney Firearms Co., North Haven, Conn.
Whitney automatic (first issued as the Wolverine).

Caliber	.22
No. of grooves and direction	6-R
Inches for 1 turn of rifling	16
Bore diameter, inches	0.2165+0.0010 − .0000
Groove diameter, inches	.2225+ .0000 − .0005
Lands and grooves equally spaced	

TABLE A-19
Winchester Repeating Arms Company, New Haven, Conn.

A. Winchester standard barrel bore and rifling dimensions—rim fire rifles under production as of Jan. 15, 1948*

Chamber	Gun model	Bore diam., in.	Rifling diam., in.	Groove width, in.	No. of grooves	Inches per turn
.22 Short	61, 62A	.219	.223	.080	4	20
.22 Short	74A, 74	.214	.219	.080	4	20
.22 Long Rifle	52 Sporting and 75	.217	.222	.085	6	16
.22 Long Rifle	52 Target, 52 Heavy, and Bull	.2170-.2175	.2223-.2229	.085	6	16
.22 Long Rifle	69A Targ. and Match	.219	.223	.080	4	16
.22 Long Rifle	61, 63, 74A	.219	.223	.080	4	16
.22 S., L., L.R.	67 Reg. and Junior†	.219	.2230-.2245	.080	4	16
.22 S., L., L.R.	47, 61, 62A, 72, and 69A Regular†	.219	.223	.080	4	16
.22 W.R.F.	61	.220	.226	.0691	6	14

*Mod. 47 not on production at this date.

†These models designed to accommodate interchangeably short, long, or long rifle cartridges.

B. Center fire rifles under production as of Jan. 15, 1948*

Chamber	Gun model	Bore diam., in.	Rifling diam., in.	Groove width, in.	No. of grooves	Inches per turn
.22 Hornet	43, 70	.217	.222	.0681	6	16
.220 Swift	70	.2190-.2195	.224	.074	6	14
.250 Savage	70	.250	.256	.0785	6	14
.257 Roberts	70	.250	.256	.095	6	10
25/35 Win.	94 Carb.	.250	.256	.0785	6	8
.270 Win.	70	.270	.277	.160	4	10
7 mm.	70	.2755	.283	.160	4	8¾
.30/30 Win.	64, 94 Carb.	.300	.308	.0942	6	12
.30/06 Sprg.	Springfield, 70	.300	.308	.176	4	10
.300 H and H Magnum	70	.300	.308	.176	4	10
.32 Win. Special	64, 94 Carb.	.315	.320	.099	6	16
.348 Win.	71	.340	.348	.120	6	12
.351 Win. S.L.	1907	.345	.351	.1083	6	16
.375 H and H Magnum	70	.366	.376	.115	6	12
.218 Bee	43	.219	.224	.074	6	16
.25/20 Win.	43	.250	.256	.0785	6	14
.32/20 Win.	43	.305	.311	.0958	6	20

*Model 43 not on production at this date.

C. Rim fire combinations in which cartridge or gun model or both have been discontinued or a change has been made in rifling dimensions since revision of June 1930

Chamber	Gun model	Bore diam., in.	Rifling diam., in.	Groove width, in.	No. of grooves	Inches per turn
.22 Short	56, 57, S.S.	.219	.224	.0665	6	24
.22 Long	90, 62	.219	.224	.0688	6	20
.22 Long Rifle	56, 57, 62, 74, 90	.217	.222	.0681	6	16
.22 S., L., L.R.	59, 60 Target†	.217	.222	.0681	6	16
.22 S., L., L.R.	06†	.217	.222	.0681	6	17
.22 S., L., L.R.	02, 58, 61, 62†	.219	.223	.080	4	16
.22 S., L., L.R.	68, 60 Reg.†	.219	.2230-.2245	.080	4	16
.22 Long Rifle	60A Target	.217	.222	.0681	6	16
.22 Long Rifle	Win. Sprg.	.218	.223	.0856	4	16
.22 W.R.F.	62, 67, 68, 90	.220	.226	.0691	6	14
.22 Auto.	03	.220	.226	.0691	6	14
.22 Short	90, 62, 72	.219	.224	.0688	6	20
.22 Long Rifle	61, 63	.217	.222	.0681	6	16
.22 Long Rifle	Springfield	.218	.223	.0854	4	16

*The 24″ twist was superseded by 20″ twist on Mar. 11, 1942.

†These models designed to accommodate interchangeably short, long, or long rifle cartridges.

(Continued)

TABLE A–19 (Continued)

D. Center fire combinations in which cartridge or gun model or both have been discontinued, or a change has been made in rifling dimensions since revision of June 1930

Chamber	Gun model	Bore diam., in.	Rifling diam., in.	Groove width, in.	No. of grooves	Inches per turn
.219 Zipper	94, 64, 55	.219	.224	.074	6	16
.22 Hornet	S.S., 54	.217	.222	.0681	6	16
.220 Swift	54	.2190-.2195	.224	.074	6	14
.250 Savage	54	.250	.256	.0785	6	14
.25-20 Win.	92, 53, 65	.250	.256	.0785	6	14
.257 Roberts	54	.250	.256	.095	6	10
.25-35 Win.	55, 64	.250	.256	.0785	6	8
218 Bee	53, 65, 92	.219	.224	.074	6	16
.270 Win.	54	.270	.277	.160	4	10
7 mm. Mauser	54	.2755	.283	.160	4	8¾
.300 Savage	70	.300	.308	.095	6	12
.30-30 Win.	55	.300	.308	.0942	6	12
.30-06 Sprg.	Sprg., 54	.300	.308	.176	4	10
.303 British	95	.303	.313	.0951	6	12
.30 Army	95	.300	.308	.0942	6	10
.308 Win.	71	.300	.308	.0942	6	12
7.65 mm. Belg.	54	.303	.3105	.176	4	10
7.65 mm. Peruv.	54	.303	.3105	.176	4	10
.32 Win.	92, 53	.305	.311	.0958	6	20
.32-20 Win.	92, 65, 53	.305	.311	.0958	6	20
.32 Win. Special	55	.315	.320	.0958	6	
9 mm. Mauser	54, 70	.350	.358	.1099	6	12
32-40 Win.	94	.315	.320	.099	6	16
32 Win. S.L.	05	.315	.320	.0989	6	16
.33 Win.	S.S., 86	.330	.338	.1036	6	12
.35 Rem.	70	.350	.358	.1099	6	16
38/55	94	.373	.379	.1171	6	18
38 Win.	92	.394	.400	.1237	6	36
38/72	95	.373	.379	.1171	6	22
40/72	95	.3995	.406	.1253	6	22
401 Win. S.L.	10	.400	.407	.1256	6	14
405 Win.	95	.405	.413	.1272	6	14
.44 Win.	92, 53	.4225	.4285	.1327	6	36
38/40 Win.	92	.394	.400	.1237	6	36

E. All these cartridges and some of the gun models were discontinued previous to revision of June 1930

Center fire ctges.	Gun model	Bore diam., in.	Rifling diam., in.	No. of grooves	Inches per turn
38 Win. Exp.	Single Shot	.373	.379	6	26
38/70 Win.	1886	.373	.379	6	24
38/72 Win.	1895	.373	.379	6	22
38/56 Win.	1886, S.S.	.373	.379	6	20
40/50 Sharps St.	Single Shot	.402	.408	6	18
40/70 " "	" "	.402	.404	6	20
40/60 Win.	1876, S.S.	.3995	.405	6	40
40/60 Marlin	Single Shot	.402	.4085	6	26
40/70 Ballard	" "	.402	.408	6	20
40/90 "	" "	.402	.408	6	18
40/90 Sharps St.	" "	.402	.408	6	18
40/65 Win.	1886, S.S.	.3995	.405	6	26
40/70 Win.	1886	.3995	.406	6	20
40/72 Win.	1895	.3995	.406	6	22
40/82 Win.	1886, S.S.	.402	.408	6	28
40/110 Exp.	Single Shot	.3995	.4055	6	28
45/60 Win.	1876, S.S.	.450	.456	6	20
45/75 Win.	1876, S.S.	.450	.456	6	20
45 Sharp	Single Shot	.452	.458	6	18

Determination of caliber from weight of bullet

The weight of a fired bullet may be useful in determining the caliber (or probable caliber) in those cases where, because of deformation, a measurement of diameter cannot be made. It is applicable only in those instances where it is clear that no appreciable amount of metal of the bullet has been lost.

An extensive compilation of weights, calibers, and types of cartridges has recently been prepared at the H. P. White Laboratory and is reproduced here by permission. The information in Table A–20 applies only to the type of ammunition usable in hand guns.

From a knowledge of the weight of a fired bullet and its type, i.e., solid or jacketed (including type of jacket), the type of cartridge from which the bullet came can often be determined, as well as the caliber. It must be pointed out, however, that in several cases there are a number of possibilities. For example, a solid lead bullet weighing 80 or 81 grains could have come from any of five different cartridges, as far as weight is concerned. Also a bullet weighing 148 to 150 grains could have come from any of four different cartridges, using weight alone as the criterion. Despite such limitations, the information contained in the table is very useful.

TABLE A–20

Determination of caliber of a fired bullet from its weight

Wt. (grains)	Type	Cartridge
15	Solid	.22 Short (gallery)
16-20	Solid	.22 BB Cap
27-30	Solid	.22 CB Cap
27-30	Solid	.22 Short
27-30	Solid	.22 Long
36-40	Solid	.22 Long Rifle
45	Jacketed	5.5 mm. Velo Dog
48-51	Jacketed	.25 Auto.
55	Jacketed	7 mm. Nambu
70-77	Jacketed	.32 Auto.
70-77	Jacketed	.35 S & W Auto.
80-82	Solid	.32 Short R.F.
80-82	Solid	.32 Short Colt
80-82	Solid	.32 Long Colt
80-90	Solid	.320 Revolver
80-90	Solid	.320 Long Revolver
84-92	Jacketed	7.62 mm. Tokarev
84-92	Jacketed	7.63 mm. Mauser
85-88	Solid	.32 S & W
89-90	Solid	.32 Long R.F.
89-92	Solid	9 mm. Parabellum, Iron
90-96	Jacketed	7.65 mm. Parabellum
90-115	Solid and Jacketed	.32-20 W.C.F.

(Continued)

TABLE A–20 (Continued)

Wt. (grains)	Type	Cartridge	Wt. (grains)	Type	Cartridge
92-97	Jacketed	.380 Auto.	160-180	Solid and Jacketed	.38-40 W.C.F.
97-101	Jacketed	9 mm. Parabellum, Iron Core	168-170	Solid	.44 Bulldog
98-100	Solid	.32 S & W Long	173	Solid	.45 Auto.
98-100	Solid	.32 Colt New Police	176-181	Jacketed	.380 Revolver MK. II
99-103	Jacketed	8 mm. Nambu	185	Jacketed	.45 Auto.
110	Solid	.38 Special	190-225	Solid	.44 S & W American
113-127	Jacketed	9 mm. Parabellum	195-200	Solid	.41 Long Colt
114-118	Jacketed	9 mm. Steyr	200	Solid	.38 Special
123-128	Jacketed	9 mm. Mauser	200-217	Solid and Jacketed	.44-40 W.C.F.
125-130	Solid	.38 Short Colt	200-230	Jacketed	.45 Auto.
125-136	Jacketed	9 mm. Bergmann Bayard	210-222	Solid	.44 Colt
128-130	Jacketed	.38 Auto.	230	Solid	.45 Webley
145-150	Solid	.38 S & W	230-255	Solid	.45 S & W
148-150	Solid	.38 Long Colt	230-255	Solid	.45 Auto-Rim
148-150	Solid	.38 Colt New Police	240	Solid	.44 Magnum
148-150	Solid	.38 Special	246	Solid and Jacketed	.44 S & W Russian
158	Solid and Jacketed	.38 Special	246	Solid and Jacketed	.44 S & W Special
158	Solid and Jacketed	.357 Magnum	250-260	Solid	.45 Colt
160-167	Solid	.41 Short Colt	265	Solid and Jacketed	.455 Revolver MK. II

(Continued)

Determination of caliber of damaged bullets

In many cases a bullet is so deformed or even fragmented that no useful measurement of its diameter can be made, hence the caliber cannot be determined by the customary procedure. B. D. Munhall of the H. P. White Laboratory, following a suggestion made to him by Lt. Ed. Crowthers of the Pennsylvania Police, has worked out a method whereby the probable original caliber and number of grooves in the barrel can be determined. Where at least one groove and one land on a mutilated bullet remain (without distortion), a measurement of their combined width may give an approximation of the original caliber and the number of grooves in the barrel from which it was fired, by using a table constructed from calculations made from manufacturers' factory specifications. Such a table, compiled by Munhall, is presented in Table A–21. The data were secured by multiplying factory land diameters and groove diameters by pi (3.1416) to get the circumferences and then dividing each of the two resulting figures by varying numbers of grooves. The tabulations here given are limited to pistol and revolver caliber determinations. Obviously, since there is overlapping of the ranges of figures in the left hand column in a number of instances, the precise answer may not always be given. As pointed out by Munhall (personal correspondence) "these tabulations are simply a guide, and such other factors as bullet weight and size of fragment must be considered." The tabulation may be considered as useful, within limitations.

TABLE A–21

Determination of caliber of fired bullet from rifling widths

(by courtesy of B. D. Munhall, H. P. White Laboratory)

Land width plus groove width (inches)	Caliber indicated	No. of grooves
.094–.101	.22, 5.5 mm., 5.6 mm.	7
.109–.118	.22, 5.5 mm., 5.6 mm.	6
.127–.132	.25, 6.35 mm.	6
.131–.142	.22, 5.5 mm., 5.6 mm.	5
.134–.141	.30, .32, 7.65 mm.	7
.152–.158	.25, 6.35 mm.	5
.154–.163	.35, .357, .38, 9 mm.	7
.157–.165	.30, .32, 7.65 mm.	6
.162–.169	.35 S & W. Auto.	6
.164–.177	.22, 5.5 mm., 5.6 mm.	4
.180–.190	.35, .357, .38, 9 mm.	6
.188–.198	.30, .32, 7.65 mm.	5
.190–.197	.25, 6.35 mm.	4
.197–.207	.45, .455	7
.201–.210	.38/40, .41	6
.216–.228	.35, .357, .38, 9 mm.	5
.218–.225	.44	6
.230–.242	.45, .455	6
.235–.247	.30, .32, 7.65 mm.	4
.242–.252	.38/48, .41	5
.262–.270	.44	5
.270–.285	.35, .357, .38, 9 mm.	4
.276–.290	.45, .455	5
.302–.315	.38/40, .41	4
.327–.338	.44	4
.345–.363	.45, .455	4

Spanish and Belgian firms who specialized in rifling of barrels

Name of gun	Type	Maker of gun
Rifled by Faustino Artiagoita, Eibar		
Apache	Automatic	Ojanguren y Vidosa
Avion	"	Bartra y Azpiri
Colon	"	Antonio Azpiri
Destroyer	"	Isidro Gaztañaga
LeDragon	"	Aguirre y Cia.
Looking Glass	"	Domingo Acha
"Azul" Oscillante	Revolver	Eulogio Arostegui
Destroyer (several models)	"	Isidro Gaztañaga
Guisasola (many models)	"	" "
Puppit	"	Ojanguren y Vidosa
Tanque	"	" " "
Rifled by J. Debroux, Liége		
Le Page	Automatic	Mre. d'Armes Le Page
Hammerless	Revolver	Théate Fréres
Lincoln	"	" "
Rifled by Echave y Arizmendi, Eibar		
Elcid	Automatic	Casimiro Santos
Martian	"	Martin A. Bascaran
Rifled by Teodoro Elcoro, Eibar		
"B. H."	Automatic	Beistegui Hermanos
Libia	"	" "
"B. H."	Revolver	" "
Rifled by D. Gillet, Liége		
Jieffeco	Automatic	Robar and DeKerkhove

Name of gun	Type	Maker of gun
Rifled by D. Gillet, Liége (Continued)		
Melior	Automatic	Robar and DeKerkhove
Rifled by Theodoro Isarra, Ermua		
Bolumburu	Automatic	Gregorio Bolumburu
Etna, Invicta, Protector, Tisan, Unis°	"	Santigo Salaberrin
Regina, Regent, Rex°	"	Gregorio Bolumburu
Vainqueur	"	Aurelio Mendiola
Rifled by J. Jamart, Liége		
Baby	Revolver	L. Ancion-Marx
Bull Dog	"	" " "
Cobolt	"	" " "
Constabulary	"	" " "
Extracteur	"	" " "
LeNovo	"	" " "
Lincoln	"	" " "
Bijou (many models)	"	D.D. Debouxtry
Rifled by Mendizabal y Barranco, Eibar		
Acier Comprime	Automatic	Apaolozo Hermanos
"A.A.A."	"	A. Aldazabal
Aldazabal	"	" "
Campeon	"	Hijos de C. Arrizabalaga
Destructor	"	Retolaza Hermanos
Errasti	"	Antonio Errasti
Especial	"	Hijos de C. Arrizabalaga

°Guns in each group are the same, but sold under different name.

(Continued)

341

Name of gun	Type	Maker of gun
Rifled by Mendizabal y Barranco, Eibar (Continued)		
Gallus	Automatic	Retolaza Hermanos
Jubala	"	Larranaga y Elartza
Liberty	"	Retolaza Hermanos
"Military"	"	" "
Paramount	"	" "
Retolaza	"	" "
Sharp Shooter	"	Hijos de C. Arrizabalaga
Stosel	"	Retolaza Hermanos
Singer	"	Francisco Arizmendi
Titanic	"	Retolaza Hermanos
Triumph	"	Apaolozo Hermanos
Walman	"	Francisco Arizmendi
Ydeal	"	" "
Constabulary	Revolver	Francisco Arizmendi
Dreadnaught	"	Antonio Errasti
Errasti	"	" "
Especial	"	" "
Goliat	"	" "

Name of gun	Type	Maker of gun
Rifled by Mendizabal y Barranco, Eibar (Continued)		
Oicet	Revolver	Antonio Errasti
Gallus	"	Retolaza Hermanos
Rifled by Orban and Gilman, Liége		
Dictator	Automatic	Liége United Arms Co.
Le Rapide	"	J. Bertrand
Monobloc	"	J. Jacquemart
Legia Demontants (made for French trade)	"	Nicolas Pieper
N. Pieper	"	" "
Pieper "Basculant"	"	" "
Pieper "Demontant"	"	" "
Hammerless	Revolver	Jannsen Fils and Co.
Lincoln	"	" " " "
Puppy	"	" " " "
Hammerless	"	Théate Fréres
Lincoln	"	" "

Manufacturers of automatic pistols

Name and (or) model	Manufacturer (or source)	Location
A. A. Auto Pistol		
Mod. 1916	Azanza y Arrizabalaga	Eibar, Spain
Action	Modesto Santos	Eibar, Spain
Adler	Engelbrecht and Wolff (for Adlerwaffenwerke —later Max Hermsdorf)	Zella St. Blasii, Germany
Aguro	Erquiaga Muguruza	Eibar, Spain
Alfa	Armero Especialistas Reunidas	Eibar, Spain
Alkar	Soc. Alkartasuna Fab. de Armas	Guernica, Spain
Alkar	Manufacture de Armas Fuego	Guernica, Spain
Alkartasuna	Soc. Alkartasuna Fab. de Armas	Guernica, Spain
"Allies"	Berasaluze Areitio-Aurtena y Cia.	Eibar, Spain
"Allies"	Domingo Acha	Ermua, Spain
Apache	Ojanguren y Vidosa	Eibar, Spain
Arizaga	Gaspar Arizaga	Eibar, Spain
Arminius	Friederich Pickert	Zella-Mehlis, Germany
"Arminius" (Spanish copy)	Gregorio Bolumburu	Eibar, Spain
Arva	Unknown	Spain
Astra (many models)	Juan Esperanza y Pedro Unceta (later Unceta y Cia.)	Guernica, Spain
Atlas	Domingo Acha	Ermua, Spain
Atlas	Tomas de Urizar y Cia.	Eibar, Spain
Audax	Mre. d'Armes des Pyrénées	Hendaye, France
Automatic	Mre. d'Armes á Feu	Liége, Belgium

Name and (or) model	Manufacturer (or source)	Location
Automatic Mod. 1924	Marked B. C. (possibly Bernedo y Cia.)	Eibar, Spain
Aut. Pistole ZKP 501 - II	Possibly Pošumavska Zbrojovka	Czechoslovakia
"Automatique Francaise"	Soc. Francaise d'Armes Automatiques	Paris, France
Avion	Bartra y Azpiri (formerly Azpiri y Cia.)	Eibar, Spain
Azul	Eulogio Arostegui	Eibar, Spain
Ballester-Molina (or Ballester-Rigaud)	Hispano Argentine Fabrica de Automoviles Sociedad Anonima	Buenos Aires, Argentina
"Basculant"	Aguirre Zamacolas y Cia.	Spain
"Basculant" (Pieper)	Nicolas Pieper	Liége, Belgium
Bayard	Anc. Etablissements Pieper, S.A. (formerly Henri Pieper)	Herstal, Belgium
Bayard-Bergmann	Anc. Etablissements Pieper, S.A.	Herstal, Belgium
Bayard-Bergmann	Haerens Tøjhus (Haerens Rustkammer)	Copenhagen, Denmark
Beholla	Becker and Holländer	Suhl, Germany
"B. H."	Beistegui Hermanos	Eibar, Spain
Benemerita	D. G. Ortega de Seija	Madrid, Spain
Beretta	Pietro Beretta (or Beretta, S.A.)	Gardone V.T. (Brescia), Italy

(Continued)

Name and (or) model	Manufacturer (or source)	Location	Name and (or) model	Manufacturer (or source)	Location
Bergmann (early models)	Eisenwerke Gaggenau, A.G. (later Bergmann's Industriewerke)	Gaggenau, Germany	Bulwark	Beistegui Hermanos	Eibar, Spain
Bergmann (pocket models)	V. Chas. Schilling (for Theodor Bergmann)	Suhl, Germany	Burgham	Mre. d'Armes des Pyrénées	Hendaye, France
Bergmann-Erben	August Menz (for Bergmann-Erben)	Suhl, Germany	Campeon (later named "Terrible")	Hijos de C. Arrizabalaga	Eibar, Spain
Bergmann-Simplex	Bergmann's Industriewerke (also made in Belgium and Spain)	Gaggenau, Germany	Campo Giro	Esperanza y Unceta	Guernica, Spain
Bernardelli	Vincenzo Bernardelli	Gardone V.T. (Brescia), Italy	Cantabria	Garate Hermanos	Ermua, Spain
			Capitan	Mre. d'Armes des Pyrénées	Hendaye, France
Bernardon-Martin	Bernardon-Martin (also Thomas Martin)	St. Etienne, France	Carl (Experimental)	J. H. Carl	Gilray, Calif.
Bernedo	Victor Bernedo y Cia.	Eibar, Spain	Cebra	Arizmendi, Zulaika y Cia.	Eibar, Spain
"B. C."Automatic	Victor Bernedo y Cia.	Eibar, Spain	Celta	Tomas de Urizar	Eibar, Spain
Bijou (same as Kaba, Okzet, and Liliput)	August Menz	Suhl, Germany	Cesar	Mre. d'Armes des Pyrénées	Hendaye, France
			J. Cesar	Tomas de Urizar y Cia.	Eibar, Spain
Bittner	Gustav Bittner	Weipert, Austria	Česka Zbrojovka	Česka Zbrojovka A.S. (later C.Z. Národni Podnik)	Strakonice, Prague, and Brno.
Björgum	Nils Björgum	Asker, Kristiana, Norway	Chanticler	I. Charola	Eibar, Spain
Bolton	Francisco Arizmendi	Eibar, Spain	Chanticler	Mre. d'Armes des Pyrénées	Hendaye, France
Boltun	Unknown	Spain	Charola-Anitua	I. Charola (for Charola-Anitua Cia.)	Eibar, Spain
Bolumburu	Gregorio Bolumburu	Eibar, Spain			
Borchardt	Ludwig Loewe and Co. (later (1897) by D.W.M.)	Berlin, Germany	Chimère Reinor	Mre. d'Armes des Pyrénées	Hendaye, France
Borealis ("Brigadier" with stock, etc.)	North American Arms Corp.	Toronto, Canada	Chinese - 7.63 and .45 (Copies of Mauser Mil. Mod.)	Shansei Province Arsenal	Shansei, China
BSW Selbstlade	Berlin-Suhler Waffen u. Fahrzeugwerke, G.m.b.H.	Berlin and Suhl, Germany	Chylewski	Soc. Industrielle Suisse (later by Bergmann and by Lignose)	Neuhausen, Switzerland
"Brigadier" (experimental)	North America Arms Corp.	Toronto, Canada	Clair	Clair Fréres	St. Etienne, France
Bristol	Gregorio Bolumburu	Eibar, Spain	Clement	Charles Ph.Clement	Liége, Belgium
Brixia	Metallurgica Bresciana Gia Tempini	Fiumegrande (Brescia), Italy	Clement	M. Neumann (Succ. to Clement)	Liége, Belgium
Broncho	A. Errasti	Eibar, Spain	Cobra	Unknown	Spain
Bronco	Echave y Arizmendi	Eibar, Spain	Colon	Antonio Azpiri	Eibar, Spain
Browning	Fab. Nationale d'Armes de Guerre (also see Husqvarna)	Herstal, Belgium	Colonial	Fab. d'Armes de Guerre de Grande Precision (Exporters)	Eibar, Spain
Browning H.P. (only)	John Inglis Co.	Toronto, Canada	Colonial	Mre. d'Armes des Pyrénées	Hendaye, France
Brunswig - Mod. 1916	Esperanza y Unceta	Guernica, Spain	Colt	Colt's Pt. F.A. Mfg. Co.	Hartford, Conn.
Bufalo	Gabilondo y Cia. (for Beristain y Cia., Barcelona)	Elgoibar, Spain	Colt Military Models	Colt's Pt. F.A. Mfg. Co.	Hartford, Conn.

(Continued)

Name and (or) model	Manufacturer (or source)	Location	Name and (or) model	Manufacturer (or source)	Location
.45 cal. Mod. 1911	Contracts (partially fulfilled) let to:		Demon "Marine"	Mre. d'Armes des Pyrénées	Hendaye, France
	Springfield Armory	Springfield, Mass.	"Demontant" (Pieper)	Nicolas Pieper	Liége, Belgium
	No. American Arms Co. (less than 100 produced)	Quebec, Canada	Destroyer	Isidro Gaztañaga	Eibar, Spain
.45 cal. Mod. 1911A1	Contracts (partially fulfilled) let to:		Destructor	Retolaza Hermanos	Eibar, Spain
			Diana	Unknown	Spain
	Springfield Armory	Springfield, Mass.	Dictator (Centaure)	Soc. Anonyme des Fab. d'Armes Reunies (Later name: Fab. d'Armes Unies de Liége)	Liége, Belgium
	Ithaca Gun Co.	Ithaca, N. Y.			
	Remington Arms Co.	Bridgeport, Conn.			
	Remington-Rand	Syracuse, N. Y.			
	Singer Manufacturing Co.	Elizabethport, N. J.			
	Union Switch and Signal Co.	Swissvale, Pa.	Dormus	Dormus (and Salvador)	Austria
Colt Military Mod. Copies	Pusan Jin Iron Works	Pusan, Korea	Douglas	Lasagabaster Hermanos	Eibar, Spain
	F.M.A.P. Domingo Mathieu	Rosario, Argentina	Dreux	Unknown	France
	Bangkok Arsenal	Bangkok, Thailand	Dreyse	Rheinische Metallwaren u. Maschinenfabrik	Sömmerda, Germany
	Kongsberg Vapenfabrik	Kongsberg, Norway			
	Fabrica de Hajuba		Duan	Fernando Ormachea	Ermua, Spain
Continental (Belgian)	M. Neumann	Liége, Belgium	Le Tout Acier	Mre. d'Armes des Pyrénées	Hendaye, France
Continental (German)	Rheinische Waffen u. Munitionsfabrik	Cologne, Germany	"DUO" DUO	F. Dušek	Opočno, Czechoslovakia
Continental (Spanish)	Tomas de Urizar y Cia.	Eibar, Spain	D.W.M.	Deutsche Waffen u. Munitionsfabriken	Berlin, Germany
Corla	Fab. de Armas Zaragoza	Mexico Puebla, Mexico	Durabel	Unknown	Belgium
Corrientes	Modesto Santos	Eibar, Spain	E.B.A.C. (Dealer)	Mre. d'Armes des Pyrénées	Hendaye, France
Cow Boy	"Fabrication Francaise"	France	Echeverria	Bonifacio Echeverria	Eibar, Spain
Criolla	Hispano Argentine Fab. de Automoviles, S.A.	Buenos Aires, Argentina	El Cid	Casimiro Santos	Eibar, Spain
			Eles	Unknown	Spain
			Elite	Mre. d'Armes des Pyrénées	Hendaye, France
Crucelegui	Hijos de C. Arrizabalaga (for Crucelegui Hermanos)	Eibar, Spain	El Perro	Lascurarin y Olasolo	Eibar, Spain
"Crucero"	Unknown	Spain	Erika	Unknown	Austria
"CZ"	Česka Zbrojovka	Strakonice, Czechoslovakia	Erma	Erma Waffenfabrik (Orig. name - Erfurter Maschinen u. Werk-zeugfabrik bei Geipel, G.m.b.H.)	Erfurt, Germany
"CZ" - DUO	Fr. Dušek	Opočno, Czechoslovakia			
Czech Mod. 22	Čs. St. Zbrojovka	Brno, Czechoslovakia	Errasti	A. Errasti	Eibar, Spain
Czech Mod. 27	Böhmische Waffen-fabrik (German name for Česka Zbrojovka)	Prague, Czechoslovakia	Especial	Hijos de C. Arrizabalaga	Eibar, Spain
Danton	Gabilondo y Cia.	Eibar, Spain	Estrella	Bonifacio Echeverria	Eibar, Spain
Defender	Javier Echaniz	Vergara, Spain	Etai	Unknown	Spain
Defense	Unknown	Spain	Etna	Santigo Salaberrin	Ermua, Spain
Delu	Fabrique d'Armes Delu and Co.	Liége, Belgium	Express	Tomas de Urizar y Cia.	Eibar, Spain
DeLuxe	Gregorio Bolumburu	Eibar, Spain	Express	Apparently also made by others unknown.	Spain
Demon	Unknown	Ermua, Spain			

(Continued)

345

Name and (or) model	Manufacturer (or source)	Location
FAR	Soc. Anon, des Fab. D'Armes Reunies	Liége, Belgium
Favorit	Unknown	Spain
Fiala Repeating Pistol	Fiala Arms and Equipment Co. (Made for Fiala by Blakslee Forging Co.)	New Haven, Conn.
Fidjeland	A. B. Schwartz - Fidjelands Gevaersyndikat	Sweden
Fiel	Erquiaga, Maguruza y Cia.	Eibar, Spain
Floria	Unknown	Spain
F.M.G. ("Famae")	Fab. de Material de Guerra del Ejercito	Santiago, Chile
Fortuna	Unceta y Cia.	Guernica, Spain
Fox	Česka Zbrojovka	Czechoslovakia
Francotte	Auguste Francotte et Cie.	Liége, Belgium
French 1935-A (S.A.C.M.)	Soc. Alsacienne de Constructions Mécaniques	Cholet, France
French 1935-S (M.A.S.)	Mre. d'Armes de Saint Etienne	St. Etienne, France
French 1935-S (M.A.T.)	Mre. d'Armes de Tuile	Tuile, France
French Mod. 35 S.M.1. (M.A.C.)	Mre. d'Armes de Chatellerault	St. Etienne, France
French Mod. 35 S.M.1. (S.A.G.E.M.)	Soc. de Applications Général Electriques et Mécaniques	France
Frommers (1901-1911)	Fegyver-es Gépygar Részvénytarsaság (Succ. by the firm Fémáru Fegyver és Gépgyár R.T.	Budapest, Hungary
Frommer - Baby	Fémáru-Fegyver-és Gépgyár R.T.	Budapest, Hungary
Frommer - Liliput	Fémáru-Fegyver-és Gépgyár R.T.	Budapest, Hungary
Frommer - Stop	Fémáru-Fegyver-és Gépgyár R.T.	Budapest, Hungary
Frommer - Mod. 29M	Fémáru-Fegyver-és Gépgyár R.T.	Budapest, Hungary
Frommer - Mod. 37M	Fémáru-Fegyver-és Gépgyár R.T.	Budapest, Hungary
Frontier	Unknown	Spain
Furor	Mre. d'Armes des Pyrénées	Hendaye, France
Gabbett-Fairfax (also called Mars)	Webley and Scott, Ltd. (later by Auto Pistol Syndicate)	London and Birmingham, England
Galesi	Industria Armi Galesi (later Armi Galesi)	Brescia, Italy

Name and (or) model	Manufacturer (or source)	Location
Gallia	Mre. d'Armes des Pyrénées (acc. to this mfgr. - but specimens are marked St. Etienne)	Hendaye, France
Gallus	Retolaza Hermanos	Eibar, Spain
Gaulois Repeating Pistol	Mre. Francaise d'Armes et Cycles de St. Etienne	St. Etienne, France
"A. G." (Gavage)	Fab. d'Armes de Guerre Haute Precision Armand Gavage	Liége, Belgium
Gecado	G. C. Dornheim	Suhl, Germany
Glisenti	Societa Siderurgica Glisenti	Carcina (Brescia), Italy
Gloria	Gregorio Bolumburu	Eibar, Spain
Grant Hammond	Grant Hammond Mfg. Corp.	New Haven, Conn.
Gueure	Maker unknown; sold by Isidore Arizmendi y Hijos	Eibar, Spain
Gustloff	Gustloff-Werke-Waffenfabrik	Suhl, Germany
Haenel-Schmeisser	C. G. Haenel Waffen u. Fahrradfabrik	Suhl, Germany
Hafdasa	Hispano Argentina Fab. de Automoviles S.A.	Buenos Aires, Argentina
Hamal	Unknown	Birmingham, England
Hamilton	Torssin and Son	Alingsòs, Sweden
Hämmerli	Hämmerli et Cie.	Lenzburg, Switzerland
Harrington and Richardson	Harrington and Richardson Arms Co.	Worcester, Mass.
Handy	Unknown	Spain
"H and D"	A. Henrion and T. Dassy	Liége, Belgium
Hartford	Hartford Arms and Equipment Co.	Hartford, Conn.
Heim	C. E. Heinzelman	Plochingen, Germany
Helfricht (or Helkra)	A. Krauser Waffen-fabrik	Zella-Mehlis, Germany
HE-MO	Unknown	Germany
Herman	Unknown	Spain
Hermetic (See Bernardon-Martin)		
"J. C. Higgins" - Mod. 80	High Standard Mfg. Co.	Hamden, Conn.
"J. C. Higgins" - Mod. 85	Mre. d'Armes des Pyrénées	Hendaye, France

(Continued)

Name and (or) model	Manufacturer (or source)	Location	Name and (or) model	Manufacturer (or source)	Location
Hijo (same as Galesi)			Kolibri	Georg Grabner	Rehberg Bei Krems a Donau, Austria
HI-Standard	High Standard Mfg. Co.	Hamden, Conn.	Kolibri (Spanish)	Hijos de Francisco Arizaga	Eibar, Spain
"H. V."	Hourat et Vie	Pau (Basses Pyrénées), France	Kommer	Theodor Kommer	Zella-Mehlis, Germany
Hudson	Unknown	Spain	Komuro	Private Mfr.	Tokyo, Japan
Hungarian Mod. 37	Fémáru-Fegyver-és Gépgyár R.T.	Budapest, Hungary	Pistolet Korovin (also called TOZ)	Tula Arsenal	Tula, U.S.S.R.
Husqvarna (Browning)	Husqvarna Vapen-fabriks	Husqvarna, Sweden	Krag (Hansen)	Nils A. Krag	Kristiania, Norway
Husqvarna (Lahti)	Husqvarna Vapen-fabriks	Husqvarna, Sweden	Krnka	Oesterreichische Waffenfabrik	Steyr, Austria
"I. A. G."	Industria Armi Galesi	Brescia, Italy	Lahti VKT L35	Valtion Kivääri Tehdas	Jyväskyla, Finland
Imperial	Tomas de Urizar y Cia. (or Gregorio Bolumburu)	Eibar, Spain Eibar, Spain	Lahti M-1940	Husqvarna Vapen-fabriks, and Forsvarets Fabriksverk	Husqvarna, Sweden Stockholm, Sweden
Ideal	Francisco Arizmendi	Eibar, Spain	La Industrial Orbea	Orbea Hermanos	Eibar, Spain
Indian	Isidro Gaztañaga	Eibar, Spain	La Lira	Garate, Anitua y Cia.	Eibar, Spain
Infallible	Warner Arms Co. and Davis-Warner Co.	Norwich, Conn. Assonet, Mass.	Lambert (Experimental)		U.S.A.
Invicta	Santigo Salaberrin	Ermua, Spain	Lampo (Automatic ejecting repeating pistol)	C. Torbuzio	Turin, Italy
Ixor	Mre. d'Armes des Pyrénées	Hendaye, France			
Izarra	Bonifacio Echeverria	Eibar, Spain	Langenhan "Selbstlader"	Fr. Langenhan	Zella-Mehlis, Germany
Jaga	F. Dušek	Opočno, Czechoslovakia	Le Basque	Unknown	Spain
Jäger	Jäger and Co.	Suhl, Germany	Le Chasseur (M.A.B.)	Mre. D'Armes Automatiques Bayonne	Bayonne, France
Jenkins Special	Unknown	Spain	Le Dragon	Aguirre y Cia.	Ermua, Spain
Jieffeco	Robar et Cie.	Liége, Belgium	Le Francais	Mre. Francais d'Armes et Cycles	St. Etienne, France
Joha	Unknown	Spain			
JO-LO-AR	Hijos de Calixto Arrizabalaga	Eibar, Spain	Le Fulgor	Chas. Ph. Clement	Liége, Belgium
Jubala	Larranaga y Elartza	Eibar, Spain	Legia Demontants	Nicolas Pieper	Liége, Belgium
Jupiter	Unknown	Spain	Le Majestic	Mre. d'Armes des Pyrénées	Hendaye, France
Kaba "Speziall"	August Menz (For Karl Bauer, Berlin)	Suhl, Germany	Le Martiny	Unknown	Liége, Belgium
"Kaba Spezial"	Francisco Arizmendi	Eibar, Spain	Leonhardt	H. M. Gering and Co.	Arnstadt, Germany
Kappora	Unknown	Spain	Le Page	Mre. d'Armes Le Page	Liége, Belgium
Kebler	Unknown	German (?)	Lepco	Unknown	Probably Spain
Kessler	F. W. Kessler	Suhl, Germany	Le Rapide	J. Bertrand	Liége, Belgium
Kimball	Kimball Arms Co.	Wayne, Michigan	Le Sans Pareil	Mre. d'Armes des Pyrénées	Hendaye, France
Kirikkale	Kirikkale Tüfek Fabrikular (sold by Makina ve Kimya Endustrisi Kurumu of Ankara)	Kirikkale, Turkey	Le Secours	Tomas de Urizar y Cia.	Eibar, Spain
			Liberty	Retolaza Hermanos	Eibar, Spain
Knoble	William B. Knoble	Tacoma, Washington	Libia	Beistegui Hermanos	Eibar, Spain
Kobra	Unknown	Germany	"Liége"	Mre. Liégeoise d'Armes à Feu	Liége, Belgium
Kohout	Kohout and Spol.	Kdyně, Czechoslovakia			

(Continued)

Firearms identification

Name and (or) model	Manufacturer (or source)	Location	Name and (or) model	Manufacturer (or source)	Location
Lightning (Orig. called Wolverine)	Whitney Firearms Co.	North Haven, Conn.	Mars	Webley and Scott, Ltd.	Birmingham, England
Lightning	Echave y Arizmendi	Eibar, Spain	Marte	Erquiaga, Muguruza y Cia. (Pat. issued to Miguel Culle y Suso)	Eibar, Spain
Lignose	Theodor Bergmann (for Akt. Ges Lignose)	Suhl, Germany	Martian	Martin A. Bascaran	Eibar, Spain
Liliput (Frommer)	Metallwaren, Waffen u. Maschinenfabrik	Budapest, Hungary	Martigny	Hijos de Jorge Bascaran	Eibar, Spain
Liliput (Menz)	August Menz	Suhl, Germany	"M.A.S." (see French Service Pistols)		
Little Tom	Wiener Waffenfabrik (Orig. by Alois Tomiška in Pilsen)	Vienna, Austria	Mauser	Mauser Werke (after 1922) (Originally Waffenfabrik Mauser)	Oberndorf a/N, Germany
Llama (many models)	Gabilondo y Cia.	Elgoibar, Spain	Maxim	Maxim and Silverman	Crayford, England
Lobo	Unknown	Probably Spain	Mayor	Francois Mayor (Pat. by E. Rochat)	Lausanne, Switzerland
Longines	Cooperativa Obrera	Eibar, Spain	Melior	Robar et Cie.	Liége, Belgium
Looking Glass	Domingo Acha	Ermua, Spain	Menta	August Menz	Suhl, Germany
Looking Glass (Hammer Mod.)	Fernando Acha	Ermua, Spain	Menz	August Menz	Suhl, Germany
Losada	Unknown	Germany	Merke	Unknown	Spain (?)
Luger	Deutsche Waffen u. Munitions Fabriken	Berlin, Germany	Merkel Olympic	Franz Merkel (formerly Udo Anschütz)	Zella-Mehlis, Germany
Luger	Waffenfabrik Bern	Bern, Switzerland	Mieg	Armand Mieg	Heidelberg, Germany
Luger	Schweizerische Industrie Ges. (Component parts only, no complete pistols)	Neuhausen, Switzerland	Mikros	Mre. d'Armes des Pyrénées	Hendaye, France
Luger	Heinrich Krieghoff Waffenfabrik	Suhl, Germany	"Military"	Retolaza Hermanos	Eibar, Spain
Luger	Mauser Werke	Oberndorf a/N, Germany	Minerve	Maker unknown; sold by Fab. D'Armes de Guerre de Grande Precision	Spain
Luger	Waffenfabrik Simson	Suhl, Germany	Minima	M. Boyer	St. Etienne, France
Luger	Vickers, Ltd.	Crayford, England	Mitrailleuse	Unknown	Probably Spain
Luger	Erfurt Gov't. Arsenal	Erfurt, Germany	Mondial	Gaspar Arizaga	Eibar, Spain
M. A. B.	Mre. d'Armes Automatiques Bayonne	Bayonne, France	Monobloc	J. Jacquemart	Herstal, Belgium
Mann	Fritz Mann (or Mann Werke)	Suhl, Germany	M. S. (Action)	Modesto Santos	Eibar, Spain
Mannlicher	First by: Fab. d'Armes Neuhausen Later by: Waffenfabrik Steyr	Neuhausen, Switzerland Steyr, Austria	Mueller	Bernard Mueller	Winterthur, Switzerland
Marina	Gregorio Bolumburu	Eibar, Spain	"Mugica" (Llama)	Gabilondo y Cia. (for J. C. Mugica, Eibar)	Elgoibar, Spain
Marke	Hijos de Jorge Bascaran	Eibar, Spain	Nambu - Commercial	Nambu Small Arms Mfg. Co., Ltd.	Tokyo, Japan
Mars Modell 1903	Bergmann's Industrie-werke	Gaggenau, Germany	Nambu - Military	Tokio Gas and Electric Co., Kokura, Koyobe, and Nagoya Arsenals	
Mars (see Gabbett - Fairfax)			Neuhausen	Schweizerische Industrie Ges.	Neuhausen, Switzerland
Mars	Kohout and Spol. (Possibly also Vilimec)	Kdyně, Czechoslovakia	New Nambu	Shin Chuo Kogyo K.K.	Tokyo, Japan
Mars	Mre. d'Armes des Pyrénées	Hendaye, France			

348

(Continued)

Name and (or) model	Manufacturer (or source)	Location	Name and (or) model	Manufacturer (or source)	Location
Niva	Kohout and Spol.	Kdyně, Czechoslovakia	Praga	Zbrojovka Praga	Prague, Czechoslovakia
Nordheim	G. v. Nordheim	Zella-Mehlis, Germany	Precision	Unknown	Spain
Obregon	Fab. de Armas Mexico	Mexico City, Mexico	Premier	Tomas de Urizar y Cia.	Eibar, Spain
Okzet (same as Bijou, Kaba and Liliput)	August Menz	Suhl, Germany	Prima	Mre. d'Armes des Pyrénées	Hendaye, France
Omega	Industria Obrera Armera	Eibar, Spain	"Princeps" Patent	Tomas de Urizar y Cia.	Eibar, Spain
Orbea	Orbea Hermanos	Eibar, Spain	Protector	Echave y Arizmendi	Eibar, Spain
Ortgies	Deutsche Werke, A.G. (originally Ortgies and Co.)	Erfurt, Germany	Protector	Santigo Salaberrin	Ermua, Spain
			PZK	Pošumavska Zbrojovka	Czechoslovakia
O.W.A.	Oesterreichische Werke gws Anstalt	Vienna, Austria	Ranger	Mre. d'Armes des Pyrénées	Hendaye, France
Oyez	Oyez Arms Co.	Liége, Belgium	Rapide-Maxima	Mre. d'Armes des Pyrénées	Hendaye, France
Padre (Galesi)	See Galesi		Regent	Gregorio Bolumburu (Also, Soc. Española de Armas y Municiones)	Eibar, Spain
Pantax	E. Woerther	Buenos Aires, Argentina			
P-38	Carl Walther	Zella-Mehlis, Germany	Regento	Gregorio Bolumburu (Also, Soc. Española de Armas y Munciones)	Eibar, Spain
P-38	Mauser Werke	Oberndorf a/N, Germany			
P-38	Spreewerk, G.m.b.H.	Berlin-Spandau, Germany	Regina	Gregorio Bolumburu	Eibar, Spain
			"Reims" Patent	Azanza y Arrizabalaga	Eibar, Spain
Parabellum (see Luger)			Reina	Mre. d'Armes des Pyrénées	Hendaye, France
Paramount	Retolaza Hermanos	Eibar, Spain	Reising	Reising Arms Co. (1922—Name changed to Reising Mfg. Corp.)	Hartford, Conn. New York, N. Y.
Pathfinder (same as Bronco)	Echave y Arizmendi (Sold in U.S. by Stoeger Arms Corp.)	Eibar, Spain			
Pederson (experimental)	Remington Arms Co. Inc.	Ilion, N. Y.	Remington Mod. 51	Remington Arms Co.	Ilion, N. Y.
Pence (experimental)	Lauf Pence	San Francisco, Calif.	Renard	Echave y Arizmendi	Eibar, Spain
			Republic	Unknown	Spain
Perfect	Mre. d'Armes des Pyrénées	Hendaye, France	Retolaza	Retolaza Hermanos	Eibar, Spain
			Rex	Gregorio Bolumburu	Eibar, Spain
Philips (experimental)	Springfield Armory	Springfield, Mass.	Rheinmetall	Rheinische Metallwaren Fabrik	Sömmerda, Germany
Phoenix	Tomas de Urizar y Cia.	Eibar, Spain	Rino Galesi	Rigarmi	Brescia, Italy
Phoenix (Ident. to Jieffeco, made by Robar and Co.)	Lowell Arms Co.	Lowell, Mass.	Roland	Francisco Arizmendi	Eibar, Spain
			Rosebush (several experimental models)	Waldo Rosebush	Appleton, Wis.
Pieper	N. Pieper	Herstal, Belgium			
Pierce-Hawkins (experimental)	Springfield Armory	Springfield, Mass.	Roth-Sauer	J. P. Sauer u. Sohn	Suhl, Germany
			Roth-Steyr	A. G. Steyr Waffen-fabriks (Also made by Fegyvergyar)	Steyr, Austria Budapest, Hungary
Pinkerton	Gaspar Arizaga	Eibar, Spain			
Pistola Automatica	Charola y Anitua	Eibar, Spain	Royal	Zulaika y Cia.	Eibar, Spain
			Ruby	Gabilondo y Cia.	Elgoibar, Spain
			Ruby	Gabilondo y Urresti	Eibar, Spain
Plus Ultra	Gabilondo y Cia.	Elgoibar, Spain	Ruby	Ruby Arms Co.	Guernica, Spain
			(Continued)		

Name and (or) model	Manufacturer (or source)	Location
Ruby	"Ruby" Arms Co. (same as Gabilondo)	Elgoibar, Spain
Ruby Type	Alkartasuna Fabrique de Armas	Guernica, Spain
Ruby Type	Zulaika y Cia.	Eibar, Spain
Ruby Type	Bruno Salaverria y Cia.	Eibar, Spain
Ruby Type	Eceolaza y Vicinai y Cia.	Eibar, Spain
Ruby Type	Hijos de Angel Echeverria y Cia.	Eibar, Spain
Ruby Type	Armera Elgoibarresa y Cia.	Eibar, Spain
Ruger	Sturm, Ruger and Co.	Southport, Conn.
S.A. Automatique	Soc. D'Armes Paris	Paris, France
S.A.C.M. and S.A.G.E.M.	See French Service Pistols M1935A	
Safei Type 31	Chinese	China
St. Hubert	Mre. d'Armes des Pyrénées	Hendaye, France
Salaverria	Iraola Salaverria y Cia.	Eibar, Spain
Salvaje M1918	Unknown	Spain
"SATA"	G. Tanfoglio and A. Sabotti	Brescia, Italy
Sauer	J. P. Sauer u. Sohn	Suhl, Germany
Savage	Savage Arms Corp.	Utica, N. Y.
Schall	Schall and Co.	New Haven, Conn.
Schmeisser	C. G. Haenel	Suhl, Germany
Schonberger	Oesterreichische Waffenfabriks A. G.	Steyr, Austria
Schouboe	Dansk Rekyriffel Syndikat	Copenhagen, Denmark
Schwarzlose	A. W. Schwarzlose	Berlin, Germany
S.E.A.M.	Soc. Española de Armas y Municiones	Eibar, Spain
Secours	Tomas de Urizar y Cia.	Eibar, Spain
Selecta	Echave y Arizmendi	Eibar, Spain
Selecta	Mre. d'Armas des Pyrénées	Hendaye, France
Sharpshooter	Hijos de Calixto Arrizabalaga	Eibar, Spain
Shiki - Mod. I (Copy Mauser M.P.)	Shansei Province Arsenal	China
S.I.G.	Schweizerische Industrie Ges.	Neuhausen, Switzerland
Simplex Pistole	Bergmann's Industrie-werke (Copies made in Belgium)	Gaggenau, Germany
Simson	Waffenfabrik Simson and Co.	Suhl, Germany
Singer	Arizmendi y Goenaga (or Francisco Arizmendi)	Eibar, Spain
Sivispacem	Soc. Española de Armas y Municiones	Eibar, Spain
Slavia	A. Vilimec	Kdyně, Czechoslovakia
Smith and Wesson	Smith and Wesson, Inc.	Springfield, Mass.
SMOK	S. Nakulski	Gniezno, Poland
Sosso (First Mod.)	Giulio Sosso	Turin, Italy
Sosso (Second Mod.)	Fabb. Nazionale Armi	Brescia, Italy
Sprinter	Gregorio Bolumburu	Eibar, Spain
Star	Bonifacio Echeverria	Eibar, Spain
Stenda	Stenda Werke Waffen-fabrik	Suhl, Germany
Steph	L. Bergeron	St. Etienne, France
Stern	Albin Wahl	Zella-Mehlis, Germany
Steyr	A. G. Steyr Waffen-fabrik	Steyr, Austria
Steyr (Pieper Pat.)	Oesterr, Waffenfabriks Ges. (Steyr-Daimler-Puch A.G.)	Steyr, Austria
Stock	Franz Stock	Berlin, Germany
Stosel	Retolaza Hermanos	Eibar, Spain
Sunngard	Harold Sunngard	Kristiania, Norway
"Super-Destroyer"	Gaztañaga, Trocaola y Ibarzabal	Eibar, Spain
Sympathique	Mre. d'Armes des Pyrénées	Hendaye, France
T.A.C.	Trocaola, Aranzabal y Cia.	Eibar, Spain
Tala	Tallares de Armas Livianas Argentinas	Bahia Blanca, Argentina
Tanque	Ojanguren y Vidosa (dealers)	Eibar, Spain
Tarn	Swift Rifle Co.	London, England
Tatra	Unknown	Spain
Tauler (same as Llama)	Gabilondo y Cia. (for G. Tauler, Barcelona)	Elgoibar, Spain
Terrible (see Campeon)	Hijos de Calixto Arrizabalaga	Eibar, Spain
Thunder - Mods. 1912, 1919	M. Bascaran (for Alberdi, Teleria y Cia.)	Eibar, Spain
Tigre	Garate, Anitua y Cia.	Eibar, Spain
Tisan	Santigo Salaberrin	Ermua, Spain
Titan	Retolaza Hermanos	Eibar, Spain
Titanic	Retolaza Hermanos	Eibar, Spain
Tiwa	Unknown	

(Continued)

Name and (or) model	Manufacturer (or source)	Location
Tokarev	Various Russian arsenals (principally Tula)	U.S.S.R.
Torpille	Unknown	Probably Spain
Touriste	Mre. d'Armes des Pyrénées	Hendaye, France
TOZ (same as Korovin)	Tulski Oruzheiny Zavod	Tula, U.S.S.R.
Triomphe	Apaolozo Hermanos	Zumorraga, Spain
Triomphe-Francais	Mre. d'Armes des Pyrénées	Hendaye, France
Triplex	Domingo Acha	Ermua, Spain
Trust	Fab. d'Armes de Guerre de Grande Precision (Exporters)	Eibar, Spain
Ttibar	Ttibar, S. R. L.	Buenos Aires, Argentina
Tula-Korovin (or TOZ) (see Korovin)		
U.A.E.	Union Armera Eibaressa	Eibar, Spain
U.A.Z. Pistol	Udo Anchütz	Zella-Mehlis, Germany
Pistolet Aut. Francais "Union"	Fabrique a St. Etienne (M. Seytres)	St. Etienne, France
Union (Spanish)	Tomas de Urizar y Cia.	Eibar, Spain
Union (Spanish)	Makers unknown; Sold by Esperanza y Unceta	Guernica, Spain
Union (U. S.)	Union Fire Arms Co.	Toledo, Ohio
Unique (French)	Mre. d'Armes des Pyrénées	Hendaye, France
Unis	Mre. d'Armes des Pyrénées	Hendaye, France
Unis	Santigo Salaberrin	Ermua, Spain
Urrejola	Urrejola Cia.	Eibar, Spain
Vainquer	Aurelio Mendiola	Ermua, Spain
Vulcain	Unknown	Spain
Vencedor	San Martin y Cia.	Elgoibar, Spain
Venus	Tomas de Urizar y Cia.	Eibar, Spain
Ver-Car	M. Seytres (Made for Verney-Carron)	St. Etienne, France
Vesta	Hijos de A. Echeverria	Eibar, Spain
Vici	Unknown	Herstal, Belgium
Victor	Francisco Arizmendi	Eibar, Spain
Victoria	Esperanza y Unceta	Guernica, Spain
Victory	M. Zulaika y Cia.	Eibar, Spain
Vilars	Unknown	Spain

Name and (or) model	Manufacturer (or source)	Location
Vincitor	M. Zulaika y Cia.	Eibar, Spain
Vindex	Mre. d'Armes des Pyrénées	Hendaye, France
Vis - 35	Fabryka Bronn Radom	Radom, Poland
Vite	Echave y Arizmendi	Eibar, Spain
Waldman	Francisco Arizmendi	Eibar, Spain
Walman	F. Arizmendi y Goenaga (and Francisco Arizmendi)	Eibar, Spain
Walther	Carl Walther (or Waffenfabrik Walther)	Zella-Mehlis, Germany (Now at Ulm-Donau)
Walther (under license)	Mre. de Machines du Haut-Rhin	Mulhouse-Bourtzwiller France
Walther (under license)	Hämmerli et Cie.	Lenzburg, Switzerland
Warnant	Pat. by L. and J. Warnant	Liége, Belgium
Webley	Webley and Scott, Ltd.	Birmingham, England
Webley-Fosbery (auto rev.)	Webley and Scott, Ltd.	Birmingham, England
Wegria-Charlier	Unknown	Belgium
Whitney (formerly Wolverine)	Whitney Firearms Co.	North Haven, Conn.
Winfield (or W.A.C. same as Le Chasseur)	Mre. d'Armes Automatique Bayonne	Bayonne, France
Wolverine (see Whitney)		
Yato	Made first at Hamada and later at Nagoya Arsenals	Hamada and Nagoya, Japan
Ydcal	Francisco Arizmendi	Eibar, Spain
Yovanovitch - Mod. 1931	Voino Tekhnički Zavod	Kragujevac, Yugoslavia
Yugoslav "VTZ"	Unknown	Probably Spain
Zaragoza (only a few made)	Fabrica de Armas Zaragoza	Mexico Puebla, Mexico
Zehna	Zehner Metallwaren-fabrik (E. Zehner Waffenfabrik)	Suhl, Germany
Zoli	A. Zoli	Gardone V.T. (Brescia), Italy
Zonda	Hispano Argentina Fabrica de Automoviles	Buenos Aires, Argentina
Zulaika	M. Zulaika y Cia.	Eibar, Spain

Manufacturers of revolvers and nonautomatic pistols

Foreign-made revolvers and nonautomatic pistols

Name and (or) model	Manufacturer (or source)	Location
Abadie	Unknown	Portugal
"Acier Comprime"	Apaolozo Hermanos	Zumorraga, Spain
Adams	Deane, Adams & Deane (and others in England)	London, England
Alamo Ranger	Unknown	Spain
Aldazabal	Hijos de José Aldazabal	Eibar, Spain
Alfa	Armero Especialistas Reunidas	Eibar, Spain
Alfa Repeating Pistol	Unknown	Germany
"American S & W"	Retolaza Hermanos	Eibar, Spain
Apache	Fabrica de Armas Garantazadas	Eibar, Spain
Arizmendi	Francisco Arizmendi	Eibar, Spain
Arminius	Friederich Pickert	Zella-Mehlis, Germany
Arriola (Copy of Colt)	Arriola Hermanos	Eibar, Spain
Astra	Esperanza y Unceta, Unceta y Cia., Astra-Unceta y Cia. (present name)	Guernica, Spain
ATCSA Special (Rev.)	Armas de Tiro y Caza, S.A.	Barcelona, Spain
ATCSA Target Pistol	Armas de Tiro y Caza, S.A.	Barcelona, Spain
Austrian Infantry (Officer's Mod.)	Raick Fréres (Dealer)	Liége, Belgium
Autogarde	Soc. Francaise des Munitions	Paris, France
Azul	Eulogio Arostegui	Eibar, Spain

352

(Continued)

Name and (or) model	Manufacturer (or source)	Location
Baby	L. Ancion-Marx	Liége, Belgium
Baby	D. D. Debouxtay	Liége, Belgium
Baby	Liége United Arms Co.	Liége, Belgium
Baby	Neumann Fréres	Liége, Belgium
Baby	Raick Fréres (Dealer)	Liége, Belgium
Bar Repeating Pistol	J. P. Sauer u. Sohn	Suhl, Germany
Benemerita	D. F. Ortega de Seijas	Madrid, Spain
"B. H."	Beistegui Hermanos	Eibar, Spain
Bernardelli	Vincenzo Bernardelli	Gardone V. T. (Brescia), Italy
Bijou	D. D. Debouxtay	Liége, Belgium
Bittner Mag. Pistol	G. Bittner	Weipert, Bohemia
Brazilian Army - Gerard System	Raick Fréres (Dealer)	Liége, Belgium
British Army Pattern	Raick Fréres (Dealer)	Liége, Belgium
"Browreduit"	Salvador Arostegui	Eibar, Spain
Bull Dog	L. Ancion-Marx	Liége, Belgium
Bull Dog	J. Bertrand	Liége, Belgium
Bull Dog	D. D. Debouxtay	Liége, Belgium
Bull Dog	Jannsen Fils et Cie.	Liége, Belgium
Bull Dog	Mre. d'Armes LePage	Liége, Belgium
Bull Dog	Liége United Arms Co.	Liége, Belgium
Bull Dog	Neumann Fréres	Liége, Belgium
Bull Dog	Raick Fréres (Dealer)	Liége, Belgium
Bull Dog	Théate Fréres	Liége, Belgium
Bull Dog	L. Dumoulin	Liége, Belgium
Calvert	John Calvert	Leeds, England
Cantabria	Garate Hermanos	Ermua, Spain
Cebra	Antonio Errasti	Eibar, Spain
Chamelot Type	Raick Fréres (Dealer)	Liége, Belgium
"C. H." Rev.	Crucelegui Hermanos	Eibar, Spain
Clement	Anc. Maison Clement	Liége, Belgium
Cobolt	L. Ancion-Marx	Liége, Belgium
Cogswell and Harrison	Cogswell and Harrison	London, England
Colt Imitations	Raick Fréres (Dealer)	Liége, Belgium
Constabler	Mre. Liégeoise d'Armes à Feu	Liége, Belgium
Constabulary Type	L. Ancion-Marx	Liége, Belgium
Constabulary Type	Francisco Arizmendi	Eibar, Spain
Constabulary Type	Jannsen Fils et Cie.	Liége, Belgium
Constabulary Type	Mre. d'Armes LePage	Liége, Belgium
Constabulary Type	Liége United Arms Co.	Liége, Belgium
Constabulary Type	Neumann Fréres	Liége, Belgium
Constabulary Type	Raick Fréres (Dealer)	Liége, Belgium
Constabulary Type	Théate Fréres	Liége, Belgium

(Continued)

Name and (or) model	Manufacturer (or source)	Location
Counet	Auguste Francotte et Cie.	Liége, Belgium
Cow Boy Ranger	Liege United Arms Co.	Liége, Belgium
Crucero	Unknown	Spain
Deane, Adams and Deane	Deane, Adams and Deane	London, England
Dek-Du	Tomas de Urizar y Cia.	Eibar, Spain
Destroyer	Isidro Gaztañaga	Eibar, Spain
Detective	Garate, Anitua y Cia.	Eibar, Spain
D'Ordnnance (Fr. Service)	French Gov't. Arsenal	St. Etienne, France
Dreadnought	Antonio Errasti	Eibar, Spain
Duan	Fernando Ormachea	Ermua, Spain
Duco	Fs. Dumoulin et Cie.	Liége, Belgium
Dutch Officer Pattern	Raick Fréres (Dealer)	Liége, Belgium
"El Cano"	Arana y Cia.	Eibar, Spain
Enfield	Royal Small Arms Factory	Enfield Lock, Middlesex, England
Escodin	M. Escodin	Spain
Esmit	Hijos de J. Arrizabalaga	Eibar, Spain
Espingarda	Edmund Machado	Rio de Janeiro, Brazil
Euskaro	Esprin Hermanos	Eibar, Spain
"Extracteur"	L. Ancion-Marx	Liége, Belgium
"F. A."	Francisco Arizmendi	Eibar, Spain
Famae	Fab. de Material de Guerra del Ejercito	Santiago, Chile
Francotte	Auguste Francotte et Cie.	Liége, Belgium
Francotte	L. Dumoulin	Liége, Belgium
French-Chamelot Pattern	Raick Fréres (Dealer)	Liége, Belgium
French Ord. Revolver	French Gov't. Arsenal	St. Etienne, France
French Ord. Revolver	L. Ancion-Marx	Liége, Belgium
French Ord. Revolver	Castelli	France
Frontier Bull Dog	Fab. National d'Armes de Guerre	Herstal, Belgium
Galand	Galand Arms Co.	Liége, Belgium, and Paris, France
Garate	Garate, Anitua y Cia.	Eibar, Spain
Gasser	Leopold Gasser	Vienna, Austria
Gasser Type	Raick Fréres (Dealer)	Liége, Belgium
Geco	August Genschow	Berlin, Germany
German Mauser Pattern	Raick Fréres (Dealer)	Liége, Belgium
German Ord. Pattern	Raick Fréres (Dealer)	Liége, Belgium

(Continued)

Name and (or) model	Manufacturer (or source)	Location
German Service Rev.	Erfurt Arsenal	Erfurt, Germany
German Service Rev.	V. C. Schilling - C. G. Haenel	Suhl, Germany
Glisenti (Italian Service Rev.)	Soc. Siderurgica Glisenti	Turin, Italy
Goliat	Antonio Errasti	Eibar, Spain
Guisasola	Guisasola Hermanos	Eibar, Spain
Hammerless (Velo Dog)	D. D. Debouxtay	Liége, Belgium
Hammerless	Jannsen Fils et Cie.	Liége, Belgium
Hammerless (Velo Dog)	Théate Fréres	Liége, Belgium
Hand Ejector	Neumann Fréres	Liége, Belgium
"Horse Destroyer"	Isidro Gaztañaga	Eibar, Spain
Hungarian Gendarmery Pattern	Raick Fréres (Dealer)	Liége, Belgium
"Illinois Arms Co."	Friederich Pickert	Zella-Mehlis, Germany
Iris	Orbea Hermanos	Eibar, Spain
Italian Service Rev.	Castelli	Brescia, Italy
Italian Service Rev.	R. Fabb. D'Armi	Brescia, Italy
Italian Service Rev.	Siderurgica Glisenti	Turin, Italy
Italian Service Rev.	Metallurgica Bresciana	Brescia, Italy
"26 Year Style" (Japanese)	Japanese Arsenal	Japan
Kobold	Albrecht Kind (Dealer)	Germany
Kobold Type	Raick Fréres (Dealer)	Liége, Belgium
Kynoch	Kynoch	Aston, England
Lebel (French Service Rev.)	French Gov't. Arsenal	St. Etienne, France
Lebel Type	Raick Fréres (Dealer)	Liége, Belgium
Lebel Type	Retolaza Hermanos	Eibar, Spain
Le Dragon	Aguirre y Cia.	Ermua, Spain
"L. E."	Larranaga y Elartza	Eibar, Spain
Lefaucheux (Pin Fire)	A. Francotte	Liége, Belgium
Lefaucheux (Pin Fire)	E. Lefaucheux	Paris, France
Lefaucheux (Pin Fire)	L. Ancion-Marx	Liége, Belgium
Lefaucheux (C. F.)	L. Ancion-Marx	Liége, Belgium
Lefaucheux (Pin and C. F.)	Mre. d'Armes LePage	Liége, Belgium
Lefaucheux (Pin Fire)	Neumann Fréres	Liége, Belgium
Lefaucheux (C. F.)	Jannsen Fils et Cie.	Liége, Belgium
Lefaucheux (Pin and C. F.)	Raick Fréres (Dealer)	Liége, Belgium

(Continued)

Name and (or) model	Manufacturer (or source)	Location
Lefaucheux (Pin and C. F.)	Théate Fréres	Liége, Belgium
Lefaucheux Mod. 1864	Kongsberg Vapenfabrik	Kongsberg, Norway
"Left Destroyer" (S & W Type)	Isidro Gaztañaga	Eibar, Spain
Le Mat	Le Mat	Paris, France
Le Novo	L. Ancion-Marx	Liége, Belgium
Le Novo	J. Bertrand	Liége, Belgium
Le Novo	Galand Arms Co.	Liége, Belgium
Le Page	Mre. d'Armes Le Page	Liége, Belgium
Le Protecteur (Palm Pistol) Turbiaux System	Unknown	France
Lewes	J. L. Lewes	England
Lincoln	L. Ancion-Marx	Liége, Belgium
Lincoln	J. Bertrand	Liége, Belgium
Lincoln	D. D. Debouxtay	Liége, Belgium
Lincoln	L. Dumoulin	Liége, Belgium
Lincoln	Jannsen Fils et Cie.	Liége, Belgium
Lincoln	Mre. d'Armes LePage	Liége, Belgium
Lincoln	Mre. Liegéoise d'Armes à Feu	Liége, Belgium
Lincoln	Neumann Fréres	Liége, Belgium
Lincoln	Raick Fréres (Dealer)	Liége, Belgium
Lincoln	Théate Fréres	Liége, Belgium
Manstopper (4 bbl.)	Charles Lancaster	London, England
Mauser M1878	Gebrüder Mauser	Oberndorf a/N, Germany
Merveilleux Rep. Pistol	Unknown	France
Merwin Hulbert Type	Raick Fréres (Dealer)	Liége, Belgium
"Mexican Model"	Mre. d'Armes LePage	Liége, Belgium
Milady	L. Ancion-Marx	Liége, Belgium
Milady	Jannsen Fils et Cie.	Liége, Belgium
Nagant	L. Nagant	Liége, Belgium
Nagant	Liége United Arms Co.	Liége, Belgium
Nagant	Tula Arsenal	Tula, Russia
Neumann	Neumann et Cie.	Liége, Belgium
New Nambu	Shin Chuo Kogyo K.K.	Tokyo, Japan
Nouveau (20 shot)	Henrion, Dassy et Heuschen	Liége, Belgium
"O. H." Iris (Colt Type)	Orbea Hermanos	Eibar, Spain
"O. H. Oscillante" (S & W Type)	Orbea Hermanos	Eibar, Spain
Oicet (Copy Colt Pol. Pos.)	Antonio Errasti	Eibar, Spain

(Continued)

Name and (or) model	Manufacturer (or source)	Location
Omega	R. S. Industrial Obrera	Eibar, Spain
Onandia	Onandia Hermanos	Ermua, Spain
Orbea	Orbea Hermanos	Eibar, Spain
Ordinanza	Vincenzo Bernadelli	Gardone V. T. (Brescia), Italy
Ordonnance (French Mod.)	Théate Fréres	Liége, Belgium
Ordonnance (Russian Mod.)	Théate Fréres	Liége, Belgium
Ordonnance (Swiss Mod.)	Théate Fréres	Liége, Belgium
"Oscilante-Azul"	Eulogio Arostegui	Eibar, Spain
Oscillanta "B. H."	Beistegui Hermanos	Eibar, Spain
"O. V."	Ojanguren y Vidosa	Eibar, Spain
Perfecto	Orbea Hermanos	Eibar, Spain
Perrin	L. Perrin et Cie.	Paris, France
Pickert	Friederich Pickert	Zella-Mehlis, Germany
Pistolet Flobert	Flobert	Paris, France
Puppit	Ojanguren y Vidosa	Eibar, Spain
Puppy	Francisco Arizmendi	Eibar, Spain
Puppy	J. Bertrand	Liége, Belgium
Puppy	Jannsen Fils et Cie.	Liége, Belgium
Puppy	Mre. d'Armes LePage	Liége, Belgium
Puppy	Liége United Arms Co.	Liége, Belgium
Puppy	Retolaza Hermanos	Eibar, Spain
Puppy	Théate Fréres	Liége, Belgium
Puppy	L. Dumoulin	Liége, Belgium
Radium (Magazine Pistol)	Gabilondo y Cia.	Elgoibar, Spain
Rast and Gasser	Rast and Gasser	Vienna, Austria
Reform (4 bbls. in line)	Unknown	Germany
Regnum (4 bbls. in line)	Unknown	Germany
Reilly	E. M. Reilly and Co.	London, England
Rural	Unknown	Spain
"S. A."	Suinaga y Aramperri	Eibar, Spain
Scott	W. & C. Scott & Son	Birmingham, England
Secret Service Special	Garate, Anitua y Cia.	Eibar, Spain
Secret Service Special	Guisasola Hermanos	Eibar, Spain
Serbian Officers Pattern	Raick Fréres (Dealer)	Liége, Belgium
Sharp Shooter	Hijos de Arrizabalaga	Eibar, Spain
Star	Bonifacio Echeverria	Eibar, Spain
St. Etienne	Mre. d'Armes St. Etienne	St. Etienne, France
St. Gotthardt	Mre. d'Armes LePage	Liége, Belgium

(Continued)

357

Name and (or) model	Manufacturer (or source)	Location
S & W Type (Tip Up)	D. D. Debouxtay	Liége, Belgium
S & W Type (Tip Up)	L. Dumoulin	Liége, Belgium
S & W Type (Tip Up)	Neumann Fréres	Liége, Belgium
S & W Type (Tip Up D.A.)	Mre. d'Armes LePage	Liége, Belgium
S & W Type (Tip Up S.A.)	Mre. d'Armes LePage	Liége, Belgium
S & W Type (Hammerless)	L. Ancion-Marx	Liége, Belgium
S & W Type (Hammerless)	Jannsen Fils et Cie.	Liége, Belgium
S & W Type (Hammerless)	Liége United Arms Co.	Liége, Belgium
S & W Type (Hammerless)	Théate Fréres	Liége, Belgium
S & W Type (Hammerless)	L. Dumoulin	Liége, Belgium
S & W (Copy of Russian Mod.)	Raick Fréres (Dealer)	Liége, Belgium
S & W (Spanish Copy)	Salvador Arostegui	Eibar, Spain
S & W (Spanish Copy)	Beistegui Hermanos	Eibar, Spain
S & W (Spanish Copy)	Antonio Errasti	Eibar, Spain
S & W (Spanish Copy)	Suinaga y Aramperri	Eibar, Spain
Spirlet	Al Spirlet	Paris, France
Swiss Federal Pattern	Raick Fréres (Dealer)	Liége, Belgium
Tanke	Orueta Hermanos	Eibar, Spain
Tanque	Ojanguren y Vidosa	Eibar, Spain
Texas Ranger	Liége United Arms Co.	Liége, Belgium
Tigre	Garate, Anitua y Cia.	Eibar, Spain
Trade	Liége United Arms Co.	Liége, Belgium
Tranter	William Tranter	Birmingham, England
Trocaola (Copy of Colt)	Trocaola, Aranzabal y Cia.	Eibar, Spain
Trocaola (Copy of S & W)	Trocaola, Aranzabal y Cia.	Eibar, Spain
Trocaola Mod. 333	Trocaola, Aranzabal y Cia.	Eibar, Spain
Tue-Tue	Galand Arms Co.	Paris, France
Velo Dog	L. Ancion-Marx	Liége, Belgium
Velo Dog	Arizmendi y Goenaga	Eibar, Spain
Velo Dog	Francisco Arizmendi	Eibar, Spain
Velo Dog	Eulogio Arostegui	Eibar, Spain
Velo Dog	"B. F."	St. Etienne, France

(Continued)

Name and (or) model	Manufacturer (or source)	Location
Velo Dog	D. D. Debouxtay	Liége, Belgium
Velo Dog	Antonio Errasti	Eibar, Spain
Velo Dog	Mre. Francaise d'Armes et Cycles	St. Etienne, France
Velo Dog	Galand Arms Co.	Paris and Liége
Velo Dog	A. Gilon	Liége, Belgium
Velo Dog	J. Lefebvre	Paris, France
Velo Dog	Mre. Liégeoise d'Armes à Feu	Liége, Belgium
Velo Dog	Mre. d'Armes LePage	Liége, Belgium
Velo Dog	Neumann Freres	Liége, Belgium
Velo Dog	D. D. Oury	Liége, Belgium
Velo Dog	Friederich Pickert	Zella-Mehlis, Germany
Velo Dog	Raick Fréres (Dealer)	Liége, Belgium
Velo Dog	Retolaza Hermanos	Eibar, Spain
Velo Dog	M. Seytres	Liége, Belgium
Velo Dog	Suinaga y Aramperri	Eibar, Spain
Velo Dog	(Many others not identified)	Belgium, France, and Spain
Warner-Counet	Théate Fréres	Liége, Belgium
Webley	P. Webley and Son	Birmingham, England
Webley	Webley and Scott	Birmingham, England
Webley (Copy)	Garate, Anitua y Cia.	Eibar, Spain
Werder Lightning	Austrian Gov't. Arsenal	Vienna, Austria

American manufacturers of revolvers and nonautomatic pistols — past and present*

Manufacturer	Types produced	Location
Aetna Arms Co.	.22 Short R.F. revolvers	New York, N. Y.
Allen & Thurber	Percussion pistols, including Underhammer and Bar hammer types	Norwich, Conn. and Worcester, Mass.
Allen & Wheelock	Percussion pistols and revolvers, "Pepper boxes"	Worcester, Mass.
Ethan Allen	Percussion pistols and R.F. revolvers	No. Grafton, Mass.
Ethan Allen & Co. (Succ. to Ethan Allen)	Rim fire revolvers and Derringers	Worcester, Mass.
American Arms Co.	Rim fire and center fire revolvers	Boston, Mass.
American Standard Tool Co.	"Hero" percussion pistols, and R. F. revolvers	Newark, N. J.
American Steam Works	"Pepper box" pistols	New York, N. Y.
N. P. Ames	Smooth bore percussion pistols	Springfield, Mass.
R. W. Amsden	Percussion dueling pistols	Saratoga Springs, N. Y.
Andrus & Osborn	Underhammer percussion pistols	Canton, Conn.
P. H. Ashton	Underhammer percussion pistols	
W. Ashton	Underhammer percussion pistols	
Henry Aston	Army smooth bore percussion pistols	Middletown, Conn.
William Aston	Underhammer percussion pistol	Middletown, Conn.

*Very early types, such as flintlock pistols, have been omitted.

(Continued)

Manufacturer	Types produced	Location
Bacon & Co.	Underhammer percussion pistols, Underhammer "Pepper boxes," and Bar hammer D.A. pistols	Norwich, Conn.
Bacon Manu-facturing Co. (Bacon Arms Co.)	"Pepper box" pistols percussion revolvers, and R. F. revolvers	Norwich, Conn.
Thomas Bailey	Percussion pistols, D.A. percussion revolvers	New Orleans, La.
Ballard & Fairbanks	D.A. rim fire Derringers	Worcester, Mass.
Blunt & Syms	Underhammer percussion pistols; Bar hammer pistols; Dueling pistols; Derringers. "Pepper boxes" and	New York, N. Y.
Brooklyn Arms Co.	Slocum revolvers	Brooklyn, N. Y.
Brown Manufacturing Co.	Rim fire pistols and Derringers	Newburyport, Mass.
Jesse S. Butterfield	Percussion Army and Navy revolvers	Philadelphia, Pa.
Cody Manu-facturing Corp.	.22 cal. Revolver	Chicopee, Mass.
Colt Pt. Fire Arms Mfg. Co. (several name changes)	Percussion type, R.F. and C.F. revolvers of many varieties; also many models of automatic pistols	Hartford, Conn.
Connecticut Arms Co.	"Teat Cartridge" pocket revolver	Norfolk, Conn.
Connecticut Arms & Mfg. Co.	Hammond's Bull Dog pistols	Naubuc (and Glastonbury), Conn.
Cooper Fire Arms Mfg. Co.	D.A. percussion belt revolvers and Navy Type revolvers	Frankford, Phila., Pa.
Crescent Arms Co.	D.A. automatic ejecting revolvers	Norwich, Conn.
Dance Bros. & Park	Percussion Army and Navy Type revolvers	Columbia, Tex.
Dardick Corporation	Revolvers	New York, N. Y.
B. and B. M. Darling	S.A. percussion "Pepper box"	Woonsocket, R. I.
Henry Deringer, Sr. and Henry Deringer, Jr.	Early Martial percussion pistols; Percussion and R.F. Revolvers; and, most notably, the "Deringer" Pistol. This was widely copied by others and came to be known as the "Derringer." Made in both single and double (superposed) barrels, in both percussion and rim fire. Its popularity in Frontier days almost rivaled that of the Colt.	Philadelphia, Pa.

(Continued)

Manufacturer	Types produced	Location
E. L. Dickinson	Rim fire revolvers	Springfield, Mass.
Eagle Arms Co.	Ellis & White's Pat. revolver	New York, N. Y.
Josiah Ells	Percussion bar hammer revolvers	Pittsburgh, Pa.
Forehand Arms Co. (Succ. to Forehand & Wadsworth) 1890–1900	R.F. and C.F. revolvers	Worcester, Mass.
Forehand & Wadsworth 1871–1890	Great variety of R.F. and C.F. revolvers; also a breech-loading Derringer	Worcester, Mass.
Andrew Fyrberg & Co.	Automatic ejecting revolver. (Reportedly made by Meriden F. A. Co.)	Hopkinton, Mass.
William Glaze & Co. (Palmetto Armory)	Revolvers	Columbia, S. C.
Great Western Arms Co.	Revolvers	Los Angeles, Calif.
Gross Arms Co.	R.F. revolvers	Tiffin, Ohio
Harrington & Richardson	R.F. and C.F. revolvers in great variety; also an automatic pistol (discontinued)	Worcester, Mass.
Hartford Arms Co.	R.F. pocket revolver	Hartford, Conn.
Hartford Arms & Equipment Co.	Repeating Pistol	Hartford, Conn.
High Standard Mfg. Corporation	Automatic pistols and revolvers	Hamden, Conn.
Hood Fire Arms Co.	R.F. revolver	Norwich, Conn.
Hopkins & Allen	R.F. and C.F. revolvers in great variety. (Revolver manufacture ceased in 1917)	Norwich, Conn.
Johnson, Bye & Co. (1871–1883)	Revolvers and pistols under many brand names	Worcester, Mass.
Iver Johnson & Co. (1883–1891)	Revolvers and pistols under many brand names	Worcester, Mass.
Iver Johnson Arms & Cycle Works Cycle Works	R.F. and C.F. revolvers in great variety	Fitchburg, Mass.
H. M. Kolb	Baby hammerless R.F. revolver	Philadelphia, Pa.
Lee Arms Co.	R.F. "Red Jacket" and other revolvers	Wilkes-Barre, Pa.
L. M. & G. H. Lester	Lester Pat. R.F. revolver	New York, N. Y.
Lindsay Manufacturing Co.	Two-shot pistols	New York, N. Y.
Little All Right Fire Arms Co.	"Little All Right" folding revolver	Lawrence, Mass.

(Continued)

Manufacturer	Types produced	Location
Lowell Arms Co. (Succ. to Rollin White Arms Co.)	R.F. revolvers	Lowell, Mass.
John P. Lower	R.F. revolvers and Derringers	Philadelphia, Pa.
Maltby, Corliss & Co.	D.A., R.F. revolvers	New York, N. Y.
Manhattan Fire Arms Co.	D.A. "Pepper boxes"; D.A. bar hammer R.F. revolvers; Belt revolvers and Navy Type revolver	Newark, N. J.
John M. Marlin	R.F. XXX Standard and S & W Type revolvers	New Haven, Conn.
Marlin Firearms Co.	Revolver—Automatic Ejecting	New Haven, Conn.
William M. Marston	D.A. "Pepper box" pistols; Percussion pistols; Percussion belt revolvers; Breech loading percussion pistols	New York, N. Y.
Massachusetts Arms Co.	Percussion pistols, percussion revolvers, and Maynard Type revolvers	Chicopee Falls, Mass.
Meriden Fire Arms Co.	R.F. and C.F. revolvers (sold under several names)	Meriden, Conn.
Metropolitan Arms Co.	Belt revolvers. (copy of Colt)	New York, N. Y.
Minneapolis Fire Arms Co.	Palm pistols	Minneapolis, Minn.
Daniel Moore (Moore's Pat. Fire Arms Co.)	R.F. belt type and Army revolvers	Brooklyn, N. Y.
O. F. Mossberg & Sons	4-Shot repeating pistol	New Haven, Conn.
National Arms Co. (Succ. to Moore's Pat. F.A. Co., and taken over later by Colt)	"Teat Cartridge" and R.F. revolvers, and all-metal Derringers	Brooklyn, N. Y.
North & Savage Simeon North	Percussion revolvers Very early percussion pistols. (Said to be first made in U.S.—First Gov't. contract in 1799)	Middletown, Conn. Middletown, Conn.
Norwich Lock Mfg. Co.	Percussion pocket revolvers	Norwich, Conn.
Norwich Pistol Co.	Vestpocket percussion pistol	Norwich, Conn.
Osgood Gun Works	R.F. revolvers (.22 and .32 combined)—Under names "Duplex" and "Monarch."	Norwich, Conn.

(Continued)

Manufacturer	Types produced	Location
Palmetto Armory	Percussion pistols	Columbia, S. C.
Alonzo D. Perry (Perry Pat. Arms Co.)	Breech-loading percussion pistols	Newark, N. J.
Plant's Manufacturing Co.	Plant cup cartridge revolvers in several models	New Haven, Conn.
Lucius W. Pond	R. F. Army and belt type revolvers (Marked "Manfd. for S & W"); and a front-loading Revolver	Worcester, Mass.
E. A. Prescott	R.F. revolver (Infringement on S & W)	Worcester, Mass.
Protector Arms Co.	R.F. .22 cal. revolvers (Like the Rupertus)	Philadelphia, Pa.
Raymond & Robitaille	Pettengill hammerless percussion revolvers in several models (Claimed to be first American-made hammerless revolver)	New Haven, Conn.
James Reid Manufactory	R.F. "My Friend" ("Knuckle Duster") and other models of revolvers; also Derringers	New York, and Catskill, N. Y.
E. Remington (and Successors)	Percussion, R.F., and C.F. revolvers in great variety; also automatic pistols.	Ilion, N. Y.
Reynolds, Plant & Hotchkiss	Plant Patent revolvers	New Haven, Conn.
Rogers & Spencer (Formerly R. Rogers and Rogers & Hearst)	Pettingill revolvers; and Rogers & Spencer revolvers	Willowdale, N. Y.
Rupertus Pat. Pistol Mfg. Co.	8-shot "Pepper boxes"; "Hero" revolver and R.F. revolvers	Philadelphia, Pa.
Thos. Ryan, Jr., Mfg. Co.	.22 cal. R.F. "Napoleon" revolver	New York, N. Y.
Edward Savage	Percussion Navy and other revolvers, in at least four models	Middletown, Conn.
Savage Revolving Arms Co. (Succ. to Edward Savage)	Percussion Navy type revolvers	Middletown, Conn.
R. F. Sedgeley (Succ. to H. M. Kolb)	Baby hammerless revolver	Philadelphia, Pa.
C. Sharps & Co.	Percussion revolver (tip up barrel); Breech-loading percussion Army revolver; 4-shot "Pepper box" (Fixed barrel, with rotating firing pin) in .22, .30, and .32 cal.	Philadelphia, Pa.
Sharps & Hankins (Succ. to C. Sharps & Co.)	Continuation of Sharps "Pepper Box," in different models	Philadelphia, Pa.

364

(Continued)

Manufacturer	Types produced	Location
C. S. Shattuck Arms Co.	Four-shot D.A. Palm pistol, in .22 and .32 cal.; also Shattuck swing cylinder revolver	Hatfield, Mass.
Sheridan Products Co.	Single shot pistol	Racine, Wis.
Otis A. Smith	R.F. and C.F. revolvers	Rock Falls, Conn.
Smith & Wesson	Volcanic pistols, and revolvers in many models. Also automatic pistols.	Springfield, Mass.
S-M Corporation	Single shot pistol	Alexandria, Va.
Springfield Arms Co.	Stevens percussion re-volvers (With Maynard's primer); Percussion and R.F. revolvers under Warner Pats.	Springfield, Mass.
Starr Arms Co.	S.A. percussion revolvers; D.A. Navy Mod. revolver	Yonkers, N. Y.
J. Stevens Arms and Tool Co. (Succ. to J. Stevens & Co.)	R. F. pistols, particularly target models	Chicopee Falls, Mass.
Alexander Stocking & Co.	S.A. percussion "Pepper boxes"	Worcester, Mass.
Sturm, Ruger & Co.	Revolvers	Southport, Conn.
Thames Arms Co.	D.A. automatic ejecting revolvers	Norwich, Conn.
Toledo Fire Arms Co.	R.F. revolvers and an automatic revolver	Toledo, O.
Union Arms Co.	Percussion pistols; Bar hammer D.A. pistols; Belt revolver; Navy type revolver and "Pepper boxes"	Hartford, Conn.
Union Fire Arms Co.	Revolvers; Riefgraber's automatic pistol; and Lefever's Semiautomatic revolver	Toledo, O
Volcanic Repeating Arms Co. (Sold out to O. F. Winchester)	Volcanic pistols	New Haven, Conn.
Walch Fire Arms Co.	Ten-shot percussion revolvers (Had 5 cylin-ders, 2 charges in each, and 2 hammers)	New York, N. Y.
Wamo Manu-facturing Co.	S.S. Pistol	San Gabriel, Calif.
James Warner	Percussion revolver	Worcester, Mass.
Wesson & Harrington (Succ. by Harrington & Richardson)	R.F. revolvers (Swing cylinder)	Worcester, Mass.
Wesson, Stevens & Miller	Leavitt's Pat. revolver	Hartford, Conn.

(Continued)

Manufacturer	Types produced	Location
Frank Wesson	R.F., S.S. Pistol, Super-posed bbl. model (Bbls. revolve) provided with sliding dagger	Springfield, Mass.
Rollin White Arms Co.	Revolver made under White patents (Smith & Wesson made a similar gun under agreement with White)	Lowell, Mass.
Eli Whitney (Sr. and Jr.) (Whitney Arms Co.)	Navy and belt type percussion revolvers	Whitneyville, Conn.

Rim fire firing pin impressions

As has been pointed out in Chapter 3 of Part I, the impressions made on the rims of cartridges fired in different makes and models of firearms are helpful at times in making a decision as to whether or not an evidence shell was fired in a particular gun, and also (in cases where no suspect gun has been submitted) in determining what make or makes and/or models could or could not have fired the evidence shell.

Not only is the size and shape of a firing pin mark important, but also its position on the rim with respect to its orientation in the chamber when fired. Furthermore the position of extractor marks and ejector marks (if present) are also of importance.

The value of a file of photographs has already been stressed. In this Appendix will be found the following:

1. A table showing the relative positions of firing pin, extractor, and ejector in a large number of automatic pistols. (Regretably most of these pistols were not available to the author at the time that it was decided to include such information.)

2. Six plates showing reproductions (mostly in the form of sketches) taken from the H. P. White "Firearms Information Service" cards, with an identification key preceding the plates.

3. Thirteen plates showing photographs taken by the author. In each case three shells were fired and photographed in order to get some idea of the reproducibility of the markings made by each gun. In some instances the markings are very reproducible, and others showed variations. In a few instances double impressions were produced by rebounding hammers or firing pins.

367

TABLE A-22

Relative positions of firing pin, extractor, and ejector marks on shells fired from .22 cal. rim fire automatic pistols

Extractor marks and ejector marks are often absent, but if present they should appear in approximately the positions indicated in this table.

Name-Model	Serial number	Pin	Extr.	Eject.	Name-Model	Serial number	Pin	Extr.	Eject.
Astra M 2000	50478	12	2	8	Hungarian-Type M 29	3258	12	3	8
" M 4000**	790004	12	2	clip	Llama M-XV**	178770	12	3	8
" "	795677	12	2	clip	" Air Lite	196431	12	3	8
Ballester Molina	54296	12	3	8	MAB Mod. F	4706	12	3	8
Beretta M 948	003053N	12	3	8	" 6¾"	4625	12	3	9
"	018631N	12	3	9	" Le Chasseur**	37	12	2	8
" 949 Olympic	955	12	3	8	Melior	L0077	12	3	8
" 1950 sh†	50236CC	12	no	8	Mikros sh	55078	12	2	clip
Bernardelli sh	1136	9	3	CP†	Pantax	785	12	2	8
" Target	686	10	3	FP†	Reising (Arms Co.)	1816	12	3	clip
" M 60	10571	12	3	8	Reising (Mfg. Corp.)	10967	12	3	clip
Colt Service Ace	3565	12	3	8	Rino lg	28859	9	3	FP
" Woodsman	113135	12	3	8	Romer	1088	10	3	FP
" Match Target	141619	12	3	8	Ruger**	7272	12	3	8
" Junior conv.	—	12	3	8	Sata	1395	3	12	CP
Erma	5752	12	3	9	Schall SS	7156	12	3	clip
" -Luger conv.	1051A	9	12	clip	SIG 47/8 conv.	40032	12	3	8
Fiala SS†	893	12	3	clip	S & W M 41	4767	12	3	9
Frommer Liliput conv.	396	12	3	8	Star Mod. F	341360	12	3	7
Galesi M 503 A	102148	9	3	CP†	" HF	519344	12	3	7
" Militar	10609	12	3	8	" Olimpic	383992	12	3	7
H-A**	93629	6	2	9	Stock	289	12	3	clip
Hammerli Walther	5103	12	3	8	Tala	0222	12	3	8
Hartford	4181	1	3	9	Ttibar	1112	8	no	FP
"	4555	1	3	9	Unique Ranger	420594	12	3	8
" SS†	1272	12	3	no	"	429402	12	3	9
Higgins M 80	663886	12	3	8	Walther PP	145620 P	12	3	9
" 85	532564	12	2	clip	" PPK	943744	12	3	9
HI Std. M A	39573	1	3	9	" "	242146K	12	3	9
" B	109833	1	3	8	" Target	1443	12	3	9
" C sh	63344	1	3	8	" Olympia	7922 O	12	3	9
" H-DM	182282	1	3	8	" -ManhurinPP	10026 B	12	3	9
" "	110587	1	3	8	" " PPK	102141	12	3	9
" "	117265	1	3	8	Whitney Wolverine**	100781	12	2	8
HI Std. Field King	472197	1	3	8	Zaragoza**	30	12	3	8

*Positions are given as numerals on a standard clock face, looking forward along barrel at base of cartridge.

**Information furnished by Clark E. Kauffman, Firearms Collector, Leesburg, Florida.

†CP indicates pin at center of cartridge base; FP — firing pin; lg — .22 long cartridge; sh — .22 short cartridge; SS — single shot.

Plate 8. Firing pin impressions on rim fire cartridges

Now practically limited to .22 cal., these have shapes, sizes, and locations which permit them to be classified into the five following groups:

1. BAR TYPE: The impression is a groove or indentation running directly across the base of the shell.

2. RECTANGULAR TYPE: The most common, but fortunately they vary in width, length, and location. Frequently the sides are not parallel, but wedge shaped.

3. ROUND TYPE: Second most common type. Vary in size, shape, and location. Ends of firing pins may be blunt (rounded), pointed, or flat.

4. SEMICIRCULAR: Similar to Type 3, but strike on edge thus producing semicircular effect.

5. SPECIAL TYPE: Less common, therefore very distinctive. Great variation, particularly in shape, but also in size and location. Impressions in this class are those having a shape which could not be classified as round, semicircular, rectangular, or bar. Measurement "A" is parallel to a tangent to the case circumference at the mark. Measurement "B" is at right angles to measurement "A".

KEY TO ABBREVIATIONS

T - top of gun
EX - extractor position
EJ - ejector position

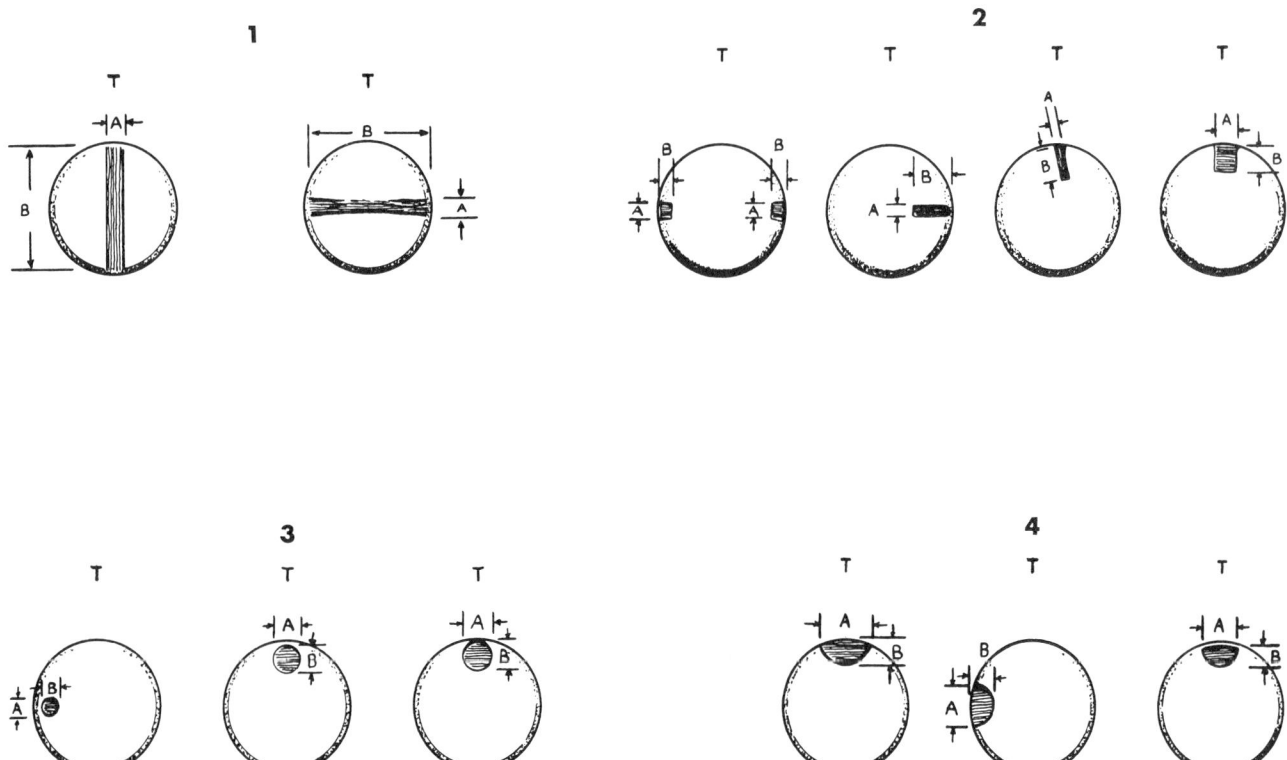

Plate 9

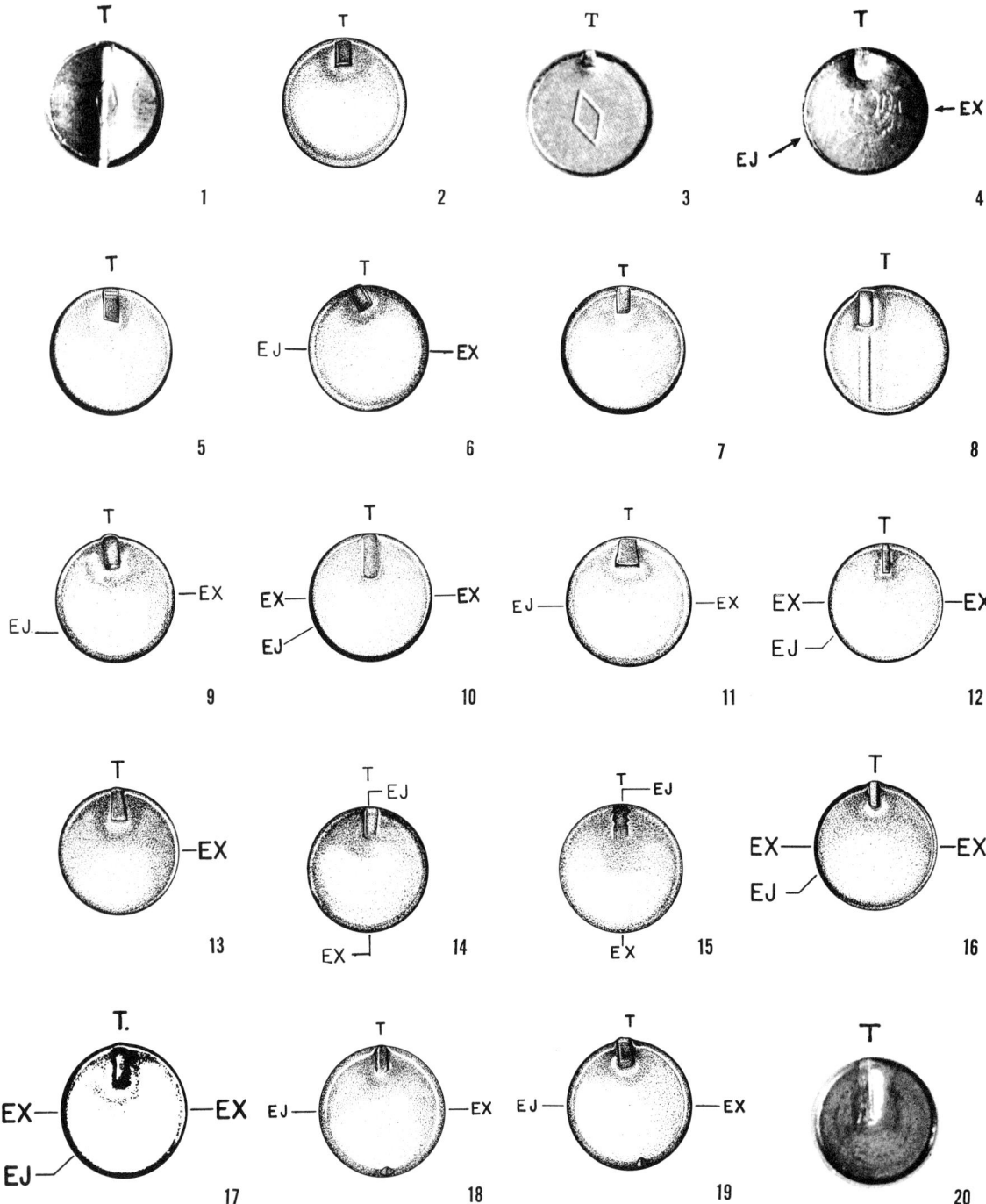

Key to Plate 9. Rim fire firing pin impressions

(Measurements of A and B are approximate)

1. Class: Bar
Cartridge: .22 L.R.

Model: None given

Size: A = .025″ B = .275″
Weapon: Gevarm Semiautomatic Rifle
Maker: Gevelot Munition Factories, Paris, France

2. Class: Rectangular
Cartridge: .22 Short

Model: 950 c.c. (Minx M-4)

Size: A = .020″ B = .043″
Weapon: Beretta Automatic Pistol
Maker: Pietro Beretta

3. Class: Rectangular
Cartridge: .22 L.R.

Model: 46-22 Thunderbird

Size: A = .020″ B = .040″
Weapon: Cody Double Action Revolver
Maker: Cody Manufacturing Corp.

4. Class: Rectangular
Cartridge: .22 Short

Model: Junior Colt Conversion Unit

Size: A = .034″ B = .098″
Weapon: Colt Semiautomatic Pistol
Maker: Made in Spain for Colt

5. Class: Rectangular
Cartridge: .22 L.R. (Also L. or S.)
Model: No. 922

Size: A = .032″ B = .060″
Weapon: H & R Revolver

Maker: Harrington and Richardson

6. Class: Rectangular
Cartridge: .22 L.R.

Model: No. 31

Size: A = .026″ B = .070″
Weapon: J. C. Higgins Automatic Rifle
Maker: High Standard Mfg. Corp. for Sears, Roebuck and Co.

7. Class: Rectangular
Cartridge: .22 L.R.

Model: W-101 Double-Nine

Size: A = .022″ B = .053″
Weapon: HI Standard Double Action Revolver
Maker: High Standard Manufacturing Corp.

8. Class: Rectangular
Cartridge: .22 L.R.

Model: No. 161 for Savage High Power

Size: A = .027″ B = .086″
Weapon: Marble Auxiliary Cartridge
Maker: Marble Arms and Mfg. Co.

9. Class: Rectangular
Cartridge: .22 L.R.

Model: 140K

Size: A = .032″ B = .073″
Weapon: Mossberg Bolt Action Rifle
Maker: O. F. Mossberg and Sons, Inc.

10. Class: Rectangular
Cartridge: .22 L.R.

Model: 144

Size: A = .026″ B = .075″
Weapon: Mossberg Bolt Action Mag. Rifle
Maker: O. F. Mossberg and Sons, Inc.

11. Class: Rectangular
Cartridge: .22 L.R.

Model: 152K

Size: A = .047″ B = .050″
Weapon: Mossberg Automatic Rifle
Maker: O. F. Mossberg and Sons, Inc.

12. Class: Rectangular
Cartridge: .22 L.R.

Model: 40-X

Size: A = .018″ B = .055″
Weapon: Remington Bolt Action Rifle
Maker: Remington Arms Co., Inc.

13. Class: Rectangular
Cartridge: .22 L.R.

Model: Fieldmaster No. 121

Size: A = .034″ B = .069″
Weapon: Remington Slide Action Rifle
Maker: Remington Arms Co., Inc.

Remarks: Firing pin acts as ejector.

14. Class: Rectangular
Cartridge: .22 Short

Model: 241-Speedmaster

Size: A = .025″ B = .063″
Weapon: Remington Semi-automatic Rifle
Maker: Remington Arms Co., Inc.

15. Class: Rectangular
Cartridge: .22 Short

Model: 241-Speedmaster

Size: A = .024″ B = .064″
Weapon: Remington Semi-automatic Rifle
Maker: Remington Arms Co., Inc.

Remarks: Typical for Serial Nos. 60067 and 60083. No. 14 above fired in specimen Serial No. 41187.

16. Class: Rectangular
Extractor Width: .064″
Cartridge: .22 L.R.

Model: Sportsmaster No. 512

Size: A = .021″ B = .055″

Weapon: Remington Bolt Action Rifle
Maker: Remington Arms Co., Inc.

17. Class: Rectangular
Cartridge: .22 L.R.

Model: Matchmaker No. 513T

Size: A = .025″ B = .060″
Weapon: Remington Bolt Action Rifle
Maker: Remington Arms Co., Inc.

18. Class: Rectangular
Cartridge: .22 L.R.

Model: No. 550

Size: A = .035″ B = .055″
Weapon: Remington Auto-loading Rifle
Maker: Remington Arms Co., Inc.

19. Class: Rectangular
Cartridge: .22 L.R.

Model: No. 550-1

Size: A = .035″ B = .055″
Weapon: Remington Auto-loading Rifle
Maker: Remington Arms Co., Inc.

20. Class: Rectangular

Cartridge: .22 Short

Model: RG-10

Size: A = .013 to .018″
B = .131 to .135″
Weapon: Röhm Double Action Revolver
Maker: Röhm Gesellschaft m. b. H., Sontheim/Brenz, Germany

371

Plate 10

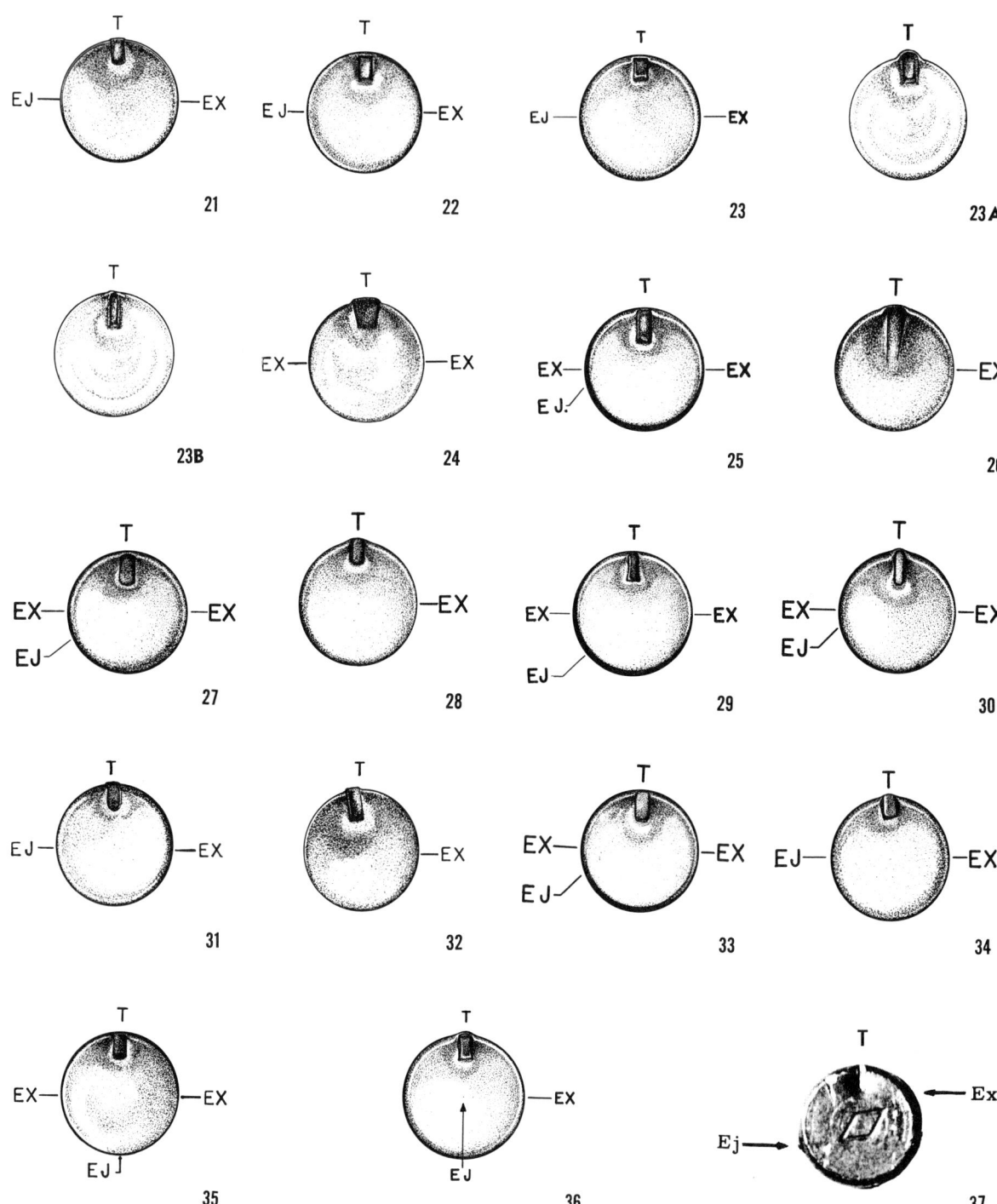

Key to Plate 10. Rim fire firing pin impressions

(Measurements of A and B are approximate)

21. Class: Rectangular
Cartridge: .22 Short

Model: 550 2 G Gallery Special

Size: A = .024″ B = .049″
Weapon: Remington Semi-automatic Rifle
Maker: Remington Arms Co., Inc.

22. Class: Rectangular
Extractor Width: .068″
Cartridge: .22 L.R.

Model: 552 Speedmaster

Size: A = .023″ B = .043″

Weapon: Remington Auto-loading Rifle
Maker: Remington Arms Co., Inc.

23. Class: Rectangular
Cartridge: .22 L.R.

Model: No. 572 Fieldmaster

Size: A = .022″ B = .033″
Weapon: Remington Slide Action Rifle
Maker: Remington Arms Co., Inc.

23A. Class: Rectangular
Cartridge: .22 Short

Model: Pocket (Hammerless)

Size: A = .008″ B = .055″
Weapon: Sable Double Action Revolver
Maker: Neumann and Co., Liége, Belgium

23B. Class: Rectangular
Cartridge: .22 Short

Model: Tackle Box

Size: A = .012″ B = .041″
Weapon: Sable Double Action Revolver
Maker: Neumann and Co.

24. Class: Rectangular
Cartridge: .22 L.R.

Model: No. 298

Size: A = .068″ B = .077″
Weapon: Savage Pump Action Rifle
Maker: Savage Arms Corp.

25. Class: Rectangular
Cartridge: .22 L.R.

Model: 6 A

Size: A = .027″ B = .061″
Weapon: Savage Semiautomatic Rifle
Maker: Savage Arms Corp.

26. Class: Rectangular
Cartridge: .22 Short

Model: "Repeating Gallery" No. 80

Size: A = .059″ B = .116″
Weapon: Stevens Slide Action Rifle
Maker: J. Stevens Arms and Tool Co.

27. Class: Rectangular
Cartridge: .22 L.R.

Model: 87B

Size: A = .036″ B = .056″
Weapon: Stevens Automatic Rifle
Maker: Savage Arms Corp.

28. Class: Rectangular
Cartridge: .22 L.R. (only)
Model: 1890 (or 90)

Size: A = .020″ B = .044″
Weapon: Winchester Pump Action Rifle
Maker: Winchester Repeating Arms Co.

29. Class: Rectangular
Cartridge: .22 L.R.

Model: No. 47

Size: A = .020″ B = .057″
Weapon: Winchester Bolt Action S.S. Rifle
Maker: Winchester-Western Div., Olin Mathieson Corp.

30. Class: Rectangular
Cartridge: .22 L.R.

Model: No. 52

Size: A = .019″ B = .065″
Weapon: Winchester Bolt Action Rifle
Maker: Win. Rep. Arms Co. and Successors

31. Class: Rectangular
Cartridge: .22 L.R.

Model: No. 61

Size: A = .020″ B = .045″
Weapon: Winchester Pump Action Rifle
Maker: Win. Rep. Arms Co. and Successors

32. Class: Rectangular
Cartridge: .22 Short

Model: No. 62 A

Size: A = .022″ B = .064″
Weapon: Winchester Pump Action Rifle
Maker: Win. Rep. Arms Co. and Successors

33. Class: Rectangular
Extractor Width: .067″
Cartridge: .22 L.R.

Model: No. 72A

Size: A = .030″ B = .057″

Weapon: Winchester Bolt Action Rifle
Maker: Win. Rep. Arms Co. and Successors

34. Class: Rectangular
Cartridge: .22 L.R.

Model: No. 74

Size: A = .029″ B = .043″
Weapon: Winchester Self-loading Rifle
Maker: Win. Rep. Arms Co. and Successors

35. Class: Rectangular
Extractor Width: .063″
Cartridge: .22 L.R.

Model: No. 75

Size: A = .027″ B = .049″

Weapon: Winchester Bolt Action Rifle
Maker: Win. Rep. Arms Co. and Successors

36. Class: Rectangular
Cartridge: 22. L.R.

Model: No. 77

Size: A = .071″ B = .056″
Weapon: Winchester Self-loading Rifle
Maker: Winchester-Western Div., Olin Mathieson Corp.

37. Class: Rectangular
Extractor Width: .064″
Cartridge: .22 L.R.
Model: Whitney (formerly Wolverine)

Size: A = .014″ B = .056″

Weapon: Whitney Auto Pistol
Maker: Whitney Firearms, Inc.

Plate 11

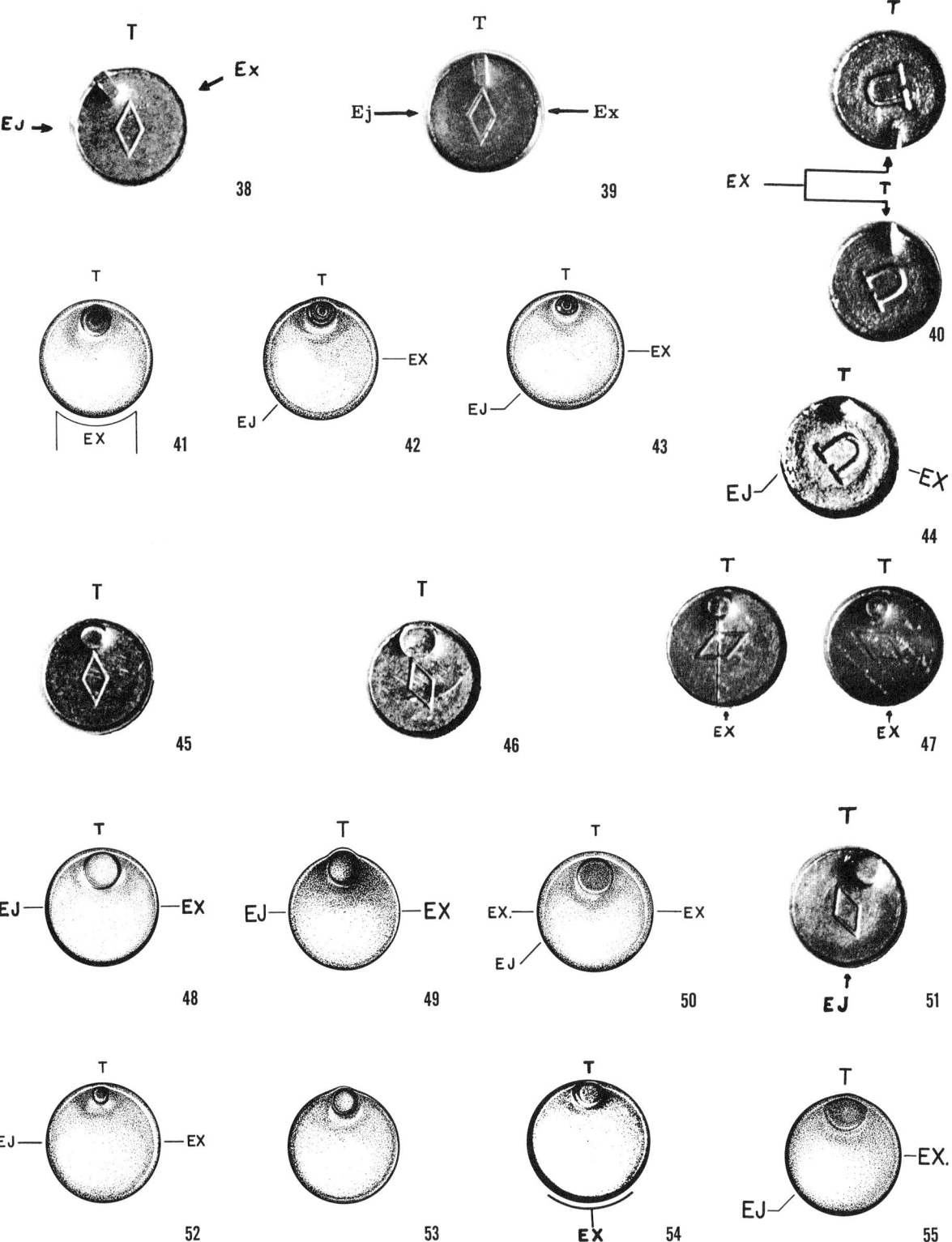

Key to Plate 11. Rim fire firing pin impressions
(Measurements of A and B are approximate)

38. Class: Rectangular
Extractor Width: .153″
Cartridge: .22 L.R.

Model: Sport

Size: A=.030″ B=.064″

Weapon: Beretta Semiautomatic Rifle
Maker: Pietro Beretta, Brescia, Italy

39. Class: Rectangular
Extractor Width: .093″
Cartridge: .22 L.R.

Model: X-5 Lightning

Size: A=.027″ B=.070″

Weapon: Ithaca Semiautomatic Rifle
Maker: Ithaca Gun Co. Inc.

40. Class: Rectangular
Extractor Width: .189″

Model: None given

Size: A=.023″ B=.070″
Weapon: "Derringer" Double Barreled Pistol
Maker: German (Distributed by Derringer Corp.)

41. Class: Round
Cartridge: .22 L.R.

Model: Martini

Size: A=.042″ B=.033″
Weapon: B.S.A. Single Shot Rifle
Maker: B.S.A. Guns, Ltd., Birmingham, Eng.

42. Class: Round
Cartridge: .22 L.R.

Model: 103.228

Size: A=.073″ B=.050″
Weapon: J. C. Higgins Bolt Action Rifle
Maker: Marlin Firearms Co. for Sears Roebuck and Co.

43. Class: Round
Cartridge: .22 L.R.

Model: No. 80

Size: A=.060″ B=.046″
Weapon: Marlin Bolt Action Rifle
Maker: Marlin Firearms Co.

44. Class: Round
Extractor Width: .134″
Cartridge: .22 L.R.

Model: SP 47/8

Size: A=.060″ B=.041″

Weapon: Neuhausen Automatic Pistol
Maker: Schweizerische Ind. Ges., Neuhausen, Switzerl.

Remarks: Spherical form. Measurements taken from top of impression.

45. Class: Round
Cartridge: .22 L.R.

Model: Single Six

Size: A=.057″ B=.050″
Weapon: Ruger Single Action Revolver
Maker: Sturm, Ruger and Co.

Remarks: Impression from guns as made prior to November 1956.

46. Class: Round
Cartridge: .22 L.R.

Model: Single Six

Size: A=.088″ B=.082″
Weapon: Ruger Single Action Revolver
Maker Sturm, Ruger and Co.

Remarks: Firing pin impressions from guns made after Nov. 1, 1956.

47. Class: Round
Extractor Width: .150″
Cartridge: .22 L.R.

Model: Knocabout

Size: A=.050″ B=.047″

Weapon: Sheridan Single Shot Pistol
Maker: Sheridan Products, Inc.

Remarks: When breech is opened or closed with cartridge in chamber and hammer in full forward position, cases are marked with characteristic scratch shown. This does not occur when closed or opened from half-cock or cocked hammer position.

48. Class: Round
Cartridge: .22 L.R.

Model: M1922M1

Size: A=.077″ B=.077″
Weapon: U.S. Springfield Bolt Action Mag. Rifle
Maker: Springfield Armory

49. Class: Round
Cartridge: .22 L.R.

Model: 1922 M2

Size: A=.075″ B=.075″
Weapon: U.S. Springfield Bolt Action Rifle
Maker: Springfield Armory

50. Class: Round
Extractor Width: .115″
Cartridge: .22 L.R.

Model: No. 416

Size: A=.071″ B=.059″

Weapon: Stevens Bolt Action Rifle
Maker: J. Stevens Arms Co., Div. of Savage Arms Corp.

51. Class: Round
Cartridge: .22 L.R.

Model: Powermaster

Size: A=.073″ B=.070″
Weapon: Wamo Single Shot Pistol
Maker: Wamo Manufacturing Co.

52. Class: Round
Cartridge: .22 L.R.

Model: 63

Size: A=.057″ B=.057″
Weapon: Winchester Selfloading Rifle
Maker: Winchester-Western Div., Olin Mathieson Corp.

53. Class: Round
Cartridge: Special Blank

Size: A=.065″ B=.065″
Weapon: Zip Chamber Auxiliary Cartridge
Maker: National Arms Co., San Francisco, Cal.

54. Class: Semicircular
Cartridge: .22 L.R.

Size: A=.075″ B=.048″
Weapon: Stoeger .22 cal. Attachment, SS
Maker: Probably made in Europe for Steoger Arms Corp., New York

Remarks: Fits all Colt guns having M1911 type frame. (Sold 1931–1934).

55. Class: Semicircular
Extractor Width: .202″
Cartridge: .22 L.R.

Model: 30 DL

Size: A=.049″ B=.049″

Weapon: Marlin Bolt Action Rifle
Maker: Marlin Firearms Co.

Plate 12

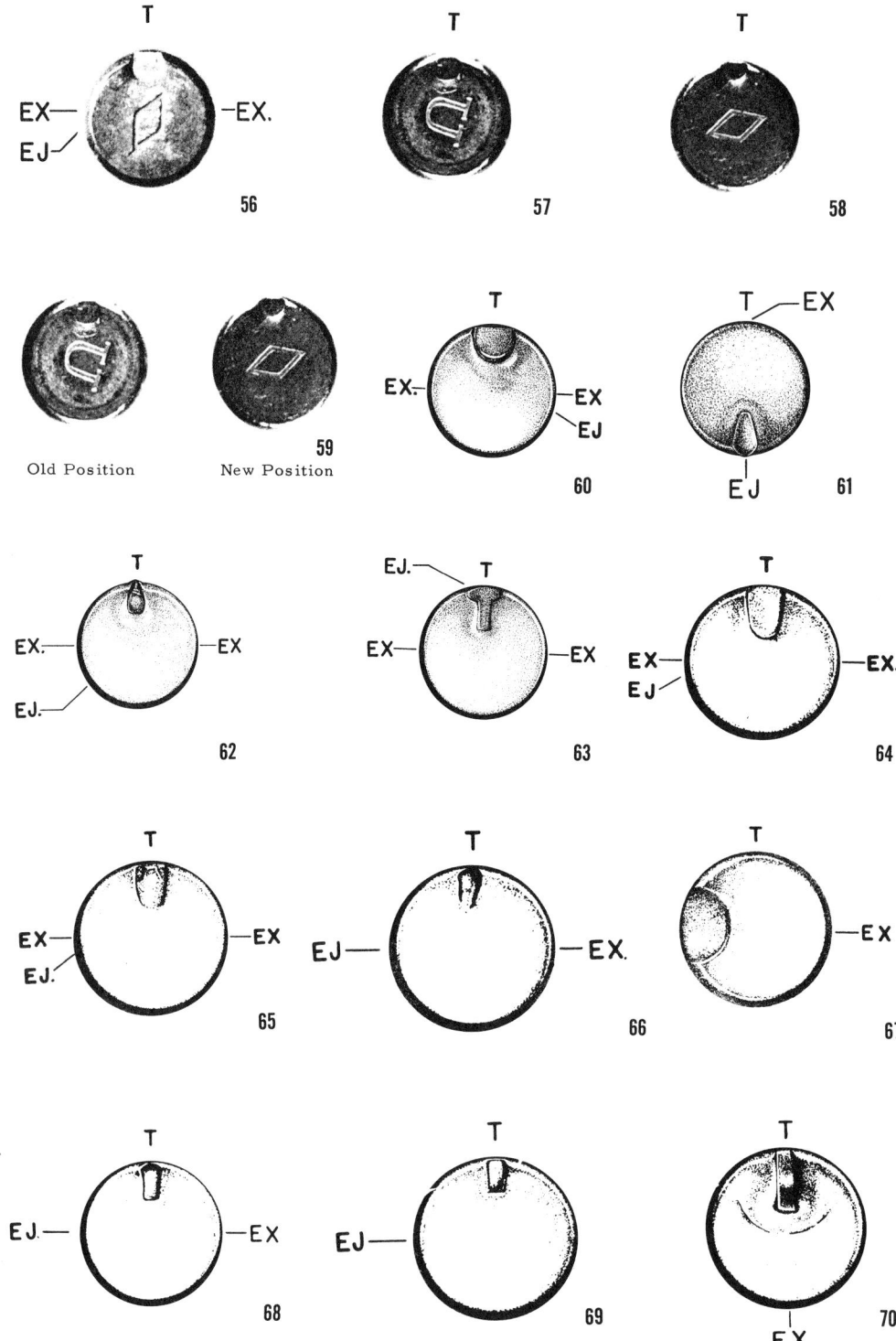

Key to Plate 12. Rim fire firing pin impressions
(Measurements of A and B are approximate)

56. Class: Semicircular
Extractor Width: .077″
(Double)
Cartridge: .22 L.R.
Model: 56

Size: A = .057″   B = .054″

Weapon: Marlin Lever Action
Rifle
Maker: Marlin Firearms Co.

57. Class: Round (or Semi-circular)
Cartridge: .22 L.R.

Model: Original K22, K22/40, and K22/46 made prior to March 15, 1948

Size: A = .055″   B = .050″

Weapon: S & W Double
Action Revolver
Maker: Smith and Wesson, Inc.

58. Class: Semicircular
Cartridge: .22 L.R.

Model: K22/46 as made after March 15, 1948

Size: A = .053″   B = .036″
Weapon: S & W Double
Action Revolver
Maker: Smith and Wesson, Inc.

59. Illustrating change in position of firing pin made by Smith and Wesson on March 15, 1948 (see No. 57 and 58 above). Firing pin bushing hole moved up .015″, thus making pin strike nearer edge of cartridge rim. Impression now definitely semicircular.

60. Class: Semicircular
Cartridge: .22 L.R.

Model: 56 Buckhorn

Size: A = .068″   B = .055″
Weapon: Stevens Bolt Action
Mag. Rifle
Maker: J. Stevens Arms Co.

61. Class: Special
Extractor Width: .123″
Cartridge: .22 L.R.

Model: 103.18

Size: A = .048″   B = .077″

Weapon: J. C. Higgins Bolt
Action Rifle
Maker: Sears Roebuck
(distributors)

Remarks: Firing pin acts as ejector.

62. Class: Special
Cartridge: .22 L.R.

Model: 37 Rangemaster

Size: A = .026″   B = .060″
Weapon: Remington Bolt
Action Mag. Rifle
Maker: Remington Arms Co.

63. Class: Special
Cartridge: .22 L.R.

Model: 29A

Size: A = .073″   B = .095″
Weapon: Savage Slide Action
Mag. Rifle
Maker: Savage Arms Corp.

64. Class: Special
Cartridge: .22 L.R.

Model: EJN 807

Size: A = .057″   B = .071″
Weapon: Western Field S.S.
Bolt Action Rifle
Maker: Jefferson Corp., New
Haven, Conn. (for Mont-gomery Ward)

65. Class: Special
Cartridge: .22 L.R.

Model: Colteer 1-22

Size: A = .052″   B = .052-.056″
Weapon: Colteer S.S. Bolt
Action Rifle
Maker: Jefferson Corp.

66. Class: Special (or Rect.?)

Cartridge: .22 Short

Model: 949 Olimpionica

Size: A = .040″   B = .041″
(Meas. of A made at top)
Weapon: Beretta Automatic
Pistol
Maker: Pietro Beretta

67. Class: Semicircular
Cartridge: .22 L.R.

Model: 75

Size: A = .125″   B = .075″
Weapon: Cooey S.S. Bolt
Action Rifle
Maker: H. W. Cooey
Machine and Arms Co., Ltd.
Cobourg, Ontario

68. Class: Rectangular
Cartridge: .22 L.R.

Model: 948 Bis Plinker

Size: A = .027″   B = .035″
Weapon: Beretta Automatic
Pistol
Maker: Pietro Baretta

69. Class: Rectangular
Cartridge: .22 Short

Model: 950 c.c. (Minx M-2)

Size: A = .029″   B = .047″
Weapon: Beretta Automatic
Pistol
Maker: Pietro Beretta

70. Class: Rectangular
Cartridge: .22 L.R.

Model: 15

Size: A = .028″   B = .081″
Weapon: Hamilton S.S.
Bolt Action Rifle
Maker: Hamilton Rifle Co.,
Plymouth, Mich.

Plate 13

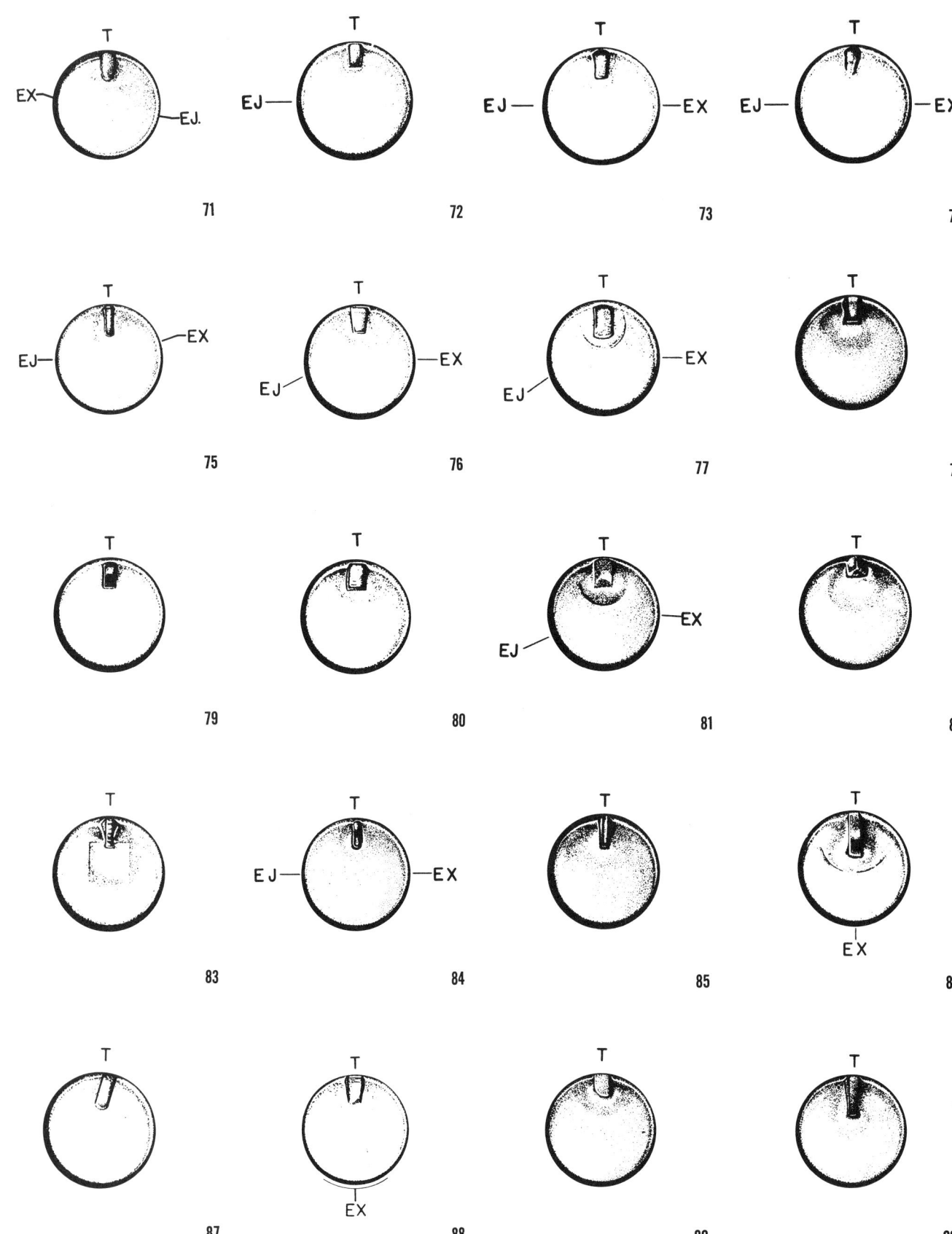

378

Key to Plate 13. Rim fire firing pin impressions

(Measurements of A and B are approximate)

71. Class: Rectangular
Cartridge: .22 L.R.

Size: A=.023″ B=.050″
Weapon: Armalite Semiautomatic Rifle

Model: Explorer AR-7

Maker: Armalite Division, Fairchild Engine and Airplane Co.

Remarks: Introduced in 1960.

72. Class: Rectangular
Cartridge: .22 Short

Size: A=.029″ B=.047″
Weapon: Beretta Semiautomatic Pistol

Model: 950 c.c. Minx M-2

Maker: Pietro Beretta

Remarks: No extractor.

73. Class: Rectangular
Cartridge: .22 L.R.

Size: A=.027″ B=.035″
Weapon: Beretta Semiautomatic Pistol

Model: 948 bis Plinker

Maker: Pietro Beretta

74. Class: Rectangular
Cartridge: .22 Short

Size: A=.040″ B=.041″
Weapon: Beretta Semiautomatic Pistol

Model: 949 Olimpionica

Maker: Pietro Beretta

Remarks: Meas. "A" made from top of impression due to rounded form.

75. Class: Rectangular
Cartridge: .22 L.R.

Size: A=.020″ B=.070″
Weapon: Brno Semiautomatic Rifle

Model: 581

Maker: Česka Zbrojovka Brno N.P.

Remarks: Post-World War II.

76. Class: Rectangular
Cartridge: .22 L.R.

Size: A=.035″ B=.057″
Weapon: Colt Semiautomatic Pistol

Model: Woodsman (Serial No. 39,189)

Maker: Colt's Pt. F. A. Mfg. Co.

77. Class: Rectangular
Cartridge: .22 L.R.

Size: A=.040″ B=.068″
Weapon: Colt Semiautomatic Pistol

Model: Woodsman (Serial No. 106,660)

Maker: Colt's Pt. F. A. Mfg. Co.

Remarks: Circular mark made by firing pin bushing.

78. Class: Rectangular
Cartridge: .22 Short or L.R.

Size: A=.037″ B=.051″
Weapon: Colt Single Action Revolver

Model: New Line

Maker: Colt's Pt. F.A. Mfg. Co.

79. Class: Rectangular
Cartridge: .22 L.R.

Size: A=.018″ B=.050=
Weapon: Colt Single Shot Pistol

Model: Camp Perry (Serial 299)

Maker: Colt's Pt. F. A. Mfg. Co.

80. Class: Rectangular
Cartridge: .22 L.R.

Size: A=.041″ B=.060″
Weapon: Colt Double Action Revolver

Model: Officers Target

Maker: Colt's Pt. F. A. Mfg. Co.

Remarks: Mark made by specimen Serial No. 7074.

81. Class: Rectangular
Cartridge: .22 L.R.

Size: A=.040″ B=.060″
Weapon: Colt Automatic Pistol

Model: Ace Target

Maker: Colt's Pt. F. A. Mfg. Co.

82. Class: Rectangular
Cartridge: .22 Short

Size: A=.044″ B=.043″
Weapon: Defiance Single Action Revolver

Model: ——

Maker: Unknown

Remarks: Based on patents issued to Wm. H. Bliss, Norwich, Conn.

83. Class: Rectangular
Cartridge: .22 Short or L.R.

Size: A=.018″ B=.042″
Weapon: Eig Double Action Revolver

Model: ——

Maker: Röhm Gesellschaft, Sontheim/Brenz W. Germany

Remarks: Mark made by gun Serial No. 240,776.

84. Class: Rectangular
Cartridge: .22 L.R.

Size: A=.011″ B=.062″
Weapon: Erma Automatic Pistol

Model: Target

Maker: Erma Waffenfabrik Erfurt, Germany

85. Class: Rectangular
Cartridge: .22 L.R.

Size: A=.009″ B=.068″
Weapon: Eureka Single Action Revolver

Model: ——

Maker: Unknown

Remarks: Made in U.S., ca. 1870–1890.

86. Class: Rectangular
Cartridge: .22 L.R.

Size: A=.028″ B=.081″
Weapon: Hamilton Single Shot Rifle

Model: No. 15

Maker: Hamilton Rifle Co., Plymouth, Mich.

Remarks: Has no ejector.

87. Class: Rectangular
Cartridge: .22 L.R.

Size: A=.030″ B=.055″
Weapon: H & R Double Action Revolver

Model: 929 Side Kick

Maker: Harrington and Richardson

Remarks: From gun Ser. No. 29,097.

88. Class: Rectangular
Cartridge: .22 L.R.

Size: A=.036″ B=.052″
Weapon: H & A Single Shot Pistol

Model: New Model Target

Maker: Hopkins and Allen

Remarks: Specimen Ser. No. 2983. Some similar models produce semicircular impressions (see No. 107).

89. Class: Rectangular
Cartridge: .22 Short

Size: A=.034″ B=.037″
Weapon: Blue Jacket S. A. Revolver

Model: No. 1

Maker: Hopkins and Allen

Remarks: Pat. date March 28, 1871.

90. Class: Rectangular
Cartridge: .22 Short

Size: A=.022″ B=.086″
Weapon: Blue Jacket S. A. Revolver

Model: No. 1

Maker: Hopkins and Allen

Remarks: Pat. date March 28, 1871.

Plate 14

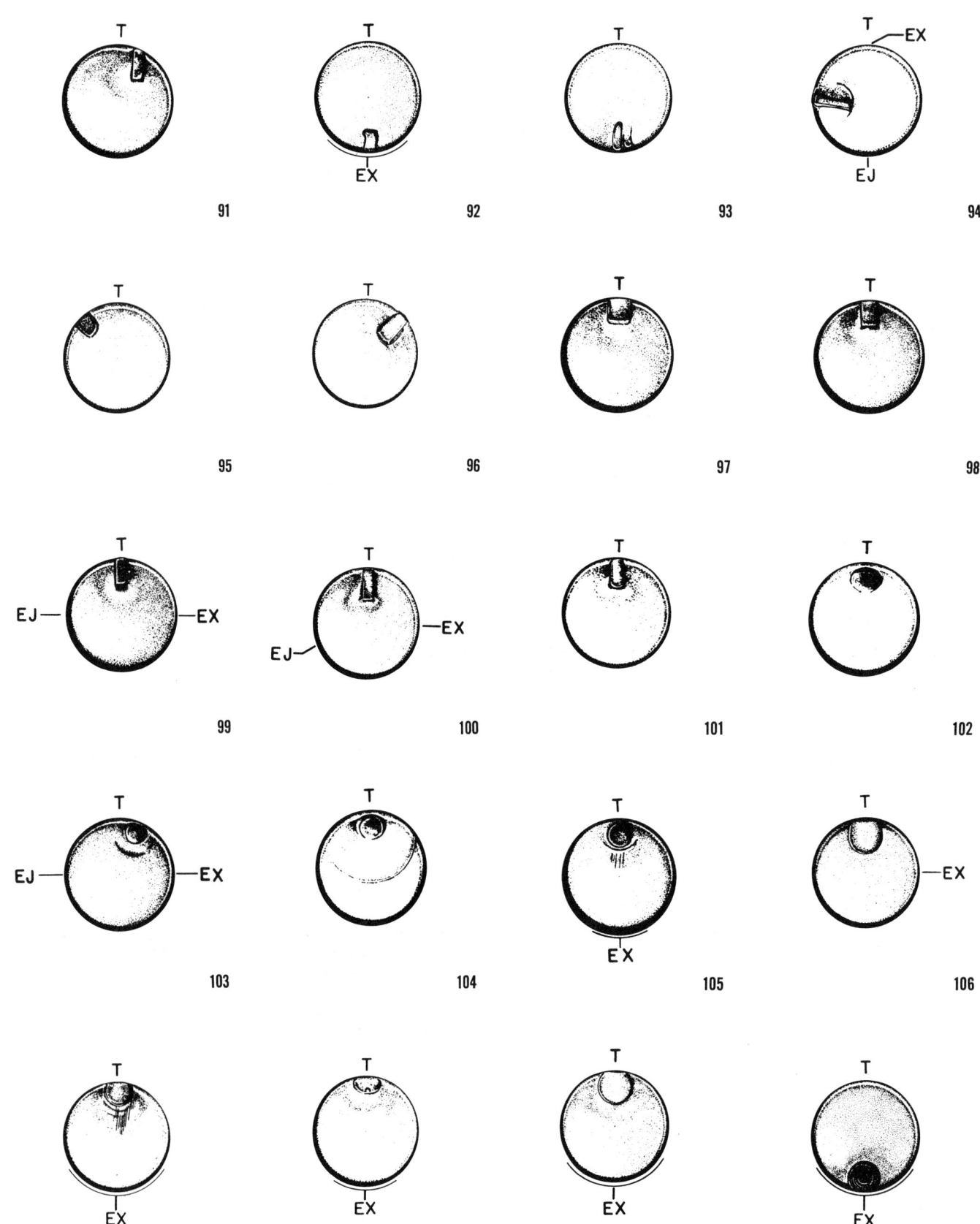

Key to Plate 14. Rim fire firing pin impressions
(Measurements of A and B are approximate)

91. Class: Rectangular
Cartridge: .22 Short
Model: ——
Remarks: Pat. date March 28, 1871.
Size: A = .015″ B = .062″
Weapon: Capt. Jack S. A. Revolver
Maker: Hopkins and Allen

92. Class: Rectangular
Cartridge: .22 Short
Model: 1911 New Baby
Size: A = .030″ B = .040″
Weapon: Kolb Double Action Revolver
Maker: Henry M. Kolb, Philadelphia, Pa.

93. Class: Rectangular
Cartridge: .22 Short
Model: Baby Hammerless
Size: A = .020″ B = .048″
Weapon: Kolb Double Action Revolver
Maker: Henry M. Kolb

94. Class: Rectangular
Cartridge: .22 L.R.
Model: ——
Remarks: Post-World War II production.
Size: A = .014″ B = .075″
Weapon: Landman Bolt Action Mag. Rifle
Maker: J. G. Landman, Preetz/Holst, Germany

95. Class: Rectangular
Cartridge: .22 L.R.
Model: Brownie
Size: A = .037″ B = .035″
Weapon: Mossberg 4-Bbl. Pistol
Maker: O. F. Mossberg and Sons
Remarks: Revolving firing pin. Impression shown on shell from lower right hand barrel.

96. Class: Rectangular
Cartridge: .22 Short
Model: ——
Size: A = .020″ B = .048″
Weapon: Sharps 4-Bbl. Pistol
Maker: C. Sharps and Co., Philadelphia, Pa.
Remarks: Revolving firing pin. Impression shown is from lower left hand barrel.

97. Class: Rectangular
Cartridge: .22 Short
Model: No. 1, Third type
Size: A = .055″ B = .061″
Weapon: S & W Single Action Revolver
Maker: Smith and Wesson, Inc.

98. Class: Rectangular
Cartridge: .22 L.R.
Model: Perfected
Size: A = .037″ B = .045″
Weapon: S & W Double Action Revolver
Maker: Smith and Wesson, Inc.
Remarks: Some specimens have round end firing pins (see No. 105).

99. Class: Rectangular
Cartridge: .22 L.R.
Model: 41
Size: A = .024″ B = .050″
Weapon: S & W Automatic Pistol
Maker: Smith and Wesson, Inc.

100. Class: Rectangular
Cartridge: .22 L.R.
Model: Sport (Pre-W.W.II)
Size: A = .018″ B = .068″
Weapon: Walther Semiautomatic Pistol
Maker: Waffenfabrik Walther Zella-Mehilo, Germany

101. Class: Rectangular
Cartridge: .22 Short
Model: ——
Size: A = .030″ B = .064″
Weapon: Rollin White S.A. Revolver
Maker: Rollin White Arms Co.

102. Class: Round
Cartridge: .22 L.R.
Model: Match 503 and 504
Size: A = .064″ B = .055″
Weapon: Hämmerli Bolt Action S.A. Rifle
Maker: Hämmerli et Cie., Lenzburg, Switzerland
Remarks: Hemispherical end to firing pin. Impression measured at top edges.

103. Class: Round
Cartridge: .22 Short
Model: C
Size: A = .074″ B = .044″
Weapon: HI Standard Semi-automatic Pistol
Maker: High Standard Mfg. Corp.

104. Class: Round
Cartridge: .22 L.R.
Model: 101
Size: A = .070″ B = .058″
Weapon: Savage Single Shot Pistol
Maker: Savage Arms Corp.
Remarks: Large arc below firing pin impression made by firing pin bushing. May not be made by all specimens of this make and model.

105. Class: Round
Cartridge: .22 L.R.
Model: Perfected
Size: A = .058″ B = .058″
Weapon: S & W Single Shot Pistol
Maker: Smith and Wesson, Inc.
Remarks: Some specimens of this model produce rectangular firing pin impressions (see No. 98).

106. Class: Semicircular
Cartridge: .22 L.R.
Model: ——
Size: A = .075″ B = .059″
Weapon: Hartford Single Shot Pistol
Maker: Hartford Arms and Equipment Co.

107. Class: Semicircular
Cartridge: .22 L.R.
Model: New Model Target
Size: A = .080″ B = .058″
Weapon: H & A Single Shot Pistol
Maker: Hopkins and Allen
Remarks: Mark made by specimen Ser. No. 2733. Similar models also make rectangular impressions (see No. 88).

108. Class: Semicircular
Cartridge: .22 L.R.
Model: New Model Target
Size: A = .067″ B = .026″
Weapon: H & A Single Shot Pistol
Maker: Hopkins and Allen
Remarks: Mark produced by specimen Serial No. 852. Rectangular marks may also be found for this make and model (see No. 88).

109. Class: Semicircular
Cartridge: .22 L.R.
Model: 855
Size: A = .070″ B = .058″
Weapon: I. J. Single Action Revolver
Maker: Iver Johnson Arms and Cycle Works

110. Class: Semicircular
Cartridge: .22 L.R.
Model: Straight Line
Size: A = .065″ B = .050″
Weapon: S & W Single Shot Pistol
Maker: Smith and Wesson, Inc.
Remarks: Made from ca. 1923 to 1927.

Plate 15

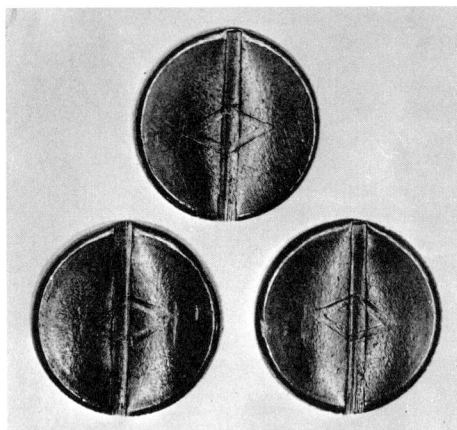

Class: BAR; RANGER RIFLE; Mod. 34-A. auto.; Box mag.; Bolt action; Serial No., none; Firing pin mark from 12 to 6 o'clock; Ex. mark, none; Ej. mark at 9 o'clock

Class: RECTANGULAR; ASTRA AUTO PISTOL; Mod. 2000; Serial No. 35546; Firing pin mark at 12 o'clock; Ex. mark at 2:30 o'clock; Ej. mark at 9 o'clock

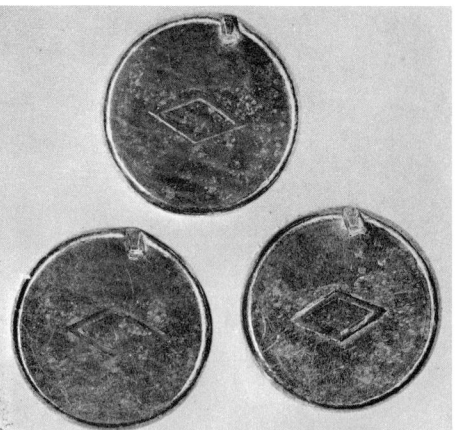

Class: RECT.; BAYARD RIFLE; Single shot; Bolt action; Serial No. 9616; Firing pin mark at 12:30 o'clock; Ex. mark at 1 o'clock; Ej. mark at 6 o'clock

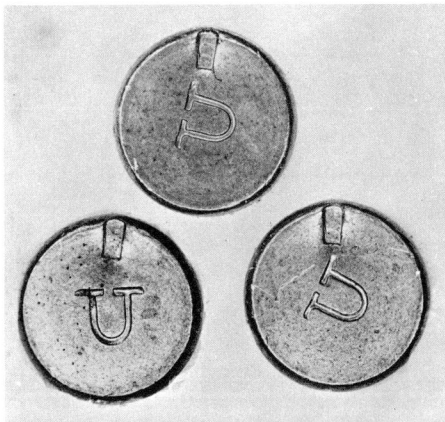

Class: RECT.; BERETTA AUTO PISTOL; Mod. 948; Serial No. 022931-N; Firing pin mark at 12 o'clock; Ex. mark at 3 o'clock; Ej. mark at 8 o'clock

Class: RECT.; COLT AUTO PISTOL; Woodsman Mod., early type; Serial No. 181219; Firing pin mark at 12 o'clock; Ex. mark at 3:15 o'clock; Ej. mark at 7 o'clock

Class: RECT.; COLT REV.; Police Mod.; Serial No. 7556; Firing pin mark at 12 o'clock. (Double impression due to rebounding hammer)

Class: RECT.; COLT AUTO PISTOL; Woodsman Mod.; Serial No. 168026-S; Firing pin mark at 12 o'clock; Ex. mark at 3 o'clock. Ej. mark at 7 o'clock

Class: RECT.; COLT AUTO PISTOL; Challenger Mod.; Serial No. 10963-C; Firing pin mark at 12 o'clock; Ex. mark at 3 o'clock; Ej. mark at 7 o'clock

Class: RECT.; DEFENDER REV.; Mod. 89; Serial No. 293; Firing pin mark at 12 o'clock

Plate 16

Class: RECT.; H&R REV.; Mod. 1896; Serial No. 83410; Firing pin mark at 12 o'clock

Class: RECT.; H&R REV.; Premier Mod.; Serial No. 48706; Firing pin mark at 12 o'clock

Class: RECT.; H&R REV.; Premier Mod.; Serial No., none; Firing pin mark at 12 o'clock

Class: RECT.; H&R REV.; Trapper Mod.; Serial No. 179947; Firing pin mark at 12 o'clock

Class: RECT.; H&R REV.; Victor Mod.; Serial No. 116062; Firing pin mark at 12 o'clock

Class: RECT.; H&R REV.; Victor Mod.; Serial No. 485466; Firing pin mark at 12 o'clock

Class: RECT.; H&R REV.; Young America Mod.; Serial No. 460; Firing pin mark at 12 o'clock. (Double impression due to rebounding hammer)

Class: RECT.; H&R REV.; Young America Mod.; Serial No. 760; Firing pin mark at 12 o'clock

Class: RECT.; H&R REV.; Young America Mod.; Serial No. 199570; Firing pin mark at 12 o'clock. (Variation due to loose cylinder)

Plate 17

Class: RECT.; H&R REV.; Young America Mod.; Serial No. 325306; Firing pin mark at 12 o'clock

Class: RECT.; H&R REV.; 1906 Mod.; Serial No. 83826; Firing pin mark at 12 o'clock

Class: RECT.; H&R REV.; Mod. 922; Serial No. P-3658; Firing pin mark at 12 o'clock

Class: RECT.; H&R REV.; Mod. "Sportsman"; Serial No. N-7162; Firing pin mark at 12 o'clock

Class: RECT.; H&R REV.; Mod. "22 Special"; Serial No. 512880; Firing pin mark at 12 o'clock

Class: RECT.; H&R REV.; Mod. "Sportsman"; Serial No. 41332; Firing pin mark at 12 o'clock

Class: RECT.; J. C. HIGGINS PISTOL; Mod. 85; Automatic; Serial No. 508255; Firing pin mark at 12 o'clock; Ex. mark at 2 o'clock. Shell is ejected off of magazine clip

Class: RECT.; J. C. HIGGINS REV.; Mod. 88; Serial No. 652749; Firing pin mark at 12 o'clock

Class: RECT.; J. C. HIGGINS REV.; Mod. 88; Serial No. 660697; Firing pin mark at 12 o'clock

Class: RECT.; J. C. HIGGINS RIFLE; Mod. 30; Automatic; Serial No. 58374; Firing pin mark at 2 o'clock; Ex. mark at 3 o'clock; Ej. mark at 7 o'clock

Class: RECT.; HI STANDARD REV.; Mod. "Sentinel"; Serial No. 10619; Firing pin mark at 12 o'clock

Class: RECT.; HI STANDARD REV.; Mod. "Double-Nine"; Serial No. 844684; Firing pin mark at 12 o'clock

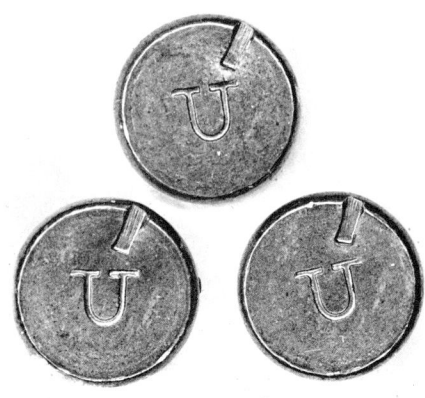

Class: RECT.; HI STANDARD PISTOL; Mod. H-D Military; Serial No. 303779; Firing pin mark at 1 o'clock; Ex. mark at 3 o'clock; Ej. mark at 7 o'clock

Class: RECT.; HOPKINS & ALLEN REV.; Mod. X.L.I.; Double action; Serial No. 5752; Firing pin mark at 1 o'clock

Class: RECT.; HOPKINS & ALLEN REV.; Mod. X.L.; Double action; Serial No. 8655; Firing pin mark at 12 o'clock

Class: RECT.; IVER JOHNSON REV.; Mod. "Sealed Eight"; Serial No. N-19909; Firing pin mark at 12 o'clock

Class: RECT.; IVER JOHNSON REV.; Mod. "Target Sealed Eight"; Serial No. N-20698; Firing pin mark at 12 o'clock

Class: RECT.; IVER JOHNSON REV.; Mod. "U. S. Revolver"; Serial No. 77287; Firing pin mark at 12 o'clock

Firearms identification

Plate 19

Class: RECT.; IVER JOHNSON RIFLE; Mod. 2-X; S.S.; Bolt action; firing pin mark at 12 o'clock

Class: RECT.; IVER JOHNSON REV.; Mod. 1900; Serial No. 18717; Firing pin mark at 12 o'clock

Class: RECT.; IVER JOHNSON REV.; Mod. 1900; Serial No. 80055; Firing pin mark at 12 o'clock

Class: RECT.; IVER JOHNSON REV.; Mod. 1900; Serial No. 98305; Firing pin mark at 12 o'clock

Class: RECT.; KOLB RE-VOLVER; Mod. 1910 Baby Hammerless; Serial No. 245; Firing pin mark at 12 o'clock

Class: RECT.; M.A.B. PISTOL; Le Chasseur Mod. Auto.; Serial No. 2603; Firing pin mark at 12 o'clock; Ex. mark at 3 o'clock; Ej. mark at 7:30 o'clock

Class: RECT.; MARLIN REV.; Mod. XX STANDARD 1873; Serial No. 2059; Firing pin mark at 12 o'clock. (Variation due to loose cylinder)

386

Class: RECT.; MARLIN REV.; Mod. XX STANDARD 1873; Serial No. 4023; Firing pin mark at 12 o'clock. (Note slant of firing pin marks)

Class: RECT.; MAUSER RIFLE; Mod., none designated; S.S.; Bolt action; Serial No. 89858; Firing pin mark at 8 o'clock; Ex. mark at 2 o'clock; Ej. mark at 9 o'clock

Class: RECT.; MAUSER RIFLE; Mod. ES 350-Ch. 51; S.S.; Bolt action; Serial No. 169703; Firing pin mark at 12 o'clock; Ex. mark at 1:30 o'clock; Ej. mark at 7:30 o'clock

Class: RECT.; MOSSBERG RIFLE; Mod. 42-A; Bolt action; Box mag.; Firing pin mark 12 o'clock; Ex. mark at 3:30 o'clock; Ej. mark at 9 o'clock

Class: RECT.; MOSSBERG RIFLE; Mod. 144; Bolt action; Box mag.; Firing pin mark at 12 o'clock. Ex. marks at 3:30 & 9:30; Ej. mark at 7 o'clock

Class: RECT.; MOSSBERG RIFLE; Mod. 151 M-B.; Automatic; Bolt action; Tubular mag. in stock; Serial No., none; Firing pin mark at 11:45 o'clock; Ex. mark at 3 o'clock, Ej. mark at 9 o'clock

Class: RECT.; MOSSBERG RIFLE; Mod. 152; Automatic; Bolt action; Box mag.; 7 shot clip; Firing pin mark at 12 o'clock; Ex. mark at 3 o'clock; Ej. mark at 9 o'clock

Class: RECT.; PREMIER RIFLE; Slide action repeater; Serial No. 14296-K; Firing pin mark at 12 o'clock; Ex. mark at 3 o'clock Ej;. mark at 8 o'clock

Class: RECT.; RANGER RIFLE; Mod. 35; S.S. Bolt action; Serial No. 370; Firing pin mark at 8:30 o'clock; Ex. mark at 3:30 o'clock; Ej. mark at 9:30 o'clock

Class: RECT.; RANGER RIFLE; Mod. 103-8; S.S.; Bolt action; Firing pin mark at 8:30 o'clock; Ex. mark at 3:30 o'clock; Ej. mark none, as firing pin acts as ejector

Class: RECT.; REMINGTON RIFLE; Mod. 6 Improved; Single shot; Rolling block type; Serial No. 496805; Firing pin mark at 3:15 o'clock; Ex. mark at 6 o'clock; Ej. mark, arm has no ejector

Plate 21

Class: RECT.; REMINGTON
RIFLE; Mod. 12; Slide action;
Serial No. 258489; Firing pin
mark at 11 o'clock; Ex. mark at
3 o'clock; Ej. mark at 8 o'clock

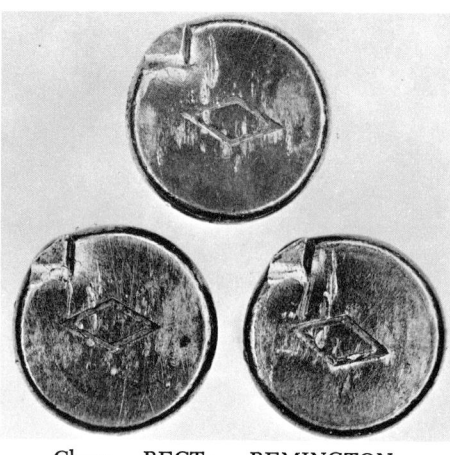

Class: RECT.; REMINGTON
RIFLE; Mod. 12; Slide action;
Serial No. 271212; Firing pin
mark at 11 o'clock; Ex. mark at
3 o'clock; Ej. mark at 8 o'clock

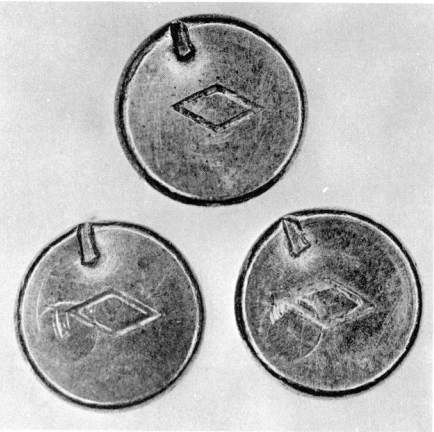

Class: RECT.; REMINGTON
RIFLE; Mod. 41-P; S.S.; Bolt
action; Serial No. 282732; Firing pin mark at 11 o'clock; Ex.
mark at 3 o'clock; Ej. mark at
8 o'clock

Class: RECT.; REMINGTON
RIFLE; Mod. 41-P; S.S.; Bolt
action; Firing pin mark at 11
o'clock; Ex. mark at 3 o'clock;
Ej. mark at 8 o'clock

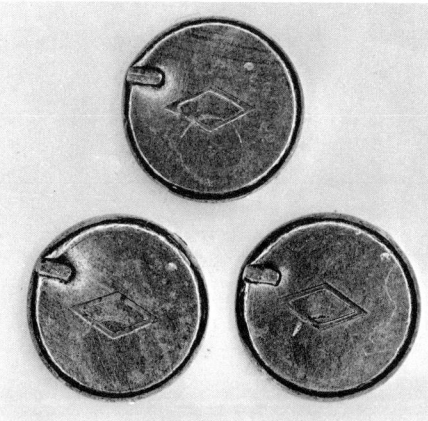

Class: RECT.; REMINGTON
RIFLE; Mod. 341-P; S.S.; Bolt
action; Serial No. 37001; Firing
pin mark at 10 o'clock; Ex.
mark at 1 o'clock; Ej. mark at
6 o'clock

Class: RECT.; REMINGTON
RIFLE; Mod. 510; S.S.; Bolt
action; Serial No. 277; Firing
pin mark at 12:15 o'clock; Ex.
marks at 3 & 9 o'clock; Ej. mark
at 7 o'clock

Class: RECT.; REMINGTON
RIFLE; Mod. 510-P; S.S.; Bolt
action; Serial No., none; Firing
pin mark at 12 o'clock; Ex.
marks at 3 & 9 o'clock Ej. mark
at 7 o'clock

Class: RECT.; REMINGTON
RIFLE; Mod. 511; Bolt action;
Box mag.; Serial No. 359; Firing
pin mark at 12:15 o'clock; Ex.
marks at 3 & 9 o'clock; Ej. mark
at 7:30 o'clock

Class: RECT.; REMINGTON
RIFLE; Mod. 514; S.S.; Bolt
action; Serial No., none; Firing
pin mark at 11 o'clock; Ex.
mark at 2 o'clock; Ej. mark at
6 o'clock

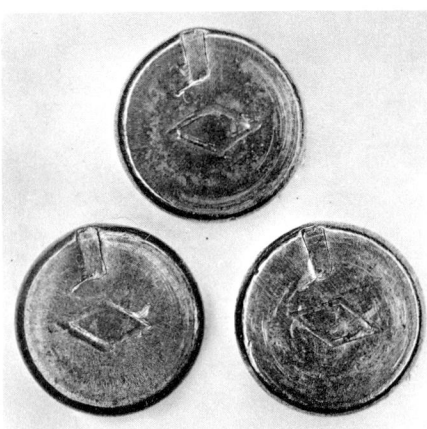

Class: RECT.; REMINGTON RIFLE; Mod. 514; S.S.; Bolt action; Serial No., none; Firing pin mark at 11 o'clock; Ex. mark at 3 o'clock; Ej. mark at 8:30 o'clock

Class: RECT.; REMINGTON RIFLE; Mod. "Nylon 66"; Autoloading; Serial No., none; Firing pin mark at 12 o'clock; Ex. mark at 3 o'clock; Ej. mark at 9 o'clock

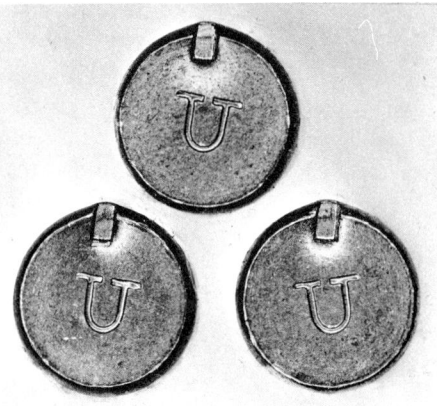

Class: RECT.; RUGER PISTOL; Mod. Standard Automatic; Serial No. 7829; Firing pin mark at 12 o'clock; Ex. mark at 3 o'clock; Ej. mark at 8 o'clock

Class: RECT.; RUGER PISTOL; Mod. Standard Automatic; Serial No. 14939; Firing pin mark at 12 o'clock; Ex. mark at 3:30 o'clock; Ej. mark at 8 o'clock

Class: RECT.; RUGER PISTOL; Mod. Standard Automatic; Serial No. 80777; Firing pin mark at 12 o'clock; Ex. mark at 3 o'clock; Ej. mark at 8 o'clock

Class: RECT.; RUGER PISTOL; Mod. Standard Automatic; Serial No. 94243; Firing pin mark at 12 o'clock; Ex. mark at 3 o'clock; Ej. mark at 8 o'clock

Class: RECT.; S&W REV.; Hand Ejector Mod. I; Serial No. 2759; Firing pin mark at 12 o'clock

Class: RECT.; S&W REV.; Mod. I. (2nd Model of); Serial No. 78988; Firing pin mark at 12 o'clock

Class: RECT.; SPRINGFIELD RIFLE; Mod. 83; S.S.; Bolt action; Serial No., none; Firing pin mark at 8:30 o'clock; Ex. mark at 3:30 o'clock. Firing Pin acts as ejector

Plate 23

Class: RECT.; SPRINGFIELD RIFLE; Mod. 83; S.S.; Bolt action; Serial No., none; Firing pin mark at 8 o'clock; Ex. mark at 3:30 o'clock. Firing Pin acts as ejector

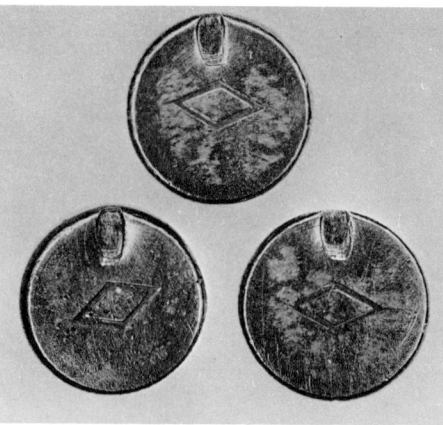

Class: RECT.; SPRINGFIELD RIFLE; Mod. 87-A; Automatic; Bolt action; Serial No., none; Firing pin mark at 12 o'clock; Ex. marks at 3 & 9 o'clock; Ej. mark at 7 o'clock

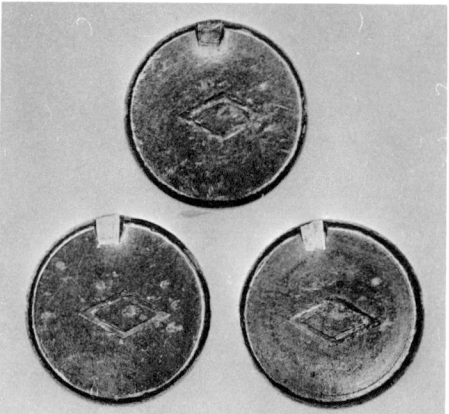

Class: RECT.; STEVENS RIFLE; "Stevens Visible Loading"; Serial No. 5743; Slide action repeater; Firing pin mark at 11:30 o'clock; Ex. marks at 3 & 9 o'clock; Ej. mark at 6 o'clock

Class: RECT.; STEVENS RIFLE; Mod. 15; S.S.; Bolt action; Serial No., none; Firing pin mark at 7:30 o'clock; Ex. mark at 4:30 o'clock; Ej. mark at 8:30 o'clock

Class: RECT.; STEVENS RIFLE; Mod. 15-A; S.S.; Bolt action; Serial No., none; Firing pin mark at 10:00 o'clock; Ex. mark at 4:30 o'clock; Ej. mark at 8:30 o'clock

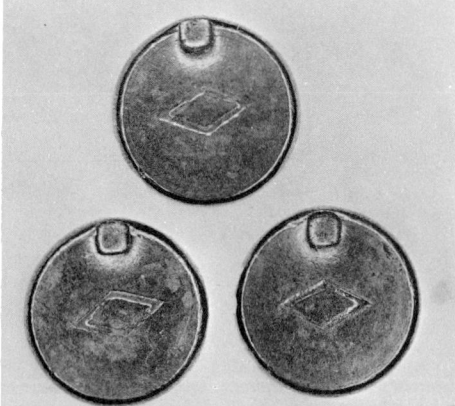

Class: RECT.; STEVENS RIFLE; Mod. 85; Automatic; Box mag.; Serial No., none; Firing pin mark at 12 o'clock; Ex. marks at 3 & 9 o'clock; Ej. mark at 7:30 o'clock

Class: RECT.; U.S. REV.; (Same as Iver Johnson Mod. 1900); Firing pin mark at 12 o'clock

Class: RECT.; WESTERN FIELD RIFLE; Mod. SD 58A; Automatic; Bolt action; Firing pin mark at 12 o'clock; Ex. marks at 3:15 & 9 o'clock; Ej. mark at 7 o'clock

Class: RECT.; WESTERN FIELD RIFLE; Mod. 46-A; Bolt action; Box mag.; Firing pin mark at 12 o'clock; Ex. marks at 3 & 9 o'clock; Ej. mark at 6 o'clock

390

Class: RECT.; WESTERN FIELD RIFLE; Mod. 93M-390A; S.S.; Bolt action; Serial No., none; Firing pin mark at 5:45 o'clock; Ex. mark at 3 o'clock. Firing Pin acts as ejector

Class: RECT.; WINCHESTER RIFLE; Mod. 47; S.S.; Bolt action; Serial No., none; Firing pin mark at 12 o'clock; Ex. marks at 3 & 9 o'clock; Ej. mark at 7 o'clock

Class: RECT.; WINCHESTER RIFLE; Mod. 61; Slide action; Serial No. 13287; Firing pin mark at 12 o'clock; Ex. mark at 3 o'clock

Class: RECT.; WINCHESTER RIFLE; Mod. 62; Slide action; Serial No. 15275; Firing pin mark 12 o'clock; Ex. mark 4 o'clock. Bar rises from below and pushes shell out

Class: RECT.; WINCHESTER RIFLE; Mod. 62; Slide action; Serial No. 24891A; Firing pin mark at 12 o'clock; Ex. mark at 4 o'clock. Bar rises from below and pushes shell out

Class: RECT.; WINCHESTER RIFLE; Mod. 67; S.S.; Bolt action; Serial No., none; Firing pin mark at 12 o'clock; Ex. mark at 6 o'clock

Class: RECT.; WINCHESTER RIFLE; Mod. 74; Auto.; Bolt action; Serial No. 221504A; Firing pin mark at 12 o'clock; Ex. mark at 3 o'clock; Ej. mark at 9 o'clock

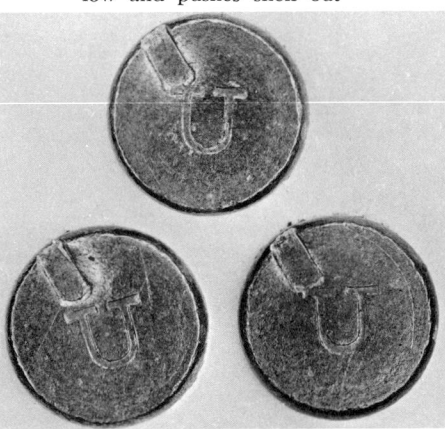

Class: RECT.; WINCHESTER RIFLE; Mod. 90; Slide action; Serial No. 603833; Firing pin mark at 11 o'clock; Ex. mark at 3:30 o'clock. Bar rises from below and pushes shell out

Class: RECT.; WINCHESTER RIFLE; Mod. 1903; Automatic; Serial No. 42297; Firing pin mark at 12 o'clock; Ex. mark at 3 o'clock; Ej. mark at 8 o'clock

Plate 25

Class: RECT.; WINCHESTER RIFLE; Mod. 1906; Slide action; Serial No. 183390; Firing pin mark at 12 o'clock; Ex. mark at 4:30 o'clock. Bar rises from below and pushes shell out

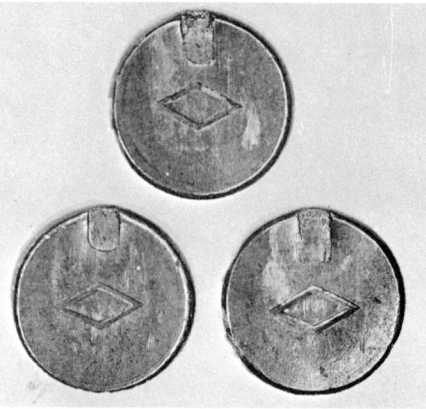

Class: RECT.; WINCHESTER RIFLE; Mod. 1906; Slide action; Serial No. 68527; Firing pin mark at 12 o'clock; Ex. mark at 5 o'clock. Bar rises from below and pushes shell out

Class: RECT.; WINCHESTER RIFLE; Mod. 1906; Slide action; Serial No. 284512; Firing pin mark at 12 o'clock; Ex. mark at 5 o'clock. Bar rises from below and pushes shell out

Class: CIRCULAR; MARLIN RIFLE; Mod. 80; Bolt action; Box mag.; Serial No., none; Firing pin mark at 12 o'clock; Ex. marks at 3 & 9 o'clock; Ej. mark at 7 o'clock

Class: CIRCULAR; MARLIN RIFLE; Mod. 80; Bolt action; Box mag.; Serial No., none; Firing pin mark at 12 o'clock; Ex. marks at 3 & 9 o'clock; Ej. mark at 7:30 o'clock

Class: CIRCULAR; MARLIN RIFLE; Mod. 81; Bolt action; Tub. magazine; Firing pin mark at 12 o'clock; Ex. mark at 3 o'clock; Ej. mark at 8 o'clock

Class: CIRCULAR; MARLIN RIFLE; Model not designated; Bolt action; Repeater; Box mag.; Serial No., none; Firing pin mark at 12 o'clock; Ex. marks at 3 & 9 o'clock; Ej. mark at 7:30 o'clock

Class: CIRCULAR; MARLIN RIFLE; Mod. 81-DL; Bolt action; Tub. magazine; Firing pin mark at 12 o'clock; Ex. mark at 3:15 o'clock; Ej. mark at 6 o'clock

Class: CIRCULAR; REISING PISTOL; Automatic; Serial No. 2251; Firing pin mark at 12 o'clock; Ex. mark at 3 o'clock. Ejects off of magazine lip

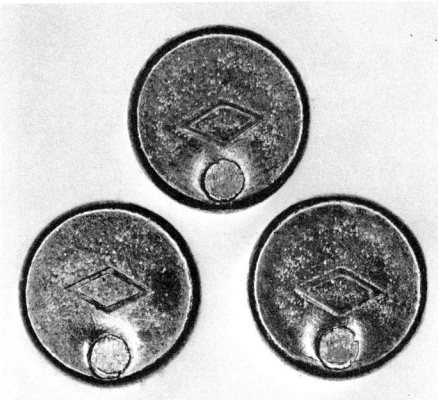

Class: CIRCULAR; REMING-
TON RIFLE; Mod. 4; Rolling
block; S.S.; Serial No. 147944;
Firing pin mark at 12 o'clock.
Block extractor leaves no mark

Class: CIRCULAR; REMING-
TON RIFLE; Mod. 4; Rolling
block; S.S.; Serial No. 184794;
Firing pin at 12 o'clock. Block
extractor leaves no mark

Class: CIRCULAR; REMING-
TON RIFLE; Mod. 4; Rolling
block; S.S.; Serial No. 387792;
Firing pin mark at 6 o'clock.
Block extractor leaves no mark

Class: SEMI-CIRCULAR; HI
STANDARD PISTOL; Dura-
matic Mod. M-101; Serial No.
494815; Firing pin mark at 12
o'clock; Ex. mark at 3 o'clock;
Ej. mark at 7 o'clock

Class: SEMI-CIRCULAR; HI
STANDARD PISTOL; Flite
King Mod.; Serial No. 435708;
Firing pin mark at 1 o'clock;
Ex. mark at 3 o'clock; Ej. mark
at 7 o'clock

Class: SEMI-CIRCULAR; HI
STANDARD PISTOL; Sport
King Mod.; Serial No. 376155;
Firing pin mark at 1 o'clock;
Ex. mark at 3 o'clock; Ej. mark
at 7 o'clock

Class: SEMI-CIRCULAR; IVER
JOHNSON REV.; Supershot
Sealed Eight Mod.; Serial No.
L-22257; Firing pin mark at 12
o'clock

Class: SEMI-CIRCULAR; S&W
REV.; Mod. Combat Master-
piece; Serial No. 315036; Firing pin mark at 12 o'clock

Class: SEMI - CIRCULAR;
RANGER RIFLE; Mod. 103-
13; Bolt action; Tubular mag.;
Firing pin mark at 12 o'clock;
Ex. mark at 3 o'clock; Ej. mark
at 7 o'clock

Plate 27

Class: SEMI - CIRCULAR;
SPRINGFIELD RIFLE; Mod.
53-B.; S.S.; Bolt action; Serial
No., none; Firing pin mark at
4:30 o'clock; Ex. mark at 4
o'clock; Ej. mark at 9 o'clock

Class: SEMI - CIRCULAR;
SPRINGFIELD RIFLE; Mod.
53-A.; S.S.; Bolt action; Serial
No., none; Firing pin at 6:30
o'clock; Ex. mark at 4 o'clock;
Ej. mark at 8 o'clock

Class: SEMI - CIRCULAR;
SPRINGFIELD RIFLE; Mod.
53-A; S.S.; Bolt action; Serial
No., none; Firing pin mark at
6:30 o'clock; Ex. mark at 4
o'clock; Ej. mark at 8 o'clock

Class: SEMI - CIRCULAR;
SPRINGFIELD RIFLE; Mod.
84-C; Bolt action; Box mag.;
Serial No., none; Firing pin
mark at 12 o'clock; Ex. mark at
3:30 o'clock; Ej. mark at 9:30
o'clock

Class: SPECIAL; MARLIN RI-
FLE; Mod. 20-A; Slide action;
Serial No., none; Firing pin
mark at 12 o'clock; Ex. mark at
3 o'clock; Ej. mark at 9 o'clock

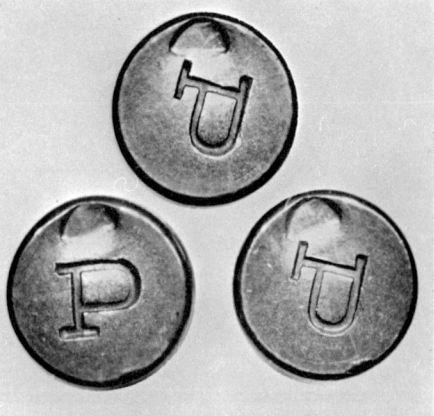

Class: SPECIAL; STEVENS
PISTOL; Stevens Single Shot
Pistol; Serial No. 13487; Firing
pin mark at 12 o'clock

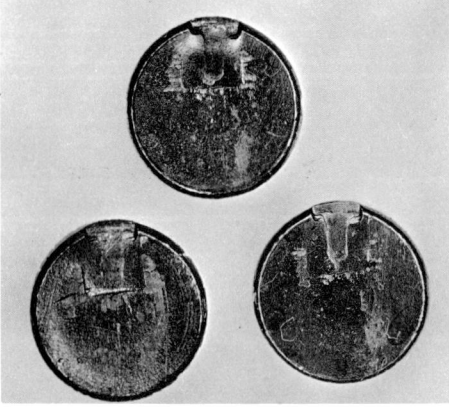

Class: SPECIAL; SAVAGE RI-
FLE; Mod. 298; Slide action;
Serial No., none; Firing pin
mark at 12 o'clock; Ex. marks
at 3 & 9 o'clock. Firing Pin acts
as ejector

Class: CIRCULAR; COLT REV.;
Mod. S.A. Frontier Scout; Serial No. 6647Q; Firing pin mark
at 12 o'clock

Class: CIRCULAR; RUGER
REV.; Mod. "Single Six"; Serial
No. 21235; Firing pin mark at
12 o'clock

German codes for manufacturers of automatic pistols

Some time prior to World War II the Germans not only started to make weapons which were forbidden by the Versailles Treaty but they also devised a system of code numbers which were assigned to the firms who were supplying material for the Government. Manufacturers names were not used.

At the close of World War I the Germans were allowed to have a "Police Army" of 100,000 men, and to equip this force Simson & Co. of Suhl were given the task of assembling Lugers from material left over at the end of the war. As this firm happened to be the 42nd on the list of Government suppliers it was assigned the code number 42, and this was used until this firm ceased its independent existence in the early or middle 1930s and was succeeded by Mauser who had taken over the manufacture of the Luger from D.W.M. Antisemitic feeling was running high in Germany at this time and Simson was forced out. The firm, now under Aryan control, continued to operate for some time, perhaps into 1937.

As Mauser had acquired a large number of parts, along with machinery, the pistols produced by them continued to bear the D.W.M. markings for some time. When the parts had been used up, these markings were discontinued and the code number 42, formerly used by Simson & Co., was used along with the marking S/42 (see Plate 28). Both markings were used until 1941 when the Germans adopted a new code system which consisted of combinations of either two or three letters. The code designation assigned to Mauser was byf, and this was used on all pistols made by this firm during the remainder of the War.

Letter codes were also assigned to firms in the occupied countries and in some cases to firms in other countries who were supplying military equipment to the Germans.

The following list contains the codes which are of major importance as far as automatic pistols are concerned. Some firms listed may not have been actively engaged in wartime production of automatic pistols but produced such before the last World War.

ac	Carl Walther, Zella-Mehlis
aek	F. Dušek Waffenerzeugung, Opočno, Czechoslovakia
ayf	Erma Waffenfabrik, Erfurt
bnz	Steyr-Daimler-Puch, A.G., Steyr, Austria
byf	Mauser Werke, Oberndorf a/N
ce	J. P. Sauer & Sohn, Gewehrfabrik, Suhl
ch	Fabrique Nationale d'Armes de Guerre, Herstal, Belgium
con	Franz Stock, Berlin
cyg	Spreewerk, G.m.b.H., Metallwarenfabrik, Berlin-Spandau
dfb	Gustloff Werke, Suhl (Made an experimental pistol only)
fnh	Böhmische Waffenfabrik, A.G., Prague, Czechoslovakia
fxo	C. G. Haenel Waffen u. Fahrradfabrik, Suhl
fzs	Heinrich Krieghoff Waffenfabrik, Suhl
jhv	Metallwaren Waffen u. Maschinenfabriken, A.G., Budapest, Hungary
jwa	Mre. d'Armes Chatellerault, Chatellerault, France
kfk	Dansk Industrie Syndikat, Copenhagen, Denmark
$\frac{SMW}{45}$	Mauser Werke, Oberndorf a/N

Plate 28. Variations in markings on Luger pistols

No. 1 (top) Made by Mauser in 1937
    2 Made by Mauser in 1935
    3 Made by Mauser in 1940

4 Made by Mauser in 1942
5 Made by Krieghoff or assembled by him
6 Made at Gov't. Arsenal at Erfurt prior
   to 1930

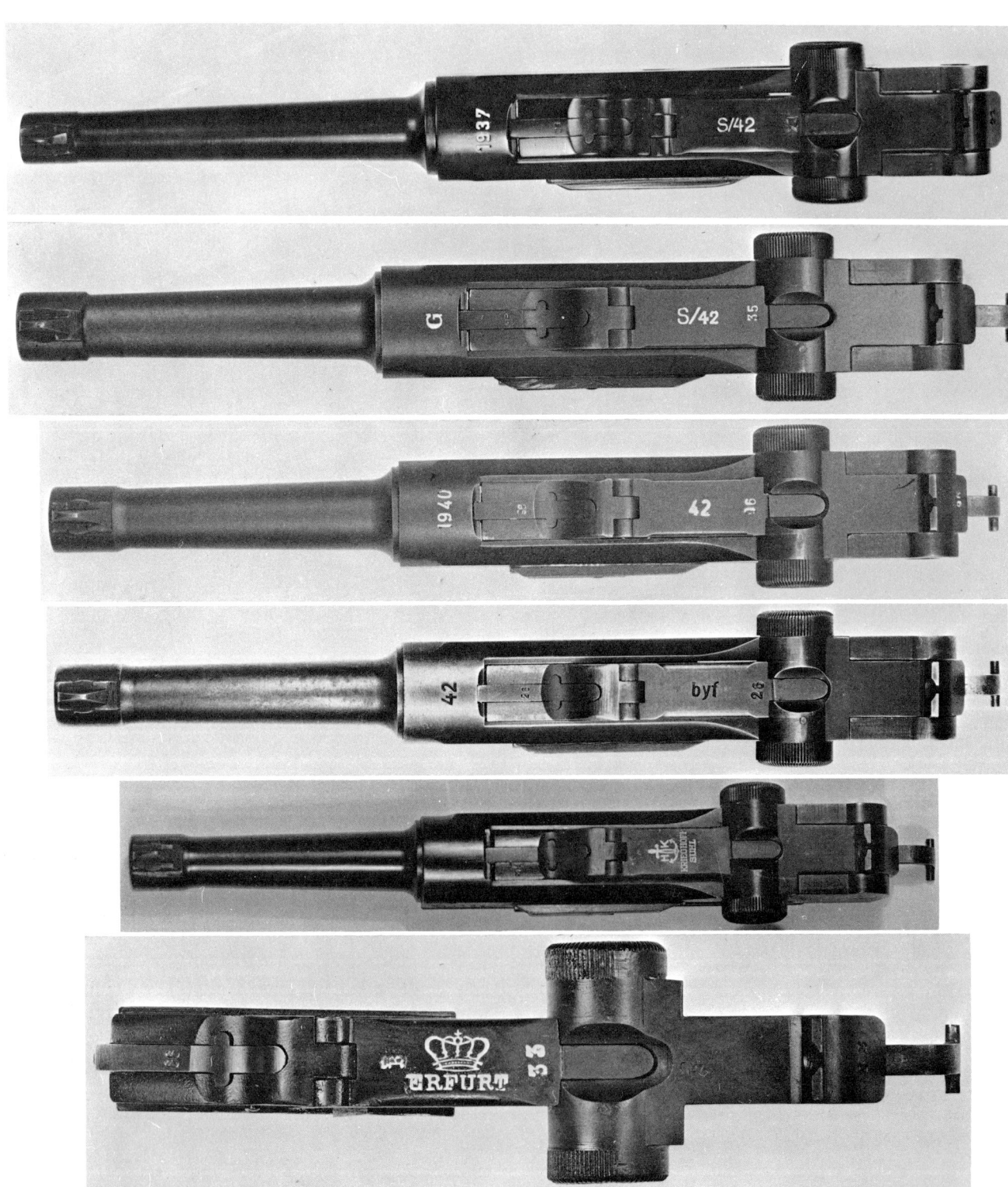

Index

398

Page

93. Note that the data for HI-Standard Mod. HD No. 194570 are repeated in line below. Delete one line.

98. 7th Item, Col. I. For Pistolet Mikros, serial number should be 73370.

98. 7th Item from bottom of page, Col. I. Serial number should be 1294.

99. Under Carl Walther—Mod. I. Delete the word "removed" and replace it with "No. 60."

101. Under Fab. de Martin Bascaran. Serial number should be 11582.

102. Line 3, Col. I of Table. Should read "A.G. Prag Werk."

103. Under Esperanza y Unceta. Groove diam. (Col. 9) for Astra Mod. 1911 should read ".3143" (not ".2143").

105. 3rd Item from bottom. Should read "Zbrojovka Praga, Prague, Czechoslovakia."

106. Under Schwarzlose. Serial number should be 245.

109. Under Bernardelli serial number 21. Remarks in last column should read, "9 mm Par. Ctge. Only a few made."

118. Col. I. Under *Caliber* 32. Name and address of manufacturer should read, "Harrington and Richardson, Worcester, Mass."

118. Col. I. Under *Caliber* 32. Spelling should be "Armero Especialistas." (in 3rd Item)

120. Under Thos. Horsley and Son. Bore diameter (8th Col.) should read ".2993" (not "2293").

127. Under Smith and Wesson. Bore diam. for D.A. 3rd Mod. Ser. No. 153209 should read ".3510" (not ".2510").

134. Col. 3. 10th Item under *6.35 mm (.25) Caliber.* Should be "Zbrojovka Praga."

Page

169. Line 4 under *Bergmann Pocket Models.* "V. Charles Schilling" should be "V. Ch. Schilling."

169. Lines 17–18, Col. 2. "V. Charles Schilling" should be "V. Ch. Schilling."

184. Col. I, 2nd line from bottom. "Českaslovenská" should be Československá."

199. Fig. 166. Legend should read, "9 mm Par." (instead of "7.65 mm Long").

267. Col. 1, 4th line from bottom. Phrase should read, "with serial numbering starting at 2000."

273. Fig. 250. Note: This is *not* a Schwarzlose, it is a Shouboe.

301. Col. 2, lines 6 and 7 of paragraph headed *Target pistol.* The phrase "rather than being a hammer model" should read, "actuated by a concealed hammer."

346. Col. 2, Item Fiel. Spelling of "Maguruza" should be "Mugurusa."

348. Col. 2, 3rd line from bottom. Delete the line, "Possibly also Vilimec."

382. Plate 15. Second and third photos are transposed. To correct, legends may be transposed.

395. Col. 2, 9th code, "cyg" should read "cyq."

395. Col. 2, code for Mauser Werke. $\dfrac{\text{"SMW"}}{45}$ should be $\dfrac{\text{"SVW"}}{45}$ and $\dfrac{\text{"SVW"}}{46}$.

395. Col. 2, 9th code, "cyg" should read "cyq." $\dfrac{\text{swp}}{45}$ Československá Zbrojovka Společnost (Czechoslovakian Arms Factory, Ltd.) Brno, Czechoslovakia.

400. Col. 1, 13th line. "V. Charles Schilling" should be "V. Ch. Schilling."